HANDBOOK of POLITICAL COMMUNICATION

HANDBOOK of POLITICAL COMMUNICATION

edited by

Dan D. Nimmo and Keith R. Sanders

SAGE PUBLICATIONS   Beverly Hills   London

For information address:

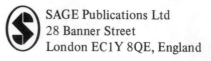

SAGE Publications, Inc.
275 South Beverly Drive
Beverly Hills, California 90212

SAGE Publications Ltd
28 Banner Street
London EC1Y 8QE, England

Printed in the United States of America

Library of Congress Cataloging in Publication Data
Main entry under title:

The handbook of political communication.

    Includes bibliographies and index.
    1. Communication in politics—Addresses, essays, lectures. I. Nimmo, Dan D. II. Sanders, Keith R.
JA74.H34   306'.2   81-9362
ISBN 0-8039-1714-7   AACR2

FIRST PRINTING

Contents

This volume is dedicated to
Dortha M. and Earl R. Sanders

Preface

IN THE 1930s a popular Hollywood film made the rounds of the nation's movie houses. The title was *Mr. Smith Goes to Washington* and the star was Jimmy Stewart. It was about Jefferson Smith, a naive and foolishly idealistic man selected to serve in the U.S. Senate. His aims were sincere, his projects grandiose. He yearned to overcome the slow, cumbersome, pork-barrel-laden legislative process with a simple credo: "Lost causes are the only ones worth fighting for."

Since 1977, when the editors of this volume first discussed the possibilities of a handbook of political communication, they have come to regard themselves as naive and foolish as the neophyte Senator Jefferson Smith. They began with a twofold aim, one as equally impossible as Smith's effort to grab the U.S. Senate by the forelock and bend it quickly to his will. They agreed that the state of the art in political communication had reached the point that it was time, first, to offer a comprehensive review of existing theories and research findings and, second, to mark the boundaries of the field. Today, a half-decade later, they recognize the persumptuous nature of their lofty aims. But, like Senator Smith, they conclude in an undaunted way that it was a cause worth fighting for; in fact, it was a cause not so lost after all.

As readers of this handbook will quickly discover, the rate of development in the field of political communication in the last three decades has long since outstripped the summarizing and synthesizing capacities of any single volume. A comprehensive statement of research approaches, methods, domains, and findings would require far more space than we have at our command. We faced the reality (and frustration) of that fact in 1978 as we labored to pare down a proposed volume of 40 essays to a publishable one of but two dozen articles. We discovered something else as well, something which at first was equally frustrating but eventually, upon reflection, most refreshing. That was the realization that the state of development of political communication as a field was in such flux that any effort to define its boundaries would be not only presumptuous but premature and misleading. Instead of residing in a fixed, static, and sterile body of knowledge, scholars find themselves living in an exciting process of emergence, one of expanding possibilities, enriching diversities, and plural options.

We believe that the essays in this volume capture what we now accept as the state of the art in political communication studies—rapid development and pluralist emergence. They are not intended as articles to provide a definitive statement of where the field is or where it is going. But they do represent a cross-section of the key theoretical approaches, areas of inquiry, and methods of study in this burgeoning field. They combine to form a summary statement on which to build, not an epitaph to a lost cause.

We are, of course, indebted to many persons who helped make this handbook possible. To begin with there are the contributors of essays to this volume. They graciously consented to participate, bore up under the exhortations of the editors to meet deadlines for various drafts, and consented to revisions. We also thank the members of a political communication seminar at the University of Tennessee-Knoxville who were the first persons exposed to drafts of the manuscripts. They provided frank assessments and all learned accordingly. The tasks of typing, retyping, and reproducing essay drafts are always tedious. We acknowledge the skills and patience of Ruth Ann Scott, Kay Parrish, Sharon Holmes, and Jackie Faughn (all of Southern Illinois University at Carbondale) in this respect. Thanks to Jan Trice Nimmo who did not ask why one editor grumbled so much. Finally, even greater thanks to Carol and Mark Sanders; their forbearance has been severely tested during the preparation of this volume.

Introduction: The Emergence of Political Communication as a Field

Dan D. Nimmo
Keith R. Sanders

A MYTHOLOGY surrounds the decade of the 1950s, one to which we in the United States are especially prone. It depicts a nation of paradoxes, defending itself against enemies foreign and domestic (fighting a cold war and Korean war abroad, undergoing a Red scare at home), yet secure in its nuclear superiority, living the golden consensus of the Eisenhower years, and witnessing its youth maturing into the "silent" generation. The paradoxes added up to an overall sense—perhaps a yearning—for order, stability, and consolidation. Viewed from a perspective of three decades hence, the 1950s offer a nostalgic glow of national calm, tranquility, and strength.

But those suffering from intellectual growing pains in the 1950s (the co-editors and most of the contributors to this volume being but a few examples) knew differently. For anyone interested in studying human behavior the times were not placid, nor the spirit serene. Something was happening in the social sciences, something exciting. More than one scholar called it a "revolution" (Truman, 1955, pp. 202-231). Others were to label it a "movement" (Dahl, 1961). Years later there would be reflections about a "paradigm change" (Kuhn, 1962). Whatever its designation, the new mood among social scientists in the 1950s espoused increasingly shared concerns and orientations. The "science" in social science was to be taken seriously. The implications of that were to turn to the physiological and biological sciences for guidelines for effective study of human affairs, to the philosophical stance of logical positivism as an orientation to the appropriate facts for study, and to empiricism for suitable techniques of data-gathering and analysis. The "social" in social science was not so honored, however; in fact, the term "behavioral sciences" seemed best suited to convey the new intent—one focusing on discovering patterns and laws of observable behavior.

Today the behavioral impetus, although not spent, is much abated. Many of its earlier unquestioned assumptions about the nature of scientific inquiry, the distinction between facts and values, the appropriateness of empirical (especially quantitative) techniques, and the social versus individualistic quality of human behavior have been challenged. Readers will find those and other assumptions and such challenges discussed throughout this volume. We take note of that impetus and the intellectual ferment of the 1950s, however, to neither honor nor bury "behavioralism." Instead, we call attention to one other facet of the behavioral climate of that and ensuing decades that left a lasting imprint on scholarly activity and, indeed, makes publication of this volume fitting, timely, and necessary. We refer to the tendency in the behavioral sciences to bring together bodies of knowledge, from whatever academic disciplines and departments they be found, and to merge them into cross-disciplinary fields hitherto investigated as offshoots of more conventional areas of inquiry. It is, of course, a tendency running throughout the development of all of the physical and biological sciences and, to some extent, has been evident in the development of the humanities as well. It dates in the evolution of the behavioral sciences, as Truman notes (1955), at least as far back as 1930, when the first edition of the *Encyclopedia of the Social Sciences* was published.

It is our contention that political communication is such an emerging field. Its piecemeal origins date back several centuries, but a self-consciously cross-disciplinary focus is of more recent vintage. Although we might with, ample justification, trace the lineage of political communication back much earlier, we think it convenient to speak of the emergence of the cross-disciplinary field as beginning in the behavioral thrust of the 1950s. For example, it is in 1956 that we find one of the first attempts to designate something called "political communication" as one of three "intervening processes" (political leadership and group structures being the other two) "by means of which political influences are mobilized and transmitted" between "formal governmental institutions, on the one hand, and citizen voting behavior, on the other hand." The editors of the volume in which that statement appeared (a reader entitled *Political Behavior* expressly intended to persuade students to employ "the political behavior approach") went on to write: "[A]lthough the body of knowledge emerging about such intervening processes ... is still gross and tentative, more reliable understanding is being acquired." Unfortunately, however, "political communication research has lagged behind similar work in other substantive fields of social science" (Eulau, Eldersveld, & Janowitz, 1956, p. 175).

As we shall see in the remainder of this introductory essay, and as exemplified in the chapters of this volume, the 1956 statement was instructive and prophetic. First, it designates political communication as a substantive field of social science. Second, however, it was a retarded field. Yet, third, even in the 1950s a body of knowledge about political communication as an intervening process was emerging. Finally, the statement defines the boundaries of the field—that is, as a process intervening between formal governing institutions and citizen voting behavior. In the 1980s political communication is even more a substantive field, but it is certainly no longer retarded, a cross-disciplinary effort at knowledge-building continues to emerge, and the boundaries of political communication have expanded considerably. The sections that follow speak to each of these points.

THE CURRENT STATE OF POLITICAL COMMUNICATION

In the quarter-century that has elapsed since research in political communication was criticized for lagging behind other substantive fields of social science, there have been noteworthy advances. These advances include not just research, but extend to political communication as a distinct domain of publication, a teaching area, a professional endeavor, a field with practical and policy applications, and a cross-national enterprise.

Research

In searching for a way to illustrate what the emerging field of political communication was all about in the 1950s, Eulau et al. (1956) relied on the republication of three case studies—one using a post facto experimental design to examine television's effects in the 1952 presidential election; another reporting a field experiment evaluating the effectiveness of propaganda techniques; and the third, a content analysis of political language. As essays in this volume attest, these concerns remain key areas and techniques of inquiry for political communication scholars: Doris Graber echoes the importance of political languages (Chapter 7), Lynda Lee Kaid focuses on political advertising (Chapter 9), Cliff Zukin examines the role of mass communication in the public opinion process (Chapter 13), and Richard Hoffstetter (Chapter 19) and Roy Miller (Chapter 20) remind us that content analysis and experimentation are very much a part of contemporary political communication research.

If, however, there was a paucity of research literature in the 1950s to illustrate the nature of political communication, that was to change rapidly. In 1972, for example, Sanders, Hirsch, and Pace compiled over 1000 entries in their comprehensive bibliography of political communication research. Two years later Kaid, Sanders, and Hirsch (1974), limiting themselves to the available research in political *campaign* communication in the United States and other selected nations, listed more than 1500 items in their bibliography. As this

Handbook's "Guide to the Literature" (Appendix A) implies, the available published and unpublished research in political communication now virtually surpasses cataloguing possibilities.

Matching the sheer quantity of research projects undertaken in political communication is an impressive diversification of the generic field. No longer regarded as simply an intervening process between formal governmental institutions and citizen voting behavior, political communication now has a wide variety of facets. Numbered among the substantive areas of the field are studies of political languages, political rhetoric, political advertising and propaganda, political debates, political socialization, election campaigns, public opinion, public policy, political movements, government-news media relations, political imagery, political symbolism, and a growing number of other research specializations. Moreover, as the chapters in this *Handbook* ably illustrate, political communication researchers are increasingly sensitive to the strengths and limitations of a variety of methodological approaches and techniques. Theoretical concerns revolve around such approaches as process, uses and gratifications, information diffusion, agenda-setting, critical theory, constructivist views, and social structure. And researchers apply a plethora of techniques to their tasks—historical, critical, content-analytical, experimental, quasi-experimental, survey, and small-sample designs. The laggard of the social sciences in the 1950s has, as the cigarette advertisement says, "come a long way, baby."

The Publication Domain

One possible indicator that a research field is obtaining a separate identity among the social sciences is the appearance of scholarly publications devoted exclusively to the research and writing of the field's specialists. This *Handbook's* appended "Guide to the Literature" offers a set of useful suggestions regarding the published efforts of scholarly specialists; hence, we need not duplicate that effort here. However, it is important to note that the field now possesses its own publication domain. Thus, *Political Communication Review* is a handy tool for scholars interested in current research trends, listings of unpublished papers, and reviews of both article and book-length research. *Political Communication and Propaganda,* a quarterly journal, is an organ publishing research of both a qualitative and a quantitative nature. Two annual volumes, *Communication Yearbook* and *Mass Communication Review Yearbook,* devote separate sections to political communication research; the former also provides an annual overview of theoretical, methodological, and research developments in the field. Finally, "political communication" has for some time been a key substantive category in publications devoted to abstracting reported research in the communication sciences, as evidenced by *Communicontents* (now no longer published) and by *Communication Abstracts.*

Teaching Political Communication

The emergence of political communication as a distinctive scholarly field encompasses more than the research enterprise. Once rarely found in a university or college catalogue, it is now increasingly commonplace to find listings of both undergraduate and graduate courses in political communication. They are not confined to a single academic department, but appear in the listings for departments of speech communication, mass communication, journalism, political science, sociology, and social psychology. Although generally taught by a specialist within the department in question, a few such courses involve the joint efforts of persons from two or more specializations. Course titles vary: "political communication," "political persuasion," "public opinion," "campaigns and voting," "mass media and politics," "political rhetoric," "political attitudes, opinions, and communication," "the sociology of mass media."

As specialized course offerings in political communication exist, so also do bibliographical guides and textbooks to serve them. For example, the publication of the American Political Science Association devoted to improving the quality of teaching in that discipline, *News for Teachers of Political Science*, has published extensive articles describing the results of a survey of types of courses in political communication offered and materials used (Blanchard & Wolfson, 1980) and course outlines and readings for courses in the mass media and American politics (Pohlmann & Foley, 1978). And clearly marking the arrival of political communication as a growth industry has been the increased competition between rival textbook authors and their respective publishers for a share of the market. The five-year period 1975-1980 witnessed the publication of core texts addressed exclusively to the political communication market (Chaffee, 1975; Kraus & Davis, 1976; Nimmo, 1978; Graber, 1980; Meadow, 1980) and a host of specialized, supplementary works. There seems little question that the textbook-monograph explosion will continue, especially with publishing houses planning specialized "topics" and "series" volumes in the field.

Professional Recognition

Scholarly and professional organizations, which once gave little thought in their planning for annual conferences to providing forums for the discussion of research in political communication, now set aside panels, plenary sessions, workshops, and other meetings for political communication scholars. Rare is the annual meeting of an internationally, nationally, or regionally based scholarly organization—in any of the social sciences—that does not conduct such sessions. Moreover, the International Communication Association provided formal recognition of political communication as a distinctive teaching and research field transcending the boundaries of separate academic disciplines when, in 1973, it accepted the founding of the Political Communication Division within its structure. The Eastern Communication Association recently did the same.

Policy Implications

As we shall note later, many of the progenitors of what has emerged as the distinctive field of political communication (e.g., rhetorical analysis, propaganda analysis, persuasion studies) provided research findings with policy applications. That heritage of a research enterprise with practical implications remains viable, as many of the chapters in this handbook clearly indicate. One example of many is noteworthy here. Also evolving since the 1950s has been a distinct profession—that of political campaign management and consulting—whose practitioners apply many of the research theories, methods, and findings to a wide range, of electoral and policy-oriented questions, such as the effectiveness of alternative campaign techniques, deriving profiles of citizens' communication habits, addressing problems in fund-raising, and legislative lobbying. Such applications are exemplified by the regularity with which newsletters of professional management and consulting firms (for example, *Campaign Insight, Campaigning Reports, Campaign Practices Report*) summarize applied political communication research or include sessions incorporating that research in their candidate training seminars.

Cross-National Growth

We have asserted that political communication as a field of inquiry is cross-disciplinary—that is, it combines the interests and skills of scholars from a wide variety of academic disciplines. Similarly, political communication is emerging as a field with a cross-national scope. In his appendix to this volume, "European Research," Richard Fitchen offers a brief sketch of some of the work being undertaken outside the United States. But the emergence of the field extends even wider. A separate volume would be required to summarize the major research and teaching programs now taking place on each continent. The ferment in political communication research of a cross-national nature can be sampled by close attention to Fitchen's contribution as well as to the efforts of Richard Lanigan (Chapter 5) and Jay Blumler and Michael Gurevitch (Chapter 17), and the materials in the "Guide to the Literature" (Appendix B).

ORIGINS AND BACKGROUNDS OF AN EMERGING FIELD

Granted, then, that as a field of inquiry political communication is in a healthy, thriving, burgeoning state. To understand how it reached that identity, and to grasp the diverse facets of this manifold field, we must look back and trace the beginnings of the various threads of intellectual concern that evolved singly, then in combination, to form the field of political communication. We need not, nor can we in such brief fashion, touch upon every line of ancestry, but we will select a few key ones for emphasis. Others are developed in many of the chapters that follow.

Interest in the interrelationship of communication and politics is scarcely new. Systematic inquiry began at least as early as the work of the Sophists and the insights provided by Aristotle in his *Politics* and *Rhetoric*. Moreover, the heritage of political communication must include classics in the arts of persuasion penned by Sun Tzu, St. Thomas Aquinas, Shakespeare, Machiavelli, and many others. And surely no student of American politics can ignore the rhetorical aspects of The Declaration of Independence, *The Federalist Papers,* or the Gettysburg Address.

Rather than pinpoint a precise era for the origins of political communication studies, it is more useful to catalogue a few of the key areas of inquiry that constitute the lineage of the field. For this purpose we select rhetorical analysis, propaganda analysis, attitude change research, voting studies, government-news media studies, functional and systems analyses, and technological change. It is important to bear in mind that in each of these areas, we frequently see investigators from a variety of academic disciplines employing a host of differing theoretical postures, research methods, and techniques. For example, anthropology and sociology stimulated interest in linguistics and symbolism, giving rise to the study of political languages; psychology and social psychology provoked interest in the subjective aspects of communication, attitude change studies, and learning—the bases of research into constructs of political discourse, the effects of mediated political appeals, and political socialization; speech communication has provided historical, critical, and quantitative analyses of messages and their reception, the bases of modern concerns with political rhetoric; political scientists undertook generations of voting studies that formed the received notions of communication's role in electoral campaigns; students of mass communication inquired into the impact of changing communication technology on social life, thus prompting concerns about the role of mass communication in altering political systems; cybernetic and systems analyses previewed the possibilities of treating entire political communities in holistic terms as communications systems of learning and control; and from philosophy stem existential, phenomenistic, and other schools of thought yielding current emphases on critical theory in political communication. In sum, bound up with the diverse substantive origins of the field are the elements lending a distinctly cross-disciplinary character to political communication inquiry.

Rhetorical Analysis

The essay by Lloyd Bitzer (Chapter 8) in this *Handbook* provides the flavor of current applications of what is perhaps the oldest and most venerable method of studying political messages, motives, and styles. From the classical writers, of which Aristotle was the most prominent, through the eighteenth-century English triumvirate of Blair (1783/1965), Campbell (1776/1963), and Whately (1828/1963), and into the twentieth century via such works as the three volumes (Brigance, 1943; Hochmuth, 1965) on *The History and Criticism of American Public Address,* much has emerged that is relevant to political communication. Indeed, since the founding of the *Quarterly Journal of Speech* in 1915, there has hardly been an issue that did not contain at least one essay on the history or criticism of public political discourse. More recently, this journal has undertaken to publish quadrennially a collection of essays on the presidential campaigns. The rhetorical tradition has kept alive and well the contributions of the ancients, elaborated and supplemented them, and, along with the behavioral trends of the 1950s, have fostered a cross-disciplinary spirit of inquiry.

Early in their presentation of the methods of rhetorical analysis, Brock and Scott (1980) traced approaches to rhetorical study through distinct perspectives. The first, which they label "traditional," has its roots in Aristotelian analysis, now appearing in neo-Aristotelian form. Brock and Scott note that the traditional perspective focuses on the speaker (source of communication) as the object of inquiry, analyzing how that speaker responds to rhetorical problems posed by the situation. Rhetoric they define as "the human effort to induce cooperation through the use of symbols" (p. 16). Students in this tradition accept the proposition that principles of sound rhetoric are discoverable, have indeed been derived, and are so stable that they transcend discrete episodes of political discourse. In Chapter 7 Doris Graber demonstrates that such a neo-Aristotelian view is still implicit in political communication inquiry as she employs it in her study of political languages.

If the traditional mode of rhetorical analysis focuses on the speaker as the essential element of inquiry, the "experiential" perspective, note Brock and Scott, denies any such essential starting point for analysis. Instead, society is regarded as in a state of process, of flux. Any analytical scheme, therefore, is arbitrary in what it examines, what it emphasizes, how it carves up chaos. It is up to the rhetorical analyst to choose among speaker, message, audience, setting, and other phases of that process of discourse. Hence, no fundamental principles of rhetoric can or do exist. The reader will find similar experiential assumptions implied in James Combs' essay on the process approach to political communication, Chapter 1.

A third perspective on rhetorical analysis, say Brock and Scott, is that of the "new rhetoric." It falls between the traditional and experiential perspectives. Like the latter, it accepts the view that society is in process; but, like the former, it believes that stable relationships can be found in human interaction. The procedure for accomplishing that is via the construction of a framework for the analysis of discourse that assumes that symbols so influence human perceptions of reality that life itself, in any social sense, is symbolic action. Again, Combs introduces such views in his essay (Chapter 1); they are also implicit in David Swanson's development of a constructivist position (Chapter 6), Herbert Simons and Elizabeth Mechling's explication of a political movements approach (Chapter 15), and Stephen Brown's focus on intensive analysis (Chapter 22).

So permanent and prominent a place has rhetorical analysis occupied in the history of studies dealing with the emerging facets of political communication that it is not surprising that the tradition itself has come under investigation and criticism. The approach has been criticized for its lack of theoretical breadth and methodological imagination (Black, 1965/1978). Trent (1975) concluded, after reviewing 54 articles on political communication appearing in national and regional journals in speech communication, that the tradition could best be extended through greater methodological awareness and sophistication. As the chapters by Bitzer (Chapter 8), Swanson (Chapter 6), Simons and Mechling (Chapter 15), and those chapters (18 to 22) in the "Methods of Study" section illustrate, these criticisms have not gone unheard. Assessing the changes that had taken place in the field between the publication of his book in 1965 and its republication in 1978, Black (1965/1978, p. ix) concluded: "There is less uniformity in the techniques of rhetorical criticism and in the sorts of subjects deemed appropriate to it, less agreement on its proper role or its ideal condition, more contention, more experiment, more confusion, more vitality."

Propaganda Analysis

At the outbreak of World War I Charles E. Merriam, frequently regarded as the father of modern political science—or at least the chief figure in training a generation of political scientists who were later to found the behavioral movement in that discipline—left his professorial duties to accept responsibility for U.S. public information programs in Italy. Out of that experience grew an interest in public opinion, propaganda, and communication. A young graduate student picked up on that interest and prepared his Ph.D. dissertation on propaganda in the world war. Merriam's former student, Herbert Lasswell, soon became the leading exponent of propaganda analysis, writing a definitive history of propaganda in World War I (1927), exploring and perfecting techniques of content analysis in World War II (Lasswell & Leites, 1949), and collaborating in a volume that clearly marked propaganda analysis a forerunner of political communication studies (Smith, Lasswell, & Casey, 1946).

The interest in propaganda stimulated by the activity surrounding the two world wars produced twin foci of inquiry—on the motives of the communicator and on the key symbols composing message content. The two merged in analysts' growing fascination with what became known as the "techniques of propaganda." In 1937 philanthropist Edward A. Filene provided financing for The Institute of Propaganda Analysis. The institute sponsored, among other things, academic research, secondary school programs in propaganda analysis, and manuals with guidelines for spotting propaganda techniques. The "seven devices of propaganda" (name-calling, glittering generalities, transfer, testimonial, plain-folks appeals, card-stacking, and band-wagon appeals) were staples for textbooks in propaganda and public opinion for decades. So venerable has been the fascination with applying and detecting propaganda techniques that in 1969 a producer of table games, the "Wff 'N Proof" organization, marketed a widely sold game based on the seven devices of propaganda, a game co-created by television actor Lorne Greene (Allen & Greene, 1969).

Today, political communication studies with a propaganda focus continue the long-term emphasis on propagandists' motives and the content of appeals. However, there is much less concern in contemporary research with direct propaganda than with the covert propagandistic content of other messages—for example, news media content and television documentaries. These studies take both an empirical bent (Efron, 1971; Hofstetter, 1976) and a speculative tone (Ellul, 1965, Schiller, 1973). Moreover, as Richard Hofstetter reports in Chapter 19, content analysis has become increasingly sophisticated, with techniques developed for measuring manifest and latent content of messages, verbal and nonverbal communication.

Attitude Change Studies

Another progenitor in the evolution of political communication studies also grew out of the period of world war, especially out of the era of World War II. At the time, the Research Branch of the Army's Information and Education Division employed a number of social psychologists to examine soldiers' attitudes and opinions, then apply those findings to the design and implementation of information, orientation, and education programs. One focus was on the effects of mass communication (chiefly military training films) on attitude change, a focus later reported in a volume prepared by Hovland, Lumsdaine, and Sheffield (1949).

Following the war, attitude change studies remained a key facet of communication research. Carl Hovland and his colleagues, through a published series of "Yale Studies in Attitude and Communication," reported numerous experimental findings dealing with the impact of a host of variables on attitude shifts: the credibility of the communicator, fear-arousing appeals, the organization of messages, personality and susceptibility to persuasion, group membership and participation, and the role of social judgment (Hovland, Janis, & Kelly, 1953; Hovland, 1957; Hovland & Janis, 1959; Hovland & Rosenberg, 1960; Sherif & Hovland, 1961). Other investigators aimed at generating theories and models of attitude change, including balance (Heider, 1946), congruity (Osgood, 1960), dissonance (Festinger, 1957), and discrepancy (Sherif, Sherif, & Nebergall, 1965) models.

It did not take long for investigators to extend their inquiries into the attitudinal effects of communication to include political attitudes. As will be noted, the early voting studies focused in part upon such matters. Yet, by the time of publication in 1960 of a now-classic review and synthesis of research of the effects of mass communication (Klapper), there were still relatively few studies solely addressing the political effects. Less than two decades later, however, that no longer was the case. In 1976, for example, an entire volume appeared which did for politics what Klapper's work had done in a more generic sense earlier (Kraus & Davis, 1976). Whereas Klapper had only 1000 studies on which to base his conclusions about mass communication's impact on behavior generally, Kraus and Davis consulted 3000 sources for effects on political behavior alone. As readers of this *Handbook* will discover, attitude change and effect studies continue to occupy a central role in inquiries into political advertising (Chapter 9), political debates (Chapter 10), political socialization (Chapter 11), elections and voting (Chapter 12), and public opinion (Chapter 13).

The Voting Studies

Systematic studies of the attitudes and forces surrounding voting behavior date back to the 1920s (Merriam & Gosnell, 1924; Rice, 1928), and communication variables were taken into account at an early stage (Gosnell, 1927). That tradition continued through three generations of voting studies that were to follow: first-generation studies of the Bureau of Applied Social Research (Lazarsfeld, Berelson & Gaudet, 1944; Berelson, Lazarsfeld, & McPhee, 1954); second-generation research led by the studies of the University of Michigan's Survey Research Center (Campbell, Gurin, & Miller, 1954; Campbell, Converse, Miller, & Stokes, 1960, 1966); and more recent, third-generation studies (Blumler & McQuail, 1969; Mendelsohn & O'Keefe, 1976; Miller & Levitin, 1976; Nie, Verba, & Petrocik, 1976; Patterson & McClure, 1976; Patterson, 1980).

This is not the place to examine in detail the complicated and multifaceted relationship between communication and voting revealed by these various studies. Chapter 12, by Garrett O'Keefe and L. Erwin Atwood, supplies readers with that summary, review, and critique. Let it suffice to say that the voting studies have provided an equivocal lineage, at least with respect to the influence of communication on voting choices. First-generation studies, designed in large measure to test the hypothesis that campaign communication did make a difference in voting, revealed that campaign appeals were less likely to convert voters than to activate, crystallize, or reinforce choices already made on the basis of some other factor, such as socioeconomic position, partisan loyalty, religion, or residence. Second-generation studies also minimize the effects of campaigns in the face of long-term, enduring partisan identifications of voters. More recent, third-generation inquiries yield a complicated interpretation of the relationship between political communication and voting behavior, one that varies depending on what uses voters made of campaign communication (see Chapter 2), how information diffuses throughout a campaign (Chapter 3), the agenda-setting role of the news media (Chapter 4), and how people construct their political views (Chapter 6). In sum, after starting with a simplistic notion of direct effects of communication on voting (the hypodermic-needle view), then adopting a minimal effects posture, voting studies now appear wed to a phenomenistic conclusion; that is, the influence of communication on voting depends on a number of phenomena operating within the field where such communication appears.

Government and the News Media

The relationship of the press to politics, the news media to government, has long been a mainstay of scholarly curiosity, fascination to and frustration of politicians, and narcissistic interest to journalists. The relationship of government and press evoked particular concern toward the end of the eighteenth century as the power of the latter began to match that of the former. English philosopher-statesman Edmund Burke, believing the press was exercising a usurping and malignant power challenging that of the House of Commons, coined the term "the Fourth Estate" to deplore the shift (Burns, 1977).

In the United States it took longer to recognize the potentially influential role the press could play independently of constitutional and extraconstitutional political institutions. One reason lay in the fact that the institutions themselves employed newspapers as direct mouthpieces of partisan interests. The press in America in the late eighteenth and early nineteenth century was essentially a party press, as witnessed by President Jefferson's providing a patronage slot on the government payroll for the editor of his party's paper. The press as challenger to governing authority would await a later era, that of "yellow journalism," toward the end of the nineteenth century. And it would not be until the publication of Walter Lippmann's classic *Public Opinion* (1922) that a serious effort to analyze the government-press relationship would be made.

Since the Lippmann era, however, the focus on government-press relations has evolved continuously, intensifying considerably in recent decades. No longer limited to discussions of print journalism, the relationship now examines the political role of all of the organs of the news media. Moreover, scholarly interest resides in specialists of a variety of academic disciplines. Hence, in the 1970s alone, for example, major book-length contributions came from political scientists (Epstein, 1973; Sigal, 1973), sociologists (Gans, 1979; Tunstall, 1970; Tuchman, 1978), and communication scientists (Shaw & McCombs, 1977; Blanchard, 1974). Moreover, apparently attempting to emulate—but not surpass—the example set by Lippmann, numerous working journalists now deem it essential at some point in their careers to assess the relationship of government and news media. The result is a sizable supply of volumes, of which those by Reston (1967), Wicker (1978), and Halberstam (1979) are representative.

Three chapters in this *Handbook* address the question of relations between politics and the news media. The first (Chapter 4), is McCombs' review and critique of research into the agenda-setting function of the news media; the second is L. John Martin's survey of the considerable body of research into the general relationship of government and the news media (Chapter 16); and the third, by Blumler and Gurevitch, views the relationship from a social-structural point of view (Chapter 17).

Functional and Systems Analyses

During the period of interest in behavioral approaches to the social sciences, one of the areas provoking considerable activity among political scientists was that of the comparative analysis of political systems. Dissatisfied with merely comparing governments (nation to nation, national to subdivision, subdivision to subdivision, etc.) by describing the institutional features of each, students of comparative politics argued that theory-building in political science would be better advanced by a new tact. That was to agree on the key functions performed by politics in any society, discover the sociopolitical structures performing those functions, then compare each structure across various societies and cultures.

In a highly influential work political scientists Gabriel Almond and James Coleman (1960) spelled out the functional requisites on which a comparative analysis of politics should rest: the "common properties of political systems" (pp. 9-58). One such function they identified as "the political communication function." "All of the functions performed in the political system" they noted, "are performed *by means* of communication." For this reason, they observed, "at first thought, it might appear that there is no political communication function as such, that communication is an aspect of all other functions." What, then, might justify the differentiation? For Almond and Coleman, it was the fact that "in the modern political system differentiated media of communication have arisen which have developed a vocational ethics of 'neutral' or objective communication" (p. 45). Such ethics require that, analytically, the dissemination of information should be treated separately from other functions. Almond and Coleman then pointed out that the separation was not unique only to modern political systems but could also apply to ancient systems—Mercury in the Greek Pantheon; duty messengers in the Old Testament; drummers and runners, medieval criers, heralds, and so on.

Picking up on this structural/functional approach to the study of political communication, a number of works have attempted to identify, isolate, and compare the institutions of political communication across national systems. For example, Fagan (1966) attempts to apply the structural/functional approach to cross-national comparisons of networks of political communication, flows of political images, determinants of communication patterns, and the influence of communication on governmental performance and political change. In a more restrictive effort, Almond and Powell (1966) compare the *functions* performed by the political communication *function* in developing nations. The essays in the volume of Nimmo and Mansfield (1981) compare the structures of government and news media relations across several political systems.

Studies derived from the Almond and Coleman model treat political communication in different ways. However, in a major treatise, Deutsch (1963) views all of government and politics as an exercise in communication and control. Deutsch thus applies cybernetics theory to the holistic analysis of political systems, emphasizing concepts of feedback, goals, purposes, learning capacities, autonomy, self-closure, and growth. Provocative though his speculations are, there have been few attempt to build upon Deutsch's work. Galnoor has made the most explicit effort, first reviewing the contours of a systems approach to political communication (1980) and applying it in the case of the Israeli political system (1981). Other works that make reference to Deutsch's model, however, either direct their attention to side issues, thus losing sight of the main thrust of a cybernetic approach (Meadow, 1980; Merritt, 1972), or base their analyses on Deutsch's earlier, more limited (1953), efforts to analyze national development as a function of trends in social communication (Merritt, 1966).

Although studies arising out of the traditions of the structural/functional and systems analyses approaches to political communication may provide considerable insight in the future, the relative absence of such investigations to date do not warrant treating either area as a separate substantive domain of study at present. Hence, readers of the *Handbook* will not find a chapter devoted to inquiries in these traditions. Such studies are, of course, represented implicitly in selected chapters, including that on the diffusion of political information (Chapter 3) by Robert Savage.

Technological Changes

The evolving interest in political communication derived from the academic spheres outlined above also emerged from a number of miscellaneous developments. It is convenient to label these changes in technology. Three merit special mention—changes in the diffusion of political information, the development of professional campaign techniques, and increased sophistication in research methodology.

Media Technology. As noted above, in the early days of the U.S. republic the press consisted primarily of partisan newspapers. Out of that era evolved periods of story journalism, sensationalist reporting, contemporary newspapers and news magazines, and the more recent emergence of electronic journalism (Nimmo, 1981). Similar trends developed in Great Britain (Johnson, 1981) and in a wide variety of other nations in Europe, North America, and Australia (Nimmo & Mansfield, 1981).

In part at least, the evolution of journalism has been a function of developments in media technology. The changes in print and the advent of sound and then visual media have certainly left marks on politics, an overall impact researchers have examined with keen interest. Few stories (even if apocryphal) so well illustrate the impact as that related of publisher William Randolph Hearst's fomenting of the Spanish-American War. Witnessing his *New York Journal* locked in a circulation fight with rival Joseph Pulitzer's *New York World,* Hearst sent artist Frederic Remington to Cuba to send back visual accounts of the insurrection against the Spanish. But Remington wired Hearst: "Everything is quiet. There is no trouble here. There will be no war. I wish to return." Hearst, undaunted, responded: "Please remain. You furnish pictures. I will furnish war" (Knightly, 1975, pp. 57-58).

If newspapers had their impact on political events, so did radio, film, and television. Scholars can scarcely ignore the role played by the electronic media in the contemporary history of either democracies or totalitarian systems. Recognizing the advantages provided by radio for mass communication, Franklin D. Roosevelt hired poets and playwrights to help him craft a Lincolnesque image to be disseminated via radio and newsreels (Jones, 1974). In the same era, Joseph Goebbels was explicit in his plans to exploit both sound and film as the media for bringing Adolf Hitler to power, keeping him there, and winning his war (Reimann, 1976).

A spate of voting studies already cited (Mendelsohn & O'Keefe, 1976; Patterson & McClure, 1976; Patterson, 1980) have explored television's impact on one facet of political life. Barber (1980) went on to argue that the evolution of media technology has created and reinforced a fundamental pattern in American electoral politics. He maintains that the media cover presidential elections in 12-year cycles, each election in the cycle evoking a predictable drama. The cycle begins with a political drama of conflict (1900, 1948, 1960, and 1972 are examples) in which campaign coverage emphasizes the divisive, cleavage-ridden side of American politics. Four years later media coverage likens the presidential campaign (1916, 1940, 1964, and 1976 are Barber's key illustrations) to a drama of conscience wherein the good and moral side of politics shows through. The final election in each cycle (for example, 1920, 1932, 1956, 1968) emerges in media coverage as a drama of conciliation—one of bringing the nation together, binding old wounds, and offering a new beginning. Much can be said in praise and criticism of Barber's Polybian thesis, but the key point is that he takes seriously the interlocking relationship of media technology to politics, even hinting that there may be a media determinism inherent in political events. Such a viewpoint goes far to promote the growth of political communication as a field worthy of serious inquiry.

Campaign Techniques. Parallel with evolving technologies of political communication have been adjustments in the techniques of political campaigning. Jensen (1980), after examining the campaign styles of all presidential elections from 1800 through 1980, noted three classifications of campaign styles and techniques, two with variations. The first, most common to campaigns in the era of the party press, was the *rally* campaign. A rally activates and reinforces party loyalties. Its goal is not to convert partisans but to mobilize one's own and overwhelm the opposition at the polls with sheer numbers. There were two variations: The army rally involved tight, military-like organizations of precinct and ward loyalists, communication to the rank and file via party newspapers (there were 1630 in the U.S. by 1850), and crowd-pleasing oratory; the missionary rally was designed to create a new movement or rebuild an old one through membership in clubs, evangelical appeals, and educational forums. In sum, the rally derived from a network of interpersonal and print communication. After the turn of this century, however, with the development of mass circulation newspapers, radio, film, and television, the *advertising* campaign became the norm. Candidates were mass marketed, brand (party) loyalties counted for less, public relations and advertising techniques came to the fore, and consumer (voter) surveys helped segment and target the market. Jensen notes that the advertising strategy first emerged in 1916; since that time an entire campaigning industry has grown around it (Agranoff, 1976; Nimmo, 1970; Rosenbloom, 1973). Finally, interspersed throughout the rally and advertising have been *crusade* (and countercrusade) campaigns. Notes Jensen (p. 49), "The dominant characteristic of the crusade is a pervasive moral fervor that animates both the standard bearer and his supporters to extirpate evil from government in the name of the people." Hence, "evil powerholders must be routed; apocalyptic doom is prophesied if the forces of evil prevail; war, social calamities, economic exploitation, or deep injustice all lie just around the corner." Crusades employ the full panoply of campaign media: mass meetings, parades, newsletters, distinctive logos, and mass communication. Conversion, not mobilization, purification, not fabrication, and moral as much as political victory are the goals.

Research Techniques. The influence of changing media technologies on politics and of changing campaign techniques on appeals via the media have both caught the fancy of an emerging community of researchers in political communication. It is doubtful, however, that the various antecedents of the emerging scholarly field would have reached confluence if the researchers themselves had not become increasingly self-conscious about the assumptions underlying their efforts, the methodologies guiding their research, and the techniques providing their evidence. One of the hallmarks of the behavioral period in the social sciences was the effort to apply hitherto neglected (and usually quantifiable) techniques to the analysis of social events. In many respects political communication research ceased to lag behind similar work in "other substantive fields of social science" (the charge made in 1956 by Eulau, Eldersveld, and Janowitz) when it, too, grew more methodologically sophisticated. As we shall see, and as amply illustrated in the chapters of this *Handbook* in the section on "Methods of Study," researchers now employ a wide range of qualitative and quantitative techniques but in an increasingly self-critical manner that looks to considerable methodological refinements in the future (consult the concluding essay in this volume, "Constructing the Realities of a Pluralist Field").

FROM DIVERSIFIED ORIGINS
TO A PLURALIST BEGINNING:
AN OVERVIEW OF HANDBOOK CONTENTS

We have described the current status of political communication as an emerging field of inquiry and traced selected aspects of its lineage. However, readers will note that we have not specified the precise substantive content of the field, nor have we defined the field's boundaries. There are reasons for that. One lies in the absence of consensus among political communication scholars regarding content and boundaries. This is not for want of proferred definitions. For example, political communication has been defined as "any exchange of symbols or messages that to a significant extent have been shaped by, or have consequences for, the functioning of political systems" (Meadow, 1980, p. 4); "cummunicatory activity considered political by virtue of its consequences, actual and potential, that it has for the functioning of the political system" (Fagen, 1966, p. 20); "the role of communication in the political process" (Chaffee, 1975, p. 15); "communication (activity) considered political by virtue of its consequences (actual and potential) which regulate human conduct under conditions of conflict" (Nimmo, 1978, p. 7); communication with actual or potential "effects on the functioning of a political state or other political entity" (Blake & Haroldsen, 1975, p. 44); and the political symbols salient in the elite press (Arora & Lasswell, 1969). To be sure, the bulk of these characterizations agree that there is some body of activity which is "communication" (but scholars do not agree what activity); another body of activity called "politics" (again, there is little agreement on what that activity is); and that when the former activity influences the latter, there is "political communication" (but once again, the nature of that influence is not a matter of concurrence).

There is another reason for avoiding the problem of precise characterization of the scholarly field. If there is a lack of consensus among students of political communication on a definition of subject matter, so also do they disagree on goals. In the spirit of the behavioral era that provided the impetus for the field's emergence, students concur that theory-building is their task; that is, the construction of a body of tested, confirmed, explanatory generalizations. But there are different visions of what shape such theory should take. Deutsch (1963) and his followers strive for a communication *theory of politics,* one that considers all political activity as systems of communication and control. Other researchers, viewing neither all of politics as communication nor all of communication as politics, aim for a *theory of political communication* (Fagen, 1966; Chaffee, 1975). The result would be a functionalist-oriented body of generalizations akin to those derived by scholars seeking a theory of political leadership, a theory of political socialization, a theory of public policy-making, and so on. Finally, there are researchers speculating that communication is political in achieving/disrupting social order; hence communication has key political dimensions—power, influence, authority, control, negotiation, symbolic transaction, and the like. Thus, a *political theory of communication* warrants aspiration (Bell, 1975; Mueller, 1973).

For a field of such disparate origins and recent vintage it is perhaps not surprising to find only superficial agreement on definitions and explicit debate on goals. And this constitutes a third reason for shunning the temptation to attempt a definitive statement of what the field of political communication is, where it is going. Decades ago a lifelong journalist and social scientist pondered the desirability of trying to define government as isolated from other forms of social activity (Bentley, 1908), a problem like trying to separate politics from communication, political communication from other varieties of communicatory activity. Bentley decided the effort was not only in vain but a dangerous exercise:

> One more question remains as to this raw material for the study of government. Ought we not to draw a distinction in advance between it and other varieties of social activity, so that we can have our field of study defined and delimited at the outset? The answer is No. Many a child, making paper toys, has used his scissors too confidently and cut himself off from the materials he needs. This is an error to avoid [p. 199].

To behave like the too-confident child in approaching political communication would be particularly foolish. The field's current immaturity and diverse antecedents make of it a pluralist endeavor that as yet defies neat characterization. As the chapters in this *Handbook* demonstrate, political communication is a field with continuously evolving theoretical approaches, subject matter areas, and methodological stances. As yet there are no fixed boundaries, hardened dogmas, methodological orthodoxies, or conventional truths. The flavor of that pluralist core of the field of political communication, we believe, pervades each of the four major sections of this *Handbook.*

Contemporary Theoretical Approaches

One can scarcely say that the youthful field of political communication research, viewed as "a system of laws" (Kaplan, 1964, p. 297), is theory-bound. Rather, as with most fields of the social sciences, political communication abounds in "quasi-theories" (Meehan, 1965) or "approaches"—that is, alternative sets of criteria employed in selecting problems or questions for investigation and relevant data (Van Dyke, 1960). Various generic classifications of such approaches exist, such as mechanistic versus organismic, structural and/or functional, systems versus process, cross-sectional versus developmental, and so on. Alternatively, approaches may be thought of as strictly tied to specialized academic disciplines—historical, anthropological, sociological, and others (Van Dyke, 1960; Budd & Ruben, 1972).

Although overt controversy has been muted, there are strong differences among political communication scholars regarding the most promising approach to take to their field. The chapters in Part I provide a sampling of those differences. Therein appear the approaches that have been most frequently employed along with two—critical and constructivist—in early stages of formulation. It is unnecessary to preview the contents of each of those chapters here, but a few words are in order to alert readers to a few fundamental differences implicit in the essays.

First, all of the chapters note the subjective nature of political communication; that is, all recognize that political communication is more than a mechanical linkage between communicators bent on transmitting messages and passive audiences which readily accept them. In short, the tradition of the hypodermic-needle approach receives short shrift. But just how large a role human subjectivity plays in political communication and how much that subjectivity is patterned or structured is a matter of dispute. Thus Combs, in the opening essay, attributes a creative role to subjectivity, going so far as to suggest that political realities are created through the communication process in a universe of the absurd. McLeod and Becker do not go so far, focusing instead on how the uses people make of political communication and the satisfactions derived from media and messages influence political conduct. Savage takes note of patterns of information diffusion through political communication, stressing a complex mingling of subjective and structural influences on those patterns. McComb's discussion of the agenda-setting facets of the political communication media raises questions of the factors shaping the subjective priorities of audiences. Lanigan, deriving his posture from recent developments in critical theory, relates linguistic structures to subjective appraisals. Swanson's concern parallels, but in key ways certainly differs with, that expressed by Combs—that is, attention to what transpires through the active constructions of messages and meanings by processors of political information.

Second, readers will note that the authors of each of the chapters in the *Handbook's* first section draw on different schools of thought in fashioning their approaches. Combs is influenced by traditions of symbolic interactionist and existential thought; McLeod and Becker are functionalist in orientation; Savage draws on a wide variety of traditions, principally agricultural sociology; McCombs reflects enduring concerns of researchers in mass communication; Lanigan draws on philosophic trends in the neo-Marxist tradition; and Swanson exploits the perspective of psychological construct theory.

Finally, we urge readers as they examine the chapters of the *Handbook* dealing with the modes and means of persuasive communication, settings of political communication, and methodology to take note of how the various assumptions, philosophical viewpoints, and disciplinary perspectives implicit in this first recur. The issues raised in any discussion of approaches to the study of political communication are fundamental and enduring. As such, they have influenced substance and methodology of the emerging field and will undoubtedly contribute to the course of the field's development in the future.

Modes and Means of Persuasive Communication in Politics

At the core of political communication is the process of persuasion—the reciprocal efforts of people to influence one another. The process takes many forms: for example, the dissemination of information (Becker, McCombs, & McLeod, 1975); manipulation (Goodin, 1980); propaganda (Ellul, 1965); and a host of other means producing a complex matrix of media, persuasive modes, and effects (McGuire, 1973).

The second section of the *Handbook* focuses on four aspects of persuasion that play a major part in contemporary political communication. First, Graber analyzes politics as a "word game," describing the types, functions, settings, and effects of political languages. In so doing she builds on a tradition of linguistic analysis which is clearly different from either that posed by Combs (Chapter 1) or Lanigan (Chapter 5), differences that again highlight the pluralist character of political communication. Second, Bitzer examines the nature and relevance of political rhetoric in the persuasive process. His stance is that of a critic, both describing and evaluating the use of rhetoric in serving political purposes. Again, readers should reflect on the differences in Bitzer's analysis and that posed in other chapters, especially by Lanigan (Chapter 5) and Brown (Chapter 22). Third, Kaid provides a detailed account of political advertising, surely one of the most pervasive modes of contemporary political persuasion. Through a discussion of the interrelations of sources, channels, audiences, and effects of political advertising, Kaid draws conclusions regarding the general character of advertising in politics and suggests gaps for future inquiry. Finally, Kraus describes the ever-increasing role of political debates in providing the governed in political systems with opportunities to evaluate and choose between those who aspire to govern. Political debates incorporate as persuasive opportunities linguistic and rhetorical devices already alluded to by Graber and by Bitzer, yet offer an alternative mode to advertising in the persuasive process.

Political Communication Settings

It is not surprising that many of subject areas that were antecedent to the development of political communication as a field of inquiry are still represented in the research of the field's scholars. Readers of the *Handbook* will find this reflected in a number of the chapters devoted to political communication settings. For example, the traditional attitude change focus remains in altered, implicit form in studies relating communication and political socialization (discussed by Charles Atkin in Chapter 11), communication in election campaigns (reviewed by O'Keefe and Atwood in Chapter 12), and mass communication to public opinion (Zukin's Chapter 13). And election campaigns provide the setting for continuing the tradition of voting studies, although taking the role of communication more seriously than did many of the earlier generation studies (Chapter 12). Finally, the focus on the relation of government to the news media is as vital a research area today as ever, as demonstrated by Martin's assessment of scholarly efforts in Chapter 16, and by Blumler and Gurevitch's more structural approach in Chapter 17.

But as political communication studies develop, new areas of investigation, either only hinted at earlier or ignored completely, are evolving. Two of those are highlighted in this volume. In Chapter 14 Cobb and Elder provide an all-too-rare review, synthesis, and critique of the role of communication in the making of public policy. Although "the policy process" has been a subject of inquiry stressed by political scientists since the mid-1960s, there has been a curious reluctance to investigate in systematic ways how communication influences policy-making. The burden of the Cobb and Elder argument is that communication is more than incidental to the policy process—indeed, it is a major dynamic of it. In Chapter 15 Simons and Mechling offer insights into another significant area of political communication, perhaps not as neglected as public policy but nonetheless underplayed in early research. That is the role played by political communication in creating, advancing, and mobilizing collective movements. Readers will note that much of what pertains to the political communication of social movements applies directly to the modes and means of political persuasion, as well as to the role of communication in political campaigns and in public opinion.

Methods of Study

In its emergence as a separate field out of the cross-disciplinary trends in the behavioral era, political communication borrowed research methods and techniques in a largely uncritical fashion from various disciplines. Rhetorical criticism emerged from speech communication, content analysis from propagandistic studies, experimental techniques from attitude change research, and large-sample surveys from the voting studies. However, as research began to accumulate in specialized areas, an awareness grew among scholars that these borrowed methods—although useful in many respects—required refinement and buttressing if they were to advance the art and science of political communication. Hence, in the past decade students of political communication have become increasingly critical of available methods, making efforts to overcome the limitations of traditional tools and reaching out for more appropriate devices.

Five contributions to the *Handbook* make critical statements regarding the leading methods currently employed in political communication research. In Chapter 18 Wander presents a wide-ranging discussion of the relationship of cultural criticism to political communication, touching on a variety of subject areas, including one of vast political relevance too often ignored: popular culture. In Chapter 19 Hofstetter provides an extensive review and critique of studies in political communication that have utilized content analysis; in the process he suggests ways for improving that venerable research method. Both laboratory and field experimentation offer promising ways to address key questions in political communication. In Chapter 20 Miller examines the possibilities and problems associated with experimental designs. The staple of the voting studies and public opinion studies was, and remains today, the method of survey research. Efforts to improve survey techniques have generally focused on problems of sampling and representativeness. However, as Bishop relates in his critique of survey research in Chapter 21, considerable attention needs to be given to other problems—question filtering, wording, meaning, and format—that suggest the failure of survey technicians to come to grips with the absence of a model explaining the cognitive processes underlying verbal reports. Finally, in Chapter 22, Brown argues that since political communication is essentially a subjective process, a great deal can be learned by applying the techniques of intensive analysis to single cases of political behavior. Employing a study of perceptions of public figures, he illustrates how that can be accomplished through the application of Q-methodology.

CONCLUSION:
CONSTRUCTING THE REALITIES
OF A PLURALIST FIELD

As fields of investigation go, political communication is obviously still in its infancy. At this stage of its development a *Handbook of Political Communica-*

tion can contribute to the field's development in two respects. First, as the chapters in this volume do, it can assess the current state of research areas, assumptions, methods, and applications. Beyond that, however, such a handbook must do more than take stock; it must point out neglected approaches, areas, and methods of inquiry and suggest where the field may direct its attention in the future. Moreover, it should raise questions about the practical applications (for campaigning, persuasion, public policy, etc.) of political communication research. Although a scholarly field, political communication has roots in practical concerns, roots that also provide future directions. We address the field's future in the concluding essay of the *Handbook*.

Finally, as an aid to readers wishing to transcend the limits necessarily placed on a single-volume statement of the boundaries of a dynamic field, two essays are appended. The first is Fitchen's brief summary of political communication study as undertaken in Europe; the second is a guide to bibliographic materials, information sources, and relevant organizations.

REFERENCES

Agranoff, R. *The management of election campaigns.* Boston: Holbrook Press, 1976.

Allen, R. W., & Greene, L. *The propaganda game.* New Haven, CT: Autotelic Instructional Materials, 1969.

Almond, G. A., & Coleman, J. F. (Eds.). *The politics of developing areas.* Princeton: Princeton University Press, 1960.

Almond, G. A., & Powell, G. B., Jr. *Comparative politics: A developmental approach.* Boston: Little, Brown, 1966.

Arora, S., & Lasswell, H. E. *Political communications: The public language of political elites in India and the United States.* New York: Holt, Rinehart & Winston, 1969.

Barber, J. D. *The pulse of politics.* New York: W. W. Norton, 1980.

Becker, L. B., McCombs, M. E., & McLeod, J. M. The development of political cognitions. In S. Chaffee (Ed.), *Political communication.* Beverly Hills, CA: Sage, 1975.

Bell, D.V.J. *Power, influence, and authority.* New York: Oxford University Press, 1975.

Bentley, A. F. *The process of government.* Chicago: University of Chicago Press, 1908.

Berelson, B., Lazarsfeld, P., & McPhee, W. *Voting.* Chicago: University of Chicago Press, 1954.

Black, E. *Rhetorical criticism, a study in method.* Madison: University of Wisconsin Press, 1978. (Originally published, 1965)

Blair, H. [*Lectures on rhetoric and belles lettres*] (2 vols.) (H. Harding, ed.). Carbondale: Southern Illinois University Press, 1965. (Originally published, 1783)

Blake, R. H., & Haroldsen, E. O. *A taxonomy of concepts in communication.* New York: Hastings House, 1975.

Blanchard, R. O. (Ed.). *Congress and the news media.* New York: Hastings House, 1974.

Blanchard, R. O., & Wolfson, L. Courses on the media, government, and public policy. *News for Teachers of Political Science,* 1980, *25,* 14-15.

Blumler, J. G., & McQuail, D. *Television in politics.* Chicago: University of Chicago Press, 1969.

Brigance, W. (Ed.). *A history and criticism of American public address* (2 vols.). New York: McGraw-Hill, 1943.

Brock, B. L., & Scott, R. L. (Eds.). *Methods of rhetorical criticism* (2nd ed.). Detroit: Wayne State University Press, 1980.

Budd, R., & Ruben, B. (Eds.). *Approaches to human communication.* Rochelle Park, NJ: Hayden Book Co., 1972.

Burns, T. *The BBC: Public institution and private world.* London: Macmillan, 1977.

Campbell, A., Converse, P., Miller, W. E., & Stokes, D. *The American voter*. New York: John Wiley, 1960.

Campbell, A., Converse, P., Miller, W. E., & Stokes, D. *Elections and the political order*. New York: John Wiley, 1966.

Campbell, A., Gurin, G., & Miller, W. E. *The voter decides*. New York: Harper & Row, 1954.

Campbell, G. [*The philosophy of rhetoric*] (2 vols.) (L. Bitzer, ed.). Carbondale: Southern Illinois University Press, 1963. (Originally published, 1776)

Chaffee, S. (Ed.). *Political communication*. Beverly Hills, CA: Sage, 1975.

Dahl, R. A. The behavioral approach in political science: An epitaph for a monument to a successful protest. *American Political Science Review*, 1961, *55*, 763-772.

Deutsch, K. *Nationalism and social communication*. Cambridge: MIT Press, 1953.

Deutsch, K. *The nerves of government*. New York: Free Press, 1963.

Efron, E. *The news twisters*. Los Angeles: Nash Publishing, 1971.

Ellel, J. *Propaganda*. New York: Alfred A. Knopf, 1965.

Encyclopedia of the social sciences. New York: Macmillan, 1930.

Epstein, E. J. *News from nowhere*. New York: Vintage Books, 1973.

Eulau, H., Eldersveld, S. J., & Janowitz, M. (Eds.). *Political behavior*. New York: Free Press, 1956.

Fagen, R. R. *Politics and communication*. Boston: Little, Brown, 1966.

Festinger, L. *A theory of cognitive dissonance*. Evanston, IL: Row, Peterson, 1957.

Galnoor, I. Political communication and the study of politics. In D. Nimmo (Ed.), *Communication yearbook 4*. New Brunswick, NJ: Transaction Books, 1980.

Galnoor, I. *The Israeli political system*. Beverly Hills, CA: Sage, 1981.

Gans, H. J. *Deciding what's news*. New York: Pantheon, 1979.

Goodin, R. E. *Manipulatory politics*. New Haven, CT: Yale University Press, 1980.

Gosnell, H. F. *Getting out the vote*. Chicago: University of Chicago Press, 1927.

Graber, D. A. *Mass media and American politics*. Washington, DC: Congressional Quarterly Press, 1980.

Halberstam, D. *The powers that be*. New York: Alfred A. Knopf, 1979.

Heider, F. Attitudes and cognitive organization. *Journal of Psychology*, 1946, *21*, 107-112.

Hochmuth, M. K. (Ed.). *A history and criticism of American public address*. New York: Russell and Russell, 1965.

Hofstetter, R. *Bias in the news*. Columbus: Ohio State University Press, 1976.

Hovland, C. I. (Ed.). *The order of presentation in persuasion*. New Haven, CT: Yale University Press, 1957.

Hovland, C. I., & Janis, I. L. (Eds.). *Personality and persuasibility*. New Haven, CT: Yale University Press, 1959.

Hovland, C. I., Janis, I. L., & Kelley, H. H. *Communication and persuasion*. New Haven, CT: Yale University Press, 1953.

Hovland, C., Lumsdaine, A. A., & Sheffield, F. D. *Experiments on mass communication*. Princeton: Princeton University Press, 1949.

Hovland, C. I., & Rosenberg, M. J. (Eds.). *Attitude organization and change*. New Haven, CT: Yale University Press, 1960.

Jensen, R. Armies, admen and crusaders: Strategies to win elections. *Public Opinion*, 1980, *3*, 44-49, 52-53.

Johnson, K. S. Political party and media evolution in the United States and Great Britain. In J. P. McKerns (Ed.), *Communications research symposium* (vol. 4). Knoxville: University of Tennessee, College of Communications, 1981.

Jones, A. H. *Roosevelt's image-brokers*. Port Washington, NY: Kennikat Press, 1974.

Kaid, L. L., Sanders, K. R., & Hirsch, R. O. *Political campaign communication: A bibliography and guide to the literature*. Metuchen, NJ: Scarecrow Press, 1974.

Kaplan, A. *The conduct of inquiry*. San Francisco: Chandler Publishing, 1964.

Klapper, J. T. *The effects of mass communication*. New York: Free Press, 1960.

Knightly, P. *The first casualty*. New York: Harcourt Brace Jovanovitch, 1975.

Kraus, S., & Davis, D. *The effects of mass communication on political behavior.* University Park: Pennsylvania State University Press, 1976.
Kuhn, T. S. *The structure of scientific revolutions.* Chicago: University of Chicago Press, 1962.
Lasswell, H. D. *Propaganda technique in the world war.* New York: Peter Smith, 1927.
Lasswell, H. D., & Leites, N. *Language of politics: Studies in quantitative semantics.* Cambridge: MIT Press, 1949.
Lazarsfeld, P., Berelson, B., & Gaudet, H. *The people's choice.* New York: Duell, Sloan and Pearce, 1944.
Lippmann, W. *Public opinion.* New York: Macmillan, 1922.
McGuire, W. J. Persuasion, resistance, and attitude change. In I. de Sola Pool, W. Schramm, F. Frey, N. Maccoby, & E. B. Parker (Eds.), *Handbook of communication.* Chicago: Rand McNally, 1973.
Meadow, R. B. *Politics as communication.* Norwood, NJ: ABLEX Publishing, 1980.
Meehan, E. *The theory and method of political analysis.* Homewood, IL: Dorsey Press, 1965.
Mendelsohn, H., & O'Keefe, G. *The people choose a president.* New York: Praeger, 1976.
Merriam, C. E., & Gosnell, H. F. *Non-voting.* Chicago: University of Chicago Press, 1924.
Merritt, R. L. *Symbols of American community, 1735-1775.* New Haven, CT: Yale University Press, 1966.
Merritt, R. L. Political science: An approach to human communication. In R. W. Budd & B. D. Ruben (Eds.), *Approaches to human communication.* Rochelle Park, NJ: Hayden Book Co., 1972.
Miller, W. E., & Levitin, T. E. *Leadership and change.* Cambridge: Winthrop, 1976.
Mueller, C. *The politics of communication.* New York: Oxford University Press, 1973.
Nie, N. H., Verba, S., & Petrocik, J. R. *The changing American voter.* Cambridge: Harvard University Press, 1976.
Nimmo, D. *The political persuaders.* Englewood Cliffs, NJ: Prentice-Hall, 1970.
Nimmo, D. *Political communication and public opinion in America.* Santa Monica, CA: Goodyear, 1978.
Nimmo, D. Mass communication and politics. In S. Long (Ed.), *Handbook of political behavior, vol. 4.* New York: Plenum, 1981.
Nimmo, D., & Mansfield, M. (Eds.). *Government and the news media: Cross-national perspectives.* Waco, TX: Baylor University Press, 1981.
Osgood, C. E. Cognitive dynamics in the conduct of human affairs. *Public Opinion Quarterly,* 1960, *24,* 341-365.
Patterson, T. E. *The mass media election.* New York: Praeger, 1980.
Patterson, T. E., & McClure, R. D. *The unseeing eye.* New York: Putnam, 1976.
Pohlmann, M. D., & Foley, T. P. Course outline and readings: Mass media and American politics. *News for Teachers of Political Science,* 1978, *19,* 5, 7, 17.
Reimann, V. *Goebbels: The man who created Hitler.* Garden City, NY: Doubleday, 1976.
Reston, J. *The artillery of the press.* New York: Harper & Row, 1967.
Rice, S. *Quantitative methods in politics.* New York: Alfred A. Knopf, 1928.
Rosenbloom, D. L. *The election men.* New York: Quadrangle, 1973.
Sanders, K. R., Hirsch, R. O., & Pace, T. *Political communication: A bibliography.* Carbondale: Southern Illinois University, School of Communication, 1972.
Schiller, H. I. *The mind managers.* Boston: Beacon, 1973.
Shaw, D. L., & McCombs, M. E. *The emergence of American political issues: The agenda-setting function of the press.* St. Paul, MN: West Publishing, 1977.
Sherif, C. W., Sherif, M., & Nebergall, R. E. *Attitude and attitude change.* Philadelphia: W. B. Saunders, 1965.
Sherif, M., & Hovland, C. I. *Social judgment.* New Haven, CT: Yale University Press, 1961.
Sigal, L. V. *Reporters and officials.* Lexington, MA: D. C. Heath, 1973.
Smith, B. L., Lasswell, H. D., & Casey, R. D. *Propaganda, communication, and public opinion.* Princeton: Princeton University Press, 1946.

Trent, J. A synthesis of methodologies used in studying political communication. *Central States Speech Journal,* 1975, *26,* 278-297.

Truman, D. B. The impact on political science of the revolution in the behavioral sciences. In R. D. Calkins (Ed.), *Research frontiers in politics and government.* Washington, DC: Brookings, 1955.

Tuchman, G. *Making news.* New York: Free Press, 1978.

Tunstall, J. *The Westminster lobby correspondents.* London: Routledge & Kegan Paul, 1970.

Van Dyke, V. *Political science: A philosophical analysis.* Stanford: Stanford University Press, 1960.

Whately, R. [*Elements of rhetoric*] (D. Ehninger, ed.). Carbondale: Southern Illinois University Press, 1963. (Originally published, 1828)

Wicker, T. *On press.* New York: Viking, 1978.

PART I

Contemporary Theoretical Approaches

CHAPTER 1

A Process Approach

James E. Combs

THE PROBLEM OF COPING with process has bedeviled thinkers since the beginnings of human self-reflection. The realities of change, the apparent passage of time, decay and death have inspired a wide variety of philosophical, theological, and poetic attempts to cope with "the empire of Time." There is a strong impulse in human thought to impose some sort of order on the processes of nature and society. Philosophers from Parmenides on have developed a tradition which either denies the reality of change or posits that change has meaning or purpose, leading to some sort of immanent good end. It is significant that theories which argue for an indeterminate, random, chance universe of meaningless becoming have never been popular. Language, and perhaps even thought itself, structures the world into identifiable entities which imbue what may be inchoate and dynamic with qualities of order and permanence. As Zeno long ago delightfully proved, the problem of permanence and change leads us into paradoxes and confusions which may be impossible to resolve. Reflect on the difficulties inherent in the statement, "The only permanent thing in the world is change."

This essay will reflect on the problem of, and the approaches to, the elusive problem of process as it has been formulated as a way to understand politics and political communication.

Central to the problem of utilizing a "process perspective" is that the concept of process is ill-defined. A glance at dictionary definitions highlights the problem: Are we talking about something that is determinate or indeterminate; continuous or discrete; a causal series or a random collocation of events; linear sequences or cycles and rhythms; a procession or a progression; psychic or material, creative or destructive, incremental or catastrophic change; the flow of continuous becoming or the individuality of discrete events; waves or particles?

The antimonies involved here are endless. If nothing else, this should remind us that the casual use of terms like "the political process" or "legislative process" are worse than useless if not conceptualized carefully.

THE CLASSICAL HERITAGE

We should also remind ourselves that conceiving politics as process has a long and rich history. Historians have long been aware of the necessity of understanding processes, and even *the* process, of history. The explanation of change over time requires some use of root metaphors of process—cycles, stages, rhythms, peaks and valleys, rise and fall, youth, maturity, and decay, and so on. Thucydides recounted the naturalistic process of the Peloponnesian war as a historical tragedy, a grand but meaningless chain of human events which led to the end of Athenian greatness. The process of the war was seen as a complex interplay of necessity and chance, of the inexorable direction of political events and decisions impelling the war toward its historical outcome, but wherein those events and decisions were ultimately "fortunate." Pericles' death was a chance event, but it played a large role in what was to be the necessary outcome. Thucydides's conception of process as combinations of antimonies—macroprocesses and microprocesses, chance and necessity, randomness and inevitability—remains the supreme example of the difficulties and power inherent in process explanations of political history.

Similarly, familiarity with some of the classical formulations of political process alerts us to the recrudescence of the problems with the concept. At least since Polybius there have been many attempts to posit historical cycles, recurrent patterns of political change over time, which either repeat themselves or succeed themselves. The elaborate theories of Spengler and Toynbee envisioned recurrent patterns to the rise and fall of civilizations. Hegel and Marx, of course, saw developmental stages in history, a process of conflict and progress over time. Weber, on the other hand, is the model of conceiving historical process as mechanism, a meaningless development of macroprocesses (e.g., the growth of bureaucracy) which are not necessarily progressive, do not fit into neat stages or cycles, or are "rational."

At the risk of collapsing many divergent views of the political macroprocess in history into our own categories, it does seem that there are five clear types of process conceptualizations we may draw from the classical tradition. First, there is the *cyclical* idea of process, in which history repeats itself in identifiable recurrences. Second, there is the *rhythmic* vision, which does not posit cycles but does see sequential patterns to historical and political change over time. Then there is the *developmental-progressive* tradition, which in various ways sees political processes bringing changes for the better through historical stages. This is the opposite of the *developmental-nonprogressive* view, which argues that one can observe and identify the major processes at work in politics, but not as part of some progressive historical pattern. Finally, there is the less popular but equally respectable view that the political process is unintelligible, insane, and ultimately *random,* part of no pattern or development that can be identified, rationality that can be imposed, or even causal chain that can be posited. This last view may be associated with existentialism, but it goes back at least to Hume in philosophy and to Machiavelli in political philosophy.

Machiavelli is the bogeyman of political philosophy, but he appears to have been the first major thinker who argued that politics was a process pure and simple, devoid of the redeemable features posited by the other thinkers we have mentioned, occurring in an impermanent and unstable world, with *fortuna* ultimately governing the outcomes of political situations and with history and politics going just somewhere. We may refer to this as the *dynamic* view of political process. The political world is beyond redemption or understanding, continuous activity in the pursuit of power, an insane struggle in changing and chance circumstances. The dynamism of the political process makes it out of control and even understanding. More than any other idea of process, this last vision is the most troublesome, since it most threatens our desire for order.

THE INFLUENCE OF
MODERN PHILOSOPHY AND PHYSICS

The idea of process has been given great impetus in modern times by the philosophical reflections inspired by the new physics and biology, especially what is loosely termed "process philosophy." The discoveries that space and time were not separate and absolute, that biological nature was dynamic and evolving, that the behavior of subatomic particles was apparently indeterminate all had their effect. Let us mention four influential thinkers in the field of process philosophy and the school of thought most associated with the idea of process: pragmatism.

Nietzsche (1954) saw life as a torrent of change and man as engaged in an endless process of Becoming. Further, he saw life revolving in cycles of "eternal recurrence," decay and revival. Bergson (1955) posited the idea of duration, which saw reality as a seamless temporal process, containing both some determining aspects from the past but also novelties stemming from intuitive creativity in the act. Like Bergson, Whitehead (1978) dealt with the meaning of process by linking it to an obscure metaphysics. Both appeared to believe in progress through the "creative advance of nature." An influential Catholic thinker, Tielhard de Chardin (1959) saw evolution as a creative force of which "the phenomenon of man" was the supreme creation. Unlike Nietzsche, these thinkers gave their notions of process theological overtones.

The pragmatists on the whole resisted the temptation to link natural and social process to divine providence. Pierce (1931-1958) developed a difficult evolutionary cosmology, a reality of "continua" in dynamic change in a universe characterized by objective chance. The more popular theories of James (1912) and Dewey (1917) continued this emphasis on dynamic evolution in nature, all with at least an implicit belief in progress. Dewey in particular argued that problems of communication were vital to the success of democracy, and that the processes of growth would be furthered by the creation of a social science at the disposal of a self-conscious "public."

MEAD'S "PHILOSOPHY OF THE PRESENT"

A work that is worth separate and more elaborate mention here is George Herbert Mead's *Philosophy of the Present* (1932/1959). This is perhaps the major attempt at a pragmatic cosmology and is based upon the philosophical and scientific heritage mentioned above. Mead is concerned with placing human action in a temporal universe of change and "openness," of both continuity and emergent novelty. To do so, he comes to a startling conclusion: If the world is process, then the reality of a past and a future must be denied. Reality exists in a present; the present, the flow of events as we experience them now, is the only reality. The past occurred, and the future will occur, but their reality is only in how they "exhibit" themselves in the present. From the perspective of the present, the past and the future have meaningful existence, not in terms of what actually occurred or might occur, but rather in terms of the uses of the past and future now. The past is "mediated" in a sense in the present, and successive presents "reconstruct" the past and the future for their own purposes. The radical relativity of past and future is a discomfiting notion, but it does make us aware of the ways in which dynamic presents reconstruct time past and time future for time present. The paradox is that even though the past is in a sense irrevocable, it is in another sense quite revocable, and is done so all the time, as with the "revisionism" of historians. We have many past pasts and will have many future futures. Mead's formulation is complex and rich and deserves detailed treatment by process theorists. He does not deal explicitly with communication, but certainly his emphasis on the extent to which the past and future are objects "known" in a present suggests that present communication about the nature and character of past and future should underscore the importance of knowledge communicated in a present.

Pragmatism was the intellectual godfather of several major developments in social science, including communications theory and the "symbolic interactionist" school (see below). If the pragmatic metaphysic has merit, then it followed that communications was central to ongoing human transactions and must be understood as process. This idea was to have influence with the famous "Chicago School" but did not become widespread in the social sciences. Nevertheless, the idea of process was to persist in social science and would be linked to the idea of communication by a small group of scholars, often working independently or without widespread influence.

With this philosophical heritage in mind, let us discuss in turn four roughly identifiable "schools" that contributed to the literature with which the student of political-process-as-communication should be familiar. We may label these schools as those encompassing "traditional" views of political process, the symbolic interactionist school, transactional analysis, and dramatism. After discussing each of these we will then offer some evaluation and suggestions for theoretical integration.

DIVERSE RECENT VIEWS OF
PROCESS IN THE SOCIAL SCIENCES

In this category we wish to include a variety of scholars whose work impinges upon the development of a process theory of political communication but which does not clearly fit into the more identifiable schools we will discuss below. However diverse, all the scholars mentioned here made their own contribution to the perspective in question.

Harold Lasswell's "developmental analysis" (Eulau, 1958) was an attempt to conceptualize a process view of politics. Lasswell was directly influenced by the pragmatists and the climate of thought at Chicago. He urged trying to understand the "unfolding manifold of events" in developmental terms, so that we may be able to anticipate the future. Society is seen as a "continuum of social change," characterized by "patterns of succession of events," throwing the "time axis—the 'from what, toward what'—into relief." This would give us perspective on the "whole manifold of events which includes the future as well as the past." Lasswell makes no assumptions about laws of change or progress, nor does he explicitly see history and politics as communication processes.

But Harold Innis (1950) did. He attempted an imaginative vision of historic change as a communication process. In particular, the technology of communication largely determines the kind of social organization dominant in a particular epoch. If the dominant mode of communication is "time-binding," such as in an oral culture, the institutions and values are likely to be traditional, sacred, and hierarchical; if it is "space-binding," such as cultures with writing, institutions and values are likely to be secular, technical and cumulative, and politically expansive. The dynamic of change can be found, then, in major innovations in communications technology. Innis's disciple, Marshall McLuhan (1962), emphasized the subjective changes in perception that communications technology brings rather than changes in social institutions (Carey, 1967). Although their work was not explicitly political, it is not difficult to see the political consequences. Innis in particular explored broad-gauge theses about the process of communication playing a central role in change, and his ideas deserve further exploration by both social scientists and historians.

The political scientist most associated with building models of political communication is undoubtedly Karl Deutsch. His *Nationalism and Social Communication* (1953) remains one of the major attempts to specify the role of communication patterns in the development of a large-scale political process—namely, the development of national identity. His more formal theoretical book, *The Nerves of Government* (1966), was an attempt to use the cybernetic model, with elements drawn from the development of communication engineering and the modeling of the human brain. But two criticisms may be leveled at this rather elaborate model of politics. First, the language has an almost Hegelian tone, with the attribution of "memory," "will," "consciousness," and "spirit" to political collectivities. Second, while the model is based on the assumption that all politics is communication, it is also biased toward a somewhat rationalistic and nondynamic vision of political reality. For Deutsch, government is a "process of steering" by which the system modifies and adjusts itself through the "feedback" of information. The tenor is benevolent and rather optimistic, and the model does not handle well the explosive dynamics of political change with the irrational and fluctuating processes familiar to political historians.

A somewhat more comprehensive attempt to construct a process model of political communication is Thomas L. Thorson's *Biopolitics* (1970). Drawing on diverse sources, Thorson argues for the creation of a theory of political process drawn from the general metaphor of evolution but in which communications plays a key role. The argument rests on a naturalism in which political processes must be seen in the context of natural development. The growth of human society and "consciousness" is a kind of "cultural DNA" in which "evolution becomes conscious of itself." Thorson has been accused of promulgating a new version of natural law, the kind associated with thought in the wake of Hegel's progressive theory of history and Darwin. Although Thorson's book does "take time seriously," there is the implication of progress through the growth of consciousness, an Aristotelian *telos* interwoven with modern developmental notions. But whether the reality of the political convulsions of history "fit" is another question. Too, whether historical and political change can be subsumed within a larger theory of natural evolution is still much debated.

Thorson's book is related to the more inclusive debate in political science over the proper approach to political explanation. This debate takes various forms—positivism versus historicism or "contextualism," hypothetico-deductive versus "paradigmatic," deductive versus inductive, universalistic laws versus relativistic hypotheses (see Gunnell, 1969; Miller, 1972). At the risk of oversimplifying a sophisticated and vigorous debate, we may say that the question of process-in-politics is central to the consequences of adopting one position or another. If one opts for the hypothetico-deductive position, questions of process become secondary, since presumably the universal laws of politics apply at all times and places. Explanation would not aim at the rhythms and spasms of political process in the inchoate process of history, but rather at the structural uniformities of politics which transcend the immediate and palpable variations of place, moment, and situation. The diverse writers discussed here at least have in common some sense of the centrality of either process or communication for politics, although not necessarily both. Yet their works form part of the legacy on which process theories of politics must build.

SYMBOLIC INTERACTIONISM

Another cornerstone of a process theory of politics may be taken from the symbolic interactionist school. George Herbert Mead (1934) is the lawgiver of this school, although the work on process mentioned above has had surprisingly little influence. But his other work contained an assumption of a process universe, and the temporal dimension of social life was to be incorporated in the work of many of his followers. Mead had argued that all of social life had to be understood as a process and that every event contained past, present, and future. Further, every event implied continuous novelty, mutuality, and negotiation. One's very self-identity is negotiated with others in ongoing communication, and a "new self" is constantly being "reconstructed" in the process of interaction. Mead's attempt to conceptualize the "social self" as a communication process is perhaps the best answer to Hume's famous skepticism about the "existence" of the self. The symbolic interactionist school has made relatively few attempts to study politics as a symbolic-interactionist process, and the great bulk of the works that treat politics as communication have seemed blissfully unaware of the "SI" school. Symbolic interaction itself has confined its interests largely to social psychology, with special attention to role behavior, reference group behavior, and substantive microsocial activities such as deviance (Manis & Meltzer, 1967; Rose, 1962). However, the symbolic interactionists are clearly one of the potential sources of a process theory of political communication.

In the spirit of the progmatic philosophy with which it was influenced, symbolic interactionism is an "active" view of human interaction, stressing the ongoing dynamics of interaction as people adjust their actions toward each other and social objects. Some have tried to avoid the "conformist" conception of role-playing, stressing instead that role-playing is a process that is continually being redefined in interaction (Turner in Rose, 1962, pp. 20-40). Others have stressed the so-called "definition of the situation," the importance of meaningful constructions put on contexts of interaction (Blumer, 1969). The centrality of this interpretive process gives this viewpoint a dynamic basis which some of the followers of Mead have retained in their writing.

The communication process is at the core of symbolic interaction. Mind, self, and society all emerge in symbolic communication between people. Mind is the process of acquiring the ability to use and actually using symbols. The self arises, develops, and is transformed in ongoing social interaction. Society is a cauldron of communicative activity. Mind, self, and society are all communication processes and not structures. The social objects of the world are not "things" but rather communication processes, symbolic entities which change over time through interaction and thus new definitions of the situation and the objects of the situation. Political symbols, for example, are communicated in the dynamic process of political activity and changed over time.

The school of symbolic interaction is something of a subculture in sociology, and both the theoretical and empirical results of the school have not satisfied everyone. Certainly it has not affected political science, nor devoted much attention to politics. But let us here discuss briefly four works associated with this school with which the student of political communication should be familiar, since they introduce concepts useful for a process theory of political communication.

First, the idea of *negotiated order* has been developed by Anselm Strauss (1978). In the spirit of Thomas Hobbes, this notion does not assume a permanent or structural basis to society, but maintains that order is constantly negotiated. Institutions, rules, laws, and so forth exist in time. Thus, different people, circumstances, and mutual communication processes give the "order" of one time and place a different character than that at another. Negotiated order—that which is "conserved" and that which is "changed"—occurs by networks of patterned communication establishing and implementing temporary modus operanti. Such "working relationships" have identifiable limits beyond which the organizational "house of cards" is in danger of collapse and must be renegotiated. What seems settled after a while becomes unstuck, and the work of concerted negotiation must be begun again.

The concept of negotiated order is useful, since it assumes a process universe in which the very relationships worked out in the seemingly most stable environments are dependent upon the maintenance of what we might call a "communication contract." People who must "work together" in whatever setting forever recreate the reality that they share by "contractual" negotiation. But the ebb and flow of communication processes gives a shared reality defined in such a contract a new array of circumstances to consider, and thus the contractual settlement can become problematic.

Communication contracts may be quite implicit, informal, and based on unspoken "understandings," but the introduction of *novelty* into communication processes may augur changes in the relationship so subtle that the participants may be only dimly aware of what has changed. Like the poets and peasants of the late medieval period in Huizinga's *Waning of the Middle Ages* (1924), communication contracts are subject to the subversion of novelty. If new messages are introduced into a negotiated order, then the order has to deal with novel elements that did not exist before.

If the above is a modified social contract theory, it shares the difficulties imputed to such theories—mainly that it omits power, coercion, and conflict. Hall (1972) has attempted to overcome this difficulty, including power relations in a discussion of political negotiated orders. For him, politics "represents the areas of social concern which reflect the undefined and unresolved issues which are deemed by participants to necessitate the creation and application of a norm." This implies the problematic outcome of negotiated interactions. The essential elements of the political process involve, in either a manifest or latent form, processes of negotiation. The communication networks that conduct the actual negotiations which "keep things going" are often informal (e.g., "old boy networks" in bureaucracies). This suggests what many observers of politics have always insisted: that the important processes are not found on organizational charts and in public declarations of "consultation" with the "proper authorities," but rather in informal, subtle, but certainly not strictly structural processes. This is not to say that structures are unimportant, only that negotiation is an active process which permeates the formal structures of government. Indeed, it reminds us that structures retain their integrity by the adaptive process through negotiations which define their "presence" in time.

A third work in the tradition of symbolic interaction of interest here is Julius Roth's *Timetables* (1963). This book examines the structuring of time in a hospital, but concludes with some worthwhile speculation about the role of timetables in other social contexts. Timetables, Roth argues, emerge in human life because people want to "structure uncertainty" by structuring their time in everyday life. In group situations, the definition of time—what constitutes a "career," what the rhythms and cycles of time are, what "reference points" are identifiable as signposts for temporal changes or ends—is crucial to the tasks and integrity of the group, as well as the behavior of its members. Indeed, one finds considerable bargaining over timetables within and between groups. Roth examined a relatively small group setting, but even there the conflicts and definitions of time-structuring were considerable. He concludes that "larger social units— even whole nations—may be seen as moving through a series of steps toward more distant goals while bargaining with other nations or social units whose interests and timing are in conflict with theirs" (p. 117).

People communicating in "political time" have reference to political and cultural timetables. Much bargaining in politics involves the timing of events with respect to some defined reference point. For example, the bargaining over the release of the American hostages in Iran in 1980-81 coinciding with the presidential election involved such an attempt to control the timing of events in relation to the political purposes of the parties involved. Elections in general are signposts which define politico-temporal changes and ends, at least as interpreted in retrospect. The elections of 1896, 1932, or 1980 "mean" something as reference points for political beginnings or endings. Elections as well as many other political events participate in the large mythical story of the political culture as it is "worked out" over time.

Some related ideas about time are discussed in Lyman and Scott's *A Sociology of the Absurd* (1970). "Human existence," they argue, "is in effect a journey upon a complex network of timetracks." They note two key dimensions of the social construction of time: the "humanistic-fatalistic" and the "continuous-episodic." In the former case, some people see themselves on time tracks they have chosen and which have elements of adventure, risk, and gamble; others see themselves on tracks that are stultifying and unchosen. In the latter case, people distinguish between long-term and short-term time tracks, temporal periods of inclusive importance and continuity and others of "enclosed" significance and duration. These dimensions can be seen in the careers of political actors and political cultures. A king or president, for instance, may see himself on a political timetrack he has chosen and over which he has considerable control; or he may—especially in times of drift or disaster—see himself as a victim of circumstance, of Machiavelli's *fortuna*. Too, politicians may have a vision of themselves as part of a long-term time track, a continuous march toward some abstract future goal; or they may see themselves captured in the "time of the present," caught in an immediate political episode from which there is no exit.

The works we have mentioned all involve symbolic communication about time, in the sense of how people do deal with time. For the symbolic interactionist, time is *mediated*. It is not a thing apart from the "definitions of temporal situations" in which people take part. Like the self and social order, time is an object of our environment; and since objects are dynamic, mediated by the communications of the actors in a given situation, understanding those mediations becomes crucial to understanding how time works in life. Thus, studying political communication about time gives us considerable insight as to the actual definition and conduct of political life in time.

THE TRANSACTIONAL PERSPECTIVE
AND POLITICAL COMMUNICATION PROCESSES

The transactional perspective is rooted in pragmatism and is not unrelated to symbolic interactionism; but it may be distinguished here because of some of its features, particularly as developed by the philosophical writings of Arthur F. Bentley. Bentley's long career began in journalism and the study of social science, evolved through various aspects of the philosophy of science, and wound up in consideration of epistemology and language. The thrust of his work was the formulation of what has come to be called "transactional" analysis, an ambitious program for inquiry that reflects the conviction that the social sciences should be grounded in the methodological advances in the natural sciences, especially physics.

The term "transaction" is distinguished by Bentley and Dewey (1949; Weinstein, 1971; Hakman, 1958) from "self-action" (things acting on their own powers), and "interaction" (things balanced in discrete and causal interconnection). "Transaction" does not abstract out essences which define some essential natural law that governs human action; nor does it posit a human nature which obeys interactional causal laws, as with chains of billiard balls hitting one another in succession. Rather, the transactional perspective posits a human condition which occurs in fields of action. The human condition does not suggest essential or universal features of human existence, but rather conditions which are a mix of the processes at work in the human world at a particular time and place. This condition is manifest in processes which display a constantly shifting structure and array of empirical phenomena. To cite Weinstein's critique of Bentley,

> neither man as an individual nor man as a fragment of humanity can be determined except as one coordinate of a domain of action including nature, culture, and social processes. Here, the natural, relational, cultural, and personal are not levels of analysis but coordinates of a domain continually undergoing change [Weinstein, 1971, p. 7].

The transactional perspective is obviously influenced by Einsteinian science, with its ideal of "unfractured observation" that understands human action in the full context of space and time, relational complexity and reciprocity, and the kaleidoscope of changing situations.

The transactional perspective, then, posits the most inclusive and complex image of man, nothing less than what Bentley called "man-in-process with environs" (1954, p. 338)—human life in an evolving cosmos of society-in-nature of which the individual is only a part. Man is a "coordinate" in the seamless loom of social and natural space-time, and to extract "causes," "motives," and other single-dimension explanations from a situation is to ignore the full constituents of that situation. The transactional perspective is a kind of ambitious contextualism which insists on no prior assumptions and careful examination of the "act-ual" activities of people as they appear. The "raw material" of the transactional approach, then, is what people do, without reference to alleged universals or deductive propositions. This is in the spirit of Peirce's "abduction," inquiry without preconceptions which must precede induction and deduction.

It became clear to Bentley that society and politics were indeed processes and that the central phenomenon of social process was communication. "We have one great moving process to study," he wrote, "and of this great moving process it is impossible to state any part except as valued in terms of the other parts"

(1967, p. 178). The transactional vision of process is relational, "interlacing," a floating cosmology in which "the continents go, and the islands" in the "fluidness," the passage of "events" (Bentley & Dewey, 1949, pp. 183-184). There are no Archimedian points on which the inquirer can stand and observe a world at stop. It is not Zeno's arrow, but rather the flight of the arrow through space and time that Bentley would observe.

Bentley's processual vision led him to considerations of language, logic, and inquiry as processes within nature. Knowledge is a dynamic process of men talking and writing in languages, and languages are no less subject to transactional analysis simply because they claim to be logical or scientific.

Bentley finally focused on the processes involved in communication. If human life is a vast relational enterprise, a loom of interlacing actions forever in the process of creation, then it must include all those forms of communication we may envision, "things-in-a-world talked about by men, men-in-a-world talking about things, a man-and-thing complex composing the knowing world of Talk" (Ratner in Taylor, 1957, p. 56). Indeed, Bentley, in his valedictory address at the age of 83, concluded that the primal raw materials of transactional inquiry were "linguistic," more precisely "actions, not of individual men, but as wave motions of the linguistic behaviors of men, advancing and receding across the centuries" (Taylor, 1957, p. 212).

Bentley's transactional perspective, then, posits the organic unity of the full communicative event. But to avoid the traditional bifurcation of the "moments" of the communication act, Bentley (1935) attempted to invent a new observation language, naming the basic human act (the Communact), or "men seen in communication," and the Communicane, which includes the "full behavioral observation" of men in communication. Bentley's recognition of the centrality of communication processes offers us a rich conceptual source for a process theory of political communication.

Although Bentley's methodological concerns were written long after his famous *Process of Government,* much of transactional analysis is implicit in that work. The book is, after all, about the "process of government" as it is manifest in group interests in a constant flow of political activity in which groupings and interests emerge, change, and disappear—that is, the actual "performed legis-lating-administering-adjudicating activities of the nation and in the streams and currents of activities that gather among the people and rush into these spheres" (1967, p. 180). Bentley conceives of groups the way communication theorists would: aggregates of men-in-action who share their joint action because they communicate to each other their commonality on some political interest. It is through communication that they share the interest and commit the activity that that makes them a group. When they do not, the group does not exist. Groups are not reified objects, but dynamic "clots" of people whose "existence" and "nature" depends on what and with whom people communicate at a given place and time. The ongoing transactions of individuals-in-action defines the activities, the "interests," of the group.

For Bentley, then, if men define group situations as real, they are real in their consequences. Groups are held together by communication, by the transactions that define symbols which the actors utilize for joint action. Group activity is "relative" to the contemporary mix—the extant "cross-sections"—which define the present and what activities the group defines as relevant to their interests. This insistence on the fluid nature of the group process is not static, as is much of group theory in political science. The transactional viewpoint is methodologically more sophisticated than the usual case studies of interest groups and is considerably more aware of the spatial-temporal setting in which the "communication nets" converge as group activity in politics.

It is central to the dynamic of groups that they share "something" in common, Bently had maintained. Exactly how this communication process operates is one of the keys to the incorporation of transactional analysis into the larger view we urge here. If groups are "communication nets," then the "reality" they create, share, and act upon becomes an identifiable and discoverable "aspect and phase" of group action. We may term this a process of "group knowing," since, as Bentley insisted, the process of knowing is constructed. If groups are a "negotiated order", then exactly how that communications work within the group to give them that quality of group knowledge is crucial.

Bormann's work on group fantasizing seems a promising line of inquiry. It is based on the discovery by Bales (1970) that small groups engage in communication in which they create dramatic realities that they more or less share and conjur with. These shared fantasies have a dramatic form, a kind of story with heroes, villains, narrative, moral, ironies and suspense, and so on. Bormann (1972) argues that these "sumbolic dramas" are also communicated to much larger groups through various media, "chaining out" among people who share the fantasy and thus participate in "group knowing." There is a sense in which these dramatizing communications "create" the group by creating a social reality, however insane or unreal, that the group shares. What this kind of idea offers is how communication links people in groups, even though they may not be physically proximate. What they share is not merely an attitude or motive, but a dramatized vision of a larger reality which they believe is occurring "out there." One can also see how group fantasizing is a process, since it involves definitions shared, interpreted, and negotiated in groups that deal with new "facts" over time by incorporating them into the symbolic reality they have created. Even though this is a "subjective" reality, it is easy to see how it is an "our" experience, transactions among members of the group. And finally, it is also clear how such a shared fantasy can be linked to action, since the fantasy is one of the activities of the group which define it as a group and direct its joint actions in politics.

Of special interest here for the communication researcher is understanding the process of the mediation of political reality. By this we mean the various group fantasies which are media-borne and become part of a "fantasy chain" that people use to "fill out" their envisioned political reality, either through interpretation and sharing of mass-mediated messages or through group-mediated messages that emanate from the group and are mass-mediated for the benefit of people not in the group. Television news, for instance, helps create group identifications by communicated mass-mediated messages which are then interpreted by members of potential groups one to another; but groups also come up with symbolic realities within groups quite independent of media cuing—such as conspiracy theories—which are subsequently "fed" by the use of other media facts and communicated to the world at large. In both cases, the stress is on what Bentley envisioned: the dynamic, shifting, and reality-creating aspects of group action.

DRAMATISTIC THEORY

It might surprise some readers that we have included dramatism in a discussion of process theories of communication, but some reflection reveals the logic. Drama is, after all, a form of communication, both among the actors on the stage and between the actors and the audience that attends the play. But how is it a process theory? Dramatism is relevant to the study of process, we argue, because in the first place the metaphor of the theater is applicable to "real life." That applicability means that the categories of the theater can be used to describe and explain communication in society. The assertion that "all the world's a stage" is an ancient and incisive idea, but one that has gained new credence in recent decades (see Combs and Mansfield, 1976; Brisset & Edgley, 1975). Dramatism is based on the insight that human life is aesthetic and that dramatic theory understands the symbolic actions in life which are manifestations of that aesthetic sense. Dramatics are a strategic resource of communication, and it should not surprise us that drama emerges in contexts of human interaction.

The man who gave impetus to the rediscovery of drama in life is Kenneth Burke (1945). Burke reminded us to see dramatics in life as a "grammar," a communicative logic which occurs in social contexts conducive to that interactional strategy. The existential logic of situations "dictates" or "transforms" the situation into one in which dramatic communications emerge. The histrionic strategies of the lover, the public speaker, or the diplomat are brought to bear in situations in which it "makes sense" or "is expected" that dramatic communication will be utilized. Burke, then, pointed up the dramatic structure-in-process, of how drama is used as a communicative resource in the social process. As two acute observers put it, "a consequence of Burke's thought was that one was enabled to see the *social process within space,* as a framed arena in which the behavior is according to the principles of drama" (Kinser & Kleinman, 1969, p. 8).

Dramatism is a process theory, then, in the sense that it understands the process by which drama emerges and is conducted in mundane life. It is related to the other theories we have discussed here. Dramatic communication involves symbolic transactions in social contexts. To use Burke's terminology, it occurs in a Scene, is conducted by Agents, involves the commiting of Acts, using various communicative Agencies (or Means) for a variety of Purposes. Dramatism sees dramatic-structure-in-time as "consisting of the dramatic performances of people in groups whose members act together in common enterprises" (Cleveland, 1969, p. 187). The negotiations of everyday life and politics are communications which cope with social process by constructing a dramatic meaning to self, others, performance, and situation.

Victor Turner has studied this phenomenon in African tribal societies. He came to see them as social process, stressing "the dynamic character of social relations", and observing "a form in the process of social time. This form was essentially *dramatic.*" Social dramas, he argues, "represent sequences of social events, which, seen retrospectively by an observer, can be shown to have structure." Structures are simply "the more stable aspects of action and inter-relationship." If one looks at the "diachronic profile" of the social drama, one sees that "structures" become known as "phases in social processes, as dynamic patterns right from the start." For Turner, " 'Processualism' is a term that includes 'dramatistic analysis' " (Turner, 1974, pp. 31-43).

Turner is not primarily interested in political processes, but his insistence that we must delineate "phases" of dramatic process as they are conducted over time is certainly applicable to politics. Take, for example, the drama of campaigns. Political campaigns are ritual dramas conducted according to well-defined polit-ical rules and sequences. The ritualization keeps them within the bounds of political civility and predictability over a specified time period. The candidate and his team must act in certain obligatory scenes and communicate certain obligatory messages in accordance with dramatic expectations of the attendant audiences. From the announcement of candidacy through the primaries and conventions and the fall campaign, culminating with the reintegrative and successive ritual of the inauguration, the politico-ritual drama of the campaign gives structure to a competitive and potentially disruptive process. The phases of the campaign are dramatic scenes in the ritual which "constrain" what are indeed dynamic processes, and *in toto* a recurrent seasonal form in the process of social time. One can point to many political processes which seem to obey these canons of phased temporal structure which constrains the actions therein into dramatic actions: diplomacy, legislative dramas, movements, and so on (Combs, 1980).

The possibilities of the dramatic "framing" for process analysis has been put to insightful use by Kinser and Kleinman in their study of "the search for aesthetic reality" in Germany, 1890-1945. They argue that this historical frame can be analyzed in terms of the struggle for cultural and political self-definition on the part of the Germans. Throughout the tremors of that period of historical process there was an agonizing search for a political "aesthetic reality" which defined the nature, roles, and purpose of the present as social drama. German mythology became an increasingly salient reference point for the flow of political discourse. This helped to shape political perceptions and to institutionalize politics as theater, symbolic enactments that transcended "normal politics." The Nazis fused past, present, and future in a spectacular political theater devoid of reality but one in which the cultural search for meaning and identity was temporarily resolved. This is an example of "history as fiction" in which deeply rooted myths become a symbolic vehicle for political self-dramatization.

The dramatistic analysis of Kinser and Kleinman offers a rich precedent for other macropolitical studies which attempt to interpret inclusive political processes as symbolic dramas occurring within a defined "reality" wherein mythic enactments are played out according to their cultural and political "logic." Such analysis is not unrelated to the fantasy theme approach mentioned above. Bormann's notion of "symbolic convergence" (1980, pp. 188-189) focuses our attention on the ways in which "human beings converge their individual fantasies, dramas, and meanings into shared symbol systems." The dramatistic perspective offers a way of giving episodic boundaries to politico-temporal processes and investigating the symbolic forms and enactments which characterize transactions within that time frame.

CONCEPTUALIZING PROCESS

The rich array of ideas about process, politics, and communication we have surveyed all illustrate the difficulty of conceptualizing the world as process. This should not surprise us, since the problem of permanence and change has plagued the mind of man since time immemorial. Recall the enduring question of Theodorus with which Socrates struggles in *Theaetetus*: "How is that possible, Socrates, either in the case of this or any other quality—if while we are using the word the subject is escaping in the flux?" The dialectic between the Heraclitian and Parmenidian polarities continues in contemporary thought. One recalls Gilbert Ryle's (1953) famous lecture on "the two chairs," the first chair the one of everyday life—solid, structured, and permanent—but the second chair—the chair of the physicist, biologist, and geologist—dynamic, turbulent, changing, and doomed to disintegration and transformation. This is not to say that the polarities are a "pseudo-problem" or a false dichotomy. Rather, it is to say that reality is always more complex, inchoate, contradictory, and inexplicable than our images and metaphors of it.

Does it then make sense to conceive of the world, and the political world in particular, as process? What is a political communication process? Each school of thought seems, when push comes to shove, to retreat into the easier and more comfortable language of inquiry that posits tangible and identifiable entities ("pressure groups"). Kress has rightly identified the root problem here to be the "law of identity," wherein persons and units must be regarded as "logical primitives" or "primary particulars" as identifiable, concrete units. But his "faith" is in the "integrity of our conceptual and linguistic systems" and the "integrity of human experience itself" (Kress, 1970, p. 243). The process theorists, of course, is not at all convinced of the "integrity" of language and experience.

Nor is the process theorist alone. If one considers the emergence of modern process thinking in light of the artistic, scientific, and philosophical trends of our century, one finds those doubts amplified. Kress himself has pointed to this in the "escape of identity in the flux" in modern art, literature, and philosophy. Twentieth century arts and letters have in large measure abandoned a sense of structure external to the actor, that any firm knowledge is possible, that the world possesses some immanent meaning or purpose. The sense of dynamism and turbulence in Nietzsche was also to be seen in Van Gogh, Joyce, Schoenberg, and the many artistic schools—surrealism, expressionism, dadaism—that have emerged in our century. When mere anarchy was indeed loosed upon the world, it was hard to retain the imagination of order and purpose that the preindustrial and prewar generations had entertained. Kress cites Mannheim's famous thesis to the effect that it is in eras of disintegration that the subtleties of process "webs of affiliation" become evident (Kress, 1966, pp. 4-5; Jacobson, 1964).

But the sciences, too, contributed to the growth of process thinking. The startling conceptualizations of subatomic physics, relativity theory, molecular biology, and so on gave impetus to process imagery. The Einsteinian revolution, along with such disturbing discoveries as the Heisenberg principle of indeterminacy, made the world seem much more complicated, interrelated, and—yes—indeterminate than had previously been thought. For example, the questions Hume raised about causality the physicists finished off. It is no wonder that Bentley said, "The continents go, and the islands." It is also no wonder that those such as he who were versed in modern science would turn to process as a new way to organize inquiry.

But, to cite Kress again, "having posited the interconnectedness of everything, how were they to restore being to a universe of becoming or, in the more earthy language of social science, how were they to make their 'cuts' " (1966, p. 6)? The conceptualization of the world as process resists making the cuts and has difficulties when identifying units. The world is not buckshot but jelly, not discrete events or units bouncing like billiard balls off of each other but intricate webs of connections which defy easy extrication. The philosophical and aesthetic revolution of the twentieth century made us aware of the "interconnectedness of everything" and thus focused inquiry onto *relations* and not objects. As Shands notes, the "revolutionary idea is most precise in its denial of the individual existence of any thing or object; the *mutuality of process* between the *putative* object and the *putative* subject is the new basis for understanding" (1967, p. 102). A communications science, then, would focus on the "concrete temporal processes of Becoming" rather than a "timeless abstract world of Being" (Toulmin, 1977, p. 159).

With that aim in mind, we must then agree with Berlo: "Reality is not a given. It is a set of rules" (1977, p. 17). The philosophical revolution of our time suggests that reality is not a snapshot of immutable fixed objects, but rather more like a portrait constantly being redone (Matson, 1964, p. 121). Reality is not a fact but a hypothesis, not only Ryle's chair of commonsense experience but also the more inclusive and dynamic other "chair" of full processual life-in-time. The idea that reality is created rather than discovered means also that it is continually re-created through the process of giving new meanings to the "rules." Thus, communication creates what we term "reality." As Watzlawick et al wrote, there are "many different versions of reality, some of which are contradictory, but all of which are the results of communication and not reflections of eternal, objective truths" (1967, p. xi).

This view of process suggests the relevance of phenomenology in giving us some understanding of the delusionary veil of *maya* which the communication process creates. Alfred Schutz and his followers have been interested in the process by which people *interpret* the worlds they occupy. This directs inquiry toward the world of social relationships—a "communicative common environment"—and the "multiple realities" that people construct and change over time. Schutz was much aware of the temporal foundation of social action and went to great pains to try to characterize the processual nature of action. The relevance of him and other phenomenologists for us here, however, is that they understand that consciousness itself—and therefore social action—occur within the "stream of experience." Since our social experience occurs in a temporal universe, interpretation is an essential pragmatic for coping with the life-world (Schutz, 1970; Rabinow & Sullivan, 1979).

The phenomenon of society-in-process has inspired some reflections by Victor Turner which are relevant here. Turner maintains that "culture has to be seen as processual" as "an endless series of negotiations among actors about the assignment of meaning to the acts in which they jointly participate." The phenomenal quality of social reality gives it an aspect of "indeterminacy," in which situational adjustments constitute processes whereby "the seemingly fixed is really the continuously renewed." He calls for a "processual symbolic analysis," which concentrates on "the interpretation of the meaning of symbols considered as dynamic systems of signifiers, signified and changing modes of signification in temporal sociocultural processes." He suggests that process theorists look at "liminal" contexts of social play which are "heavily invested with cultural symbols, particularly those of ritual, drama, and other powerful performance genres" (Turner, 1974).

The view these thinkers represent suggests for us some themes that are crucial to our purpose. First, process is a "god-term," an existential condition of temporality and change which "encapsulates" the social world and the acts of communication in it. Social reality is dynamic and mediated by the "processors" who must act in it. Reality is constantly being constructed and re-created by people jointly involved in acts of "processing," using symbolic communication to reinvest the "rules" of a communicative common environment with interpreted meanings. If it is the case that communication creates our realities, then Berlo is correct to assert that "Communication is Make-believe, but Make-believe is Real" (1977, p. 19). He suggests that we conceive of communication as a social game, in that "it involves players, outcomes, and rules and regulations of play. The rules define the game, and changes in the rules change the game" (1971, p. 21).

A POLITICAL SCIENCE OF THE ABSURD

The attempt to conceive of the political world as a process of communication must include an attempt to place such inquiry in a larger philosophical context. Our assumptions and conclusions about the nature of communication, process, and politics would have to be combined in a coherent position from which our specific investigations of political processes would derive. Let us state a position here which logically flows, we contend, from the intellectual legacy and "connections" we have summarized.

It seems to the author that such a theory might characterize a "political science of the absurd." This term is appropriated from Lyman and Scott's seminal book (1970, pp. 1-30). They draw from the same intellectual sources as we have here—existentialism and phenomenology, symbolic interactionism and dramatism, ideas about life as a game and on time tracks. The fundamental underpinnings of what they have to say is the logical conclusion one should draw from conceptualizations of a process universe.

Their work is doubly relevant because it begins with Machiavelli, perhaps still the most perceptive analyst of the "logic" of politics. Machiavelli's world is a process universe in which one attempts, through communication, to play the political game well in the wake of all the entropic and insane processes which occur. Machiavelli simply assumes, as do Lyman and Scott, that the world has no objective meaning and that politics is one of the arenas of society in which people dramatize meanings through political communication. Political communication is a pragmatic art, an attempt to conquer fortune by the political *virtu* of symbolic action. Politics is a process of events-in-time, episodes which must be "re-created" and mastered each time, in a political universe in which the actor has complete control over events and the "rules" that characterize events (Orr, 1969). Political make-believe involves interpretations derived from symbolic transactions in which political meanings are dramatized.

The concept of absurdity, of course, is derived from the existentialists, and Camus in particular (Camus, 1955; Weinstein, 1980). A process vision of the political universe is consistent with existentialist absurdity. Indeed, absurdity is a manifestation of communication. The absurdity of politics is a condition of the confusions, misinterpretations, paradoxes, disinformations, conflicting meanings, multiple realities, and pathologies of communication. This position assumes that politics is a social arena in which man strives for meaning in a meaningless world, wherein man attempts to construct political meanings out of his own fantasies in an endless effort to make an ever-changing reality conform to his expectations. Political actors communicate to try to apply "rules" to a world in which entropic and centrifugal processes are forever changing the rules. As Machiavelli's Prince understood, the political actor can count on absurdity, both the constancy and inconstancy of changes which alter political situations and thus what can or must be communicated in them. Politics is indeed a make-believe world, a world mediated at odds with multiple realities and stubborn facts.

The existential nature of communication has been alluded to by Watzlawick et al. in their seminal *Pragmatics of Human Communication* (1967). They note the confluence of communication studies and existentialism as proposing similar relationships between man and reality: [Man is] thrown into an opaque, formless, meaningless world out of which man himself creates his situation. His specific way of 'being-in-the-world' therefore is the outcome of his choice, is the meaning *he* gives to what is presumably beyond objective human understanding" (Watzlawick et al., 1967, p. 262). The processes of politics give political Princes very imperfect knowledge over and control of the dynamics of what happens and what people communicate to each other they believe is happening. Political choice becomes, as Sartre suggests, a condemnation, since the absurdity of choices, and the often tragic consequences of choices, makes the game seem insane. In this view, politics is less like the sanitary world of "systems theorists" and the like and more like *Catch-22*. If politics is drama, then it is the political theater of the absurd.

In an excellent commentary on *Catch-22,* Ramsey (1968) notes that in the literature of the absurd

> the apparently ordered surface of reality is torn away to reveal the chaos and unreason beneath. . . . [T]raditional reason is revealed as unreason because it supposes an ordered, rational world. Sanity in the traditional sense is really insanity; that is, if sanity is the ability to come to terms with reality, then it is insane to act as if the world is coherent and rational [p. 228].

A process view of political communication would see politics as an important and consequential form of human activity that occurs in an incoherent and irrational universe. The "surface reality" of politics, like war, is communicated in symbolic terms which clothe power; but when the Emperor has no clothes, the full implications of living in a chaotic and unreasonable world become all too apparent.

If we can accept this thoroughly existential view of political life, then the concepts that some of the writers we have mentioned in this essay developed converge as a world-view. Process suggests an irreversible, "open" universe of ongoing communication, in which the "stream" of action—the remembered past, the immediate present, and the anticipated future—are acted upon in what Watzlawick et al. call "the perennial now" (1967, p. 240). Political events are mediated in symbolic interaction and thus are, as Bentley insists, interconnected reciprocal transactions occurring in dynamic space-time. Politics is an absurd drama of political communication in which individuals and groups dramatize fantasized rhetorical visions of political symbols and stories. Since is is impossible to transcend the politico-communicative reference point, action occurs in a condition of uncertainty. The political man-in-process-with-environs is condemned to act in a political universe in which its very temporality and unknownability make coping with it adequately chancy. Indeed, it may be the case that the political actor must communicate in "bad faith" because that is a condition of political communication: dramatic rhetoric communicated to audience groups with intent to shape the fantasies and actions of those engaged in the political "moment." But since no political actor, however powerful, can ultimately control the processes of political communication—such as group fantasies which emerge over time—the very process which creates and maintains political power also may alter or destroy it, since Princes have imperfect control over entropic and centrifugal processes created in new aggregates of political communication. The intent of one's political messages are not necessarily the consequence: Interpretive processes intervene in the temporal interval.

We should remind ourselves that politics is quite serious, autonomous, and pragmatic; indeed, it is a major task for a process theory of political communication to specify the nature and conduct of politics according to the "logic" peculiar to that form of action. In this view, communication games—interpersonal, economic, organizational, and so on—take on a "logic" that is identifiable as appropriate to that realm and indeed that particular situation. Political logic, then, is an intentional communicated act in a political situation designed for pragmatic purposes in the face of power relations and the dynamics of political process. Political logic is a logic-in-use, what seems to be the political thing to do at a point in time and space. One uses political logic to play the game, to communicate those pragmatic messages which might turn fortune in your favor by grasping the dynamics of an "open" political situation.

SOME CONCLUDING QUESTIONS

This essay has ranged over a wide array of ideas and has taken a position requiring further investigation. What remains to be done here is to point to some philosophical issues and research vistas which are suggested by a process vision of political communication. The previous section tried to link a process view of politics to existential absurdity. The power of that stance is clearly dependent upon the articulation of that viewpoint, specifying the implications of such a view both for research and political pragmatics.

The philosophical and poetic vision of existentialism turns on a conception of reality. Some existentialists, such as Sartre, have posited a subjectivism that denies the possibility of firm knowledge of an objective reality independent of our own knowledge of it. Others envision a chance universe, devoid of meaning and order, which we in some sense know and which exists objectively. In any case, man is a "stranger" in this world. But the explanatory power of a political science of the absurd is enhanced if we can say something about what political reality is. Is the political world chaos? In what sense do we "create" political reality in our subjective images, or does it exist "out there"? What is the role of communication in the construction of reality?

It may seem contradictory to posit that reality is both extant and created, but process analysis permits us to do no other. The difficulty is best conceptualized as transactional (Bentley & Dewey, 1949), wherein the knower and the knowing are not bifurcated and the process of knowing is a reciprocal communication between subject and object. Organism-environment are involved in a constant process of mutual communication. Reality includes the extant processes of nature-and society-in-time as well as the reciprocating process of the individual consciousness attempting to imagine, construct, and communicate reality as he experiences it. Both dimensions of political reality come within the purview of process analysis. The process of politics-in-time includes vast networks of political communications, in which process takes on its macrocosmic meaning as a "real" accumulation of events involving many actors and shaping the course of political history. But the process of politics-in-time is also mediated by the microcosmic meanings as equally real "mediated" events for individuals. Political reality is an ongoing dynamic of communicative transactions at both levels and with both meanings.

Indeed, it is the concept of communication itself that permits us to take an inclusive stance on these difficult questions. For the idea that reality is chaotic stems from our inability to order sensory data into a coherent pattern, and our sense that the world is devoid of meaning originates in our efforts to evaluate it. This does not mean that the world is inherently chaotic or a void, but it does mean that our experience with it is communication-dependent. Following Bentley, our existence is an ongoing process of knowing through communication. Following Machiavelli, those knowings are dynamic, communications which are time-dependent. A process universe is "many-evented," temporal communication events occurring in "the roaring loom of time" (Mead, 1959, p. 21).

The temporal process of communication then gives us the sense of absurdity. The political dynamics of our century has directed our knowing toward the many events which define the political nature of our times. And our knowledge of political reality has been "mediated" not only by the grotesque shape of events but also by the breadth of perspective that new means of communication brought to us. If the political world has seemed many-evented and proceeding at an awesome pace, this undoubtedly derives from our individual historical consciousness. If both self and objects seem to lack firm identity anymore, surely this is linked to an awareness of impermanence and dynamism. The subjective jumble that produced surrealism, absurdist fiction, and existentialist philosophy derived from, and helped to shape, whatever we can know of the objective reality of the twentieth century. Our aesthetic, if not our rational, expression envisioned reality transformed from structure to process, in which what was "real" to us was not permanence but change. What was identifiable in ourselves was that we existed as a passing event, as a temporal process in our very beings.

Such thinking gave impetus to focus on the phenomenon of process, and also the importance of communication in human relations. Together they form a powerful vision of what happens in politics. A process approach to political communication thinks reality dynamic, devoid of teleological reason but not completely unknowable or chaotic. But its dynamism makes for continual change in subjective and objective reality which makes understanding and control problematic. Human communication in such a world is always inadequate, unequal to explaining, understanding, or controlling the dynamics of politics. Thus, we must turn to symbolic dramas as metaphors, creating fantasy worlds we imagine to exist out there. That there is a gap between what we believe to exist and what does is obvious, but it ensures that whatever political logic we bring to contemporary political reality is absurd, since it may have only an incidental and certainly not a direct relationship to the processes occurring out there. Political communication is absurd, then, in that it expresses a form of human estrangement from the world—that is, our inability to communicate adequately in the presence of a larger process universe that seems inherently irrational.

Such a philosophical position requires more elaborate discussion than is possible here, but it underscores the importance of philosophical underpinnings for the development of political communication theory. For whatever observations we make of the process of political communications are "theory-dependent," standing or falling on the powers of the imaginative explanations that extend us beyond the limits of our own existence. As Bentley would urge us, we cannot shrink from the complexity of the inexhaustible transactions that characterize the world of political communication, or from the task of asking what knowledge of specific politico-communicative processes tell us about the theoretical context we have argued for.

So what sort of research questions should be, and indeed can be, addressed given this perspective? Recognition of the philosophical assumptions of an existential universe does not negate the study of actual processes, and indeed this essay has referred to many studies which form the precedents for successful inquiries. The key to process studies is in focus on the processes themselves and in careful interpretation as to what processes are under way in a given historical period. A temporal framing then focuses analysis on what we might call the aesthetics of experience in that time-frame; that is, what symbolic dramas are being conducted in politics at that time. The symbolic "rules" which obtain in the process in question can be subjected to aesthetic interpretation as to their meanings for the people involved in the relevant transactions. In other words, to understand a political process requires the study of the communications which define the situation for those involved. Such analysis offers a happy marriage of aesthetic interpretation and behavioral rigor, as in the aforementioned fantasy theme analysis. Although such research cannot ultimately settle the philosophical questions raised here, it can specify dramas of political existence as people communicate in the dynamic processes of political life.

One recurrent political process, observable in both large-scale and small-scale settings, is entropy, or how communication rules which obtain in a symbolic drama over time run down, come apart, or devolve to disorder (Rifkin, 1980). This question is of interest to both academics and politicians, since it involves the intriguing question of whether man can ultimately control or reverse entropic processes. The study of actual "declines and falls" should offer insight into the symbolic dramas associated with such processes and the extent to which that they are absurd, in the sense that political orders cannot control their own historical fate. Can the introduction of new political symbols, or new interpretations of old symbols, delay, impede, or reverse the dissipation or disintegration of a political order? How does political communication shape and reflect the processes of political change? These are not idle questions, since cognizance of the role of political communication in the dynamics of politics may make the difference between drift and mastery in the onrush of unfolding events. In that sense, the "communication arts" could be used by politicians as a communicative *virtu* against the chancy processes of political *fortuna*.

"One has to stay with process a little," wrote Jacobson (1964, p. 21), "to learn its ways before issuing to it commands of obedience." We have tried here to give the concept some "commands," linking it with the existential notion of absurdity. But such a vision involves intellectual risks and perhaps even a "leap of faith." For example, our perception that political communication processes are in some sense absurd not only may be historically conditioned, but may also reveal an inability to grasp the higher meaning of human history because of our lack of breadth of perspective in which absurdity itself either dissolves or takes on a new meaning in the larger view. Such ideas bring us breathlessly close to metaphysics, but it is only in addressing such questions that communication theory achieves its promise and our vision of politics as a dynamic of people communicating-in-process is enhanced.

REFERENCES

Bales, R. F. *Personality and interpersonal relation.* New York: Holt, Rinehart & Winston, 1970.

Bentley, A. F. *Behavior knowledge fact.* Bloomington, IN: Principia Press, 1935.

Bentley, A. F. Kennetic inquiry. *Science,* 1950, *112,* 775-783.

Bentley, A. F. *Inquiry into inquiries: Essays in social theory.* Boston: Beacon, 1954.

Bentley, A. F. Epilogue. In R. W. Taylor (Ed.), *Life, language, law: Essays in honor of Arthur F. Bentley.* Yellow Springs, OH: Antioch Press, 1957.

Bentley, A. F. *The process of government.* Cambridge, MA: Belknap Press, 1967.

Bentley, A. F. *Relativity in man and society.* New York: Octagon Books, 1968.

Bentley, A. F., with Dewey, J. *Knowing and the known.* Boston: Beacon, 1949.

Bergson, H. *An introduction to metaphysics.* Indianapolis: Bobbs-Merrill, 1955.

Berlo, D. K. Communication as process: Review and commentary. In B. D. Ruben (Ed.), *Communication yearbook I.* New Brunswick, NJ: Transaction Books, 1977.

Blumer, H. *Symbolic interactionism: Perspectives and method.* Englewood Cliffs, NJ: Prentice-Hall, 1969.

Bormann, E. G. Fantasy and rhetorical vision: The rhetorical criticism of social reality. *Quarterly Journal of Speech,* 1972, *58,* 396-407.

Bormann, E. G. *Communication theory.* New York: Holt, Rinehart & Winston, 1980.

Brisset, D., & Edgley, C. (Eds.) *Life as theater: A dramaturgical sourcebook.* Chicago: AVC, 1975.

Burke, K. *A grammar of motives.* Englewood Cliffs, NJ: Prentice-Hall, 1945.

Camus, A. *The myth of Sisyphus and other essays.* New York: Vintage Books, 1955.

Carey, W. Harold Adams Innis and Marshall McLuhan. *Antioch Review,* 1967, 5-39.

Cleveland, L. Symbols and politics: Mass communication and the public drama. *Politics,* 1969, *4,* 186-196.

Combs, J. *Dimensions of political drama.* Santa Monica, CA: Goodyear Publishing, 1980.

Combs, J., & Mansfield, M. (Eds.) *Drama in life: The uses of communication in society.* New York: Hastings House, 1976.

Cragan, J. F., & Shields, D. C. *Applied communication research: A dramatistic approach.* Prospect Heights, IL: Waveland Press, 1980.

Deutsch, K. W. *Nationalism and social communication: An inquiry into the foundations of nationality.* Cambridge: MIT Press, 1953.

Deutsch, K. W. *The nerves of government.* New York: Free Press, 1966.

Dewey, J. *Creative intelligence.* New York: Holt, Rinehart & Winston, 1917.

Eulau, H. H. D. Lasswell's developmental analysis. *Western Political Quarterly,* 1958, *11,* 229-242.

Fagen, R. R. *Politics and communication.* Boston: Little, Brown, 1966.

Fisher, W. R. A motive view of communication. *Quarterly Journal of Speech,* 1970, *56,* 131-139.

Gunnell, J. G. Deduction, explanation, and social scientific inquiry. *American Political Science Review,* 1969, *63,* 1233-1246.

Hakman, N. Bentley's transactional view of politics. *Social Science,* January 1958, 36-43.

Hall, P. M. A symbolic interactionist analysis of politics. *Sociological Inquiry,* 1972, *42,* 35-75.

Holton, G. Constructing a theory: Einstein's model. *American Scholar,* 1979, *48,* 309-340.

Huizinga, J. *Waning of the middle ages: Study of the forms of life, thought & art in France and the Netherlands in the 14th & 15th centuries.* New York: St. Martin's Press, 1924.

Huizinga, J. *Homo Ludens: A study of the play element in culture.* Boston: Beacon, 1950.

Innis, H. A. *The bias of communication.* Toronto: University of Toronto Press, 1951.

Innis, H. A. *Empire and communication.* Oxford: Clarendon Press, 1950.

Jacobson, N. Causality and time in political process: A speculation. *American Political Science Review,* 1964, *58,* 15-22.

James, W. *Essays in radical empiricism.* New York: Longmans, Green, 1912.

Kinser, B., & Kleinman, N. *The dream that was no more a dream: A search for aesthetic reality in Germany, 1890-1945.* New York: Harper Colophon, 1969.

Kress, P. J. Self, system, and significance: Reflections on Professor Easton's political science. *Ethics,* 1966, *77,* 1-13.

Kress, P. F. *Social science and the idea of process: The ambiguous legacy of Arthur F. Bentley.* Urbana: University of Illinois Press, 1970.

Lyman, S. M., & Scott, M. B. *A sociology of the absurd.* New York: Meredith Corporation, 1970.

McLuhan, M. *The Gutenberg galaxy.* Toronto: University of Toronto Press, 1962.

Manis, G., & Meltzer, B. N. (Eds.). *Symbolic interaction.* Boston: Allyn & Bacon, 1967.

Matson, F. W. *The broken image: Man, science, and society.* Garden City, NY: Doubleday, 1964.

Mead, G. H. *Mind, self, and society.* Chicago: University of Chicago Press, 1934.

Mead, G. H. *Philosophy of the present.* LaSalle, IL: Open Court Publishing, 1959. (Originally published, 1933)

Miller, E. F. Positivism, historicism, and political inquiry. *American Political Science Review,* 1972, *66,* 796-817.

Nietzsche, F. *The portable Nietzsche* (W. Kaufmann, ed.). New York: Viking Press, 1954.

Orr, R. Time motif in Machiavelli. *Political Studies,* 1969, *17,* 145-159.

Pierce, C. S. *Collected papers.* Cambridge, MA: Harvard University Press, 1931-1958.

Rabinow, P., & Sullivan, W. M. (Eds.). *Interpretive social science.* Berkeley: University of California Press, 1979.

Ramsey, V. From here to absurdity: Heller's 'Catch-22.' In B. Whitebread (Ed.), *Seven contemporary authors.* Austin: University of Texas Press, 1968.

Rifkin, J. *Entropy.* New York: Viking Press, 1980.

Rose, A. M. *Human behavior and social processes.* Boston: Houghton Mifflin, 1962.

Roth, J. A. *Timetables*. Indianapolis: Bobbs-Merrill, 1963.

Ryle, G. *Dilemmas*. London: Cambridge University Press, 1953.

Schutz, A. *On phenomenology and social relations* (H. R. Wagner, ed.). Chicago: University of Chicago Press, 1970.

Shands, H. C. Outline of a general theory of human communication: Implications of normal and pathological schizogenesis. In L. Thayer (Ed.), *Communication: Concepts and perspectives*. Washington: Spartan, 1967.

Strauss, A. *Negotiations: Varieties, contexts, processes, and social order*. San Francisco: Jossey-Bass, 1978.

Taylor, R. W. *Life, language, law: Essays in honor of Arthur F. Bentley*. Yellow Springs, OH: Antioch Press, 1957.

Thorson, T. L. *Biopolitics*. New York: Holt, Rinehart & Winston, 1970.

Teilhard de Chardin, P. *The phenomenon of man*. New York: Harper & Row, 1959.

Toulmin, S. From form to function: Philosophy and history of science in the 1950s and now. *Daedalus*, 1977, *106*, 143-162.

Turner, R. H. Role-taking: Process versus conformity. In A. Rose (Ed.), *Human behavior and social processes*. Boston: Houghton Mifflin, 1962.

Turner, V. *Dramas, fields, and metaphors: Symbolic action in human society*. Ithaca, NY: Cornell University Press, 1974.

Watzlawick, P. et al. *Pragmatics of human communication*. New York: W. W. Norton, 1967.

Weinstein, M. *New ways and old to talk about politics*. Paper presented at the meeting of the Midwest Political Science Association, Spring 1971.

Weinstein, M. Camus: The absurdity of politics. In B. Barber & M.J.G. McGrath (Eds.), *The artist and political vision*. New Brunswick, NJ: Transaction Books, 1980.

Whitehead, A. N. *Process and reality* (corrected edition, D. R. Griffin & D. W. Sherburne, Eds.). New York: Free Press, 1978.

CHAPTER 2

The Uses and Gratifications Approach

Jack M. McLeod and Lee B. Becker

RESEARCHERS SUFFER from a weakness common to the rest of mankind: We like to use labels. One of the labels receiving extensive use in recent years is "uses and gratifications research." This label has served the legitimate purpose of alerting others to an increasingly important approach to communication research. But labels have their limits. Unlike the labels on consumer products, researchers' labels have no mandate to systematically disclose their contents. Lacking careful specification, the label may take on whatever meaning suits the user. So it is with "uses and gratifications," which as a label appears to have a kind of Rorschach-like quality such that neither its proponents nor its critics have reached agreement about some of its most basic characteristics.

To many of its adherents, the uses and gratifications approach is a welcome escape from the dead end of traditional "hypodermic" effects analysis, while other supporters see it as a logical extension and refinement of the analysis of message effects. Its critics are also divided on this point. Some see the approach as merely descriptive and lacking in responsiveness to social consequences of existing media content, while others write it off as just more of the "same old stuff" of empirical audience effects research. Similarly, there are widely divergent views as to its grounding in theory. While some of its critics attack uses and gratifications for being atheoretical, others score it for being hopelessly ensnared in the sterile morass of functional theory. At least some of its supporters agree with its functional roots but find this a happy home; others accept its lack of unifying theory but see it therefore as an eclectic shelter for those of varying theoretical persuasions. Still other followers seem not to be concerned with theory at all and simply use its measures as a handy additive to tune up their empirical predictions.

The antecedents of audience uses and gratifications is another area where little agreement is evident. Some critics have attacked the approach for failing to identify the social structural roots of human needs, sometimes arguing for the supremacy of structural factors over the "trivial redundancy" of what gratifications people say they seek from media. Researchers following the demand to study social structural antecedents of audience uses and gratifications may do so at their peril, however, for other critics have warned that such investigation robs the individual audience member of his/her autonomy. Finally, the relationship of uses and gratifications to public policy evokes a wide range of opinion. It has been attacked as having a conservative bias in being used mainly to justify the status quo of mass media content; other critics argue that it is too visionary regarding change in media content, citing as evidence the discrepancy between what people say they want and what media fare they actually watch. Its defenders are similarly divided, some focusing on the multiple functions served by existing media content while others see gratifications sought as guides or constraints on possible improvements in media formats.

The ambiguity of the uses and gratifications label does not set it off from other approaches to political communication research. No approach to our knowledge has provided the necessary ingredients on the label: well-explicated concepts with unambiguous operational definitions, clearly stated assumptions and theoretical statements leading to testable hypotheses. However, uses and gratifications researchers have provided sufficient empirical evidence to begin to make some sense out of the confusion. That is what we are attempting here. As we shall see, the label subsumes a lot of sins, as well as some research offering new insight into the ways audience members use the mass media and are affected by them.

HISTORY OF USES AND GRATIFICATIONS RESEARCH

Research conducted under the uses and gratifications label has a common concern with the uses audience members make of the mass media as well as the gratifications sought and received from such use. The research is social psychological in focus and employs functionalist terminology in its presentation.

To understand the current uses and gratifications research it is necessary to learn something of the tradition's history. For while modern research has moved beyond the confines of the early research activity, much remains from that early period. The first studies were published at the start of World War II and focused on radio and its entertainment content: quiz programs (Herzog, 1942), classical music (Suchman 1942), and soap operas (Herzog, 1944; Warner & Henry, 1950). These were extended to newspapers in studies of children's use of comics (Wolfe

& Fiske, 1949) and the functions of newspaper reading (Berelson, 1949). All but the last of these studies followed the strategy of isolating a particular type of content and identifying a need or set of needs satisfied by that content for a given group of people. In many cases the function served was latent or non-obvious, in the sense that its satisfaction was not implied by the manifest media content. However, only Berelson's (1949) finding that the activity of reading was missed to a greater degree than was news content during a newspaper strike was germane to the field of political communication research.

The thrust of political communication research during the 1940s and '50s was not a positive one. Rather, it developed in response to the failures of mass persuasion campaigns of the postwar period. Specifically, it developed in those years when communication research moved out of the laboratory and into the field. It was stimulated by the failure to replicate the media effects of the laboratory in the real world. The conclusion reached in the pioneering Columbia University voting studies was that the campaign effects of the mass media were limited almost entirely to reinforcing "predispositions" and, to a minor degree, to mobilizing those less interested in the campaign (Lazarsfeld, Berelson, & Gaudet, 1948; Berelson, Lazarsfeld, & McPhee, 1954). The stance of the audience member as portrayed in these studies was a defensive one in selecting only supportive information and avoiding discrepant information.

The uses and gratifications research and the voting studies had a number of things in common: Both were products of the Lazarsfeld et al. group at Columbia University; they shared the common vocabulary of functionalism; and each represented a refocus of attention from mass media institutions and their content to an attribution of an increased share of power to the audience. But nowhere in the voting studies do we see the application of the uses and gratifications research strategies employed earlier with the entertainment content of radio. Katz (1979) noted another important difference in portrayals of audience members in the two types of studies. The voting studies and the statements of limited effects models that followed (Klapper, 1960) depicted the audience member in a negative light. Although he/she was more autonomous than as cast by the earlier powerful-media "hypodermic" effects models, the person was active only in the sense of seeking consonant and avoiding discrepant information. The uses and gratifications research presents a much more positive image. The person follows his/her interests, choosing media content according to needs and synthesizes that content to satisfy those needs.

It is important to note that both the Columbia uses and gratifications and voting research languished after the 1950s. The earlier flow of gratifications studies slowed to a trickle, and the Columbia voting research ended with a shift in attention to the University of Michigan national voting studies in 1952. Because the Michigan studies dealt only minimally with mass media uses until the 1974 election, there was little opportunity to meld the uses and gratifications approach into political communication research. Unfortunately, too, the tentative inferences of Lazarsfeld et al. about limited effects of the mass media and audience avoidances had become virtual laws despite the fact that the original data were obtained prior to the advent of television and that subsequent research cast doubt on the power of selective exposure (Sears & Freedman, 1971).

From 1950 on, the dominant trend was away from a concern with the political consequences of media use and toward a market orientation. While there was less concern with the gratifications sought and received from the mass media, studies of the use of entertainment media—particularly television—continued. Steiner (1963) used data showing discrepancies between critical attitudes toward commercial entertainment programming and its extensive use to argue the case for the status quo. Mendelsohn (1966) treated audience uses of mass entertainment more substantially. Even today some of the most important recent treatments of audience uses of media have concentrated on their entertainment content. Noteworthy examples are the analyses of audiences by Goodhardt, Ehrenberg, and Collins (1975), Wober's (1980) work for the Independent Broadcasting Authority in Britain, and Frank and Greenberg's (1980) work on American television.

Despite a long separation, the uses and gratifications approach and more traditional lines of political communication research were yet to converge. This was brought about by Blumler and McQuail (1969) in their seminal study of the 1964 British general election. Blumler has continued this work in studies of more recent British elections (Blumler, 1974, 1975; Blumler & McLeod, 1974) and still more recently in a cross-national study of the first direct election to the European Community Parliament (Blumler & Fox, 1980). The research has stimulated several U.S. replications and extensions, about which more will be said later.

More generally, the uses and gratifications approach has enjoyed a marked increase in interest among mass communication researchers. The publication in 1974 of the Blumler and Katz volume *The Uses of Mass Communications* served to summarize much of the work in the area. Of particular value to American researchers was the infusion of European thought and research in the book. This stimulated renewed activity from the uses and gratifications perspective and paved the way for some much-needed cross-national research between the United States and other nations.

While, as noted above, much of the recent research has dealt with audience uses of the entertainment fare of the mass media, significant work also has been undertaken to examine the motivations behind use of the news content of the various media. Noteworthy examples include Levy (1978), who deals with television news, and several numbers in the News Research Reports of the American Newspaper Publishers Association which examine motivations behind use of the various types of newspaper content.

What is perhaps more significant, the resurgence of interest in the uses and gratifications research has occurred just at the time that many communication researchers have begun to reexamine the conclusion of Klapper and others that the mass media have minimal effects (see Blumler & McLeod, 1974; Clarke & Kline, 1974; Becker, McCombs, & McLeod, 1975; and Patterson & McClure, 1976). The particular promise of the uses and gratifications perspective as a means of integrating the massive and minimal media effects positions into something of a middle-ground position has led to its receiving increased attention. Perhaps it is in this role as an integrative component in an effects model that the uses and gratifications perspective offers its greatest promise to the study of political communication.

COMPONENTS OF USES AND GRATIFICATIONS RESEARCH

There is, to be sure, no coherent uses and gratifications theoretical perspective. Rather, there exist various formulations of just what should be included in any eventual theory carrying this label.

Common to all formulations is the notion that audience members must be viewed as active processers rather than passive receivers of media messages. In contrast to the common laboratory situation, where receivers can be manipulated to attend to a particular message, audience members in the real world exercise considerable freedom in their use of the mass media.

In positing that audience members are selective, proponents of this notion of an active audience hold that media behavior reflects prior interests and preferences. Blumler (1979) noted that at least three other views of audience activity exist in the literature. First, some hold that media behavior is utilitarian, and by "active" it is simply meant that audience members use the media most useful to them. Others view media behavior as intentional, directed by prior motivation. In this view, media behavior is seen as motivated behavior. Finally, some have used the notion of activity to represent imperviousness to influence. Bauer's (1964) formulation of an "obstinate audience" is consistent with this final position. While it is Blumler's contention that it is now time to treat the caveat of an active audience as an empirical question and to disentangle some of these different meanings, it is sufficient here to note that although uses and gratifications researchers have in common a concern with audience activity, not all define audience activity similarly.

Working within this framework of an active audience, researchers have explored differing components of the relationship between the content of the mass media and audience members. The various concerns of uses and gratifications researchers have been identified by Katz, Blumler, and Gurevitch (1973a) as dealing with "(1) the social and psychological origins of (2) needs, which generate (3) expectations of (4) the mass media or other sources, which lead to

(5) differential patterns of media exposure (or engagement in other activities), resulting in (6) need gratifications and (7) other consequences, perhaps mostly unintended ones." Investigators have dealt more extensively with one component of this integrative model than with others. For example, much of the recent research on newspaper readership taking a uses and gratifications perspective has focused on items 2, 3, 4 and 5. The work of McLeod and Choe (1978), Stevenson (1979), Weaver, Wilhoit, and Reide (1979) and Becker, Fruit and Collins (Note 1) is illustrative. Only infrequently have researchers concerned themselves with all components of the model.

We have argued elsewhere (McLeod & Becker, 1974) for a media effects model—labeled a transactional model—which fully incorporates the uses and gratifications paradigm. The model draws on the arguments of Davison (1959), Bauer (1964), Weiss (1969), and others, who have argued that to understand media effects one must understand that, in Bauer's words, communication is "a transactional process in which two parties each expect to give and take from the deal approximately equitable values."

The transactional model, which can be seen as representing a reasonable synthesis of the hypodermic and limited effects models of media effects, may be able to escape the unwarranted simplicities of each of the parent models. Proponents of a hypodermic model have held that message characteristics are most important in understanding effects, while those arguing for a limited effects position hold that audience characteristics are most significant. A transactional model recognizes that effects probably can be understood best by combining knowledge of message characteristics and the level of exposure given them with an understanding of *orientations* of the audience members to those messages.

We intentionally used the term "audience orientations" in this formulation rather than audience motives or gratifications sought from the media because motives or gratifications sought are only part of what audience members bring to the effects equation. Other variables which suggest themselves are audience assessments of the credibility of the media, dependence on a particular medium for a given type of content, and level of attention paid to a particular type of content.

The transactional model, of course, is not a complete picture of how audience motives should be incorporated into communications research. A fuller model would need to take into consideration the antecedents of motives, the dynamics linking motives to media behavior, as well as the consequences of the media behavior (modified by the motive state). Figure 2.1 presents the outlines of such a complete model.

The components of such a model, of course, can be found in the writings of many others, including Katz et al. (1973a), McGuire (1974), Rosengren (1974), Blumler (1979), Katz, Gurevitch, and Haas (1973b), Frank and Greenberg

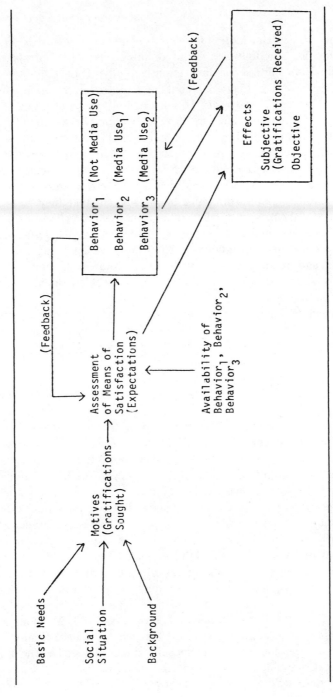

Figure 2.1: A Uses and Gratifications Model

(1980), and Kippax and Murray (1980), to name just a few. It is offered here not as something new, but as a means of integrating what has appeared elsewhere, both in the political communications and other contexts.

The model shown in Figure 2.1 contains a distinction between *motives* and one of its antecedents, *basic needs*. This distinction, comparable to that made by Rosengren (1974), is not shared by all those working in the uses and gratifications tradition. As explified by Katz et al. (1973a), most prefer to use only the term "needs" in subsuming both concepts. Yet there are some good reasons for separating the two. The assessment of basic needs lies in the domain of psychologists and physiologists who have found them poorly measured by the individual's self-report. Motives seem a bit easier to measure, in that they go beyond the internal state of the person to imply action, thus making a closer theoretical link to media use. Certain other commonly made contrasts between *needs* and *motives* argue for their separation; the latter are viewed as being less physiologically based and more amenable to conscious awareness, more focused and directed to some behavioral resolution, more problem-oriented, and more specific to the situation.

Motives can be defined as expressed desires for gratification in a given class of situations (for example, in presidential election campaigns). Operationally, we will refer to them as *gratifications sought*. They are seen as originating in the person's basic needs, in his/her social structural background, and in the current social situation. These motives direct behavior, but the behavior is—at least in the mature individual—informed by an assessment of the various means by which satisfaction can be obtained. We refer to these as *expectations*, as rough probabilities of satisfaction assigned by the person to various behaviors. The result of these directed assessments of expectations is the selection of an option. Various mass media sources are only some among many possible behavioral options. The selection of a given option, of course, also is constrained by the availability of the various options (such as cost or ease of use).

The behavior selected to achieve satisfaction may have various effects. One class of these outcomes is indexed by the person's *subjective* evaluation of how well the behavior satisfied each motive or gratification sought. We call these *gratifications received*. These subjective evaluations are faithful to the spirit of the uses and gratifications approach in asserting the importance of the audience member in evaluating media effects. Examples of comparisons of both gratifications sought and received in the same investigation are rare (see Sanders & Chalfa, Note 2; Palmgreen, Wenner, & Rayburn, 1980; McLeod, Bybee, & Durall, in press). Too often it is assumed that what is sought from media must somehow have been received from exposure to the mass media. The importance of the subjective evaluations of gratifications received should not make us lose track of more *objective* criteria of media performance, such as gains in knowledge and political participation. These are particularly important when the social system, rather than the individual, is the unit of analysis.

A hypothetical case serves to illustrate the dynamics of the model. An individual may, as a result of some social discourse at his or her place of work, seek information about some ongoing political issue. The information, simply put, would have social utility. That motive directs the individual to consider the means of satisfaction. Based on what the individual knows from past experiences, several means present themselves. The individual could talk to his/her spouse in an attempt to learn about the political issue or debate. Or he/she could consult one or several of the media. If the spouse has been judged to be uninformed about such matters in the past, that option would seem unacceptable. If newspapers have provided needed information in the past (while perhaps television has not), newspapers might be sought out. More specifically, certain kinds of stories in the newspaper might be hunted for. The experience the individual gains for these efforts, of course, will serve to inform future choices in similar situations.

Use of the newspaper, of course, would be expected to have certain effects. In this hypothetical case, it should lead to an increase in information stored by the individual about the problem and/or to a subjective feeling of becoming better informed. But the motivation for the use of the media also has consequences. A person seeking to relax after a hard day at work might also read stories about the problem of interest to our hypothetical character. But, given the different motivations, it certainly seems clear that the person motivated to learn about a specific problem would indeed learn more about it than a person with an entirely different motivation. Yet their use of the medium—even the extent to which they read specific stories might well be the same.

Empirical evidence to support this model is not available in simple form, though numerous studies have shown support for various elements. For example, work of Blumler (1979) cited above, as well as that of Becker, Fruit, and Collins (Note 1) in a nonpolitical context, have provided evidence that needs have their origin in the social situation. Dimmick, McCagin, and Bolten (1979) have summarized the data on life-span changes in media use patterns in a way consistent with this position. Studies linking needs and media use have been cited in various places throughout this chapter. The recent works of Frank and Greenberg (1980) and Kippax and Murray (1980) serve as two nonpolitical examples.

THEORETICAL ISSUES

While there is considerable agreement that the uses and gratifications approach developed from functional theory in sociology and that its terminology reflects its origins, there is much less agreement as to what role these roots play today. Although space does not permit elaborate description here, it may be useful to review briefly the historical background to functionalism.

Functionalism developed during the nineteenth century, particularly in France, as a rejection of utilitarian economic theories in favor of the rapidly emerging biological theories of Darwin and others that seemed especially relevant to the disarray of societies brought about by the industrial revolution. It was tempting to draw an analogy between living organisms and societies and to treat each as self-regulating systems tending toward homeostatis and equilibrium. Societies, too, were seen as having basic needs or requisites which must be met to maintain equilbrium and ensure survival. Durkheim, Radcliffe-Brown, and Malinowski are the most central figures of early functionalism. The early work suffered greatly from imputing purpose (teleology) to societies and from the tautologies of unwisely assuming functions from the existing order of things.

The two most prominent exponents of functionalism in this century were Robert Merton (1968) and Talcott Parsons (1951). Merton is the more important to the history of mass communication research in that, as a Columbia University sociologist, he influenced many students with media interests. Parsons, of less direct relevance for our field, is best known for his highly abstract attempts to develop elaborate metatheoretical category systems for the analysis of cultural, social, and personality systems. His muddy prose may have had much to do with the demise in popularity of functionalism during the 1960s, as did a demand by others to make sociology more relevant to social change.

Stinchcombe (1968, p. 80ff.) presents a lucid presentation of a functional explanation as one in which "the *consequences* of some behavior or social arrangement are essential elements of the *causes* of that behavior." Motivation or wanting is a common expression of that type of explanation. He goes on to say that "uniformity of the consequences of action but a great variety of the behavior causing those consequences" (or equifinality) is an indicator of a functional sequence. The underlying model has three parts. A homeostatic variable (H) is one which tends to be stable even though there are forces to change it. These forces—tensions or difficulties (T)—come from outside the system to upset H. The third component comprises the behaviors of structures (S) that are selected out or reinforced through evolution, satisfaction, and the like because of their ability to maintain H. As applied to our model, H might be the surveillance motive to maintain one's reputation as an informed citizen. During normal times (as in a precampaign period) this might be satisfied by modest levels of newspaper reading and news viewing (S). But during times of rapid change (for example, in the heat of the presidential campaign), the strength of tensions (T) might build, making it increasingly difficult to continue to be well informed; as a result, new Ss in the form of debate watching, reading of magazines, and so on might supplant the standard behaviors having the maintenance of H as their consequence.

Some other concepts of functionalism are pertinent to the uses and gratifications approach. Some of the functions served are *latent,* in that they are not obvious from the nature of the behavior (S). For example, the intake of political information may serve the social motive of maintaining the person's social status rather than the more obvious goal of serving intrinsic informational motives. The concept of equifinality suggests that several *alternative* behaviors may serve the same functions and that there may be a succession of behaviors serving a given function. Various news sources serving surveillance motives is an example of functional alternatives, while the replacement of moviegoing with television viewing illustrates the latter. Not all behaviors can be said to serve some specific function, as for example dial-twisting behavior or leaving the television set on because it's too much effort to turn it off. More theoretically interesting are those behaviors which are *dysfunctional* with respect to some criterion. Watching the two candidates spar during the debates may have served to confuse and disenchant many viewers who were seeking clarification on issue stands.

Inherent in functional theory are certain characteristics that separate it from various other types of theory. First, the biological analogy and the homeostatic principle make it more amenable to the analysis of social control problems than it is to the study of how systems change. Critics such as Elliott (1974) and Swanson (1979) see this as leading to a conservative analysis of the mass media and, at worst, to a defense of the status quo of existing media content. Its defenders see no inherent reason why change cannot be studied within the functionalist model if the criteria are specified and the identification of dysfunctions is possible. A second inherent characteristic is that locus of change inevitably comes from outside the system (T). Critics see this as ignoring the possibility of tensions arising from contradictions within the system, while defenders say that internal weaknesses can be accounted for by the inability of the system to devise structures to maintain equilibrium (for example, no media source is found to satisfy the gratifications sought by the audience member).

Beyond the inherent theoretical problems of the functional model, critics have made a number of other charges about the theoretical grounding of the uses and gratifications approach. Various critics have charged it with being lashed to the sinking ship of functionalism, with being both atheoretical and ahistorical, with being conservative in its research strategies, with being indifferent to the realities of social structure, and with failing to deal with parts of the mass communication process other than the audience.

What can we say in response to such charges? To the assertion that uses and gratifications is inextricably linked to the declining functionalism, several comments can be made. We must understand that functionalism is not a highly constraining theoretical straightjacket. Rather, it is a way of looking at and conceptualizing social phenomena in the manner presented above (Timasheff & Theodorson, 1976). While it is true that functionalism as a paradigm has lost popularity, it still has many adherents, and its functional terminology finds its way into many research examples not acknowledging such origins. Some, like

Katz (1979), are happy to retain such identification. To the extent that latent functions are involved, we can see a direct parallel to the heart of all research activity and much journalistic activity as well—the unmasking of surface appearances to get at underlying processes of what is really going on. Perhaps the most common counterargument to the tie with functionalism is that the uses and gratifications approach need not be constrained by its historical roots and that many theoretical positions may find a home here (Blumler, 1979). If that is the case, then researchers need to pay more attention to consciously bringing other alternative theoretical perspectives into research guided by the gratifications approach.

The charges that uses and gratifications is atheoretical and ahistorical are harder to refute. There are many empirical statements, but it is difficult to find many clear theoretical statements in the literature. There seems to be more "postdiction" than prediction, in the sense that tensions and media behaviors are combined ex post facto to infer motives or needs. But the scarcity of testable theoretical statements is no less true of other competing research perspectives: theories of conflict, exchange, symbolic interaction, diffusion, and so on.

There is also much truth to the ahistoric nature of uses and gratifications research. Trend data and cohort analyses have not appeared in the literature, but the gathering of empirical data on gratifications itself does not have a long history. There is at least one example in the work of Blumler that suggests that the gathering of comparable data across time might be fruitful. The British research showed a marked decline between 1964 and 1974 in the extent to which the reinforcement gratifications were sought, a trend that may be tied to fundamental changes in the political system (Blumler, Note 3).

Perhaps the strongest attack on uses and gratifications research centers on its alleged conservative status quo tendencies. It is possible to assemble an impressive array of examples from this approach that come to some strong conclusions about the ways the audience use and motive patterns make difficult the alteration of media content. But it is also possible to find examples to the contrary, as for example Mendelsohn's (1974) examination of how uses and gratifications research might be used to foster changes in content. It seems fair to say that the functionalist model, because of its homeostatic nature and social control focus, leads easily but not inevitably to answering conservative questions. This being the case, it seems necessary for those using the approach to expend extra effort to come to grips with the issues of change.

The measurement of gratifications sought need not be the end of the research problem; discrepancies between what is sought and the extent to which gratifications are actually received provide a basis for experimenting with change. Critics and proponents alike have paid inadequate attention to this difference between seeking and receiving, even assuming the two are synonymous. McLeod et al. (in press) examined this possibility that audiences' motives are simple reflections of what they get. If this were the case, then gratifications sought and received should exhibit similar factor structures and should be highly correlated. McLeod et al. examined data for gratifications sought from the presidential campaign generally and for the rated helpfulness of the 1976 presidential debates. Similar factor structures were shown for the Surveillance-Vote Guidance factor but not for the two remaining factors. Further, several of the 11 items showed strong correlations between seeking and helpfulness, but none was so high as to assert that the two sets of questions were measuring the same thing. The researchers also looked at the relationship between debate viewing and ratings of helpfulness while controlling for gratifications sought. While the correlations averaged less than those for seeking by helpfulness, there was evidence that debate viewing affected gratifications received substantially for 4 of the 11 items and marginally for 4 others. It is clear that gratifications sought are by no means synonymous with gratifications received.

There is general agreement that little attention has been paid to the social structural antecedents of motive patterns. That little attention is too much attention since the thought of social and psychological factors affecting motives and, hence, the meaning of messages is threatening to some constructivist essayists (Swanson, 1979). Such deterministic thinking is thought to violate the autonomy of the individual and the active process of constructing meaning from media messages (Carey & Kreiling, 1974). We see no necessary contradiction between the postulate of an active audience and the search for social structural antecedents of motives. Because the combination of social situation, background, and basic needs as measured within our current capabilities probably accounts for less than half the variance in the strength of any motivational factor, the "variable analytic" social scientists can keep their half, leaving the rest for the uniqueness of the individual. As for the importance of studying the active processing of messages by the audience member, there is no quarrel. Most studies of the impact of media exposure and gratifications sought have used effects too far removed from the actualities of information processing.

At the other extreme is the larger number of critics who scorn uses and gratifications for failure to uncover more fully the social and psychological antecedents of motives. Elliott (1974, p. 255) goes even further to assert that "there is something fundamentally illogical in the claim that basic human needs are differentially located through society" and that "there seems every reason to declare the needs redundant and to go back to social and psychological factors as direct explanations of behavior." Elliott's point about basic human needs makes sense according to our definition of *basic human needs,* but only if they are distinguished from *motives,* which we see as a combination of those basic needs as interpreted according to the person's background and social situation.

We see no problem in conceiving of motives as affected by social and psychological factors and propose they should also influence the person's expectations, media use, and gratifications received. Indeed, the study of the equivalence of media impact across social structural strata—the "effects gap"—is an important empirical question (McLeod, Bybee, and Durall, 1979). But before we consign gratifications sought to the dustbin of redundant variables, we should go beyond argument to examine research findings. First, nowhere in the various programs of research (Blumler, Brown, & McQuail, Note 4; Blumler & McLeod, 1974; Becker, 1976, 1979; Becker et al., Note 1; McLeod & Becker, 1973; McLeod et al., 1979; McLeod, Luetscher, & McDonald, Note 5) do we find any evidence for declaring gratifications redundant. Social structural factors simply do not *strongly* predict levels of gratifications sought. Education is moderately related to Surveillance motives, but other social class indicators and demographic variables do less well. Second, although the social structural variables predict political knowledge and other effect variables, their control does not eliminate the influences of gratifications sought on political outcomes. Again, the claim of redundancy is unwarranted. Rather than engaging in more polemical discussions, we might spend more time gathering empirical evidence for how social structure and motivational factors relate and how they may interact to produce political effects.

The final charge, that uses and gratifications research has focused attention on the audience at the expense of understanding the rest of the mass communication process, deserves serious consideration. Perhaps the approach does depict the audience as too powerful if it can be inferred that almost any need can induce any media behavior, which, in turn, provides any gratification (Weiss, 1976). But careful reading of political research in the gratifications tradition does not support such a sweeping assertion. It does seem fair, however, to say that the existing research has not tied motives either to specific message characteristics or to proximate message effects. Nor has the uses and gratifications approach connected audience motives to the perceptions of reporters or to the processes of news gathering. We could, for example, ask reporters and editors what gratifications they seek from sources, what their readers are seeking and obtaining, and so on. If the early uses and gratifications research amplified the power of the audience as a corrective to the previous overemphasis on the power of media messages, then surely future research in this tradition can afford to present a balanced view where neither messages nor the audience is supreme.

METHODOLOGICAL APPROACHES AND ISSUES

Perhaps the thorniest problems confronting uses and gratifications researchers are in the area of operationalization. Measures of elusive audience characteristics such as motives, expectations, and satisfaction are crucial, yet few obvious strategies for dealing with such audience-oriented concepts present themselves. Measures of the social and psychological origins of the motives, the patterns of media exposure, and potential effects are more in the mainstream of communications research, and earlier experiences can serve as a guide. Even here, however, solutions may seem deceptively obvious.

Most of the concern to date with methodological problems in the uses and gratifications area has been with measurement of audience needs, or the motives guiding media use behavior. Becker (1979) has identified three distinct measurement strategies in the literature. First, researchers can make inferences about audience motives by measuring some separate, yet related, variable or variables. In the research of Kline, Miller, and Morrison (1974) on audience uses of family planning information, for example, motives were inferred from locator variables such as age and sex. Female respondents were assumed to have different motives than male respondents, and older adolescents were assumed to have different information needs than younger adolescents.

The second and more common strategy for measuring motives (gratifications sought) is to rely on self-reports of audience members. Indeed, Katz et al. (1973a) hold that implicit in the uses and gratifications model is the assumption that audience members are "sufficiently self aware" to be able to report to the researcher on their interests and motivations. As a result, researchers have employed either open-ended questions accompanied by appropriate probes or lists of motivations—often developed from earlier probings—to determine the level of a particular type of motivation of an audience member. Becker (1979) reports results of both open-ended and closed-ended probes of this sort, most explicitly tied to the political content of the mass media.

A third strategy available to gratifications researchers—but one seldom employed—is to manipulate in field or laboratory settings the needs or motivations of the subjects. For example, subjects could be instructed to attend to a visual message in order to learn as much as possible of its contents or in order to learn as much as possible of the technique used to generate the message. Comparisons then could be made between the two groups of subjects on relevant dependent variables, such as information acquisition or task enjoyment.

Each of these strategies—measurement by inference, by self-report, or by manipulation—assumes some knowledge on the part of the researcher of the population motivations governing audience behavior. Each also assumes some understanding by the researcher of the relationship between motives and specific media or alternative satisfying behaviors. Measurement of a motive that is unlikely to be satisfied by use of a given medium may be rendered useless should that medium not be available to respondents or subjects as a means of satisfaction. Finally, all three strategies assume the researcher adequately understands the relationship between positive motivations, which lead audience members to certain media use behaviors, and negative forces, which result in nonuse of the media.

The inferential approach to measurement of needs is limited additionally by the requirement that researchers have the ability to identify some surrogate—either a cause, an effect, or a spurious covariate—which can be used to specify the motive. If the surrogate is a cause or an effect, the researcher has to argue that the link is strong enough to rule out serious contamination due to problems of multiple causation. If the surrogate is spuriously related to the motive, the researcher must be willing to argue that the relationship is stable enough to exist without serious variations across situation. The inferential strategy, then, assumes a rather high level of theorizing about the relationships between motivations and other variables.

The self-report strategy is plagued by problems resulting from the differential abilities and desires of respondents to verbalize answers to rather difficult questions about motivations as well as to recognize controlling motivations when they are suggested by the researcher. Certain motives are socially more acceptable than others. And better-educated respondents would be not only more likely to recognize governing motives but also better prepared to explain motives and the resulting assessments of the media's abilities to satisfy them.

There is considerable evidence from research on human behavior to suggest that there are serious limits on the extent to which people can report insights into the causes of their own behavior. Despite efforts to generate checklists of gratifications sought from the open-ended responses of audience members, the closed-ended self-report questions still may be considered to reflect imposed researcher's concepts. The respondent's answers to them thus may be transitory and represent invalid responses made to nullify the investigator. If so, the responses should correlate poorly when the same gratification items are repeated at some future time. This possibility, in technical terms *stability reliability*, has not been tested in the published literature. McLeod and McDonald (Note 6) analyzed measures of gratifications sought in data obtained at two time points 12 months apart. The test must be considered a conservative one because not only was the time lag long, but the referents to the two sets of items were quite different. The first data set, collected in October 1979, used "news about current events and politics" as the referent, whereas the October 1980 study dealt with "presidential campaigns." In the question wording, the first interview schedule used "public officials" in contrast to "presidential candidates" of the more recent study. Despite these differences, an average correlation of more than +.30 was shown for the five items across the 12-month lag (n = 245, $p < .001$). This coefficient was higher than the average correlation between gratification items on the same dimension at each time point and considerably greater than the synchronous associations between media exposure and the gratification items. The stability of individual gratification items appears sufficiently strong to rule out the possibility that audience members give frivolous responses to the gratifications sought items.

Validity, like reliability, has not been examined very carefully by researchers using the uses and gratifications approach. Face validity, the examination of items to see if they seem to be measuring the underlying gratification, seems to be as far as most research goes. Pragmatic validation has not been used systematically even though opportunities exist. Construct validation, evaluation of the items through the testing of hypotheses, has been thwarted by the failure to integrate gratifications into communication theory and to examine their effects. The most systematic attempt was by McLeod and Becker (1974), who found rather clear support for the validity of gratifications sought items tested against the criteria of political effects. Subsequent research cited in the Motives and Effects section has given added support to the construct validity of the measures originally developed by Blumler and McQuail (1969).

Four further comments can be made regarding the validity of gratifications sought lists. First, an impressive array of examples of validation of gratification statements in nonpolitical areas has been assembled by Blumler (1979). These at least indirectly support the utility of self-report measures for political content. Second, the existing set of a dozen statements has been found to be applicable to a wide variety of respondents not only in the United States but in several Western European countries as well (Blumler, Ewbank, Cayrol, Geertz, & Thoveron, 1978; Blumler & Fox, 1980). Third, efforts to expand the existing list of statements through open-ended questioning has not been fruitful in revealing previously untapped areas of need (Becker, 1979). It appears that, at least within our existing methods of eliciting needs, the present lists appear to be nearly exhaustive. Finally, validity appears strongest if we deal with dimensional relationships to other variables and avoid the direct interpretation of levels of individual gratification items. Not only may social desirability affect the level of response (more or less equally for all respondents if the measure is valid), but previous satisfaction could lead to an understatement of the extent of seeking.

Numerous problems also beset the manipulation of motivation in the laboratory. It is difficult to devise instructions that adequately stimulate audience motives without at the same time informing subjects of the purpose of the experiment. In other words, those instructions most likely to stimulate relevant motives may also render the findings trivial, for subjects may simply act out the scenario inferred from the researcher's instructions. The best procedures for manipulation no doubt require a sophisticated understanding of the antecedents of the governing motives.

Some previously unreported data from a pilot study conducted by the second author and his graduate students serves to illustrate the experimental strategy as well as the potentially illuminating nature of the results. The subject matter of the experiment is political in at least an international sense.

Seventy subjects recruited from an introductory-level journalism course were randomly assigned to one of three task conditions intended to manipulate

TABLE 2.1   Results of Pilot Experiment on Manipulation of Information
             Motive

	Condition			
	Group 1 (Test)	Group 2 (Essay)	Group 3 (Control)	Sign. of One-Way F
Mean use of public affairs periodicals in minutes	5.29	4.00	2.21	.05
Mean use of entertainment periodicals in minutes	3.29	5.63	5.04	NS
Mean no. of distinct pieces of information in essay	1.58	4.86	2.75	.05
Mean no. of words in essay	67.58	103.45	53.42	.05
Mean knowledge score	3.88	4.05	4.08	NS
Mean no. of pictures able to be described	.67	.50	.13	.05
N	24	22	24	

various motives. Subjects were run in small groups of approximately five subjects. In each case, subjects were told upon arrival for the experiment that there
was a 10- to 15-minute delay and that they would have to wait in a lounge area
until it was time to begin. The lounge area consisted of a series of chairs around
a coffee table, on which were placed equal numbers of public affairs periodicals
(*Time, Newsweek,* the *New York Times* week in review section) and entertainment periodicals (*Cosmopolitan, People,* and *Us*).

In the first task group, subjects were informed prior to their wait that the
experiment they would be involved in would include a test "on what you know
about the current situation in Pakistan." The second group was informed it
would be required to write an essay "explaining your opinion on what the U.S.
policy should be on giving military aid to Pakistan." The third group was given
no indication of the content of the experiment.

The study was conducted in the winter of 1980, after the U.S. Embassy in
Pakistan had been burned out while the U.S. was contemplating ways of
countering the Soviet invasion of Afghanistan. The public affairs periodicals
available to the students dealt with Pakistan in some fashion, though usually
only indirectly in stories about the crisis and U.S. policy alternatives. The
entertainment periodicals did not deal with the Pakistan issue at all.

Group 1 (Test) subjects were expected to have a need for information of a
general sort (facts and details), while Group 2 (Essay) subjects were expected to
need information of value to them in making a decision regarding U.S. policy

toward Pakistan. Subjects in Group 3 (Control) were not expected to have a need for information beyond the general curiosity common to all groups.

Subjects actually waited in the room for 10 minutes before they were given posttest instruments which asked them to write an essay and answer specific questions about Pakistan. During the 10-minute wait their media use behavior was observed through a one-way mirror.

The data in Table 2.1 show the general nature of the findings. As expected, both the test and essay subjects used the public affairs media more than did those subjects in the control condition, though there was no significant difference in use of the entertainment media. The essay group did write lengthier essays and use more distinct pieces of information in doing so than did those in other groups. And both the Test and Essay groups recalled more information about the pictures dealing with Pakistan in the magazines than did the control subjects. On the crucial measure of knowledge, which consisted of 10 objective questions about details of the Pakistani situation, no differences appeared.

The data suggest that experimental manipulation of the motives of audience members is possible through simple task situations analogous to those that can arise in a social situation. Those motives then led audience members to assess the media available to them and make selections, presumably as the result of past experiences. The media behaviors then seem to have some consequences, but not independent of the motivations that led to their selection. The essay group, for example, was lower in use of the public affairs media than the test group, but the members clearly obtained information from their use which benefited them in the essay task which those in the test condition did not obtain. Finally, the consequences of the use and motivation may not always be the obvious ones. This is illustrated by the differential abilities in recalling details of pictures. Those in the test and essay situations were significantly better able to recall these materials than those in the control groups, despite the fact that the control group was no lower than those in the other two groups on overall knowledge.

USES AND GRATIFICATIONS RESEARCH
IN POLITICAL COMMUNICATION

One of the basic issues underlying the assemblage of the materials for a volume such as this one results from uncertainty about the unique character of the subject matter—in this case, political communication. For a discussion of the uses and gratifications literature, the questions can probably best be rephrased as follows: Is the uses and gratifications model a political one?

The answer is almost certainly a negative one. While the formulation historically did develop out of the political and public opinion research of the Columbia group, it quickly turned away from political matters. As noted above, perhaps the largest amount of current research activity in the United States is of a decidely commercial and entertainment nature.

Yet there are two distinct ways the uses and gratifications model speaks to political concerns. First, audience members do make use of those materials in the mass media usually thought of as political. For example, the 1976 and 1980 U.S. presidential debates attracted large audiences. Similarly, political commercials and the political appeals of the parties in such countries as Britain attract the attention of significant segments of the audience. Presumably, such use of the political content of the mass media is governed by audience motives similar in at least general nature to the motives which generate use of the entertainment content of the media or the general public affairs content of the media.

Researchers should be cautious, however, in defining a priori what is political. An assumption of the uses and gratifications model is that audience members have considerable latitude in determining what kinds of content and which media can be used to satisfy a given need. And the audience member may have a considerably different view of what is meant by "politics" than the researcher. For example, unemployment often is viewed by communication researchers as a political issue. For the respondent, however, unemployment may be defined solely in terms of family economics, devoid of what would seem to the researcher to be obvious political connections.

The second way uses and gratifications research can take on a decidedly political nature is through effects analysis. Though uses and gratifications research was born out of frustration with existing analyses of media effects, it has not been devoid of an interest in media effects. As the reviews of Katz et al. (1973a) and Weiss (1969) make clear, many researchers in this tradition saw the inclusion of audience motivations and needs as a way of better understanding media effects. Many media effects, of course, are decidedly political.

Despite this promise, relatively little empirical work has actually addressed the question of how audience motives can assist in an understanding of the media's impact on audience members. Some of the research which has spoken to this matter is presented below.

ILLUSTRATIVE STUDIES IN POLITICAL COMMUNICATIONS

The existing studies in the uses and gratifications area dealing with politics in one of the two ways discussed above can be classified into five categories. First are the studies that have attempted to isolate empirically the audience motives likely to have relevance for the study of audience uses of political material. The second group of studies has attempted to determine the antecedents of these motives. The third type examines audience evaluations of the various media's abilities to meet the needs, while the fourth group of studies has examined the actual linkages between audience needs and use of materials judged to be political in nature. The final group of studies has dealt with political effects of the media.

Identification of Relevant Motives

Blumler and McQuail (1969), working with a list of items developed after extensive open-ended probings, presented eight different motivations for use or nonuse of the political content of the media. Audience members were thought to be using the mass media for *vote guidance, reinforcement* of decisions already made, general *surveillance* of the political environment, *excitement,* or because of their *anticipated utility* in future interpersonal communication situations. Motives for avoiding political materials were because of a feeling of *alienation,* because of *partisanship,* or because it was not found to provide needed *relaxation.*

Subsequent use of these items, however, has shown that they do not always have empirical independence; Becker (1979) concluded that while conceptual distinctions may be possible, it may not be possible empirically to isolate the distinct role of some of these individual motivations in a particular analysis. Empirically, audience motives seem to cluster somewhat consistently into three groups: (1) those representing informational needs, (2) those representing diversionary needs, and (3) those relating to more specific personal needs. Blumler (1979) and Katz (1979) have referred to these as "cognitive," "diversion," and "identity" needs.

Antecedents of Motives

At least three studies have dealt explicitly with te antecedents of the motives underlying use of the political content of the media. The findings would have to be treated as suggestive at best. Becker, McLeod, and Ziemke (Note 7) and Stroman and Becker (1978), for example, found in analyses of the 1974 national Michigan voting study that demographic variables, with the possible exception of education and race, were not good predictors of audience motives. Such variables as partisanship, feelings of political efficacy, and political trust were related positively to several of the *cognitive* measures of motives, but here the problem of a tautology surfaces, as it is not clear whether the measures of the motives and the measures of political orientations are tapping distinct yet empirically related concepts or the same general orientation.

Blumler (1979) found that researchers may be rewarded for going beyond the traditional types of measures of social circumstances in looking for the antecedents of motives. For example, ownership of a telephone was found to be negatively related to the diversion and personal identity motives, and this finding was more striking for some groups (such as house-bound groups) than for others. In general, Blumler argued, the data suggest researchers should pursue three types of antecedents of motives: (1) normative influences, socially imposed by such things as age, sex, and social class; (2) socially distributed life chances, such as frequency of social contacts through work settings or social organizations; and (3) the subjective adjustment or reaction of the audience member to his or her situation, indexed through such variables as work satisfaction.

Evaluations of Media's Abilities to Provide Satisfaction

Mendelsohn and O'Keefe (1976) have provided the most extensive examination of U.S. audience members' evaluations of the ability of the mass media to satisfy political needs. While the analyses are limited to a comparison between television and newspapers, they show that audience members can and do make distinctions among the media. Newspapers were rated more highly overall in terms of their ability to satisfy cognitive or informational motives associated with the campaign. There were few differences among various demographic groups in this assessment.

Distinctions among media sources were also found by McLeod et al. (in press) in examining the ratings of helpfulness (gratifications received) in judging the candidates' stands on issues and their personal qualities in the 1976 presidential campaign in Madison, Wisconsin. Newspaper news was rated at least as high with respect to clarifying issues stands; however, the newspaper fell well behind television when illustration of personal qualities was the criterion. Debates were intermediate in gratifications received on both criteria, finishing well ahead of magazines and campaign brochures.

The helpfulness of the presidential debates was further analyzed for nine other criteria in the righthand portion of Table 2.2. The debates appear relatively effective in satisfying motives in several areas: in clarifying the candidates' issue stands, in presenting their personal qualities, in pointing out their weak points, and in suggesting what they would do if elected. As discussed earlier, these also tend to be those criteria most sought after by voters (as shown in the left portion of Table 2.2). Other needs seem to be poorly provided by the debate format: They were not very helpful in providing information about who was going to win, in making the campaign exciting, and in giving supportive or useful information that could be used in communication with others. Fortunately, all of these were gratifications not heavily sought by voters. An exception to this pattern can be seen for "helping to make up your mind"; 66 percent were seeking help but only 14 percent found the debates very helpful.

The McLeod et al. research was consistent with Mendelson and O'Keefe (1976) in finding few demographic differences. Younger respondents, however, were somewhat more likely than their elders to find the debates helpful overall and, more specifically, to find the candidates' weak points and to obtain things to talk to others about. Some situational differences were also found. Those respondents who had made their presidential choice prior to the first debate were more likely to obtain supportive information about their own positions and their candidate's strong points; voters deciding during the debate period were more likely than early deciders or those deciding in the last 10 days of the campaign to report that the debates aided them in their decision. These last findings contribute to the validity of these self-report measures.

TABLE 2.2 Reasons for Paying Attention to Presidential Campaigns (Gratifications Sought) and Perceived Helpfulness of 1976 Presidential Debates (Gratifications Received)

	Percent Seeking in Presidential Campaigns:			Percent Reporting Debates as Helpful:		
	A Lot	A Little	Not at all	Very	Somewhat	Not at all
Surveillance-Vote Guidance						
To see how the candidates stand on the issues	86	13	1	31	44	25
To help you make up your mind how to vote in the election	66	25	9	14	50	36
To see what the candidates would do if elected	52	34	14	21	54	25
Contest-Excitement						
To judge the personal qualities of the candidates	46	47	7	29	46	25
To judge which candidate is likely to win the electio.ı	23	46	31	6	48	46
To enjoy the excitement of the election race	16	40	44	10	41	49

(Continued)

TABLE 2.2 Continued

	Percent Seeking in Presidential Campaigns:			Percent Reporting Debates as Helpful:		
	A Lot	A Little	Not at all	Very	Somewhat	Not at all
Communication-Utility						
To get information that agrees with your position	24	49	27	9	55	36
To use what you learn in political discussions	19	51	30	9	52	39
To give you something to talk about with others	15	50	35	12	49	39
Other items						
To judge the candidates' weak points	45	44	11	26	60	14
To remind you of your candidate's strong points	31	48	21	19	53	28
N 353						

In addition to measuring the gratifications sought and the gratifications received from debates, the Wisconsin research also asked a subset of respondents (n = 97) interviewed before the debates how helpful they *expected* the upcoming debates to be regarding learning issue stands and personal qualities of candidates. Comparisons of marginals revealed that the predebate expectations were rather close to the levels of helpfulness reported after the debates. Estimates of help in learning issue stands were a few points higher than the postdebate ratings, while those for personal qualities were almost identical to the subsequent evaluations. Correlations between the predebate expectations and the postdebate ratings, however, revealed only moderate accuracy. The predebate expectations predicted postdebate helpfulness ratings at only slightly better than chance levels. Underestimation as well as overestimation of debate helpfulness was common.

Adoni (1979), in a study which can be viewed as a political extension of the work of Katz et al. (1973b) on general audience evaluation of the motive-satisfying capabilities of the media, found that Israeli high school students saw clear distinctions among the various media. For example, newspapers, television, and radio were perceived as useful for the development of civic attitudes toward the political system. Books were perceived as most helpful in developing national orientations. Cinema was generally evaluated poorly as a means of developing political values.

Linkages Between Motives and Media Use

Becker (1976) found that general measures of motives for using political content of the media predicted attention given the televised 1973 Senate Watergate Hearings, even after party affiliation and normal public affairs television use were held constant through statistical control. The findings were stronger for older voters than for younger ones. Surveillance was generally the best positive predictor of exposure to the hearings, while a motive for relaxation was the best negative predictor.

McLeod et al. (in press) have provided the most detailed examination of audience motives and viewing of one specific set of political events. Using the extent of viewing of the 1976 presidential debates as the criterion, it was found that the seeking of 6 of the 11 gratification items shown in Table 2.2 were significantly related to debate viewing at the zero-order (without controls for other variables) level. Strongest prediction came from the seeking of excitement (.24), of personal qualities (.21), and of stands on issues (.20). Few differences were found for age, but time of decision analyses revealed much larger differences largely in the directions anticipated. Early deciders' viewing was most influenced by wanting to enjoy the excitement of the election race (.26); judging personal qualities showed the strong association for those deciding during the debate period (.29), while the debate viewing of those deciding very late in the campaign was best predicted by wanting to make up their minds (.39).

With the same Wisconsin data set, McLeod, Durall, Ziemke, and Bybee (1979) used regression analysis to isolate predictors of debate watching, campaign news exposure, and use of partisan political materials. For debate watching, the zero-order correlations with both surveillance-vote guidance and contest-excitement were significant for both young and older respondents, while communication utility reached marginal levels in both cases. After controls for a variety of demographic, political, and media use items were introduced, however, the block of gratification factors was shown to be nonsignificant, accounting for only two percent of the incremental (that not accounted for by controls) variance. The most important determinant of debate viewing turned out to be the person's customary use of public affairs content in television and newspapers. Because the gratifications sought were introduced late in the analysis, it could be argued that their role in affecting debate viewing was as mediating processes reflecting the combined impact of a large number of social and political forces.

The McLeod et al. (1979) analyses of campaign news media use revealed a much stronger role for gratifications sought than was found for debate watching. Surveillance-vote guidance was related to campaign media use for the young, while the contest-excitement factor proved to be strong for older respondents. The latter factor and, to a lesser extent, surveillance-vote guidance, predicted use of partisan media content among both age groups.

Motives and Effects

Audience motives have been used in effects analysis in two ways: (1) as contingent conditions in examining the relationships between such variables as exposure and some criterion effect, and (2) as either supplementing or interacting with exposure to produce an effect.

The introduction by McLeod, Becker, and Byrnes (1974) of audience motives in the study of the hypothesized agenda-setting influence of the press is illustrative of the first strategy. The data were supportive of such an inclusion, showing that audience members motivated by the seeking of information were generally *less* likely to show an agenda-setting effect—that is, to show a pattern of issue concerns similar to those of the newspaper they read—than those without such motivation. The less motivated "scanners" were more likely to pick up the newspaper's agenda. McCombs and Weaver (Note 8) and Weaver (1977) have used variables at least conceptually similar to those of McLeod et al. and concluded that audience orientations were likely to play a role as contingent conditions in agenda-setting analysis. The McLeod et al. and McCombs and Weaver analyses seem to be in conflict, however, in that those *low* in motivation showed greater agenda-setting effect for the former, while those *high* in need for orientation (and information) were more affected for McCombs and Weaver. The two teams of researchers used differing measures of audience orientations, however, and the conflict may result from this. Weaver (1980) has examined the issue of comparability of measures in a non-agenda-setting context and found some evidence to support such an interpretation.

Blumler and McQuail (1969), in their analyses of the 1964 British general election, illustrate the second strategy. They found that the strength of motivation (a summation of seeking various individual gratifications) played different roles in mediating the impact of political communication. In some comparisons, the effects of exposure were magnified by motivation, while in others a diminishing impact was apparent. The various effects of strength of motivation tended to be interactive rather than simply supplementary to media exposure. That is, the combined effects of exposure and motivation were most often either greater or less than that expected from the addition of their individual effects. Further, their analyses of specific gratifications revealed different types of mediation, vote-guidance playing a role varying from that of reinforcement, for example.

McLeod and Becker (1974) conducted the most elaborate study to date of the construct validity of self-report measures of gratifications sought. The set of five gratifications sought factors, together with three factors comprised of reasons for avoiding political communication, accounted for significant increments of variance beyond that predicted by television public affairs exposure for a variety of 1972 political campaign effects criteria: issue accuracy, probability of voting, campaign interest and activity, and discussion of the campaign. For many of these campaign effect criteria, additional analyses found evidence supportive of the validity of individual gratifications sought factors, even after controlling for education, political interest or activity, and television public affairs exposure. The results gave strong encouragement to a media exposure-gratifications sought political effects model that was clearly *additive* rather than interactive. Thus, in contrast to the predominant findings of the earlier Blumler and McQuail (1969) research, media exposure tended to predict political effects equally at all levels of gratifications sought; conversely, the extent of exposure did not alter the strength of the relationship between gratifications sought and campaign effects.

These findings were generally replicated by Becker (1976) and McLeod, Brown, Becker, and Ziemke (1977), as well as in a recent study of the role of gratifications sought in a between-campaign period (McLeod et al., Note 5). In this last study, the seeking of surveillance (issue positions and qualities of elected officials and their performance) from media coverage of current events and politics predicted knowledge of the ongoing economic crisis and placing of blame for inflation. This held even after controls for education, age, and a variety of televisions' and newspapers' exposure measures were introduced. Communication utility (the seeking of excitement, discussion, and talk with others and consonant information) predicted blaming a variety of sources for inflation but was not significantly tied to economic knowledge. For both gratification factors, the relationships to political outcomes proved to be additive rather than interactive. Relatively few interactions between either gratification sought factor and the various television newspaper and television exposure measures reached statistical significance. This was in strong contrast to two other orientational measures, attention level and media reliance, which revealed a much higher proportion of significant multiplicative interactions (levels of effects departing from a simple addition of exposure and gratification effects) when multiplied by the media exposure measures. The dominance of additive over interactive models for gratification-exposure effects which has characterized recent research findings should be carefully replicated with other criteria and media exposure measures and under differing conditions and locales.

Audience motives also may produce effects indirectly through the stimulation of media use, which in turn may affect political outcomes. Mendelsohn and O'Keefe (1976) found that time of vote decision was related to the extent of dependence on the media for information. Those voters having made their decision early in the campaign were more likely to report depending on the media for information about the campaign than were late deciders. Time of decision was related more directly to specific gratifications sought by McLeod et al. (in press), who found that early deciders were more likely than others to seek information about their candidate's strong points and other supportive information and to want excitement from media content.

A LOOK TO THE FUTURE

We began this chapter with a review of the present ambiguity in the label "uses and gratifications" research. It is impossible to say whether this ambiguity will continue in the future with research going on in its unorganized, if productive, fashion. Perhaps it should go on in its present course. Variety and eclecticism may be the best we can hope for in political communication research. But a more directed future is also possible where research findings would be more cumulative and some theoretical integration could be achieved. We can speculate about the conditions that might produce a more organized future for uses and gratifications.

First, there would be considerable benefit if the concepts of motivation and media use were to be used more consistently. It would be foolish to argue for some academy-like regulation of conceptual and operational definitions. It would be useful, however, to at least make distinctions between basic human needs and motives, and among gratifications sought, expectations, and gratifications received. Even the seemingly straightforward concept of "media use" has widely varied meanings, including exposure time, intake of various types of media content, and what the person expects to get from the media. The inclusion of the various types of gratifications and media use within the same investigations could aid in empirically clarifying definitions.

Second, there seems to be agreement among theorists of varied perspectives that a uses and gratification approach would benefit if a closer tie were made between differing patterns of gratifications sought and the meanings and interpretations given specific media messages. Present research has tended to use general classes of messages (such as news viewing) and larger units of effects (for example, knowledge). Closer connection between specific messages and more proximate effects could specify more closely the mediating effects of motives. Such research might also have the latent function of narrowing the gap between the social scientists in the uses and gratification tradition and exponents of popular culture and others working from perspectives of the humanities.

Third, those doing uses and gratifications research might well abandon equating of effects research with the hypodermic all-powerful media model and attempt to investigate the consequences of various patterns of media use and motivation. This frees the approach from the circularity of assuming what people need is what they watch and vice versa. Without evaluative criteria for determining how well media content satisfies motives, the approach can too easily fall back into the trap of a conservative status quo. Perceptions of how well various media sources and other nonmedia behaviors provide gratifications can become an important basis for media evaluation and planning. As indicated, gratifications received should be measured independently from gratifications sought, from expectations that various sources can satisfy what is sought, and from media exposure patterns.

The integration of uses and gratifications into media effects research should not be limited to measuring impact solely by subjective criteria, however. The perception of being informed, for example, may be an illusion of the clever packaging of media content. More objective criteria, less dependent on the self-report of the audience member, are also needed to strengthen the evaluative process.

Fourth, more systematic attempts could be made to develop broader and more complex models of the role of uses and gratifications. More attention should be paid to the question of how exposure to various types of media content combine with motives to produce effects. Most previous research indicates the effects are simply additive, but more theoretically interesting interactions could be uncovered. Little is known at present about how past experience feeds back to expectations of satisfaction and to the structure of motives. In general, the model presented in this chapter would benefit from new research at each relationship designated by an arrow in Figure 2.1.

Fifth, uses and gratifications research could move closer to social theory if it went beyond its present largely individual focus to consider its relevance to social systems. As discussed earlier, the locations in social structure of motive patterns and of the ability to use media content to achieve satisfaction is an inadequately researched issue. Surely the harsh realities of being poor, of living in decaying cities, and the like have some connection to media uses and gratifications and their effects. Integration into more general social theory also requires more systematic examination of the relationship between the use and gratification patterns of the audience and the production of messages in the mass media. Political communication research might extend this connection to the communication activities of various government officials and to election candidates as news sources.

Finally, uses and gratifications research on political communication may have to come to grips with the discrepancy between researchers' focus on political concepts and contexts for motives and the widespread indifference to these topics and issues among the audience. What is important to the political communication researcher is not salient to the average audience member. Politics is a word falling into increasing disfavor and may not serve as the frame of reference for the disaffected and indifferent citizens as they regard the realities of their everyday lives. Perhaps new methods, more sensitive to the perspectives of the people we study, are needed to resolve this apparent contradiction. Its solution should act as a challenge for future political communication researchers to better understand the meaning of an active audience.

REFERENCE NOTES

1. Becker, L. B., Fruit, J. W., & Collins, E. L. *Motivations and media use: Exploring the linkage.* Paper presented at the Midwest Association for Public Opinion Research annual meeting, Chicago, 1979.

2. Sanders, K. R., & Chalfa, J. J. *Washington behind closed doors: Its uses and effects.* Paper presented at the Eastern Communication Association meeting, Philadelphia, 1979.

3. Blumler, J. G. Electoral volatility: *Examining communication and change among young voters.* Paper presented at the World Association for Public Opinion Congress, Montreux, Switzerland, 1975.

4. Blumler, J. G., Brown, J. R., & McQuail, D. *The social origins of gratifications associated with television viewing.* Unpublished manuscript, Centre for Television Research, Leeds, England, 1970.

5. McLeod, J. M., Luetscher, W. D., & McDonald, D. G. *Beyond mere exposure: Media orientations and their impact on political processes.* Paper presented at the Association for Education in Journalism annual meeting, Boston, 1980.

6. McLeod, J. M., & McDonald, D. G. *Some test-retest reliability coefficients of media use and gratification measures.* Unpublished manuscript, Mass Communications Research Center, Madison, Wisconsin, 1981.

7. Becker, L. B., McLeod, J. M., & Ziemke, D. A. *Correlations of media gratifications.* Paper presented at the American Association for Public Opinion Research annual meeting, Asheville, North Carolina, 1976.

8. McCombs, M. E., & Weaver, D. H. *Voters' need for orientation and use of mass communication.* Paper presented at the International Communication Association annual meeting, Montreal, 1973.

REFERENCES

Adoni, H. The functions of mass media in the political socialization of adolescents. *Communication Research,* 1979, *6,* 84-106.

Bauer, R. A. The obstinate audience. *American Psychologist,* 1964, *19,* 319-328.

Becker, L. B. Two tests of media gratifications: Watergate and 1974 elections. *Journalism Quarterly,* 1976, *53,* 26-31.

Becker, L. B. Measurement of gratifications. *Communication Research,* 1979, *6,* 54-73.

Becker, L. B., Collins, D. L., & Fruit, J. W. Personal motivations and newspaper readership. *ANPA News Research Report No. 26,* 1980.

Becker, L. B., McCombs, M. E., & McLeod, J. M. The development of political cognitions. In S. H. Chaffee (Ed.), *Political communication: Issues and strategies for research.* Beverly Hills, CA: Sage, 1975.

Berelson, B. What "missing the newspaper" means. In P. F. Lazarsfeld & F. N. Stanton (Eds.), *Communication research, 1948-49.* New York: Duell, Sloan and Pearce, 1949.

Berelson, B., Lazarsfeld, P., & McPhee, W. *Voting.* Chicago: University of Chicago Press, 1954.

Blumler, J. G. Mass media roles and reactions in the February election. In H. R. Penniman (Ed.), *Britain at the polls: The parliamentary election of February, 1974.* Washington, DC: American Enterprise Institute for Public Policy Research, 1974.

Blumler, J. G. The role of television in British politics. In H. J. Oyer (Ed.), *Human communication: International and cross-cultural implications.* East Lansing: Michigan State University Press, 1975.

Blumler, J. G. The role of theory in uses and gratifications studies. *Communication Research,* 1979, *6,* 9-36.

Blumler, J. G., Ewbank, A., Cayrol, R., Geertz, C., & Thoveron, G. A three-nation analysis of voters' attitudes to election communication. *European Journal of Political Research,* 1978, *6,* 127-156.

Blumler, J. G., & Fox, A. D. The involvement of voters in the European elections of 1979: Its extent and sources. *European Journal of Political Research,* 1980, *8,* 359-385.

Blumler, J. G., and Katz, E. (Eds.). *The uses of mass communications: Current perspectives on gratifications research.* Beverly Hills, CA: Sage, 1974.

Blumler, J. G., & McLeod, J. M. Communication and voter turnout in Britain. In T. Leggatt (Ed.), *Sociological theory and survey research.* Beverly Hills, CA: Sage, 1974.

Blumler, J. G., & McQuail, D. *Television in politics.* Chicago: University of Chicago Press, 1969.

Carey, J. W., & Kreiling, A. L. Popular culture and uses and gratifications: Notes toward an accommodation. In J. G. Blumler & E. Katz (Eds.), *The uses of mass communication: Current perspectives on gratifications research.* Beverly Hills, CA: Sage, 1974.

Clarke, P., & Kline, F. G. Media effects reconsidered. *Communication Research,* 1974, *1,* 224-240.

Davison, W. P. On the effects of communication. *Public Opinion Quarterly,* 1959, *23,* 343-360.

Dimmick, J. W., McCagin, T. A., & Bolten, W. T. Media use and the life span. *American Behavioral Scientist,* 1979, *23,* 7-31.

Elliott, P. Uses and gratifications research: A critique and a sociological alternative. In J. G. Blumler & E. Katz (Eds.), *The uses of mass communication: Current perspectives in gratifications research.* Beverly Hills, CA: Sage, 1974.

Frank, R. E., & Greenberg, M. G. *The public's use of television.* Beverly Hills, CA: Sage, 1980.

Goodhardt, G. J., Ehrenberg, A.S.C., & Collins, M.A. *The television audience: Patterns of viewing.* Lexington, MA: D. C. Heath, 1975.

Herzog, H. Professor quiz: A gratification study. In P. F. Lazarsfeld & F. N. Stanton (Eds.), *Radio research, 1941.* New York: Duell, Sloan and Pearce, 1942.

Herzog, H. What do we really know about daytime serial listeners? In P. F. Lazarsfeld & F. N. Stanton (Eds.), *Radio research 1942-1943*. New York: Duell, Sloan and Pearce, 1944.

Katz, E. The uses of Becker, Blumler and Swanson. *Communication Research*, 1979, *6*, 74-83.

Katz, E., Blumler, J. G., & Gurevitch, M. Uses and gratifications research. *Public Opinion Quarterly*, 1973, *37*, 509-523. (a)

Katz, E., Gurevitch, M., & Haas, H. On the use of mass media for important things. *American Sociological Review*, 1973, *38*, 164-181. (b)

Kippax, S., & Murray, J. P. Using the mass media: Need gratification and perceived utility. *Communication Research*, 1980, *7*, 335-360.

Klapper, J. *The effects of mass communication*. New York: Free Press, 1960.

Kline, F. G., Miller, P. V., & Morrison, A. J. Adolescents and family planning information: An exploration of audience needs and media effects. In J. G. Blumler & E. Katz (Eds.), *The uses of mass communications: Current perspectives on gratifications research*. Beverly Hills, CA: Sage, 1974.

Lazarsfeld, P., Berelson, B., & Gaudet, H. *The people's choice*. New York: Columbia University Press, 1948.

Levy, M. R. The audience experience with television news. *Journalism Monographs, No. 55*, 1978.

McGuire, W. J. Psychological motives and communication gratification. In J. G. Blumler & E. Katz (Eds.), *The uses of mass communication: Current perspectives on gratifications research*. Beverly Hills, CA: Sage, 1974.

McLeod, J. M., & Becker, L. B. Testing the validity of gratification measures through political effects analysis. In J. G. Blumler & E. Katz (Eds.), *The uses of mass communications: Current perspectives on gratification research*. Beverly Hills, CA: Sage, 1974.

McLeod, J. M., Becker, L. B., & Byrnes, J. E. Another look at the agenda setting function of the press. *Communication Research*, 1974, *1*, 131-166.

McLeod, J. M., Brown, J. D., Becker, L. B., & Ziemke, D. A. Decline and fall at the White House: A longitudinal analysis of communication effects. *Communication Research*, 1977, *4*, 3-22.

McLeod, J. M., Bybee, C. R., & Durall, J. A. Equivalence of informed political participation: The 1976 presidential debates as a source of influence. *Communication Research*, 1979, *6*, 463-487.

McLeod, J. M., Bybee, C. R., & Durall, J. A. Gratifications sought and received as criteria for mass media evaluation. *Journalism Quarterly*, in press.

McLeod, J. M., Durall, J. A., Ziemke, D. A., & Bybee, C. R. Expanding the context of debate effects. In S. Kraus (Ed.), *The great debates 1976: Ford vs. Carter*. Bloomington: Indiana University Press, 1979.

McLeod, J. M., & Choe, S. Y. An analysis of five factors affecting newspaper circulation. *ANPA News Research Report, No. 10*, 1978.

Mendelsohn, H. *Mass entertainment*. New Haven: College & University Press, 1966.

Mendelsohn, H. Some policy implications of the uses and gratifications paradigm. In J. G. Blumler & E. Katz (Eds.), *The uses of mass communication: Current perspectives on gratifications research*. Beverly Hills, CA: Sage, 1974.

Mendelsohn, H., & O'Keefe, G. J. *The people choose a president*. New York: Praeger, 1976.

Merton, R. K. *Social theory and social structure*. New York: Free Press, 1968.

Palmgreen, P., Wenner, L., & Rayburn, J. Relations between gratifications sought and obtained: A study of television news. *Communication Resarch*, 1980, *7*, 161-192.

Parsons, T. *The social system*. New York: Free Press, 1951.

Patterson, T. E., & McClure, R. D. *The unseeing eye*. New York: Putnam, 1976.

Rosengren, K. E. Uses and gratifications: A paradigm outlined. In J. G. Blumler & E. Katz (Eds.), *The uses of mass communication: Current perspectives on gratifications research*. Beverly Hills, CA: Sage, 1974.

Sears, D. O., & Freedman, J. L. Selective exposure to information: A critical review. *Public Opinion Quarterly*, 1971, *31*, 545-553.

Steiner, G. A. *The people look at television.* New York: Alfred A. Knopf, 1963.

Stevenson, R. E. Newspaper readership and community ties. *ANPA News Research Report No. 18,* 1979.

Stinchcombe, A. L. *Constructing social theories.* New York: Harcourt Brace Jovanovich, 1968.

Stroman, C., & Becker, L. B. Racial differences in gratifications. *Journalism Quarterly,* 1978, *55,* 767-771.

Suchman, E. An invitation to music. In P. F. Lazarsfeld & F. N. Stanton (Eds.), *Radio research, 1941.* New York: Duell, Sloan and Pearce, 1942.

Swanson, D. L. Political communication research and the uses and gratifications model: A critique. *Communication Research,* 1979, *6,* 37-53.

Timasheff, N. S., & Theodorson, G. A. *Sociological theory.* New York: Random House, 1976.

Warner, W. L., & Henry, W. E. The radio day time serial: A symbolic analysis. *Genetic Psychology Monographs,* 1948, *37,* 3-71, and in B. Berelson & M. Janowitz (Eds.), *Reader in public opinion and communication.* New York: Free Press, 1950.

Weaver, D. H. Political issues and voter need for orientation. In D. L. Shaw & M. E. McCombs (Eds.), *The emergence of American political issues.* St. Paul, MN: West Publishing, 1977.

Weaver, D. H. Audience need for orientation and media effects. *Communication Research,* 1980, *7,* 361-376.

Weaver, D. H., Wilhoit, G. C., & Reide, P. Personal needs and media use. *ANPA News Research Report No. 21,* 1979.

Weiss, W. Effects of the mass media of communication. In G. Lindzey & E. Aronson (Eds.), *The handbook of social psychology vol. 5.* Reading, MA: Addison-Wesley, 1969.

Weiss, W. Review of the uses of mass communications: Current perspectives on gratifications research. *Public Opinion Quarterly,* 1976, *40,* 132-13.

Wober, J. M. *Needs and satisfactions of the TV audience.* London: Independent Broadcasting Authority, 1980.

Wolfe, K. M., & Fiske, M. Why children read comics. In P. F. Lazarsfeld & F. N. Stanton (Eds.), *Communications research, 1948-49.* New York: Harper & Row, 1949.

CHAPTER 3

The Diffusion of Information Approach

Robert L. Savage

ON FEBRUARY 15, 1981, U.S. Senate Minority Leader Robert Byrd appeared on the radio interview program, *Capitol Cloakroom*. The Senator repeatedly refused to respond to the interviewers' queries regarding likely budget cuts to be proposed in President Reagan's upcoming address to the U.S. Congress, saying that he had not yet seen the celebrated, but apparently elusive, "black book" prepared by the President's budget director. Byrd's statement came after a virtual blitz in the nation's media for several preceding days in which a large volume of messages presumably revealed most, if not all, of the contents of the "black book." While the document itself remained mysterious, it contained no mysteries for very long.

Indeed, media reports beginning more than a week prior to the President's address had announced impending cuts or elimination of a wide variety of governmental programs, including agencies funding scientific research and cultural programs, foreign aid, farm price supports, health program, the Urban Development Action Grant (UDAG) program, the Comprehensive Employment and Training Act program, and a wide array of social services. Support for and objections to these reductions, both generally and specifically, were also being reported. Congressmen typically announced general support for the proposals, although Democrats were perhaps somewhat more ambiguous. A major business organization, the U.S. Chamber of Commerce, also announced its unreserved support. Specific objections also rolled in, such as local government officials complaining about threats to UDAG, labor leaders concerned about federal employee cutbacks and restrictions on unemployment compensation, prominent entertainment figures alarmed about the prospects of the National Endowment for the Arts, and even federal administrators such as health officials decrying the possible elimination of the National Health Service Corps.

101

Whatever the reason that an important congressional leader such as Senator Byrd somehow did not come into contact with the "black book," it is best left to historians and political biographers to ponder. Of much greater interest to political communication scholars is the fast and furious *spread* of a large volume of political information. Certainly, the White House had disseminated much of this information in a piecemeal fashion to various public and private interest groups and to media reporters as well. Allegedly, the "black book" itself made the rounds of Capitol Hill (although it may have made a late appearance in the Senate Minority Leader's office). Moreover, all these events occurred prior to the "big event" itself, the President's address on the evening of February 18, which largely confirmed the accuracy of earlier reports on the book's likely contents. The lines of battle for and against Reagan's proposals continued to form in the weeks following as actors already in the fray spread the word of the positions they would subsequently adopt and as new actors, either just becoming aware of the proposals, finally obtaining sufficient information to judge (Senator Byrd presumably among others), or withholding evaluations until the President's total package was personally delivered, also adopted stances.

Such rapid spreading of the word about a highly publicized set of events in a modern nation with advanced communications technology and strong organizational development is no great surprise, particularly when interest focuses on the various elite elements involved as described above. Moreover, there may well have been widespread popular dissemination across the nation if the swelling mailbags arriving in congressional offices are accepted as an indication of such dissemination. The importance of the little scenario, however, lies in what it may reveal about underlying processes of political communication in a society. It suggests the importance of such questions as: How do particular people or groups become aware of particular political matters? What factors contribute to the acceptance or rejection of political ideations? Are there basic contours in a given political system that shape who learns what and when? These questions and others that might be formulated about political communications point to the fact that information *moves* through space and time. One theoretical approach to political communication that capitalizes on the notion of movement, albeit from a variety of research traditions and methodologies, is *diffusion.*

DIFFUSION AS AN APPROACH TO
THE STUDY OF POLITICAL COMMUNICATION

Diffusion has been variously defined (see Graber, 1976, pp. 44-45; Katz, 1965, p. 28; Naroll, 1964; Rogers & Shoemaker, 1971, pp. 18-38), but generally all conceptualizations of this communication phenomenon systemically link a number of elements pointing to the spread of some communicable property through space and time from one agent to another. More precisely, we may define diffusion as the adoption of a communicable element, symbolic or artifactual, over time by decision-making entities linked to some originating source by channels of communication within some sociocultural system. As Brown (1977) has described, this conception of the "movement" of information is generally isomorphic with other phenomena involving movement as diffusion combines six interrelated elements: an area or environment, a temporal dimension, an item being diffused, nodes of origin and of destination, and paths of movement and influence, or other relationships between these nodes. As a consequence, diffusion research occasionally adopts analogies and/or methods from such types of "movement" research as epidemiology, cybernetics, and sociometry. At the same time, diffusion research is typically focused on one or more narrowly defined elements that are being diffused, elements that are highly visible and of intrinsic interest to the researchers, often resulting in much more empirical, inductive studies than those in other types of "movement" research. Still, this systemic character heightens the utility of the diffusion perspective in political communication research, especially as it sensitizes researchers to all those elements in the communication process leading to *decisions*, or, as they are more often styled, *adoptions*.

Because diffusion is most often viewed as a process culminating in a decision, it has often been described as a series of activities reflecting more or less sequenced phases or stages of communication in which messages have varying effects at different points in time beginning with attention arousal and ending in adoption or rejection (Graber, 1976, pp. 43-67). While this phasal character of diffusion is not always clearly evident in separate and sequential steps, the focus on behaviors across time leading to a decision more strongly emphasizes the temporal character of human communication than do other theoretical approaches. At the same time, this temporal aspect of diffusion leads to research problems that are not easily soluble, problems that will be examined later in considering diffusion modeling.

A second consequence of the focus on decision-making is that adoption units, the nodes of destination, or, in a broader communication sense, the communicatees or audience become more problematic. In determining the appropriate unit of analysis, researchers must closely consider what entities, from individuals to aggregates as abstract as cultures, are the behaving units which make decisions. For example, the decision to adopt a given policy innovation in municipalities may lie with voters, legislative bodies, bureaucratic agencies, or some combination thereof. Such variations in decision units may raise serious doubts about the applicability of generalizations on policy difusion across cities. (However, such variations might well be included in the research design.) But another problem for communication research arises here inasmuch as adoption decisions frequently have requisites that are extraneous to communication behaviors. This is notably the case where economic resources are required prior to an adoption. An example might be an instance where a governmental agency is interested in bringing about the adoption of some technological innovation requiring a particular source of power, only to discover that potential adopters do not have access to such power sources. At the same time, a given research concern may stop short at an "earlier" stage—for example, initial awareness or information-seeking—where such a problem may be irrelevant. Political communication research utilizing the perspective must, then, be sensitive to this phasal character of diffusion.

To some extent, the determination of the appropriate "stage" of diffusion may be shaped by the character of the element(s) being diffused. Political communication studies have focused on the diffusion of policies (for example, Davis, 1930; McVoy, 1940; Sutherland, 1950; Walker, 1969, 1971; Becker, 1970; Landes & Solomon, 1972; Gray, 1973, 1974; Collier & Messick, 1975; Bingham, 1976; Eyestone, 1977; Foster, 1978; Savage, 1978, in press; Hamm & Robertson, 1981), rumors (see Allport & Postman, 1947; Shibutani, 1966), news events and campaign messages (see Greenberg, 1964; Tichenor, Donohue, & Olien, 1970; Funkhouser & McCombs, 1971; Atkin, 1972; Mendelsohn, 1973; Ostlund, 1973; Placek, 1974; Zukin, Note 1, technology (for example, Pred, 1973; Frantzich, 1979), and violence (see Huff & Lutz, 1974; Most & Starr, 1980). Studies of the diffusion of rumors, news events, and campaign messages are more likely to focus on attention arousal and information-seeking effects, while those concerned with policies, technology, and violence are more likely directed to the decision stage.

While such temporal concerns are essential, location is just as essential. Indeed, the diffusion perspective is especially distinctive in this regard for, as Sopher (1972, p. 333) points out, "in much social theory, essentially nonspatial, society may be said to extend uniformly in space." A very graphic, although minor, example of the importance of location was uncovered by Greenberg (1964), who found that the last person in his sample from a Northern California city to learn of John Kennedy's assassination had been many hours away at sea at the time of the first news report. More important, location may be associated with considerable differences in economic resources and development and in cultural patterning that function together with physical geography to constitute distinctive syndromes of characteristic human behavior.

Location may also be associated with the degree of homophily among entities toward which messages are directed. This is especially crucial in studies of individuals where interpersonal ties are involved in the diffusion process, for some degree of heterophily, or "weak ties" (Liu & Duff, 1972), is needed to maintain the chain of communication. If all people in a given area are essentially similar, many new ideas might go relatively unnoticed, as the prevailing pattern of social assumptions holds that "everyone thinks like me."

Location may also be critically associated with the number of decoders in the communication process. To the extent that entities are less centrally connected in prevailing communication channels, the more times a given message may be decoded by others the higher the likelihood of distortion. This distortion process has been particularly well documented in studies of rumor (see especially Allport & Postman, 1947; also Graber, 1976, p. 38-41, for a succinct discussion of distortion problems arising from multiple decoders).

Finally, location may be of prime importance with regard to the essential mode of diffusion itself. That is, in the broadest sense, information may be moved through space either by transmission of messages via a variety of media or by the transfer (relocation) of individuals. For example, the diffusion of messages from Nazi Germany via radio and other media to Czechoslovakia prior to its invasion was aided and abetted by the Sudeten Germans who were sympathetic to ideas of the Motherland even after their emigration from Germany. Political diffusion studies most often look to a transmission model of diffusion, but a relocation model can be an important tool in understanding political communication patterns in some circumstances.

The discussion to this point has centered on prime elements explicitly presented in diffusion mdocls and on the utility of these for political communication research. The most important feature of the diffusion perspective, however, is an implicit consequence flowing from such models, an emphasis on *social change*. Certainly, if the meanings of messages lie, as Boulding (1956) argues, in the changes produced in people's images of their environments, then all communication theories are concerned with social change. However, a focus on the spread of "new ideas" and the decision processes associated with their acceptance places social change up front as a concern in diffusion research. This concern is fraught with potential disadvantages, however, as well as having obvious utility.

A particular problem pointed to in recent years is the association of particular research traditions with the diffusion of distinct categories of items—for example, rural sociology and its attendant interest in the acceptance of new farm practices and technologies. Such traditions of research are often associated more or less intimately with existing social mechanisms for diffusion, as, again, the rural sociology tradition of diffusion research in the United States (where it began) was initially caught up in the existing agricultural extension system. Thus, diffusion researchers have often held an implicit belief that the innovations or new ideas they study have impacts on individual and collective welfare, typically believing that these innovations are beneficial and that the purpose of diffusion research is to promote their acceptance (see the arguments of Yapa, 1976; and Brown, 1977, pp. 36-37). Thus, resistant potential adopters are

viewed as "laggards," as less "innovative," or, in the case of news diffusion
studies, as shirkers from their obligations as citizens in a democracy. Yet, the
acceptance of change always entails *risk* (Weeks, 1970; Rogers & Shoemaker,
1971, pp. 12-13). Diffusion research could well benefit from emphasizing this
notion of risk and placing less emphasis on the notion of *resistance* to change.
To be sure, diffusion studies have found perceived risk to be an important
variable in the adoption of new ideas, but have generally treated it as simply one
more "barrier" to innovation.

A more useful approach would be that taken by Chaffee (1975), who
conceptualizes the diffusion of political information as a system of communication parallel to the political system. He follows Easton's (1953, 1965a, 1965b)
model of a political system, arguing that different groups of people within a
community play divergent roles depending on where they are located relative to
supports and demands for the system. Hence, their communication needs as they
perceive them entail differing priorities and risks. Stephenson (1967) points to
the fact that much information that people attend to through the mass media is
just not instrumental to them; it will just not *work* for them regardless of their
awareness, interest, or accuracy of perception. At the same time, such information may *play* for them as a cathartic agent, as a means of establishing or
maintaining social identity, and the like. Broadly, then, political diffusion
research should look to conceptions of the political order, such as Easton's, and
to the pragmatics of human communication for fresh insights into the availability and willingness of behavioral units to serve as receptacles of diffusion. None
of these suggestions should be taken to mean that the findings of established
diffusion research traditions should be ignored. Quite the contrary; for there is a
rich body of literature that is highly suggestive for future political communications research.

DIFFUSION RESEARCH TRADITIONS AND
THE EMERGENCE OF DIFFUSION MODELS

The empirical, inductive bias in much diffusion research is not a result of a
low level of theoretical analysis; diffusion modeling is actually a special case of a
more general functional model of the communication process which specifies a
source sending a message to some receiver(s) through some channel(s) having
some consequent effect(s). Indeed, some very sophisticated statistical and mathematical modeling attempts, with varying degrees of success, are extant (see
Bartholomew, 1973, pp. 295-380; Bramhall, 1960; Dodd, 1956; Gale, 1972;
Hagerstrand, 1967; Mahajan, Haynes, & Kumar, 1976; Stouffer, 1960; see also
Frisch & Hammersley, 1963). The bias results, instead, from the historical
emergence of diffusion research within specific scientific disciplines as noted
above (Rogers & Shoemaker, 1971, pp. 45-70; Katz, Levin, & Hamilton, 1963).

Moreover, these instances have generally arisen in response to relatively specific problems with, at least initially, little cross-fertilization from other diffusion "traditions." Initial similarities flow from the isomorphism inherent in moving messages through space and time. At the same time, many differences emerge across these traditions due to their various original foci.

Thus, anthropological diffusion emphasizes the compatibility of new ideas with existing cultural patterns (for example, Niehoff, 1966). Rural sociology (see Campbell, 1966; Young & Coleman, 1959), initially concerned with promoting certain farm practices to American farmers, focused on the individual adoption process, looking to social barriers that impede "innovativeness" on the part of these "clients." Later, as the rural sociology tradition acquired a greater cross-national perspective, cultural barriers came to occupy a comparable status with social barriers. Educational and medical sociologists developed similar traditions given their concern with such special groups of clients (for example, Miles, 1964; Coleman, Katz, & Menzel, 1966). A marketing tradition also emerged with similar research interests but with a more general category of clients, consumers (see Cohen, 1962; Arndt, 1968). Geographers, without a specific client focus, emphasized spatial considerations, pointing to the social-physical structures of communication potentialities (Hagerstrand, 1967; Brown, 1968). Social psychology, while focused on the receivers of diffusing messages, emphasized perceptual processes and, to a lesser extent, motivation (for example, Allport & Postman, 1947; Shibutani, 1966). More recently, various fields of inquiry that may be lumped together as "decision sciences" have become concerned with organizational constraints that impede or promote learning of new ideas (see Sapolsky, 1967, 1968). Communication research alternatively has tended to focus on the extent and veridicality of information flow (see Allen & Colfax, 1968; Atkin, 1972), thus having as much interest in attention arousal and learning as in adoption (persuasion?).

The diffusion perspective in political communication research at present reflects most of these interests due to the heterogeneity of its parent disciplines—political science, political sociology, mass and speech communication—and to the variety of types of diffusing elements that are studied—news events, campaign messages, policies, and so on—and receivers—individuals, organizations, and communities at varying levels of aggregation. Moreover, except for news dissemination studies, the current political communication literature explicitly making use of the diffusion perspective is as yet small in volume. Thus, the relevance of the accumulated diffusion literature in the more established traditions for understanding political communication remains somewhat problematic.

Still, some empirical regularities widely substantiated across traditions of diffusion research should be given careful and even systematic attention by political communication scholars. Perhaps the most often noted regularity is the S-curve pattern of adoption of new ideas over time. Most simply, the S-curve is a graphic portrayal of the cumulative tendency for many items to be accepted by a small number of early adopters, a much larger number during some "middle" range of time, and by a small number again during late stages, assuming complete acceptance across the entire population. Yet, as Chaffee (1975, pp. 88-89) aptly notes, this curve is a cumulative representation of our old friend, the normal or bell-shaped distribution, so useful in statistical analysis as a random model. Thus, considered in isolation, the S-curve is of little interest, as it suggests that nothing has an effect on the diffusion rate; the interesting cases are those elements whose diffusion rates deviate from the S-curve (see Chaffee, 1975, pp. 89-92, for a discussion of these deviant patterns).

If an S-curve is found, however, it cannot simply be concluded that there are no systematic factors affecting diffusion, for movement occurs through not only time but space as well. Diffusion research points likewise, then, to certain regularities in spatial patterns of distribution, notably what may be called "hierarchy" and "neighborhood" effects. The hierarchy effect occurs where early adoptions are located in central places that are not necessarily connected to one another. Thus, for example, studies of the diffusion of policy innovations among the American states strongly indicate the important role of some states as "regional centers," or innovators, in the spread of many new policies (McVoy, 1940; Walker, 1969; Savage, 1978, in press). Where this occurs there is likely to be a neighborhood effect in which the policies adopted by the regional centers diffuse later in a gradient fashion across successively adjoining states within their regions. These spatial regularities may occur independently, however; McVoy (1940) shows a hierarchy effect in the case of the establishment of state highway departments wherein they diffused steadily westward and southward from the urban northeast. And a classic example of the neighborhood effect is Key's (1949) "friends-and-neighbors" voting pattern in the American South where two or more candidates are supported most strongly in their home counties with declining support more or less gradually as the distance from these centers grows greater.

Another important regularity often found is a multistep flow of communication (see Lazarsfeld, Berelson, & Gaudet, 1948; Berelson, Lazarsfeld, & McPhee, 1954; Katz, 1957) in which some members of an audience for a diffusing message learn of it directly from the propagating source and others learn second-hand from those directly exposed. Operationally, most research uncovering a two-step or multistep flow of information utilizes the mass media as the original source, calling audience members who are directly exposed and who pass the message on to others' "opinion leaders." Recent news dissemination research suggests that the much-heralded "two-step" hypothesis has been too easily accepted by communication scholars and that other patterns may be more important depending on the type of news event reported (see, for example, Ostlund, 1973).

Beyond these models or analogues of time, space, and the communication structure, the model most commonly utilized in diffusion research is one that describes the individual decision-making process flowing primarily from the rural sociology tradition. This model posits the stages of the adoption process whereby a potential adopter becomes *aware* of a new idea, seeks additional *information,* then *evaluates* this knowledge in terms of its utility for him/her and usually subjects the diffusing element to *trial,* resulting in a *decision* to adopt or reject. The model further posits that the decision is affected by receiver characteristics such as personality, social traits, perceived need, and the like; by social system variables such as norms and communication integration; and by perceived characteristics of innovations such as relative advantage, compatibility, complexity, trialability, and observability. The voluminous literature utilizing this model has led to the formulation of 103 generalizations about the innovation-decision process, which have received differing degrees of substantiation in empirical research studies (Rogers & Shoemaker, 1971, pp. 347-385). Many of these generalizations have special relevance for political communication; but, again, political diffusion studies have less often derived from the client-focused research traditions and are still too few for a thorough assessment.

Criticisms of diffusion models in recent years have primarily focused on the innovation-decision model so pertinent to the client-focused traditions. Two of these criticisms relate to empirical concerns and another finds normative fault with certain consequences flowing from these research traditions. The objections are essentially (1) confusion of adopter and observer points of view in assessing adopter-innovation compatibility; (2) the emphasis on communication receivers, the "demand" side of diffusion, has led to overlooking the "supply" side (that is, the role and structure of diffusion agencies); and (3) the implicit assumptions of the client-focused approach about the inherent beneficiality of innovations leading to an overemphasis on "innovativeness" have contributed to further gaps between "haves" and "have-nots" in developing areas.

Thio (1971) first pointed to the gap in studies of adopter-innovation compatibility between the point of view of the adopter and that of the observer. While, in a given analysis, the observer's stress on functional requirements in an innovation being compatible with the cultural, social, and sociopsychological characteristics of the adopter may not essentially conflict with the adopter's symbolic interpretations of those compatibilities, the possibility of conflict is nonetheless there. Thio's concern is simply to stress the primary importance of the adopter's point of view. For example, in news dissemination studies, a concern often voiced flows from the functional requirement of "being informed" as a cultural characteristic of the good citizen in a democratic society. On the other hand, particular groups of citizens may well interpret their roles in a larger context of role complexes in which the citizen role is part-time at best. "Being informed" beyond the specific needs of more basic social roles could well be beyond their understanding of the "good citizen," culturally defined as a rational, *self*-interested individual, not to mention social and sociopsychological constraints. Chaffee (1975, pp. 103-104) has also pointed to such problems in examining political communication patterns from a systemic conception of the polity.

Geographer Lawrence Brown (1969, 1975, 1977; Brown & Philliber, 1977; Sagers & Brown, 1977; see also Rosenberg, 1972) has been the most persistent critic of a "demand"-oriented conception of diffusion, arguing that there is a compelling need to counterbalance this with "supply" considerations. Certainly, client-focused traditions have recognized the important role of the "change agent," but all too often this agent is approached only in the context of the immediate connection with the client. Even news dissemination studies tend to focus on media-audience relationships, with little or no accounting of media infrastructure as an important aspect in producing diffusion results.

In looking at a great many situations in which diffusion occurs, Brown has revealed many instances where the infrastructure of diffusion propagators is critical for the quantity and/or quality of diffusion. He points out that with the adoption of new ideas, frequently two stages of activity, both of a "supply" variety, occur before the innovation-decision process, the "demand" side, is fully underway. Initially, there is the establishment of one or more diffusion agencies, followed by the establishment of the innovation itself; that is, the strategy and other actions that facilitate adoption. Brown has suggested two idealized propagation structures, mononuclear and polynuclear, recognizing that real situations are likely to entail some combination of both. The importance of this conceptualization is especially evident in the study of policy diffusion.

Eyestone (1977) has criticized existing comparative studies of policy diffusion among American states, showing the differences in assumptions that are called for where the national government plays no role (pluralistic model)—a polynuclear propagation structure in Brown's terminology—or the national government uses grants as carrot-and-stick incentives for the states (federal model)—polynuclear diffusion with central propagator support. There are other structural possibilities in the American federal system as well. One important difference Eyestone found, however, is that the federal model tends to result in a much faster diffusion rate and, perhaps, is more likely to continue to completion than where the diffusion structure is pluralistic.

Actually, Brown's market and infrastructure model of diffusion supply does not go far enough. Indeed, he may be a prisoner of the same assumptions in the client-focused diffusion studies he decries. That is, as conceptualized, the market and infrastructured model does not clearly allow for a situation where two or more new ideas or innovations are in direct conflict, each with their own supply structures. Such a modification would be particularly relevant for political communication research for which conflict is inherently at issue. Nimmo's *The*

Political Persuaders (1970), although not written in the context of the diffusion perspective, would be a good starting point, for example, in developing a model for the diffusion infrastructure for contemporary campaign politics. Once again, that old refrain of the need for more research must be sung, for the existing political diffusion studies are too sparse to determine the need for other models of diffusion supply infrastructure where other types of politial "innovations" are at issue (but Siune & Kline, 1975; and Chaffee, 1975; are suggestive regarding media structure and its role in diffusion).

The other major criticism of client-focused research traditions, the development perspective which points to the likelihood of increasing gaps between "innovators" and "laggards," is a much more recent concern. Moreover, most political communication research has been conducted in "developed" nations. The relevance of concerns from this perspective for political communication scholars is not yet so pressing but will likely manifest itself in the not-too-distant future. Instructive starting points for addressing those concerns would be the work of specialists in development administration (see especially Riggs, 1964).

Indeed, much that is known about diffusion processes in politics lies scattered in works that are not explicitly studies of political communication. In the following section some representative studies making use of the diffusion perspective, explicitly or implicitly, are presented to demonstrate its utility and richness for political analysis.

SOME APPLICATIONS OF
THE DIFFUSION APPROACH
IN POLITICAL COMMUNICATION

Findings from political diffusion studies have been frequently introduced here as examples, but the richness of possibilities for political analysis of the diffusion perspective does not emerge in such casual examples. Instead, more detailed reviews of some representative studies are offered below. At the same time, some caveats are in order. In the first place, the studies selected do not conform to any statistical approximation of the actual emphases as to topics, models, or procedures utilized across all political diffusion studies. In this regard, news dissemination studies are easily the most numerous but will receive little attention here precisely because they are widely recognized. Nor do these studies represent the "best" studies of political diffusion in terms of analytical rigor or methodological precision. Indeed, as some of them utilize the diffusion perspective only implicitly, that is, they focus on diffusion phenomena without the "trappings" of diffusion modeling, such rigor and precision must be precluded. Finally, not all the possibilities afforded by the foregoing review of diffusion traditions and models will be represented, either because some have not actually been utilized in political studies or, quite possibly, some have escaped this author's attention. Still, this sample should convey the rich and useful potentialities of the diffusion approach for political communications research.

One important diffusion study that has had a seminal impact in political science is Walker's (1969) study of the diffusion of policy innovations among American states. His analysis points to many of the typical concerns of traditional diffusion research, yet utilizes data not commonly applied in this fashion (but see the earlier studies by sociologists Davis, 1930; McVoy, 1940; and Sutherland, 1950). Walker utilized the dates of legislative adoption of a wide array of policies that had been adopted by states at different times to compute a score of policy innovativeness of each state. He then correlated this index with a variety of social, economic, and political indicators, establishing the basic characteristics of "innovators" and "laggards." Not surprisingly, innovative states were found to be more wealthy, larger, and urban. Walker also Q-factored the original adoption scores for the separate policies in order to examine the likelihood of regional patterns of policy adoption. Indeed, regional blocs of states did emerge. He further hypothesized that policy diffusion among the states reflects communication patterns of emulation and competition, and that time lags are decreasing due to the activities of not only the national government but also those of a variety of national organizations of state officials. Certainly, the adoption data used in this study were at best only indirectly indicative of such communication patterns, but Walker (1971) subsequently provided survey evidence in a study of state administrators that did provide some confirmation of these patterns. The seminal character of Walker's policy diffusion work is attested to by a growing number of studies that directly trace their roots to his 1969 essay (see Note 2; Note 3; Clarke & Dodson, 1978; Note 4, Note 5; Eyestone, 1977; Foster, 1978; Gray, 1973, 1974; Savage, 1973, 1975, 1978, in press). Most important, Walker sensitized political scientists to understanding communication as spatial and temporal patterning.

Frantzich (1979), on the other hand, harks to the client-focused traditions of diffusion research by focusing on the innovation-decision process set; however, within a very elite corps of political figures, the U.S. House of Representatives. His study examines the adoption of a modern technology application—computer use—among the members of this body, popularly perceived as a highly conservative institution, in an attempt to determine the characteristics of those most prone to adoption. He finds that innovative congressmen are more likely to perceive a need for the innovation, but this need seems prompted by their greater social marginality within Congress. Hence, they exhibit higher risk-taking behavior. From this study a distinctive profile of the "innovator" in this conservative elite body emerges; he is a young Republican from a very competitive district who has little previous experience in elective office and has been in Congress only a few terms. Frantzich's findings recall an early study of innovation diffusion in China, where Fei (1946) found a similar group of marginals, the compradors who were outcasts in port areas, to be the only important sources of innovations in a society where the other elements, peasants and gentry, were generally very conservative in their orientation to change. This study of diffusion in an American legislative body especially points to the role of perceived risk in promoting political diffusion.

Another interesting application of the innovation-decision model is Zukin (Note 1). He applied the model to voting decisions in the 1972 presidential election, utilizing responses to a national survey by the University of Michigan Survey Research Center to indicate acceptance of the innovation (a vote for the challenger, George McGovern) and as surrogate measures for four attributes of innovations that have been found to be important in client-focused diffusion research. These attributes are *relative advantage,* operationalized as a summed value of the responses to the open-ended questions indicating reasons for support of or opposition to McGovern and Nixon; *compatibility,* defined in terms of an ordinal scale combining partisan identification and the response to a seven-point scale indicating the degree of support for the statement "I like McGovern; *complexity,* operationalized as a scale indicating knowledge of McGovern's issue stances; and *observability,* indirectly measured as disapproval of Nixon's performance as President, since respondents could not actually observe McGovern performing in the office. As predicted, after controlling for education and income, Zukin found that relative advantage, compatibility, and observability were all strongly and positively related to the vote for McGovern. Complexity, however, was unrelated. A regression model with the four attributes as independent variables explained 59.3 percent of the variance in the vote for McGovern, considerably better than the level generally found with the six-component model emanating from earlier SRC studies (Stokes, 1966; Note 6). While the validity of the four attribute measures is somewhat problematic, the empirical strength of the diffusion concept of innovation attributes combined with its theoretical import suggests the utility of a future voting study with hand-tailored innovation attribute measures rather than the secondary ones Zukin was forced to rely on.

The studies detailed to this point are concerned with "demand" or adopter aspects of diffusion. No political diffusion studies currently exist which deal explicitly with "supply" considerations. Their importance, however, is nicely explicated in Levine's (1972) analysis of American public planning. In reviewing the failure to achieve major aims of the national government's urban renewal policy, notably the *replacement* of much-blighted housing, Levine points to infrastructural elements utilized by national policy makers in the diffusion of this complex innovation. While the policy clearly presented its aims and provided impressive incentives for local actions, the structure for implementation (diffusion) of the policy was left to be developed by state and local officials in concert with private developers. This infrastructure was little understood by national officials, who failed to recognize that such intermediary change agents would impose their own values where the requirements of the innovation were ambiguous. As a consequence, lesser numbers of luxury housing units arose to replace a much larger number of dilapidated housing units. This is not to argue that if national officials had been aware of diffusion concepts they would have avoided such latent consequences. After all, Brown's important work on the market and infrastructure model of diffusion came much later. But Levine's implicit recognition of the role of the diffusion infrastructure is a valuable warning not only to policy makers but to policy analysts as well.

One final work that is of particular importance not only for its seminal importance in the study of American politics but also for its contribution to the study of political communication is Elazar's (1966) examination of the historical roots and development of subcultural variations in American politics. Its importance for political communication research derives from its focus on diffusion through relocation rather than transmission. Elazar describes three political subcultures having their origins in distinctive areas along the Atlantic Coast during colonial times. Due to a variety of factors—physical geography, economic utilities, historical accidents, and so on—characteristic settlement patterns during the westward expansion of the nation led to a sectionally stratified diffusion of these subcultures in which each group moved more or less directly westward, albeit with many minor deviations, such as the Moralistic Scotch-Irish element moving through the Southern Appalachians and the Traditionalistic Southerners flowing into many valleys of the Mississippi River's tributaries. Along with their material possessions, these population subgroups carried their value orientations and characteristic political practices and institutions which have continued to have important political consequences, including the basic modes of political communication and organization, to the present time (see Elazar, 1970; Savage, 1973).

Moreover, Elazar (1966) points to the role of fundamental settlement patterns in bringing about the peculiar mixes of political subcultures and the resultant patterns of conflict and community in localized areas. While the classic land frontier produced the north-to-south stratified overlay of the three political subcultures with the minor historical and geographic variations, new settlement patterns (diffusion through relocation) produced many localized variations on this theme of political subcultural patterning. The period of urban-industrial concentration brought urban and rural folk together but also brought about major resettlements of particular population groups from one subcultural region to another. Later, the emergence of a metropolitan-technological era resulted in an explosion of groups across the countryside. As is all too well recognized, these eras of resettlement did not simply bring about a return to the settlement patterns of earlier times. Instead, the United States today finds certain groups concentrated and other groups extended in characteristic patterns that not only have ominous policy implications but affect basic patterns of political communications as well. And as settlement patterns will almost certainly alter in their essential nature in the future, Elazar's work points to the need for further study of political diffusion through relocation.

CONCLUSION

Rogers and Shoemaker (1971) concluded their review of the massive diffusion literature with a considerable number of emerging generalizations. Only a relatively small number of studies reviewed by them were concerned directly with politics, however; thus, the applicability and relevance for political communication of the generalizations enumerated there remains open. Further, a major taxonomic effort will be required to organize diffusion concepts for application to political communication research due to the heterogeneity of research interests arising from the variety of what is diffused, the varying levels of social aggregation of senders and receivers, and the complexity of public and private agencies in political diffusion infrastructures. This essay has, in part, argued for the utility of such an effort, however Herculean.

It is tempting to follow the example of Chaffee (1975) and sketch an agenda for future research in political diffusion. Yet, since his analysis of the diffusion of political information was largely limited to the mass communication diffusion research tradition, with its focus on the spread of awareness and knowledge of news events, needed lines of research are more evident than where political diffusion is defined much more broadly, as it has been here. Assuredly, many such suggestions have been presented in the sketch of the diffusion approach presented above, but no systematic agenda for research are apparent. At the same time, certain problems in the existing political diffusion literature should receive more attention in the future, such as (1) Are diffusing messages causes or effects of human actions? (2) What latent and/or dysfunctional consequences follow from existing diffusion patterns? (3) Have political communication scholars using the diffusion approach begun to apply it to all relevant forms of political information?

With regard to cause and effect, the diffusion research traditions seem uniformly to approach diffusion as a causal process. Yet, some studies of the diffusion of political information suggest that, at least under some circumstances, diffusion is the effect. Landes and Solomon (1972), for example, found that, contrary to the prevailing notion that compulsory school attendance laws raised educational levels of the populations of American states, in fact such laws were the result of higher educational levels to begin with. A related problem is revealed by Becker (1970), who points out that rapidity of adoption was the cause of centrality in information networks among local health officials, not the result of that centrality. These research results pose problems for research designs and for practical applications that must be considered in the future.

The developmental perspective mentioned above has pointed to the dusfunctional consequences of diffusion applications in less modern societies where innovators are helped to become even more innovative, thereby increasing the gap between them and those who are less innovative. Tichenor et al. (1970) offer evidence of a similar disparity emerging in the United States, a "knowledge gap" among categories of potential consumers of mass media information. What can and should political communication researchers do to address this problem?

Finally, the richness of the diffusion approach for political communication inquiry flows in large part from the variety of diffusing elements that have been studied. Yet, the spread of much politically relevant information occurs in the form of mythic propositions through interpersonal channels, distinct from the more concrete messages flowing from media-reported news events, campaign pitches, or even the more ambiguous rumor mill. To what extent do people pass along such messages as "The United States has entered its declining years as an economic and military power?" This mythic proposition does spread, perhaps slowly and erratically; but the channels, the occasions, the basic social contours of its diffusion remain draped in shrouds. Political communication inquiry, from a diffusion approach or any other theoretic orientation, still lacks any hard knowledge of everyday political discourse, a realm of myth, and—yes—of fantasy.

REFERENCE NOTES

1. Zukin, C. *Voting in 1972: An application of an innovation diffusion model to the political system.* Presented at the annual convention of the International Communication Association, 1976.

2. Allen, R., & Clark, J. *State policy adoption and innovation: Lobbying and education.* Presented at the annual meeting of the Southwestern Political Science Association, 1979.

3. Clarke, S. E. *Growing and learning: The incidence of state growth management innovations.* Presented at the annual meeting of the Southern Political Science Association, 1977.

4. Daniels, M. R. *Domestic violence policy and the American states: An analysis of the variation and speed of formulation.* Presented at the annual meeting of the Western Political Science Association, 1980.

5. Daniels, M. R. *Physicians' assistance programs as health care delivery mechanisms: An analysis of the formulation, variation and speed of legislative adoption.* Paper presented at the annual meeting of the Midwest Political Science Association, April 1980.

6. Kagay, M., & Caldeira, G. *I like the looks of his face: Elements of electoral choice, 1952-1972.* Presented at the annual meeting of the American Political Science Association, 1975.

REFERENCES

Allen, I. L., & Colfax, J. D. The diffusion of news of LBJ's March 31 decision. *Journalism Quarterly,* 1968, *45,* 321-324.
Allport, G. W., & Postman, L. *The psychology of rumor.* New York: Holt, Rinehart & Winston, 1947.

Arndt, J. Selective processes in word-of-mouth advertising. *Journal of Advertising Research,* 1968, *8,* 19-22.

Atkin, C. K. Anticipated communication and mass media information-seeking. *Public Opinion Quarterly,* 1972, *36,* 188-199.

Bartholomew, D. J. *Stochastic models for social processes* (2nd ed.). London: John Wiley, 1973.

Becker, M. H. Sociometric location and innovativeness: Reformulation and extension of the diffusion model. *American Sociological Review,* 1970, *35,* 267-282.

Berelson, B. R., Lazarsfeld, P. F., & McPhee, W. N. *Voting: A study of opinion formation in a presidential campaign.* Chicago: University of Chicago Press, 1954.

Bingham, R. D. *The adoption of innovation by local government.* Lexington, MA: D. C. Heath, 1976.

Boulding, K. *The image: Knowledge in life and society.* Ann Arbor: University of Michigan Press, 1956.

Bramhall, D. F. Gravity, potential, and spatial interaction models. In W. Isard (Ed.), *Methods of regional analysis.* New York: John Wiley, 1960.

Brown, L. A. *Diffusion processes and location: A conceptual framework and bibliography.* Philadelphia: Regional Science Research Institute, 1968.

Brown, L. A. Diffusion of innovation: A macroview. *Economic Development and Cultural Change,* 1969, *17,* 189-211.

Brown, L. A. The market and infrastructure context of adoption: A spatial perspective on the diffusion of innovation. *Economic Geography,* 1975, *51,* 185-216.

Brown, L. A. *Diffusion research in geography: A thematic account.* Studies in the Diffusion of Innovation # 53. Columbus: Department of Geography, Ohio State University, 1977.

Brown, L. A., & Philliber, S. G. The diffusion of a population-related innovation: The planned parenthood affiliate. *Social Science Quarterly,* 1977, *58,* 215-228.

Campbell, R. R. A suggested paradigm of the individual adoption process. *Rural Society,* 1966, *31,* 458-466.

Chaffee, S. H. The diffusion of political information. In S. H. Chaffee (Ed.), *Political communication: Issues and strategies for research.* Beverly Hills, CA: Sage, 1975.

Clarke, S. E., & Dodson, M. L. Growth management innovation in the South. *UNC Newsletter,* 1978, *63,* 22-28.

Cohen, R. A theoretical model for consumer market prediction. *Sociological Inquiry,* 1962, *32,* 43-50.

Coleman, J., Katz, E., & Menzel, H. *Medical innovation: A diffusion study.* Indianapolis: Bobbs-Merril, 1966.

Collier, D., & Messick, R. E. Prerequisites versus diffusion: Testing alternative explanations of social security adoption. *American Political Science Review,* 1975, *69,* 1299-1315.

Davis, A. J. The evolution of the institution of mothers' pensions in the United States. *American Journal of Sociology,* 1930, *35,* 573-582.

Dodd, S. C. Testing message diffusion in harmonic logistic curves. *Psychometrika,* 1956, *21,* 191-205.

Easton, D. *The political system.* New York: Alfred A. Knopf, 1953.

Easton, D. *A framework for political analysis.* Englewood Cliffs, NJ: Prentice-Hall, 1965. (a)

Easton, D. *A systems analysis of political life.* New York: John Wiley, 1965. (b)

Elazar, D. J. *American federalism: A view from the states.* New York: Crowell, 1966.

Elazar, D. J. *Cities of the prairie.* New York: Basic Books, 1970.

Eyestone, R. Confusion, diffusion, and innovation. *American Political Science Review,* 1977, *71,* 441-447.

Fei, H. T. Peasantry and gentry: An interpretation of Chinese social structure and its changes. *American Journal of Sociology,* 1946, *52,* 1-17.

Foster, J. L. Regionalism and innovation in the American states. *Journal of Politics,* 1978, *40,* 179-187.

Frantzich, S. E. Technological innovation among members of the House of Representatives. *Polity,* 1979, *12,* 333-348.

Frisch, H. J., & Hammersley, J. M. Percolation processes and related topics. *Journal of the Society for Industrial and Applied Mathematics*, 1963, *11*, 894-919.

Funkhouser, G. R., & McCombs, M. E. The rise and fall of news diffusion. *Public Opinion Quarterly*, 1971, *35*, 107-113.

Gale, S. Some formal properties of Hagerstrand's model of spatial interactions. *Journal of Regional Science*, 1972, *12*, 199-217.

Graber, D. A. *Verbal behavior and politics.* Urbana: University of Illinois Press, 1976.

Gray, V. Innovation in the states: A diffusion study. *American Political Science Review*, 1973, *67*, 1174-1185.

Gray, V. Expenditures and innovation as dimensions of "progressivism": A note on the American states. *American Journal of Political Science*, 1974, *18*, 693-699.

Greenberg, B. S. Diffusion of news of the Kennedy assassination. *Public Opinion Quarterly*, 1964, *28*, 225-232.

Hagerstrand, T. *Innovation diffusion as a spatial process.* Chicago: University of Chicago Press, 1967.

Hamm, K. E., & Robertson, R. D. Factors influencing the adoption of new methods of legislative oversight in the U.S. states. *Legislative Studies Quarterly*, 1981, *6*, 133-150.

Huff, D. L., & Lutz, J. M. The contagion of political unrest in independent black Africa. *Economic Geography*, 1974, *50*, 352-367.

Katz, E. The two-step flow of communication: An up-to-date report on an hypothesis. *Public Opinion Quarterly*, 1957, *21*, 61-78.

Katz, E. Diffusion of innovation. In D. E. Payne (Ed.), *The obstinate audience.* Ann Arbor: Foundation for Research on Human Behavior, 1965.

Katz, E., Levin, M. L., & Hamilton, H. Traditions of research on the diffusion of innovation. *American Sociological Review*, 1963, *28*, 237-252.

Key, V. O. *Southern politics in state and nation.* New York: Alfred A. Knopf, 1949.

Landes, W. M., & Solomon, L. C. Compulsory schooling legislation: An economic analysis of law and social change in the nineteenth century. *Journal of Economic History*, 1972, *32*, 54-91.

Lazarsfeld, P. F., Berelson, B., & Gaudet, H. *The people's choice.* New York: Columbia University Press, 1948.

Levine, R. A. *Public planning: Failure and redirection.* New York: Basic Books, 1972.

Liu, W. T., & Duff, R. W. The strength in weak ties. *Public Opinion Quarterly*, 1972, *36*, 361-366.

Mahajan, V., Haynes, K. E., & Kumar, B. *Modeling the diffusion of public policy innovations among the U.S. states.* Studies in the Diffusion of Innovation # 35. Columbus: Department of Geography, Ohio State University, 1976.

McVoy, E. C. Patterns of diffusion in the United States. *American Sociological Review*, 1940, *5*, 219-227.

Mendelsohn, H. Some reasons why information campaigns can succeed. *Public Opinion Quarterly*, 1973, *37*, 50-65.

Miles, M. B. *Innovation in education.* New York: Teacher's College Press, Columbia University, 1964.

Most, B. A., & Starr, H. Diffusion, reinforcement, geopolitics, and the spread of war. *American Political Science Review*, 1980, *74*, 932-946.

Naroll, R. Diffusion. In J. Gould & W. L. Kolb (Eds.), *A dictionary of the social sciences.* New York: Free Press, 1964.

Niehoff, A. *A casebook of social change.* Chicago: AVC, 1966.

Nimmo, D. *The political persuaders.* Englewood Cliffs, NJ: Prentice-Hall, 1970.

Ostlund, L. E. Interpersonal communication following McGovern's Eagleton decision. *Public Opinion Quarterly*, 1973, *37*, 601-610.

Placek, P. J. Direct mail and information diffusion: Family planning. *Public Opinion Quarterly*, 1974, *38*, 548-561.

Pred, A. R. *Urban growth and the circulation of information: The United States system of cities, 1790-1840.* Cambridge: Harvard University Press, 1973.

Riggs, F. W. *Administration in developing countries: The theory of prismatic society.* Boston: Houghton Mifflin, 1964.

Rogers, E. M., & Shoemaker, F. F. *Communication of innovations: A cross-cultural approach* (2nd ed.). New York: Free Press, 1971.

Rosenberg, N. Factors affecting the diffusion of technology. *Exploration in Economic History,* 1972, *9,* 3-33.

Sagers, M. J., & Brown, L. A. *An economic history perspective on innovation diffusion.* Studies in the Diffusion of Innovation # 51. Columbus: Department of Geography, Ohio State University, 1977.

Sapolsky, H. M. Organizational structure and innovation. *Journal of Business,* 1967, *40,* 497-510.

Sapolsky, H. M. Science advice for state and local government. *Science,* 1968, *160,* 280-284.

Savage, R. L. Patterns of multilinear evolution in the American states. *Publius,* 1973, *3,* 75-108.

Savage, R. L. The distribution and development of policy values in the American states. In D. J. Elazar & J. Zikmund II (Eds.), *The ecology of American political culture: Readings.* New York: Crowell, 1975.

Savage, R. L. Policy innovativeness as a trait of American states. *Journal of Politics,* 1978, *40,* 212-224.

Savage, R. L. *The states as experimental laboratories: Policy innovations and their diffusion.* CFS Notebook, in press.

Shibutani, T. *Improvised news: A sociological study of rumor.* Indianapolis: Bobbs-Merrill, 1966.

Siune, K., & Kline, F. G. Communication, mass political behavior, and mass society. In S. H. Chaffee (Ed.), *Political communication: Issues and strategies for research.* Beverly Hills, CA: Sage, 1975.

Sopher, D. E. Place and location: Notes on the spatial patterning of culture. *Social Science Quarterly,* 1972, *53,* 321-337.

Stephenson, W. *The play theory of mass communication.* Chicago: University of Chicago Press, 1967.

Stokes, D. Some dynamic elements of contests for the presidency. *American Political Science Review,* 1966, *60,* 19-28.

Stouffer, S. A. Intervening opportunities and competing migrants. *Journal of Regional Science,* 1960, *56,* 144-156.

Sutherland, E. H. The diffusion of sexual psychopath laws. *American Journal of Sociology,* 1950, *56,* 144-156.

Thio, A. O. A reconsideration of the concept of adopter-innovation compatibility in diffusion research. *Sociological Quarterly,* 1971, *12,* 56-68.

Tichenor, P. J., Donohue, G. A., & Olien, C. N. Mass media flow and differential growth in knowledge. *Public Opinion Quarterly,* 1970, *34,* 159-170.

Walker, J. L. The diffusion of innovations among the American states. *American Political Science Review,* 1969, *63,* 880-889.

Walker, J. L. Innovation in state politics. In H. Jacob & K. N. Vines (Eds.), *Politics in the American states: A comparative analysis* (2nd ed.). Boston: Little, Brown, 1971.

Weeks, J. Uncertainty, risk, and wealth and income distribution in peasant agriculture. *Journal of Development Studies,* 1970, *7,* 28-36.

Yapa, L. S. *Innovation diffusion and economic involution: An essay.* Studies in the Diffusion of Innovation # 40. Columbus: Department of Geography, Ohio State University, 1976.

Young, J. N., & Coleman, A. L. Neighborhood norms and the adoption of farm practices. *Rural Sociology,* 1959, *24,* 372-380.

CHAPTER 4

The Agenda-Setting Approach

Maxwell E. McCombs

THE METAPHOR OF AGENDA-SETTING, which has recently been of much interest to mass communication researchers, is a succinct statement about the social impact of the mass media. It captures the idea so long cherished by social scientists that the mass media have a significant impact on our focus of attention and what we think about. While this basic notion of mass communication influence has coexisted for more than a half-century with other ideas about the effects of mass communication, its initial empirical exploration (McCombs & Shaw, 1972) was fortuitously timed. It came at that time in the history of mass communication research when disenchantment both with attitudes and opinions as dependent variables and with the limited effects model as an adequate intellectual summary was leading scholars to look elsewhere. This metaphor of an agenda-setting role of the media captured a significant portion of the shift in thinking about long-term effects of mass communication on knowledge and awareness.

Part of the richness of metaphor as a style of communication is that it allows each individual to make his or her own translation of the comparison. Metaphor preserves the richness of each individual's unique experience. Metaphoric description encourages creative thinking. In the case of empirical research on the agenda-setting role of mass communication, the fact that the central concept guiding this research is expressed as a metaphor has encouraged a broad variety of operational definitions and data.

In the early periods of research on any idea, diversity and creativity are highly desirable. Their presence proves the fruitfulness of the guiding scientific concept. As James Conant (1951) emphasized in *Science and Common Sense*, the fruitfulness of an idea or concept—the extent to which it generates new research and new questions—is a principal criterion for the evaluation of scientific work.

By this criterion, agenda-setting has made a significant contribution to mass communication research, a contribution that has been recognized in recent years by the inclusion of agenda-setting among the ideas discussed in major overviews of mass communication (Dennis, 1978: Emery & Smythe, 1980; Kraus & Davis, 1976). But the diversity of all this research has been an embarrassment of riches when it came to preparing a succinct statement on the agenda-setting role of mass communication.

In a recent review of the literature, James Winter (1981) pessimistically noted that "the drive for total innovation has overwhelmed the scientific prerequisite of at least partial replication." Each new investigator has gone his or her own way with little regard to previous conceptualization or operationalization of the agenda-setting metaphor. This dearth of replication in the research literature leaves many alternative explanations for the variations in the empirical findings.

Social science research is very much a laissez-faire activity, but at some point progress demands the existence of a degree of theoretical order. Continued proliferation of empirical fragments adds footnotes which have career value, but it adds little to the cumulative value of the research in the absence of a theoretical map orienting researchers to the roads they are traveling.

This chapter will sketch several theoretical maps which are implicit in the research to date on agenda-setting. Since progress in social science research typically means the slow process of making explicit that which was previously implicit, the first step here is to construct an explicit map of the *phenomenon* labeled "agenda-setting." Social scientists interested in agenda-setting, the impact of press coverage on the perceived salience of issues by the public, have studied several different, albeit related, agenda-setting concepts. While the metaphor and basic ideas are the same, the actual empirical observations are quite distinct.

FOUR CONCEPTS OF AGENDA-SETTING

Part of the broader topic of public opinion and mass communication, most agenda-setting research focuses on the influence coverage of public issues in the news media has on the audiences of these mass media. While some research has considered agenda composed of items other than public issues, the dominant focus in agenda-setting research has been on issues.

The modal research strategy in the past has been to examine the principal *set of issues* before the public. Fortunately, the public agenda seems to be an oligopoly limited to approximately a half-dozen major concerns at any particular moment, so these attempts at capturing the full array of issues before the public have been largely successful. Most of the studies following this strategy have used cross-sectional designs to describe the set of issues on the public agenda and content analysis to describe the media coverage of these issues. The convergence of the two agendas is then examined. A few studies following this strategy have extended the descriptions of the public and press agendas across time through the use of panel designs (Shaw & McCombs, 1977; Tipton, Haney, & Baseheart, 1975). While this has obvious advantages for testing the causal assertions of the agenda-setting hypothesis, it also greatly increases the logistical complexity of the research.

An alternative approach is to narrow the focus of the research to a *single issue,* taken either at a single point in time or traced across time through a longitudinal design. While the latter design yields extensive comparisons between the mass media coverage and the rise and fall over time among the public of the salience of the issue under study, the use of a cross-sectional design at a single point in time (for example, the typical public opinion poll) would require some kind of internal comparison of the data in order to test the agenda-setting hypothesis (for example, differences in the salience of the issue among high and low users of television news).

These two options—examining a set of issues or a single issue—define the researcher's observations of the mass media and the audience. The decision made here determines the issue category or categories to be measured in both the content analysis and survey(s). But this decision on the substantive focus of the investigation, a single issue or set of issues, does not settle the question of how the public agenda is to be analyzed.

There are additional options to be weighed. Agenda-setting can be described either in terms of *aggregate* data from a population or in terms of *individual* data from a population. For example, in the original McCombs and Shaw study, the public agenda was described in terms of the proportion of the total sample who designated each issue as the most important issue. The issue endorsed by the largest proportion of voters was ranked number one on the public agenda. The issue endorsed by the next largest proportion of voters was ranked number two on the agenda, and so on.

In a longitudinal design for analysis of a single issue, the proportion of survey respondents designating that particular issue as most important is the score at that point in time for the issue. In both examples, the marginals of the survey data provide the scores for the issue(s) on the public agenda.

In contrast to these macroscopic approaches, some studies have taken a more microscopic approach and used individual data for analysis of an issue or a set of issues. One can compare how the rating of a single issue changes for each individual respondent across time; or one can collect a rank-ordering, or some other set of ratings, for an entire set of issues for each individual. In both of these examples, the *individual* is the unit of analysis, whereas in the previous examples based on aggregate data the *issue* was the unit of analysis.

To summarize, the first decision to be made in designing a study of the agenda-setting role of the press is whether to study a *single issue* or a *set of*

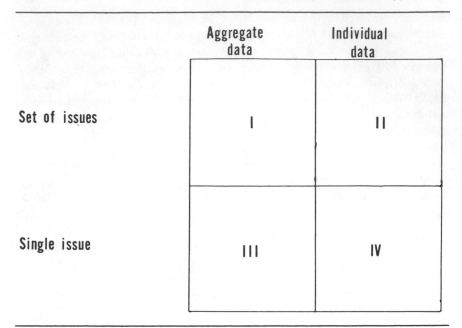

	Aggregate data	Individual data
Set of issues	I	II
Single issue	III	IV

Figure 4.1: A Typology of Agenda-Setting Research

issues. The second decision is whether to use the *issue(s)* or the *individual* respondents as the unit of analysis.

The combination of these two decision points, illustrated in Figure 4.1, yields four possible modes of studying the agenda-setting influence of the press. Put another way, the four cells of Figure 4.1 are four definitions of the agenda-setting role of the press.

ORGANIZING THE LITERATURE

This typology also can be used to organize the existing research literature on agenda-setting. To date, the vast majority of this literature falls into Category I. Here, for example, falls the original McCombs and Shaw investigation and their subsequent study of the 1972 presidential election, reported in *The Emergence of American Political Issues.* (Shaw & McCombs, 1977). In both of these studies press coverage of the issues of the day was compared to the ranking of these same issues' importance by the voters. In other words, the major set of issues on the press agenda was compared to the public's aggregate agenda of issues.

The principal difference in the two studies was the scope of public opinion explored. In the initial study of the 1968 presidential election only undecided voters were interviewed. McCombs and Shaw assumed that if the press did influence voters' perceptions of what were the important issues of the day, this influence was more likely to be discernible among undecided voters. In 1972 this initial restricted look at a cross-section of voters was expanded into a panel study of a general voter population.

A different approach to agenda-setting research, but one still having Category I characteristics, was taken by Funkhouser (1973) in his analysis of the major issues of the 1960s. He examined 14 major issues from that decade, again comparing press coverage with aggregate public opinion statistics. In addition to providing support for the basic hypothesis asserted in the agenda-setting metaphor, Funkhouser also demonstrated the active nature of the press in this process. Press coverage and the world as perceived by the public showed greater convergence with each other than either did with the actual environment. Press attention—and public opinion—on such issues of that decade as the Vietnam war, campus unrest, and urban riots peaked well before the historical climax of these events. While the press is constrained by what is happening in the real world, its coverage is not isomorphic.

Yet another approach was taken by Benton and Frazier (1976), who analyzed two levels of information-holding on a single issue, the economy. The public agendas in that study consisted of proposed solutions to economic problems and rationales for proposed solutions. Although their analysis is representative of Category I agenda-setting research, their detailed examination of a single issue foreshadows additional research strategies to be discussed shortly.

Research in Category II continues the examination of the entire set of major issues before some public, but shifts the unit of analysis to the individuals making up that group. A recent example of this type of analysis is found in Stevenson and Ahern's (Note 1) reanalysis of the 1972 Charlotte data (Shaw & McCombs, 1977). However, they were unable to detect any evidence of agenda-setting at this level of analysis (also see Weaver, Auh, Stehla, & Wilhoit, Note 2). There is some evidence of agenda-setting in McLeod, Becker, and Byrnes's (1974) comparison of issue saliences among individual readers of two newspapers with strikingly different agendas for six major issues of that period. However, evidence supportive of the agenda-setting hypothesis emerged only when a number of contingent conditions were examined (such as respondents' ages, level of interest in politics, and major source of political news). The importance of specifying the conditions under which agenda-setting effects are stronger or weaker is a point which will be taken up again in this chapter.

Category III defines a different arena of activity. Since it has been acknowledged from the very outset that agenda-setting is not a universal influence affecting all issues among all persons at all times, a number of investigations have sought to gain some control over the array of competing forces producing the issue patterns typical of Category I or II by narrowing their focus.

An early study by Siune and Borre (1975) was based on an issue-by-issue matching of the voters' agenda with the mass media agendas. The 45 observation points underlying the correlations reported there were based on a combination of nine issues and five partisan groupings. A more recent study by Eyal (Note 3) illustrates the value both of examining specific issues and more tightly controlling for relevant contingent conditions. Eyal distinguished empirically as well as conceptually between obtrusive issues—those with which people have personal contact—and unobtrusive issues—those remote concerns of public opinion for which the media are the primary, and often only, sources. Pursuing a Category I strategy for each of these subsets of issues, Eyal found no agenda-setting effects whatsoever for the obtrusive issues, but effects of considerable magnitude for the unobtrusive issues. This fragmentation of the full set of issues in the press and before the public represents a transition toward Category III analysis with its tighter focus. Eyal's study also represents a transition toward greater specification of the contingent conditions affecting agenda-setting.

In a trend-setting investigation fully representative of Category III, Winter and Eyal (in press) examined the agenda-setting impact of the press on the civil rights issue from 1954 to 1976. In another study, Winter, Eyal, and Rogers (Note 4) investigated three separate issues—inflation, unemployment, and national unity—in a Canadian setting. Both studies documented significant agenda-setting effects on public opinion.

By concentrating on a single issue, investigators following the strategy of Category III can more sharply focus their efforts at measurement and analysis of the contingent conditions affecting the magnitude of the agenda-setting relationship. Such contingent conditions as the amount and nature of media exposure or interpersonal discussion can be more tightly measured when only a single issue is under the microscope.

Finally, the typology in Figure 4.1 defines the possibility of another research strategy, Category IV. While no full-scale examples are available for citation, and the possibilities in Category IV remain essentially unexplored at this time, some indication of this line of research in comparison to the other three types can be found in Graber's (1980) analysis of public response to crime news coverage.

OPERATIONAL DEFINITION OF THE CONCEPT

The idea of agenda-setting influence by the mass media is a relational concept specifying a positive—indeed, causal—relationship between the emphases of mass communication and what members of the audience come to regard as important. In other words, the salience of an issue or other topic in the mass media influences its salience among the audience. Stated in terms of "effects," the basic concept of an agenda-setting function of mass communication is itself a two-variable hypothesis.

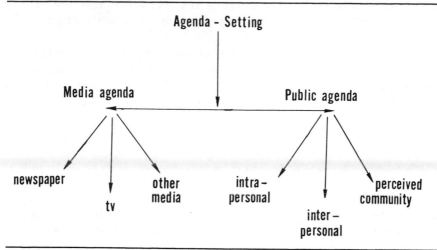

Figure 4.2: Concept of Agenda-Setting

It is the conceptual development and operationalization of these two variables (press coverage and public opinion) defining the basic concept of agenda-setting which introduces the first bits of complexity in grasping the phenomenon and its expanding research literature.

Press Agenda

While most researchers have used quantitative content analysis procedures to generate frequency counts as their measure of the press agenda, there is also the question of which mass media to include in each study. Most studies have included both newspapers and television because these are the dominant mass communication channels for news. At first, newspapers and television were used in tandem simply as replications of the press agenda. But recent work has begun to outline distinct agenda-setting roles for these two mass communication channels.

Shaw and McCombs (1977) found that newspapers were the prime movers in defining the agenda of issues for Charlotte, North Carolina voters during the 1972 presidential campaign. Issues emphasized by the newspaper in the late spring and early summer exerted a major influence on what voters regarded as the major issues during the fall campaign. But it is an influence shared with fall television coverage. During the fall campaign television played a spotlighting role, exerting a short-term influence on the perceived importance of a few issues on the agenda. The net result was that the television agenda was more strongly correlated with the voter agenda in the fall than was the newspaper agenda. Just the opposite had been true across time, from early summer to the fall. A replication of these patterns was found by Tipton et al. (1975) in their study of a state election. They also found an agenda-setting effect across time for newspapers, but not for television.

More recently, a longitudinal study of voters at three Northeastern and Midwestern sites during the 1976 presidential election year (Weaver, Graber, McCombs, & Eyal, 1981) documents the impact of situational factors, represented by the three geographic locations and the voters' educational and occupational backgrounds. Each of these factors affected the roles of television and newspapers in setting the agenda of issues in the presidential campaign. For highly educated individuals who are likely to have white-collar jobs, both media exerted agenda-setting influence early in the campaign year. However, as time passed, the agenda-setting effect of both media diminished. In those geographic locations where the population is of low educational level and more likely to have blue-collar jobs, the impact of the two media was mixed in the early period of the election year. But later on the agenda-setting effects of newspapers gave way to television's spotlighting impact.

The empirical evidence to date is no more than a tentative description of distinct agenda-setting roles for newspapers and television. No explanation has been given for these apparent differences. Among the alternative explanations for the appearance of empirical differences in the correlations between the public agenda and various mass media agendas are demographic variations in the news audiences of network television and the daily newspapers and differential patterns of news coverage. With their larger newshole, newspapers can feature articles in the back pages early in an issue's life cycle. Television coverage is more like the front pages. Over time the newspaper reader is likely to be exposed to mentions of most issues many more times than is his counterpart in the TV news audience.

Public Agenda

The diversity in the literature on the public agenda is even greater than the apparent diversity of newspapers' and television's agenda-setting roles. Much of the discussion to date has centered on the distinction between the *intrapersonal agenda* (usually operationalized in terms of what each individual considers personally most important) and the *interpersonal agenda* (usually operationalized in more overtly behavioral terms of what each individual talks about most often with others). Considerations of personal opinions and beliefs about what are the most important issues of the day follow in the half-century tradition of Gallup and other public opinion polls (Smith, 1980). This was the conceptualization of the public agenda used by McCombs and Shaw (1972) in their original study. Alternative conceptualizations of the public agenda in terms of what people actually talk about follow in the tradition of speech communication, unobtrusive measures of public opinion via eavesdropping on public conversations (Bogart, 1972, p. 160; Smith, 1972), and the flawed, but persistent, concept of a two-step flow of communication (Katz & Lazarsfeld, 1955).

While explicit comparison of the intrapersonal and interpersonal versions of the public agenda reveals considerable convergence, it is far from complete (McCombs, 1978). Many topics of great personal concern are never prominent topics of discussion with family or friends. A great deal of the content of daily conversation consists of the trivial and topics of passing moment, not the abiding and pressing public issues of the time.

This study of public opinion among college students also found that for only a single issue—Watergate—did a majority of students most frequently talk about the same issue they considered personally most important. At the other extreme, only about ten percent of the students who regarded energy and environmental issues as personally most important said it was their most frequent topic of discussion. Overall, just over half of the students most frequently discussed *and* considered personally most important the same public issue.

In this specific example of public opinion, Watergate was the principal reason for the discrepancy between these two versions of the public agenda. While more than two-thirds of the students talked more frequently about Watergate than any other public issue of the time, less than half considered Watergate the issue of greatest personal concern. This disparity between the focal points of conversations and personal concerns points up largely unexplored distinctions between types of public issues. What characteristics ensure spontaneous discussion of some issues, while others are relegated largely to the sphere of private concern?

In addition to the question of the extent to which versions of the public agenda converge, there also is the important empirical question of the extent to which each one is shaped by the press agenda.

Press Influence

The primary evidence on the causal impact of press coverage comes from cross-lagged correlational analysis of panel design data. These designs allow us to separate press coverage and the public agenda across time, a first step in establishing causality. An early study of the issues in a statewide election (Tipton et al., 1975) found strong relationships between newspaper coverage and the frequency with which issues were mentioned by the public. Although the differences in the cross-lagged correlations were in the right direction, both the agenda-setting correlations and their reciprocals exceeded the baseline statistic for significance, so no conclusion can be drawn in favor of the causal impact of press coverage on the public agenda.

Stronger evidence for the impact of newspaper coverage on the public agenda comes from a study of the 1972 presidential election (Shaw & McCombs, 1977). In that study of Charlotte, North Carolina voters there were significant differences in the strengths of the cross-lagged correlations favoring the causal version of the agenda-setting hypothesis. Interestingly, both studies just cited found strong correlations between the public agenda and newspaper coverage, but not television coverage.

More recently, these effects across time were traced in a panel study conducted across the entire 1976 election year (Weaver et al., 1981). Drawing data from a longer timespan, this study found that the period of the campaign year had a major impact on the agenda-setting influence of newspapers and television, especially with regard to unobtrusive issues not directly experienced by most voters.

The influence of both newspapers and television was significant during the spring primaries, the period when the shape of the political year begins to emerge and personal interest in politics begins its quadrennial rise. The agenda-setting influence of both media was less during the summer, and least during the traditional fall campaign.

Overall, the length of time required for these agenda-setting effects to manifest themselves in the public agenda seems to shift with the political seasons. In addition, the agenda-setting impact of television appears to be short-range—the spotlighting of key issues—while newspapers are the prime movers in setting the public agenda across a longer span of time. For example, Eyal (Note 3) found that the modal time frame for significant agenda-setting correlations was a 14-week period during the spring of 1976 for newspapers, but only six weeks for television. By late summer both media demonstrated significant effects across a six- to eight-week period.

Methodologically, the time frame for an agenda-setting study consists of three elements:

- duration of the media agenda: the number of days of media content analyzed to yield a measure of the independent variable;
- duration of the public agenda: the number of days which elapse during the collection of data on the public agenda, the dependent variable;
- timelag: the number of days which elapse between the last day of media content examined and the first day of data collection from the public. In the literature this ranges from zero to nine months.

Variations in these elements of the research calendar introduce variation in the findings regardless of the underlying trends in public and press expressions of issues.

As empirical investigations have probed the causal hypothesis stated by the idea of agenda-setting, we have come to realize that the variety of time periods involved in election and nonelection settings, the kind of news media examined, and the nature of the issues themselves are all critical variables delimiting the boundaries of the agenda-setting concept.

FROM CONCEPT TO THEORY

Even when considered from an effects perspective, the agenda-setting role of the press is not a universal influence. As we have already seen, some issues are far more susceptible than others to the agenda-setting influence of the press (Eyal, Note 3). Almost from the very beginning of this research tradition, scholars have speculated about those characteristics of the mass media, their messages, their audiences, and the social setting of mass communication which facilitate or inhibit the agenda-setting influence of the press. These concerns about limiting conditions—and the empirical research exploring them—begin the process of creating a *theory* of agenda-setting. Some studies, such as those already cited as examples of the four modes of observing agenda-setting, or of the various operational definitions of the press and public agendas, examine the basic *concept* of an agenda-setting role of the press. Other studies either assume this relationship or go beyond it to link the basic concept with other variables. Typically, these additional variables are hypothesized to facilitate or inhibit agenda-setting influence. Introducing these variables yields the first connected pieces in a larger intellectual jigsaw puzzle which we can label a *theory* of agenda-setting. So, on the one hand, we have the concept of agenda-setting, which is itself a hypothesis; on the other we have a broader theory of agenda-setting.

Neither the concept nor the theory of agenda-setting is an assertion that the mass media are the sole source of influence on the perceived salience of public issues. Indeed, the development of a theory of agenda-setting explicitly begins the complex job of specifying the many factors which converge to define the public agenda of the day, the focal points of public opinion. It also is important to remember at this point that both the concept and theory of agenda-setting are concerned only with the focus of public opinion, the salience of public issues. Agenda-setting is not concerned with the distribution of opinion on these issues, the proportions of the public favorably, unfavorably, and neutrally disposed toward various resolutions of these issues.

THEORY OF AGENDA-SETTING

The basic concept of agenda-setting, outlined in Figure 4.2, can be placed in a number of different contexts. Here we will follow the mainstream of this research tradition and review those variables defining the context upon which the potency of agenda-setting influence on *public issues* is contingent. No one contends that agenda-setting is an all-powerful effect of mass communication reminiscent of the old hypodermic theory of mass communication. Agenda-setting effects often have been demonstrated, but they are not of consistent and major magnitude in all circumstances.

Contingent Conditions

This theoretical approach—making explicit the variables which facilitate or inhibit agenda-setting—brings together the long-dominant *effects* tradition of mass communication research and its more recent intellectual competitor, *uses-and-gratifications* research. In the tradition of effects research, the basic concept of agenda-setting asserts a direct, powerful effect of the mass media on public opinion. But a broader theory of agenda-setting modifies this assertion by recognizing that the ways people use mass communication affect its role and impact on public issues.

One of the major theoretical frontiers now being explored is specification of the contingent conditions which constrain or enhance the agenda-setting role of the mass media. These contingencies arise from the *nature of the issues* on the agendas of the press and public and from the *characteristics of the mass media audiences*.

Recent research not only has shifted to the analysis of single issues (Category III and IV research in Figure 4.1) because their rise and fall display different trajectories; it also has shifted its focus because of a distinction in the very nature of issues. As previously noted, Eyal (Note 3) divided issues into two categories:

- obtrusive issues, which are directly and personally experienced by most individuals (such as inflation), and
- unobtrusive issues, which are almost the exclusive domain of the mass media (for example, the Iranian hostage situation).

He found agenda-setting effects only for the set of unobtrusive issues. Similarly, Zucker (1978) and Winter (Note 5) analyzed a variety of individual issues and found agenda-setting only for unobtrusive issues. In an analysis of Syracuse voter opinion during the 1980 presidential election, Blood (Note 6) has abandoned the notion of a researcher-designated dichotomy in which an issue is either obtrusive or unobtrusive. Instead, he has conceptualized this distinction as a continuum on which each individual locates each issue. For example, the issue of economic recession was highly obtrusive to some voters in 1980 and relatively unobtrusive to others. These explorations of the nature of issues promise to be a rich frontier for agenda-setting theory and public opinion research.

However, the majority of contingent conditions empirically explored to date are attributes of the audience. Winter (1981) suggested that the original agenda-setting study by McCombs and Shaw (1972) set the stage for this development by focusing exclusively on undecided voters, a group assumed to be most susceptible to press influence. Following that lead, others have examined the impact on agenda-setting by the press of numerous individual differences:

- amount of exposure to the mass media (McClure & Patterson, 1976; Weaver, McCombs, & Spellman, 1975; Mullins, Note 7);

- frequency of interpersonal discussion (Miller, Erbring, & Goldenberg, 1980; Weaver et al., 1975; Atwood, Sohn, & Sohn, Note 8; Shaw, Note 9);
- level of need for orientation, a motivational variable (Weaver, 1977; Weaver et al., 1981; McCombs & Weaver, Note 10); and
- demographic characteristics, including sex, education, and income (Moreno, Ramirez, Schael, & Vernon, Note 11).

Transactional Model of Contingent Conditions

While the proliferation of studies exploring the contingent conditions of agenda-setting effects represent the ad hoc development of theory, a more systematic approach is desirable. To illustrate one line of theoretical development, a possible *transactional model of contingent conditions* is outlined here.

In a transactional model the outcomes of exposure to the contents of the mass media are seen as the result of a bargain struck by two *active* participants, the mass media and the individuals in their audiences. From a transactional point of view, influence results both from the content of the mass media *and* from the social situation in which that content is scanned by each individual in the audience. In contrast, for example, to the traditional social categories approach of demographic analysis, which looks at the uniformities of behavior, a transactional model is an individual differences approach.

The first component in the model described here is that set of attitudes, beliefs, and motivations documented in the mass communication literature as predictors of media use and information-seeking. Interest in politics, a desire to keep up with what is going on in the world, and the need for information useful in daily life are examples of variables which determine the frequency of exposure to various media, how much of their content is perused, and the degree of close attention to specific bits of content. Such variables and their behavioral consequences define the news media *scanning behavior* of each individual. This scanning behavior incorporates the agenda-setting transaction as a by-product. That is, the perceived salience of an issue is one outcome of the individual's scanning behavior. However, rather than making a simple "effects" prediction that the priorities of the media will become the priorities of the public, this transactional model assumes individual differences both in this scanning behavior and the degree of attunement to the priorities of the mass media agenda.

Past efforts at describing and exploring transactions between individuals and the mass media typically have examined a single component or dimension of the transaction. For example, the extensive work in the agenda-setting literature on *need for orientation* represents one psychological dimension of the transactions between audiences and mass media. Grunig (Note 12) has suggested that need for orientation *and* low involvement are the two key contingent conditions for the agenda-setting influence of the press. But any major, systematic effort at building agenda-setting theory should encompass the widest possible range of variables involved in these transactions.

Another major variable found in the agenda-setting literature on the contingent conditions represents a social influence on mass media scanning behavior and its agenda-setting consequences. The variable is *interpersonal communication*. Nowhere is the grab bag mixture of operational definitions used in agenda-setting research better illustrated than in this research. As a result, a number of studies indicate that increased interpersonal discussion reduces the agenda-setting influence of the press while an equal number of studies show just the opposite, the facilitation of agenda-setting by interpersonal discussion.

While the wide variety of study designs and operational definitions employed in these studies yield many alternative explanations for the different results, Winter (1981) notes that an especially important factor is the topic tapped by the measures of interpersonal communication. Some studies measured the frequency of interpersonal communication on specific issues mentioned by survey respondents. Others measured the discussion of politics generally.

This variation in the literature on interpersonal communication and agenda-setting underscores an important characteristic of any transaction models constructed to describe the larger context of human behavior surrounding the use of the mass media. For some situations and purposes it may be desirable to construct single-issue transaction models which consider need for orientation, frequency of interpersonal communication, prior experience, current level of interest, and so on for a specific issue. In other cases the goal may be a transaction model focused on a broad set of issues.

While need for orientation, frequency of interpersonal communication, and the nature of one's experience are the three variables extensively documented to date as major candidates for a transaction model of agenda-setting, the general literature on mass communication suggests a host of other variables which might help illuminate the specific agenda-setting transaction, as well as help specify the general dimensions of how people use mass communication.

Conceptual Domains

The concept of agenda-setting is not limited to the relationship between the salience of topics in the mass media and the salience of those topics to members of the audience. In addition to providing cues about the salience of topics— objects, if you will—the mass media also differentiate between the saliency of various attributes of these topics or objects. Not every attribute of a person, issue, idea, or event in the news is considered newsworthy. Even among those attributes selected for mention in the news, all are not accorded equal treatment. Just as the objects in the news have different saliences, so the attributes of those objects also have different saliences. Benton and Frazier (1976), in a study of the economic issue, and Cohen (Note 13), in a study of an environmental issue, have demonstrated that the influence of the mass media on the perceived salience of attributes of issues in the news is equal to its influence in placing the issues themselves on the public agenda.

Consideration of agenda-setting in terms of the saliences of both objects and their attributes subsumes several similar ideas found in the communication literature. The concepts of status-conferral, image-making, and stereotyping all concern the salience of objects and/or attributes (McCombs, Note 14).

Just as the original metaphor of an agenda of objects has been extended to embrace an agenda of attributes for an object, the metaphor of an agenda of issues has been extended in recent research to include candidates (Becker & McCombs, Note 15), their images (Weaver et al., 1981), and politics in general (McCombs & Weaver, Note 16) as agenda items.

Translating research strategies and hypotheses based on an array of issues to a focus on an array of candidates is straightforward. Such a translation and extension puts to empirical test the popular notion that the press determines the front-runners in the out-of-power party's process of selecting its presidential contender.

The original idea of an agenda of issues and the modification expressed in the idea of an agenda of candidates both maintain the concept of an agenda-setting function of the press as a central part of political communication. But political communication is just one small segment of the communications spectrum. For most Americans, politics occupies center stage, if at all, during a few brief weeks each election year.

To continue our metaphor, politics is just one item on the larger agenda of personal concerns. For most persons it is found high on the personal agenda only for a short time during election year. A key political role of the press—indeed, a key agenda-setting role—is the movement of politics onto the agenda and to a prominent position during election year (McCombs & Weaver, Note 16; Weaver et al., 1981).

To sum up, the agenda-setting influence of the press can be examined for three kinds of agenda items: public issues, political candidates, and politics per se. For the first two, both an array of objects (the issues or the candidates themselves) or an array of the attributes of one of these objects can be the subject of agenda-setting research. This is a total of five distinct political domains for the concept of agenda-setting. Strictly speaking, these five domains are elaborations of the basic concept. But they have been included here in the section on theory because the full nexus of variables defining the agenda-setting role of the press should be considered in research on these domains.

Substantive Domains

Much of the empirical agenda-setting research has concentrated on political communication during election campaigns. Since this is the oldest, continuing field of research within mass communication, dating from at least the 1940 Erie County study (Lazarsfeld, Berelson, & Gaudet, 1944), it is an appropriate locus for work on agenda-setting. However, the time is at hand for a major extension of the concept of agenda-setting and its theoretical elaborations to noncampaign settings (see, for example, Gilberg, Eyal, McCombs, & Nicholas, 1980; and Graber, 1980) and to topics other than public issues. Not only has the empirical research to date emphasized public issues of the moment, this research has concentrated almost exclusively on the mass media-audience interface. But exchanges of information and the creation of awareness are not limited to transactions between the mass media and their audiences. Individuals, groups, and institutions inform each other. Within the various news media, for example, there are thousands of daily transactions. The concept of agenda-setting could revitalize inquiry into such communication phenomena as those traditionally labeled "two-step flow" (Katz & Lazarsfeld, 1955) or "gatekeeping" (Snider, 1967; White, 1950). For example, reanalysis of the Mr. Gates data by McCombs and Shaw (1976) documents a significant agenda-setting influence role for the wire services.

A shift to intrapress agenda-setting could enhance our knowledge in a number of ways. It would link the last decade's high scholarly interest in news reporting and news organizations to a long tradition of audience research. Moreover, it would shift attention from effects per se to the broader social function of mass communication. As a social function, the idea of agenda-setting represents an intersection of Lasswell's (1948) surveillance and correlation functions of mass communication. From this broader societal perspective, examination of the correspondence between the press and public agendas seeks answers to different questions. It is not so much concerned with the influence of one agenda on the other as it is with the relevance of one for the other. Is the information in the press relevant to the concerns and activities of the public, a question increasingly raised in newspaper research? As Chaffee (Note 17) has observed.

> As a hypothesis regarding effects of the news media, agenda-setting has had limited success. On the other hand, as a general functional requirement of society, agenda-setting is practically indispensable. We should be evaluating the news media in terms of fulfilling that kind of function, and not falling into the old persuasional trap of looking for media influence and directional effects. The societal function of the press is not to direct and channel people's behaviors and perceptions in specific ways, but to help us to organize our activities and knowledge so that we can work in a coherent way on problems that are common to many people, communities, etc.

News media are private and powerful institutions with their own values and traditions. The concept of an agenda-setting function of mass communication prompts us to consider critically the fit of journalistic practices to the changing needs of American society.

CONCLUSION

In addition to a vast accumulation of empirical findings, the first decade of research into the agenda-setting role of the mass media also has contributed a number of opening gambits toward a theoretical grasp of this topic. Two of these opening gambits which need to be elaborated over the next few years initially can be expressed as simple questions: "Why do people attend to the news media?" "Which message elements do they attend to?" Important leads to the theoretical answers to these two general questions already appear in the literature.

In seeking to determine why people use the mass media, previous discussions of agenda-setting have linked it with both the social (Lasswell, 1948) and psychological functions (Blumler & McQuail, 1969) of surveillance of the environment. A promising and more specific lead to a theoretical understanding of surveillance is found in the work to date on need for orientation. Posited as the psychological equivalent of "nature abhors a vacuum," the concept of a need for orientation asserts that individuals strive to maintain a current map of their physical and intellectual surroundings.

Of course, it seems clear that the strength of this characteristic will vary vis-a-vis different objects of attention. Even in regard to the same objects of attention, the level of this need also consistently will vary among individuals. Some people have more intellectual curiosity than other people. And one may be more curious about some things than another.

If need for orientation provides a theoretical explanation for why people attend to the news media and why they sometimes absorb the media's cues about the salience of various topics, then these expected variations in curiosity across topics and individuals suggest that the agenda-setting effects of the mass media will be enhanced or reduced by

— the topics and message content under consideration;
— personal characteristics of audience members; and
— the behavioral setting (which includes the relevant public agenda under examination).

In short, need for orientation may provide the key theoretical concept around which the other individual, social, and media variables defining each communication transaction can be fruitfully organized.

Elaboration of a transactional model, which includes consideration of each individual's scanning behavior, also brings us to the second question: Which message elements do audience members attend to? In other words, out of the vast package of variables which each mass media message represents, which ones actually are attended to? Which variables provide the cues from which audience notions of salience are constructed?

Most of the agenda-setting research to date follows the historical lead of quantitative content analysis in assuming that the *frequency* with which a topic or item is mentioned is the key characteristic. While it was appropriate for the early research to rely on this heritage from the content analysis tradition, future research should probe more fully the nature of the cues used by the audience to establish the salience of a topic in their mind.

These two questions are not the only strategic ones requiring attention in the second decade of research on agenda-setting. But they do illustrate the importance and value of probing more deeply into the individual and media characteristics pertinent to the agenda-setting phenomenon. One of these questions asks about people and why they use mass media. The other asks about the important characteristics of the media messages.

None of this is to suggest that the variety of tactical questions touched on in this chapter are undeserving of researchers' time. More attention is needed to the question of the relative roles of newspapers and television news, the timelag involved in the learning process described by agenda-setting, the design of Category III and IV studies which yield causal evidence, and similar tactical questions. But the careful replication and extension of our knowledge on these and other research topics can best proceed in the context of basic theoretical questions about audiences and mass communication.

One of the exciting aspects about research based on the concept of agenda-setting is the integration of a number of long-standing mass communication concerns within a single conceptual framework. Continued pursuit of these lines of agenda-setting research will reveal whether the integration simply results from parallel metaphors or from theoretical integration at a higher level of abstraction.

In any event, consideration of agenda-setting, whether from an "effects" perspective or from a broader social perspective, directs our attention to the origins and foundations of public opinion and to the critical role of the press in the laying of those foundations (Westley, 1976; DeWeese & McCombs, Note 18). Tracing the evolution of public opinion is a key theoretical task for political communication.

REFERENCE NOTES

1. Stevenson, R., & Ahern, T. *Individual effects of agenda-setting.* Paper presented at the meeting of the Association for Education in Journalism, Houston, Texas, 1979.

2. Weaver, D., Auh, T. S., Stehla, T., & Wilhoit, C. *A path analysis of individual agenda-setting during the 1974 Indiana Senatorial Campaign.* Paper presented at the meeting of the Association for Education in Journalism, Ottawa, Canada, 1975.

3. Eyal, C. *Time frame in agenda-setting research: A study of the conceptual and methodological factors affecting the time frame context of the agenda-setting process.* Unpublished doctoral dissertation, Syracuse University, 1980.

4. Winter, J. P., Eyal, C., & Rogers, A. *Issue specific agenda-setting: Inflation, unemployment, and national unity in Canada, 1977-1978.* Paper presented at the meeting of the International Communication Association, Acapulco, Mexico, 1980.

5. Winter, J. P. *Differential media-public agenda-setting effects for selected issues, 1948-1976.* Unpublished doctoral dissertation, Syracuse University, 1980.

6. Blood, R. W. *Unobtrusive issues and the agenda-setting role of the press.* Doctoral dissertation, Syracuse University, forthcoming.

7. Mullins, L. E. *Agenda-setting on the campus: The mass media and learning of issue importance in the '72 election.* Paper presented at the meeting of the Association for Education in Journalism, Fort Collins, Co., 1973.

8. Atwood, L. E., Sohn, A., & Sohn, H. *Community discussion and newspaper content.* Paper presented at the meeting of the Association for Education in Journalism, University of Maryland, July-August 1976.

9. Shaw, E. F. *Some interpersonal dimensions of the media's agenda-setting function.* Paper presented at the conference on the Agenda-Setting Function of the Press, Syracuse University, October 1974.

10. McCombs, M. E., & Weaver, D. H. *Voters' need for orientation and use of mass media.* Paper presented at the meeting of the International Communication Association, Montreal, 1973.

11. Moreno, L. M., Ramirez, I. A., Schael, D. C., & Vernon, C. R. *Importancia tematica en prensa y publicode la ciudad de Mexico,* (Thesis). Universidad Iberoamericana, Departamento De Communicacion, Mexico, 1977.

12. Grunig, J. E. *A simultaneous equation model for intervention in communication behavior.* Paper presented at the meeting of the Association for Education in Journalism, Houston, Texas, 1979.

13. Cohen, D. *A report on a non-election agenda-setting study.* Paper presented at the meeting of the Association for Education in Journalism, Ottawa, Canada, 1975.

14. McCombs, M. E. *Elaborating the agenda-setting influence of mass communication.* Bulletin of the Institute for Communication Research, Tokyo, Japan: Keio University, Fall 1976.

15. Becker, L., & McCombs, M. E. *U.S. primary politics and public opinion: The role of the press in determining voter reactions.* Paper presented at the meeting of the International Communication Association, West Berlin, Germany, 1977.

16. McCombs, M. E., & Weaver, D. H. *Voters and the mass media: Information seeking, political interest, and issue agendas.* American Association for Public Opinion Research, Buck Hill Falls, PA, 1977.

17. Chaffee, S. *Comments on agenda-setting research.* Presented at the meeting of the International Communication Association, Acapulco, Mexico, 1980.

18. DeWeese, L. C. III., & McCombs, M. E. *Systematic identification of emerging public concerns.* Paper presented at the meeting of the Midwest Association for Public Opinion Research, Chicago, 1977.

REFERENCES

Benton, M., & Frazier, P. J. The agenda-setting function of mass media at three levels of "information molding." *Communication Research,* 1976, *3*, 261-274.

Blumler, J. G., & McQuail, D. *Television in politics.* Chicago: University of Chicago Press, 1969.

Bogart, L. *Silent politics: Polls and the awareness of public opinion.* New York: John Wiley, 1972.

Conant, J. *Science and common sense.* New Haven, CT: Yale University Press, 1951.

Dennis, E. *The media society.* Dubuque, IA: William C. Brown, 1978.

Emery, M., & Smythe, T. *Readings in mass communication: Concepts and issues in the mass media* (4th ed.). Dubuque, IA: William C. Brown, 1980.

Funkhouser, G. R. The issues of the sixties: An exploratory study in the dynamics of public opinion. *Public Opinion Quarterly,* 1973, *37,* 62-75.

Gilberg, S., Eyal, C., McCombs, M., & Nicholas, D. The state of the union address and the press agenda. *Journalism Quarterly,* 1980, *57,* 584-588.

Graber, D. *Crime news and the public.* New York: Praeger, 1980.

Katz, E., & Lazarsfeld, P. F. *Personal influence.* New York: Free Press, 1955.

Kraus, S., & Davis, D. *The effects of mass communication on political behavior.* University Park: Pennsylvania State University Press, 1976.

Lasswell, H. The structure and function of communication in society. In L. Bryson (Ed.), *The communication of ideas.* New York: Institute for Religious and Social Studies, 1948.

Lazarsfeld, P. F., Berelson, B., & Gaudet, H. *The people's choice.* New York: Columbia University Press, 1944.

McClure, R. D., & Patterson, T. E. Setting the political agenda: Print vs. network news. *Journal of Communication,* 1976, *26,* 23-28.

McCombs, M. E. Public response to the daily news. In L. K. Epstein (Ed.), *Women and the news.* New York: Hastings House, 1978.

McCombs, M. E., & Shaw, D. L. The agenda-setting function of the mass media. *Public Opinion Quarterly,* 1972, *36,* 176-187.

McCombs, M. E., & Shaw, D. Structuring the "unseen environment." *Journal of Communications,* 1976, *26,* 18-22.

McLeod, J. M., Becker, L. B., & Byrnes, J. E. Another look at the agenda-setting function of the press. *Communication Research,* 1974, *1,* 131: 166.

Miller, A., Erbring, L., & Goldenberg, E. Front page news and real-world cues: Another look at agenda-setting by the media. *American Journal of Political Science,* 1980, *24,* 16-49.

Shaw, D. L., & McCombs, M. E. *The emergence of American political issues.* St. Paul, MN: West Publishing, 1977.

Siune, K., & Borre, O. Setting the agenda for a Danish election. *Journal of Communication,* 1975, *25,* 65-73.

Smith, A. L. Life in wartime Germany: Colonel Ohlendorf's opinion service. *Public Opinion Quarterly,* 1972, *36,* 1-7.

Smith, T. America's most important problem—A trend analysis, 1946-1976. *Public Opinion Quarterly,* 1980, *44,* 164-180.

Snider, P. "Mr. Gates" revisited. A 1966 version of the 1949 case study. *Journalism Quarterly,* 1967, *44,* 419-427.

Tipton, L. P., Haney, R. D., & Baseheart, J. B. Media agenda-setting in city and state election campaigns. *Journalism Quarterly,* 1975, *52,* 15-22.

Weaver, D. H. Political issues and voters need for orientation. In D. L. Shaw & M. E. McCombs (Eds.), *The emergence of American political issues: The agenda-setting function of the press.* St. Paul, MN: West Publishing, 1977.

Weaver, D., Graber, D., McCombs, M. E., & Eyal, C. *Media agenda-setting in a presidential election: Issues, images, interest.* New York: Praeger, 1981.

Weaver, D., McCombs, M. E., & Spellman, C. Watergate and the media: A case study of agenda-setting. *American Politics Quarterly,* 1975, *3,* 458-72.

Westley, B. Setting the political agenda. What makes it change? *Journal of Communication,* 1976, *26,* 43-47.

White, D. M. The "Gate Keeper": A case study in the selection of news. *Journalism Quarterly,* 1950, *27,* 383-390.

Winter, J. P. Contingent conditions in the agenda-setting proces. In *Mass communication review yearbook* (Vol. II). Beverly Hills, CA: Sage, 1981.

Winter, J. P., & Eyal, C. An agenda-setting time frame for the civil rights issue, 1954-1976. *Public Opinion Quarterly,* in press.

Zucker, H. G. The variable nature of news media influence. In B. D. Ruben (Ed.), *Communication yearbook 2* (B. D. Ruben, ed.). New Brunswick, NJ: Transaction Books, 1978.

CHAPTER 5

A Critical Theory Approach

Richard L. Lanigan
with the assistance of Rudolf L. Strobl

THE YEARS 1967 to 1969 are now a memory. Yet, memories shape commitment. Persons commit themselves, as the French say, to *l'histoire*. People are the story of the moment that vehemently marks out a value choice that should be lived through in society. This social living through, this history, becomes for most a reminiscence. For a few, it is a memory. The memory is that consciousness and reflective capability by which we come to make personal choices of social consequence. Our memory is critical of our actions: Each person values society by participating in it. Indeed, this is the nature of government and the function of politics. But when action fades into habit, memory becomes an uncritical reminiscence to be forgotten in the familiarity of institutions or lost in fear. The years 1793 and 1794 are such a reminiscence. Only the student of political history has a memory which instantly pieces together the puzzle which was the infamous Reign of Terror by the Committee of Public Safety in the Paris Commune.

The political years 1967-1969 are a guaranteed memory, never to be lost to reminiscence. Rarely has such a brief moment of history been recorded so meticulously and analyzed so critically for its story. Two extraordinary examples are the critical case study analyses of the October 27, 1968 demonstration against the Vietnam war in London, England (Halloran, Elliot, & Murdoc, 1970) and that of the "May Movement" by French students in Paris from November 1967 to June 1968 (Schnapp & Vidal-Naquet, 1969/1971). The 1967-1969 years exist as a paradigm case in the evolution of a critical theory of political communication. They signal not a new reign of terror displaying the collision of theory and praxis, but a renaissance of humane discourse, a *Selbstbesinnung* or

141

critical self-awareness of the political meaning attached to social science research—the discovery of ideology as a level of meaning in research per se (Frankfurt Institute for Social Research, 1956/1972). These years announce a rebirth of concern by European and Latin American scholars with the power of discourse in all modes of human life and the social responsibilities that attach to the exercise of that power. As Schnapp and Vidal-Naquet (1969/1971, pp. 2, 49). suggest, *La Commune Étudiante*'s failed university strike demand for a return to the method of oral examination and the abolition of written examinations illustrates the critical theory perspective. That is, "the dream of a society that would be pure speech characterized the movement, but it was just that: a dream, since in reality 'pure speech' can only lead to 'pure action,' another dream of the movement." Thus Max Horkheimer (1968/1972, p. v), founder of the Frankfurt Institute for Social Research, reminds us:

> Men of good will want to draw conclusions for political action from the critical theory. Yet there is no fixed method for doing this; the only universal prescription is that one must have insight into one's own responsibility. Thoughtless and dogmatic application of the critical theory to practice in changed historical circumstances can only accelerate the very process which the theory aimed at denouncing. All those seriously involved in the critical theory, including Adorno, who developed it with me, are in agreement on this point.

Memories shape commitment, but we must make our commitments critically.

WHAT IS CRITICAL THEORY?[1]

Following upon Horkheimer's remark about method and application, it is now apparent why it is necessary to begin this essay with an exercise in critical thought about a memorable event in political communication, the 1967-1969 epoch. Critical theory variously evokes denotations and connotations of a long tradition in German philosophy and sociology that is essentially located in a Marxist or neo-Marxist orientation and is historically referenced by the work of the Frankfurt Institute for Social Research (Horkheimer, 1968/1972; Adorno, 1969/1976; Jay, 1973; Schroyer, 1975). At the more recent end of this German tradition, the work by Jürgen Habermas (1970b, 1971a, 1971b, 1973, 1975, 1979b), who is currently Director of the Max-Planck-Institut at Starnberg, specifically focuses critical theory on the problem of communication, although this is not an exclusive direction in German social science (Merton & Gaston, 1977). The result, over the long term, is a growing diversity of application (Rogers, 1981). While originally a calculated attack on philosophic and scientific positivism, critical theory now has become a questioning of, and qualitative approach to, the study of communication in a world dominated by quantitative methodologies and the social perspective of an advanced industrial society modeled on the United States. This new, "second force" in critical theory shares the problematic determined by the older German "first force" school of thought whose spokespersons have been a majority in Germany and a minority in the United States. But this second force, which is often non-Marxist, owes its motivation to a number of grass-roots efforts—a political legacy of the 1967-1969 period—to move the academy into the community. I shall mention only the most important of these efforts, leaving the majority to citation.

In Europe, the second force effort began at a plenary session of the 1969 conference of the European Association of Experimental Psychology held in Belgium at the University of Louvain.

> On the one hand, there was genuine respect for much that has been achieved through the well-tried methods of clear-cut empirical hypotheses and their experimental testing. On the other hand, many felt that an unquestioned acceptance of the assumptions—social, scientific and philosophical—underlying much of this research was a heavy price to pay for achieving a modicum of "scientific respectability" and even for making *some* gains in knowledge. It is possible that the "student revolution"—very much in evidence in the spring of 1969—had something to do with these conflicts [Isreal & Tajfel, 1972, p. 2].

The culmination of these and subsequent discussions was the publication of a now classic book edited by Joachim Isreal and Henri Tajfel, *The Context of Social Psychology: A Critical Assessment.*

Representative of a similar mood in Latin and South America was the publication of "Ideology and Social Sciences: A Communicational Approach" by Eliseo Veron (1971), then director of the Research Program on Social Communication at the Torcuato Di Tella Institute, Center for Social Research in Buenos Aires, Argentina. In this important article, Veron speaks in the voice of second force critical theory: "From the point of view of communication theory, ideology is a level of meaning, and this implies that it is a structural condition of production of messages within a human language system, including scientific communication" (p. 74). This critical judgment derives from the fact that "in science, the ideological level of meaning stems from all those options in the construction of scientific language that are not decidable in terms of the formal rules of scientific procedure. This field, as everyone knows, is very wide in the social sciences today" (p. 70).

At nearly the same time in Great Britain, a profoundly personal, yet parallel, statement was issued by Trevor Pateman with the private (he refused complicity with commercial publishing houses) publication of *Language, Truth, and Politics: Towards a Radical Theory for Communication.*

> Of course, since I was a Ph.D. student in Philosophy, I was meant to get on with a conceptual rather than a substantive analysis, and the impossibility or emptiness of doing such a thing is one reason why this book exists and

not a thesis shelved in the Library of the University of London. In any case, this book refocuses the problem of consciousness in a communicational perspective [Note 1, p. 26].

Finally, I should note that the once clear line existing between what I have called the first force, German, and the second force strain in critical theory is now becoming blurred. If I can characterize the overall movement or development of critical theory, it is to say that first force critical theory began with the Marxist problematic (that is, a theoretically defined problem) of social interaction and has developed a movement toward the problem of language (Apel, 1967, 1972, 1972/1980; Habermas, 1971b, 1976; McCarthy, 1978; Dallmayr & McCarthy, 1977). By contrast, second force critical theory began later in various countries besides Germany and often with a non-Marxist concern for the problem of language—in particular the political nature of speech or language use—and moved to the problematics of society, especially those directly associated with the definition of situation within a speech community (Giglioli, 1972; Sandywell et al., 1975; Smart, 1976; Poster, 1979; Fiske & Hartley, 1978; Bisseret, 1979; Blake, 1979; Cotteret, 1979; Grossberg, 1979; Harms, 1980; Jacobson, 1980; Kress & Hodge, 1979; Lemert, 1979). An especially good illustration of this second force orientation and of the empirical, qualitative method used by critical theorists is Mueller's (1973) study of the political sociology of language. He begins his dialectic analysis with the data specifying the rewriting of standard German dictionaries and encyclopedias by the Nazis and subsequent modifications by the East Germans. This paradigm case is then used as a standard by which to generalize criteria inductively for comparative (dialectical) analysis with other data such as linguistic stratification in social classes and subsequent mass media appeals designed for maintaining these classes. Mueller's analysis is particularly useful for American political communication scholars, since he offers a very readable account of empirical research ranging over German and American mass media, voters, and political authority from a critical theory perspective.

At the risk of oversimplification, let me suggest that the empirical qualitative approach of critical theory, especially in its second force context, consists of the following process: (1) a paradigm case of empirical data is examined because it displays certain overt normative features; (2) a set of inductive generalizations is made from the paradigm case (that is, a theoretical exemplar is constructed); (3) the exemplar is used to locate and specify new data (often linguistic) which is, at least by first perception, value free or "objective"; and (4) the ideological value inherent in the "objective" data is discovered and its actual value commitment exposed because of the exemplar. Where the critical theory is informed by a Marxist perspective, we need to add a fifth step, which consists of a demand for ideological correction of the "objective" situation by restoring decision-making power and control to the people whose actions constitute that situation. Such a demand usually rests on an analysis showing that the apparent "objective" situation exists as an institutional force that systematically frustrates an individual's ability to act otherwise. The extent to which the Marxist perspective is required by the second force critical theorists has prompted in part the republication and translation of classic articles by first force authors (Adorno, 1969/1976; Horkheimer, 1968/1972; Frankfurt Institute for Social Research, 1956/1972) and new commentaries by their adherents and critics (Bernstein, 1978; O'Neill, 1976; Bologh, 1979; Jung, 1979).

In order to explicate the key issues with respect to the development of a critical theory perspective on political communication, I propose to divide the remainder of the essay into three parts. The first section is a brief discussion of the HISTOMAT exemplar of Wulf D. Hund and Horst Holzer, which is a characteristic illustration of second force critical theory emergent in contemporary Germany. The second section discusses the communication model offered by Jürgen Habermas largely because this model is the best effort by a first force critical theorist and typifies the Frankfurt School *theoretical* grounding. This theoretical position is to be distinguished from the technical, philosophical position articulated by Karl-Otto Apel (1972/1980), which I shall note at relevant points of analysis. And third, I offer a critique of Habermas's model of universal pragmatics as a philosophy of political communication.

ELEMENTS OF A NEO-MARXIAN THEORY
OF COMMUNICATION[2]

In recent years the work of German sociologists Wulf D. Hund (1980) and Horst Holzer (1973) began to attract increased international attention alongside of the work by Habermas. Hund and Holzer are principally known for their writings on media theory and their orientation on historical-dialectical materialism (HISTOMAT). Their work is strongly rooted within the philosophical tradition of German social thought. It brings together the insights of critical theory and contemporary Marxist philosophy and can be called *neo-Marxian* in orientation. This approach proceeds from the basic societal contradictions to be found in mass media production, distribution, and consumption. For example, it underscores, more emphatically than critical theory, the antagonism of interests existing between capital and labor in media production; and it points to the commodity character of media products as an instrument of manipulation via mass communications. In addition, this approach assigns a fundamental role to the historical conditions of development and traces the emergence of mass communications back to the needs of the capitalistic model of production (Bisky, 1976). In this view, the antagonism between capital and labor manifests itself in the subjugation and dependence of media producers to media capital— that is, in the placement of the producers at the bureaucratic disposal of owners.

The conditions of capitalist media production based on profit maximization considerations are seen as leading to increased concentration and monopolization. Thus, the commodity character of the media determines the selection of the content in accordance with the criteria of saleability and attractiveness to ensure profit maximization.

The indictment of *manipulation* is directed against those media products, such as sensationalist press reportage, that divert the attention of the mass audience from their objective interests and basic needs, from "the basic orientations rooted in specific fundamental conditions of the possible reproduction and self-constitution of the human species, namely *work* and *interaction*" (Habermas, 1968/1971a, p. 196). The accusation *in flagrante delicto* also encompasses the consumption of pure entertainment material for regenerative and recuperative purposes, as well as advertising that creates artificial needs and thereby produces delusions of a harmonious and homogeneous society. To recapitulate, this media theory can be described as a historically and dialectically determined analysis of mass communication, specifically in terms of the antagonism between capital and labor in media production. From this antagonism results the commodity character of media production and distribution which is closely related to manipulation through mass communication consumption. Such an analysis calls for a proletarian-emancipatory alternate *publicality* (a neologism meaning the sphere where communications take place) utilizing the achievements of the bourgeois media under transformed structures of control.

Such a media theory aims essentially at the *democratic* transformation of the prevailing conditions in the entire scope of mass communications. While first force critical theory, which also has the same aims, tends to offer nothing more than abstract postulates and generalizations, neo-Marxian media theoreticians specify the aims of such a new media theory. In addition, they are proposing a long-term strategy for the *democratization of the mass media* which has the following political goals:

(1) changing the content of the mass media so that materialism and communication are not distorted as consumerism and persuasion (discussed below in the critique of Habermas) which has permeated deeply into the consciousness of the employees and wageearners;

(2) dismantling of the capitalist system and thereby the existing structures of mass communication and the subsequent creation of a political, proletarian *publicality* (Negt & Kluge, 1972);

(3) worker participation in all areas of mass media production (on the editorial, technical, and administrative levels); liberation of the workers in media production from subjugation and dependence on the providers of capital;

(4) transferring media control from private owners to producers, expropriation of privately run media businesses, decentralization and demonopolization of media firms and their transformation into socialized institutions open to participation on the entire allocative and operational spectrum;

(5) the formation of advertising and publicity cooperatives to distribute advertisements and publicity orders to all affiliated media on an equal basis and thereby to prevent concentration of communication powers; and

(6) the political activization of the masses for communicative emancipation and the development of communicative competence—that is, action oriented toward reaching understanding (Habermas, 1968/ 1971a)—in the spontaneous creation of media programs through public articulation of objective societal needs and interests.

Hund and Holzer have been sharply critical of the traditional bourgeois mass communication research and its theories. According to them, the bourgeois communication research accepts mass media as tools of domination and the state of *speechlessness* in societal communication as given—that is, the lack of individual participation illustrated, for example, by the issue of "local access" in cable television licensing. They refer to it as administrative, directed, and bureaucratically enacted research: Its findings and conclusions serve only those who are already dominating the existing order for the *consciousness industry*. Furthermore, it presumes the dualism of subject and object and the divergence of *what is* from *what ought to be*. Bourgeois media theory is thus seen as a theory of domination.

Critical and neo-Marxian media theoreticians, on the other hand, focus on the mass media as instruments of liberation (Negt, 1978; Negt & Kluge, 1972). They see them as a means through which the objective and authentic interests of the masses can be articulated. Their communication research reflecting this perception centers on the social state of the media, culture, and the educational system in the context of conflicts between social strata, rather than within the media. These theoreticians reject the distinction between what is and what ought to be. Science is seen not as something separate from daily experience, but as a process which should contribute in form and substance to the proletarian context of life which itself organizes the experiences of the masses in a specific way. The objective of critical and neo-Marxian communication research therefore is not the *distribution* of mass communications through mass media, but an absolute societal *communication* itself through the exchange of information about the objective interests and needs of the masses.

As a final point of emphasis, Hund and Holzer's philosophical orientation and thought based on *historical-dialectical materialism* (HISTOMAT) pertains to social research generally and to communication research specifically at the following three levels (Hahn, Note 3):

(1) HISTOMAT contains as a dialectic and materialistic philosophical theory of society the basic solution of *epistemological* problems which we find in sociological research and which stem from certain peculiarities of this research and from social reality. This applies especially to the materialistic determination of the relationship subject-object.

(2) HISTOMAT represents the basic solution of general *theoretical* questions which sociological research centers on and with which sociological research is connected through a number of special theoretical assertions. HISTOMAT offers the basic theoretical framework, terminology, and categories which also make possible the scientific analysis of single problems in an empirical way.

(3) These two relationships are at the same time essential parts of the *methodological* function of HISTOMAT in relation to sociological research in terms of the use of certain logical procedures.

Habermas provides a theoretical discussion of these issues in Part Two of his *Knowledge and Human Interests* (1968/1971a), while Mićunović (1979) provides a specific illustration in his analysis of "Bureaucracy and Public Communication."

HABERMAS'S MODEL OF UNIVERSAL PRAGMATICS

In the latest essay describing universal pragmatics, which extends the discussion of an earlier working position (Habermas, Note 4; 1976), Habermas (1979b) explains that the object of such a pragmatics is "to identify and reconstruct universal conditions of possible understanding [*Verstandigung*]." As he further notes, such an analysis concerns the general presuppositions of communicative action which is fundamental to working out the problem of *understanding*. What makes the model of universal pragmatics one of political communication is the forthright declaration: "Thus I start from the assumption (without undertaking to demonstrate it here) that other forms of social action—for example, conflict, competition, strategic action in general—are derivatives of action oriented to reaching understanding [*verstandigungsorientiert*]" (1979b, p. 1). The axiological context for action Habermas outlines is thus inclusive of all the normal subtopics of axiology: politics, ethics, and morality (Habermas, 1979a). In particular, we might characterize the universal pragmatics model as one of communicative ethics in which the standard constructs of communication theory are displayed: intention, punctuation, convention, and legitimation. It is a viewpoint Habermas (1979b, p. 2) confirms by stating: "I shall develop the thesis that anyone acting communicatively must, in performing any speech action, raise universal validity claims and suppose that they can be vindicated [or redeemed: *einlosen*]."

Intention

Habermas (1970a) locates intention, the object of consciousness experience to be analyzed, in the general theory parameters of psychoanalysis. Explicitly he argues that psychoanalytic theory gives the researcher (1) a preconception of the structure of nondistorted ordinary communication; (2) an attribution of the systematic distortion of communication to the confusion of two developmental levels of symbols organization, the prelinguistic and linguistic; and (3) a theory of deviant socialization to explain the origin of deformation. The model of logic Freud provided in his analysis of thought, discourse, and behavior is widely recognized by European scholars, while Anglo-American researchers tend to discount Freud's work as empirically represented in its questionable contemporary use as a successful therapeutic procedure. In terms of Habermas's work in particular and European scholarship in general, it is well to recall that the Freudian heritage is the *logic model* (an exemplar) that is utilized to focus on new problems, issues, or data. The best detailed discussion of Freud in this context is Wilden (1972b), wherein the Freudian semiotic model of condensation and displacement is specifically related to the theory constructs which constitute information theory and communication theory (cybernetics) and which are exemplified in the technology of digital and analogue computers.

On this psychoanalytic base, Habermas builds a parallel set of theoretical propositions that indicate the meaning parameters in *normal communication*. First, in the case of nondeformed language games, there is a congruency of all three levels of communication as presented in the psychoanalytic model above. Second, normal communication conforms to intersubjectively recognized rules; it is public in this sense. Third, speakers are aware of the categorical difference between subject and object in normal speech. Fourth, normal communication provides a contextual situation in which an intersubjectivity of mutual understanding, which guarantees ego-identity, develops and is maintained in the relation between individuals who acknowledge one another. Fifth, " normal speech is distinguished by the fact that the sense of substance and causality, of space and time, is differentiated according to whether these categories are applied to the objects within a world or to the linguistically constituted world itself, which allows for the mutuality of speaking subjects" (1970a, p. 212).

Punctuation

The boundary limitation for the analysis of normal communication results from two postulates Habermas draws from his set of five propositions. He argues that psychoanalysis in the study of communication relies on a genetic connection beyond successive phases of human symbol organization. First, "the archaic symbol-organization, which resists the transformation of its contents into grammatically regulated communication, can only be disclosed on the basis of the data of speech pathology and by means of the analysis of dream material" (1970a, p. 212). Second, the symbol organization the psychoanalyst utilizes is a theoretical construct in that it genetically precedes language. In brief, Habermas goes on to suggest that such a theoretical construct presumes a theory of communicative competence modeled on Chomsky's model of linguistic competence/performance.

Habermas's theory of communicative competence is a combination of the problem as defined by psychoanalysis and the method of ordinary language analysis suggested by the conceptual analysts: Austin (1962), Grice (1967), and Searle (1967, 1969). In particular, Habermas (1979b) adopts Searle's general formulation of the speech act theory and applies it in the social context of communication (Sullivan, 1978). That is, an interpersonal model of communication at the performance level is generalized to a model of social discourse (as a legitimation process) at the competence level. In this generalization of social levels from the individual to the mass, Habermas maintains the ideal speech situation as a construct—that is, Searle's model where the interpersonal communication is always logical, literal, and contextually unambiguous. Let me simply indicate that there are serious problems in maintaining such an ideal in the analysis of empirical social research (Wellmer, 1976).

Habermas offers the following set of theoretical propositions which correspond at the social level to those which Searle (1967, 1969) presents for the interpersonal speech act. (1) The personal pronouns and their derivatives form a reference system between potential speakers. The identity of meanings, the foundation of every communication, is based on intersubjectively valid rules—at least two speakers understand the meaning of a symbol on the basis of reciprocal recognition. (2) The deictic expressions of space and time, as well as articles and demonstrative pronouns, form the reference system of possible denotations. (3) Forms of address (vocative), forms of social contact (greeting), of speech introduction and speech conclusion, indirect discourse, questions and answers, are performatory in that they are directed at the act of speaking as such. (4) The performatory speech acts form a system which finally enables us to mark the basic differentiations which are fundamental for any speech situation. Thus system relations are formed between (a) being and appearance; (b) being and essence; and (c) fact and value—that is, what is and what ought to be.

Convention

The summary result that Habermas's model of communication achieves is a specification of the social levels of communication and the parallel validity claim that can be based on speech acts as rule-governed behavior with social import. By examining the formation and transformation of speech acts, Habermas (1976) arrives at two levels of communication. First is the *level of intersubjectivity,* at which the speaker and hearer, through illocutionary acts, bring about an interpersonal relationship which allows them to achieve mutual understanding. Second is the "level of objects in the world, or states of affair about which they would want to achieve a consensus in terms of the communicative role as laid down in the level of intersubjectivity" (p. 159).

In principle, therefore, every competent speaker has the responsibility of choosing among three modes of social communication (Habermas, 1979b, p.

58): first, communication to state a proposition which can be illustrated in the propositional attitude of a nonparticipating third person who hears a speech act; second, communication to stress an interpersonal relationship as such, as illustrated in the performative attitude of a participant conforming to the expectations of a second person; or third, communication to express an intention as such (that is, speaker presents himself before others). Each form of communication carries a claim to validity that is situationally recognized for its value (Hooft, 1976).

Legitimation

Habermas makes an explicit connection between communication and axiology, both in terms of how human communication leads to ethnical judgments about persons and in terms of the social aesthetic (moral) values which dominate personal existence. Ultimately, his concern is with the special connection in communication by which personal ethics and social aesthetics form political norms of existence: social legitimation. Fiske and Hartley (1978) provide a useful empirical illustration of Habermas's view in their analysis of a British Broadcasting Corporation "News at Ten" program in which the main story is coverage of British troops in Northern Ireland. Their study provides a typical second force cirtical analysis in which the intended (by BBC programmers) visual and oral information message(s), a "social aesthetic" for Habermas, are structurally semiotic and thereby substantially perceived as norms of the "reality" of the situation, the "political norm of existence" for Habermas. In short, a political norm is offered as "information," thereby distorting the actual political situation and obviating the viewers' opportunity to judge as individuals. Instead, mere viewing of the political norm message makes it legitimate information; this is social legitimation.

In careful propositional language, Habermas (1975) suggests that "only *communicative ethics* guarantees the generality of admissible norms and the autonomy of acting subjects solely through the discursive redeemability of the validity claims with which such norms appear" (p. 89). Communication is an action which, we should recall, deals with theoretical facts, values which have a pragmatic effect because they are formed in speech acts. In this context, Habermas advances three basic *pragmatic universals* (levels of understanding that emerge in human action) which are derived from the linguistic universals apparent in all speech communication.

First, "each specific language offers a reference system which permits a sufficiently reliable identification of something in the world about which one would want to make propositions." Second, "each specific language offers a *system* of personal pronouns and a system of speech acts with the aid of which we can bring about interpersonal relationships." And third, "each particular language offers a *system of intentional expressions* for the self-presentation of subjectivity which, in spite of the degree of variation of its expression in particular languages, reflects the system of ego-delimitations" (p. 161).

For Habermas, then, social and political legitimation of personal and public action, whether technically instrumental or communicative, result in the formation of a communication ethic. That is, the rational society which manifests a universal pragmatics is a transformation of "the communication community [*Kommunikationgemeinschaft*] of those affected, who as participants in a practical discourse test the validity claims of norms, and, to the extent that they accept them with reasons, arrive at the conviction that in the given circumstance the proposed norms are 'right' " (p. 105). A parallel argument in non-Marxist terms is made by Apel (1967, 1972/1980).

In short, the critical theory model begins with an axiological pragmatics (legitimation) of speech communication which is based on the logical notion of ideal speech acts (convention). For Habermas, as a critical theorist, speech acts are part of the symbol formation process (punctuation) that derives its epistemological stages of development from the metaphysical approach of Freudian psychoanalysis and its theory of consciousness (intention). Thus, a theory of a rational society is an ideal generalized from a theory of normal communication in the rational person (Habermas, 1979b, pp. 67-68). The resultant implications of the critical theory approach for political analysis and research as they relate to the traditional American view of empirical research are explored at length in the now classic essay by Reid and Yanarella (1974) entitled "Toward a Post-Modern Theory of American Political Science and Culture: Perspectives from Critical Marxism and Phenomenology."

A CRITIQUE OF HABERMAS AND CRITICAL THEORY

Marx and Practical Consciousness

The concept and sometime slogan of "dialectical materialism" is, for all the caution of liberal politics in the West, intimately tied to the theory and practice of human communication. As Wellmer (1971, p. 87) remarks,

> Only because Marx could rely on a revolutionary tradition, in which the intentions of achieving the freedom of the individual and personal happiness were already more or less clearly bound up with the idea of a public political arena constituted by citizens able to communicate with one another without coercion, and with the idea of *public* freedom and *public* happiness, was the young Marx's critique of Hegel able to become a criticism of the ideology of the bourgeois constitutional state of the advanced Western type.

The very concerns of "dialectical materialism" and "communication" are contemporary paradigms (Hickson & Jandt, 1976) of what Habermas (1970a) calls *distorted communication.* As Marx suggests, "the chief defect of all previous materialism (including Feuerbach) is that things [*Gegenstand*], and reality, and the sensible world, are conceived only in the form of *objects* [*Objekt*] *of observation,* but not as *human sense activity,* not as *practical activity,* not subjectively" (Bottomore & Rubel, 1963, p. 82; Smythe, Note 5). Or as Apel (1972, p. 3) asserts, "in my opinion, the chief question still is: whether it does or does not make a difference for the philosophy of science that in the human sciences, the *object* of science is also the *subject* of science, namely human society as a communication community." It is no surprise, then, that the technological consciousness of postindustrial democracy reifies, as a pragmatic of argumentation (Apel, 1975, p. 247), the concepts of materialism and communication (thereby distorting them) into *consumerism* and *persuasion,* respectively.

In the analysis that follows, I would like to illustrate the sense in which critical theory functions as a "militant philosophy" in the defense of communication as a human activity constituting the person as a subject in society. In addition, I would like to argue that critical theory as exemplified in the proposal by Habermas (1970b, 1976, 1979b, Note 4) for a "universal pragmatics" is grounded in the phenomenology of communication. Here I take the phenomenology of communication to be the subjectivity inherent in the existential speech act that makes consciousness a social product—that is, the constitution of the *Kommunikationsgemeinschaft.* Finally, my analysis attempts to raise the issue of the creation of values by positing a speech act phenomenology within the wider context of a universal pragmatics, which is a theme in the current research of Habermas (1979b, pp. 66-68). In the development of these three themes, I hope to illustrate the appropriateness of Marx's contention that

> language is as old as consciousness, language *is* practical consciousness, as it exists for other men, and thus as it first really exists for myself as well. Language, like consciousness, only arises from the need, the necessity of intercourse with other men. Where a relationship exists, it exists for me; the animal has no "*realtions*" with anything, has no relations at all. For the animal, its relation to others does not exist as a relation. Consciousness is therefore from the very beginning a social product, and remains so long as men exist at all [Bottomore and Rubel, pp. 85-86].

In short, I wish to point out that the necessary dialectical materialism that communication creates is *not* consumerism grounded in persuasion. Rather, communication accounts for the dialectic in society by which individual persons constitute their consciousness of a lived-world (*Lebenswelt*) by the practical activity of speaking for themselves and others in the emancipatory process of identity, an authentic social existence. Interpersonal communication is thereby the legitimation of society as humanly lived (Lefebvre, 1966/1968, p. 66). As Merleau-Ponty (1964, p. 130) suggests, "Marxism is not a philosophy of the subject, but it is just as far from a philosophy of the object: it is a philosophy of history [*l'histoire*]."

Militant Philosophy

"For the first time since Hebel, militant philosophy is reflecting not on subjectivity but on intersubjectivity," says Merleau-Ponty (1964, pp. 133-134) of Marx's insistence on the critique of the "objects of observation" which ignore the dialectic between the subject and the lived-world. At this point, we need to remind ourselves that human communication is itself an object of observation—a fundamental grounding. This is to say that metacommunication is a condition of human interaction in which communication is the methodology utilized to critique itself with attending implications for the description and explication of consciousness as bounded by society. In more familiar terms recalling the example of consumerism and persuasion, I am saying that a critical analysis of communication by a human communicator can lapse into reifying communication as language behavior (an object of consumption; the method of positivism) and into reifying the person as cognition (an object of persuasion; the method of ordinary language philosophy).

Habermas (1971b) correctly draws attention to the danger of reification by pointing out the appropriate social distinction between *purposive-rational action* (variously referred to as "instrumental") and *communicative action.* In this context, purposive-rational action is a condition of persuasion; that is, the state of affairs in which a preconceived metacommunication constitutes what communication is or can be—hence assigns a negative value to the emergence of an individual act in society. This negative value (consumerism) emerges in most cases as the *role* of the person in society as prescribed by society (metacommunication). By contrast, communicative action is a condition of emancipation (from the domination of persuasion), the state of affairs in which communication regulates what metacommunication is or can be—thereby assigning a positive value to the engagement of persons in individual acts (parole). The positive value is the generation of authentic existence (*parole parlante*) within the interpersonal boundaries (*langue*) of the social group (Habermas, 1979b, p. 6).

At this point it is helpful to review the technical comparison Habermas (1971b, pp. 91-93) draws between purposive-rational action and communicative action because the distinction drawn illustrates what I have previously characterized as the "inductive" method of critical theory generally. In the former case,

> instrumental action is governed by *technical rules* based on empirical knowledge. In every case they imply conditional predictions about observable events, physical or social. These predictions can prove correct or incorrect. The conduct of rational choice is governed by *strategies* based on analytic knowledge. They imply deductions from preference rules (value systems) and decision procedures; these propositions are either correctly or incorrectly deduced.

In contrast, Habermas continues,

> By "interaction," on the other hand, I understand *communicative action*, symbolic interaction. It is governed by binding *consensual norms,* which define reciprocal expectations about behavior and which must be understood and recognized by at least two acting subjects. Social norms are enforced through sanctions. Their meaning is objectified in ordinary language communication. While the validity of technical rules and strategies depends on that of empirically true or analytically correct propositions, the validity of social norms is grounded only in the intersubjectivity of the mutual understanding of intentions and secured by the general recognition of obligations.

I have previously (Lanigan, 1979b) made the argument that communication is by definition a speech act which succumbs to ambiguity when restricted to the status of an *action.* That is, interpersonal actions at any semiotic level are burdened by a good or bad ambiguity. Or, as Habermas (1979b, pp. 31-34) is forced to concede, the predictions of purposive-rational action prove correct or incorrect. Likewise, communicative actions are enforced or not by sanctions. In either case, the action is legitimized by the presence or absence of conative meaning (Habermas, 1979b, p. 58). That is, a group expectation (social state of affairs) constitutes a negative value (it is a metacommunicative condition) of ambiguity—any result is held in question. Although Habermas contends that "learned rules of purposive-rational action supply us with *skills,* internalized norms with *personality structures,*" we do not escape the metacommunication context. Our speech act may be the product of skill—for example, in the expression of an argument—or the act may reflect our personality structure, as in the perception of another's argument. Yet, the action is still Marx's object of observation in which the preconditions of communication (metacommunication) constitute inauthentically the human act. In short, the ethical rhetoric (authentic discourse) is dominated by rhetorical ethics (inauthentic discourse).

On reflection, then, it is apparent that critical theory is a militant philosophy in the problematic shift from an exclusive concern with subjectivity (bad ambiguity when counterposed to objectivity) to an inclusive concern with intersubjectivity (good ambiguity). Yet, the militancy of critical theory is subdued by the reification of practical activity as an object of analysis—which Marx warns against. Resolution of the problematic is, however, possible in the larger project of the philosophy of communication.

Phenomenology of Communication

Communication as a focus of phenomenological analysis is problematic when our analysis is limited to the "effects" of discourse at the interpersonal level. That is, the conception of communication as an action forces the analysis into a consideration of the causality of "meaning" (purposive-rational action) or "behavior" (communicative action). What is wanted, by contrast, is an account of the conditions for the *performance* (as production) of communication. Here the focus is on the *dialectic* of semantics, syntactics, and pragmatics in the sense of a semiotic phenomenology. In this context, semantics constitutes *capta*, or that which is taken to be the case (hypothesis). Syntactics accounts for *data*, or that which is given as being the case (hypostasis). And pragmatics is the realm of *acta*, or that which is done as the case (hermeneutic). The communication problematic advanced by Habermas is a digital logic that attempts to counterpose *capta* (communicative action) against *data* (purposive-rational action). I am, therefore, in disagreement with the confirming interpretation which Wellmer (O'Neill, 1976, pp. 248-249) ascribes to Habermas: "As epistemological categories, consequently, 'instrumental' and 'communicative' action represent the distinction between nomological and instrumental knowledge, on the one hand, and hermeneutic and reflective knowledge on the other. Correspondingly, they also reflect the methodological distinction between the 'natural sciences' and 'Geisteswissenschaften.'" This confusion is another instance of allowing familiar methodology to confuse the levels of communication and metacommunication— that is, the analogue distinction between a prereflective and reflective process (act) on the one hand and a preconscious and conscious act on the other. While there is a categorical opposition between the prereflective/reflective and the preconscious/conscious that is binary in process, it is not a dignital function in effect (as Habermas and Wellmer impute). It is thus ironic that Habermas (1975, p. 10; 1979b, p. 41) proceeds to argue for an "outer nature" (instrumental actions) and an "inner nature" (communicative actions) on the basis that

> linguistic communication has a double structure, for communication about propositional content may take place only with simultaneous metacommunication about interpersonal relations. This is an expression of the specifically human interlacing of cognitive performances and motives for action with linguistic intersubjectivity. Language functions as a kind of transformer; because psychic processes such as sensations, needs and feelings are fitted into structures of linguistic intersubjectivity, inner episodes or experiences are transformed into intentional contents—that is, cognitions into statements, needs and feelings into normative expectations (percepts and values).

In this argument there is an equivocation that is generated in the following sequence of analysis. Nomological knowledge proceeds according to prescribed *rules* of reasoning which in consequence become *tools* (instruments) for legitimate description (*explication*). Hermeneutic analysis describes the instrumental nature of legitimation and in consequence prescribes the reasoning that must be found in rules (legitimate *explanation*).

The equivocation occurs at two points in the argument. One is the concept of rules. Nomological knowledge relies on constitutive rules that entail regulative rules; explication entails (logically) explanation. In similar fashion, hermeneutic knowledge relies on the use of regulative rules which may be asserted as (but are not) constitutive; explanation can be made to explicate. In this sequence of events, we make the false assumption that rules define a state of consciousness ("inner nature"), rather than specify the relational process between the preconscious and the conscious. And, we also incorrectly assume that rules indicate the emergence of the reflective from the prereflective as a static condition ("outer nature"). In point of fact, then, Habermas tends to make the instrumental-communicative action distinction rest on "action" as an object of observation, where observation is defined by *rules conceived as normative conditions*—that is, abstractions reified as perceptions (the *form* of the object of observation for Marx).

The second part of equivocation concerns the concepts of nomological and hermeneutic judgment as they bear on the disjunction between the *Naturwissenschaften* and the *Geisteswissenschaften*. Where the process of observation is reified into the "state" of observation, we extend the ambiguity of rules (abstractions) utilized as conditions (perceived experience). It is widely assumed that this reification is legitimate in the physical sciences, since they are *data* based, whereas the reification is illegitimate in the human sciences, since they are *cupta* based. As Habermas (1968/1971a, pp. 140-141) puts the issue,

> the cultural life context is formed on a level of intersubjectivity that is presupposed by the attitude of strictly empirical science but cannot be analyzed by it. If this is so, we are confronted by the question whether the cultural sciences in fact do not proceed within a different methodological framework and are not constituted by a different cognitive interest than the natural sciences comprehended by pragmaticism.

Of course, the point at issue is the nature and function of *acta*. (By identifying the problem as one of pragmatics, Habermas is entirely correct—even if we contest his conclusions.)

When we pay close attention to the place of action in the process of observation, we cannot dispose of the observer, the human agent. In this sense, the methodology of the natural and human sciences participates in the same process of legitimation. The dialectic is such that the natural scientist moves from the nomological to the hermeneutic as a *process* of legitimation, while the human scientist moves from the hermeneutic to the nomological as a *process* of value ascription. The point is that the dialectic process, "while directionally [descriptively] different [binary] is analogical ['nature'] and not digital in consequence ['inner' or 'outer']" (Wilden, 1972a, 1972b).

In short, the process of observation must be thrown over in preference to the observer, as Marx suggests. The practical activity of consciousness must be located in the person; we must focus on the *act* rather than the *action* (*data/*

capta). In this sense, act is the name we can apply to the universal pragmatic that takes account of reified actions: nomological consciousness reified as *data* and hermeneutic consciousness reified as *capta,* where "reification" is rule-governed hypostasis (meaning) and hypothesis (behavior). Before we take up the issue of pragmatics in the universal pragmatic, we need to discuss the ideal situation which is preconceived in the concept of "universal" as Habermas (1970b, 1979b, p. 29) derives it from the thesis of *communicative competence.*

Speech Act Phenomenology

The discussion of speech acts (Austin, 1962; Searle, 1967, 1969; Lanigan, 1977) is a record of shifting perspective between the contexts of information theory (data) and communication theory (capta). Habermas locates this shifting argument within the "ideal" situation of language behavior by contrasting *linguistic competence* (according to Chomsky) with *communicative competence.* While this move provides a certain amount of technical insight about human communication theory, I believe it is ultimately an unsatisfactory direction that falls victim to the very objection it is fleeing: "the idealization of pure communicative action would have to be reconstructed as the condition under which the authenticity of speaking and acting subjects can be imputed as well as verified" (Habermas, 1971/1973, p. 19).

According to Habermas (1970b, pp. 361, 367):

> "Linguistic competence" is Chomsky's name for the mastery of an abstract system of rules, based on an innate language apparatus, regardless of how the latter is in fact used in actual speech. This competence is a monological capability; it is founded in the species-specific equipment of the solitary human organism. For such a capability to be a sufficient linguistic basis for speech, one would have to be able to reconstruct the communication process itself as a "monological" one. The information model of communication is suitable for this purpose.

In contrast to the Chomsky theory of linguistic competence, which must assume an information theory model of human discourse (*langue* is reified as *langage*), Habermas argues that "on the contrary, in order to participate in normal discourse the speaker must have at his disposal, in addition to his linguistic competence, basic qualifications of speech and symbolic interaction (role-behavior), which we may call *communicative competence.* This communicative competence means the mastery of an ideal speech situation." Habermas (1970b, p. 369) further clarifies this thesis by suggesting that "communicative competence is defined by the ideal speaker's mastery of the dialogue-constitutive universals, irrespective of actual restrictions under empirical conditions." Thus, Habermas's proposal is the reification of *parole* as *langue* (which is assumed to be a reification of *langage* via linguistic competence).

The contribution Habermas makes to the ongoing analysis of speech acts is that he recognizes the *semiotic* requirement that communication be analyzed as the interaction of persons at the syntactic, semantic, and pragmatic levels. In this view, he advances beyond the work of Searle, who restricts his analysis to an information theory model grounded in a "monological" syntactics and developed as a "dialogial" semantics. However, Habermas accepts the same conditions of analysis Searle does by assuming the necessity of an ideal speaker in an ideal situation. This procedure repeats the mistake outlined above, in which rules are conceived as conditions of behavior and not inversely. "Ultimately, Habermas would want to argue, such communicative equality could only exist on the basis of real *social* equality. Here the theory of communication (aimed at truth) turns into political theory: the ideal speech situation becomes the ideal decision situation of Rousseau's *Social Contract*" (Pateman, Note 6, p. 6). In addition, the assumption of the "universal" perspective of the ideal speaker/situation does violence to the very concept of pragmatics. "Since most, if not all, signs have as their interpreters living organisms, it is a sufficiently accurate characterization of pragmatics to say that it deals with the biotic aspects of semiosis, that is, with all the psychological, biological, and sociological phenomena which occur in the functioning of signs" (Morris, 1938, p. 30; see also Lanigan, 1972). The lesson of Saussure that *parole, langue,* and *langage* are dialectically human communication is ignored by the technical approach Habermas takes.

I have argued elsewhere (Lanigan, 1977) that a complete speech act analysis that includes a theory of communicative competence that *legitimizes* human interpersonal communication must be approached as a phenomenology of human interaction. In other words, an adequate account of communicative competence in a communication situation requires a "dialogical" consideration of pragmatics as the ground for syntactics and semantics. This is another version of the argument that acta (*parole*) must be the key for interpreting data (*langage*) and capta (*langue*). The social product of communication becomes the authenticity of a person speaking. Thus, the person legitimizes the act of communicating, rather than the false consciousness of the action defining the person—the mistake of positive behaviorism is thereby avoided.

It is necessary to point out that Habermas is quite aware of the difficulty attending to the notion of a "universal" in pragmatics as applied to speech acts. As he suggests (Habermas, Note 4, pp. 11-12, 1976, 1979b),

> First, we would have to show that the structural change of world-views obeys an inner logic, such that the systematic variation of a basic pattern can be reconstructed. Over and above this, it would have to be possible to derive from the social evolution of world-views a universalistic morality based on the basic norms of speech and the ideas of the responsibly acting person developed in the model of pure communicative action. Then we could comprehend all divergent concepts of the person and the expressions

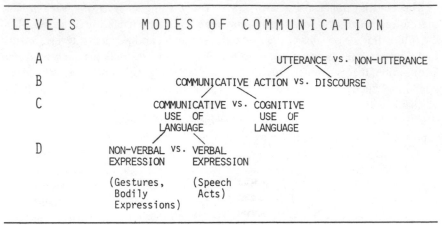

LEVELS   MODES OF COMMUNICATION

A   UTTERANCE vs. NON-UTTERANCE

B   COMMUNICATIVE ACTION vs. DISCOURSE

C   COMMUNICATIVE vs. COGNITIVE
                        USE OF   USE OF
                        LANGUAGE   LANGUAGE

D   NON-VERBAL vs. VERBAL
             EXPRESSION   EXPRESSION

             (Gestures,   (Speech
              Bodily   Acts)
              Expressions)

Figure 5.1: Choice Levels in Modal Communication According to Lanigan

of persons as modifications of the one universal idea of responsibility similar to those that guide us in relating to children.

The consequence of this view of the idealization of the communication situation is in fact pragmatic to the extent that it allows Habermas to hypostatize levels of *choice* between various modes of communication. Choice is a fundamental concept here because it accounts for the "inner logic" that is possible among the pragmatic rules governing communication, such as social and cultural variation, psychological condition, and so on. In addition, this "levels" model of the communication act suggests the conditions under which the authenticity of communicating (morality) may be "imputed as well as verified."

There are four levels of choice between the different modes of communication. "On condition of free choice, every choice at a higher level eliminates choices at the next lower level." Habermas (Note 4, p. 25) offers the schema presented in Figure 5.1 as an illustration of his model. As a matter of information, we should note that this working schema (and its variations [Habermas, 1979a, p. 196, 1979b, pp. 40, 209]) of the modes of communication offered by Habermas already exists in large measure in the *Model of Sign Production* formulated by Eco (1976, p. 217). Eco divides the physical labor required to produce expressions into progressively higher levels of communication beginning with "recognition" advancing to "ostension" and then on to the level of "replica" and finally "invention." Eco's concern focuses on the production of "aesthetic texts" in which the hermeneutic of human sign production exemplifies an authentic social product in language—that is, signification in human code systems.

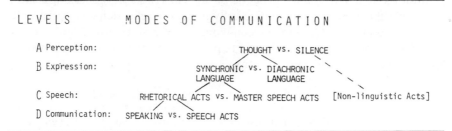

Figure 5.2: Choice Levels in Modal Communication According to Habermas

However, both Habermas and Eco take the restrictive view that dialogical communication in its pragmatic stance does not provide a basis for authentic choice where that choice is restricted to "freedom" in a social rather than personal sense. At the same time, they are unable to remove their analysis from the constrictions of the universal pragmatic that seems to be required for a transition from the problem of subjectivity to intersubjectivity in the analysis of communication as a *system*. I believe this difficulty results in part from the failure to recognize the semiotic, rather than formal (Habermas, 1979b, pp. 8-9), link between perception and expression (Lanigan, 1979a). Perception is the social level that results from the infrastructure of expression, variously constituted by speech and communication acts (Lanigan, 1979b). My position is illustrated in the schema in Figure 5.2 using the same general structure that Habermas presents.

The perspective in this formulation is, of course, a specification the dimensions of authentic choice as manifest in communication. As such, the social product of communication is produced by the *inclusion* of the choices at a lower level when the choice at a higher level is made. This position is clearly phenomenological in terms of social choice and existential in terms of personal choice. The arguments supporting this schema and analysis, which are technical and lengthy, have already been made elsewhere (Lanigan, 1977). In short, I believe Habermas offers a successful, parallel argument for social free choice in his discussion of social legitimation (which we will take up below) in his concept of *communicative ethics,* even though his analysis must still treat the person as an idealization in a like situation.

The Politics of Semiology

Habermas (1973/1975, p. 10) argues that "linguistic communication has a double structure, for communication about propositional content may take place only with simultaneous metacommunication about interpersonal relations. This is an expression of the specifically human interlacing of cognitive performance and motives for action with linguistic intersubjectivity." Speech acts then perform the function of a hermeneutic assessment for society. Speaking creates values; yet those values may not be overtly present to reflection on a social scale (what is a prudent act?), and the conscious values may be articulated but not known (what is an act in good faith?). In point of fact, the communication ethic is largely preconscious and prereflective.

> Only *communicative ethics* guarantees the generality of admissable norms and the autonomy of acting subjects solely through the discursive redeemability of the validity claims with which norms appear. That is, generality is guaranteed in that only norms that may claim generality are those on which everyone affected agrees (or would agree) without constraint if they enter into (or were to enter into) a process of discursive will-formation [Habermas, 1973/1975, p. 89].

In short, when communicators engage in communication acts that are both reflective and conscious (therefore *political*), they create values that morally link the subjective and the intersubjective. The semiotic connection of the personal and the interpersonal guarantees that the act joins, at one level, the preconscious and the reflective (expression). Yet again, the conscious and the reflective join (speech), as do the preconscious and prereflective (communication). Thus, the semiotic link that unites person and society is also the one that unites the modes of communication with pragmatic values. Recall Marx's assertion that "language *is* practical consciousness."

On the social level, Habermas (1979b, p. 49) provides an excellent statement of the political nature of semiotic analysis as the problem communicative action must address.

> It is a consequence of the fundamental contradiction of the capitalist system that, other factors being equal, either
>
> — the economic system does not produce the requisite quantity of consumable decisions, or;
> — the administrative system does not produce the requisite quantity of rational decisions, or;
> — the legitimation system does not provide the requisite quantity of generalized motivations, or;
> — the socio-cultural system does not generate the requisite quantity of action-motivating meaning.
>
> The expression "the requisite quantity" refers to the extent, quality, and temporal dimension of the respective system performances (value, administrative decision, legitimation, and meaning).

It should not be difficult to see that in the phenomenological schema I presented above, Level A: "perception" is equivalent to Habermas' "socio-cultural system"; Level B: "expression," equal to "legitimation system"; Level C:

"speech," equivalent to "administrative system"; and Level D: "communication," equal to "economic system." In making these ratios I want to assert the connection between authenticity of choice and language use/speech as a social product; that is, the Marxian thesis that "human sense activity" becomes a social product with personal value. Human communication is per se a political act (Cushman & Dietrich, 1979).

To the extent that there is a system failure in a postindustrial capitalist society, there is a crisis of human identity. There is moral and political alienation and domination. The causality of this value interest in the person/society link is, as Habermas senses, contained in the *communication codes* that link the observation of action with the act of observing. The operative concept here is "code" where action, act, value, and interest are joint products of emancipation (Lanigan, Note 7). In this instance, "code" is the concept discovered by Merleau-Ponty that a primary characteristic of *human* communication is *parole parlante*: the speaking which is a speech act (communication ethic) and the speech act which is speaking (authentic communication).

> In the language of the Geisteswissenschaften we could say: The possibility that linguistic signs have meaning cannot be understood without presupposing a "meaning-intention" which expresses itself in the signs. In other words, not even the facts of science are facts for the unchanging "subject as such" (of "the language as such"), but they are constituted in a concrete and therefore historically determined human horizon of meanings [Apel, 1967, p. 33].

In conclusion, let me suggest that the critical theory approach to a communication theory of society, initiated in the development of the speech act theory and the hermeneutic phenomenology of communication, represents a starting point in the analysis of the fundamental relationship between persons and societies. From Marx we gain an insight based on the nature of person and moral value. The fundamental grounding of emancipation from consumerism and persuasion as reified in social institutions is linked inseparably to the discovery of the communication community (*Kommunikationgemeinschaft*) as a source of authenticity and interpersonal legitimation. Thus, "the greatness of Marxism lies not in its having treated economics as the principal or unique cause of history but in its treating cultural history and economic history as two abstract aspects of the same process" (Merleau-Ponty, 1964, p. 107).

NOTES

[1]Portions of the analysis presented in this essay are based on "Critical Theory as a Philosophy of Communication," a paper I presented on May 30, 1977 at the International Congress for Communication Science, West Berlin, Germany. Also, portions are based on "Communication Models in Philosophy: Review and Commentary" in *Communication*

Yearbook 3 ed. Dan Nimmo (New Brunswick, NJ: Transaction Books/International Communication Association, 1979).

[2]This section was written by Rudolf L. Strobl independently of any knowledge of the other sections written by Richard L. Lanigan. This section was adapted and included by Lanigan to provide a concrete indication of a current model not generally known to researchers who lack fluency in German. For a more detailed discussion of a historical-dialectical materialist analysis of communication, see Strobl (Note 2).

REFERENCE NOTES

1. Pateman, T. *Language, truth, and politics: Towards a radical theory for communication.* Private printing, (2nd ed.), 1980. (Available from Jean Stroud, P.O. Box 12, Lewes East, Sussex BN7 1AZ, United Kingdom.)

2. Strobl, R. L. *Recent European critical thought: Emergence of a theory of communication.* Paper presented to the Seminar on Communication Theory from Eastern and Western Perspectives, East-West Communication Institute, Honolulu, Hawaii, December 15-23, 1980. (Available from the author, Dept. of Communication, University of Hartford, West Hartford, CT 06117).

3. Hahn, E. *Historischer Materialismus and marxistische Soziologie.* Berlin, Ost, 1968.

4. Habermas, J. *Gauss lectures at Princeton university* (J. J. Shapiro, trans.). Unpublished manuscript held by the New School Library, New School for Social Research, New York City, 1971.

5. Smythe, D. W. *Communications: Blind spot of Western Marxism.* Unpublished paper, revised copy, February 1976. (Available in the *Canadian Journal of Political and Social Theory*, 1977, *1*, 1-27.)

6. Pateman, T. *Habermas and the critique of communication: An introduction.* Unpublished paper, 1976. (Available from the author, Education Area, University of Sussex, Falmer, Brighton BN1 9RG, Sussex, United Kingdom.)

7. Lanigan, R. L. *Philosophy of communication: Essays on phenomenology, semiology, speech act theory, critical theory, and rhetoric.* Manuscript in preparation, 1981.

REFERENCES

Adorno, T. W. et al. *The positivist dispute in German sociology.* New York: Harper & Row, 1976. (Originally published, 1969)

Apel, K.-O. *Analytic philosophy of language and the geisteswissenschaften.* Dordrecht, The Netherlands: D. Reidel, 1967.

Apel, K.-O. The a priori of communication and the foundation of the humanities. *Man and World*, 1972, *5*, 3-37.

Apel, K.-O. The problem of philosophical fundamental-grounding in light of a transcendental pragmatic of language. *Man and World*, 1975, *8*, 239-275.

Apel, K.-O. *Towards a transformation of philosophy.* Boston: Routledge & Kegan Paul, 1980. (Originally published, 1972)

Austin, J. L. *How to do things with words.* New York: Oxford University Press, 1962.

Bernstein, R. J. *The restructuring of social and political theory.* Philadelphia: University of Pennsylvania Press, 1978.

Biskey, L. *Zur Kritik der bürgerlichen Massenkommunikationsforschung.* Berlin, Ost: Deutscher Verlag der Wissenschaften, 1976.

Bisseret, N. *Education, class language, and ideology.* London: Routledge & Kegan Paul, 1979.

Blake, C. Communication research and African national development. *Journal of Black Studies*, 1979, *10*, 218-229.

Bologh, R. W. *Dialectical phenomenology: Marx's method.* Boston: Routledge & Kegan Paul, 1979.

Bottomore, T. B., & Rubel, M. (Eds.). *Karl Marx: Selected writings in sociology and political philosophy.* Harmondsworth, England: Penguin, 1963.

Clavel, P., Forester, J., & Goldsmith, W. (Eds.). *Urban and regional planning in an age of austerity.* Elmsford, NY: Pergamon, 1980.

Cotteret, J.-M. Televised debates in France. *Political Communication Review,* 1979, *4,* 1-18.

Cushman, D. P. & Dietrich, D. A critical reconstruction of Jürgen Habermas' holistic approach to rhetoric as social philosophy. *Journal of the American Forensic Association,* 1979, *16,* 128-137.

Dallmayr, F. R., & McCarthy, T. (Eds.). *Understanding and social inquiry.* Notre Dame: University of Notre Dame Press, 1977.

Eco, U. *A theory of semiotics.* Bloomington: Indiana University Press, 1976.

Fiske, J., & Hartley, J. *Reading television.* London: Methuen, 1978.

Frankfurt Institute for Social Research. *Aspects of sociology* (J. Viertel, trans.). Boston: Beacon Press, 1972. (Originally published, 1956)

Giglioli, P. P. (Ed.). *Language and social context.* Harmondsworth, England: Penguin, 1972.

Grice, H. P. Meaning. In P. F. Strawson (Ed.), *Philosophical logic.* London: Oxford University Press, 1967.

Grossberg, L. Marxist dialectics and rhetorical criticism. *Quarterly Journal of Speech,* 1979, *65,* 235-249.

Habermas, J. On systematically distorted communication. *Inquiry,* 1970, *13,* 205-218. (a)

Habermas, J. Towards a theory of communicative competence. *Inquiry,* 1970, *13,* 360-375. (b)

Habermas, J. *Knowledge and human interest* (J. J. Shapiro, trans.). Boston: Beacon Press, 1971. (a) (Originally published, 1968)

Habermas, J. *Towards a rational society: Student protest, science, and politics.* Boston: Beacon, 1971. (b) (Essays included originally published, 1968 & 1969.)

Habermas, J. *Theory and practice* (J. Viertel, trans.). Boston: Beacon, 1973. (Originally published, 1971)

Habermas, J. *Legitimation crisis* (T. McCarthy, trans.). Boston: Beacon, 1975. (Originally published, 1973)

Habermas, J. Some distinctions in universal pragmatics: A working paper. *Theory and Society,* 1976, *3,* 155-167.

Habermas, J. Aspects of the rationality of action. In T. F. Geraets (Ed.), *Rationality today/La Rationalité Aujourd'hui.* Ottawa: University of Ottawa Press, 1979. (a)

Habermas, J. *Communication and the evolution of society* (T. McCarthy, trans.). Boston: Beacon, 1979. (b) (Essays included originally published, 1976)

Halloran, J. D., Elliot, P., & Murdock, G. *Demonstrations and communications: A case study.* Harmondsworth, England: Penguin, 1970.

Harms, L. S. Appropriate methods for communication policy science: Some preliminary considerations. *Human Communication Research,* 1980, *7,* 3-13.

Hickson, M., & Jandt, F. E. (Eds.). *Marxian perspectives on human communication.* Rochester, NY: PSI Publishers, 1976.

Holzer, H. *Kommunikationssoziologie.* Reinbek bei Hamburg: Rowohlt, 1973.

Hooft, S. van Habermas' communicative ethics. *Social Praxis,* 1976, *4,* 147-175.

Horkheimer, M. *Critical theory: Selected essays* (M. J. O'Connell et al., trans.). New York: Seabury Press, 1972. (Originally published, 1968)

Hund, W. D., & Kirchhoff-Hund, B. *Soziologie der Kommunikation: Arbeitsbuch zu Struktur und Funktion der Medien: Grundbegriffe und exemplarische Analysen.* Reinbek bei Hamburg: Rowohlt, 1980.

Isreal, J., & Tajfel, H. (Eds.). *The context of social psychology: A critical assessment.* New York: Academic Press, 1972.

Jacobson, R. E. Communication as complement: The practical gap. *Journal of Communication,* 1980, *30,* 219-221.

Jay, M. *The dialectical imagination: A history of the Frankfurt School and Institute of Social Research, 1923-1950.* Boston: Little, Brown, 1973.

Jung, H. Y. *The crisis of political understanding: A phenomenological perspective in the conduct of political inquiry.* Pittsburgh: Duquesne University Press, 1979.

Kress, G., & Hodge, R. *Language as ideology.* London: Routledge & Kegan Paul, 1979.

Lanigan, R. L. *Speaking and semiology: Maurice Merleau-Ponty's phonomenological theory of existential communication.* The Hague and Paris: Mouton; Hawthorne, NY: Walter de Gruyter, 1972.

Lanigan, R. L. *Speech act phenomenology.* The Hague: Martinus Nijhoff; Atlantic Highlands, NJ: Humanities Press, 1977.

Lanigan, R. L. A semiotic metatheory of human communication. *Semiotica,* 1979, *27,* 293-305. (a)

Lanigan, R. L. The phenomenology of human communication. *Philosophy Today,* 1979, *23,* 3-15. (b)

Lefebvre, H. *The sociology of Marx* (N. Guterman, trans.). New York: Vintage Books, 1968. (Originally published, 1966)

Lemert, C. C. *Sociology and the twilight of man: Homocentricism and discourse in sociological theory.* Carbondale: Southern Illinois University Press, 1979.

McCarthy, T. *The critical theory of Jürgen Habermas.* Cambridge, MA: MIT Press, 1978.

Merleau-Ponty, M. *Sense and non-sense* (H. L. & P. A. Dreyfus, trans.). Evanston: Northwestern University Press, 1964.

Merton, R., & Gaston, J. (Eds.). *The sociology of science in Europe.* Carbondale: Southern Illinois University Press, 1977.

Mićunović, D. Bureaucracy and public communication. In M. Marković and G. Petrović (Eds.), *Praxis: Yugoslav essays in the philosophy and methodology of the social sciences* (Joan Coddington, trans.). Boston: D. Reidel, 1979.

Morris, C. W. *Foundations of the theory of signs.* Chicago: University of Chicago Press, 1938.

Mueller, C. *The politics of communication: A study in the political sociology of language, socialization, and legitimation.* New York: Oxford University Press, 1973.

Negt, O. Mass media: Tools of domination or instruments of liberation? Aspects of the Frankfurt School's communication analysis. *New German Critique,* 1978, *15,* 61-80.

Negt, O., & Kluge, A. *Offentlichkeit und Erfahrung: Zur Organisationsanalyse von bürgerlicher und proletarischer Öffentlichkeit.* Frankfurt am Main: Edition Suhrkamp, 1972.

O'Neill, J. (Ed.). *On critical theory.* New York: Seabury Press, 1976.

Poster, M. *Critical theory of the family.* New York: Seabury Press, 1979.

Reid, H. G., & Yanarella, E. Toward a post-modern theory of American political science and culture: Perspectives from critical Marxism and phenomenology. *Cultural Hermeneutics,* 1974, *2,* 91-166.

Rogers, E. M. The empirical and the critical schools of communication research. In M. Burgoon (Ed.), *Communication yearbook 5.* New Brunswick, NJ: Transaction Books, 1981.

Sandywell, B. et al. *Problems of reflexivity and dialectics in sociological inquiry: Language theorizing difference.* London: Routledge & Kegan Paul, 1975.

Schnapp, A., & Vidal-Naquet, P. *The French student uprising November 1967-June 1968: An analytical record* (Maria Jolas, trans.). Boston: Beacon, 1971. (Originally published, 1969)

Schroyer, T. *The critique of domination: The origins and development of critical theory.* Boston: Beacon, 1975.

Searle, J. R. Human communication theory and the philosophy of language: Some remarks. In F.E.X. Dance (Ed.), *Human communication theory: Original essays.* New York: Holt, Rinehart & Winston, 1967.

Searle, J. R. *Speech acts: An essay in the philosophy of language.* New York: Cambridge University Press, 1969.

Smart, B. *Sociology, phenomenology and Marxian analysis: A critical discussion of the theory and practice of a science of society.* London: Routledge & Kegan Paul, 1976.

Sullivan, W. M. Communication and the recovery of meaning: An interpretation of Habermas. *International Philosophical Quarterly,* 1978, *18,* 69-86.

Veron, E. Ideology and social sciences: A communicational approach. *Semiotica,* 1971, *3,* 59-76.

Wellmer, A. *Critical theory of society.* New York: Herder & Herder, 1971.

Wellmer, A. Communication and emancipation: Reflections on the linguistic turn in critical theory. In J. O'Neill (Ed.), *On critical theory.* New York: Seabury Press, 1976.

Wilden, A. Analog and digital communication: On the relationship between negation, signification, and the emergence of the discrete element. *Semiotica,* 1972, *6,* 50-82. (a)

Wilden, A. *System and structure: Essays in communication and exchange.* London: Tavistock; New York: Harper & Row (Import), 1972. (b)

CHAPTER 6

A Constructivist Approach

David L. Swanson

CONSTRUCTIVISM is a substantive theory of human communication which has become increasingly visible in the past several years and has generated programmatic research investigating a diverse array of communication contexts, processes, competencies, and effects. It is only recently, however, that a constructivist approach to the study of political communication has been explicitly formulated. This essay identifies the nature and significance of the problem to which a constructivist approach to political communication is primarily addressed, briefly outlines the constructivist conception of political communication and summarizes results of some recent studies of political communication based on this conception, and explores implications of the constructivist view for certain major issues in political communication research.

THE PROBLEM: HOW DO VOTERS
UNDERSTAND POLITICAL COMMUNICATION?

The election campaign is, of course, the most intensely studied of the contexts in which political communication occurs. Researchers have been especially attracted to this context for a variety of reasons, including its obvious social importance, its practical advantages (for example, it is a neatly bounded universe of discourse and action which eventuates in clear behavioral choices and outcomes), and the general belief that the nature and significance of political communication might be seen with particular clarity in the campaign setting.

The character of political communication research has been shaped by its focus on election campaigns. Following the traditional conception of the goal of scientific inquiry, research has sought to provide explanations of election results.

And the special commitment of students of political communication has been to understanding the influence of messages on those results.

Although the body of voting behavior and political communication research that has accumulated over the past four decades is extraordinarily diverse in its foci, theoretical orientations, and research methods, it may be given a particular reading that will underscore a thesis of this essay: Understanding how citizens interpret or create the meaning of political messages has been and continues to be a major theoretical and empirical problem in political communication research. This reading, admittedly a gloss of a strikingly heterogeneous literature, stresses two threads running through the evolution of this 40-year research effort. One such thread is an enduring conviction that an at least implicit conception of the process by which persons somehow understand political messages must be part of any satisfactory explanation of the influence (or noninfluence) of political communication. The second thread, less easily discernible than the first, exposes an ordering principle underlying the way in which political communication research has evolved. That ordering principle is progressive movement in the direction of seeing the relationship between political messages and persons' understandings of those messages as increasingly problematic.

In order to understand these threads and, thereby, the centrality of voters' interpretive processes to the study of political communication, it is necessary to characterize some of the major research traditions in this field.

Interpretive Processes in the Effects Tradition

The effects tradition in voting behavior and political communication research began with the sociologically oriented panel studies of Lazarsfeld and his associates (for example, Lazarsfeld, Berelson, & Gaudet, 1944; Berelson, Lazarsfeld, & McPhee, 1954) and was extended and refined in the largely attitude-oriented national surveys conducted by what was then known as the Survey Research Center of the University of Michigan (see Campbell, Gurin, & Miller, 1954; Campbell & Cooper, 1956; Campbell, Converse, Miller, & Stokes, 1960). The effects tradition was based on roughly this model of how voting choices are made: A person's demographic/sociological background and circumstances lead the person, under normal conditions, to form certain appropriate long-term nonpartisan (sense of citizen duty, sense of political efficacy, etc.) and partisan (feeling of identification with a political party) attitudes. Long-term nonpartisan attitudes strongly influence the degree to which the person is likely to be interested and participate in election campaigns and voting. Long-term partisan attitudes guide the acquisition or formation of short-term attitudes (toward, for example, the candidates and issues in a particular election) in such a way that the short-term attitudes are likely to be consistent with and supportive of long-term partisanship.

The effect of this process, which was schematically represented in the familiar "funnel of causality" (Campbell et al., 1960), is that "party labels enable people to organize their perceptions and preferences" in particular elections (Sears, 1969, p. 348). As a result, long-term partisanship was conceived to be the most important immediate determinant of citizens' voting choices. As Nimmo (1977) noted, summarizing this model, "the stable political attitudes of audience members, not political communication, shaped behavior" (p. 447).

In the host of studies confirming the critical influence of long-term partisanship, the overwhelming effect of political communication on voting decisions was found to be reinforcement of persons' preexisting partisan loyalties, leading to the formulation of the "law of minimal consequences" as a description of political communication's impact (see McCombs, 1972, pp. 174-177). This "law" held that political communication had a minimal independent effect on voters' decisions because, in usual conditions, such messages merely activated long-term predispositions and crystallized them into behavioral choices.

The key elements in the effects model's conception of how political communication works were identified more precisely by McCombs (1972): "reinforcement has been adjudged the dominant effect of political mass communication. And selective exposure and selective perception are the concepts commonly used to explain this outcome" (p. 174). The selectivity hypotheses may be characterized as follows:

> The key assumption of the selectivity hypotheses was that the act of attitude holding motivates persons, as a general rule, to maintain that attitude by acquiring supportive information and avoiding nonsupportive information. Exposure to mass communication was conceived to be usually voluntary, and persons were expected to decline opportunities for voluntary exposure to what they expected to be nonsupportive information. Further, perception of information was conceived to be, within limits, malleable, and persons exposed to what would generally be regarded as nonsupportive information were expected to "misperceive" the information in order to cause it to lose its nonsupportive quality. Susceptibility to persuasion in political campaigns was generally believed to be symptomatic of either an absence of strongly held political attitudes, in which case psychological defenses would not be practiced, or of "cross-pressures," conflicts among political attitudes that would prevent the consistent practice of psychological defenses [Swanson & Freeman, Note 1, p. 3].

For present purposes, the important thing to notice is that in the effects tradition's conception of political communication, voters' perceptions and interpretations of political messages are seen as essentially controlled by voters' preexisting political attitudes. Sears's (1969) review of the effects tradition concluded, for example, that "consistency pressures often make evaluations of new information little more than creatures of predispositions" (p. 348).

Similarly, Natchez (1970) explains: "Party identification . . . is responsible for the way in which people (selectively) perceive politics. What new information voters receive is integrated in terms of their previously established partisan attitudes" (p. 577).

This analysis of the effects tradition has been necessary in order to show why it is not necessarily correct to view the tradition as lacking any real conception of how political communication works, beyond the simple notation that reinforcement is its usual result. Fundamentally, voters' understandings of political messages are *not* deemed to be unimportant or unrelated to their voting choices in the effects model. Rather, these understandings are believed to be determined by voters' partisan attitudes, such that knowledge of attitudes is treated as equivalent to knowledge of how voters interpret the meanings of political messages. Thus, there was no special reason for effects tradition researchers to investigate directly the processes by which perceivers interpret political messages because "persons who hold similar attitudes relevant to a message were assumed to employ similar cognitive procedures in processing the message" (Swanson & Freeman, Note 1, p. 2).

Another way of phrasing the same point—a phrasing which speaks more directly to the thesis argued here—is to observe that the effects tradition's model of voting viewed voters' understandings of political communication as unproblematic. Hence, voters' interpretive processes and meanings were studied indirectly through examination of political attitudes and their relation to behavior. Nimmo's (1977) statement of this view is especially clear: "people react to political stimuli in fixed, stable, almost conditioned ways on the bases of enduring predispositions" (p. 447).

Challenging the Claim that Interpretive Processes Are Attitude-Determined

In the latter half of the 1960s, an impressive body of research results began to accumulate which seriously questioned whether partisan attitudes determine voters' understandings of political messages in the way that the effects tradition had claimed. Much of this research reported findings that contradicted the motivational and behavioral claims of the selectivity hypotheses (for example, Freedman & Sears, 1965; Sears & Freedman, 1967; Sears, 1968; Steiner, 1962). Additionally, credible accounts of political information seeking and use were forwarded that made no substantive reference to partisan attitudes (see Atkin, 1972; McCombs & Shaw, 1972; Swanson, 1976).

As a result of this and other research, it became clear that the process by which perceivers interpret and evaluate political communication warranted more direct theoretical and empirical attention and could no longer be understood as the simple result of certain sociological and attitudinal antecedents. As Weisberg and Rusk (1970) concluded from an examination of the effects tradition, "We still know very little about the psychological dimensions of meaning involved in how an individual perceives, reacts to, and evaluates a set of candidates. We know little about the more general organizing concepts a person uses in developing the specific perceptions and reactions described in contemporary voting and public opinion surveys" (p. 1167). In short, it was apparent that voters' interpretive processes constituted a major problem in political communication research.

Alternative Views of Interpretive Processes

As we would expect, much posteffects tradition theorizing and research in political communication has explicitly recognized the centrality of voters' interpretive processes. Three such lines of work will be briefly discussed here because they both illustrate major ways of responding to the problem of interpretive processes and allow us to see how the problem remains a troublesome one.

Agenda-Setting Research. Since its initial statement by McCombs and Shaw in 1972, the agenda-setting hypothesis has generated an impressive quantity of empirical research. The details of this research need not concern us here. For our purposes, it is sufficient to note the major claim of the hypothesis: By the quantity and quality of the attention they give to topics covered in the news, the news media influence their audiences' judgment of the relative importance of those topics. The role of the agenda-setting phenomenon in a comprehensive conception of mass communication's effects is described by McCombs and Shaw (1977): "the chain of effects that result from exposure to mass communication has a number of links preceding attitude and opinion change. . . . [I]n recent years scholars interested in mass communication have concentrated on earlier points in the communication process: awareness and information. Here the research has been most fruitful in documenting significant social effects resulting from exposure to mass communication" (pp. 4-5).

Agenda-setting research may be conceived of as responding to the problem of interpretive processes by shifting focus from how persons understand the meaning of messages to a prior concern, how persons judge the importance of topics treated in messages. Such a shift may help to illuminate the nature and use of interpretive processes by examining precursors to or early stages in those processes, but it does not inquire directly into how understandings of messages' meanings are created.

Symbolist and Interactionist Views. More direct attempts to understand persons' interpretive processes in political communication research have been based on what Nimmo (1977) terms "an alternative characterization of political audiences": "the viewpoint is of a citizen who actively takes account of political messages, creates meaning through a process of imagery and imagination, and constructs a line of meaningful conduct in response" (p. 447). Included among recent views embracing this conception of political communication and its audiences are symbolist/dramaturgical (Combs, 1980; Combs & Mansfield, 1976; Graber, 1976; Nimmo & Combs, 1980) and symbolic interactionist (Nimmo & Savage, 1976; Nimmo, 1978) positions. All of these views see the process of understanding the meaning of political messages as a major problem for theorizing and, in this sense, exemplify the ordering principle we have claimed underlies the general evolution of much political communication research.

To be sure, the claims made by these views, although related, are quite different. Nevertheless, two observations about these views as a group may be offered that will advance the present analysis. First, these views conceive of how political messages come to have meaning and be understood as a more public or social process than the social-psychological, individual-oriented effects tradition. While the effects tradition sees meaning as created by individuals who are governed by attitudes, these views understand meaning as either created and accomplished in a process of social interaction and negotiation (interactionist views) or produced through the invocation or selection of transsituational, usually culturally embedded, structures such as myths (symbolist views). Hence, these views offer a major reconceptualization of the nature of meaning in political communication research.

The second observation to be made about these views is that, in general, they are descriptive and theoretical frameworks that are not conceptually connected to concrete empirical research methods. That is, the question of how these general conceptions may be accurately and precisely translated into research practices is a difficult one. An example may help to clarify this problem. Q-methodology is a research procedure often employed by devotees of interactionist and symbolist views in political communication (for example, Nimmo & Savage, 1976). Yet there is no clear or explicit conceptual connection between this procedure and the theoretical views under whose aegis they are employed. The absence of such a connection creates some difficulty in determining the extent to which research results confirm or are readily interpretable in terms of the particular theoretical position being employed. One might make equally plausible arguments for a quite diverse array of research methods—including quantitative procedures such as Q-methodology, qualitative methods such as participant-observation, and interpretive-evaluative critical methods such as some schools of rhetorical criticism—as the methodological results of these views. But these methods are grounded in conflicting assumptions about such matters as the nature of objects of study and the aims and requirements of systematic scholarly observation. The inevitable result is some confusion in the movement from theory to observation to interpretation.

At this point in their development, then, it appears to be the case that symbolist and interactionist views in political communication offer explicit conceptions of how political messages are understood by their audiences, but have not yet been sufficiently or clearly elaborated at the methodological level.

The Uses and Gratifications Approach. The uses and gratifications approach appears to grow out of the same "alternative characterization of political audiences" that undergirds symbolist and interactionist views of political communication. In contrast to those views, however, the uses and gratifications approach returns to an essentially social-psychological level of analysis and offers a relatively well-formulated procedure for conducting empirical research (see Blumler & Katz, 1974). This procedure recognizes the importance of voters' interpretive processes for understanding political communication.

> Perception is ultimately the key element in the uses and gratifications position. Audiences' perceptions of goals and expectations of media sources of gratification are thought by many to determine differential patterns of media consumption. Correlatively, the manner in which particular messages are used and whether they prove gratifying is assumed to be determined, at least in part, by how those messages are interpreted or given meaning by audience members in the active process of perception. Presumably, it is this active view of persons, including their active perceptual or interpretive processes, which unifies the widely variant forms of uses and gratifications research [Swanson, 1977, p. 219].

It is thus curious that the approach has thus far been unable to convert voters' interpretive processes for understanding political messages into an empirical question suitable for direct investigation (Blumler, 1979). Instead, "the typical uses and gratifications research design investigates nearly every stage in the process—need, goal or expectation, media exposure, consequence of exposure (gratification)—*except* the perceptual activity of interpreting or creating meaning for messages" (Swanson, 1977, p. 220). By so doing, "uses and gratifications researchers are leaving the presumed link which ties together their vision of the mass communication process unexplored" (p. 220). Thus, like researchers in the effects tradition, uses and gratifications researchers are forced to make inferences about perceivers' understandings of messages based on examination of the presumed antecedents and consequents of those understandings. In the uses and gratifications approach, however, audience members' understandings of messages are not assumed to be controlled by the partisan attitudes that are the cornerstone of the effects tradition's conception of political communication.

Conclusion

This highly selective and interpretive review of political communication study yields several conclusions concerning the status of voters' ways of understanding political messages as a theoretical and empirical problem. First, researchers appear to agree that any satisfactory account of the nature and influence of political communication must include an explanation of how persons understand and ultimately act on political messages. Second, many researchers have come to reject the effects tradition's view that persons' understandings of political messages are controlled by sociologically grounded partisan attitudes. As a result of this rejection, coming to grips with how political messages are understood has become a major agenda item for theorists and researchers. Attempts to do so, however, have not proven fully satisfactory. It is this problem to which a constructivist approach to political communication is chiefly addressed.

A CONSTRUCTIVIST APPROACH TO
POLITICAL COMMUNICATION

The general constructivist approach to the study of human communication has been presented in detail elsewhere (for example, Delia, 1977; Delia, Note 2; Delia, O'Keefe, & O'Keefe, in press). Accordingly, it will not be outlined here. For present purposes, it is sufficient to note that a constructivist approach to political communication is an application of the broader constructivist theory of communication to a particular context and that the approach thus shares the substantive claims of the general theory, along with its interpretive orientation as a philosophical anthropology (see Delia & Grossberg, 1977, esp. p. 36) and its Weltanschauungen philosophy of science (see O'Keefe, 1975, and Delia, 1977).

Fundamentally, a constructivist approach to any domain sees persons as approaching the world through processes of interpretation which channel their activity and organize their behavior. Applied to the political domain, the constructivist approach conceives of behavior, such as voting, as meaningful action grounded in voters' beliefs about the political world. These beliefs, in turn, are viewed as the results of particular interpretive processes by which, among other things, political messages are understood. Through these interpretive processes, campaign communication is seen as influencing persons' beliefs and, thereby, their political behavior.

As we have seen from an examination of alternatives to the effects tradition, constructivism's basic focus on interpretive processes is not unique. The most forceful advocates of an interactionist position, for example, argue that "we have ignored what is essential to candidate imagery—*interpretation,* or the ways people construct a subjectively meaningful reality (or image) from the transactions of their predispositions with the campaign stimuli that bombard them" (Nimmo & Savage, 1976, p. 102). Rather, constructivism finds its distinctiveness in the particular conception of the nature, uses, and results of interpretive processes that is embedded in its substantive theory. Following is an elaboration of relevant portions of this substantive theory, along with a review of research that has thus far been completed in the constructivist approach to political communication.

Basic Elements of Political Perception

In the constructivist approach, *constructs* are seen as providing the fundamental means by which persons discriminate among political actors and events in the process of perception. These discriminations or contrasts (for example, honest-dishonest, Republican-Democrat, serves the people-serves special interests) function to identify what are, for a particular perceiver, relevant dimensions of political actors and events. Persons understand or form impressions of political actors and events by placing or locating them along these dimensions relative to other actors and events.

The cluster or group of such constructs used by a perceiver to understand political objects of perception is referred to as the perceiver's "political construct subsystem." The term "subsystem" is used to indicate that persons may develop particular groups of constructs for use in various domains of their experience—the political domain, the interpersonal domain, and so on—and that these subsystems jointly constitute persons' overall construct systems. As the basic elements of political perception, political construct subsystems are the starting point of a constructivist approach to political communication.

Admittedly, many accounts of political communication also proceed from at least implicit assumptions about the nature of perception, as we have seen. Hence, such labels as "strong partisans," "independents," "image-oriented voters," and "issue-oriented voters" which are commonly found in these accounts are believed to identify systematic differences in the way various groups of voters perceive campaign messages (Swanson, Note 3). Yet, as we have also seen, most such accounts lack any formal conception of the nature and form of perceptual or interpretive processes and, as a result, have been unable to transform these assumptions into concrete empirical research questions. One important feature of a constructivist approach, hence, is that it is equipped by its substantive theory to directly investigate the basic elements of political perception, political construct subsystems.

One set of questions that might be asked about these construct subsystems has to do with their content: What sorts of discriminations or contrasts do persons normally make when perceiving political actors and events; and are there systematic differences between persons in the kinds of discriminations that are made? Several coding systems have been adapted or created for classifying particular constructs and, more generally, political construct subsystems on the basis of their content (see Freeman, Note 4, Note 5). One such system codes constructs used to perceive political candidates into seven different categories, based on their content:

> (1) constructs regarding *personal qualities,* such as "friendly" and "honest"; (2) constructs regarding *personal background,* such as "southerner" and "religious upbringing"; (3) constructs regarding *political background,* such as "former Congressman" and "little experience in government"; (4) constructs regarding *political ideology,* such as "conservative," "Democrat," and "favors new federal programs and big government"; (5) constructs regarding *specific issue stands,* such as "favors zero-based budgeting," "advocates strong national defense," and "opposes

national health insurance programs"; (6) constructs regarding *campaign style*, such as "has support from labor," "is fuzzy on the issues," and "enjoys talking to voters"; and (7) constructs which do not fit into any category are termed *other* [Freeman, Note 5, p. 26].

Coding systems such as this seek to identify common foci among particular constructs that have been elicited from perceivers by various free-response techniques, consistent with the methodological tenets of the substantive theory of constructivism (see Delia et al., in press).

Application of these coding systems has led to several tentative conclusions concerning the content of constructs used in the political domain. For example, the discriminations that have often been thought to be major determinants of voters' impressions and evaluations of candidates—party labels, political philosophy, positions on issues—constitute a minority of the constructs actually used in the political domain. These categories subsumed less than eight percent of a sample of nearly 1500 constructs analyzed by Mihevc (Note 6). Similar results were found in a study by Freeman (Note 7). Nor do the constructs perceivers use fall conveniently into the general categories of "issue" and "image," at least in the minds of the perceivers themselves. Freeman (Note 4) found that subjects were unable to classify 42 percent of their own constructs into either of these categories, believing instead that the constructs were relevant to both categories or to neither category.

Systematic differences in the content of persons' political construct subsystems have been formulated in the notion of *political specialism*. Political specialists are persons who discriminate among, say, political candidates largely by using constructs that are specifically political in their content. These constructs concern such things as the candidates' political backgrounds, stands on political issues, political ideologies, and campaign styles. Political nonspecialists are persons who discriminate among political candidates largely by using constructs that are also employed in, for example, the interpersonal domain. Constructs of this type concern such things as candidates' personal qualities—the same things persons think about when forming impressions of personal acquaintances. As used here, the concept of political specialism is similar in some respects to the notion of political experts developed by Fiske and Kinder (in press). Concerned chiefly with the development and use of political information-processing schemas in the study of social cognition, these researchers contend: "Political experts should be set off from the rest of us by the nature of the schemas available to them; by the ease by which such schemas are employed in the various tasks set by political cognition." According to Fiske and Kinder, "through practice experts acquire more—and more complexly organized—knowledge."

Interestingly, political specialism has thus far not been found to be related to political partisanship or to interest in politics (Swanson & Freeman, Note 1).

That is, persons who strongly identify with a political party or who are strongly interested in politics do not appear to be more likely than others to develop specifically political subsystems of constructs for discriminating among political candidates. This suggests, among other things, that it is tenuous to draw inferences about the basic elements of voters' perceptual processes from knowledge of voters' partisan political attitudes. Further, although observers might be tempted to conceive of the difference between specialists and nonspecialists as the difference between conventionally understood "issue voters" and "image voters," such a conception does violence to the way perceivers view their own constructs and draw implications from them (Freeman, Note 4; Jackson, Note 8).

It seems to be the case, then, that systematic differences do exist in the content of constructs used in the political domain, and that these differences are not adequately subsumed within the orthodox categories used to distinguish presumably distinctive groups of political perceivers—issue/image, partisan/nonpartisan, interested/disinterested, and so on.

A second set of questions one might ask about political construct subsystems has to do with their structure or degree of differentiation. Persons who have highly differentiated subsystems incorporating relatively large numbers of constructs are said to be politically complex perceivers. Such persons form impressions of, for example, political candidates by locating or placing the candidates on a considerable number of different perceptual dimensions. Those who are said to be politically noncomplex perceivers, in contrast, rely on a relatively small number of constructs to discriminate among political actors and events. The result of this structural difference between groups of political perceivers is that there are related systematic differences in the ways these groups perceive political objects and in the impressions that are consequently formed.

Overall, the complexity of political construct subsystems seems to be less than that of interpersonal construct subsystems, perhaps reflecting persons' relative lack of experience with political matters. The average number of constructs used by persons in the political domain—across a wide variety of populations ranging from college students to political party precinct workers—has repeatedly been found to be about half the average number of constructs used by persons in the interpersonal domain (Swanson & Delancey, Note 9). However, the levels of complexity of a given perceiver's construct subsystems in these two domains appear to be related. A modest but significant relationship between complexity in the interpersonal and political domains has been found in several studies (Freeman & Garrison, Note 10; Swanson & Delancey, Note 9).

Despite what we might expect, complexity in the political domain has thus far not been found to be related to political specialism (Freeman, Note 4, Note 5; Swanson & Freeman, Note 1). That is, the relative differentiation of one's subsystem for construing political actors and events has not been found to be related to the extent to which the content of one's political constructs is specifically political in nature. Similarly, political partisanship has not been found to be related to political complexity (Swanson & Freeman, Note 1).

The conclusion that appears to emerge from all of this is, again, that there are indeed systematic differences between persons in the basic elements of political perception—political construct subsystems—but that these differences are not entirely what conventional accounts stressing the presumed influence of political attitudes and interest on perception would lead us to expect.

Political Beliefs and Attitudes

In the constructivist view, the application of constructs to political actors and events produces context-relevant beliefs about those actors and events. Hence, particular beliefs about a candidate (for example, the candidate is honest, well-intentioned, but ineffectual) are determined by the specific constructs employed by the perceiver and by the perceiver's placement of the candidate along the dimensions described by those constructs. Impressions of political candidates consist of beliefs about the candidates produced in just this way. Research examining the content and structure of political constructs, therefore, also illuminates the content and origin of perceivers' beliefs about political actors and events. In the constructivist conception, it is these beliefs which are the immediate determinants of persons' political behavior.

Political attitudes, on the other hand, are conceived to be generalized evaluations of, for example, a political party or candidate. Because the constructivist conception sees context-relevant beliefs as the bases of behavior, generalized evaluations or attitudes are of interest only insofar as they relate to or somehow affect these beliefs. Constructivism's view of the relationship between attitudes and beliefs has been presented in detail by O'Keefe (1980). As he explains, "Generalized evaluations of objects [attitudes] can serve as organizing principles for beliefs by providing criteria for evaluative consistency" (p. 123). That is, attitudes may function as principles by which perceivers can maintain evaluative consistency among their beliefs. Each belief about an object can be, in effect, checked against the overall attitude to determine the belief's evaluative consistency with the generalized evaluation. This view of political attitudes is, on its surface, similar to the effects tradition's conception of political partisanship as an anchor point or perceptual-cognitive shortcut which directs the formation of short-term attitudes in particular elections (see, for example, Polsby & Wildavsky, 1968, p. 16).

However, the constructivist analysis suggests an important refinement in the traditional conception. In this analysis, "persons with relatively more developed systems of personal constructs within a given domain will be less likely to rely upon a principle of evaluative consistency within that domain than will persons with relatively less developed cognitive systems in that domain" (O'Keefe, 1980,

p. 123). In other words, the degree to which political attitudes do, in fact, direct the formation of political beliefs should vary, depending on the relative differentiation or complexity of a person's system for construing political actors and events. In this analysis, politically noncomplex perceivers' beliefs about political candidates or parties should be strongly influenced by and reflective of their generalized evaluations, or attitudes, toward the candidates or parties. Politically complex perceivers, on the other hand, may be expected to hold beliefs that are evaluatively inconsistent with their political attitudes. Thus, systematic differences in attitude-belief evaluative consistency should exist between complex and noncomplex political perceivers.

Following O'Keefe and Della's (in press) results in the interpersonal domain, Swanson and Delancey (Note 9) found significant differences of just this kind in the evaluative consistency of beliefs about political figures between complex and noncomplex perceivers. Noncomplex perceivers' beliefs about political figures do seem to be strongly connected to and reflective of their attitudes or generalized evaluations of those figures, while complex perceivers hold beliefs that are often evaluatively inconsistent with their attitudes toward those figures.

This analysis may have important implications for the way we should understand the nature and function of political attitudes, and for the kinds of conclusions concerning persons' probable beliefs about political objects we may draw from knowledge of their attitudes toward those objects. Research summarized previously suggested that knowledge of a person's partisan attitudes does not allow us to draw any particular inferences about the content or structure of the process by which that person will discriminate among political objects and, for example, form impressions of candidates. Now there seems to be reason to believe, in addition, that knowledge of a person's political attitudes, by itself, is uninformative concerning the evaluative consistency of that person's related beliefs. Simply, cognitively complex and cognitively noncomplex perceivers give researchers different kinds of information when these perceivers respond to standard political attitude scales.

Political Attitudes and Political Behavior

As we have seen, the constructivist approach views context-relevant beliefs as the immediate determinants of behavior in the political domain, as in other domains. Because noncomplex political perceivers rely more heavily on evaluative consistency principles (attitudes) in deriving their beliefs about political actors and events, we expect the attitudes of these persons to relate more closely to or be more reliably reflected in their political behavior than we do for relatively more complex political perceivers. Swanson and Delancey (Note 9) found significant differences of this kind in the relation of attitudes toward political candidates and behavioral intentions toward those candidates between complex and noncomplex political perceivers.

In our analysis, politically noncomplex perceivers acquire, through the process described above, a set of beliefs about a political candidate that are more evaluatively consistent (favorable or unfavorable) than are the beliefs formed by more complex perceivers. Because these beliefs direct and are implemented in behavior, the attitudes (generalized evaluations) of noncomplex perceivers relate more closely to political behavior than is the case for complex perceivers. But it is important to stress that "the constructivist analysis denies that attitudes are important direct determinants of behavior; in our view, the immediate determinants of behavior are context-relevant beliefs" (O'Keefe, 1980, p. 122). And, as we have seen, "these beliefs are the product of the application of systems of personal constructs to events" (p. 122).

Structural differences in perceptual processes thus seem to influence the role of political attitudes in directing political behavior, such that the predictions we can make about a person's political behavior based on knowledge of the person's political attitudes are quite different, depending on the person's level of cognitive development or differentiation in the political domain. This formulation has clear implications for such general questions as the sense in which we might think of political attitudes as somehow "causing" political behavior, and how it is that political communication might affect the beliefs that are the bases of persons' political behavior.

Beyond the attitude-behavior relation, other differences in political behavior have been linked to structural and content-related properties of persons' political construct subsystems. For example, political complexity has been found to be positively related to such behaviors as registering to vote and the frequency with which one discusses politics with one's associates (Freeman, Note 7; Swanson & Freeman, Note 1). Similarly, political specialism has been found to be positively related to such forms of political activity as contributing money to campaigns, working in campaigns, and attending political meetings (Swanson & Freeman, Note 1).

Thus, attributes of persons' perceptual processes for understanding the political domain of experience appear to influence not only the status and function of those persons' political attitudes but also a range of political behaviors.

Media Preferences

Content-related attributes of perceivers' political interpretive systems have been related to perceivers' media preferences in following a campaign. Freeman (Note 5) found a significant relationship between political specialism and media preference: "Individuals who followed Campaign '76 via print media rather than television and radio employed relatively more constructs which were specifically political in nature when forming impressions of candidates" (p. 30).

However, no such relationship has yet been found between political complexity and the specific communication media that are followed for information about a political campaign. That is, "political complexity does not determine or have a strong influence on whether one follows the campaign on television or via the print media" (Freeman, Note 5, p. 29).

Current Work: Orientations to and
Effects of Campaign Communication

Obviously, constructivist research in the political domain to date has been essentially exploratory and descriptive. It has sought to establish the fundamental applicability of the substantive theory of constructivism to the political domain and, in so doing, has further confirmed the substantive theory itself.

Currently, however, projects are underway that seek to explore the particular implications of constructivism for understanding the nature and effects of campaign communication more directly. The projects, involving data collected during the 1980 presidential campaign, differ from earlier work described here in two major ways. At the theoretical level, a particular model of how campaign communication works is being employed. This model is based on constructivism's root assumption that the purpose of constructive/perceptual processes is, ultimately, to orient persons to their worlds. Persons apply, retain, abandon, or revise their constructs largely on the basis of whether those constructs seem to serve adequately this orientational function and, thereby, provide understandings that allow persons to take effective action in their various domains of experience.

Based on this root assumption, current projects conceptualize the relationships between cognitive/perceptual processes and the effects of campaign communication in roughtly this way: Political construct subsystems are assumed to both give rise to and reflect various kinds of what might be thought of as general orientations to a political campaign. Campaigns are, among other things, arenas or domains in which choices must be made from among an array of actions that might be taken. The lines of action persons may anticipate taking in or as a result of a political campaign vary widely, as we know. A political campaign may cue some persons that information will need to be sought and digested thoughtfully before a responsible decision can be made on a question of great personal and societal importance. A campaign may serve as a signal to other persons that it will soon be time to perform civic duty and vote for some candidate, chosen by the easiest means available. For some, a political campaign may be anticipated as an opportunity to witness real-life, dramatic conflict between competitors playing for high stakes and to bet on the winner, while for others a campaign may be anticipated as an unwelcome intrusion into normal, daily life.

In one sense, these general orientations might be conceived as identifying intended uses or functions of paying attention to campaign communication and, thereby, following a political campaign. Certainly we would expect these orientations to be related to and displayed in persons' political construct subsystems and, as a result, to determine the particular ways persons understand political messages, frame impressions of candidates, and, in general, form beliefs about the campaign that direct their ultimate behavior. Thus, we are exploring such general orientations to campaigns as summary labels for and synthesizing concepts that identify distinctive general patterns of political interpretation or perception.

Importantly, there seems to be no good reason to suppose that differences in these general orientations should be related to such "standard" determinants of political perception as partisanship, interest, issue-orientation, and the like. Nearly all possible combinations of these "standard" determinants could be accommodated within nearly all of the general orientations described above.

We further hypothesize that these general orientations, and the cognitive elements and processes they subsume, influence persons' political communication behavior, including the extent and manner of information-seeking about a campaign and the uses to which persons anticipate putting information. Additionally, once persons are exposed to campaign-related messages, their perceptions or interpretations of those messages should be structured by the particular content of their political construct subsystems. Thus, viewers of a campaign debate who discriminate among candidates chiefly on the basis of the candidates' personal qualities would be expected to construct a different "meaning" for the debate from the meaning constructed by viewers who discriminate between candidates largely on political issue-related grounds. Continuing, these personally constructed meanings of campaign messages should determine the beliefs that are formed about the candidates and the campaign and that are the basis of eventual voting choices. Finally, the results of campaign communication—including formation and change of beliefs, changes in the political construct subsystem itself (for example, as additional constructs are acquired during the campaign), maintenance or change of political attitudes, and ultimate behavior—should be explicable in terms of the interaction of persons' general orientations to the campaign and relevant features of their political construct subsystems.

Methodologically, projects now under way employ a longitudinal design in which relationships specified in the general model described above were monitored throughout and following the 1980 campaign. This type of design is obviously essential if changes over time are to be discerned.

Clearly, the constructivist approach to political communication has only now reached the point of being able to probe the research questions that lie at the core of any conception of campaign communication's effects. To be sure, most of the general research questions themselves are not unique to a constructivist approach. For example, the notion that a person's intended use of information will affect his or her voluntary exposure to messages plays a central role in the uses and gratifications approach to mass communication research (see Swanson,

1977). However, the formulation outlined above is unique in specifying the concrete ways in which intended uses or, more generally, orientations relate to the particular manner in which messages are interpreted and to the sense that is made of them. The constructivist approach to political communication is thus best understood not as an adjunct to other conceptions and research traditions, but rather as a comprehensive and substantive theory which is equipped to deal directly with one of the major problematics of political communication research: the interpretive processes by which perceivers understand political messages, form resultant beliefs, and act on those beliefs.

IMPLICATIONS OF THE CONSTRUCTIVIST APPROACH
FOR SELECTED ISSUES IN
POLITICAL COMMUNICATION RESEARCH

The constructivist conception of political communication outlined above may be extended to suggest some ways of thinking about a number of major issues in this research field that might prove helpful. Some of the most important of these issues are discussed below.

Analyzing Political Message Content

An enduring problem in the study of political communication has concerned how—and why—to analyze the content of political messages. Common sense suggests that if different kinds of messages have different effects on voters, as is widely believed, then something about the content of those messages must be related to their effects. Hence, it is important to develop useful ways of analyzing message content. As we have seen, researchers have remained convinced that political messages do play some role in voters' political behavior. Yet researchers have been in something of a quandary over just how to analyze the content of these messages in fruitful ways.

Early in the effects tradition, for example, message analysis was essentially limited to noting which candidate or party was favored by the message and relating voters' exposure to messages favoring one side or the other to their voting choices. Later, topics dealt with in messages were catalogued in order to see, for example, whether voters exposed to these messages "learned" the topics—issue positions, party affiliations, and so on. This approach to message analysis continues in the work of Patterson and McClure (1976) and Patterson (1980). These well-known studies have analyzed campaign news coverage and campaign commercials in order to determine the topics treated in the messages and the relative amounts of attention devoted to each topic in the universe of such messages across a campaign. Essentially the same procedure for message analysis has been followed by agenda-setting researchers (such as Shaw & McCombs, 1977).

This is a very simple and general way of analyzing messages. The relative simplicity of the current state of political message analysis results, in large part, from the lack of any formal, theoretical conception of how the details of message content impact on voters' interpretations of messages in ways other than information gain (topic recognition or association with a particular candidate) or judgments of topic salience or relative importance. A constructivist conception of political communication might provide the basis for a somewhat more substantive and detailed analysis of political messages and a more elaborate view of the possible consequences of message content. For example, the point is frequently made that campaign news coverage focuses on the "horse race" aspects of campaigns (see Patterson, 1980; Patterson & McClure, 1976). "Horse race" coverage might be conceived of as reflecting what was earlier described as a particular general orientation to campaigns. Analyzing the content of such coverage in order to identify the specific constructs it employs in describing candidates and events would more clearly and precisely reveal the nature of its content. Further, a possible effect of "horse race" coverage might be to stimulate news viewers to add to their political construct subsystems dimensions of perception that reflect the "horse race" orientation. Or perhaps viewers whose political construct subsystems contain no such dimensions may tend to ignore or overlook the "horse race" orientation of campaign news. The conclusion suggested by this example is that, at the level of general orientations, a constructivist approach might provide the basis for detailed message analysis and empirical study of the effects of the content (rather than merely the topic or valence) of messages on voters' perceptions of candidates and campaigns.

At a level more specific than general orientations to campaigns, constructivism offers a conception of the way messages' emphases on particular qualities of candidates may affect voters' impressions of and ultimate actions toward those candidates. As we know, this concern with the strategic implications of the relative salience of attributes of topics or candidates has interested agenda-setting researchers for some time (see Shaw & McCombs, 1977). A constructivist conception would suggest that the attributes which political messages ascribe to candidates might affect some voters' perceptions and resultant beliefs about the candidates by, in effect, instructing the voters how to locate the candidates along the dimensions described by the attributes. Or, for voters who do not include a particular attribute among their political constructs, messages stressing that attribute might stimulate persons to add the attribute to their political constructs. What is being described here, of course, is a concrete, theoretically grounded way of addressing the long-troublesome "stimulus-determined" versus "perceiver-determined" controversy concerning the effect of political communication (see, for example, McGrath & McGrath, 1962; Sigel, 1964).

Both of these examples—one general, one particular—illustrate some of the ways a constructivist approach might enhance the ability of political message analysis to contribute to empirical research concerning the effects of political communication.

Exploring Alternative Conceptions
of Political Belief Systems

Compelling negative findings concerning partisan attitudes' control of political communication behavior and voting choices constituted a serious challenge to the effects tradition's view of political behavior, as we saw earlier. One way researchers and theorists have sought to accommodate these findings is by forwarding alternative conceptions of the nature and results of political communication of the kind reviewed in the first section of this chapter. A second general line of response—concerned more with understanding non-partisan-based voting behavior itself than with the role of communication in such behavior—has focused on identifying kinds of persons or groups whose voting behavior seems least influenced by partisanship and offering accounts of ways these voters differ from traditional partisans. Hence, many studies following this second line of response begin by identifying, for example, ticket-splitters (see DeVries & Tarrance, 1972) and compare them to the effects tradition's conception of partisan voters along what are thought to be relevant dimensions.

These attempts to explain the bases of nonpartisan voting have produced a variety of conceptions of political attitude and belief systems that stand in contrast to the effects model. One such alternative conception that has received wide currency is Pomper's (1975) "responsive voter." This voter, although often possessing some feelings of partisanship, is particularly responsive to the elements of specific elections—issues, candidates, pressing concerns at the moment—in making voting choices. As a consequence of this responsiveness, the responsive voter's electoral biography shows considerable partisan variability as issues and conditions change. Pomper's account of the responsive voter is, at base, a description of a particular kind of political attitude and belief system.

Similarly, Nie, Verba, and Petrocik (1976) argue that the decline in partisanship's influence on voting behavior has been accompanied by and is related to a rise in the consistency of voters' issue-related beliefs, an increasing tendency of voters to conceive of political matters in ideological terms, and other presumed signs of relatively sophisticated analytic processes. According to these authors, "there has been a major increase in the level of attitude consistency within the mass public. Not only has constraint increased among traditional attitudes but also as new issues have merged in the 1960's, they have been incorporated by the mass public into what now appears to be a broad liberal/conservative ideology" (p. 123).

From the viewpoint of this chapter, one problem with alternative accounts of political attitude and belief systems is that they are post hoc formulations resting on the same sort of indirect, correlational evidence that proved so misleading in the effects tradition. In both of the formulations mentioned, research evidence consists chiefly of secondary analyses of aggregate data collected in the institutionalized national voting studies. Voters' concerns are inferred from their behavior and their responses to various standardized attitude and issue scales. Post hoc reconstructions of belief systems not rooted in any formalized or precise theory inevitably have a certain problematic quality that has been repeatedly demonstrated in the history of political communication research.

More to the immediate point, however, is that these formulations lack any conception of the relation of political messages to beliefs and action in the political domain. Although Nie et al. (1976) claim that the public's increasing conceptual sophistication results, in part, from the increasing sophistication of contemporary politics and political discourse—"the way in which citizens conceptualize the political realm is dependent on the political content to which they are exposed" (p. 121)—these researchers' position offers no basis for testing their claim. In general, arguments for the existence of alternative genres of political attitude and belief systems tend to suffer from the lack of any formal theoretical framework that would allow direct investigation of their claims and from the absence of a conception of political communication's role in the formation and implementation of political attitudes and beliefs.

A constructivist approach might offer useful ways of addressing these difficulties. The approach's substantive theory and attendant research methodology allow direct examination of the content of political beliefs and of their precursors, political constructs. Use of constructivist research methods thus could allow straightforward examination of whether genres of alternative political belief systems of the kind proposed in these post hoc accounts seem to exist and to guide political behavior in the way that authors of these accounts suppose. And, of course, constructivist methods would free persons interested in pursuing alternative political belief systems from the present necessity of relying only on indirect indices of the ways, for example, ticket-splitters process or understand campaign messages, form or alter their political beliefs, and frame voting decisions.

CONCLUSION

At this early stage in its development, the constructivist approach seems to offer promise as a means of better understanding one of the enduring research questions of political communication: How do persons come to understand political messages? In addition, the constructivist approach appears to suggest some useful ways of addressing a variety of other important concerns, such as the influence of political attitudes on behavior, the ways particular features of political messages may impact on persons' understandings of political actors and events, and so on.

At the same time, it should be clear that a constructivist approach deflects attention from certain kinds of phenomena and research questions that are of interest to scholars who work with different substantive theories. Reified social and political forces that are independent of individual citizens' understandings of them, objective content of campaign messages which directly impacts on voters' behavior, and the like cannot be studied from the substantive theory of constructivism because, according to that theory, such phenomena are chimerical.

At present, the promise of a constructivist approach to political communication is difficult to assess fully because of the largely exploratory and foundational nature of research thus far completed. The more comprehensive projects now under way should help to clarify the nature and magnitude of the contribution that a constructivist approach may make to understanding political communication. As is always the case, however, the final judgment of an approach's usefulness will come not only from theoretical discussions but also, and perhaps more importantly, from detailed evaluation of the ongoing program of systematic research generated by the approach.

REFERENCE NOTES

1. Swanson, D. L., & Freeman, D. N. *Political construct subsystems as an approach to political communication: A preliminary report.* Paper presented at the annual conference of the Central States Speech Association, Kansas City, Missouri, 1975.

2. Delia, J. G. *The research and methodological commitments of a constructivist.* Paper presented at the annual conference of the Speech Communication Association, Minneapolis, Minnesota, 1978.

3. Swanson, D. L. *Campaign '76: What we need to know.* Paper presented at the annual conference of the Speech Communication Association, New York, 1973.

4. Freeman, D. N. *Personal construct theory, political perception, and mass communication: The judgmental dimensions employed in the evaluation of political figures based on mass media messages.* Unpublished doctoral dissertation, University of Illinois at Urbana-Champaign, 1976.

5. Freeman, D. N. *A constructivist approach to political candidate perception.* Paper presented at the annual conference of the Eastern Communication Association, Ocean City, Maryland, 1980.

6. Mihevc, N. T. *The dimensions of political judgment: An analysis of political figure constructs.* Unpublished manuscript, University of Illinois at Urbana-Champaign, 1973.

7. Freeman, D. N. *Political knowledge, political complexity, and the perception of political figures.* Unpublished manuscript, University of Illinois at Urbana-Champaign, 1975.

8. Jackson, S. A. *A constructivist analysis of the perception of political candidates.* Paper presented at the annual conference of the Speech Communication Association, Washington, D.C., 1977.

9. Swanson, D. L., & Delancey, C. A. *Cognitive complexity and individual differences in the strength of the attitude-behavioral intentions relationship in the political domain.* Unpublished manuscript, University of Illinois at Urbana-Champaign, 1980.

10. Freeman, D. N., & Garrison, J. P. *The generalizability of cognitive complexity in the political domain.* Unpublished manuscript, Auburn University, 1979.

REFERENCES

Atkin, C. K. Anticipated communication and mass media information-seeking. *Public Opinion Quarterly,* 1972, *36,* 188-199.

Berelson, B. R., Lazarsfeld, P. F., & McPhee, W. N. *Voting.* Chicago: University of Chicago Press, 1954.

Blumler, J. G. The role of theory in uses and gratifications studies. *Communication Research,* 1979, *6,* 9-36.

Blumler, J. G., & Katz, E. (Eds.). *The uses of mass communications.* Beverly Hills, CA: Sage, 1974.

Campbell, A., Converse, P. E., Miller, W. E., & Stokes, D. E. *The American voter.* New York: John Wiley, 1960.

Campbell, A., & Cooper, H. C. *Group differences in attitudes and votes.* Ann Arbor, MI: Survey Research Center, 1956.

Campbell, A., Gurin, G., & Miller, W. E. *The voter decides.* Evanston, IL: Row, Peterson, 1954.

Combs, J. E. *Dimensions of political drama.* Santa Monica, CA: Goodyear, 1980.

Combs, J. E., & Mansfield, M. W. (Eds.). *Drama in life.* New York: Hastings, 1976.

Delia, J. G. Constructivism and the study of human communication. *Quarterly Journal of Speech,* 1977, *63,* 66-83.

Delia, J. G., & Grossberg, L. Interpretation and evidence. *Western Journal of Speech Communication,* 1977, *41,* 32-42.

Delia, J. G., O'Keefe, B. J., & O'Keefe, D. J. The constructivist approach to communication. In F.E.X. Dance (Ed.), *Comparative human communication theory.* New York: Harper & Row, in press.

DeVries, W., & Tarrance, V. L., Jr. *The ticket-splitter.* Grand Rapids, MI: Eerdmans, 1972.

Fiske, S. T., & Kinder, D. R. Involvement, expertise, and schema use: Evidence from political cognition. In N. Cantor & J. Kihlstrom (Eds.), *Personality, cognition, and social interaction.* Hillsdale, NJ: Lawrence Erlbaum, in press.

Freedman, J., & Sears, D. Selective exposure. In L. Berkowitz (Ed.), *Advances in experimental social psychology* (Vol. 2). New York: Academic Press, 1965.

Graber, D. A. *Verbal behavior and politics.* Urbana: University of Illinois Press, 1976.

Lazarsfeld, P. F., Berelson, B., & Gaudet, H. *The people's choice.* New York: Duell, Sloan and Pearce, 1944.

McCombs, M. E. Mass communication in political campaigns: Information, gratification, and persuasion. In F. G. Kline & P. J. Tichenor (Eds.), *Current perspectives in mass communication research.* Beverly Hills, CA: Sage, 1972.

McCombs, M. E., & Shaw, D. L. The agenda-setting function of mass media. *Public Opinion Quarterly,* 1972, *36,* 176-187.

McCombs, M. E., & Shaw, D. L. The agenda-setting function of the press. In D. L. Shaw & M. E. McCombs (Eds.), *The emergence of American political issues.* St. Paul, MN: West Publishing, 1977.

McGrath, J. E., & McGrath, M. F. Effects of partisanship on perceptions of political figures. *Public Opinion Quarterly,* 1962, *26,* 236-248.

Natchez, P. B. Images of voting: The social psychologists. *Public Policy,* 1970, *18,* 553-588.

Nie, N. H., Verba, S., & Petrocik, J. R. *The changing American voter.* Cambridge, MA: Harvard University Press, 1976.

Nimmo, D. Political communication theory and research: An overview. In B. Ruben (Ed.), *Communication Yearbook 1.* New Brunswick, NJ: Transaction, 1977.

Nimmo, D. *Political communication and public opinion in America.* Santa Monica, CA: Goodyear, 1978.

Nimmo, D., & Combs, J. E. *Subliminal politics.* Englewood Cliffs, NJ: Prentice-Hall, 1980.

Nimmo, D., & Savage, R. L. *Candidates and their images.* Santa Monica, CA: Goodyear, 1976.

O'Keefe, D. J. Logical empiricism and the study of human communication. *Speech Monographs*, 1975, *42*, 169-183.

O'Keefe, D. J. The relationship of attitudes and behavior: A constructivist analysis. In D. P. Cushman & R. D. McPhee (Eds.), *Message-attitude-behavior relationship.* New York: Academic Press, 1980.

O'Keefe, D. J., & Delia, J. G. Construct differentiation and the relationship of attitudes and behavioral intentions. *Communication Monographs,* in press.

Patterson, T. E. *The mass media election.* New York: Praeger, 1980.

Patterson, T. E., & McClure, R. D. *The unseeing eye.* New York: Putnam, 1976.

Polsby, N. W., & Wildavsky, A. B. *Presidential elections* (2nd ed.). New York: Scribner's, 1968.

Pomper, G. *Voters' choice.* New York: Dodd, Mead, 1975.

Sears, D. O. The paradox of de facto selective exposure without preferences for supportive information. In R. P. Abelson, E. Aronson, W. J. McGuire, T. M. Newcomb, M. J. Rosenberg, & P. H. Tannenbaum (Eds.), *Theories of cognitive consistency: A sourcebook.* Chicago: Rand McNally, 1968.

Sears, D. O. Political behavior. In G. Lindzey & E. Aronson, (Eds.), *The handbook of social psychology, Vol. 5: Applied social psychology*, (2nd ed.). Reading, MA: Addison-Wesley, 1969.

Sears, D. O., & Freedman, J. L. Selective exposure to information: A critical review. *Public Opinion Quarterly,* 1967, *31*, 194-213.

Shaw, D. L., & McCombs, M. E. (Eds.). *The emergence of American political issues.* St. Paul, MN: West Publishing, 1977.

Sigel, R. S. Effect of partisanship on the perception of political candidates. *Public Opinion Quarterly,* 1964, *28*, 483-496.

Steiner, I. D. Receptivity to supportive versus nonsupportive communications. *Journal of Abnormal and Social Psychology,* 1962, *65*, 266-267.

Swanson, D. L. Information utility: An alternative perspective in political communication. *Central States Speech Journal,* 1976, *27*, 95-101.

Swanson, D. L. The uses and misuses of uses and gratifications. *Human Communication Research,* 1977, *3*, 214-221.

Swanson, D. L. Political communication research and the uses and grafications model: A critique. *Communication Research,* 1979, *6*, 37-53.

Weisberg, H. F., & Rusk, J. G. Dimensions of candidate evaluation. *American Political Science Review,* 1970, *64*, 1167-1185.

PART II

Modes and Means of
Persuasive Communication in Politics

CHAPTER 7

Political Languages

Doris A. Graber

INTRODUCTION

Politics is largely a word game. Politicians rise to power because they can talk persuasively to voters and political elites. Once in power, their daily activities are largely verbal—commands, dialogues, debates, formulation of proposals, laws, orders, decisions, and legal opinions. The skill with which they wield the tools of political discourse, adapting them to the needs of various audiences and the goals to be achieved, determines their success. What are these tools? How are political languages used in different political settings?

Verbal and Nonverbal Languages

Political languages share the major properties of all languages. They are means for translating observations and ideas into vocal and visual symbols. They are also means for transmitting these observations and ideas to others who may understand them if they are familiar with the symbol codes employed for the message.

While language frequently takes the form of verbal symbols, there are also many ways of communicating through nonverbal symbols. These nonverbal symbols carry a major share of the communication burden—better than 60 percent in face-to-face communications (Harrison, 1966). These either supplement the words or convey meanings without words. For instance, the meaning of spoken words can be modified and enhanced by their tone, pitch, timber, inflection, and rhythm. These paralinguistic properties can convey the confidence or insecurity that speakers may feel about their remarks. They can convey anger or joy, honesty or deceitfulness, national or social origins. A speaker's body language, whether through posture, hand movements, facial movements, or positioning in relation to other speakers, can supplement what is said (Birdwhistell, 1970).

Political activities can also convey messages. They have therefore been called "rhetorical icons" (Chesebro, 1976). In the realm of international politics, for instance, the boycott of the 1980 Moscow Olympics by numerous Western countries conveyed their dismay and disapproval of the Soviet Union's invasion of Afghanistan. In an American presidential election, a vote for a third-party candidate who has no chance to be elected may constitute a clear protest against the quality and programs of the candidates who are likely to win. A politician's presence at a neighborhood rally may signify his or her interest in the cause, even if he or she does not utter a sound. A country's massing of troops along its borders may be mute testimony to its fears about military threats from its neighbors.

By and large, what makes verbal and nonverbal language *political* is not a distinctive vocabulary or form. Rather, it is the substance of the information it conveys, the setting in which this information is disseminated, and the functions that political languages perform. When political actors, in and out of government, communicate about political matters, for political purposes, they are using political language. In similar manner, physicians use the language of medicine when they interact with patients, or scientists use the language of science when they communicate about their professional concerns.

Given different settings, the same words may belong to different languages and may mean diverse things (Pool, 1980; Lerner, 1980). As Justice Holmes said so well, "A word is not a crystal, transparent and unchanged; it is the skin of a living thought and may vary greatly in color and content according to the circumstances and the time in which it is used" (1918, p. 425). During the Watergate period of the Nixon presidency, for example, John Dean, counsel to the president, warned Richard Nixon: "We have a cancer within, close to the Presidency, that is growing. It is growing daily. It's compounded, growing geometrically now, because it compounds itself" (Watergate Transcripts, Note 1). The meaning conveyed by this statement about the political forces gathering to destroy the President's political future was quite different than the meaning conveyed by a statement about cancer made by a physician to a patient, or the meaning given to geometrical growth by a mathematician.

The Potency of Political Languages

Several features of political discourse endow it with special potency. Three in particular stand out when one observes major actors on the political scene plying their craft. They relate to its content, its message senders and receivers, and its modes of dissemination (Graber, 1976).

First, the subject matter of political discourse generally deals with public affairs of concern to large numbers of people. The interested public may be the political community of a village, a city, a county, or an entire nation. The subject matter may range from the trivial—like the color of a license plate—to the gravest issues—such as matters of peace and war, of economic security or deprivation, of freedom or bondage. Such issues, and the particular ways in which they are structured through political discourse, affect not only the political community collectively but individual lives as well, often drastically.

Second, political discourse is likely to be significant because it involves major elites whose official positions put great resources for action at their disposal. Major politicians have privileged access to information and the power to affect the public issues they are discussing. The manner in which they formulate these issues strongly influences how these issues will be perceived. These perspectives and subsequent proposals on matters such as tax policy, public services for the jobless, or military draft legislation may become blueprints for action.

The impact of politicians' discourse is also enhanced because the mass media, conscious of their importance, disseminate it widely to important audiences. Most of the daily news published in newspapers and audiovisual media concerns political affairs (Graber, 1980). In this manner, the words and actions of political leaders often reach audiences numbered in millions. These audiences are of two types: political influentials and average people. When political leaders send messages, political influentials listen and take these messages into account. Political language thus affects thoughts and actions at the highest levels of political life.

Average people listen as well. What politicians communicate becomes part of general discourse and helps to shape public opinion. Public opinion, in turn, may provide, or fail to provide, legitimation for public action. Major programs, involving citizen action, such as fighting a war, conserving scarce resources, or mustering votes for elections, cannot succeed unless public opinion becomes mobilized through verbal and nonverbal appeals.

Political discourse thus is extremely important because it deals with the major problems of public life. It describes them and, in the process, shapes them. Verbal images become the major form in which political reality is grasped. They become the basis for official action or inaction, and for the public's feeling of optimism or pessimism, content or discontent, about the course of political life.

It is frequently said that facts or ideas are powerful, rather than the words that express them. But facts and especially ideas cannot become powerful until they become known. In most cases, this requires language that is appropriately formulated to convey these facts and ideas so that they appear important in very specific ways to receptive audiences. Without language, facts and ideas are mute, unable to generate thought and communicate meanings.

MAJOR FUNCTIONS OF POLITICAL LANGUAGES

We shall first discuss the major functions performed through political languages in a general way. Then we shall examine how and for what purposes these functions are performed in a variety of different settings. These differences may involve audience size and composition, which may range from small, informal groups to large, formal assemblies or worldwide audiences reached only through the mass media. They may involve subject matter and goals which may vary from the politician's banter about a fund-raising dinner to the careful formulations of a law by Congress or a legal opinion by the Supreme Court.

We shall pay only limited attention in this chapter to the forms of presentation of verbal symbols. This is no reflection on the significance of form to the efficacy of message transmission. Messages may fail to receive the attention they merit if they are poorly presented. Poor presentation may spring from deficient encoding—a message sender's inability to present the message clearly enough to the audience so that the intended meanings are conveyed. It may also spring from unattractive modes of presentation—a shrill, jarring speaker or a boring, uninspiring one would be examples. Senator Eugene McCarthy uncovered a serious flaw in President Carter's ability to communicate when he called him "an oratorical mortician who inters his words and ideas beneath piles of syntactical mush" (Wooten, 1978). Messages may also fail in impact because they are presented at the wrong time, in the wrong place, and to the wrong audience, which is unreceptive to the message's meaning.

Because appropriate encoding is so important to the impact of messages, the effectiveness of politicians is very heavily judged by their ability to generate clear messages. Powerful communicators become political stars, while verbal ineptitude often becomes equated with general ineptitude. President Eisenhower's fuzzy, frequently tangled speech, for instance, gave him the image of a bungler. In Eisenhower's case, as in many others, the inference was incorrect. Recent evidence shows that he was a clear thinker who could express ideas concisely. His fuzziness was a clever, deliberate ploy to sound ignorant to avoid answering sensitive questions (Greenstein, 1979).

The major functions performed by political language can be grouped under five headings: (1) information dissemination, (2) agenda-setting, (3) interpretation and linkage, (4) projection to future and past, and (5) action stimulation. We shall discuss each separately, although most public discourse involves combinations of these functions.

Information Dissemination

EXPLICIT INFORMATION

The most obvious function performed by political language is information dissemination about the state of the polity and the roles played by various political actors. Politicians continually provide their colleagues, subordinates, and the public with formal and informal reports about their activities and the problems faced by the political units for which they have responsibility or with which they interact. These reports may involve simple descriptive statements or value judgments couched in the form of generalizations, comparisons, and inferences. Information may be disclosed in an informal conversation, an interview with reporters, a press conference, a state-of-the-state or state-of-the-union message, or a formal report of an agency's annual activities.

The availability of such information is crucial because, for the most part, people cannot experience the world of politics directly. The bulk of their knowledge must be based on verbal images. People use these verbal images to form political perceptions and to guide their formal and informal political actions. Images conveyed through verbal and nonverbal symbols, rather than reality, thus turn the wheels of the political world.

CONNOTATIONS

Messages usually convey much more than the explicit information expressed by their literal meaning and serve a variety of purposes beyond a mere exposition of events. Words as such may be "condensation symbols"—words that evoke a multitude of cognitive and affective meanings for the receivers (Baas, 1979). For Jews, mention of the state of Israel, for instance, may generate visions of the Promised Land, of a haven from religious persecution, of a place rich in the history of their faith. "Welfare state," "Founding Fathers," Hippie," and "busing" all are condensation symbols or "code words" that carry a broad array of meanings with them whenever the words are spoken to audiences familiar with the code. At times, such meanings may not be apparent from an examination of the words as such. For instance, investigations of public reactions to the word "busing" have shown that it carries images of forced racial integration, violence in schools, and long journeys for tiny tots. These images explain hostile reactions to the concept in the 1970s and 1980s, even though busing has long been a normal, well-accepted feature of many American school systems. (Sears, Hensler, & Speer, 1979).

Words may also carry connotations—special meanings that define relationships or processes. Addressing a person by a nickname thus connotes familiarity and the speaker's equal or superior status. Talking of "correctional facilities" implies that inmates will be taught to mend their ways during their stay, a meaning missing from the term "prison." In fact, manipulating perceptions through euphemisms—words that connote desirable meanings—is a widely practiced political art. Genocide can then become a Hitler's "final solution," feeble-minded students turn into "exceptional children."

INFERENCES

Verbal messages are also the raw material for inferences—for reading between the lines to capture unintended or unexpressed meanings. Likewise, messages may reveal patterns and trends. They may tell many things about the situation in which message senders find themselves, about their appraisals of these situations and about the message senders themselves.

For example, verbal exchanges in public assemblies can reveal patterns of alignments. Perusal of the debates of the Arab-Israeli conflict in the United Nations readily reveals the lines of political cleavage in that body (Graber, 1969). With some experience, observers can even infer the political orientations of various countries from their messages. The public language of communist societies, for example, differs materially from the public language of noncommunist societies. A message referring to "the toiling and exploited classes of the United States of North America" would hardly be expected from a noncommunist country (Kennan, 1956, pp. 512-513). Similarly, when unemployment among American workers is attributed to the defects of the capitalist system, rather than market forces, technological obsolescence, and worldwide inflation, one may well infer that a member of the Soviet bloc is speaking.

Changes in the stream of messages over time may indicate that the conditions revealed by earlier messages have changed. For instance, monitoring the pronouncements of leaders of the radical movement in the United States clearly shows that their concerns and approaches have changed since the 1960s. Judging from their rhetoric, most have returned to the establishment fold.

Political messages can provide clues to the message sender's perspectives on reality. A report about a prison riot which identifies participants by race, age, and social status indicates that these personal factors are deemed significant aspects of the event. By contrast, a report that stresses prison and community conditions and social neglect would indicate that the sender is primarily concerned with social causes of the riot.

Words may provide clues to the senders' honesty and dishonesty, their feelings of security or insecurity, their rigidity or flexibility. Imagery used in political rhetoric may permit inferences about the psychological makeup of the speaker. Psychologically oriented biographies therefore often use verbal analysis to assess the character of the biographee. Even the manner of language use may carry messages about social origins and personal characteristics. Certain clues, such as mishandling of established pronunciations and tenses, may become commonly accepted signs that indicate low social and educational status. Conversely, the mere fact that people can handle language expertly, in written or spoken form, is deemed an indication of intelligence (Bernstein, 1971).

Messages may also provide clues about events which are not readily accessible to observers. A news story telling about the dispatch of ambulances to an isolated plant involved in a labor dispute may indicate that violence has taken place. In war time, messages announcing that bread and meat will be rationed in a distant enemy's country permit inferences that food is in short supply.

SYMBOLIC MEANINGS

Words may also be purely symbolic, so that the act of speaking, rather than the words, conveys the meaning. The mere fact that the activities of some people are reported through the mass media, or recorded in writing, carries the message that these people are important. Casual banter and greetings provide other examples: They are symbols of friendliness and politeness, rather than meaningful exchanges of information. Politicians occasionally deny the significance of their achievements as a sign of modesty. Negotiators may make strong demands merely as a show of firmness and courage. Religious invocations and much of the formal language of courts are largely symbolic, designed to invoke the picture of serious proceedings conducted in established and hallowed forms.

Agenda-Setting

The word "agenda" is derived from the Latin *agere* which means "to act." When politicians select certain topics for discussions, be they political issues and events, or the activities of other politicians, these topics have a chance to move to the center of public attention. Once they become matters of public attention—usually through mass media publicity—they are likely to become matters of public action as well. If, for instance, needs for public child care centers or for tariffs to protect the textile industry from cheap foreign imports are widely discussed by political leaders, legislative or executive action becomes probable. This is particularly true if discussion by political leaders receives extensive and sustained mass media publicity and if it is preceded, accompanied, or followed by discussion by members of the general public.

THE HALO EFFECT

Why does this happen? There is a halo effect through which the importance of the speaker rubs off on the subjects to which the speaker pays attention. Significant issues may languish in the shadows until a prominent political figure brings them to light by talking about them. This halo effect becomes magnified through the wide publicity journalists give to the words of politicians. Journalists may even become surrogate politicians by raising issues on their own, directly or indirectly, by aggressive questioning of public figures. The combination of linkage to an important person and wide publicity through the mass media lends an aura of importance to situations, events, and people, even when trivialities and minor figures are involved.

Conversely, events, issues, and personalities ignored by politicians and the media are unlikely to become part of the political agenda—the plan for action. The civil rights movement provides pertinent examples. It received little verbal attention from prominent political leaders before the 1960s. Since then it has become a major topic of public discourse and action, with verbal lulls paralleled by pauses in action.

CONTROL OVER INFORMATION DISSEMINATION

Politicians' motivations for including or excluding people and issues from political dialogue are diverse. But even after many subjects for discussion have been deliberately eliminated, a huge pool of potential topics remains. This pool must be pared down to manageable proportions because time and energy resources of message senders and their audiences are finite. Political leaders can devote attention to only a limited number of concerns. The print and electronic media can cover only a fraction of these. Audiences have still smaller appetites for political information.

The choices that must be made may be purely a matter of chance. Time and circumstances may determine which potentially significant public issues are mentioned by politicians and receive wide publicity. Alternatively, choices may be made consciously, based on the political and social priorities of political leaders and of media personnel. Whatever seems most important to the message senders may receive their attention and become part of political discourse. The reasons may range from matters of grand policy to petty personal motivations and concerns for specific audiences, or attempts to divert attention from sensitive topics. Wise politicians choose their topics carefully, keeping the ultimate payoffs in mind (Cook, 1980).

They may also choose omissions carefully to keep certain matters silent in order to deny them the importance and action potential that spring from public expression. Whenever feasible, politicians try to avoid attention to touchy subjects which are likely to alienate and alarm supporters or lead to demands that may be difficult to meet. Politicians also draw the cloak of secrecy over their misdeeds and failures, and over the laudable achievements of their enemies.

When politicians lose control over information dissemination, the consequences can be disastrous. President Nixon's inability to stop dissemination of the Watergate tapes cost him the presidency. Leakage of information about America's military unpreparedness in 1980 forced the Carter administration to release information prematurely about new weapons developments.

The ability to control the topics for public discussion at the national level is a prized political asset. Although it is widely dispersed, it remains unavilable to large numbers of aspirants to the role of national agenda-setter. However, many political elites are able to set agendas in narrower settings which, in turn, may affect the national political agenda. Chairmen of congressional committees, for instance, may have nearly complete control over the topics to be discussed by their committees. Mayors and city councilmen may control local political agenda-setting on matters, such as transportation or welfare policy, which have national implications.

Control over the discussion agenda is especially valuable for politicians at election time. To a large extent, political campaigning is the art of projecting one's preferred political discussion agenda on the political stage to make oneself look good and the opponent look bad. Congressmen who have made fine records in promoting labor legislation will want to choose labor policy as their political battleground, rather than the poor showing they may have made on tax reduction or securing pork barrel projects for their districts. If they can focus the campaign on issues which show them in a favorable light, reelection chances and the opportunities to act on their agendas may be good.

Interpretation and Linkage

REALITY CREATION

In the process of calling attention to situations, people, and events—or in addition to it—political elites interpret the political scene. They explain the significance of events, indicate their causes and interrelation with other events, and pass judgments about the merits of particular situations. They also justify their own actions by linking them to sound motives, goals, and developments. All this can be done explicitly or implicitly through arranging the data of politics into a variety of patterns. For example, public officials may explicitly state that the discovery of a new fuel source is a significant event which will ease domestic fuel shortages and reduce reliance on imports. They may claim that government financial support of geological and chemical research was responsible for the discovery. They may predict that expected reductions in imports will lower the domestic inflation rate and increase the value of the dollar.

Alternatively, officials may imply significance by likening the discovery to a major relevant event, such as the discovery of gold in California in 1848. Such an "analogic linkage" conjures up visions of enormous profits made rapidly by early arrivals on the scene, as well as tragic reversals and misfortunes. Instead of using an analogy or metaphor, the linkage may be "conceptual"—to the idea that the fuel discovery is another triumph of American knowhow. This concept suggests that there is ground for optimism that America's energy problems can be solved through traditional American ingenuity and persistence.

The linkages speakers choose to make, explicitly or implicitly, to causes, concepts, or analogies shape the meaning and impact of their messages (Merelman, 1966; Borman, 1973; Miller, 1979). Using the previous example, the message announcing the new fuel may not receive positive linkages. It may be said that the discovery is insignificant, unlikely to reduce fuel shortages, and that government fuel research has been unproductive. Announcement of the new fuel may be labeled a cheap political trick designed to lull the public into a false sense of security and to enhance the reputation of the current administration. Discovery of the new fuel may be likened to the alchemist's age-old futile quest to produce gold—an analogy that implies that the new project is a miserable failure.

The example illustrates how different realities can be created from the same set of facts by verbally endowing the facts with different meanings. Depending on which interpretation or, to use a different term, which "definition of the situation" becomes accepted by politicians and their publics, beliefs and actions based on them can be diametrically different. To use another example, if draft card burning is defined as a juvenile prank, a mild warning may suffice; if it is defined as a crime which threatens the nation's military security, harsh penalties may be in order. Similarly, if poverty is linked to human laziness, obvious remedies are far different than if poverty is blamed on a faulty social system (Edelman, 1977).

CONTROL OVER DEFINITIONS

The potency of verbal definitions of political situations springs from the fact that they become bases for beliefs and actions, even though they are not readily verifiable. Meanings, motives, and evaluations are mental constructs with no counterpart in physical reality. Even if there are factual situations and events that could be examined to illuminate disputed interpretations, it is not feasible for most people to check them. They lack the time, opportunity, and skills to make their own assessments. They even find it difficult to analyze and understand the unexpressed assumptions and experiences that lie behind the perspectives submitted to them by political elites. In fact, most of the time, people are unaware that clashing interpretations and evaluations spring from incompatibilities of the authors' preconceived ideas. Just as the blind men of legend identified an elephant as a snake, a wall, or a tree trunk, depending on the part they touched, so politicians verbally highlight different parts of problems, warranting different labels (Nimmo & Combs, 1980).

Because verbal definitions become the reality on which actions are based, the individuals or groups whose often self-serving definitions are accepted benefit politically. For the most part, these groups are the established political elites whose status permits them to control definitions and, through them, the public's perspectives and opinions. Through this power, they can make serious social and political problems seem trivial, and trivial problems seem serious. They can also enhance their own images as public benefactors, strengthening their hold on power. As Stokeley Carmichael, the civil rights leader, said so eloquently during the civil rights struggle: "The power to define is the most important power that we have. He is master who can define" (Bosmajian & Bosmajian, 1969).

While multiple and clashing political realities are activated during political struggles, many significant political realities are shared by members of political communities. These realities have been communicated to people from childhood onward. Collectively, they constitute the specific world views which social scientists call shared "political socialization" (Mueller, 1973). Continuous socialization creates "reality sleeves"—series of fixed perspectives and interpretations view and interpret ongoing events. Such shared perspectives and interpretations provide a basis for feelings of mutual interest and belonging within a society. This sense of community is essential for the development and maintenance of allegiance to political communities. When it is lacking, civil strife and even breakup of political entities may ensue. This is an ever-present danger for societies where cultural diversity impairs common socialization (Meadow, 1980).

MANIPULATION OF EXPECTATIONS

Another important facet of reality creation involves the manipulation of expectations. Politicians announce benchmarks by which their achievements and political events are to be judged. In the process, they determine whether the judgment will be positive or negative. For instance, when a mayor pledges that local tax increases will be limited to 10 percent during the current term of office, expectations are set. A rise of 5 percent will be small, a rise of 15 percent disappointingly large. Had decrease been mentioned, a rise of 5 percent might seem outrageous. Similarly, if a president announces that one million men will have to be drafted into the armed forces, an actual draft of two million will appear high. Had the announcement named a three million target, a two million draft would seem low.

Manipulation of expectations through verbal pronouncements is a common political tactic, particularly at election time. Politicians frequently understate their expected margins of victory to make actual figures seem more impressive; they may overstate obstacles facing them so that their successes appear to be more impressive. They may claim that inflation is inevitable or that a 10 percent unemployment rate is normal so that social problems become expected and accepted without protest.

Political messages even create nonexistent realities which nonetheless shape action. If, for instance, a crowd believes a false report that a policeman has wantonly shot their leader, it may go on a rampage. The fact that nothing of the kind has occurred pales in importance. If a public official's statement about tax policy is misinterpreted by the media, the actual intent of the speaker matters less than media interpretations. People will base their reactions on the news stories rather than the actual event which lies beyond their ken.

DEFINING INTERPERSONAL RELATIONSHIPS

Besides interpreting the meanings of events, definitions of the situation may also define relationships among individuals. As Murray Edelman points out in an essay on the political language of the helping professions:

> But the psychiatrist who defines a patient as psychopathic or paranoid, or the teacher who defines a student as a slow learner or a genius, creates a relationship that is far more fundamental and influential for both professional and client. It tells them both who they are and so fundamentally creates their social worlds that they resist evidence that the professional competence of the one or the stigmatizing or exalting label of the other may be unwarranted. For both, the label tends to become a self-fulfilling prophecy and sometimes immune to falsifying evidence (1977, p. 74).

Projection to Future and Past

The third major function of political languages is the projection of the past as well as the future. This is the realm of words, par excellance. The past, which no longer exists except for the physical monuments it has left behind, can be recreated in words that may or may not bear an accurate resemblance to what has actually occurred. The same holds true for word pictures of the future which depict, with more or less accuracy, the shape of things to come. No reality testing is possible at the time of prediction because future events have not occurred as yet. Yet politicians predict future developments as if they were preordained or could be produced without fail through proposed human action.

INFORMAL PROJECTIONS

In fact, a large part of political talk deals with matters of the past and future. Such projections are vastly influential because they become guides for current action. The past presumably produces patterns and evidence of tested experiences, while visions of the future are glimpses of anticipated outcomes of current and prospective activities. Projecting the future may involve foretelling the effects of various policy options or making claims that one course of action will lead to disaster while another will produce success. It may involve promises of all kinds about future political activities and articulation of visions of miracles to come. Political campaigns are veritable marathons of political pledges of future performance where each candidate tries to outdo opponents.

All such projections are, of course, subjective and often self-serving. They vary from elite to elite and at different historical times. Hence, every generation produces its revisionist historians who upgrade and downgrade the reputations and achievements of past political leaders and attach new meanings and motivations to their deeds. This task is so useful for political manipulation that George Orwell's mythical dictatorship, described in *Nineteen Eighty-Four*, provided for a "Ministry of Truth" charged with day-to-day falsification of the past (1949).

FORMAL PROJECTIONS

Often verbal plans for future action are elaborate and presented in highly structured forms. Political parties, for instance, will spend considerable time to put together platforms which contain a large array of promises of actions they intend to take in the future and principles by which they pledge to be guided. These platforms usually encompass the full range of political activities that a party expects to span, if and when it finds itself in the seat of power.

Rather than presenting platforms intermittently to coincide with elections, parties may develop complete ideological blueprints. These outline how political leaders view the world and the social forces shaping it, and how, based on this vision, they intend to act to transform it. Karl Marx's *Das Kapital* is but the most prominent example of this genre of political document. Couched in the figures of speech and allusions which have become familiar trademarks of Marxist political language, *Das Kapital* analyzes the past from a Marxist perspective and predicts the future based on Marxist projections of political trends.

Twentieth-century economic development plans are more recent versions of the ideological blueprint. Political leaders in many countries project state-guided economic and social developments over a period of years. Subsequently, they may promulgate three-, four-, or five-year plans of economic development and initiate policies designed to reach the projected goals. Alternatively, the plan may be a purely symbolic expression of hopes that insiders know to be vain.

If messages about the future were purely academic exercises, their accuracy or inaccuracy might not matter too much. But since they frequently become guides for political action, they may determine the very future which they predict. Success in painting believable futures often becomes an admission ticket to political office. Once in office, the blueprints for action that the most persuasive politicians have publicized may be interpreted as commitments to action. At the very least, if the agenda of promises does not become the actual blueprint for action, it may serve as a constraint on policies in violation of the blueprint, lest damaging charges of broken promises be brought.

Action Stimulation

DIRECT APPEALS

The link between verbal projection and action is only one of many examples of the use of language to spur or guide action. Messages can command people to act. They may be couched either in the form of legislation or court orders or in the form of executive directives or in less formal orders conveyed verbally or in writing. Even if the message receivers are not persuaded that the orders are sound, they will usually obey them out of the respect accorded to the source and to public authority in general. This is particularly true if the verbal commands are shrouded in the trappings of legitimacy—a law, a court order, or a public proclamation.

Messages may persuade or implore people to act. They may take the form of a plea to an electorate to vote for particular candidates, to support a charity drive, or to refrain from using scarce resources wastefully. They may come in the shape of a lobbyist's presentation to a legislative body or a government agency's attempt to popularize its programs so that prospective clients will use it. The success of these messages in producing the desired overt behavior determines whether policies succeed or fail.

Major political changes are generally heralded by verbal expressions. A revolution may begin with a dramatic, inciting verbal formulation of grievances—of the suffering of suppressed peoples at the hands of their oppressors. This may be followed by a call to action, to revolt, to secede, to fight. The American Declaration of Independence was such a call. So is the Communist Manifesto. If armed action becomes necessary, the call to arms must be stirringly expressed. People will willingly fight and die to make the world safe for democracy or socialism, or for the true faith—concepts that have verbal reality only. They will not fight and die in the name of mundane goods or paltry privileges.

MOOD CREATION

Words are also spurs to action when they produce policy-relevant moods, such as hope or fear, pride in country, cynicism, mutual hatred, or a sense of community and nationhood. Such moods are particularly important during times of crisis. When disasters strike, such as floods, hurricanes, major explosions, or public riots, political leaders must calm the public and restore a sense of hope and optimism. During the early days of the Great Depression of the 1930s, when fear and panic moods contributed to the collapse of the economy, President Franklin Roosevelt's fireside chats helped restore the public's confidence which was essential to recovery. Moods of confidence are crucial even in normal times to keep the economy on an even keel. The stockmarket rises with hopes and sinks with fears, as does consumer buying and investing.

The creation of proper moods is also important in political settings where people interact verbally. For instance, important public functions are begun with prayers to set a mood of solemnity. In large assemblies, like the Congress, codes of polite speech preserve an atmosphere of decorum which then prevents open strife which could make agreement and the orderly conduct of business difficult. When tense negotiations take place during bargaining sessions between hostile groups, the mediator will often inject a joke to put the parties at ease and generate a more relaxed atmosphere. At times, it may be advantageous to encourage displays of open hostility in hopes that the release of pent-up hatreds will be followed by moods of calm and conciliation.

WORDS AS ACTION SURROGATES

Messages may become a substitute for action, turning, in the process, into the action itself. Thus politicians may threaten harm, promise support, or blame an enemy. The threat or promise or fear of blame may have an impact akin to that of the potential action, provided it is believed by significant audiences. For instance, a threat that troops will take over if workers in a defense plant remain on strike may end the strike. The actual troop movement need not take place at all—in fact, it may never have been intended—verbal action alone accomplishes the result.

Likewise, international treaties of alliance frequently promise that parties to the treaty will support each other in wartime. The mere existence of this promise may deter would-be aggressors who fear that they will be opposed by all parties to the treaty. American pledges to defend Western Europe serve as part of the protective shield of that area against aggression by the Soviet Union. American pledges to defend Japan have contributed to that country's willingness to keep its own military commitment to a minimum. These are significant political consequences springing from promises.

Blame and accusations are extremely potent political weapons as well. The government may find it inadvisable to proceed against dissident groups at home or to use force against weak countries abroad because it might be blamed and condemned for proceedings against defenseless opponents. Such condemnation could alienate its supporters and allies and strengthen the appeal of its opponents. Accusations that individual politicians or public agencies have been granting illegal favors or that they have acted imprudently or beyond their legal powers may lead to severe political penalties, regardless of the merits of the charges.

WORDS AS SYMBOLIC REWARDS

Words can also take the place of action when they convey symbolic satisfactions. The political world is frightening to many people who feel at the mercy of forces beyond their control. They hope that political leaders will cope with major problems like air and water pollution, the safety of the work place, the opportunity to work for decent wages, and the chance to purchase necessities at affordable prices. Politicians promise, in language rich in familiar political symbols, that solutions for these problems are possible and on the way.

The promises symbolize concern and appropriate action to anxious audiences. They are reassured and calmed. Political demands and protests are stilled. The promises may also be convertible into support for political leaders in the expectation that fulfillment hinges on keeping the promise-maker in power. Because mere promises to cope with threatening situations are such valuable tools in the politician's kit, political elites routinely play on the public's fears. They alert people to real and putative dangers and then promise salvation, contingent on people's continued support.

Symbolic reassurance may go beyond mere promises that problems will be solved, to pledges of formal investigations. If carried out, such investigations further reassure audiences that the problems are receiving proper attention. Subsequent reports symbolize progress toward the problems' solution, even when there is no follow-up action.

Symbolic reassurances may take the form of public hearings. Here people have a chance to express their views on issues that concern them. This gives them the comforting feeling that their views are important to political leaders. Even when subsequent action bears no relation to the ideas brought out in the hearing, the feeling persists that there has been consultation with the public and thereby democratic participation in politics.

In this manner, symbolic reassurances make it possible for politicians to quiet the fears and demands of their publics with words and avoid actions that may be difficult, impossible, or undesirable. For the publics, bought off and soothed with empty talk, false expectations and unwarranted complaisance may be the dangerous consequences. Economic hardships, air and water pollution, and

outrageous delays in the court system are accepted because politicians are able
to substitute verbal for instrumental satisfactions (Edelman, 1977).

THE IMPACT OF SETTINGS ON
POLITICAL LANGUAGES

The settings in which political language occurs vary in three major ways.
These are the degree of openness and visibility of the speech event, the numbers
of speakers who are interacting, and the primary purposes of the speech effort.
Various combinations of these factors require the uses of different language
forms to reach the speakers' goals.

We shall begin the discussion with the "oratory setting." It involves a public
and visible event. A single message sender, who expects to speak without
interruptions by other speakers, seeks to inform or persuade audiences with a
formal speech. Next we will analyze the major characteristics of the "bargaining
setting" where speakers, interacting in small groups, remote from publicity,
strive to strike political bargains with each other. Finally, we will examine the
"debate setting." Here interactive discourse takes place in public locations
among members of large groups. The ostensible purpose is to reach agreement
among group members, but it frequently becomes subordinated to a variety of
other goals. Although the settings are discussed separately, the language modes
and goals which characterize each setting are not exclusive to it. Oratory may
occur in a bargaining or debate setting and interactive dialogue may occasionally interrupt a formal speech. Likewise, the goals most commonly sought in one
setting may sometimes be motivating forces in other settings as well.

The Oratory Setting

The most consequential feature of the oratory setting is the ability of the
orator to control the speech situation fully. Oratory is essentially a solo performance rather than an interactive one. The orator can develop lines of reasoning
and present them as planned, generally without concern about instant, point-by-
point rebuttal. Since commonly only major authority figures—heads of governmental units, clergy, or academics—address large audiences at length about
political issues, public oratory carries great weight and is potentially highly
influential. Its major purposes generally are to inform, arouse, and possibly
persuade. Orators may report on the state of a political unit and projected
policies. They may try to stir enthusiasm for enlistment in the armed forces or
for participation in a community venture. They may seek to make converts for a
particular political ideology or movement.

LANGUAGE STYLES

The form political language takes in an oratory setting is generally hortatory.
This is a language style that uses florid appeals to high ideals and the glorious

past to create the impression that powerful and knowledgeable leaders are discussing important issues that deserve public attention. The figures of speech may be trite and predictable, yet they are almost guaranteed to stir favorable sentiments because they appeal to human ideals and noble aspirations. The audience may know that much of the appeal is ritualistic and "mere rhetoric." But it is aroused nonetheless by stirring appeals because people want and often need to believe what they hear. As Murray Edelman remarked: "That talk is powerful is not due to any potency in words but to the needs and emotions in men" (1964, p. 114). Through inspiring language large numbers of people can be successfully exhorted to believe, accept, and act in prescribed ways.

The hortatory style is quite distinct from other language styles used in political discourse. Administrative language, for instance, which is designed to regulate and command, abounds in complex definitions and circumlocutions. It orders audiences to behave in prescribed ways, without impelling them to act through appeals to high principles. Legal language, in turn, differs from hortatory language by using technical rather than inspirational symbols. It does not persuade, but tends to intimidate the average reader or listener by conveying an impression of esoteric learnedness and attention to minute detail (Edelman, 1964).

RATIONAL AND NONRATIONAL APPEALS

The hortatory language style of political orators varies in character depending on the appeals used to interact with the audience. Forms range from the oratory of the statesman to the oratory of the charismatic leader and the harangues of the demagogue. A single speech may combine elements of all three styles in varying proportions. No style is firmly linked to a particular approach to politics so that statesmen may, at times, talk like demagogues and demagogues may speak like statesmen.

The underlying characteristic of a statesman's oratory is an appeal to reasoned argument, eschewing appeals to emotions such as love or pride, fear or prejudice. Salient aspects of a situation are presented clearly and in moderate language. Value judgments are submitted on an intellectual plane, rather than trivialized through slogans and simplistic explanations (Graber, 1976).

By contrast, charismatic rhetoric appeals to deeply held emotions and ideals shared by large numbers of people. Charismatic speakers can articulate these emotions and ideals in ways that make their audiences feel they have a spokesman who is expressing their most deeply felt needs. The audience identifies with such speakers and has faith in whatever they may urge. In ancient Greece, Demosthenes exemplified this style, while Cicero used a stateman's oratory. Hence, "when Cicero finished speaking, the people said, 'How well he spoke'— but when Demosthenes had finished speaking, people said, 'Let us march!' " (Allport, 1967, p. 218).

Demagogic rhetoric also appeals to emotions, but on a baser level. Speakers may stir prejudice, hatred, bigotry. They may exorcise social evils to show that they are on the side of the angels, without suggesting any practical remedies. They have little concern for truth, fairness, or balance. Appeals are opportunistic, judged solely by their effectiveness. As is also true of charismatic rhetoric, delivery style serves to evoke emotions. It may be a preacher's harangue, an avalanche of honeyed words, or a controlled, taut whisper which makes the audience feel it is privy to important secrets. It may be the polished verbiage of experts or pseudo-experts, designed to convey their expertise. Or it may be plain words, uttered in colloquial style and the prevailing dialect, which demonstrates that the speakers, like their audiences, are just ordinary folk.

THE DECLINE OF POLITICAL ORATORY

In modern times, traditional statesmen's oratory has become rare. A mixture of charismatic and demagogic rhetoric, garbed in the trappings of rationality, has taken its place. Attempts to persuade through logical reasoning have given way to attempts to manipulate audiences through psychological tactics. Speakers identify with audience needs and predispositions and then link their goals to those of the audience. Speeches conceal and distort information, lull people into a false sense of security or impotence, and prevent thought rather than stimulate it (Corcoran, 1979).

In the age of television, the acting ability of the orator has become even more important than verbal skills. The drama of politics now is performed on a stage that millions can view simultaneously and instantaneously (Combs, 1980; Burke, 1966; Duncan, 1962). This emphasis on visual information has restored non-verbal symbols to a primacy previously enjoyed only in the preliterate age of human history (Corcoran, 1979). Modern American audiences have also developed a preference for quick, instant gratification so that long speeches are no longer tolerated.

The debasement of oratory and public disenchantment with it are reflected in the fact that political speeches are rarely publicized in their entirety. Rather, the public receives excerpts or summaries. The preferred forms of public discourse are press conferences or interviews where no single theme controlled by the orator is fully developed. Instead, interviewers ask an array of disjointed questions. Public figures are forced to respond to issues raised by the questioners, rather than presenting their own well-developed arguments. Their answers must be squeezed into tiny time capsules, putting a premium on glibness and superficiality. Their messages are judged heavily, and often predominantly, by the nonverbal symbols expressed through body language, facial expressions, and voice quality, and through the general images of capability and trustworthiness that speakers are able to convey.

The Small Group Bargaining Setting

PREDOMINANCE AND PURPOSES

Small group bargaining is particularly important in politics because most political decisions, especially in a democracy, are made by small groups (Graber, 1976). Large public assemblies do much of their work through committees and subcommittees which have a limited number of members. If they find themselves the object of press curiosity, they may retreat into closed "executive" sessions whenever delicate matters are to be discussed.

Likewise, much of the work of the executive branch of government is done by small committees. These may be ad hoc committees, created to deal with particular problems, or permanent committees, established to make routine decisions and plan the work of the executive branch. Even at top levels of government, in times of acute crisis, when decisions must be swiftly made by the chief executive, the small group bargaining process prevails. Advocates who hold diverse views gather to bargain, build coalitions, and ultimately reach compromises (George, 1980). This was true, for instance, for decision-making in the Cuban missile crisis and the Bay of Pigs invasion and even for President Lyndon Johnson's very personal decision to leave the presidency after one term (Phillips, 1966).

The primary purpose of bargaining language in the small group setting is to reach a decision. Bargaining language offers "a deal, not an appeal." It concentrates on "an exchange of *quid pro quo's*" among a small group of people, remote from the glare of immediate publicity (Edelman, 1964, p. 146). Deals lack the drama and heroics which are the hallmarks of public rituals and performances. They do not involve exhortations to approve political action unconditionally, without a tangible, specified reward. Rather, their essence is compromise: a willingness to make concessions, to grant and accept favors and rewards, to reach agreement. Even when their goals are entirely legitimate and aboveboard, their consummation is not deemed suitable for performance on an open stage for all the world to see.

VERBAL CLIMATE FACTORS

To reduce the chances for unwanted publicity, major bargaining sessions frequently are held behind closed doors in geographically remote settings (Lall, 1966; Young, 1968). The peace negotiations conducted by President Jimmy Carter, President Anwar Sadat of Egypt, and Prime Minister Menachem Begin of Israel behind closed doors at the secluded mountain retreat of Camp David, Maryland, in September 1978 are an example. In such a setting, bargainers need not worry about the images they are presenting to the press and public, or about the effects of their words on outside audiences. They do not have to impress their constituents by firm statements of nonnegotiable positions, which are so

common in open meetings. Instead, they can concentrate on reaching compromises.

In small bargaining groups, the verbal climate is generally kept at a fairly even
keel to foster an atmosphere of mutual trust and commitment to a common task
and to avoid rifts which might jeopardize the bargain (Speier, 1980). Expressions
of disagreements and dissatisfactions are inhibited. Language is cautious and
compromising. There are fewer deceptions and threats than is true of public
settings, and the opponents' motives are less likely to be impugned. This is true
because it is far more difficult to attack and deceive a fellow human being with
whom one is meeting face-to-face in a setting that implies equality of the
participants, than it is to threaten a distant opponent. In the small group setting,
one restrains those behaviors that one does not wish to be reciprocated. This
means controlling personal invective, steering clear of topics and conceptualizations that might obstruct the group's progress, and limiting verbal input to allow
others to participate in the discussion. Of course, these norms are not universally
observed. In fact, at times, they are deliberately violated when a party believes
that it can thereby intimidate the opposition (Graber, 1976).

Small groups make it easier to assess one's collaborators or opponents. In the
more intimate setting, it becomes far simpler to communicate attitudes, expectations, and relevant personality traits through verbal and nonverbal symbols.
Immediate feedback makes it possible to adjust the flow of verbal interaction
more quickly to directions likely to bring about agreement. Misunderstandings
and uncertainties can be cleared up promptly. Group members are likely to
develop personal ties and patterns of deference and command that may prevent
individuals from expressing hostilities linked to conflicting official positions.
Occasionally, the opposite may happen as well. Intimate contact may produce
great friction in small groups so that outbursts occur that might be restrained in
a public setting where people try harder to appear dignified.

CONTROLS OVER DISCUSSION FLOW

While discussions in small groups may be conducted informally, they can also
be tightly controlled so that they proceed in more orderly and purposive fashion
than is generally true of larger assemblies. A carefully selected agenda can be
established to make sure that potentially disruptive items are excluded or
minimized. Discussion can be focused on topics likely to produce compromise,
in a sequence designed to develop momentum toward agreement. The sequence
of discussion is crucial because each prior verbal exchange becomes the setting
for subsequent exchanges. This is particularly true at the start of negotiations
because the mood that is created initially may determine the ultimate bargaining
outcomes. An agenda that places some items of agreement first, or that contains
initial items that can be readily sacrificed, may produce a good setting for
subsequent conflict resolution. The scope of the agenda must be confined to

those items that are "negotiable"—which means those items for which the parties prefer agreement and the concessions that it may require to no agreement at all. This is the "manifest contract zone" or "bargaining zone" concept described by game theorists (Stevens, 1963).

The essence of the bargaining process lies in the verbal formulation of problems so that they become amenable to solution and in the presentation of a variety of alternative formulations by members of the group. Through verbal interactions these alternative proposals are narrowed to a single, mutually acceptable choice that usually represents an amalgamation of various views. The final compromise must be phrased extremely carefully to convey shadings of meanings acceptable to opposing sides and to blur conflicts that may still remain after bargaining has been concluded. Because the needs and perspectives of various parties to the bargain frequently differ, they may phrase separate justifications and explanations of bargaining outcomes to gain approval and support from their constituencies.

EFFECTIVENESS OF SMALL GROUP BARGAINING

The ultimate effectiveness of verbal tactics in producing agreement depends, to a large degree, on the context in which bargaining occurs. Obviously, the subject matter of bargaining is highly important. A serious international conflict, for instance, is far less likely to be resolved than is a disagreement about a minor domestic policy change. The fact that a bargaining situation may be part of a continuous, established system of interaction in which many subsequent encounters are expected is also important. The need for future dealings is likely to make the parties more willing to compromise.

Overall, small group bargaining is a highly effective verbal process. The records of a number of international and national crises reveal that when small group bargaining was used along with attempts to reach decisions in larger, more formal groups, the face-to-face negotiations accomplished their purposes better. This was true in the Cuban missile crisis, the Berlin airlift, and the Taiwan Strait crisis of 1958. It was also true of the Vietnam peace negotiations, where formal sessions proved irrelevant while informal sessions succeeded. Domestically, presidential meetings with labor groups have been more productive of accommodations than have public exhortations.

The Debate Setting

The debate setting provides a cross between the oratory setting and the bargaining setting. As in the oratory setting, verbal behavior occurs in a public place before a large, live audience, and often an even larger media audience. As in the bargaining setting, talk, which may range from formal speeches and debates to informal discussions, is interactive. Its ostensible major purpose is to produce agreements. For most assemblies, these agreements concern laws, regulations, and resolutions which deal with major aspects of political and personal

life. Public assemblies include legislative assemblies of various kinds, international bodies like the United Nations and its major agencies, and public mass
meetings and political conventions. The constraints imposed on debate by the
public nature of the meetings vary depending on the extent of their visibility and
the chance that their deliberations will be publicized in full.

MAJOR FUNCTIONS OF ASSEMBLY DEBATES

The functions performed by debate in public assemblies are diverse and the
verbal tactics vary accordingly. Traditionally, the primary function of public
debate in public assemblies has been to air the views of members on matters of
official concern to the body and to frame and adopt public policies. Because of
the difficulty of reaching compromises and agreements in the glare of modern
publicity, this goal now is rarely accomplished. Parliaments no longer act as great
deliberative bodies where the merits of policies are debated in the grand manner.
Rather, real bargaining takes place in small groups which gather, often ahead of
time, to reach decisions and agreements. Most so-called debates in public
assemblies have become little more than oratorical exercises that precede or
follow decision-making.

While most decision-making has moved to a different forum, several major
aspects of the public debate function remain intact. Agenda-setting is one. Public
assemblies provide a highly visible forum where ideas may be aired to attract
attention and set the agenda for public discussion and subsequent political
bargaining and action. Ideas which receive no public airing are less likely to
become matters of concern and action by the body.

The way issues are verbally defined in the public setting is likely to shape the
discussion and chances for agreement. If policy adoption is the goal, appropriate
linkages must be made and divisive aspects excluded from public discussion. For
instance, measures proposing aid to primary and secondary schools have been
repeatedly defeated in Congress when the touchy issue of aid to parochial
schools became part of the debate (Eidenberg & Morey, 1969). Some issues are
so sensitive that there is great reluctance to discuss them at all because debates
may arouse such hard feelings that policy-making about the issue becomes
impossible. Legalized abortion and prostitution are examples. Such issues are
better handled in small group settings without prior or subsequent public debate.

Debate may also be used to record motivations and justifications for projected or past actions. The consequences of the choices of particular justifications may be momentous. For instance, experienced political analysts contend
that Soviet interventions in the affairs of Eastern European countries have been
greatly facilitated by borrowing the rationale for American intervention in Latin
America. When foreign policy debates in Congress and the executive branch
stressed that countries are justified in keeping competing ideologies out of their
immediate geographical sphere of influence, the logic was not lost on America's

adversaries. The Brezhnev Doctrine, used to justify Soviet intervention in various parts of the world, "faithfully echoes official U. S. pronouncements made during the covert overthrow of the governments of Guatemala, the Cuban missile crisis, and the invasion of the Dominican Republic" (Franck & Weisband, 1972, p. 6).

The problem of coping with a multiplicity of diverse audiences simultaneously poses a very serious challenge for speakers in public assemblies. Usually they cannot limit the numbers and kinds of audiences to which their discourse will be broadcast. An American representative to the United Nations may speak simultaneously to colleagues in that assembly, to the American public, and to widely scattered audiences in hundreds of other countries throughout the world. The necessity to keep all of these audiences in mind may force speakers to modify what they might otherwise want to say to their immediate target audiences. It frequently tempts them to talk in the vaguest generalities in hopes that the remarks will be interpreted in a variety of favorable ways by different audiences.

Besides setting the agenda for action and defining the parameters of public issues and the rationales for political decisions, debates in public assemblies shape and reveal the divisions among political combatants. They bring out supporters and opponents on various sides of each question and herald the lines of arguments each side is likely to pursue in solving policy disputes. Debate may also be directed toward building morale and an *esprit de corps* so that the assembly can act in unison. Alternatively, debate may be designed to build loyalty for certain individuals, groups and issues, and diminish it for others. Such personal loyalties can be crucial to the passage or defeat of various measures.

RESTRAINTS ON LANGUAGE USE

The need to maintain an atmosphere of civility conducive to continuous working relationships forces members of public assemblies to keep verbal exchanges moderate, despite conflicting interests and personalities. To assure such moderation, most assemblies have well-observed formal and informal rules for verbal interchanges by their members. Besides regulations to keep the debate within the bounds of available time and to allow a variety of viewpoints to be aired, they include a host of rules designed to foster an atmosphere of politeness.

Personal attacks and derogatory remarks about a member's religion or ethnicity are scorned. Members' motivations or intelligence may not be impugned. Expressions of opposition are tactfully phrased in florid language. If feasible, arguments are made on procedural rather than substantive grounds because members are less likely to have an emotional stake in procedures. When intemperate, emotional language is used, it is generally interpreted as a sign that the speaker is unwilling to reach a compromise about the issues in question. In fact, reports of the use of intemperate language, even in off-the-record sessions, have been grounds for breaking off negotiations (Graber, 1976).

Political language employed in public settings is strongly affected by the twin constraints of instant publicity and instant response and rebuttal. Aware that they are performing on a public stage, debate participants strive mightily to maintain a favorable public image. They try to present themselves as persons of strength, dignity, and lofty ideals who discuss matters of public policy on a plane of high principle and according to the accepted norms of the body. They also want to appear as staunch defenders of the legitimate interests of their constituents. At the same time, they restrain their remarks because they do not wish to be embarrassed by rebuttals from colleagues who can readily point to weaknesses in arguments, hyperbole, contradictions, half-truths, and outright lies.

Speakers also know that their remarks provide settings for fellow debate participants and therefore must be structured to produce desirable interactions. The ground must be laid for arguments by later speakers, supporters as well as opponents. However, in contrast to the oratory setting, the flow of arguments often is difficult to guide in a debate setting. Fellow assembly members may bring out matters which a given speaker would prefer to keep quiet. The interactive nature of debates also limits speakers' topic choices because their preferred topic and line of argument may have been preempted by other speakers.

The attempts to create favorable images make for a good deal of posturing which may impair the chances for genuine bargaining and compromises. During the public debate, policy positions may be stated in terms of morality and such widely sanctioned principles as the right of free speech, national honor, or the rule of law. Because matters of principle are involved, this makes it difficult to abandon these positions later. Disabling rigidity results.

The pressures toward posturing are partly counteracted by the opportunities for instant rebuttal which may show the weakness and emptiness of a speaker's remarks. Moreover, speakers may fear that their pronouncements before a sizable audience will be interpreted as commitments which may later force them into unwanted actions. But despite such restraints on distortions and exaggerations, public debate is likely to contain more empty rhetoric than verbal interchanges in less public settings. No wonder that it does not rate very highly as a medium for accurate information transmission!

OPERATIONAL FUNCTIONS

Besides their major functions, public debates also serve ancillary and less obvious purposes. These are frequently of equal or even greater political significance than the ostensibly primary goals. Secondary functions relate to the operation and impact of the assembly's affairs, to the personal and professional needs of the speakers, and to the concerns of outside audiences who are not part of the formal debating process.

One of the most important ancillary functions of debates in public assemblies is the dissemination of information to assembly members. Because assemblies usually lack formal internal communications systems, various speakers weave information about issues under discussion or about extraneous issues more or less skillfully into their debates. To ferret out and publicize information some members might wish to conceal, parliaments have developed various formal and informal procedures, such as legislative hearings and question hours. Speakers may also find it useful to convey information designed to confuse their colleagues and to obscure issues they do not want made clear.

The arguments advanced in public assemblies may be designed to go beyond the immediate political situation to building a permanent record for future legal interpretation and action. This is possible because it is common practice to publish complete transcripts of assembly debates. Members are free to present their understandings and interpretations of certain proceedings which may then influence subsequent policy execution. Members can explain their motivations so that these may not be misconstrued. They can also indicate their opposition to certain measures and thereby dissociate themselves from any future consequences.

In countries with a parliamentary form of government, where voting follows strict party lines, debate may be the only opportunity for members to air dissent. The debate then becomes an important means to record intraparty differences and gauge opportunities for future modifications of the policy in question. Parliamentary debates in the British House of Commons about Britain's relations with the European Common Market provide a number of examples (Richards, 1967).

Verbal maneuvers may also serve several tactical goals in the conduct of assembly business. Most dramatically, they may be used to delay assembly action or to stop it entirely. Filibustering in the U. S. Senate is the best-known example. Lengthy, often irrelevant speeches are used to physically exhaust the opposition and kill off the business under consideration. Even short of filibustering, measures are often talked to death by exhausting the membership's patience to listen or by talking past the expected end of a session when members are eager to leave. Under these circumstances, members may agree to either kill or pass a measure merely because they are weary of listening or eager to get home. At times, debate may be deliberately prolonged to give time for additional supporters to gather or for the opposition to rally and defeat a measure which might have passed otherwise (Gross, 1953).

EGO SUPPORT FUNCTIONS

Much speech-making in public assemblies can also be credited partially or totally to the speakers' desire for ego inflation (Gregor, 1971). People like to hear themselves talk in public settings. It makes them feel important and allows them to impress their audiences with their wit and wisdom. People talk for catharsis—to let off steam. Talk may support their friends or pay off a political debt. It may further their political fortunes and keep them in the political limelight.

It is impossible to tell from the form of speeches made in public assemblies whether they serve the assembly's primary functions or whether they are wholly or partly motivated by the speakers' desires to gratify their egos. However, studies of debate participation in the U. S. Congress indicate that the desire for ego inflation is generally restrained. There are few idle talkers. The norm that those who participate in debates should have special knowledge about the subject matter at hand apparently serves to limit the opportunities for indulging ego concerns (Lehnen, 1969).

APPEALS TO EXTERNAL AUDIENCES

In many instances, the primary purpose of debate in public assemblies is the desire to appeal to outside audiences. Speakers tailor the form and substance of their arguments accordingly. In an effort to use language that is likely to attract substantial media coverage, they may make their arguments overly simplistic or overly sensational and emotional. During public hearings, the desire to attract attention may lead to flamboyant, inflammatory claims, hostile and misleading questions, and character assassinations. Such verbal misfeasance, which can have serious adverse consequences, is generally absent from small group bargaining settings (Barth, 1955).

The purposes of appeals to outside audiences are varied and parallel the purposes sought for internal audiences. The chief object may be to disclose information and specific interpretations of this information. Speakers may also wish to build external support or opposition for certain policies. For instance, much of the congressional debate on the Vietnam war was designed to mobilize public support or opposition for specific policies. Members who could not win majority support for their views in the assembly could nonetheless aspire to win victories through their appeals to external publics.

Some public debates are scheduled primarily to convey propaganda messages to external audiences, even though the officially stated purpose indicates otherwise. Many past arms limitations conferences provide examples. Bargaining in such conferences becomes little more than "parallel monologues in which the basic appeals are made to the galleries of world public opinion, rather than across the table to the opposition" (Jensen, 1963, p. 522). Each side tries to impress the public with the reasonableness of its arguments and the justice of its causes. Pressure anticipated from external publics is expected to soften the stands of balky negotiators or, at the very least, to damage their public image. While this does happen, a more likely consequence of publicized propaganda exchanges is a hardening of positions of the negotiators, as happened in U.S.-North Vietnamese negotiations during the Vietnam war.

The need to consider debate impact on external audiences may inhibit the substance as well as the tone of debates. If respected speakers repeatedly cast doubts on the ability of public officials to cope with a country's problems, large publics may become convinced that their government is functioning poorly. Erosion of public trust weakens the political system. To maintain public trust, speakers therefore are often tempted to conceal facts that might betray governmental incompetence and national weakness or to make unwarranted reassuring statements. These may lull the public into false confidence, delaying or preventing a reevaluation and recasting of public policies.

THE IMPACT OF PUBLIC DEBATES

Thus, public debates need to be assessed in terms of their ancillary effects as much as, and often more than, by their chief purpose. They may have succeeded even when their official purpose fails. However, many public debates do indeed fail in most of their purposes. This is true because the bulk of debating in public assemblies falls on deaf ears. Audiences tune out, even when they are interested in public affairs, because they realize that most debates are ritualistic, manipulative, and lacking in important substance. They know that the real work of an assembly goes on elsewhere.

Moreover, there is a surfeit of public dialogue of all kinds since, in an age of mass literacy and mass communication, the manipulation of the symbolic rather than the material environment has become particularly tempting. Through the mass media, audiences are swamped with information, most of it touted as important. Given the difficulty of knowing in advance what is wheat and what is chaff, general audiences are likely to restrict their limited listening time to messages from the most powerful political figures in the country. Much of the political dialogue remains unheard, except by a limited number of specially interested listeners.

In the final analysis, then, the impact of political messages hinges on the willingness of general and special audiences to listen and on their ability to interact with these messages. Political elites may be able to couch their messages and ideas in appropriate language forms. They may have important things to say. But if the audience does not listen, words have as little force as the breath that utters them.

REFERENCE NOTE

1. Watergate Transcripts, March 21, 1973. Washington, DC: Government Printing Office.

REFERENCES

Allport, G. W. Psychological models for guidance. In F. W. Matson & A. Montague (Eds.), *The human dialogue: Perspectives on communication.* New York: Free Press, 1967.
Baas, L. R. The constitution as symbol: The interpersonal sources of meaning of a secondary symbol. *American Journal of Political Science,* 1979, *23,* 101-138.

Barth, A. *Government by investigation.* New York: Viking Press, 1955.

Berstein, B. *Class, codes and control* (2 vols.). London: Routledge & Kegan Paul, 1971.

Birdwhistell, R. *Kinesics and context: Essays on body motion communication.* Philadelphia: University of Pennsylvania Press, 1970.

Bormann, E. G. The Eagleton affair: A fantasy theme analysis. *Quarterly Journal of Speech,* 1973, 143-159.

Bosmajian, H., & Bosmajian, H. *The rhetoric of the civil rights movement.* New York: Random House, 1969.

Burke, K. *Language as symbolic action.* Berkeley: University of California Press, 1966.

Chesebro, W. J. Political communication. *Quarterly Journal of Speech,* 1976, *62,* 289-300.

Combs, J. E. *Dimensions of political drama.* Santa Monica, CA: Goodyear, 1980.

Cook, T. E. Political justifications: The use of standards in political appeals. *Journal of Politics,* 1980, *42,* 511-537.

Cocoran, P. E. *Political language and rhetoric.* Austin: University of Texas Press, 1979.

Duncan, H. D. *Communication and social order.* New York: Bedminster Press, 1962.

Edelman, M. *The symbolic uses of politics.* Urbana: University of Illinois Press, 1964.

Edelman, M. *Political language: Words that succeed and policies that fail.* New York: Academic Press, 1977.

Eidenberg, E., & Morey, R. D. *An act of Congress: The legislative process and the making of education policy.* New York: W. W. Norton, 1969.

Franck, T., & Weisband, E. *Word politics: Verbal strategy among the super powers.* New York: Oxford University Press, 1972.

George, A. *Presidential decisionmaking in foreign policy: The effective use of information and advice.* Boulder, CO: Westview Press, 1980.

Graber, D. A. Perception of Middle East conflict in the United Nations, 1953-1965. *Journal of Conflict Resolution,* 1969, *13,* 454-484.

Graber, D. A. *Verbal behavior and politics.* Urbana: University of Illinois Press, 1976.

Graber, D. A. *Mass media and American politics.* Washington, DC: Congressional Quarterly Press, 1980.

Greenstein, F. I. Eisenhower as an activist president: A look at new evidence. *Political Science Quarterly,* 1979, *94,* 575-599.

Gregor, A. J. *An introduction to metapolitics.* New York: Free Press, 1971.

Gross, B. M. *The legislative struggle.* New York: McGraw-Hill, 1953.

Harrison, R. Nonverbal communication: Explorations into time, space, action, and object. In J. H. Campbell & H. W. Hepler (Eds.), *Dimensions in communication.* Belmont, CA: Wadsworth, 1966.

Holmes, O. W. *Towne v. Eisner,* 245 U. S. 418, 1918.

Jensen, L. Soviet-American bargaining behavior in the postwar disarmament negotiations. *Journal of Conflict Resolution,* 1963, *7,* 522-541.

Kennan, G. F. *Russia leaves the war.* Princeton: Princeton University Press, 1956.

Lall, A. *Modern international negotiation: Principles and practice.* New York: Columbia University Press, 1966.

Lehnen, R. G. Behavior on the Senate floor: An analysis of debate in the U. S. Senate. *Midwest Journal of Political Science,* 1969, *11,* 505-521.

Lerner, D. The revolutionary elites and world symbolism. In H. D. Lasswell, D. Lerner & H. Speier, (Eds.), *Propaganda and communication in world history* (Vol. 2). Honolulu: University Press of Hawaii, 1980.

Meadow, R. G. *Politics as communication.* Norwood, NJ: Ablex, 1980.

Merelman, R. M. Learning and legitimacy. *American Political Science Review,* 1966, *60,* 548-561.

Miller, E. F. Metaphor and political knowledge. *American Political Science Review,* 1979, *73,* 155-170.

Mueller, C. *The politics of communication: A study in the political sociology of language, socialization, and legitimation.* New York: Oxford University Press, 1973.

Nimmo, D., & Combs, J. E. *Subliminal politics: Myths & mythmakers in America.* Englewood Cliffs, NJ: Prentice-Hall, 1980.

Orwell, G. *Nineteen-eighty-four.* New York: Harcourt Brace Jovanovich, 1949.

Phillips, G. *Communication and the small group.* New York: Bobbs-Merrill, 1966.

Pool, I. De Sola. The language of politics: General trends in content. In H. D. Lasswell, D. Lerner & H. Speier (Eds.), *Propaganda and communication in world history (Vol. 3).* Honolulu: University Press of Hawaii, 1980.

Richards, P. *Parliament and foreign affairs.* Toronto: University of Toronto Press, 1967.

Sears, D. O., Hensler, C. P., & Speer, L. K. Whites' opposition to "busing": Self-interest or symbolic politics? *American Political Science Review* 1979, *73,* 369-384.

Speier, H. The communication of hidden meaning. In H. D. Lasswell, D. Lerner & H. Speier (Eds.), *Propaganda and communication in world history* (Vol. 2). Honolulu: University Press of Hawaii, 1980.

Stevens, C. *Strategy and collective bargaining negotiations.* New York: McGraw-Hill, 1963.

Wooten, J. T. The president as orator: His deliberate style appears to run counter to the inspiration he seeks to instill. *New York Times,* January 26, 1978.

Young, O. *The politics of force: Bargaining during international crisis.* Princeton: Princeton University Press, 1968.

CHAPTER 8

Political Rhetoric

Lloyd F. Bitzer

IF STUDY OF PAST AND PRESENT political rhetoric merely commits us to consider bombastic language, sophistic word tricks, and deceptive speech, we should abandon this subject to those who analyze errant forms of communication. If review of classical theories of political rhetoric leads us only to resurrect arcane notions that have little bearing on contemporary political communication, then we should leave to historians the study of ancient texts and turn to other matters. However, the practice of political rhetoric is far more than uses or misuses of language; it is the engagement of motives, principles, thoughts, arguments, and sentiments in communications—an engagement which functions pragmatically to form attitudes and assist judgments regarding the broad range of civic affairs. Political rhetoric serves the art of politics at every turn, both as a mode of thought and as an instrument of expression and action. The classical theories of political rhetoric provide for us rich principles and distinctions won through dialectical struggle with hard problems of government and civic affairs: Where is the location and what is the use of power and authority? Where and what are the sources of premises? To what extent must political discourse exhibit truth and moral quality? Therefore, any inquiry into political thought and communication should undertake the subject of political rhetoric with appreciation of its proper definition and attention to the contributions of its foremost theorists.

This chapter begins with a sketch of the kind of rhetoric which links easily and naturally with political thought and action. Thereafter topics and problems relevant to the study of political rhetoric are taken up, and along the way concepts useful to critics, theorists, and students are surveyed.

THE CONCEPT OF RHETORIC

Rhetoric has received virtually uninterrupted study for nearly 2500 years—from the time of Plato and Aristotle to the present. Until print became a practical medium of communication, rhetoric and public speaking throughout most of these centuries were nearly synonymous. Numerous definitions strongly imply this historic connection: Quintilian, for example, defined rhetoric as "the art of speaking well" (1958). In discussions of rhetoric, theorists spoke typically of public speaking or oratory; they explained the talents and duties of the speaker, the types of speeches, and the methods of invention, arrangement, style, memory, and delivery by which a speech could be created and presented to an audience. After the advent of print, almost every book on rhetoric was composed with reference to speaking or writing. Modern and contemporary theorists regard rhetoric broadly as a method of inquiry and communication applicable to spoken and written discourse, as well as to broadcasting, film, and other media.

Common to all rhetorics is consideration of methods and techniques whereby expression and communication can be rendered effective. Beyond this element, however, different theories focus on other skills and ends. The sophistic rhetoric of ancient Greece portrayed by Plato's dialogues and other classical sources emphasized the persuasive power of the speaker and his discourse for the producing of intended effects. Plato, after refuting that view, called for a rhetoric devoted to the health of the soul—both the soul of the individual and the collective soul of the polis. His noble rhetor would be physician to the audience, the medicine being those truths, values, and persuasive messages sufficient to keep the audience in health or return it to health. While the sophists focused on the speaker's influence and Plato on the audience's well-being, Aristotle conceived rhetoric as a kind of method and communication leading to reliable judgments about practical and civic matters. Cicero and Quintilian, taking a broader view, regarded rhetoric as the theory of communication; still, politics was its principal stage. In Quintilian's view, the finished orator and the ideal statesman were identical. Thus, his *Institutes of Oratory* served both as the manual of instruction for the orator—"the good man speaking well"—and as the educational program for the Roman citizen. Numerous writers, focusing particularly on the resources of language and style, have identified the strategies and figures of language which contribute to clarity, appropriateness, energy, beauty, and other qualities (Howell, 1956).

Chaim Perelman and Kenneth Burke, the two twentieth-century theorists whose views command the widest study, assign wide scope and basic functions to rhetoric. Perelman (1969) holds rhetoric to be the theory and practice of all argumentation which aims to secure the persuasion and conviction of audiences in political and other humane fields and also in the sciences. Rhetoric is at work whenever a writer or speaker seeks through argument to secure the assent of others to theses he advances. Burke's theory commences not with attention to argumentation, but to the nature of man as the symbol-using animal. Says Burke (1962): "Rhetoric as such is not rooted in any past condition of human society. It is rooted in an essential function of language itself . . . ; the use of language as a symbolic means of inducing cooperation in beings that by nature respond to symbols." In this view, rhetoric seeks to promote cooperation by use of symbolic, linguistic, and other strategies of identification. This is enough to suggest that in Western thought rhetoric has been assigned various ends; it has been brought to the service of politics, religion, science, literary achievement, social intercourse, personal relations, and salesmanship.

The most influential rhetorics, the classical theories of ancient Greece and Rome, show three characteristics especially important to our purpose. First, they were strikingly political in conception and practice. All the major writers— Isocrates, Plato, Aristotle, Cicero, Quintilian—thought that politics was the principal locus for rhetorical thought and communication, and therefore they designed their theories for use by political agents. In the second place, their rhetorics were significantly normative. Each theorist was a reformer seeking to correct defects in political oratory and recommending methods and principles to improve practice. Plato penned history's most famous attack on rhetoric when, speaking through Socrates in *Gorgias*, he denounced sophistic rhetoric as a mere sham art, a kind of "cookery," a means of making the worse appear the better, and a "knack" which substitutes appearance for reality and probability for truth. Aristotle complained that his sophistic predecessors failed to invest rhetoric with sufficient rational character. Quintilian (1958) took pains to explain that his rhetoric aimed not at victory but at "speaking well," by which he meant saying what ought to be said—and speaking in such a way that posterity will judge the speech right, fit, becoming. These and other rhetorics incorporated regulative principles for the purpose of encouraging, though never guaranteeing, that messages and decisions would be informed by fact and wisdom and would serve the public interest. Finally, these theories treated rhetoric as an art, or systematic method, the object of which was to guide practice toward the best activity permitted by circumstances, and they assigned it tasks of the first order. Thus Aristotle defined rhetoric as the art or faculty of discovering the available means of persuasion in any given case; and he placed it alongside dialectic, the two being the arts, or organons, by which we come to judgments about subjects and problems in the field of the contingent. Of all the classical theorists, Aristotle was the most philosophical, rigorous, and at the same time the most concerned with the political realm. This chapter draws heavily from his work.

In agreement with the tradition just reviewed, we regard rhetoric as a method of inquiry and communication which functions to establish judgments, primarily in areas of practical and humane affairs, for ourselves and for the audience addressed. All persons use rhetoric to some extent, since they try to ground judgments on investigation and seek the agreement of other minds through communication. However, many do not take the trouble to acquire competence in handling subjects and problems, and consequently they often embrace viewpoints and seek to persuade others to adopt viewpoints that are weak in conception and shallow in value. It is obvious that we need to judge and persuade not on the basis of whimsy, falsehood, or inadequate information and methods, but rather on the basis of purposeful deliberation which employs as much truth as the subject admits and proceeds systematically through methods of investigation, evaluation, and communication suited to the subject, the audience, and the purpose. This rhetoric differs from both propaganda and the craft of persuasion. The former implies inculcation of beliefs in the absence of critical deliberation, while rhetoric insists on rational justification. The craft of persuasion reduces truth and value to the role of tactic for the sake of making people believe or do what the communicator desires, while rhetoric is committed to truth and value as regulative principles.

SKILLFUL INQUIRY AND COMMUNICATION

The notion of political rhetoric often reminds us of messages which stand out because of factors such as intrinsic importance or uniqueness, situational urgency, and short- or long-term influence, or because of the communicator's extraordinary skill, eloquence, or courage in the face of danger. Thus our anthologies contain such touchstones as the Declaration of Independence, the Federalist Papers, Milton's *Areopagitica,* Henry's Liberty or Death speech, Lincoln's Second Inaugural, Churchill's wartime addresses, and Martin Luther King's "I Have A Dream" speech. Such memorable works are only dots on a vast landscape, however. For each impressive speech by an Edmund Burke, ten thousand routine speeches also played their parts well or ill. And for each political speaker or writer who crafted a message, there were countless audience members engaged by those messages who exercised their own rhetorical skills in tasks of interpretation, argumentation, and judgment.

Every citizen who deliberates and creates messages about civic affairs—estimating ends and means, selecting arguments and evidence, weighing factors of advantage, justice, and virtue—engages in political rhetoric. And this activity of deliberation and message-making constitutes genuine political rhetoric even when self-addressed. Indeed, we should acknowledge that one of the most important competencies of the citizen is the ability to deliberate skillfully for himself, as well as for others. Walter Lippmann (1966) once reminded educators that every citizen's education ought to include an art of judging rightly. "Now that we live in a time when, as Huey Long truly said, every man is a king, it is still the prime function of education to instruct and to train the future rulers of the state." A critical task of scholarship, he concluded, is discovering "what should be taught to the future rulers of a modern state" and how citizens can "acquire that capacity of judging rightly which is the essence of wisdom." The competence to "judge rightly" should apply not only to eloquent political communications but also to the mundane; to normal communication settings as well as to private deliberation of civic matters by an individual; to the tasks of the message maker's audience as well as to the message maker.

Skill in political rhetoric must involve union of inquiry and communication. The separation of the two is both dangerous and unphilosophical. If political rhetoric were regarded simply as skillful communicative behavior, then the focus of theory, research, and instruction would go almost inevitably to such matters as causal linkages between communicative behaviors and their effects, while such matters as thought, the soundness of arguments, and the foundation of positions would be short-circuited. Politics is too important and its stakes too large for us to allow its fortunes to be committed to a theory of communication divorced from inquiry—in short, to a know-nothing rhetoric. This is one of the reasons Plato rejected the sophistic rhetoric of his time: It purported to teach tactics of persuasion to political agents who had neither motive nor means to discover the truth or probable truth of matters on which they spoke; thus it amounted to a rhetoric of ignorance, dangerous to its users and to the public. The separation of inquiry and communication is also unphilosophical. Political discourse makes claims and urges judgments about policies and actions which deserve to stand or fall on the strength of the evidence and proofs that support them. This is the very essence of rational thought. For this reason Aristotle held that the essential element of rhetorical discourse is proof, while all else is accessory. Moreover, if we view political rhetoric as a system comprised of many competing messages, we should hold that its proper function is "deliberation," using the word in its general sense of inquiry on a large scale. For example, deliberation is the proper function of all the messages in congressional committee hearings, public speeches, newspaper and magazine articles, and formal debates on the question of ratifying Panama Canal treaties.

Classical rhetoricians, particularly the Romans, tried to assure complete education regarding the whole art of political deliberation by dividing rhetoric into five essential parts—invention, arrangement, style, memory, and delivery. According to the *Rhetorica ad Herennium,*

> invention is the devising of matter, true or plausible, that would make the case convincing. Arrangement is the ordering and distribution of the matter, making clear the place to which each thing is to be assigned. Style is the adaptation of suitable words and sentences to the matter devised. Memory is the firm retention in the mind of the matter, words, and arrangement. Delivery is the graceful regulation of voice, countenance, and gesture.

These five covered practically all the concepts, rules, and methods concerning both inquiry and communication.

Theorists did not slight the first part—invention; indeed, they copiously detailed its task of discovering, creating, and judging the subject matter of discourse. Most of Aristotle's *Rhetoric* was concerned with invention, leading Quintilian to complain that Aristotle neglected the other four parts. Presupposing the speaker's wide learning and information about the subject at hand, theorists of invention provided systems of topics to aid the speaker. For example, an advocate and a prosecutor preparing to defend and accuse a party at trial—either in a formal judicial setting or in the court of public opinion—were advised to examine the basic causes of human action, which Aristotle identified and characterized as chance, nature, compulsion, habit, reason, passion, and desire. Topics were provided to guide inquiry in relation to types of discourse— deliberative, forensic, and epideictic; modes of proof—logos, ethos, and pathos; kinds of disputes—conjectural, definitional, qualitative, and procedural; arguments, according to kinds, forms, premises; audiences, according to various factors including age and social standing. The topics, singly and in combination, were heuristic methods by which to probe in the right places.

SUBJECT MATTER

The territory of political rhetoric implies some idea of the "public's business," or public affairs, and this phrase in turn implies some identity of the "public." (Bitzer, 1978). What, then, is the public, and what is the public's business? We borrow answers from John Dewey's *The Public and Its Problems*. Seeking to account for the origin of the state, Dewey distinguished between public and private actions and identified public business according to the seriousness and duration of the consequences of public action.

> We take then our point of departure from the objective fact that human acts have consequences upon others, that some of these consequences are perceived, and that their perception leads to subsequent effort to control action so as to secure some consequences and avoid others. Following this clue, we are led to remark that the consequences are of two kinds, those which affect the persons directly engaged in a transaction, and those which affect others beyond those immediately concerned. In this distinction we find the germ of the distinction between the private and the public. When indirect consequences of an action are confined, or are thought to be confined, mainly to the persons directly engaged in it, the transaction is a private one [Dewey, 1927, p. 12].

In Dewey's view, then, the consequences of some transactions are short-lived, nonrecurring, and of only minor significance; they do not require attention and control. But other transactions produce consequences that are widespread and enduring; and to the extent that they affect persons other than oneself for good or evil, the transactions and their consequences amount to the public's business. Moreover, Dewey identified as the public that class of persons significantly affected by public transactions and their consequences. The state and its machinery—laws, courts, offices, and so on—come into existence for the purpose of caring for and conducting the public's business.

We may say that political rhetoric deals with matters thought to constitute the public's business—that is, all transactions and their consequences which significantly affect the public or its parts. This includes the notion of possessions, since the public acquires things of value which need protection and nurture. Possessions in the physical sense are obvious—public lands and buildings, for example, as well as such things as clean air and water. But the public also possesses much in the realm of language and thought—laws, principles, authoritative documents, values, symbols, and other elements of its mythos— which may require protection or shoring up because these, in whole or in part, are essential to the public's character and stable identity.

Ambiguous areas rather than sharp lines separate political from other kinds of rhetoric. In the first place, persons disagree over whether some transactions are actually public; whether a public transaction has or will have significant consequences; whether an alleged possession is a legitimate possession of the public; and whether a possession deserves protection or nurture. The fact that disagreements on such points attain stature as serious public issues indicates the centrality of political rhetoric even on questions of what constitutes the business of the public. In the second place, human motives and activities are often mixed in such a way that it is difficult to find the line between essentially political rhetoric and religious, aesthetic, or social rhetoric. Finally, even discourse that in its function appears to be essentially religious or philosophical or purely entertaining will often produce effects—sometimes distant—on beliefs and attitudes relevant to the public's business. This is one reason why some critics argue that the state should control activities and discourses that appear not to be political in nature.

To observe that political rhetoric is about subject matter which affects the public and is the public's business is not to say that rhetoric itself is a discipline or science with content in the sense that political science, physics, and psychology have content. Aristotle held explicitly that rhetoric must be understood as a general art (akin to dialectic, or logic) consisting not of knowledge about specialized fields but of classifications, topics, methods, lines of argument, probabilities, prudential rules, and so on. This general art is widely applicable to matters which .come before citizens for judgment when there is no special discipline or science to guide choice. This point is important for two reasons: First, as a matter of theoretical cleanliness, rhetoric should be distinguished from other arts and sciences. (Readers of Plato's *Gorgias* will recall that Gorgias, muddled in his thought, momentarily confused rhetoric with mathematics.) Second, and more important practically, we should not try to prove a proposition that belongs to physiology by using rhetoric, or vice versa; in either case, a gross methodological error would be involved. It is erroneous to set out to establish by means of rhetoric that a fetus has or has not certain physiological characteristics, and equally wrong to seek to prove, by using methods and knowledge of physiology, that moral laws were or were not violated by destruction of a fetus.

Thomas DeQuincy held that rhetoric deals mainly with matters which lie in that vast field "where there is a *pro* and a *con*, with the chance of right and wrong, true and false, distributed in varying proportions between them" (1967, p. 91). Aristotle meant approximately the same thing when he said rhetoric deals with matters that are contingent rather than necessary, questions which might be answered one way or another, with problems which permit probable rather than certain conclusions. We do not deliberate rhetorically, he said, about absolute certainties or about matters that are fixed by nature. In other words, rhetoric applies to contingent and probable matters which are subjects of actual or possible disagreement by serious people, and which permit alternative beliefs, values, and positions.

Rhetorical subjects, then, are mainly probable, contingent, interest-laden, and frequently in contention. These characteristics mark the central realm of activity for rhetoric, which is the practical world of human affairs. Here rhetoric labors between the challenge and the fitting response, the imperfection and the remedy, the crisis and the calm. This, Kenneth Burke colorfully remarked, is the area of the human barnyard—the big scramble. Some arts and disciplines shun strife, discord, practical interests, and effects: They work quietly, removed from the practical business of life and free from the burdens of decision and action. Rhetoric, however, is geared for human affairs, and much of its work lies in the bustle and jostling of political and social deliberations, in courtrooms, assemblies, and in controversies of many kinds. Unlike the sciences, which may be said to deal with the realm of truth, rhetoric deals with the realm of action where truth and feeling, actuality and motive, problems, uncertainties, hopes, and visions all play a role in the formation of judgment and action.

Characteristically, political subject matter engages interests, values, emotions, and aspirations. As a natural consequence, messages designed for persuasion in courts, assemblies, political campaigns, and public ceremonies make their way on arguments linked to valued premises, facts linked to interests, descriptions and visions linked to emotions, and on language which rouses and satisfies appetites by means of its form as well as its substance. Political rhetoric which presents itself as dispassionate, purely objective, or empirical only disguises the operating forces of valuation. Even those empirical public opinion polls issued during presidential campaigns engage partisan motives and function persuasively, notwithstanding their authors' protestations of scientific and journalistic purity.

The fact that human valuation interacts with contingent subject matter helps explain why political rhetoric must ever remain unscientific—that is, why it will refuse to be held to statements of the true-false variety. Values and interests will exert such force that persons contending in the same context and about the same subject will disagree in what they perceive and say, a political speaker will be inconsistent from one situation to another, and the perceived truth of political discourse will vary markedly across contexts. This variable quality would be of little note, perhaps, if political rhetoric were inconsequential. But in fact the consequences are as large as the health of the state and the well-being of each and every citizen.

Political rhetoric has served good ends and bad, used intelligence and defied it, and harnessed the noblest of motives and the worst. It has aided the triumph of magnificent causes; but it has also furthered the reign of despots and promoted massive lies and injuries. In short, political rhetoric is dangerous. This is why practically every theorist of rhetoric has labored to identify and define principles, methods, and standards which, if observed, would bring political rhetoric under the influence of a rationality suitable to practical action, thus making it as good as it can be.

ACTION AND RHETORICAL PROOF

A fundamental question is whether political persuasion is essential to the human enterprise or some part of it. This is not to ask whether it is sometimes useful in a purely utilitarian sense: Political persuasion may be useful and yet lack centrality if it is only an incidental aspect of life capable of being eliminated with no significant loss and no alteration in the nature of the human being or the human community. Let us say that political persuasion must be counted as essential if it is necessary to civic cooperation and decision-making. Should it fail this test, we would doubt its centrality.

Now, we might define man as the communicating animal, thus calling attention to the fact that communicability is essential to being human. This conception, however, does not bear closely enough on the question of whether political persuasion is essential: It is possible that human beings must communicate, but need not engage in political persuasion. Or we might hold the view that political and other kinds of persuasion are essential because those things we count as believable—from facts to laws of nature, from preferences to maxims of moral conduct—in the final analysis are objects of agreement which received that status through processes of persuasion (Ziman, 1968). But this view encounters theoretical and commonsense objections: For example, few of us are prepared to reduce facts and truths of the physical universe to the status of objects of agreement. We are inclined to think that distinctions should be made between is and ought, actuality and possibility, necessity and contingency, motion and action, and between scientific method by which we come to know and judge things capable of precision and certainty on one hand and other modes of proof and persuasion by which we properly judge and act with some degree of confidence regarding uncertain matters on the other.

One way to place political rhetoric within the whole scheme of human endeavor begins with the great fact of division. As Kenneth Burke remarks, "if men were not apart from one another, there would be no need for the rhetorician to proclaim their unity. If men were wholly and truly of one substance, absolute communication would be of man's very essence." But individuals are at odds with one another; and so also are groups, cultures, and generations. The human condition is shot through with divisiveness, separation, competition. This condition explains why the key notion in Burke's theory of rhetoric is identification, which "is affirmed with earnestness precisely because there is division. Identification is compensatory to division." Rhetoric functions through language, a kind of symbolic action, to "induce cooperation in beings that by nature respond to symbols." Human agents with competing motives, interests, meanings, and truths find themselves at odds, sometimes radically so; but at the same time they share those same elements in some degree as a condition of their common understanding and humanity. There is, then, a constant condition of both division and community; our efforts to bridge gaps, even when successful, sometimes create others; and some of our most exhausting labor toward cooperation only anticipates division, as when we take great pains to rally ourselves for war. Rhetoric's function is essentially pragmatic—to find common meaning, unifying symbols, and ways of acting together, thus promoting cooperation.

It is but a small step from the general notion of cooperation to the specific notion of political cooperation, which involves strategies of identification and ways of inducing joint action that relate to political life and, indeed, make political life possible. Says Burke (1962): "Identification ranges from the politician who, addressing an audience of farmers, says, 'I was a farm boy myself,' through the mysteries of social status, to the mystic's devout identification with the source of all being" (pp. 522, 546-547, 567). Strategies of identification, at once strategies of persuasion, are at work when divergent purposes or interests are linked, when the material and formal features of arguments bring minds to agreement on premises and conclusions, when meanings, images, and other resources of language bring us to the same thoughts and feelings, and when the regimens to which we submit succeed in harmonizing our actions. All of this takes place in the realm of action and symbolism, not in the realm of motion and physicality. In the absence of political persuasion, only motion or force might impose some discipline on the physical aspects of persons; but it could never produce a community of minds.

Aristotle's placement of rhetoric among the arts and sciences and his conception of the mission of political persuasion result from a line of reasoning different from Burke's. The main reason for the difference is that Aristotle holds judgment to be rhetoric's chief concern: Properly speaking, the audience is a judge, and the object of rhetorical transactions involving speakers and listeners is to produce reliable judgments. His concern is announced at the very beginning of the *Rhetoric* with the complaint that his sophistic predecessors placed an inappropriate emphasis on appeals to the emotions, and that this emphasis put the audience into the wrong emotional condition, thus warping their judgment: "It is not right to pervert the judge by moving him to anger or envy or pity—one might as well warp a carpenter's rule before using it." Aristotle knew that a speaker's powerful delivery and clever style can exert persuasive force; but, he said, these should not be persuasive—they should neither pain nor please, because the case should be won on the strength of the proofs. In rhetoric, only the proofs—logos, ethos, and pathos—are essential; everything else is accessory.

Logos (logical proof) refers to the probity of thought and the convincing quality of evidence and arguments, ethos (ethical proof) to the credibility and integrity of the speaker, and pathos (emotional proof) to the emotional condition of the audience. When an audience is persuaded to accept a speaker's position, all three types of proof are usually operative: The audience accepts as reliable the information and arguments set forth by the speaker (logos); the audience considers the speaker to be trustworthy, expert, authoritative (ethos); and the audience experiences interests or emotions that influence the judgment it makes (pathos). Thus, "the orator must not only try to make the argument of his speech demonstrative and worthy of belief; he must also make his own character look right and put his hearers, who are to decide, into the right frame of mind" (Aristotle, 1946, p. 1377a). Proofs of these types are called "artistic" when they are generated by the speech itself, and "inartistic" when they already exist and are operative.

Much of the first and second books of Aristotle's *Rhetoric* treat these kinds of proof. In amplifying logos, Aristotle treats the two broad forms of rhetorical argument—enthymeme, or the rhetorical syllogism, and example, the rhetorical induction. In addition, he discusses the materials of which enthymemes are made (probabilities, infallible signs, fallible signs, and examples), the premises appropriate to deliberative, forensic, and epideictic speeches, constructive and refutative arguments, sound and sophistical arguments, and 28 lines or patterns which commonly occur, such as arguments from precedent, from cause, from good and evil consequences, from opposites, and so on. He makes it clear that logical proof in rhetoric differs from proof in science: The former is less logically rigorous; it ordinarily achieves probability rather than certainty; it must engage premises credible to the audience as a condition of persuasion; and, of course, it deals with matters that are contingent rather than necessary. Ethos has reference to the speaker's trustworthiness or character as a ground of proof. The three constituents of ethos are said to be universal: In the first place, the speaker must display intelligence or knowledge; second, he must be perceived as a person of high moral character; and finally, it must be apparent that he has the best interests of his audience at heart. Aristotle indicates that there is a close tie between ethos and the virtues: The person of highest ethos will be one believed to possess the virtues in the highest degree, among which are knowledge and prudence as well as good will. Pathos is taken up in Book 2, where Aristotle discusses each emotion in detail. "The emotions," he writes, "are all those feelings that so change men as to affect their judgments, and that are also attended by pain or pleasure." Here, then, is one clear reason for the extensive discussion of pathos: The judgment of an audience will be influenced by emotion. His discussion includes the emotions of anger, calmness, friendship, enmity, fear, confidence, shame, shamelessness, kindness, unkindness, pity, indignation, envy, and emulation. At the outset he indicates the pattern of discussion for each emotion. With respect to anger,

> here we must discover (1) what the state of mind of angry people is, (2) who the people are with whom they usually get angry, and (3) on what grounds they get angry with them. It is not enough to know one or even two of these points; unless we know all three, we shall be unable to arouse anger in any one. The same is true of the other emotions. So just as earlier in this work we drew up a list of useful propositions for the orator, let us now proceed in the same way to analyze the subject before us.

At the conclusion of his discussion, Aristotle says: "This completes our discussion of the means by which the several emotions may be produced or dissipated, and upon which depend the persuasive arguments connected with the emotions" (1946, pp. 1378a, 1388b).

This brief account of Aristotle's notion of rhetorical proof leaves unanswered the question, Why are these kinds of proof—these ways of persuasion—essential to political life? Furthermore, while Aristotle recommends that the speaker know the emotions and use emotional proof—for example, to make an audience angry—he nevertheless complains that his predecessors erred by recommending and using pathos. On the surface, this amounts to an incompatibility. The search for Aristotle's view of the essential role of rhetorical proof, including the proper influence of feelings and emotions, takes us to his *Nicomachean Ethics* and *Politics,* both of which, he remarks, are closely linked to rhetoric.

First, rhetoric is put squarely to the service of politics, as a part of it and as an instrument. At the beginning of the *Ethics,* after explaining that ethical studies aim to determine what the good is, Aristotle links ethics to politics: The latter, as the "master science," considers the conditions under which human beings can achieve the good life. Oratory is said to be contained in politics, and to serve as one of its "most honored capacities" along with strategy and household management.

Second, the three problems Aristotle says are paramount in politics—problems about the good, the just, and the noble—coincide with the concerns of his three types of rhetoric: deliberative concerned with the good or expedient, forensic with the just, and epideictic with the noble or praiseworthy.

Third, in the *Politics* (Books 2 and 3) Aristotle explains that deliberation by the many is in the interest of the state. Individuals by themselves tend to form imperfect judgments, influenced in part by defects of prudence, virtue, and emotion; however, "the many, of which each individual is but an ordinary person, when they meet together may very likely be better than the few good, if regarded not individually but collectively, just as a feast to which many contribute is better than a dinner provided out of a single purse." Again: "Now any member of the assembly, taken separately, is certainly inferior to the wise man. But the state is made up of many individuals . . . [and] a multitude is a better judge of many things than any individual." These and similar comments indicate that judgment appropriate to political affairs ordinarily is better when it results from deliberation involving many minds rather than one or a few.

Fourth and most important, the *Ethics* (chiefly Books 2 and 6) explains the rationale underlying the three forms of rhetorical proof—a rationale that draws heavily on Aristotle's notions of practical wisdom, the nature of action, and the golden mean.

(a) Practical wisdom, one of five intellectual excellences or virtues, is concerned with the field of action, aims at good action, deals with matters about which human beings deliberate and particularly with "what is just, noble, and good for man," and is critical to judging rightly: "No choice will be right without practical wisdom and virtue. For virtue determines the end, and practical wisdom makes us do what is conducive to the end." The "man of practical wisdom is *ipso facto* a man of good character."

(b) Good choice in the field of action involves reasoning and desire, and both must be right. Such choice differs from decisions in science and theoretical disciplines: "In the kind of thought involved in theoretical knowledge and not in action or production, the good and the bad state are, respectively, truth and falsehood." On the other hand, "in intellectual activity concerned with action, the good state is truth in harmony with correct desire."

(c) How can desire, emotion, and the choice of ends be said to be correct? Aristotle answers that a choice, desire, or emotion is correct when it hits the right point between extremes of excess and deficiency, a point "relative to us" and dependent on circumstances. "We may thus conclude that virtue or excellence is a characteristic involving choice, and that it consists in observing the mean relative to us, a mean which is defined by a rational principle, such as a man of practical wisdom would use to determine it. It is the mean by reference to two vices: the one of excess and the other of deficiency." It is important to note that there is a mean regarding emotional experience, although selecting the mean is difficult—"it is a hard task to be good." With respect to anger, for example, "anyone can get angry," but the problem is directing anger "to the right person, to the right extent, at the right time, for the right reason, and in the right way." Thus, the moral virtues involve desire and emotion, as well as a rational principle; and these factors are essential in practical wisdom and deliberation.

Why, then, must the three modes of rhetorical proof be used? Because deliberations about the contingent and actionable require engagement of practical wisdom, virtue, and the right emotional experience, else judgment cannot be reliable. Logos, the rational element, is always required; so is ethos, the virtuous character, which is no other than the combination of excellences by which speaker and audience select the mean and aim at the right end; and pathos is required because the right emotional condition is critical to judging correctly.

Finally, why is political persuasion essential? Because when persuasion is right—involving the three modes of proof in a process of deliberation—we come to reliable judgments about matters which must be decided and which can be decided rationally in no other way. Ideally, everyone involved in political deliberations would possess practical wisdom.

MESSAGES AND SITUATIONS

The territory of contemporary political rhetoric is diverse. It ranges from campaign rallies, with their hoopla and extravagance, to the most somber deliberations in capital offices; from robust persuasive speeches in quest of victory to quiet, informative discourses meant to assist decision-making; and from passionate speeches of competing advocates to reflective statements by judges and critics on what is legally and morally just. The territory varies from press reporting and commentary to symbol-rich ceremonies of public life; from the fervent speeches of the civil rights movement to the threat-backed advocacy of special interest groups; from the televised state-of-the-union address aimed at millions to the self-deliberations of a single constituent; and from the highest congress to the local school board.

All of these messages are political in the sense that they either conduct the public's business or they bear on it. Into the former class fall the most obvious types, such as debates and deliberations in assemblies by citizens and their representatives, as well as public persuasion to rally citizen support outside such assemblies. A wide range of messages bear on the public's business—for example, some press reporting and commentary and other informative messages, social and political criticism, ceremonial discourses, and, in some cases, literary and philosophical works. The messages comprising contemporary political campaigns certainly bear on the public's business, and sometimes they conduct it. A chief characteristic of campaign rhetoric is that it aims to decide who will conduct public affairs; this explains why it plays so much on the themes of the candidates' personal character and competence.

Novels and other poetic works typically create a fictive context that is sufficient to render meaningful the utterances and actions of characters; thus our understanding of a novel or drama seldom requires study of its author's actual historical situation. Philosophical and other theoretical works typically make explicit the arguments and data needed to establish conclusions and perspectives. But political messages, unlike literary and theoretical discourses, link so closely to historical situations that we must understand details of the situation as a condition of understanding the meaning of the message. For example, on January 28, 1980, prior to important presidential primary elections in the East in which he was a candidate, Senator Edward Kennedy presented a televised speech to the people of New England. He prefaced his speech with a short message on the subject of Chappaquiddick. That brief but critically important message will be nearly unintelligible to persons unfamiliar with the Chappaquiddick incident and with Kennedy's misfortunes in the 1980 campaign. The message presumed the audience's knowledge of events, including numerous attacks on his character during the weeks preceding the speech, and its persuasive strategy made appeals to unstated presumptions and values in the audience. Anyone who examines political messages outside familiar contexts will be struck by the fact that context and message are so interactive that they can scarcely be separated: The real message, one might say, is a construction consisting of meanings supplied jointly by speaker and audience; it will seldom be explicit or even fully implied by the speaker's utterances.

Most political messages occur in specific historical situations and are essentially responsive to them. Political speakers find themselves in situations that present problems, crises, obstacles, or other kinds of exigencies which they seek to modify by addressing messages to mediating audiences—that is, to audiences which have sufficient power to modify the exigencies. In a normal situation, the speaker or writer perceives an *exigence* whose positive modification needs or requires the assistance of a message (or a campaign of messages) to engage *constraints*—facts, laws, principles, arguments, feelings, values, emotions, attitudes, motives—that are sufficient to persuade one or more *mediating audiences* to positively modify the exigence. In the absence of an exigence, there would be no motive to speak; in the absence of constraints, messages could not be effective; in the absence of a mediating audience, messages would be futile. Exigence, constraints, and mediating audience thus are the essential constituents of political situations in which discourse is invited.

When political situations are experienced as forceful or urgent, agents are inclined to respond rhetorically, although sometimes the agent does not respond and the situation, lacking response, atrophies to a point where any message would be too late. In the prior example of Senator Kennedy, the exigence—the obstacle to his success in New England primaries—was the public's perceptions about weaknesses in his character, perceptions recently aroused or generated in large part by journalists. He obviously sensed a need to respond by addressing the New England audience capable of modifying the exigence by providing a strong vote in his favor. His analysis was probably correct, but his failure to overcome the Chappaquiddick problem in that instance can be traced to his inability to find and use adequate proofs and other constraints. Kennedy's character exigence, and the situation given focus by it, persisted throughout his presidential campaign. At a broader level, we may observe that a presidential candidate's campaign develops around a set of exigencies, ranging from public issues to personal traits, and that the candidate's speeches on the stump and on special occasions consist largely of commonplaces, or set units of discourse, meant to modify the exigencies. However, in the progress of a campaign new, unanticipated exigencies and situations arise, such as one's own blunders or crisis events over which one has no control.

The exigencies to which political speakers respond are sometimes anchored in external reality, such as rampant inflation or unemployment, but at other times their location is in thought, such as the presence in some people of a dangerous intention or belief. In any case, genuine exigencies involve a real condition, whether physical or mental, coupled with one or more human interests. It is obvious that speakers and writers sometimes seek to modify unreal or fictional exigencies. This may result from misperception, ignorance, playfulness, or strategy. A common practice in political campaigns is to fabricate or purposely exaggerate an exigence (the "missile gap" in the 1960 presidential campaign) for the strategic purpose of creating an issue favorable to victory. The enthusiasm of a political agent often leads to exaggeration, but a fault in moral character leads to creation of a strategic fiction. We should notice also that persons with competing interests may disagree on the actuality of an exigence even when they perceive almost the same facts; this is because interest is a component of every exigence (Bitzer, 1968, 1980).

The dominant types of political rhetoric are those which conduct the public's business. We acknowledge Aristotle's identification of three broad types, while noting that these admit of many combinations and permutations arising from the particularities of situations. Aristotle defined the three types—deliberative, forensic, and epideictic—in terms of the kind of judgment characteristic of each: a judgment about what is expedient or good—deliberative rhetoric; a judgment about what is just or right—forensic; and a judgment regarding what is noble or worthy—epideictic. In ancient Athens the scenes of the three were the assemblies, courts, and ceremonial occasions; but, obviously, messages in all categories go beyond these scenes today.

Political discourse is deliberative when it calls for a judgment concerning the well-being of the public or some part of it. The end-term or ruling value is well-being, or some synonymous term such as the "good" or the "expedient," and the purpose in speaking is either to secure advantageous things by persuading the audience that a policy or proposal or remedy will be advantageous or by dissuading the audience from a course of action likely to lead to injurious consequences. Most political discourse of the normal sort is deliberative: legislators, school board members, political leaders of all kinds usually address audiences on matters of future policy—what should or should not be done. The arguments draw premises from the audience's stock of maxims and beliefs about what constitutes its own or the public's interest. And the speaker who anticipates disputes regarding his proposal is advised by Aristotle to consider four stock issues of deliberation—that is, four places where disputes can occur: What he proposes either can or cannot be done; what he proposes would or would not be just; what he proposes would or would not be advantageous; and what he claims regarding the degree or quality of advantages may be disputed.

Discourse is forensic, or judicial, when it calls for a judgment relative to justice. This ordinarily occurs in response to some denial or violation of law, moral principle, cultural value, and the like. The end-term or ruling value is justice, and the purpose in speaking is to secure a judgment that some act, purpose, or policy is or was just or unjust. The speaker draws premises from conceptions, values, and rules subordinate to justice (laws, constitutions, maxims of conduct) in order to prove the case. The obvious forensic scene is the courts, but numerous other contexts invite this kind of discourse—committee hearings, for example. Often, too, messages conveyed through essays and books judge past events—for instance, those written about President Nixon's conduct in the Watergate incident. There are four stock areas or topics of dispute in forensic discourse, according to Aristotle: an act was or was not done; it was or was not harmful; it did or did not cause the degree of harm attributed to it; and it was or was not justified. The clear cases for forensic deliberation lie in the past; and one cannot judge as right or wrong, lawful or unlawful, what has not yet occurred, except hypothetically. Yet some deliberative proposals involve elements of justice, and for that reason Aristotle's topics of deliberative dispute include the matter of justice. An example would be a congressional debate on whether to reinstate the selective service draft: the issue would be decided in part on a criterion of expediency, but also on whether a draft is ethnically, racially, or socially discriminatory—a question of justice.

Discourse is epideictic when it serves to show that an act, belief, person, institution, or thing deserves approval and praise because it is worthy, or disapproval and blame because it is unworthy. Aristotle said that the end-terms of epideictic are the honorable and the dishonorable (or the noble and the base); that the means are praise and blame; and that the principal topics are virtues and vices. These terms, interpreted broadly, cover all instances of epideictic discourse. There are many kinds of occasions, prompted by events and traditions, when speakers are called upon to praise someone or something—to pay tribute, celebrate, dedicate, approve, commend, compliment, endorse—or when they are called upon to do the opposite, to blame someone or something—to disapprove, belittle, defame, depreciate, reprove. The discourse of praise includes eulogies, commemorative addresses, speeches of celebration, and declarations of ideals. The aspirations, sentiments, and values treated by such messages permit eloquent style, bordering on poetry. Epideictic rhetoric is seldom argumentative; rather, it displays and amplifies the subject's virtuous traits, or vicious ones. The ideals and feelings expressed by the speaker are usually latent in the audience; the speaker gives voice to ideas and sentiments, hopes and aspirations, ideals and judgments which the audience would express if it could. The audience in epideictic situations neither decides and acts with regard to future well-being nor determines the justice of acts; rather, if conditions are right, it responds to the epideictic message with a sympathetic "yes"—it shares in praising or in blaming the subject.

Epideictic units of discourse may be employed in either deliberative or forensic messages: In deliberative, a speaker may wish to prove that a proposed action is desirable because it is honorable as well as expedient; and in forensic, the speaker may wish to strengthen his client's defense by proving that the client is virtuous as well as innocent of the alleged injustice.

Aristotle's view of the function of epideictic discourse in the state is indicated at the close of the *Ethics,* where he laments that the task of developing moral and intellectual virtues, or excellences, among citizens is very difficult. Yet, he remarks, citizens must have a capacity to apprehend what is right, and to judge rightly. It will be difficult, and perhaps impossible, to develop citizen virtues by means of teaching and argument, because most people are under the sway of emotion: "A man whose life is guided by emotion will not listen to an argument that dissuades him, nor will he understand it." What is required is this: "There must first be a character that somehow has an affinity for excellence or virtue, a character that loves what is noble and feels disgust at what is base." We assume from this and other statements of similar kind that the broad function of epideictic discourse is to cultivate and preserve those aspirations, values, beliefs, and habits which form the public's virtues and which are requisite to competent deliberation by the public in civic affairs as well as to the happiness of citizens as individuals.

Campaign rhetoric, broadly conceived, is deliberative; it asks for a judgment by citizens regarding whether one or another candidate would best administer public affairs. When substantive issues are particularly salient, campaign discourse may also decide matters of policy; but the stuff of ordinary campaigns consists of arguments, position statements, testimonials, commercials, and other materials relating to the prudence, good character, and right intentions of the candidate—to the image. This means that much campaign rhetoric, although mainly deliberative in function, works its way by taking up the topics of epideictic: by celebrating the virtues of a candidate, citing his past good deeds, and showing that on selected issues he displays prudence. And, in opposing a candidate, speakers try to show that prudence, character, and intentions are suspect. Thus, discussion of issues (deliberative) tends to be subsumed under discussion of images (epideictic). Occasionally, forensic themes of guilt or innocence enter, as they did in 1980 regarding the candidacy of Edward Kennedy.

It is important to notice that a significant part of campaign rhetoric centers on mistakes: The candidate makes an erroneous statement, or he says something contradictory, or he expresses a judgment showing lack of prudence—lack of practical wisdom. The opposition quickly dramatizes the mistake—a sign the guilty politician is unfit for office; and the press often gives a mistake front-page headlines. One example was President Gerald Ford's mistake in the second debate with Jimmy Carter in 1976. Responding to a panelist's question, Ford declared that the countries of Eastern Europe are not under the domination of the Soviet Union. That mistake dominated campaign rhetoric for about five days, until Ford admitted he had not said what he meant. During the same campaign year, Jimmy Carter suffered for weeks because of a lack of prudence in agreeing to a *Playboy* magazine interview and in the interview using language offensive to millions. What explains the attention given to such mistakes? For the competing candidates, serious mistakes obviously provide points of easy attack. For the press, mistakes are sometimes the most newsworthy matters to report. And it surely is true that a voter often enjoys learning that a candidate has made a major error: For voters, mistakes count as evidence that their assessment of a candidate is correct. But the importance of mistakes in campaign rhetoric rests on a more basic point: The public forms fairly reliable judgments about candidates by observing their mistakes—especially their flaws in reasoning, character, and prudence. Most voters are not well educated about details of issues and legislation, although they should be; consequently, most are not good judges of a candidate's pronouncements on complicated issues. But most voters do have sound views on the constituents of logical reasoning, good character, and prudence. Thus, when a candidate makes a mistake of reasoning, or of practical wisdom, or a mistake resulting from a flaw in character, the public is quick to recognize and, by and large, competent to judge it. Mistakes provide the public with tests of candidates' intelligence, character, and prudence, which accounts for why they play a most important role in campaigns.

Although Aristotle's *Rhetoric* did not provide for a class of *informative* discourse, we should do so, because the occasions for messages that inform the public are abundant. Furthermore, there exist professionals, established message forms, and industries for the purpose of presenting information to the public. The end-term or ruling value of informative discourse must be truth, or knowledge; the purpose of messages is to state and defend what is true, or deny and refute what is false. When argument is unneeded, the means are affirmation and denial, and when argument is required, the means are proof and refutation. Units of informative discourse occur subordinately in deliberative, forensic, and epideictic messages. However, in pure instances of informative discourse, information is generated and conveyed not because it serves the ends of goodness, justice, or nobility, but simply because it is truth the audience should know or would want to know—it relates to their interests. News reporters and analysts in their reports and explanations do not seek primarily to improve the well-being of their audience or to uphold the just or noble, although sometimes their discourse has these effects; they seek to provide news, interpretations, and conclusions which are true and of interest to the public. It seems self-evident that a competent public must receive a steady supply of information that is reliable and relevant to its real or perceived interests, and that "news" in the broad sense should answer that need.

Journalists have been at work for generations as reporters, interpreters, seers, agitators, critics of government, and advisors. But today's journalists, swelled by broadcasters, assisted by new technologies, and involved in the competitive merchandising of news, constitute a new class of orators. Although they would prefer not to be called orators, or rhetoricians, in fact the term fits: They form a profession of communicators including the prestige commentators and news analysts, anchorpersons, reporters, editors, and all who convey news to the public through television, radio, newspaper, and magazine. Their message-making is voluminous; they have easy access to the most available and effective channels of public communication—channels already linked to audiences prepared to read and hear them; they win our trust more easily and securely than do politicians; and perhaps the journalists, rather than the preachers and politicians, have become the dominant speakers in our political life. Whether the orators of news have an art of inquiry and communication adequate to their mission is a question of large importance.

TOWARD POLITICAL COMPETENCE

A sound theory of political rhetoric regards the audience as neither a terminal receiver of messages nor a passive object to be manipulated, but as an active, participating agent in deliberations. Reliable deliberations require a competent audience no less than a competent speaker, because each is a center of information, interest, and intelligence with the capacity to influence the other; and neither is assumed to be generally wiser than the other. The best audience will be the one possessing the most practical wisdom, skill, and knowledge relevant to the case at hand. Recognition of these principles is implicit in our efforts to elect wise and skillful men and women to legislative bodies, and in our expectations that biased or impractical speakers and audiences will produce biased or impractical decisions.

It follows that, ideally, a speaker would always address the audience most competent to judge the matter about which he speaks, and as a rule would not ask an incompetent audience to decide or act. However, sometimes the most competent audience is unavailable or powerless, and the situation virtually requires persuading an audience that is biased, misinformed, or otherwise incompetent. A speaker who persuades such an audience may have to use premises drawn from its field of beliefs and commitments even though these grounds of assent would be rejected by a more competent audience. For responsible speakers, such occasions pose an obvious dilemma, sometimes escaped by designing a message that would be acceptable to the most competent audience and at the same time is persuasive to the audience addressed. Occasionally the dilemma cannot be escaped, and with reference to it Quintilian remarked that the advocate might need to deceive a bad judge in order to make justice prevail.

What is the ideal condition of deliberation? Chaim Perelman provides an ideal involving address to the "universal audience," a pivotal concept in his theory of rhetoric and argumentation. The universal audience refers to a class of ideal hearers or readers to whom an arguer appeals as the perfectly reasonable and impartial audience. This audience would not be influenced by such things as flattery, prejudices, local conventions, private preferences, falsehoods, and invalid reasoning. It would be influenced instead by fact and truth, by reality, and by faultless reasoning. Statements and arguments which win the assent of the universal audience secure authoritative confirmation as true and sound. In other words, the universal audience is a model or standard of perfection; it provides "a norm for objective argumentation." Any actual audience may be evaluated in terms of how nearly it approximates this ideal. Furthermore, any message may be evaluated in terms of how much of it would be accepted by the universal audience: "In general, a speaker or writer who desires to win the adherence of the universal audience will give up arguments that this audience—as he conceives it—would find inadmissible, even when he is addressing a particular audience. He will deem it almost immoral to resort to an argument which is not, in his own eyes, a rational one." The universal audience is never fully realized in an actual, or particular, audience, but exists as an ideal formulated by the speaker or by a group, profession, or culture. All normal persons are capable of membership in the universal audience at some times and on some matters provided they accept only what is true and reasonable. But when preferences, values, and aspirations exert influence, this audience ceases to be "universal" (Perelman & Olbrechts-Tyteca, 1969, pp. 13-14).

Aristotle's portrait of persons ideally suited to political deliberation has features we have already noticed. First, they have the commitment to rationality, fact, and truth mentioned by Perelman. However, their excellence is displayed chiefly in deliberations about matters contingent, indeterminate, and actionable, when choice necessarily involves pleasure and pain, emotion, and preference. In the second place, therefore, Aristotle's ideal agents exercise their perfected moral and intellectual virtues, chiefly practical wisdom, for the purpose of deliberating well and making reliable choices. Third, this class of persons, limited to those having practical wisdom, is small in number relative to the whole population because only a few people possess the essential qualities.

Shifting from the ideal to the real, let us ask, What sort of group actually deliberates about and decides most of the public's business? For the most part, the public's business is conducted by what we may call assigned-function organizations—that is, organizations of persons elected or appointed to perform functions mandated by law, custom, or decree of a parent organization. Such organizations include legislative assemblies, commissions, school boards, special committees, juries, judicial panels, and the like. Members deliberate among themselves; also they are addressed by speakers from outside their ranks. Among the characteristics of the assigned-function organization are these: (1) It has an assigned jurisdiction or area of concern; that is, it is established to handle a class of problems or exigencies. (2) It is duty-bound to fulfill its functions expeditiously, faithfully, and with a view to the public interest. Frequently the organization's adherence to these goals is enforced by rules. (3) It usually has considerable duration. A jury may serve for weeks or months, and some governmental bodies have continued existence even while membership changes. (4) As a consequence of these characteristics, the organization tends to be well informed about matters within its scope, motivated by the right interests, and guided by familiar principles and methods. (5) Its members ordinarily are selected because of known qualifications; or, if elected, there is at least the possibility that electors will select members on recognition of their knowledge and skill. At any rate, as a result of working together for a period of time, they come to possess common knowledge and interests, and so they come to have even greater homogeneity. (6) As its experience increases, this organization becomes increasingly stable and self-confident and settles into more and more uniform procedures. (7) It has power which it appreciates and protects, and so it resists efforts to change its power, methods, and standards; also, often laws and conventions establish protections to allow the organization to do its work without undue pressures from outside. Owing to these characteristics, the assigned-function organization is far more competent than citizens selected at random. Political entities entrust to such organizations the conduct of important categories of public business. Legal decisions, legislation, policies, and similar matters result from their deliberations.

If we look for organizations and groups that conduct the public's business through somewhat formal deliberation, we can find none except assigned-function organizations. Other groups, it is true, are addressed by political speakers and sometimes make decisions—such groups as special-interest organizations, institutional and elite audiences, and the public at large; but it is very doubtful that these engage in the kind of political deliberation that would make their decisions right. The reason genuine deliberation sometimes occurs outside assigned-function organizations is either that some sponsors and speakers take special pains to promote it or that the individual citizen initiates deliberation alone or with associates.

Two facts seem ominously important. The first is that the public at large is not a deliberative organization, and the second is that great numbers of citizens live out their lives having never participated in rigorous political deliberation. Perhaps the whole public cannot become a deliberative body, and perhaps most individuals cannot become competent citizens; if so, then maybe it is a good thing that assigned-function organizations conduct the public's business. On the other hand, assigning the duties of citizenship to a few persons may actually cultivate an even larger class of incompetent citizens.

A third important fact is that political messages addressed to the general public are ordinarily shallow—a description applicable to campaign discourse, presidential messages, and some press reporting and commentary, to name a few examples. Analysis of those messages will show that they seldom invite deliberation, and we may suspect the reason traces to the fact that they are meant to engage a public that is not prepared to deliberate.

There are, then, large problems for all who hold that the public should be competent and that political communication should engage it responsibly in processes of decision-making. The problems we have noted relate to political rhetoric on local and national scales, which at once reminds us that the problems of political competence are larger. In fact, we should conceive the whole of mankind as a single massive public whose vital interests are at stake, who require proper representation in assemblies empowered to conduct their business, and who need to acquire an art of judging rightly as citizens of the world. A daring political strategy assisted by the most artful communication will be needed to create a competent world community out of the divisions that now exist.

REFERENCES

Aristotle. *Rhetoric* (W. R. Roberts, trans.). Oxford: Clarendon Press, 1946.
Aristotle. *Politics* (B. Jowett, trans.). Cleveland: Fine Editions Press, 1952.
Aristotle. *Nicomachaean ethics* (M. Ostwald, trans.). Indianapolis: Bobbs-Merrill, 1962.
Bitzer, L. F. The rhetorical situation. *Philosophy and Rhetoric, 1*, 1968.
Bitzer, L. F. Rhetoric and public knowledge. In D. M. Burks (Ed.), *Rhetoric, philosophy and literature: An exploration*. West Lafayette: Purdue University Press, 1978.

Bitzer, L. F. Functional communication: A situational perspective. In E. E. White (Ed.), *Rhetoric in transition: Studies in the nature and uses of rhetoric.* University Park: Pennsylvania State University Press, 1980.

Burke, K. *A grammar of motives and a rhetoric of motives.* Cleveland: World Publishing, 1962.

DeQuincey, T. In F. Burwick (Ed.), *Selected essays on rhetoric.* Carbondale: Southern Illinois University Press, 1967.

Dewey, J. *The public and its problems.* Chicago: Swallow Press, 1927.

Howell, W. S. *Logic and rhetoric in England, 1500-1700.* Princeton: Princeton University Press, 1956.

Kennedy, G. A. *Classical rhetoric and its Christian and secular tradition from ancient to modern times.* Chapel Hill: University of North Carolina Press, 1980.

Lippmann, W. L. Speech presented at a convocation sponsored by the Center for the Study of Democratic Institutions, Beverly Hills, California, in *The Capital Times,* Madison, Wisconsin, May 9, 1966.

Perelman, C., & Olbrechts-Tyteca, L. *The new rhetoric: A treatise on argumentation.* Notre Dame: Notre Dame University Press, 1969.

Plato. *The Dialogues* (B. Jowett, trans.). New York: Random House, 1937.

Quintilian. *Institutes of oratory* (H. E. Butler, trans.). Cambridge: Harvard University Press, 1958.

Rhetorica ad herennium (H. Caplan, trans.). Cambridge: Harvard University Press, 1954.

Ziman, J. *Public knowledge: The social dimensions of science.* Cambridge: Cambridge University Press, 1968.

CHAPTER 9

Political Advertising

Lynda Lee Kaid

> All advertising, whether it lies in the field of business or of politics, will
> carry success by the continuity and regular uniformity of application. . . .
> The great masses of the people . . . will more easily fall victims to a great
> lie than to a small one [Hitler, 1940, pp. 240, 313].

Political advertising and political propaganda are undoubtedly as old as
communication itself. From earliest times, governments and leaders, both in and
out of power, have found it advantageous to advertise their accomplishments.
It is, however, probably fair to say that the modern preoccupation with the
effects of such efforts owes its genesis to the development of mass channels of
communication. It is also undoubtedly true that political advertising is the most
controversial and, perhaps, most feared form of political communication. Political advertising and propaganda have been accused of many evils, including the
creation of Hitler's Third Reich, the selling of candidates like soap, the creation
of candidate images which bear no relation to reality, and the destruction of the
political system by emphasizing personalities over issues.

While political advertising and propaganda can and do operate in almost any
setting in which government/political systems and their leaders/spokesmen must
compete for the approval, tolerance, and/or votes of a populace, the unique
characteristics of political advertising as it operates through mass channels in
democratic systems to woo voters during election campaigns have merited the
greatest scholarly, as well as popular, attention in recent years. Consequently,
the following analysis will make no effort to trace the long history of political
propaganda in other settings or to consider the transmission of political messages
through channels other than the mass media.

That political advertising of this type—through mass channels in electoral settings—occupies a preeminent role in our political system is at least partly a result of the increasing dominance of broadcast media, particularly television. In 1956, for instance, both parties spent a combined total of over $9 million on radio and television time in the presidential campaign (Dreyer, 1964). Only 16 years later, in 1972, broadcasters sold over $56 million worth of time to candidates for various political offices (Szybillo & Hartenbaum, 1976). In the 1976 general election, the two major party candidates for president spent $17 million on television ads alone (Devlin, 1977). Whether the lies be great or small or lies at all, most modern politicians clearly believe in the success of regular uniformity of application.

Explicit definitions of political advertising are not prevalent in the political communication literature. In fact, perusal of the literature seems to indicate that most scholars and practitioners use the term to mean simply "advertising whose content is political," and this may be a most convenient description. In order to highlight certain characteristics of political advertising, I suggest that political advertising might be considered the communication process by which a source (usually a political candidate or party) purchases the opportunity to expose receivers through mass channels to political messages with the intended effect of influencing their political attitudes, beliefs, and/or behaviors.

The unique element of this definition is, of course, the *purchased* or *paid* nature of the communication. The paid aspect of political advertising is particularly important because it gives the source the right to control the form and content of the message. This characteristic of political advertising and the assumptions that accompany it have resulted in a strong distinction between "advertising" and "news" in the political arena. Throughout the literature this distinction is described as a dichotomy between paid and unpaid media, purposive and nonpurposive communication, controlled and uncontrolled media, intentional and unintentional communication.

The other elements of the above definition are, of course, a mere application of the famous Lasswell (1948) explication of communication as "Who Says What to Whom in What Channel with What Effect." After a brief discussion of the implications of past and current political communication theory and an overview of the legal and regulatory environment in which political advertising operates, this analysis will consider the current state of research in political advertising in regard to sources, messages, channels, receivers, and effects. A discussion of methodological concerns and suggestions for future research will be offered as a conclusion.

THEORETICAL IMPLICATIONS

A few studies of political advertising predate the classic empirical voting behavior studies (Berelson, Lazarsfeld, & McPhee, 1954; Campbell, Converse,

Miller, & Stokes, 1960; Lazarsfeld, Berelson, & Gaudet, 1944) to which most modern political communication scholars trace the genesis of their discipline, but these few studies clearly operate from the same theoretical perspective. Known alternately as the "direct effects," the "hypodermic needle," or the "bullet" models, most early research was based on the premise that message stimuli would have direct and uniform effects on the audiences to which they were directed. The demise of this perspective requires little elaboration. Most such research found little support for a direct effects interpretation of political media or messages. resulting in the adoption of the "limited effects" model. Joseph Klapper (1960) is widely credited with the first comprehensive articulation of the limited effects position when he declared that the mass media generally serve as reinforcing agents and generally have few effects, political or otherwise, because they operate through a nexus of mediating factors (primarily audience predispositions resulting in selective exposure, attention, retention, and perception). Excellent reviews of the specifics of the progression from direct to limited effects perspectives in the study of political communication can be found elsewhere (Atkin, 1980; Kraus & Davis, 1976; Martin, 1976; Sanders, 1978, Sears & Whitney, 1973).

Recently, researchers have begun to wonder if the direct effects perspective was rejected prematurely. Kraus and Davis (1976) have identified several characteristics of the early research (in which limited effects were found) which seem to reduce the utility of that research when applied to modern political communication. Among the most important limitations are that (1) such studies fail to treat the mass media as serious variables, (2) most studies predate the domination of television in politics, and (3) audience predispositions such as party identification seem to be weakening. Other scholars suggest that the preoccupation with affective rather than cognitive/informational effects may have obscured findings (McCombs & Shaw, 1972) and/or that more attention should be paid to the "functions" which political communications serve for receivers (Blumler, Katz, & Gurevitch, 1974).

These criticisms of early work apply to political advertising research as well as to other political communication research. Two other criticisms of the research on which the limited effects model is based are particularly relevant here. First, most such research was based on presidential elections and therefore focused on situations in which voter involvement and interest and candidate familiarity could be expected to be high. Second, none of this research treats political advertising as distinct from other media information. The research reviewed later in this analysis clearly substantiates the view that political advertising does have distinct, identifiable effects on audience beliefs, attitudes, and behaviors; and much of this evidence is predicated on completely opposing assumptions—that low levels of involvement in some election situations combine with the nature of advertising, particularly on television, to result in considerable voter impact.

LEGAL AND REGULATORY ENVIRONMENT

Most federal regulations of political advertising govern the broadcast media. Many states have individual statutes which prohibit anonymous political advertising or the distribution of anonymous literature, although some authorities have suggested that such laws may be unconstitutional under Talley v. California (Jones & Kaid, 1976).

The broadcast media operate under different constraints. The Federal Communications Act of 1934, as amended, requires broadcasters to sell equal time to all legally qualified candidates for federal office. When a station sells time to any candidate—whether for local, state, or federal office—the station must make the time available at the lowest unit rate. In addition, stations must keep records of all ads and their sponsorship, and Federal Communications Commission regulations require all ads to carry disclaimers, indicating who paid for the ad. Any broadcast entity is expressly prohibited from exercising censorship of any kind over the content of political advertising (National Association of Broadcasters, 1976).

Political commercials are not regulated to ensure truth or prohibit distortion of deception as is product advertising (Spero, 1980). Beyond traditional libel suits, which are difficult to sustain where public figures are concerned, a candidate's only recourse against deceptive or untruthful advertising is appeal to the voluntary procedures of the Fair Campaign Practices Committee. In recent years, a substantial percentage of the complaints received by this body have concerned advertising through radio, television, newspapers, or other media (Archibald, 1971).

Congress has tried other methods of regulating political advertising. The Federal Election Campaign Act of 1971 (PL 92-225) responded to concerns about high broadcast advertising expenditures by setting maximum limits of ten cents per voter which could be spent by presidential, Senate, or House candidates on advertising. Up to 60 percent of this total could be used for broadcast media (Congressional Quarterly, 1971). Subsequent reforms and amendments superseded these requirements by setting overall spending limits for primary and general elections at various electoral levels (Agranoff, 1976), but all of these spending limits were declared unconstitutional by the 1976 Buckley v. Valeo decision. Only a presidential candidate who accepts federal financing can constitutionally be held to spending limits. This decision should be interpreted as invalidating any state expenditure limits, as well (Jones & Kaid, 1976).

The fact that political advertising is subject to so little regulation is partly responsible for the popular concerns about its use. Current laws simply provide no check on the form or content of such messages, leaving considerable opportunity for abuse. There is considerable opportunity for current and future research to serve as a guide for policy changes in this area.

SOURCE

The major focus of political advertising research has been on the receiver and on the effects, with very little attention to source credibility, status, or attractiveness (Nimmo, 1978); although considerable attention has been paid to candidate image as it is perceived by voters or as it is affected by messages.

Popular speculation on this topic indicates that many fear political television advertising has increased the success of attractive, movie-star-type candidates. The election of Ronald Reagan as President will undoubtedly, though perhaps wrongly, be cited as supporting this view. The assumption underlying this concern is that the public may be misled by a glib performer who substitutes style for the substance we should expect from candidates for public office. This concern rests on the premise that the preceived nature of the source has an effect on voter behavior, a proposition which has not been empirically demonstrated in political advertising research, although there is some indirect evidence to be found in the more general body of research on source credibility (McGuire, 1968).

The use of neutral or nonpartisan groups or individuals has often been recommended in television ads because such sources are presumed to be perceived as objective (Hy, 1973). Research by Andreoli and Worchel (1978) lends some credence to this belief. In an experimental study, the researchers found that high credibility sources such as a newscaster or a former, retired politician were generally more effective than a current officeholder or a candidate.

The accuracy of message perception in political ads apparently is also related to source credibility. Meyer and Donohue (1973) reported that students are more likely to misperceive the content of political radio commercials for highly credible sources. These inaccuracies are in the direction of the subject's own position on the issues involved, indicating that the subject reads favorable positions into the messages of favored candidates. This relationship is somewhat less strong when television, rather than radio, political ads are considered, although more misperceptions occur for high credibility sources on high salience issues than on low salience issues (Donohue, 1973b).

MESSAGE

Message variables have generated somewhat more concern than have source variables in political advertising research, although little research has considered the content characteristics of political ads or attempted to relate content to effects (Sanders & Kaid, 1978). Studies which consider the content of political ads fall into two basic categories, those which offer impressionistic, descriptive analysis of advertising content and strategies and those which offer systematic content analyses. In the former category, Tucker (1959) analyzed the radio and television advertising in the 1956 Oregon Senate campaign between Wayne

Morse and Douglas McKay, concluding that part of Morse's success may have been due to his wide assortment of program lengths and formats and to his superior ability to project positive "personality" characteristics. A similar effort by Rose and Fuchs (1968) considered the film techniques and content of television spots used by Reagan and Brown in the 1966 California gubernatorial contest. Here, the opposite strategy appeared most successful, since winner Reagan used simple production techniques and issue-oriented spots. Devlin's (1973, 1977) careful analyses of the techniques and content of the television commercials used by both candidates during the 1972 and 1976 presidential elections provide useful data on campaign strategies and on the intended effects of such advertising.

Only political advertising on television or in newspapers has been subjected to systematic content analysis, and in both cases the results have been surprising in light of popular criticism of political advertising as a purveyor of nonsubstantive, issueless information. Mullen (1963a, 1963b, 1968) conducted a series of content analyses of newspaper ads in presidential and senatorial campaigns. Using a sample of 1231 ads appearing in 90 newspapers during the last two weeks of the 1960 presidential campaign (Mullen, 1963b) and a sample of 1864 ads in the 1964 presidential campaign (Mullen, 1968), he compared number and size of ads for each candidate, the use of pictures, and the appeals contained in the aids. In both cases, the candidates' ads contained large numbers of appeals related to domestic and foreign issues. In a more limited study of the use of newspaper ads in 1960 Senate campaigns, Mullen (1963a) used similar techniques and found a significantly higher use of pictures by Senate candidates than by presidential candidates and a tendency for Senate candidates to use more vague appeals.

Had Mullen used categories which reflected use of candidate personality, image, or qualifications content, his work would be easier to compare with two subsequent newspaper advertising analyses. An analysis of 849 ads used in presidential campaigns between 1932 and 1960 in a small Midwestern daily newspaper found that the candidate was the central or comparison theme in 78 percent of all the ads. The candidate alone was featured 49 percent of the time, the candidate with an issue 23 percent, the candidate with the political party 6 percent, issues alone 15 percent, and party alone only 7 percent (Humke, Schmitt, & Grupp, 1975). In an analysis of 820 ads for 1970 senate, gubernatorial, and congressional candidates in 23 states, Bowers (1972) found issues constituted 46 percent of the assertions in the ads compared to 37 percent candidate personality and 8 percent various other assertions. Within each level of race, only congressional candidates concentrated more on candidate characteristics than on issues.

There is no question that this differentiation between issue and image has been the focus of concern about the content of political advertising. This concern has its roots in the classic democratic voting theory assumptions that votes should be rational and, therefore, based on issues (Berelson, 1966; Jano-witz & Marvick, 1970). The accusation that political advertising, particularly on television, concentrates on candidate image rather than issues has generated tremendous popular controversy over advertising in campaigns at all levels. Yet content analyses of television ads do not indicate that their overall content warrants such concern.

Joslyn (1980) selected a sample of 156 television ads which were chosen not randomly, but to ensure balance in terms of partisanship, level of race, geo-graphic origin, electoral outcome, and candidate incumbency status. He found that 57.7 percent of the ads had issue content, although much of this was not specific issue positions. Only 47.4 percent mentioned candidate qualifications, and even fewer (39.7 percent) made a group-related appeal.

Recent studies of the 1972 presidential campaign have also indicated that the concern about image concentration in political television commercials may be overblown. McClure and Patterson (1976) report that 42 percent of all television ads used during this campaign were primarily issue-oriented and another 28 percent contained substantial issue information. Hofstetter and Zukin (1979) suggest an even higher percentage of issue content in these ads—85 percent of each candidate's ads included some issue information. Both studies compared the issue content of televised political ads to the issue content of televised news and found news to be inferior as a conveyor of issue information. In addition, Buss and Hofstetter (1976) found that television spots use ordinary logical styles, 90 percent of which are "cognitive maneuvers," such as using an example or making a distinction between two preceding notions. None of this research offers very compelling reasons for indicting the content of political ads.

One of the most interesting controversies in political commercials is related to the image content of spots. The question is whether candidate images are a result of what a candidate projects (and, therefore, message- or stimulus-determined) or a result of what a voter projects onto the candidate (perceiver-determined). Nimmo (1976) suggested that neither approach is sufficient alone and that a combination offers the most useful explanation of candidate image formation. Nonetheless, several studies have attempted to determine if one approach may be superior to the other. Brownstein's (1971) operationalization of the contro-versy pitted nonambiguous message commercials against the ambiguous, image-oriented commercials and found subjects in the experiment were more likely to misperceive the candidate (and vote for a candidate who was incompatible with their own predispositions) when they viewed an ambiguous spot. He concluded, however, that both approaches are useful predictors of candidate evaluation and vote choice. Baskin's (Note 1) less complex experiment simply analyzed subject responses to several 30-second ads (with no systematic message manipulation) and concluded that candidate image is more likely message- or stimulus-determined.

Most other research in which message variables play a role make some effort to compare the effect of two or more differing message characteristics. Related to the issue-image controversy, Kaid and Sanders (1978) conducted an experimental study of political television commercials which compared issue spots with image spots. They found that issue spots resulted in higher candidate evaluation, while image spots elicited more recall of information in the spot. A short (60-second) issue spot also resulted in the highest likelihood of voting for a candidate. In a 1935 Pennsylvania election, Hartmann (1936) compared the effect of Socialist party leaflets using "rational" appeals with those using "emotional" appeals and found the latter more effective.

The length of political messages on television has also been a subject of controversy, with some advertising agency personnel and political practitioners joining in proposals to set a minimum time of five minutes for television spots (Szybillo & Hartenbaum, 1976). This controversy has prompted only limited research. Swanson's (1973) survey of a small Illinois sample during the 1972 election validated that shorter television spots result in higher audience exposure and that the retention loss from such spots is only about half of that for longer (30-minute) programs. In a telephone survey of a larger sample in Florida during the same campaign, O'Keefe and Sheinkopf (1974) concluded that, since more long spots were used in 1972 and since voters could not seem to recall many campaign issues, long spots must not be very effective. However, this study provides no measure of differential exposure to long and short spots and should not be interpreted as a true test of the question. In an experimental study, Kaid and Sanders (1978) found that 5-minute spots resulted in higher candidate evaluation than 60-second spots but that content recall was not higher for the longer spot.

Of incidental interest is the finding by Donohue (1973a) that television political ads in color are judged as being of significantly higher quality and aesthetically more pleasing than the same commercials in black and white. These effects seem particularly strong for female viewers.

CHANNEL

Channel variables would seem to be one of the most theoretically and practically interesting variables in the study of political advertising, yet little directly applicable research has been done in this area. Marshall McLuhan's (1964) provocative speculations about "hot" and "cool" media, along with the widespread popular belief that different media have different effects, should have been sufficient stimulation for such research.

For the dissemination of political advertising messages, political candidates and parties use many mass channels and formats, including radio, television, newspapers, direct mail, magazines, billboards, various signs, brochures, bumper stickers, buttons, and other paraphernalia. The greatest expenditures generally go for advertising of the first four types, although lower-level races often rely on the other (mostly print channel) formats listed, and the increased ability to target and regionalize has made magazine ads more attractive to politicians (Muller, 1978).

Some survey research has provided evidence of the influence of varying channels. As sources of political information, television and newspapers are seen in different dimensions by voters. Atwood and Sanders (1975) found that, with the television medium, voters do not differentiate news from advertising, a situation which does not occur with newspapers. In one of the few surveys to consider multiple types of advertising (magazine ads, brochures, billboards, direct mail, as well as television, radio, and newspaper ads), DeVries and Tarrance (1972) found that ticket-splitters rate all advertising as much less influential in making vote decisions than news-format information. In a rating of 35 potential types of influence, the highest ratings awarded any advertising formats were given to newspaper ads, brochures, and television ads which ranked twenty-second, twenty-third, and twenty-fourth, respectively. In a survey of voters in a state senate campaign, Kaid (1976) found that of 12 political advertising variables, newspaper ads and brochures had a higher correlation with the vote than did radio ads, billboards, bumper stickers, and other advertising.

None of the survey data reported above provides an authentic test of channel variation, since none holds other communication variables, such as message content, constant. For this reason, experimental studies should be more successful at isolating channel differences, but to date the only experimental studies that have considered channel variables have discovered no effects attributable solely to differences between radio and television ads (Cohen, 1976) or among radio, television, and newspaper versions of the same ad (Andreoli & Worchel, 1978; Brownstein, 1971).

Apparently, however, channel variables appear to interact with the source of a political advertisement. Cohen (1976) found that some candidates are simply more effective on radio, and some are more effective on television. Andreoli and Worchel (1978) present findings demonstrating that source trustworthiness interacts with the medium such that low credibility sources (candidates) are least effective on television while high credibility sources (newscasters) are most effective on that medium.

RECEIVER

Since a major tenet of the limited effects perspective in political communication was the belief that receiver predispositions mediated the effects of political messages, considerable attention has been focused on the selective processes which might operate in political advertising. Most of the concern has centered on partisanship or candidate preference as a reason for selective exposure or perception, since voting behavior research has stressed the importance of partisan identification as a long-term force (Campbell et al., 1960).

One of the practical arguments in favor of short political spots on television has been that they might overcome selective exposure tendencies of the receiver because of their length and positioning within entertainment programming. Since the limited effects position was outlined by Klapper (1960), there has been increasing justification for questioning the legitimacy of receiver exposure patterns based on a predisposition to consonant information (Freedman & Sears, 1965). In the area of television political advertising, this principle should be discarded. Atkin, Bowen, Nayman, and Sheinkopf (1973) provided the first empirical demonstration of this when they studied the 1970 Wisconsin and Colorado gubernatorial elections and found that availability of television spots overcame partisan selectivity. Subsequently, researchers have found that voters did not consciously avoid exposure to communications for opposition candidates or parties in the 1972 presidential election (Bowers, 1977; Hofstetter & Buss, 1980; Mendelsohn & O'Keefe, 1976; Surlin & Gordon, 1976; Swanson, 1973, 1976).

Despite the expectation that longer political programs might be more subject to partisan selective exposure (Schramm & Carter, 1959), it now appears that even receiver exposure to programs of 30 minutes or so is not a result of partisan selectivity (Mendelsohn & O'Keefe, 1976; Swanson, 1973; Hale, Kaid, & Fahey, Note 2). Overall, it appears that frequency of television viewing may be a better predictor of exposure to political television ads than any partisan predisposition of the receiver, although limited evidence suggests the possibility that attention and/or retention may be selective (Atkin et al., 1973; Surlin & Gordon, 1976).

Whether this lack of selectivity is true for exposure in other media has been the subject of too little research to allow an informed conclusion. There is some evidence that political direct mail may be subject to partisan selective exposure (Bartlett, Drew, Fahle, & Watts, 1974), but there is little reason to believe this applies to other print media.

Once a receiver is exposed to a political advertising message, however, there is some evidence that selective perception can be a powerful obstacle to persuasion (Sears & Whitney, 1973). Conclusions from both laboratory experiments and survey research are in accord that partisanship and/or candidate/issue compatibility can result in misperceptions of political advertising content. In experimental studies of radio ads (Meyer & Donohue, 1973) and television ads (Donohue, 1973b), subject predispositions resulted in inaccurate interpretations of political advertising content, with source credibility and/or issue salience interacting with the degree and type of misperception. Mendelsohn and O'Keefe (1976) found a somewhat different, but no less selective, process operating in their 1972 presidential election survey when they discovered selective preception in the evaluation of characteristics of favored candidates' commercials.

The question of whether candidate images are message/stimulus-determined or perceiver/receiver-determined has been discussed briefly above; and, while limited research has indicated some support for a message-determined view, this is by no means a settled question in political communication research. Nimmo and Savage's (1976, p. 8) definition of image as "a human construct imposed on an array of perceiver attributes projected by an object, event or person" clearly demonstrates their belief that a candidate's image is multifaceted and dynamic, an interaction between what a candidate projects and what a voter perceives. The question with which political advertising research must be concerned, then, is: In what ways do receiver characteristics affect this interactive, dynamic process as political advertising messages are received/perceived?

Several theoretical positions bear on this question, but little research has evaluated them. For instance, Stephenson's (1967) play theory of mass communication maintains that people engage the media primarily for the purpose of entertainment or "subjective play." In terms of political media, Stephenson's concept would suggest viewers expose themselves to political media to enjoy the drama and conflict of politics; and advertising—particularly typical television formats—may be the supreme method of dramatization for a political candidate and, therefore, a highly effective means of persuasion (Combs, 1980). Certainly, many practitioners feel that the ability to stir emotions and to evoke feelings through dramatic television spots is the key to voter response (Schwartz, 1974).

This belief that voters may be more engaged in entertainment than in information-seeking when viewing television advertising is related to the research on how the involvement level of receivers affects political advertising reception. Much of this research has its basis in Zajonc's (1968) findings that increased exposure to a stimulus enhances evaluation of that stimulus, particularly under conditions where three or more stimuli are repeated three or more times and where stimuli are relatively unfamiliar. Krugman's (1965) application of this concept to advertising is well known. His contention is that, with repeated stimuli (product advertising), behavioral change may precede attitudinal change, since the audience lets down its guard to television commercials due to low levels of involvement. Krugman has called this process "learninig without involvement."

The usefulness of these perspectives in political advertising has been carefully outlined by Rothschild (1978). In political advertising, the level of receiver involvement is the key concept. Under conditions of high voter involvement, one can expect that attitudes must be affected before behaviors change. On the other hand, when voter involvement is low, a voter may receive information from candidate ads without evaluating the message or source carefully and may therefore display behavioral effects prior to attitude change. This position would suggest that the adoption of a limited effects perspective was partly due to the fact that most early research occurred in limited situations—that is, presidential elections which were probably high in involvement and in message/source familiarity. Atkin (1980) posited a contextual framework for analyzing campaign persuasion which is quite similar. He suggests that communication impact is a result of the degree of campaign definition (extent to which attributes are available to distinguish candidates), the level of voter involvement, and the stage of voter decision-making. Thus, the greatest media impact could be expected in situations/elections where there is low voter involvement, low campaign definition, and high predecisional uncertainty.

One experimental study and several survey research projects have considered the effects of levels of voter involvement on reactions to political advertising— again, usually televised advertising. The most comprehensive treatment of the factors involved occurred in Rothschild and Ray's (1974) experiment, which used a factorial design, varying number of repetitions of the commercials (0-6), type of election (national, congressional, and state legislative), and level of voter involvement (low, zero-order, high). The results indicated that repetition of ads increased recall for all three types of elections, but the effect was much more pronounced at state legislative and congressional levels, with little effect on attitude but some effect on vote intention. Low levels of involvement proved to have a clear relationship to increased political advertising effects.

These experimental findings have had almost unanimous confirmation in survey projects. Hofstetter and Buss (1980) found that when voter involvement was low, paid advertising stimulated turnout and caused changes in candidate preference during the 1972 campaign. Both spots and longer paid television programs, along with other media sources, were associated with increased political knowledge and issue information, and this relationship was stronger for voters with low, rather than high, involvement (Hoffstetter, Zukin, & Buss, 1978). McClure and Patterson (1974) reported similar findings in that same election. Additional confirmation has been provided by an innovative application of laboratory techniques to analysis of aggregate election data. Using data from the 1972 congressional primaries (which can easily be classified as low involvement), Grush, McKeough, and Ahlering (1978) divided all races into categories according to how well they satisfied laboratory research conditions relating message exposure (amount of media expenditures) and stimuli familiarity (candidate visiblity and incumbency). Using regression and path analysis, the researchers then substantiated a strong relation between amount of advertising expenditure and election outcome, particularly in cases where candidates were novel and unfamiliar.

Results which run counter to these findings were produced by Mulder's (1979) study of political television advertising in the 1975 Chicago mayoral race, where high/low voter involvement did not appear to be an intervening variable.

One word of caution in interpreting all of these results is in order—it is clear that consistent definitions and measures of "involvement" are not present throughout.

Few receiver variables other than selectivity and involvement have received much attention in political advertising research. Limited consideration has been given to the effects of various demographic characteristics of voters. Illustrative is the research of Surlin and Gordon (1976, 1977), who report that voters with higher education and higher socioeconomic status also found political spots which attacked the opposition to be more unethical but more informative than did respondents with midsocioeconomic status (Surlin & Gordon, 1977). Patterson and McClure (1976) also compared demographic groups, finding that women and those with lower education, lower incomes, and high and low ages were exposed to more television spots during the 1972 election.

Because of the receiver-orientation of the uses and gratifications perspective, the resurgence of interest in this theoretical position in mass and political communication could have been expected to spawn interesting research on receiver variables in political advertising. To date, however, efforts using this paradigm to evaluate political advertising have been limited.

Blumler and McQuail's (1969) original effort to derive patterns of audience gratifications in the 1964 British general election was based on voter responses to televised party programs. Although such programs in Britain are generally longer than spot announcements and are not candidate-purchased, they bear similarities to American political advertising. Blumler and McQuail found that reasons related to surveillance, vote guidance and reinforcement, and excitement were the dominant factors in voter exposure to political programming. Few have tried to apply or extend these concepts in relation to political advertising in the United States. Swanson (1976) reported that voters attend to political ads because they think the information will be useful. Hale et al. (Note 2) discovered that voter reasons for watching a 30-minute television advertisement during the 1976 presidential primaries were similar to those found by Blumler and McQuail.

Advertisements may perform important functions for campaign and party workers. Not surprisingly, such individuals tend to pay more attention to ads than the average voter and report that ads bolster their morale and confidence and provide substantive information on their candidate and his qualifications (Sheinkopf, Atkin, & Bowen, 1972, 1973). Perhaps of greater interest have been the few findings that indicate that voter gratifications can interact with a political advertising message to determine the nature of the effect such ads will produce (McLeod & Becker, 1974; Hale et al., Note 2).

EFFECT

In the years immediately following the pervasive spread of the limited effects perspective, it was considered somewhat unsophisticated and, perhaps, uninformed, to believe that political advertising—or other political communications for that matter—had any effects. It is ironic that the adoption of this perspective in scholarly circles coincided with gigantic increases in expenditures for political advertising, particularly in the television medium. Political practitioners clearly did not and do not now share scholarly reservations about the effects of political advertising (McGinniss, 1969; Napolitan, 1972; Steinberg, 1976; Wyckoff, 1968).

Throughout this analysis many reasons have been mentioned for questioning the assumptions on which the limited effects perspective rests. One more reason seems necessary here. Early direct effects researchers may have been inordinately restrictive in their definition of *effects,* concentrating primarily on affective and behavioral effects with little attention to cognitive effects.

Cognitive Effects

Much of the renewed interest in the direct effects of political advertising owes its roots to increased interest in cognitive effects. Researchers have been increasingly excited about the ways political advertising appears to increase voter knowledge and awareness of issues.

In the 1964 British elections, Blumler and McQuail (1969) identified surveillance as a key motive for voter exposure to political programs; and subsequent research in the United States has clearly demonstrated that political advertising can result in substantial information acquisition. Patterson and McClure (1976) documented the fact that political television ads in the 1972 presidential election caused substantial changes in voter beliefs, and other surveys have confirmed a positive relationship between advertising exposure/attention and levels of political information and knowledge in that election (Hofstetter & Buss, 1980; Hofstetter, Zukin, & Buss, 1978; Mendelsohn & O'Keefe, 1976). These associations appear valid in lower-level races as well. Kaid (1976) reported that, in a state senate race, political advertising in the print media resulted in voter issue awareness; while Mulder (1979) found exposure to television ads was correlated with issue concerns in a mayoral election, and Atkin and Heald (1976) isolated high correlations between exposure and attention to radio and television ads and knowledge about candidates and issues in a 1974 Michigan congressional campaign. Political advertising may also play a role in political socialization, since even children appear to gain knowledge about candidates from political advertising (Atkin, 1977).

It should not be surprising that political advertising has such direct effects on information gain. Viewed from the perspective of Anthony Downs's (1957) economic theory of voting, a voter would find the "cost" of acquiring information via advertising, particularly television spots, to be very low.

Agenda-setting functions have also been theorized for political advertising. It may be possible for a candidate to use his political advertising to communicate an agenda of issues to the public. Such results have been noted for newspaper ads in 1970 senate and gubernatorial campaigns (Bowers, 1973), in a 1972 state campaign (Kaid, 1976), and for a 30-minute paid program by Ronald Reagan in the 1976 Texas presidential primary (Hale et al., Note 2). Much lower associations, however, were reported when comparing voter issue agenda with candidate television advertising agenda in the 1972 presidential election (Bowers, 1977). As in all agenda-setting findings, it is important to remember that the *direction* of the causal relationship is not clear here. It has not been possible to ascertain if political advertising actually structures voter agenda or whether the advertising simply reflects those issues which opinion polls indicate are voter concerns.

Affective Effects

Affective components of advertising effects have most often taken the form of evaluations of political candidates. Various measuring techniques have been utilized, with the overall goal of determining the degree of positive feeling toward the candidate or identification with his personality/image attributes.

The evidence that political advertising affects candiate evaluation has been less convincing than the evidence for cognitive effects. Patterson and McClure (1976) reported little change in candidate images from 1972 presidential television ads, a result confirmed by Hofstetter et al. (1978). In the 1976 primary elections, viewers of a 30-minute paid program did not evaluate the presidential candidate involved more positively after viewing (Hale et al., Note 2). However, at lower election levels, exposure to broadcast advertising has been correlated with candidate evaluation (Atkin & Heald, 1976; Mulder, 1979), although direct mail advertising has not produced such favorable results for the candidate (Miller & Robyn, 1975). Positive affects toward candidates have also been reported to result from repetition of simple audio ads for candidates. Becker and Doolittle (1975) found a curvilinear relationship between frequency of advertising repetition and affect toward candidates—that is, moderate exposure/repetition produces higher affect than low or high exposure.

Behavioral Effects

The most common behavioral effects purported to result from political advertising are vote decisions and increased turnout. Obviously, other behavioral possibilities abound. A voter could be stimulated to seek additional information (Becker & Doolittle, 1975), to contribute money to a campaign, to try to persuade other voters, and so on. Only turnout and vote decision effects are considered here. The evidence for these behavioral effects generally takes one of three forms.

The first and least convincing evidence for behavioral effects of political advertising results from asking voters how important political advertising is to their vote decisions. By this measure, ads are not a major factor in the vote decisions of most ticket-splitters (DeVries & Tarrance, 1972), nor are they considered important by a majority of all voters (Mendelsohn & O'Keefe, 1976; Atkin et al., 1973). On the other hand, a substantial number of late deciders seem to perceive ads as helpful in finally arriving at a vote decision (Atkin et al., 1973).

A second type of evidence relating political advertising to voting behavior analyzes aggregate spending and voting data. Although Prisuta's (1972) analysis of Michigan legislative candidates found no relation between broadcast advertising expenditures and electoral outcomes (perhaps due to low overall broadcast usage), most other studies have demonstrated some relationship between advertising expenditures and winning elections, particularly in primaries and at electoral levels below the presidency (Dawson & Zinser, 1971; Grush, McKeough, & Ahlering, 1978; Jacobson, 1975; McClenaghan, 1980; Palda, 1975; Wanat, 1974). Early studies of direct mail showed it to be effective in stimulating turnout (Eldersveld & Dodge, 1954; Gosnell, 1927) and in influencing voters to support a 1953 ballot item in Ann Arbor, Michigan (Eldersveld & Dodge, 1954). It is, of course, difficult to argue for a direct causal relationship with evidence of this type.

A third type of evidence derives from specific survey and experimental research on political advertising. Here, too, the results have been mixed. Interestingly, the early empirical voting studies did not separate political advertising from other political media, and it is therefore impossible to evaluate their findings here (Berelson et al., 1954; Lazarsfeld et al., 1944).

The behavioral effects of political advertising in the print media have received no more attention than have other print media effects. Only two modern studies make more than an incidental attempt to measure print advertising effects. Miller and Robyn (1975) conducted a well-designed field experiment of direct mail effects in a congressional primary, finding no significant effects on turnout or candidate vote. This indicates that direct mail effects may be less strong in candidate election situations than in the nonpartisan and ballot efforts reported above (Eldersveld & Dodge, 1954; Gosnell, 1927). Kaid's (1976) survey of the effect of 12 political advertising variables (mostly print media variables) in a state senate campaign found that the advertising variables accounted for 18-19 percent of the overall variance in the vote, but for only 3 percent of the unique variance.

The evidence for vote decision and turnout is stronger for television ads. Hofstetter and Buss (1980) have found a positive association between late campaign exposure to spots and longer paid programs and vote turnout and changing candidate preferences. This association for voters in the 1972 presidential election was stronger for voters with low levels of involvement. Experimental studies have also found some effects on vote decisions from television ads, particularly when the advertising is issue-oriented (Dyson & Brownstein, 1979; Kaid & Sanders, 1978).

A few conclusions seem warranted by the above review of sources, messages, channels, receivers and effects of political advertising:

1. Contrary to popular criticism, political advertising contains a substantial amount of *issue* information.

2. In political advertising communications, channel variables probably interact with source variables such that some sources (usually candidates) are more effective on one medium than on another.

3. Political advertising on television overcomes partisan selective exposure but may be subject to selective attention, retention, and perception.

4. Political advertising is more effective when the level of voter involvement is low. This tends to be particularly true at electoral levels below the presidency.

5. Political advertising, particularly on television, may have its greatest effects at the cognitive level, increasing knowledge about candidates and issues.

6. There is also persuasive evidence that political advertising, particularly on television, has behavioral effects, directly influencing voting behavior.

METHODOLOGY

Methodological problems plague much of the research above. Most of us are never satisfied with any methodology, and the criticisms and suggestions here are offered in the hope that they will prove helpful to future researchers. The validity of survey research on political advertising continues to suffer from weak measures of receiver exposure. Most such studies rely on voter recall of advertising exposure, a particularly defective measuring device for stimuli which may have effects because they are not purposely sought and tend to operate at low involvement levels. Patterson and McClure (1976) have made some inroads with this problem by using diaries in which voters record their overall television viewing. Future researchers would do well to consider this approach and, finances allowing, to adopt other Nielsen approaches such as audimeters to determine exactly what and how much political advertising stimuli a voter receives. A voter might even record all media input (newspapers read, radio listening, television viewing, and so on) over a specified period in an overall media diary. This approach would not only allow more accurate measures of exposure, but could also provide the data to deal with another prevalent problem in survey research: the failure to correlate media message content with effects.

At this stage in the development of political advertising research, the laboratory and field experiment probably hold the key to isolating important variables and to generating more specific hypotheses for subsequent testing in survey situations. Such research has also been guilty of not going far enough to ensure valid results. One pervasive problem has been the poor and unrealistic quality of stimulus material. Some researchers have used simple slides, short audio messages without music, or actors representing candidates in simple face-on commercials. Stimuli need to approximate more closely the sophistication of current radio and television advertising production, and the experimenter should attempt to provide a more realistic viewing environment for exposure. This latter problem might be solved through innovative uses of cable and closed-circuit television systems now available in many areas, allowing subjects to view the stimuli in a home viewing environment. Both problems might be offset by adopting on-air testing methods used by product advertising research (Clancy & Ostlund, 1976), thus combining survey and experimental methods.

Laboratory researchers might also consider some of the interesting *measures* of advertising effectiveness used by product advertising researchers—galvanic skin responses, brain waves, eye movement, pupil dilation, and so on. Laboratory researchers could also attempt to improve external validity by adapting field experimental techniques or by recruiting subjects other than college students. Since the major randomness question in experimental research is the random assignment of subjects to experimental/stimulus conditions, researchers might consider using civic or other adult groups as population pools.

SUGGESTIONS FOR FUTURE RESEARCH

The foregoing analysis of research points up some areas where future research in political advertising is needed, and a few of these are briefly highlighted below.

1. More research is needed on how source variables affect political advertising reception. What aspects or elements of source credibility relate to cognitive, affective, and behavioral effects? With the increased role of women in the political system, consideration might be given to whether sex of the source makes a difference in perceptions of political advertising.

2. Channel variables have been seriously neglected. We do not know if messages with similar content are more effective when presented via a print, radio, or television medium. We do not know if issue information is communicated better through one channel and image information better through another channel. The possible questions of theoretical and practical value are almost endless in this area.

3. We need much more research on the ways in which message characteristics affect perceptions of political advertising. Research is needed on the effects of image-versus-issue messages, on the impact of varying cognitive styles of message presentation, and on the relative value of ethical, emotional, or logical proof

offered by a political message. The possible interaction of these message characteristics with source, channel, and receiver variables should also be studied.

4. The ways receivers process information from political ads and the functions such stimuli provide needs more attention. The uses and gratifications perspective (see Chapter 2 of this volume) offers much hope in this area but that hope has been unfulfilled at this point. Particularly fruitful would be additional efforts to link functions with effects, perhaps with message characteristics as an intervening variable.

5. Several unanswered research questions are of more practical and policy interest than theoretical interest but should be mentioned here. Does the content of political television advertising messages interact with surrounding program content? For instance, are political spots about crime problems more effective during detective shows than during situation comedies? Are there identifiable differences between effects of long and short spots? Would requiring candidates to appear in all television spots result in differences in effects or audience perceptions?

These suggestions are, of course, only illustrative, not exhaustive. Scholars are just beginning to explore in systematic fashion the infinite number of questions raised by earlier researchers, and there is much yet to be done. There are, however, few issues more fundamental to a democratic society than those pertaining to the process of transferring political power from one government to another. It is no exaggeration to note that political advertising in the modern political campaign is at the very heart of that process.

REFERENCE NOTES

1. Baskin, O. *The effects of televised political advertisements on candidate image.* Paper presented at the International Communication Association Convention, Portland, April 1976.
2. Hale, K., Kaid, L. L., & Fahey, J. *Measuring the impact of a televised political program: Combining three research perspectives.* Paper presented at the Speech Communication Association Convention, Washington, D.C., December 1977.

REFERENCES

Adamany, D. Financing national politics. In R. Agranoff (Ed.), *The new style in election campaigns* (2nd ed.). Boston: Holbrook Press, 1976.

Agranoff, R. (Ed.). *The new style in election campaigns* (2nd ed.). Boston: Halbrook Press, 1976.

Andreoli, V., & Worchel, S. Effects of media, communicator and message position on attitude change. *Public Opinion Quarterly,* 1978, *42,* 59-70.

Archibald, S. J. *The pollution of politics.* Washington, DC: Public Affairs Press, 1971.

Atkin, C. K. Effects of campaign advertising and newscasts on children. *Journalism Quarterly,* 1977, *54,* 503-508.

Atkin, C. K. Political campaigns: Mass communication and persuasion. In M. E. Roloff & G. R. Miller (Eds.), *Persuasion: New directions in theory and research.* Beverly Hills, CA: Sage, 1980.

Atkin, C. K., Bowen, L., Nayman, O. B., & Sheinkopf, K. G. Quality versus quantity in televised political ads. *Public Opinion Quarterly,* 1973, *37,* 209-224.

Atkin, C. K., & Heald, G. Effects of political advertising. *Public Opinion Quarterly,* 1976, *40,* 216-228.

Atwood, L. E., & Sanders, K. R. Perceptions of information sources and likelihood of split-ticket voting. *Journalism Quarterly,* 1975, *52,* 421-428.

Barlett, D. K., Drew, P. B., Fahle, E. G., & Watts, W. A. Selective exposure to a presidential campaign appeal. *Public Opinion Quarterly,* 1974, *38,* 264-270.

Becker, L. B., & Doolittle, J. C. How repetition affects evaluations of information-seeking about candidates. *Journalism Quarterly,* 1975, *52,* 611-617.

Berelson, B. Democratic theory and public opinion. In B. Berelson & M. Janowitz (Eds.), *Reader in public opinion and communication.* New York: Free Press, 1966.

Berelson, B., Lazarsfeld, P., & McPhee, W. *Voting.* Chicago: University of Chicago Press, 1954.

Blumler, J. G., Katz, E., & Gurevitch, M. Utilization of mass communication by the individual. In J. G. Blumler & E. Katz (Eds.), *The uses of mass communications.* Beverly Hills, CA: Sage, 1974.

Blumler, J. G., & McQuail, D. *Television in politics.* Chicago: University of Chicago Press, 1969.

Bowers, T. A. Issue and personality information in newspaper political advertising. *Journalism Quarterly,* 1972, *49,* 446-452.

Bowers, T. A. Newspaper political advertising and the agenda-setting function. *Journalism Quarterly,* 1973, *50,* 552-556.

Bowers, T. A. Candidate advertising: The agenda is the message. In D. L. Shaw & M. E. McCombs (Eds.), *The emergence of American political issues.* St. Paul, MN: West Publishing, 1977.

Brownstein, C. Communication strategies and the electoral decision making process: Some results from experimentation. *Experimental Study of Politics,* 1971, July, 37-50.

Buss, T., & Hofstetter, C. R. An analysis of the logic of televised campaign advertisements: The 1972 presidential campaign. *Communication Research,* 1976, *3,* 367-392.

Campbell, A., Converse, P. E., Miller, W. E., & Stokes, D. E. *The American voter.* New York: John Wiley, 1960.

Clancy, K. J., & Ostlund, L. E. Commercial effectiveness measures. *Journal of Advertising Research,* 1976, *16,* 29-34.

Cohen, A. Radio vs. TV: The effect of the medium. *Journal of Communication,* 1976, *26,* 29-35.

Combs, J. E. *Dimensions of political drama.* Santa Monica, CA: Goodyear, 1980.

Congressional Quarterly. *Dollar politics* (Vol. I). Washington, DC: Congressional Quarterly, Inc., 1971.

Dawson, P. A., & Zinser, J. E. Broadcast expenditures and electoral outcomes in the 1970 congressional elections. *Public Opinion Quarterly,* 1971, *35,* 398-402.

Devlin, L. P. Contrasts in presidential campaign commercials of 1972. *Journal of Broadcasting,* 1973, *18,* 17-26.

Devlin, L. P. Contrasts in presidential campaign commercials of 1976. *Central States Speech Journal,* 1977, *28,* 238-249.

DeVries, W., & Tarrance, V. L. *The ticket-splitter.* Grand Rapids, MI: Eerdmans, 1972.

Donohue, T. R. Viewer perceptions of color and black-and-white paid political advertising. *Journalism Quarterly,* 1973, *50,* 660-665. (a)

Donohue, T. R. Impact of viewer predispositions on political TV commercials. *Journal of Broadcasting,* 1973, *18,* 3-15. (b)

Downs, A. *An economic theory of democracy.* New York: Harper & Row, 1957.

Dreyer, E. C. Political party use of radio and television in the 1960 campaign. *Journal of Broadcasting,* 1964, *8,* 211-217.

Dyson, J. W., & Brownstein, C. N. Campaign information, attitudinal voting and the electoral context: An experimental investigation. *Experimental Study of Politics,* 1979, *7,* 1-19.

Eldersveld, S. J., & Dodge, R. W. Personal contact or mail propaganda: An experiment in voting turnout and attitude change. In D. Katz (Ed.), *Public opinion and propaganda.* New York: Dryden Press, 1954.

Freedman, J. L., & Sears, D. O. Selective exposure. In L. Berkowitz (Ed.), *Advances in experimental social psychology* (Vol. II). New York: Academic Press, 1965.

Gosnell, H. *Getting out the vote.* Chicago: University of Chicago Press, 1927.

Grush, J. E., Mc Keough, K. L., & Ahlering, R. F. Extrapolating laboratory research to actual political elections. *Journal of Personality and Social Psychology,* 1978, *36,* 257-270.

Hartmann, G. W. A field experiment on the comparative effectiveness of "emotional" and "rational" political leaflets in determining election results. *Journal of Abnormal Psychology,* 1936, *31,* 99-114.

Hitler, A. *Mein Kampf.* Reynal and Hitchock Publishers, 1940.

Hofstetter, C. R., & Buss, T. F. Politics and last-minute political television. *Western Political Quarterly,* 1980, *33,* 24-37.

Hofstetter, C. R., & Zukin, C. TV network news and advertising in the Nixon and McGovern campaigns. *Journalism Quarterly,* 1979, *56,* 106-115, 152.

Hofstetter, C. R., Zukin, C., & Buss, T. F. Political imagery and information in an age of television. *Journalism Quarterly,* 1978, *55,* 562-569.

Humke, R. G., Schmitt, R. L., & Grupp, S. E. Candidates, issues and party in newspaper political advertisements. *Journalism Quarterly,* 1975, *52,* 499-504.

Hy, R. Mass media in election campaigns. *Public Administration Survey,* 1973, *20,* 1-6.

Jacobson, G. C. The impact of broadcast campaigning on electoral outcomes. *Journal of Politics,* 1975, *37,* 769-793.

Janowitz, M., & Marvick, D. The quality of the electorate's deliberation. In E. Crotty (Ed.), *Public opinion and politics: A reader.* New York: Holt, Rinehart & Winston, 1970.

Jones, C. A., & Kaid, L. L. Political campaign regulation and the constitution: Oklahoma's campaign contributions and expenditures act. *Oklahoma Law Review,* 1976, *29,* 684-711.

Joslyn, R. A. The content of political spot ads. *Journalism Quarterly,* 1980, *57,* 92-98.

Kaid, L. L. Measures of political advertising. *Journal of Advertising Research,* 1976, *16,* 49-53.

Kaid, L. L., & Sanders, K. R. Political television commercials: An experimental study of type and length. *Communication Research,* 1978, *5,* 57-70.

Klapper, J. *The effects of mass communication.* New York: Free Press, 1960.

Kraus, S., & Davis, D. *The effects of mass communication on political behavior.* University Park: Pennsylvania State University Press, 1976.

Krugman, H. E. The impact of television advertising: Learning without involvement. *Public Opinion Quarterly,* 1965, *29,* 349-356.

Lasswell, H. D. The structure and function of communication in society. In L. Bryson (Ed.), *The communication of ideas.* New York: Harper & Row, 1948.

Lazarsfeld, P. F., Berelson, B., & Gaudet, H. *The people's choice.* New York: Duell, Sloan and Pearce, 1944.

McCleneghan, J. S. Media and non-media effects in Texas mayoral elections. *Journalism Quarterly,* 1980, *57,* 129-134, 201.

McClure, R. D., & Patterson, T. E. Television news and political advertising: The impact on voter beliefs. *Communication Research,* 1976, *1,* 3-31.

McCombs, M. E., & Shaw, D. L. The agenda-setting function of mass media. *Public Opinion Quarterly,* 1972, *36,* 176-187.

McGinniss, J. *The selling of the president 1968.* New York: Trident Press, 1969.

McGuire, W. J. The nature of attitudes and attitude change. In G. Lindzey & E. Aronson (Eds.), *The handbook of social psychology* (Vol. III). Cambridge, MA: Addison-Wesley, 1968.

McLeod, J., & Becker, L. Testing the validity of gratifications measures through political effects analysis. In J. G. Blumler & E. Katz (Eds.), *The uses of mass communications.* Beverly Hills, CA: Sage, 1974.

McLuhan, M. *Understanding Media.* New York: New American Library, 1964.

Martin, J. L. Recent theory on mass media potential in political campaigns. *Annals of the American Academy of Political and Social Science, 1976, 427,* 125-133.

Mendelsohn, H., & O'Keefe, G. J. *The people choose a president: Influences on voter decision making.* New York: Praeger, 1976.

Meyer, T. P., & Donohue, T. P. Perceptions and misperceptions of political advertising. *Journal of Business Communication, 1973, 10,* 29-40.

Miller, R. E., & Robyn, D. L. A field experimental study of direct mail in a congressional primary campaign: What effects last until election day? *Experimental Study of Politics, 1975, 4,* 1-37.

Mulder, R. The effects of televised political ads in the 1975 Chicago mayoral election. *Journalism Quarterly, 1979, 56,* 336-340.

Mullen, J. J. How candidates for the senate use newspaper advertising. *Journalism Quarterly, 1963, 40,* 532-538. (a)

Mullen, J. J. Newspaper advertising in the Kennedy-Nixon campaign. *Journalism Quarterly, 1963, 40,* 3-11. (b)

Mullen, J. J. Newspaper advertising in the Johnson-Goldwater campaign. *Journalism Quarterly, 1968, 45,* 219-225.

Muller, N. J. Political advertising in national magazines. *Practical Politics, 1978, 2,* 16-20, 28.

Napolitan, J. *The election game and how to win it.* New York: Doubleday, 1972.

National Association of Broadcasters. *Political broadcast catechism* (8th ed.). Washington, DC: Author, 1976.

Nimmo, D. Political image makers and the mass media. *Annals of the American Academy of Political and Social Science, 1976, 427,* 33-44.

Nimmo, D. *Political communication and public opinion in America.* Santa Monica, CA: Goodyear, 1978.

Nimmo, D., & Savage, R. L. *Candidates and their images.* Santa Monica, CA: Goodyear, 1976.

O'Keefe, M. T., & Sheinkopf, K. G. The voter decides: Candidate image or campaign issue. *Journal of Broadcasting, 1974, 18,* 403-411.

Palda, K. S. The effects of expenditure on political success. *Journal of Law and Economics, 1975,* 745-771.

Patterson, T. E., & McClure, R. D. *The unseeing eye.* New York: Putnam, 1976.

Prisuta, R. H. Broadcast advertising by candidates for the Michigan legislature: 1970. *Journal of Broadcasting, 1972, 16,* 453-459.

Rose, E. D., & Fuchs, D. Reagan vs. Brown: A TV image playback. *Journal of Broadcasting, 1968, 12,* 247-260.

Rothschild, M. L. Political advertising: A neglected policy issue in marketing. *Journal of Marketing Research, 1978, 15,* 58-71.

Rothschild, M. L., & Ray, M. L. Involvement and political advertising effect: An exploratory experiment. *Communication Research, 1974, 1,* 264-285.

Sanders, K. R. A critique of contemporary approaches to the study of political communication. In R. Davis (Ed.), *Proceedings of the 1975 Speech Communication Association summer conference.* Falls Church, VA: Speech Communication Association, 1978.

Sanders, K. R., & Kaid, L. L. Political communication theory and research: An overview, 1976-77. In B. Ruben (Ed.), *Communication yearbook II.* New Brunswick, NJ: Transaction Books, 1978.

Schramm, W., & Carter, R. F. Effectiveness of a political telethon. *Public Opinion Quarterly, 1959, 23,* 121-126.

Schwartz, T. *The responsive chord.* Garden City, NY: Anchor Press/Doubleday, 1974.

Sears, D. O., & Whitney, R. E. Political persuasion. In I. de Sola Pool et al. (Eds.), *The handbook of communication.* Chicago: Rand McNally, 1973.

Sheinkopf, K. G., Atkin, C. K., & Bowen, L. The functions of political advertising for campaign organizations. *Journal of Marketing Research,* 1972, *9,* 401-405.

Sheinkopf, K. G., Atkin, C. K., & Bowen, L. How political party workers respond to political advertising. *Journalism Quarterly,* 1973, *50,* 334-339.

Spero, R. *The duping of the American voter: Dishonesty and deception in presidential television advertising.* New York: Lippincott/Crowell, 1980.

Steinberg, R. *Political campaign management: A systems approach.* Lexington, MA: D. C. Heath, 1976.

Stephenson, W. *The play theory of mass communication.* Chicago: University of Chicago Press, 1967.

Surlin, S. H., & Gordon, T. F. Selective exposure and retention of political advertising. *Journal of Advertising Research,* 1976, *5,* 32-44.

Surlin, S. H., & Gordon, T. F. How values affect attitudes toward direct reference political advertising. *Journalism Quarterly,* 1977, *54,* 89-98.

Swanson, D. L. Political information, influence and judgment in the 1972 presidential campaign. *Quarterly Journal of Speech,* 1973, *59,* 130-142.

Swanson, D. L. Information utility: An alternative perspective in political communication. *Central States Speech Journal,* 1976, *27,* 95-101.

Szybillo, G. J., & Hartenbaum, R. F. Political advertising and the broadcast media. *Journal of Advertising,* 1976, *5,* 42-46.

Tucker, D. E. Broadcasting in the 1956 Oregon senatorial campaign. *Journal of Broadcasting,* 1959, *3,* 225-243.

Wanat, J. Political broadcast advertising and primary election voting. *Journal of Broadcasting,* 1974, *18,* 413-422.

Wyckoff, G. *The image candidates.* New York: Macmillan, 1968.

Zajonc, R. B. Attitudinal effects of mere exposure. *Journal of Personality and Social Psychology,* 1968, *9* Monograph Supplement, 1-27.

CHAPTER 10

Political Debates

Sidney Kraus and Dennis K. Davis

TELEVISED PRESIDENTIAL DEBATES began as an innovation in the 1960 election campaign between John F. Kennedy and Richard M. Nixon. They appeared in four confrontations (Kraus, 1962) carried by both radio and television. For various reasons, some political and some legal, 16 years elapsed before another set of presidential debates occured.

In 1976, President Gerald Ford and challenger Jimmy Carter appeared together in three debates. Also in that year we witnessed the first vice-presidential debate. The Robert Dole-Walter Mondale debate came about largely as a response to events which heightened public awareness of the importance of the vice-presidency.

The 1980 election campaign, characterized by a series of critical events (Kraus & Davis, 1976), included five Republican primary debates and two debates in the general election period—Ronald Reagan first debated John Anderson and later confronted President Carter. Carter's appearance marked the first time a candidate participated in televised debates in two successive presidential campaign years. Reagan's quest for the presidency recorded the first time that a candidate debated in both primaries and the general election.

There were, then, nine televised presidential debates in general elections of three campaigns and one vice-presidential debate. In 1976, a series of public forums were held which featured Democratic candidates for the presidency, while in 1980 a series of five Republican primary debates was staged.

Since the 1960 televised debates, social scientists, political pundits, political party leaders, and even television critics have discussed the effects of that innovation on the American political system. This debate over televised debates has centered on the relative value of these contests as a permanent and major part of the election process. It has been argued that debates further undermine an already quite threatened two-party system (Bishop, 1980), that they have not been true debates (Auer, 1962; Bitzer & Rueter, 1980), that they encourage an all-too-prevalent "horse race" syndrome by focusing media and scholarly attention on "who won" (Katz & Feldman, 1962), and that they stress personality (image) traits at the expense of substance (issue positions; see Katz & Feldman, 1962).

On the positive side, there are those who advocate the continuation of debates as a systemic part of the election process (Kraus, 1979; Chaffee, 1978; Germond & Witcover, 1979; Karayn, 1979; Mitchell, 1979; Broder, 1981). Based on reviews of scholarly research, both Kraus and Chaffee conclude that the overall role of debates in presidential elections is positive. Chaffee attaches "a rather high net value to the debates as an emerging insitituion," while Kraus calls for institutionalizing them. Germond and Witcover, suggest, "as the first priority, the decision of whether to participate in televised presidential and vice-presidential debates should be taken out of the hands of the candidates and away from their yardstick of self-interest and the debates should be given institutional status." Karayn would provide for their continuance with the formation of a special, autonomous commission "chartered by Congress and comprised of representatives from wide-ranging . . . groups . . . funded directly by the Congress or by the Federal Election Commission." Mitchell echoes Karayn's view by recommending the establishment of a Presidential Debates Committee. Broder feels that the debates should be in the hands of the political parties, beginning with a commitment to debate before candidates are selected.

Given these contrasting views on the usefulness of televised presidential debates, it is not likely that the issue of institutionalizing debates will be easily resolved. Our intent will be to consider this issue in light of democratic theory and empirical research findings. We have focused our attention exclusively on the role of debates in national presidential elections. Readers interested in debates at other levels should consult *The Reporter* (1962) and a Markle Foundation Report (1977). Only in the closing portion of this chapter do we address questions of debate scheduling, format, and content. While these questions are important, we believe the overriding concern should be on whether or not debates in any form are appropriate during presidential elections. There have now been debates in three national elections. A firm precedent for such debates has been established. As a society we have had time to reflect on the usefulness of such debates. We can draw on the evidence of several hundred debate studies and several major books to aid our evaluation of them.

This chapter will present a reasoned argument favoring institutionalization of debates. This argument will be structured around two fundamental questions. First, *are televised debates consistent with classical democratic theory?* Second, *do voters learn useful information about candidates and what they stand for by viewing debates?* These questions are interrelated because if voters learn about candidates from debates, this can enable them to make more responsible voting decisions. Democratic theory is grounded on the assumption that people can be trusted to make informed choices of candidates if they are given the right to do so. In seeking answers to these questions we have first examined the tenets of democratic theory. We have contrasted democratic theory with elitist theory. We have concluded that the creation of more democratic political institutions inevitably entails risks which can be justified only by a commitment to democratic ideals. Often, the arguments against democracy can be better defended than those favoring it.

In seeking to evaluate how and why voters learn from debates we have examined the empirical research since 1960. We found that much of the early research supported the view that people used the debates selectively to confirm what they already believed. This research was consistent with the dominant theoretical perspective of the 1950s and 1960s—elite pluralism. This perspective is inconsistent with democratic theory because it assumes that a just and stable social order does not require that all citizens be informed and responsible voters. Selective reinforcement of prejudiced, irrational views is justified so long as persons holding such views are constrained by their ties to pluralistic groups and traditional social institutions. More recent research supports a transaction theory view of the political order. Mass communication is found to play an increasingly important role in politics generally and political campaigns in particular. Televised debates appear to be an important form of political communication for modern campaigns. Evidence suggests that debates serve some groups of voters quite well. Debates may provide a means of making our society more democratic.

DEMOCRATIC THEORY AND
TELEVISED PRESIDENTIAL DEBATES

The current constroversy over the role of televised debates echoes earlier arguments about the enfranchisement of new groups of voters. In these disputes democratic theorists were challenged by advocates of elitist theory. Elitist theorists argued against extending the right to vote to new groups which were presumed to be incapable of choosing good leaders. In extreme cases, they argued that elections are an unnecessary and risky means of choosing leaders. Only a social elite should be entrusted with this difficult and vital task. Alexander Hamilton took an elitist position when he argued: "It is an unquestionable truth that [people] do not possess the discernment and stability necessary for systematic groverment" (Elliot, 1888).

Defenders of elections and of extending the right to vote to every citizen argued that these steps would improve the operation of government; legitimate government, in that the will of citizens would directly affect government;

encourage the personal development of voters through election participation; and act as a check on the power of leaders. Madison advocated "the fundamental principle that men cannot be justly bound by laws in making of which they have no part" (Farrand, 1911).

This debate between elitist and democratic theorists cannot be conclusively decided. Pomper (1970) points out that

> confidence in the ballot rests on a fundamental moral judgement. The basic premise of a democratic system is self-respect for everybody. . . . If the ideal is to maintain self-respect for everybody permanently, everybody must help govern. The knowledge of self-direction is acquired in no other way than the having of it in important affairs of life. . . . Participation in meaningful elections is the political corollary of a moral presumption of individual worth [p.11].

Democratic theorists often express optimism concerning the educability of average citizens. They believe that it is unrealistic to force people to demonstrate their competency to act responsibly *prior* to giving them the right to act. When people have the power to act, they can be expected to learn how to act responsibly. For this reason, efforts to make societies more democratic inevitably entail risks. People may abuse new rights before they learn how to exercise them. But such risks are necessary if democracy is to succeed as a form of government.

Since its founding, the United States has provided a "laboratory" for the testing of democratic theory. The right to vote has gradually been extended to tenants, working men, slaves, women, and those 18 to 21 years old. We now elect U.S. senators directly, and the electoral college system of selecting presidents has become an anacronism. All of these changes gave voting rights to persons who, by objective standards, were poorly prepared to exercise these rights responsibly. Our nation has survived these tests. With the passage of time, newly enfranchised groups have demonstrated their capacity to vote as responsibly as more elite groups. Pomper (1970) argues that one reason why the American system has survived such tests is that our elections put leaders in office but do not mandate that these leaders enact specific policies on a wide range of issues. Thus, the elitist fear of "mob rule" has proved incorrect. After reviewing much data on elections and subsequent government action, Pomper (1970) concluded:

> The portrait of the American voter . . . is consistent with the expectations of democratic political theorists. . . . The political structure of the United States allows the voters to make vital decisions on the choice of rulers, while restricting [their] influence over specific government decisions. . . . This is precisely the role the electorate is best able to perform [p. 95].

CONTEMPORARY POLITICAL THEORY:
ELITE PLURALISM VS. TRANSACTIONISM

Few contemporary American political theorists espouse an elitist position, but some are committed to positions that question the degree to which the average voter can be trusted to act responsibly. One of the most popular of these positions has been labeled "elite pluralism" (Berelson, Lazarsfeld, & McPhee, 1954). This perspective developed out of efforts to reconcile the findings of surveys of voters taken in the 1940s and 1950s with democratic theory. These surveys revealed that most vote decisions were determined by long-held commitments to political parties and by influence exercised by leaders of pluralistic groups, especially political parties. Mass communication was found to be of minimal importance. Its role in politics was largely one of reinforcing existing beliefs and attitudes. The elite pluralists argued that the stability of the American political system could be traced to the actions of group leaders and to political prejudices formed in childhood. The most important groups were the political parties which were responsible for socializing persons to politics and for structuring elections so that relatively ignorant and apathetic voters could participate but only in carefully restricted ways. The two-party system was seen as the essential institution which prevented the United States from suffering the political conflicts which destroyed European societies during the 1930s and 1940s.

Many political scientists who accept elite pluralism are increasingly disturbed by recent research which suggests that the influence of political parties is waning while the power of mass media is rising. Elsewhere (Kraus & Davis, 1976) we have documented these trends and have argued that positive rather than negative consequences can result. We proposed a transaction theory which assumes that as citizens acquire increasing skill in using mass media, they will be able to enter into more direct, two-way transactions with their political leaders. Elections can be viewed as providing some of the most important opportunities citizens have for engaging in transactions with their leaders. Elections require leaders to seek the consent of the governed. The actions and opinions expressed by voters during campaigns provide leaders with useful insights into their hopes and needs. The electorate can communicate to campaigning politicians in many ways other than through the ballot box. Campaign appearances and political polls provide a continuous flow of communication. Even the failure of persons to vote provides a message to leaders. For better or worse, the mass media seem to have gradually taken on the role of brokers in election campaigns. Media professionals aid in developing campaign messages, gatekeep transmission of messages, and commission the polls and create commentary which purport to reveal what the public thinks about their would-be leaders.

Elite pluralists find such a media-centered vision of the election process alarming. They believe that political parties, not the mass media, should provide the mechanism by which politicians and the public are connected. Some argue that a media-centered election process is a symptom of a mass society in which leaders can be forced to appeal to and cater to the worst desires of average voters. Such an election process could inevitably result in the rise of demogogues who promise anything to get elected. Because these demogogues are not controlled by political parties, they will not excercise power responsibly. Pluralist groups may no longer be able to insulate elites from the irrational will of the masses. The consequences of such developments are predicted to be tragic.

It must be admitted that the fears of elite pluralists are to some extent warranted. Like the fears of elitist theorists, their views are based on a harsh and pessimistic interpretation of undisputable facts. It is possible for them to point to a variety of research findings to substantiate their concerns about John Q. Voter. When the media-brokered transactions that go on during modern election campaigns are closely examined, there is much to be concerned about. Many researchers have decried the influence of media-transmitted images on voters. One controversial but widely accepted analysis of the 1972 election campaign (Patterson & McClure, 1976) found that people learned more from television advertising than from television news. Based on much more extensive research on the 1976 campaign, Patterson (1980) concluded that people learned very little about issues from television news. He found some evidence to support the argument that the way the television networks chose to cover primary elections may have been responsible for the nomination of Jimmy Carter by the Democrats. Carter was apparently much more successful in using the media to reach voters in the early primaries, and once he attained the status of the "front-runner" it was very difficult for other candidates to overtake him. A bandwagon effect may have operated in the later primaries, which assured him of victory.

However, not all present trends are objectionable. Along with the demise of political party control and the increased role of television, we have seen an increase in issue voting. We believe this is in keeping with democratic theory. Issue voting may require making rather complex vote decision based on a large amount of recently learned and categorized information. It can be contrasted with a simple vote decision based on party loyalty. Asher (1980) concludes that

> while the amount of issue voting may still not be impressively high, particularly with respect to the tenets of classical democratic theory, the important thrust of the revisionist literature is that the electorate is capable of making issue-related decisions. . . . It is unreasonable to demand issue voting from citizens when the parties themselves do not offer meaningful, clearly stated choices [p. 131].

EMERGENCE OF NEW POLITICAL INSTITUTIONS

While we do not wish to argue that a media-influenced election process is ideal, we are willing to be optimistic about future developments. It can be argued that we are currently in an important transition period which could ultimately lead to the development of more democratic political institutions. If these institutions are developed wisely, they could serve to structure the transactions between the public and political leaders in ways consistent with the ideals of democratic theorists. Televised debates could be one of the many such new institutions which might also include (a) a system of regional primaries, (b) a formalized, perhaps publicly financed and controlled opinion polling institute, (c) a Federal Elections Commission with expanded powers and responsibilities, and (d) a formalized means of creating media policies for campaign coverage combined with empirical research to evaluate the usefulness of those policies.

We raise the possibility of such new institutions only to suggest that there are many innovative ways in which leader-voter transactions can be restructured in the future. Our commitment to democratic theory as well as to transaction theory leads us to believe that important new institutions may be necessary. We are as concerned about the current situation as are elite pluralists, but for different reasons. Change is clearly necessary if we are to facilitate the transmission and reception of those forms of information average citizens can use to make decisions which maximize their personal interests and the interests of society. We are convinced that informed consent—voting based on information—will become an increasingly important basis for modern democracies. Such a development is consistent with democratic theory. New political institutions which encourage and facilitate informed consent could create a new era in democracy.

Too often the advocates of elite pluralism are forced to conclude that the flow of information to the general public should be restricted because people cannot be trusted to use this information wisely. They would rather people voted on the basis of long-standing but often ill-formed political commitments, rather than risk permitting them to vote on the basis of current information. We have nothing against political parties as stabilizing institutions, but we are suspicious of those who defend party practices which serve to discourage use of information and encourage votes based on emotional commitments. We are quite disturbed when the defenders of political parties feel compelled to argue that in order to decrease "further erosion of the two party system" televised debates should not become a "permanent fixture in our presidential campaigns" (Bishop, 1980). Such arguments seem to be based on blind faith in the importance of powerful parties for maintenance of democracies, rather than a realistic appraisal of what parties are actually doing to create new and better forms of democracy.

Below, we have sought to make a thorough and realistic appraisal of the usefulness of televised debates. Our appraisal is limited because there are many important questions concerning debates which research has not yet addressed. Our appraisal necessarily centers on the questions of how well the debates motivate and inform voters because these have been studied. On the basis of this appraisal we have drawn some conclusions about debates which have guided our development of policy recommendation.

EMPIRICAL RESEARCH ON TELEVISED DEBATES

In the years since the first televised presidential debates in 1960, there have been several hundred studies of the effects of these debates. Several authoritative summaries of this research exist (Katz & Feldman, 1962; Sears & Chaffee, 1979; Chaffee, 1978). This review of research is not comprehensive. Our purpose is to assess the usefulness of the debates for voters. We have reinterpreted existing studies and viewed findings in innovative ways. Effects research is often conducted within rather narrow research traditions and is guided by currently fasionable hypotheses. We are concerned with exploring the implications of research findings for transactionist and democratic theory.

Becker, McCombs, and McLeod (1975) argue that most research on political communication effects can be divided into two broad categories: affective research, which seeks to understand the influence of political communication on enduring attitudes and emotions, and cognitive research, which considers how people learn discrete amounts of information from political messages. During the 1950s and 1960s, political communication research focused on affective effects. Researchers sought to explain whether political propaganda could influence attitudes. The power of mass media to create affective effects was contrasted with the power of other social institutions to create these effects. Elsewhere (Kraus & Davis, 1976) we have summarized the key findings of this research. Traditional social institutions such as the family, church, schools, work, and social groups (including political parties) were found to have considerable influence, while the power of mass media was found to be minimal.

This research on affective effects was consistent with elite pluralism. In summarizing an elaborate voter survey, Berelson et al. (1954) argued that the power of traditional social institutions to dominate political attitudes served as a vital means of stabilizing American society. These social institutions served to moderate political conflicts and prevent short-term, intense, and highly polarized political messages from disrupting vote decisions. Berelson's ideal political man was a political moderate who was not very interested in politics. He relied on leaders to provide him with information and to tell him how to vote. He used mass media selectively, seeking out messages to reinforce his existing attitudes and avoiding those which might produce changes. While such citizens could hardly be labeled responsible voters according to classical democratic theory, Berelson et al. argued that this was not important. So long as the society as a whole was democratically organized, individual citizens did not have to behave as rational informed voters. Much of the early research on debates studied affective effects. This research produced little that was inconsistent with the findings for other types of mass communication.

Recently, researchers have begun to focus on cognitive effects of mass communication (Becker et al., 1975). Several new research approaches have emerged which have this focus. These approaches consider how and why learning of factual information about political issues, parties, or candidates takes place. Socialization research has traced political learning among children and found that television is often a quite important source of new information (Kraus & Davis, 1976). Information-seeking or message discrimination studies have considered how adults guide their acquisition of knowledge based on more or less consciously held interests, not on the basis of unconscious attitudes (Donohue & Tipton, 1973). Uses and gratifications research has gone even further in arguing that people actively use media to serve explicit purposes and that when they do, the learning which takes place can be personally meaningful (Blumler & Katz, 1974).

Such cognitive-based research approaches are consistent with transaction theory and classical democratic theory. These approaches assume that the things people learn from mass media can be important to their lives. It is assumed that people can be rational in their use of media and can use what they learn from the media to increase their ability to make rational decisions. Voters who actively seek to acquire information during campaigns should be in a better position to make reasonable and responsible vote decisions.

Debate Effects: Cognitive versus Affective

The 1960 debate took place at a time when most researchers were interested in affective effects. They were concerned with finding out whether this new form of mass communication was more powerful than previous political messages. Would the debates prove capable of changing attitudes which party propaganda could only reinforce? Some researchers speculated that only voters who had no strongly held political attitudes would be influenced. Such "independent" voters might be swayed by the images and rhetoric of debates. In their review of the 1960 research, Katz and Feldman (1962) were skeptical about the power of debates. They term two studies which did not find selective exposure to be "extraordinary" and argue that there is "plenty of other evidence to illustrate the workings of selective perception in audience reaction to the debates." They point out that research has "all but dispelled the myth of the 'independent voter' " and declare that "the truth is that people who make up their minds late in the campaign are likely to have very little interest in the election. Independent voters are far less likely to hear the debates."

Some of the most important contradictions between the 1960 and 1976 debate research findings may stem from an increased focus on cognitive effects. In a study which contrasts greatly with the typical 1960 research, Chaffee and Choe (1980) report that about 40 percent of their respondents in a statewide sample in Wisconsin could be labeled politically independent. These voters tended to make their vote decision during the campaign (but before the last two weeks), were more likely to use mass media to follow the campaign, and were especially likely to watch the televised debates. These voters were found to be quite unstable in their voting preferences, often voting for candidates they did not prefer before the general election campaign. The authors conclude that "in the absence of precommitment, those exposed to the campaign will make their decisions primarily on the basis of campaign-specific information." Tom Patterson (1980) also reports little evidence that viewers routinely engaged in selectivity while viewing television news. "Voters have a slight preference for some types of news, but it is based as much on their interests as a psychological need for reinforcing information." He found the debates most likely to provide useful information for "citizens of moderate and low interest" who had not already learned the information from other sources.

Nevertheless, some researchers in 1976 reported findings similar to those of 1960. Support for selective reinforcement of attitudes was most likely to be found by those who conducted experiments. Slagter and Miller (1978) report findings from an experiment conducted using students at the Southern Illinois University. They conclude that "selection biases were about twice as strong as any effects due to the content of the debate."

Interest, Exposure, and Learning

In his book, *The Mass Media Election,* Patterson (1980) developed a perspective on political learning which is useful in summarizing debate effects research and in seeking an answer to the question about learning from televised debates which we raised above. Patterson based his approach on an analysis of panel data gathered from 1200 voters during the 1976 campaign. Patterson probed how voters make their decisions by considering relationships between political interests (rather than attitudes), exposure to political communication, and changes in political cognitions. He found the interrelationships between these factors to be quite complex. Preexisting interests do not always determine why voters will be exposed to political communication or constrain what will be learned from such exposure. Unintended or uninterested exposure to political messages can create new political interests. Learning can occur after brief exposure to messages or only after repeated exposure to many message. In general, interested persons will seek out more political information and will learn more efficiently from it, while less interested persons will avoid information and need repeated exposure to many messages. In general, interested persons will seek out more political information and will learn more efficiently from it, while less interested persons will avoid information and need repeated exposure to learn even simple facts.

The picture of modern elections Patterson describes is quite consistent with the media-centered transactionist perspective we have described. Campaigns in which media are active tend to result in more people being exposed to political messages and stimulate a greater diversity of political interests. Increased political learning takes place. But the consequences of these newly formed political interests, new patterns of exposure to political messages, and higher levels of political information are not clear. These new interests have not necessarily replaced old interests but typically are added to them. Some of the newer interests are quite trivial, such as an interest in the election as a horse race or in the psychohistory of candidates. Other interests appear to have more value, such as increased interest in issues featured in media coverage (McCombs & Shaw, 1977). Voters also seem to be taking more interest in candidates' stands on issues. Similarly, questions can be raised about new patterns of exposure. Patterson reports evidence that the media succeeded in hyping the early primary caucuses and elections and attracted an extraordinary amount of attention to relatively insignificant contests. It can be argued that such increased attention may be detrimental to the political process. On the whole, the mass media may be inspiring increased attention to significant as well as insignificant events, and the value of this could prove to be important. Finally, the type of political learning which takes place can also be questioned. Many voters absorb facts which have no purpose for them. Others learn useful facts but don't know how to apply them. Patterson appears to be unconvinced that much of the learning which takes place during campaigns is actually very useful to people.

Below, our review will focus on the three factors discussed by Patterson. We will be concerned with identifying which types of voters find the debates to be useful because they (a) arouse certain political interests, (b) enable these interests to be easily acted on, and (c) facilitate specific forms of political learning. Essentially, what we will be arguing is that debates make it easier for some voters to make vote decisions which they themselves experience as responsible. We will conclude by seeking to answer the questions we raised above concerning the flow of information, use of information, initiation of significant communication, and vote decision-making. In doing this we will assess whether debates can contribute to an evolution of democratic politics in the United States.

Interests

Many critics of televised political communication have argued that such communication has generally served to trivialize election politics. It is argued that ideological conflicts between competing interest groups have been reduced to horse races. Similarly, candidates are no longer presented as tough leaders of national parties, but as nice persons who happen to belong to one party or another. Substantive political issues tend to be ignored in favor of the latest opinion poll data or pseudoevents staged by the candidates. Patterson (1980) argued that the values of television news professionals lead them to create what he calls "campaign issues" which are clear-cut and can be easily presented in 30 seconds. He contrasts such campaign issues with policy issues which require much more time to present and are of less intrinsic interest for viewers.

Historically, debates have served as a means of formalizing partisan political conflict and structuring it in a way which forces participants to reveal partisan positions on issues. Participants have the opportunity to argue for the merits of their ideological views and to criticize those of their opposition. The most classic American debates between Lincoln and Douglas centered on the issue of slavery and the competing ideologies surrounding this issue. Televised debates would appear to offer the possibility of overcoming the inherent flaws of routine televised political communication. To what extent is this true?

Existing research on debates suggests that a wide variety of interests are aroused, some clearly more likely to be useful than others. Every televised presidential debate has been of interest as an event in itself. Katz and Feldman (1962) report a Gallup poll found "55 percent of a national sample of adults looking forward to the debates with 'a lot' of interest." As the 1960 debates went on, audience interest was found to increase (p. 193). A survey by Deutsch-mann found that 77 percent of those who saw the debates sought additional information about them. Katz and Feldman summarize a variety of findings concerning why people were interested by commenting: "There is no doubt that the immediate response, at any rate, was to the drama of the combat and to the rhetoric. Just as the audience responded to the rhetoric more than to the statistics, so they responded to the personalities more than to the issues."

In 1976, research findings suggest that voter interest in the debates was initially high and then declined as the debates proved more boring than expected. Roper surveys (Robinson, 1979) found an important decline in debate interest over time. Fifty-three percent planned to watch the first debate, but only 41 percent planned to watch the third. Prior to the third debate, only 17 percent labeled the debates "very interesting," while 35 percent considered them "rather dull." A survey conducted in Akron, Ohio, by Garrett O'Keefe and Harold Mendelsohn (1979) asked persons why they would be interested in watching the debates. Ninety percent said that learning issue stands was "very important," 75 percent said learning what the candidates are like as people was "very important," and 65 percent expected to get help in deciding between the candidates. After the debate only 25 percent reported learning about issue stands and about the candidates as people from the debates. Many expressed disappointment. But "the majority of those watching the debate said they wanted to find out more about the candidates as a result of viewing, and nearly half said their interest in the campaign had been increased." Thus, while viewing of the debates may not have created more interest in the debates, such viewing may have encouraged further interest in the campaign. Robinson (1979) reported Roper surveys which found campaign interest increasing as the debates progressed.

Exposure

Clearly, the debates inspired interest among diverse groups of voters. But to what extent did this interest translate into debate viewing? Do debates tend to be viewed only by partisans seeking reinforcement, or does a broader cross-section of Americans attend to them? Ratings data from 1960 and 1976 suggest that the audiences for the debates were quite large: Katz and Feldman (1962) report that 60 to 65 percent of the total adult population watched the first debate. Nielsen estimated that the audiences for the second and third debate may have been larger even though fewer sets were turned on. Sears and Chaffee (1979) report that for the 1976 debates 70 percent watched some part of the first or second debate while 60 percent watched the third. But Sears and Chaffee are somewhat skeptical about the attention actually given to the debates by all of these viewers. They argue that "a more sensible measure of meaningful attention might be the 20 percent who read any columns or editorials or the 29 percent who read any news stories analyzing the third debate."

Other researchers provide more precise informationn about the types of people who watched or read about the debates. Miller and MacKuen (1979) analyzed data from a national sample of 2875 persons studied by the Survey Research Center at the University of Michigan. They report that the best predictor of exposure to the debates was overall political interest. Debate exposure was only weakly related to such demographic variables as social status, education, and race. These relationships became even weaker among persons who viewed more than one debate, which suggests that the debates had the ability to inspire interest for further viewing among most viewers. Miller and MacKuen conclude: "The lack of a strong relationship between any demographic characteristics and debate watching leads us to the conclusion that the debates were equally utilized as an information source by all groups in society." The authors reported that partisan political interest is related to continued viewing of the debates. Forty percent of strongly partisan voters watched all four debates, and only 12 percent failed to watch any. By comparison, of voters who categorized themselves as politically independent, only 24 percent watched all four debates, while 23 percent failed to watch any. While these differences are significant, it is important to note that significant numbers of independent voters did watch one or more debates. The "mythical independent voter" of 1960 was very much in evidence in the audience for televised debates.

Similar findings are reported by researchers who studied samples of voters in Wisconsin and Iowa. McLeod, Durall, Ziemke, and Bybee (1979) report that in

Madison, political interest was much more strongly related to debate viewing than was partisanship when other demographic and communication variables were controlled for in a multiple regression analysis. Also, use of the mass media for public affairs news was strongly related. Becker et al. (1979) reported in an Iowa study that the best predictors of attention to the debates were TV news use, campaign interest, political activity, and education. In their multiple regression analysis, they found strength of partisanship to be *negatively* related to debate exposure. Chaffee and Choe (1980) studied a statewide sample in Wisconsin and found that 40 percent of their sample consisted of people who decided how to vote while the debates were being staged. This group tended to be politically independent, more dependent on mass media for political information during the campaign, and more likely to view the debates. This group was larger than the 30 percent who made up their minds before the debate or the 30 percent who decided after the last debate.

All of these findings cast doubt on the notion that debates are of use only to partisan voters who have already decided how they will vote. Nor do debates serve merely to help voters learn images or acquire information which is consistent with their preexisting attitudes. Many persons view the debates who do not have strong partisan attitudes or well-developed political beliefs. We believe these findings suggest that debates are most likely to be used by two types of voters. One of these types fits the conceptions of elite pluralism. These voters have strongly developed attitudes which dominate their use of the debates. The debates merely serve as another source of partisan communication which helps them become more convinced of the desirability of their party's candidate and the weaknesses of his opponent.

But the other voter type is a newly emerging voter (see Nie, Verba, & Petrocik, 1976, for a similar argument) who lacks firm ties to political groups and whose political attitudes are not polarized. In some respects these voters seem to be less responsible than partisan voters. They make up their minds about candidates late in campaigns. They become interested in the campaign later and choose to follow these campaigns largely through mass media. It seems likely that media events such as televised debates may be important in activating the political interests of such voters. They do not attend party rallies or engage in other party activity. Their ability to be responsible voters seems to depend heavily on whether they receive useful campaign information from the mass media and then process this information wisely. Below, in our review of findings which consider how voters used the information in the debates, we have focused our attention on the use made of information by independent voters.

Learning and Decision-Making

The research on the 1960 debate largely focused on whether changes in perceptions of candidates' attributes or issue stands occurred as a result of viewing. Evidence of selectivity was reported. Studies by Carter (1962), Lang and Lang (1962), Kraus and Smith (1962), and Deutschmann (1962) reported some evidence that Democrats had learned more favorable things about Kennedy and unfavorable things about Nixon. These findings were reversed for Republicans. However, in nearly all instances, the evidence of selectivity was weak. Kraus and Smith report no marked changes of any kind in perceptions of issues or of candidate attributes. Lang and Lang report some rather dramatic improvements in perceptions of Kennedy in their highly Democratic New York panel but few attendant declines in Nixon's image. Carter found evidence of learning of issue positions even among persons opposed to these positions. He comments that in the debates the opposition had a chance to be heard even if it was not believed. None of the studies of the 1960 debates was designed as a straightforward evaluation of the knowledge learned from watching the debates. In general, researchers asked questions concerning issues which they knew had partisan significance; such issues were likely to be selectively perceived and recalled. Other less partisan issues were ignored. Carter's test of issue knowledge was the broadest, encompassing 16 items, and his study produced the clearest rejection of the selective exposure and perception hypotheses.

Studies of the 1976 debate have produced the most useful evidence on learning from the debates. While the majority of researchers have concluded that the debates produced useful forms of learning; several researchers have registered their doubts. Below we have summarized learning about the candidates and their positions on issues. In general, these two types of learning have been found to be highly correlated. Gains in both types of knowledge tend to occur simultaneously. However, in most cases, learning about candidates was found to occur much more commonly than learning about issues or issue positions.

Two studies report the most optimistic findings concerning learning from the debates. Based on a national sample of 2875 voters who were interviewed over the period when the debates occurred, Miller and MacKuen (1980) found that the number of comments about candidates increased steadily and was at least partly attributable to the debates. Mention of domestic issues increased sharply after the first and third debates, which dealt with these issues, while mentions of foreign issues increased sharply after the second debate on foreign policy. The researchers divided voters into three groups based on the amount of attention they paid to politics; they found that persons who were more attentive to politics were able to make more comments about candidates but that persons at all three levels of attentiveness showed increases in comments during the time of the debates. These increases were found even after education and partisanship were controlled. The findings for issue learning were less impressive but suggested that a modest amount of learning could be taking place. The researchers conclude that short-term changes in candidate evaluations can be linked to the debates. However, they are reluctant to speculate about what role these changes may play in determining the outcome of elections. They note only that such learning does increase the likelihood that votes might be decided on the basis of consciously held and rationally considered information.

Chaffee and Choe (1980) are more optimistic about the usefulness of debates. Their statewide sample of 164 Wisconsin voters permitted them to draw several interesting conclusions about learning. They pinpointed what they considered significant gains in knowledge of issue positions across a variety of issues. In general, the proportion of persons who did not know candidate positions declined from about 20 percent to less than 10 percent during the period of the debates. They argue that the persons who benefited most from the debates were those who made their vote decision during the campaign period. Forty percent of their panel consisted of these campaign deciders, who possessed moderate education and social status but were low in partisanship. Chaffee and Choe argue that in elections where large numbers of such voters are present, the heavy flow of information created by debates can be influential. Dennis and Chaffee (1978), in another analysis of the same data set, found evidence that the debates helped voters to clarify issue positions and bring their knowledge of these into conformity with their party affiliations and candidate images. They argued that in this way the debates may have increased the importance of issues for vote decisions.

Three other studies attribute modest political learning to the debates. Becker, Sobawale, Cobbey, and Eyal (1978) interviewed 1300 persons in the Syracuse, New York, area five times over the course of the campaign. Their comparison of debate viewers with nonviewers found that viewers showed significant gains in knowledge about candidate stands on issues even when education was taken into account. Davis (1979) reports results from a panel survey of 298 persons in Cleveland, Ohio. This study found that the candidate attribute perceptions of persons who made late or hard vote decisions were most strongly affected by mass media in general and debate viewing in particular. There was some evidence that the debates increased the acceptability of Ford among heavily Democratic Cleveland residents. Hagner and Rieselbach (1978) analyzed data from a national sample of 442 persons and found evidence that voter perceptions of candidates changes significantly during the debate period but that, in general, these changes were consistent with preexisting impressions. Carter voters developed more uniformly favorable impressions of him, while Ford voters developed more favorable impressions of their candidate.

Three studies are pessimistic about the learning initiated by the debates. The most detailed of these studies is reported by Graber and Kim (1979) and is based on 9 to 10 intensive interviews with 165 persons in four cities. The researchers acknowledge that their measurement of learning was quite rigorous, but they argue that it is a valid index of whether anything of use was learned. After each debate respondents were asked what they learned about the candidates and the issues. Very few persons reported learning a lot. Moderate levels of learning tended to be limited to perceptions of candidates, not to understanding of issues. The greatest amount of learning occurred among persons who had high interest in politics but little time available to follow the campaign. The debates may have allowed these persons to reduce the knowledge gap between themselves and persons who had high interest and more available time. Persons with low levels of political interest learned very little despite the fact that they did not know much initially. Graber and Kim concluded that debates seem likely to increase the gap in knowledge between persons of high and low interest. Bishop, Oldenick, and Tuchfarber (1978) draw similar conclusions based on interviews with 898 persons in the Cincinnati area. They comment that the knowledge-rich get richer as a result of the campaign, while those who are knowledge-poor gain little. They argue that debates are unlikely to be useful until basic intellectual capacities are increased and current media use patterns changed.

McLeod et al. (1979) interviewed a panel of 95 voters in Madison, Wisconsin and found tht the debates had little direct influence on learning but did stimulate interest in the campaign and increase partisanship.

CONCLUSIONS

This review of research permits us to be cautiously optimistic about the usefulness of televised presidential debates. No research has located any clearly detrimental debate effects. Perhaps the most plausible argument against debates which can be based on existing research is that debates accomplish little which is not already done by other forms of political communication. Why bother to create yet another campaign event? This argument can cite the 1960 research which suggested that people tend to use the debates to reinforce what they already believe. While more recent research has not completely rejected such notions about selective reinforcement, it is becoming increasingly clear that political interests are developed, media content chosen, and information learned which cannot be predicted by preexisting attitudes, especially when these attitudes are not strongly held. An increasing number of voters are less certain about their political attitudes and less committed to political parties. Many of these voters seek to base their vote decisions on information derived from campaign communication. There is empirical evidence that such persons are turning to the debates for the information they desire. For voters with moderate to strong interest in politics, the debates provide an opportunity to "catch up" on information they may have missed from other sources.

Other debate researchers admit that the debates do transmit innovative information to some voters, but they argue that the debates do not serve apathetic or poorly informed persons. They tell us that the "information-rich get richer" but the poor do not. While such findings were contradicted by other research, these researchers raise a potentially important criticism of the debates. Could debates increase the gulf between politically active and informed persons in our society and those who are not? What might the consequences be of such a gulf? It is likely that this is a gulf which has long existed. Comparison of early and recent voting research suggests that in the 1940s and 1950s, more voters were apathetic and uninformed than at present. Nie et al. (1976) argued that voters increasingly are basing their vote decisions on information about political issues and issue stands. Debates alone are not capable of transforming persons into model voters. But it can be argued that if the present trend is toward more rational voting by more individuals, debates can contribute to this trend. The very existence of debates as national campaign events suggests that we as a society condone rational voting and seek to encourage it through events we believe make such voting easier. If debates can serve to legitimize rational voting, then apathetic, uninformed voters might be motivated to close the gap. Debates offer no magical cure for the knowledge gaps in our society, but, along with other developments in political institutions, they could lessen rather than aggravate these differences.

One other argument is frequently raised by debate critics. Debates constitute yet another intrusion of mass media into political campaigns at the expense of political parties. Research suggests that the best evidence of this intrusion lies in the large number of persons who say they will make their vote decisions only after viewing the debates. Presumably, such persons have decided to allow themselves to be influenced by a campaign event which is not controlled by the parties. However, as currently structured, the parties and the candidates retain much greater control over the content of the debates than they do over most other forms of mass communication. Only advertising allows them greater control. Most candidates have used the debates as an opportunity to repeat old campaign speeches before a national audience. Intrusion arguments would seem to be better directed against campaign news coverage where the values and interests of news professionals clearly restrict the ability of the candidates to communicate as they choose. No one has suggested that we should eliminate news coverage of campaigns, but this would seem to be more warranted than elimination of debates. Perhaps one reason debates appear to be so intrusive at present is that they are alway scheduled on an ad hoc basis. The parties, the candidates, and the public are never certain whether they will take place at all until the candidates appear at the debate site. This problem could be remedied by institutionalizing debates, which is what we have advocated.

DEMOCRATIC THEORY AND PUBLIC POLICY

We have outlined the relationship between democratic theory and televised presidential debates. Democratic theory highlights the importance of rational, informed voting by all responsible citizens. It also stresses the necessity of permitting all persons to vote, even those who appear to be incapable of casting responsible votes. At the heart of democratic theory lies a moral conviction that people can be trusted to educate themselves to act responsibly when they are given the power to act. Democratic theory is a normative theory. It tells us what an ideal democratic society should look like and how its citizens should act. It provides a standard against which any contemporary social order can be measured. Democratic theory does not tell us how to create more democratic social orders, but it does tell us how well we have succeeded at any point in time. When we measure our own society against the ideals of democratic theory, it fails in many ways. This need not be a source of pessimism, however, so long as our social order continues to develop and to revere the ideals of democratic theory. The danger of theories like elite pluralism is that they imply that it is all right to compromise the standards of democratic theory so long as the political order is stable. Only the leaders of pluralistic groups need to be informed and politically active; others can get by merely by following the leaders' directions.

A firm commitment to democratic theory involves a radical conviction, a belief in the necessity for ongoing social changes so long as the ideals of democracy remain unrealized. Such a conviction underlies our proposal for the institutionalization of debates. We see this proposal as one of many steps which can and should be taken to reform election politics. Our basic justification for institutionalizing debates lies in the usefulness such debates may have for some voters. We have concluded that televised debates can increase what voters know about candidates and issues. Therefore, debates can enable our society to take another step toward realization of the democratic ideal that all citizens are capable of voting responsibly based on knowledge, not on prejudices.

Three groups of voters appear most likely to be directly served by the institutionalization of debates. Perhaps the most important of these groups is comprised of those persons who are moderately interested in politics and whose interest is a function of campaign events. Such voters typically have weak party affiliations and make vote decisions late in campaigns. For this group, debates can provide a catalyst to increase their concern about the election. For these persons, the hooply that typically surrounds televised debates may serve a legitimate purpose. It may stimulate an involvement in the debates which becomes an ongoing interest in the election. For such voters the timing of debates is usually ideal. Party conventions usually occur too early, while last-minute advertising campaigns are too late to aid in making vote decisions. Debates enable these moderately interested voters to get involved late but still learn as much about candidates as persons who have been involved longer. There is evidence that this voter group is increasing in size and that institutionalization of debates might serve to reinforce this trend. This group may offer the best hope of making steady progress toward the realization of democratic ideals.

A second group of voters has been identified as seekers of political information and often as ticket-splitters. This group has strongly developed political interests which are unlikely to be strengthened by debates, except during the primaries. By the time debates are held during general elections, these voters are likely to have learned as much information as they feel is necessary. However, the debates could serve a useful prupose by providing them with a brief, well-organized summary of pertinent information. Such a presentation could help these voters to draw some final conclusions from available information or to rethink conclusions they have already reached. Voter studies (DeVries & Tarrance, 1972) suggest that the number of such voters is also increasing. Institutionalization of debates might reinforce this trend and help them to make more responsible decisions.

Voters in the third group, party affiliates, use the debates to confirm or reinforce their voting predispositions. Such voters are selective in using most forms of political communication during campaigns. However, there is some evidence that while debates encourage positive perceptions of the candidate for one's own party, they do not necessarily encourage one to develop negative perceptions of the opposing candidate. In some cases, positive impressions of opposing candidates may develop. Debates seem unlikely to deepen partisan divisions beyond those which already exist. Research findings suggest that even though such voters acquire information selectively, they can vote more responsibly when they have more information available. Availability of information about candidate stands on issues can lead to voting based on issues rather than merely on impressions of candidate attributes.

The relative size of these three voter groups is likely to fluctuate from election to election. Events unique to each campaign period may dramatically increase or decrease the size of each group. While the trend in past elections has been for the first two groups to increase and the third to decrease, these trends might easily stop or reverse.

In 1976, for example, it is argued that the debates were unnecessary because most people had already made up their minds about who to vote for. Yet, the Roper poll (1976) of August 28-September 4 gave Carter 28 percent, Ford 14 percent, and the undecided vote was 56 percent. Discussions about debates sometimes avoid such pertinent facts (Mitchell, 1979) because of a tendency to rely on the findings of voter research in the 1940s. As we have already noted, this early research concentrated on affective effects which may have been more prevalent in an earlier era when most persons had strong party affiliations (Kraus & Davis, 1976). Others, such as Karayn (1979), have defended debates by noting that "half the electorate is a significant segment of the population to be uncommitted." He believes that voters, committed and uncommitted, watch the debates, make choices based on them, and are generally more informed as a result of viewing them.

DECIDING DEBATE POLICY

Evidence that voters watch debates and use them differently in assessing candidates, deciding for whom to vote or confirming their original choice, should provide the motivation for policymakers to include debates in presidential elections. The fact that not all voters are served equally well by debates or that most do not find debates to be decisive factors in forming vote decisions should not discourage policymakers from acting. Ultimately, the decision about institutionalizing debates must rest on democratic values. We believe there is sufficient evidence to conclude that debates would improve our political system.

While we strongly favor institutionalizing debates, we recognize that much can be done to improve the manner in which debates are staged. We believe that debates can be structured in ways which improve their ability to increase voter interest, encourage consideration of issues and stimulate voter turnout. Efforts should be made to devise and test such changes in structure.

For example, we know very little about the relationship of debate format to issue learning. Classical debate purists have argued that the 1960, 1976, and 1980, presidential encounters were not debates, just glorified press conferences (Auer, 1962; Bitzer & Rueter, 1980). However true those observations may have been, the fact is that voters have learned from watching even poorly structured debates. Perhaps the question of debate format should be discussed in light of *all* campaign activities on television. Mitchell (1979), in reviewing questions about format for policy considerations, suggested that "whether the debates are the candidates' only television exposure other than their own paid political advertisements or whether they are to be complemented by other types of television programming must be a factor in deciding on format."

The mix of political communication activities and coverage in campaigns may be more influential on voters than any single event or report. It is legitimate to ask what correspondence exists between a televised presidential debate and the media reports before and after. But the question often is limited to the accuracy of media reports rather than to determine the combined impact of debates and media reports about debates on voters. Lang and Lang (1978) found that persons exposed to media reports of the first Ford-Carter debate were more likely to be favorably impressed by Ford's performance.

We should be concerned about the interaction of different events within a campaign. Polling, for example, may have an indirect impact on debate format. Reporters or columnists for prominent newspapers may turn the candidates' strategies in a direction which ultimately affects the number and timing of debates. Minor party and independent candidates' nonparticipation may (and, in

1976, did) affect the way in which major candidates are asked and do participate in televised debates. The influence of such extraneous events on the debates can only be minimized through decisions to fix a more or less permanent schedule for debates throughout the general election period. But the consequences of such a fixed schedule must be carefully considered.

These and other considerations—sponsorship, participation of minor and independent candidates; financing, debate spacing, and method of determining issues to be discussed—deserve both research and policy-making attention, especially if we wish to argue that debates should be continued.

Thus, while much remains to be decided concerning televised debates, we believe that it is now possible to conclude objectively that debates should be institutionalized. It may be true that the American public is not yet ready to make adequate use of debate content. It may be true that the current format of televised debates leaves much to be desired. But, as we noted earlier, in creating more democratic social orders, it is sometimes necessary to take risks. Faith in the willingness and ability of average voters to vote responsibly if given the means to do so argues for institutionalization.

REFERENCES

Asher, H. B. *Presidential elections and American politics,* Homewood, IL: Dorsey Press, 1980.

Auer, J. J. The counterfeit debates. In S. Kraus (Ed.), *The great debates.* Bloomington: Indiana University Press, 1962.

Becker, L., McCombs, M., & McLeod, J. The development of political cognitions. In S. Chaffee (Ed.), *Political communication.* Beverly Hills, CA: Sage, 1975.

Becker, L., Sobowale, I., Cobbey, R., & Eyal, C. Debates' effects on voters' understanding of candidates and issues. In G. Bishop, R. Meadow, & M. Jackson-Beeck (Eds.), *The presidential debates.* New York: Praeger, 1978.

Becker, S., Pepper, R., Wenner, L., & Kim, J. Information flow and the shaping of meanings. In S. Kraus (Ed.), *The great debates: Carter vs. Ford, 1976.* Bloomington: Indiana University Press, 1979.

Berelson, B., Lazarsfeld, P. F., & McPhee, W. *Voting.* Chicago: University of Chicago Press, 1954.

Bishop, G. F. Book review of S. Kraus (Ed.), *The great debates: Carter vs. Ford, 1976. Public Opinion Quarterly,* 1980, 44.

Bishop, G., Oldenick, R., & Tuchfarber, A. The presidential debates as a device for increasing the "rationality" of electoral behavior. In G. Bishop, R. Meadow, & M. Jackson-Beeck (Eds.), *The presidential debates.* New York: Praeger, 1978.

Bitzer, L., & Reuter, T. *Carter vs. Ford: The counterfeit debates of 1976.* Madison: University of Wisconsin Press, 1980.

Broder, D. Editorial *Cleveland Plain Dealer,* June 14, 1981.

Carter, R. Some effects of the debates. In S. Kraus (Ed.), *The great debates.* Bloomington: Indiana University Press, 1962.

Chaffee, S. Presidential debates—Are they helpful to voters? *Communication Monographs,* 1978, *45,* 330-346.

Chaffee, S. H., & Choe, S. Y. Time of decision and media use during the Ford-Carter campaign. *Public Opinion Quarterly,* 1980, *44,* 52-69.

Davis, D. The vote decision process. In S. Kraus (Ed.), *The great debates: Carter vs. Ford, 1976.* Bloomington: Indiana University Press, 1979.

Dennis, J., & Chaffee, S. Legitimation in the 1976 U.S. election campaign. *Communication Research*, 1978, *5*, 371-394.

Deutschmann, P. Viewing, conversation and voting intentions. In S. Kraus (Ed.), *The great debates*. Bloomington: Indiana University Press, 1962.

DeVries, W., & Tarrance, V. *The ticket-splitter*. Grand Rapids, MI.: William B. Eerdmans, 1972.

Donohue, M., & Tipton, L. A conceptual model of information seeking, avoiding and processing. In P. Clarke (Ed.), *New models for communication research*. Beverly Hills, CA: Sage, 1973.

Elliott, J. (Ed.). *Debates on the adoption of the Federal Constitution, Vol. II*. New York: Burt Franklin Research and Source Series 109, 1888.

Farrand, M. (Ed.). *The records of the Federal Convention of 1787, Vol. II*. New Haven, CT: Yale University Press, 1911.

Germond, J. W., & Witcover, J. Presidential debates: An overview. In A. Ranney (Ed.), *The past and future of presidential debates*. Washington, DC: American Enterprise Institute, 1979.

Graber, D., & Kim, Y. Why John Q. Voter did not learn much from the 1976 presidential debates. In B. Ruben (Ed.), *Communication yearbook 2*. New Brunswick, NJ: Transaction Books, 1978.

Hagner, P., & Rieselbach, L. The impact of the 1976 presidential debates: conversion or reinforcement? In G. Bishop, R. Meadow, & M. Jackson-Beeck (Eds.), *The presidential debates*. New York: Praeger, 1978.

John and Mary Markle Foundation. Campaign debates '78: report of the campaign '78 debate survey project. Unpublished report, 1977.

Karayn, J. The case for permanent presidential debates. In A. Ranney (Ed.), *The past and future of presidential debates*. Washington, DC: American Enterprise Institute, 1979.

Katz, E., & Feldman, J. J. The great debates in the light of research: A survey of surveys. In S. Kraus (Ed.), *The great debates*. Bloomington: Indiana University Press, 1962.

Kraus, S. (Ed.). *The great debates: Background, perspective, effects*. Bloomington: Indiana University Press, 1962

Kraus, S. (Ed.). *The great debates: Carter vs. Ford, 1976*. Bloomington: Indiana University Press, 1979.

Kraus, S., & Davis, D. Critical events analysis. In S. Chaffee (Ed.), *Political communication*. Beverly Hills, CA: Sage, 1975.

Kraus, S., and Davis, D. *The effects of mass communication on political behavior*. University Park: Pennsylvania State University Press, 1976.

Kraus, S., & Smith, R. K. Issues and images. In S. Kraus (Ed.), *The great debates*. Bloomington: Indiana University Press, 1962.

Lang, K., & Lang, G. Reactions of viewers. In S. Kraus (Ed.), *The great debates*. Bloomington: Indiana University Press, 1962.

Lang, G., & Lang, K. The formation of public opinion: Direct and mediated effects of the first debate. In G. Bishop, R. Meadow, & M. Jackson-Beeck (Eds.), *The presidential debates*. New York: Praeger, 1978.

McCombs, M., & Shaw, D. The agenda setting function of the press. In D. Shaw & M. McCombs (Eds.), *The emergence of American political issues: The agenda setting function of the press*. St. Paul, MN: West Publishing, 1977.

McLeod, J., Durall, J., Ziemke, D., & Bybee, C. Expanding the context of effects. In S. Kraus (Ed.), *The great debates: Carter vs. Ford, 1976*. Bloomington: Indiana University Press, 1979.

Miller, A., & MacKuen, M. Learning about the candidates. The 1976 presidential debates. *Public Opinion Quarterly*, 1979, *43*, 326-346.

Mitchell, L. M. *With the nation watching. Report of the Twentieth Century Fund task force*. Lexington, MA: D. C. Heath, 1979.

Nie, N., Verba, S., & Petrocik, J. *The changing American voter*. Cambridge, MA: Harvard University Press, 1976.

O'Keefe, G., & Mendelsohn, H. Media influences and their anticipation. In S. Kraus (Ed.), *The great debates: Carter vs. Ford, 1976.* Bloomington: Indiana University Press, 1979.

Patterson, T. E. *The mass media election: How Americans choose their president.* New York: Praeger, 1980.

Patterson, T. E., & McClure, R. D. *The unseeing eye.* New York: Putnam, 1976.

Pomper, G. *Elections in America: Control and influence in democratic politics.* New York: Dodd, Mead, 1970.

Robinson, J. P. The polls. In S. Kraus (Ed.), *The great debates: Carter vs. Ford, 1976.* Bloomington: Indiana University Press, 1979.

Roper Reports. New York: Roper Organization, 1976, Vols. 76-79.

Sears, D., & Chaffee, S. Uses and effects of the 1976 debates: An overview of empirical studies. In S. Kraus (Ed.), *The great debates: Carter vs. Ford, 1976.* Bloomington: Indiana University Press, 1979.

Slagter, R., & Miller, R. The impact of the 1976 presidential debates on candidates' images: An experimental study. Paper presented to the Midwest Political Science Association, Chicago, Illinois, April 1978.

The Reporter. The little debates. December 6, 1962, pp. 36-38.

PART III

Political Communication Settings

CHAPTER 11

Communication and Political Socialization

Charles K. Atkin

ALTHOUGH FORMAL PARTICIPATION in the political system is reserved for adult citizens, the nature of involvement is significantly shaped by political socialization processes during the preadult years. This chapter examines the role of mass communication and social interaction in young people's learning about politics, focusing on responses to political content in the mass media and the communicatory aspects of family influence. This review describes major concepts and theories and presents empirical findings from the extensive research literature dealing with communication and socialization to politics.

Political socialization is typically defined as a developmental process by which children and adolescents acquire cognitions, attitudes, values, and participation patterns relating to their political environment (Hyman, 1959; Langton, 1969; Hess & Torney, 1967). Several societal agents have been identified as key transmitters of political orientations from generation to generation, particularly parents, school, peers, and the mass media.

Since Hyman (1959) provided the impetus for this field, there have been hundreds of investigations examining how young people learn political information, develop attachment to the political system, and form partisan attitudes. Research indicates that the socialization process typically begins with vague emotional allegiances and personalized identification with authority figures such as the president and police officers. According to studies in the 1950s and early 1960s, children's views are characterized by an idealized conception of leaders (Greenstein, 1960; Hess & Torney, 1967). However, this may have been an artifact of the "happy days" era and the unique charisma of Eisenhower and Kennedy, since subsequent investigations have shown a more differentiated and less benevolent set of attachments (Sears, 1975; Dennis & Webster, 1975). The declining idealization is often attributed to reactions to civil rioting, the Vietnam war, and Watergate (Niemi & Sobieszek, 1977; Dennis & Webster, 1975).

After developing the capacity to think abstractly in late childhood (see, for example, Kohlberg, 1969), a sophisticated understanding of political ideas and institutions emerges. As a child moves into adolescence, a more rational and knowledgeable conception of political roles, processes, and institutions replaces affect for individual personalities, and some distrust and cynicism begins to grow (Greenstein, 1968; Niemi & Sobieszek, 1967). Although it can be argued that political socialization covers the entire life span (Brim & Wheeler, 1966), most attention has focused on these preadult stages of learning.

Political scientists have proposed a number of frameworks for conceptualizing this process. Easton and Hess (1962) approached political socialization from a systems theory perspective. Their parsimonious input-output conversion model posits various demands and supports as the primary inputs to the political system. One important means of support is the continuous political indoctrination of incoming members of the society.

A similar macrolevel emphasis has been utilized by scholars working from Parsons's structural-functional theory (Mitchell, 1962; Almond & Verba, 1963). This perspective holds that a key element in societal pattern maintenance is conformity to prescriptions of the cultural system. Therefore, youth must be inculcated with a desire to fulfill role expectations of society concerning normative political behavior.

Most political scientists have taken the individual as the primary unit of analysis in an attempt to explain the child's acquisition of political orientations. Greenstein (1965) provided the most useful microlevel scheme in his rephrasing of Lasswell's basic question: Who learns what from whom under what circumstances with what effects? The current research literature has generally focused on several *agents* influencing certain *cognitive, affective,* and *behavioral* dependent variables for various subgroups of preadults.

A wide variety of criterion variables have been examined, including political knowledge, beliefs, efficacy, trust, interest, party identification, support for the system, partisan attitudes, participatory norms, and overt behavior (including everyday interpersonal discussions and exposure to political media content). Most scholars agree that political orientations acquired in the preadult years, particularly adolescence, have important implications for subsequent adult behavior (Cook & Scioli, 1972; Sears, 1975).

The two socialization agents most centrally involved in the informal communication of political orientations—parents and the mass media—have been treated quite differently in traditional political socialization research. Early researchers focused narrowly on the family as the major agent of political learning, and the conventional wisdom still attributes to the family the primary role in socializing the child to politics.

Until the 1970s, most researchers did not even consider the mass media as potential agents of political socialization; the few studies which included media variables treated political exposure as a criterion of socialization rather than an independent influence on the child. Chaffee, Ward, and Tipton (1970) speculate that the basis for ignoring the media role was the classic "limited effects" model of mass communication effects on adult voting behavior. They argue that it is inappropriate to apply these principles to preadult socialization, where a young person is forming rather than defending political predispositions; indeed, recent evidence casts doubt on the validity of such principles for adult voters.

This chapter focuses on the role played by the mass media and parents. The examination of mass communication will concentrate on the news media, supplemented by a brief consideration of entertainment effects. Then the contribution of the family will be considered, with the emphasis on parent-child communication about politics. As a preliminary step to examining the impact of the news media, the next section reviews the evidence on young people's exposure to news content.

NEWS EXPOSURE PATTERNS

Since news content provides the bulk of politically relevant information in the mass media, it is important to examine young people's patterns of news exposure. A number of recent studies demonstrate considerable consumption of hard news, particularly among teenage groups. The exposure data from these investigations will be reviewed in detail, followed by a brief assessment of the predictors of news consumption.

There are several reasons to study children's news exposure behavior. First, exposure is a necessary condition for direct media impact on political orientations (although some indirect effects occur via interpersonal channels). Second, patterns of news consumption established in the preadult years are likely to carry over into adulthood, providing a continuing basis for political effects on voters. Finally, exposure behavior is a criterion of political socialization, one indicator of the extent of youthful involvement in politics.

The most comprehensive survey measured exposure in a large, representative national sample of 6- to 17-year-old youths. Gollin and Anderson (Note 1) administered questionnaires to more than 1000 students, with equal numbers drawn from early elementary school grades (age 6-8), late elementary school (age 9-11), junior high school (age 12-14) and high school (age 15-17).

When asked if they ever read newspapers, the proportion replying affirmatively rises sharply from 33 percent in early elementary school to 61 percent in late elementary school, and increases more gradually to 75 percent of the junior high students and 82 percent of those in high school; these figures are closely validated by observations of the mothers. The proportions of students reporting newspaper exposure "every day" or "most days" is much lower, but follows the same pattern of increase, from 7 to 24 to 43 to 52 percent across the four age levels. The biggest jump occurs around age 10 to 12, when reading skills are typically mastered. The number of minutes spent reading newspapers per day is 14, with the oldest age group spending twice as much time as the youngest children.

Among those who ever read a newspaper, content exposure patterns were measured. Front-page news ranks second only to comics, with 40 percent of the sample reporting that they read it "most of the time." Sports, entertainment listings, and soft news features rank ahead of the other types of serious news stories: 26 percent of the readers say they are exposed to local news, 16 percent to national news, 10 percent to foreign news, and 4 percent to editorial page material. Averaging across these five categories, the proportion reading "most of the time" increases from 5 percent in early elementary school, to 12 percent in late elementary school, to 26 percent in junior high school, to 32 percent in senior high.

Gollin and Anderson also measured exposure to the other three major media. About one-third of the students report watching TV news "most days." By age level, viewers include 13 percent of early elementary children and 23 percent in the late elementary group. News viewing reaches the 40 percent level in both junior and senior high school age groups. Listening to radio news "yesterday" is slightly more extensive, rising from 12 to 26 to 43 to 55 percent across the four age levels. When asked if they had read *Time* or some other newsmagazine during the past month, 16 percent of the late elementary students, 25 percent of the junior high students, and 35 percent of the senior high students replied positively.

Another large-sample national survey focused on high school seniors (ages 17-18). According to Jennings and Niemi (1974), newspaper news and TV news exposure is fairly equivalent: 46 percent report daily reading and 38 percent daily viewing, and an additional 31 percent read the newspaper two or three times per week and 32 percent watch TV news that often. Daily radio news exposure occurs among 43 percent of the seniors, and 15 percent listen to radio newscasts two or three times per week.

Drew and Reeves (1980a) measured TV, radio, and newspaper news exposure among children in the third through seventh grades (ages 8-13). National TV newscast viewing is reported by one-third of the sample (11 percent "almost every day" and 21 percent "sometimes"), with slight increases by age level. A higher proportion say they watch the local news (14 percent almost daily, and 32 percent occasionally), but much of this focuses on sports and weather portions of the newscast. Exposure to the news portion of the local newscast rises from 7 percent of the third graders to 27 percent of the seventh graders. In addition, almost three-fourths of all age groups view the child-oriented "In the News" segments interspersed among Saturday morning cartoons.

The Drew and Reeves study found widespread radio news listening, with almost-daily exposure by 27 percent and occasional exposure by 33 percent. Regarding newspapers, 33 percent say they read almost every day and 28 percent, sometimes; however, some of this merely represents comic strip reading. Readership of the front page increased from 9 percent in the third grade to 34 percent in the seventh grade.

In the most detailed survey of children's television news exposure patterns, Atkin (1978) administered questionnaires to elementary school students (ages 6-11) and interviewed their mothers. The amount of viewing depends on which source and measurement technique is considered. When asked for generalized reports on news viewing, the children tend to give high estimates, when the questions refer to concrete recent viewing experiences, somewhat lower levels are reported by the children; when mothers are asked to describe their children's general exposure, even more conservative figures are obtained. One-third of the children claim that they watch the national news programs "almost every day," and an additional one-third indicate that they watch "sometimes." On the other hand, just 8 percent of the mothers say their children view daily, and about two-fifths report occasional viewing of national news. (Furthermore, just one-fourth of these mothers say their children pay close attention while viewing the news). Diary reports obtained from the children show that two-fifths watched national newscasts the day before; most viewed "some" rather than "all" of the newscast.

Reported levels of local news viewing are slightly higher, with weather and sports portions most popular. Exposure to the Saturday morning "In the News" mini-newscasts is very high. Nearly half of the children say they watch "alot," and diary reports show an average of one-third watching each segment. The mothers corroborate these data: more than half say their children pay close attention when the "In the News" segments appear. Exposure to national, local, and children's TV news increases moderately with age level.

The Atkin survey also tapped radio news listening. Two-thirds of the elementary school children say they have ever listened to radio newscasts. Using diaries, 40 percent report hearing a newscast on the previous day (including 14 percent who had heard one, 7 percent two, 6 percent three, 7 percent four, and 6 percent five or more). Proportions exposed show a gain from 24 percent in kindergarten and first grade to 58 percent in fourth and fifth grade.

A newspaper feature parallel to the televised "In the News" newscasts is the "Mini Page" insert appearing in dailies with nine million circulation. A survey in one market showed that 79 percent of the late elementary school children read this page (Bittner & Shamo, 1976).

A number of studies have provided less elaborate data on TV news viewing. Egan (1978) showed elementary school students pictures of newscasters and asked about exposure. Two-thirds view at least occasionally; one-fourth of the sixth graders say they watch "almost every day." Stories about crime and disaster are most avidly viewed, while presidential and government news are least popular. McLeod, Atkin, and Chaffee (1972) found that one-third of junior high school students view the news "often." Another survey of junior high students indicates that half watch at least two or three times per week (McIntyre & Teevan, 1972). Other surveys demonstrate somewhat less extensive news viewing (Schramm, Lyle, and Parker, 1961; Lyle & Hoffman, 1972). The Nielsen ratings show that the average news program attracts about half as many child and adolescent viewers as the typical prime-time entertainment program (Comstock et al., 1978).

There is also evidence of considerable viewing during political campaign periods, especially among adolescents (Chaffee, Ward, & Tipton, 1970; McLeod, O'Keefe, & Wackman, Note 2; Roberts, Hawkins, & Pingree, 1975). For example, one study of the 1976 presidential "Great Debates" showed that more than half of the junior and senior high school students watched the broadcasts, averaging almost a half-hour of viewing time per debate (Hawkins, Pingree, Smith, & Bechtolt, 1979). Late elementary school students surveyed during a presidential primary election campaign estimate they watched an average of eight televised political commercials, and half report paying full attention to these messages. When asked how often they had seen TV news stories about the presidential candidates, one-fourth responded "very often" and one-third "pretty often" (Atkin, 1977).

Aside from informal exposure, many young people have access to the print news media via the schools. About half of the students surveyed by Gollin and Anderson (Note 1) received youth-oriented newsweeklies such as *Weekly Reader* or *Junior Scholastic* in their classrooms. In addition, about half of the daily newspapers in the country provide copies of their papers to schools, primarily for social studies and civics classes. Two-fifths of the students have used either these classroom newspapers or have been assigned to read the newspaper outside school.

Looking across these varied research findings, a tentative portrait of youthful news consumption can be drawn. The young child is typically introduced to news via television, beginning with child-oriented newscasts on Saturday morning and the sports and weather portions of adult news programs. Superficial exposure to hard news on local and national newscasts occurs fairly regularly among one-third of elementary school children; however, daily exposure and attentive viewing are rare, and public affairs content is not popular. National and local news viewership doubles during the junior and senior high school years, including two-fifths who watch almost every day.

Newspaper reading begins later in elementary school, after initial contact with the comics, sports, or child-oriented pages. Frequent newspaper exposure increases from one-sixth of elementary school children to one-half of high school students. While front-page news is widely read, most politically relevant national and international news tends to have limited appeal; even among high school students, less than one-third read these stories frequently.

Radio news listening occurs on a daily basis for one-third of elementary school children and almost half of those in junior and senior high school. The latest and least consumed medium is newsmagazines, which are read at least monthly by one-fourth of junior high students and one-third of high school students.

Reasons for News Exposure

Beyond these bare statistics on news viewing, listening, and reading, what are the factors that explain why young people are exposed? The model of exposure decision-making proposed by Atkin (1973) serves as a framework for understanding media consumption patterns. Mass media exposure is considered a cost-benefit tradeoff, where the individual weighs various uses and gratifications from message content and channel processing against expenditures such as money, time, mental effort, and psychological dissonance. The most prominent gratification benefits are pleasurable enjoyment and interest satisfaction derived from substantive content, and the improvement of unpleasant states (such as loneliness, social conflict, problems, and boredom) derived from the mere act of consuming media channels, particularly television. Utilitarian benefits primarily involve message content that provides relevant information to gain knowledge, aid decision-making, or guide behavior.

Content gratifications from hard news appear to be restricted for youthful audiences, since public affairs interest is limited and fantasy programming is more entertaining. Indeed, very few children cite TV news as their favorite type of program (Atkin, 1978; Lyle & Hoffman, 1972). Drew and Reeves (1980a) found that TV news is not well liked by 8- to 13-year-olds: 11 percent like it "alot" and 36 percent "a little." A more positive rating is given by high school students; equal proportions agree, disagree, and respond neutrally to the statement "I like to watch news and public affairs programs on television" (Prisuta, 1979a). For young children, the child-oriented "In the News" mini-newscasts are fairly well received: one-third say they like the segments "alot" and almost half express "a little" liking (Atkin, 1978). The best-liked parts of the newspaper are the comics, sports, puzzles, and games, rather than serious news content (Gollin & Anderson, Note 1).

Reflecting the importance of content gratifications in producing exposure, Atkin (1978) found that those children who do enjoy the news are much more likely to view; news liking is the most powerful predictor of exposure to all types of TV news, with correlations above +.30. Furthermore, Drew and Reeves (1980a) discovered that those seeking "internal" gratifications from news viewing (greater motivation to view for fun, excitement, and curiosity) tend to have greater news exposure. Pertinent to this discussion is evidence showing a positive association between news exposure and political interest, which will be presented later in this chapter. Since topical interest and content exposure are usually related in a reciprocal fashion, part of the association is probably due to inherent interest stimulating exposure to media messages.

The act of processing news from media channels is not likely to be a major contributor to gratification benefits, since hard news constitutes such a small portion of the message flow. Relatively few minutes per day are devoted to these messages. The more pervasive entertainment content (especially TV shows and radio music) plays a much bigger role in satisfying needs to escape boredom, problems, and the like.

The major factor on the benefit side appears to be instrumental utilities. Exposure should be greater to the extent that young people perceive that news content provides useful information (for example, for conversations or school assignments) or the act of exposure elicits external reinforcement. Although researchers have not addressed this point thoroughly, there is some evidence supporting the utility explanation (Prisuta, 1979a; Gollin & Anderson, Note 1; Atkin, 1978; Drew & Reeves, 1980a; Egan, 1978; Jennings & Niemi, 1974; Hawkins, Pingree, & Roberts, 1975; Roberts et al., 1975).

Several elements on the cost side are quite significant in accounting for news exposure. The stage of cognitive development is obviously important in providing sufficient mental ability to decode, comprehend, and integrate hard news messages; in particular, facile reading skills are a key determinant of newspaper exposure. Regular availability of the newspaper in the home is a basic contributor to reading, according to Gollin and Anderson (Note 1). In a parallel fashion, accessibility to TV news is governed by inertial flow from lead-in programs. Atkin (1978) found that exposure to TV programs aired immediately prior to the news is a significant predictor of news viewing. The association between parent and child news viewing can be partly interpreted in terms of accessibility factor, too. Clearly, sheer exposure to musical entertainment on the radio yields greater exposure to the embedded newscasts. Therefore, the minimal costs of acquiring and processing news content leads to greater exposure.

These uses, gratifications, and cost components help explain some of the demographic correlates of news exposure obtained by researchers. The recurrent finding that exposure monotonically increases with age can be understood in terms of greater benefits due to increased public affairs interest, interpersonal communication about news topics, and involvement in social studies school work, along with more sophisticated processing skills that decrease mental effort expenditures. The higher level of news exposure among boys than girls (Atkin, 1978; Gollin & Anderson, Note 1; Prisuta, 1979a) may be due to differential development of intrinsic public affairs interest and interpersonal discussion as children become socialized into traditional sex roles. This explanation may also apply to differences in exposure according to race and socioeconomic status;

combined with the greater monetary and mental costs experienced by youth from disadvantaged backgrounds, news reading is especially limited. Whites and higher-SES youth are exposed more often to hard news in the print media, and the gap widens with age as differential socialization and processing capabilities unfold. For example, high-income elementary school children are 6 percent more likely than low-income children to read newspapers; this gap between income subgroups increases to 13 percent in junior high school and to 28 percent in high school. Similarly, the white-black difference in newspaper reading increases with age level from 1 to 15 to 37 percent (Gollin & Anderson, Note 1).

Finally, there are indications of a news exposure syndrome across media. Atkin (1978) found moderate intercorrelations among viewing of national, local, and children's TV news, and between news viewing and both radio news listening and newspaper news reading. In the Gollin and Anderson survey, there are strong associations among measures of newspaper, TV, and radio news exposure. This evidence suggests that there are cross-media content factors which provide similar interest and enjoyment gratifications and instrumental utilities.

MASS MEDIA EFFECTS

The central subject addressed in this chapter concerns the effects of the mass media on young people's political orientations. The socialization criteria are categorized into cognitive, affective, and behavioral dimensions. The cognitive effects primarily involve awareness and knowledge gain derived from news media content. In the affective domain, criterion variables include evaluative ratings of political actors and institutions and interest in public affairs. The key behavioral outcomes are interpersonal communication about political matters and participation in campaign activities. Following the description of news media effects, the impact of entertainment and advertising content on some of these variables will be considered.

In approaching the study of news effects, researchers have placed little emphasis on explicit theoretical models and processes. The research appears to be guided by a simple stimulus-response perspective, where exposure to news directly influences orientations in a manner corresponding to the manifest content of the news messages. The major factor is the nature of stimulus attributes, such as frequency of presentation, visibility and personalization of roles and institutions covered, positive versus negative treatment of subject-matter, and arousal value of the presentational style. For instance, if political campaign coverage in newspapers presents extensive information about certain candidates and issues, it is expected that exposed young people will cognitively acquire this basic content; or if a president is portrayed unfavorably in TV newscasts, then negative affective responses are anticipated. The precise psychological mechanisms producing these effects have been ignored, although the mere exposure theory that repetition causes liking for objects has been assessed (see Atkin, 1977).

A few investigators have explored developmental differences in response, hypothesizing that the stage of cognitive sophistication serves as a mediator in the learning process (see Atkin & Gantz, 1978; Drew & Reeves, 1980b). Thus, the same news messages may have different effects on younger versus older audiences. For example, teenagers possessing a more mature information-processing capacity and a fuller understanding of politics are predicted to acquire complex political information more broadly and deeply than do children; older youth with a more internalized sense of moral development are expected to apply more critical judgments to political actors in forming attitudes.

Other demographic, attitudinal, and social variables have also been examined as mediators of effects. Among the background characteristics, race and socio-economic status have been studied in a few investigations (see Dominick, 1972; Gollin & Anderson, Note 1). Initial levels of affective orientations have been considered to mediate subsequent responses to new information, although very little evidence pertains to this set of antecedents (see Conway, Stevens, & Smith, 1975; Hawkins et al., 1979). Finally, several researchers have focused on the interpersonal communication environment as it affects news impact (Tolley, 1973; Roberts et al., 1975). It is expected that the structure and ideological climate of the family will provide interpretive guidance for incoming media messages, serve as a constraining or facilitating context for responding to news, and directly counteract or support attitudinal effects. Despite their emphasis on indirect two-step flows of influence in early voting research, political socialization researchers have not assessed the role of parents as opinion leaders who might relay content to nonexposed offspring.

The uses and gratifications perspective has been applied sparingly by functionalists who stress a more active role for the individual receiver in reacting to media content (see Drew & Reeves, 1980a, 1980b). To the extent that different audience members approach political messages with varying needs and motivations (for example, for excitement, understanding, diversion, conversational utility, or partisan defensiveness), differential knowledge gain or attitude change is predicted. Key intervening variables are attentional focus, selective perception, believability, and news enjoyment.

Methodologically, four basic types of evidence have been presented in the research literature. The first approach relies on the respondent to provide self-reports of perceived effects (see Dominick, 1972; Coldevin, 1972). For example, the child may be asked to estimate the degree to which campaign information has been gained from various media and nonmedia sources, or to indicate whether a particular opinion has been shaped by media coverage. While this technique allows for measurement of subtle or subjective changes resulting from media exposure, the main problem is the dubious validity of such reports: The individual may be unaware of certain effects, may misestimate the degree of impact or misattribute the source of some effects, or may distort actual responses in a socially desirable direction.

A second method widely used in political socialization research is the correlational field survey (see Johnson, 1973; Gollin & Anderson, Note 1). Researchers typically measure a variety of relevant variables and analyze the interrelationships among them. In the simplist approach, amount of news media exposure is used as a predictor of socialization criteria such as level of political knowledge or participation. More elaborate studies include additional antecedent or intervening variables in multiple regression or contingent correlation analyses. The correlational survey is advantageous because the array of naturally occurring variables measured in this design tend to have high external validity and can be subjected to analyses that allow the investigator to determine linkages. The primary shortcoming concerns the inference of cause-and-effect between variables that are apparently associated, since a positive correlation may be due to reverse causation or common antecedent conditions (for example, an obtained correlation between news reading and political interest may be accounted for by interest producing exposure, or may be a spurious artifact of age or socioeconomic status simultaneously influencing each variable). Several researchers have employed panel survey designs with multiple data-gathering points over time, in an effort to trace causality flows (see Chaffee et al., 1970; Atkin & Gantz, 1978).

A third approach involves aggregate analytical methods that combine trend analysis and content analysis (see Dennis & Webster, 1975; Hawkins et al., 1975). Periodic or historical changes in the level of a political orientation, as measured in surveys, are compared to the nature of news content presented over time. For example, increases in political cynicism during the years of the Watergate scandal may be attributed to mass media news coverage. While this approach is valuable for tracing gradual naturalistic changes in fundamental affective orientations during times of unusual media treatment of political developments, there is no basis for isolating the direct contribution of news exposure.

The fourth and least frequently used method is the experiment, where exposure to news content is manipulated by the researcher (see Atkin & Greenberg, 1974; Cohen, Wigand, & Harrison, 1976). Despite the advantage of clear-cut causal inference, this approach has limited applicability because of external validity problems. In particular, experiments involve forced rather than voluntary exposure to political messages, and immediate rather than long-term measurement of basic socialization variables. Quasi-experimental designs provide a more valid basis for studying naturalistic media effects but have been ignored by most investigators.

Due to the methodological weaknesses of studies assessing the role of mass communication in political socialization, caution must be exercised in drawing inferences of effects and extrapolating findings to the real world. Nevertheless, the convergence of evidence based on a variety of methods and investigations serves as a sound basis for making conclusions about certain types of effects in the following sections.

Cognitive Effects

A large number of studies have examined the impact of news on elementary cognitive variables such as awareness, knowledge, and images of politics. The first set of investigations to be reviewed are correlational surveys, beginning with four studies that employed a panel design. In describing survey findings, the degree of relationship will be represented by reference to specific correlation coefficients or by descriptive terms such as a "strong" relationship (that is, coefficients above +.35), moderate relationship (ranging from +.25 to +.35), mild relationship (+.15 to +.25), or slight relationship (+.05 to +.15).

The first major study examining mass communication and political socialization was conducted during the 1968 presidential campaign. Chaffee et al. (1970) administered questionnaires to adolescents in both May and November. They found that public affairs media exposure via newspapers and TV is correlated moderately with political knowledge at each point in time. Analyzing cross-lagged correlations across the six-month period, they discovered that May public affairs media use correlates +.33 with November knowledge levels. This coefficient exceeds both the opposite time-order relationship and a baseline figure representing chance association, indicating a causal influence.

Atkin and Gantz (1978) interviewed elementary school children in 1973 and resurveyed a subsample one year later. Political knowledge was measured by items asking for identification of leaders (for example, Nixon, Ford, and Kissinger), cities and countries in the news (such as Washington, China, and Vietnam), and issues (Watergate, POWs, and inflation). News viewing is mildly related to knowledge for older elementary students; controlling for grade, sex, race, and academic ability, the correlation at Time 1 is +.23. The relationship is negligible for those in the early elementary grades, however. When Saturday morning news viewing is assessed, the partial correlation is +.12 for the older group and +.06 for younger children. Over-time analyses indicate that news exposure is the predominant causal variable in the relationship, particularly for Saturday morning newscast viewing.

Chaffee (1977) described media-relevant evidence derived from an eight-year panel survey conducted by political scientists Jennings and Niemi. A national sample of high school seniors was interviewed in 1965 and reinterviewed in 1973 as young adults. In the high school wave, there is a +.26 correlation between public affairs newspaper reading and political knowledge. Although the association between 1965 newspaper use and 1973 knowledge is significant, it is not as strong as the reverse causal linkage. Broadcast exposure did not appear to have a causal impact on subsequent knowledge.

In the other panel survey, Hawkins et al. (1975) questioned a sample of late elementary school students and junior high school students during the 1972 presidential campaign and again in 1973 during the Watergate scandal. They found that prior exposure to the news media is moderately related to subsequent knowledge about Watergate.

A survey of late elementary children showed that heavier TV news viewers are moderately more likely to perceive that the two major parties represent different special interest groups, and that Congress is the chief lawmaking branch of government (Conway et al., 1975).

In a national sample of elementary, junior, and senior high school students, Gollin and Anderson (Note 1) measured awareness of several public officials and issues. Controlling for age level, those who read newspapers regularly are better able to identify Anwar Sadat (19 percent correct), compared to occasional readers (10 percent) and nonreaders (6 percent). There are only slight differences for the widely recognized former President Carter. Averaging data for the issues of inflation, ERA, and SALT, correct answers are given by 22 percent of regular newspaper users, 17 percent of occasional users, and 10 percent of those who do not read. The strength of relationship is not appreciably higher for the older than the younger age groups. These researchers also created a brief test of knowledge about the political system and its constitutional underpinnings (for example, the limits of presidential power and the rights of free speech). Regular readers score one point higher than nonreaders on the five-point scale.

A recent survey focused on political knowledge in elementary school (Atkin & Neuendorf, Note 3). An index was constructed from items measuring name recognition of pictures of political figures (such as Ayatollah Khomeini, Ronald Reagan, and Margaret Thatcher), identification of that person's position, and awareness of recently publicized attributes or events involving each leader. Knowledge is correlated +.21 with national news viewing, based on number of days per week viewed and amount of time watched per broadcast.

Learning from both news and candidate advertising was explored during the 1976 presidential primary campaign. Atkin (1977) measured frequency of watching national news programs and attention to campaign stories. Knowledge about presidential candidates Carter, Reagan, and Ford is correlated moderately with news viewing within the overall elementary school sample; the correlation is stronger among older children (+.40) than younger ones (+.19). Candidate knowledge is correlated mildly with the frequency and intensity of exposure to campaign commercials; the older students (+.28) apparently learn more from political ads than do younger students (+.19).

Eight other surveys show evidence consistent with the pattern of findings from the investigations described above. In each case, an index of political knowledge is mildly associated with exposure to televised and/or newspaper news content (Hirsch, 1971; Johnson, 1973; Tolley, 1973; Hawkins, 1974; Rubin, 1976, 1978; Hawkins et al., 1979; Jackson-Beeck, 1979). These researchers surveyed samples from a variety of SES backgrounds and age levels, ranging from early elementary school to high school. The strongest relationships are found for high school seniors (Hawkins, 1974; Johnson, 1973). No consistent differences occur for newspaper versus television news predictors.

The self-report method has been employed in numerous political socialization studies. The evidence consistently shows that young people perceive that they learn more from the mass media in general and television in particular than from alternative information sources.

Chaffee et al. (1970) asked junior and senior high students to rate introspectively the four primary socialization agents according to degree of importance in providing information on two specific current topics. On the basis of self-reports on a six-point rating scale, the mass media are clearly the leading information source (mean = 5.6), compared to teachers (3.9), parents (3.3), and friends (2.6). Furthermore, students who relied primarily on the mass media score substantially higher on an index of political knowledge than those indicating that parents, teachers, or peers are the most important source.

In a survey.of junior high school students, Dominick (1972) found that the mass media are the primary sources of information about the president (83 percent citing a media source), Vice-President (84 percent), Congress (59 percent), and the Supreme Court (50 percent). In each case, TV is most often mentioned, followed by newspapers. Dominick also asked respondents to name the "best place to go for information about candidates and issues." The top-rated source is newspapers (50 percent), with television (20 percent) and parents (12 percent) trailing far behind. He reported that children from low-income homes, particularly boys, are more reliant on television and less dependent on parents, compared to middle-income children.

Another sample of junior high school students surveyed by Rubin (1976) gave similar responses when asked for political information sources: TV is cited by 79 percent for learning about the President, by 78 percent for federal government information, and by 58 percent for politics in general.

Introspective reports have been employed to determine sources of information about foreign affairs. Hollander (1971) examined five basic agents of socialization to international conflict, particularly the Vietnam war. High school seniors were asked specific questions about the nature, causes, and consequences of war. When told to identify the sources used as a basis for this knowledge, the students cite the mass media in three-fifths of the cases; among the media, TV is clearly most crucial, with newspapers cited next most often. The school, family, friends, and church are secondary in importance as sources of information.

Using a similar approach, Coldevin (1972) asked high school students to define and describe their international political cognitions. In identifying their most important sources for this information, respondents report relying primarily on the mass media, especially television. The school is next most often cited, followed by family and friends.

Tolley (1973) also found that television is the primary information source for the Vietnam war among elementary and junior high children, relative to parents, teachers, and peers.

Television ranks first as a source of knowledge about the topics of Watergate and Skylab in a self-report survey of late elementary and junior high students (Hawkins, 1974). Another survey of younger students shows TV leading the list of sources of learning about foreign peoples (Lambert, 1967).

Finally, several experimental studies have dealt with cognitive effects. Atkin and Greenberg (1974) divided classrooms of Florida high school students into two groups. One group was shown six hour-long videotapes from a PBS series reporting news about the Florida legislature; the control group was not exposed. Those seeing the series had much higher scores on a knowledge quiz pertaining to legislative business and operation.

Drew and Reeves (1980b) manipulated the context of a brief news story about controversies surrounding a modern arts museum in Paris; it was presented either within a regular adult newscast or during a children's program. The context makes no difference in learning story content: Regardless of experimental treatment, the junior high students learned more than the late elementary students in the sample. The most interesting finding is that those perceiving the function of TV news as informational rather than entertainment tend to exhibit much greater information gains from exposure.

An experiment by Cohen, Wigand, and Harrison (1976) compared learning by elementary children watching a videotape containing six TV news stories of either a political or dramatic human-interest nature. Information recall after viewing is far greater for the dramatic news events (for example, jailbreak, fire, or train wreck) than the political news items.

There is also one quasi-field experiment testing knowledge gain. Alper and Leidy (1969) assessed the impact of the TV program "National Citizenship Test," which used a quiz format to present information about U.S. constitutional law. The program portrayed short, dramatic scenes to demonstrate lawful and unlawful activities (such as police entering a suspect's home and a speaker criticizing the government). High school students who watched the broadcast at home were compared with a matched sample measured before the show was aired. On a knowledge test covering program material, viewers score 14 percent higher than the comparison group.

In conclusion, this array of findings suggests that the mass media produce an important impact on the cognitive aspects of political socialization. The convergence of evidence from the correlational, self-report, and experimental studies indicates that television news and public affairs programming is the leading source of information, especially for children; newspapers also appear to make a significant contribution for adolescents. The self-report surveys show that television and other media learning is relatively greater than from other sources, such as family, peers, and teachers.

Affective Effects

A broad range of political affect variables have been investigated by researchers in the past decade. The largest body of evidence pertains to interest in political affairs. Eight studies show relationships between news exposure and interest, ranging from mildly to strongly positive.

In Atkin and Neuendorf's sample of elementary students, TV news viewing is correlated +.47 with interest in the President's activities and +.55 with interest in Iranian events. Drew and Reeves (1980a) report that interest in city, state, national and presidential affairs is associated +.28 with local news watching and +.18 with national news watching among late elementary and junior high students. High school students who were shown the series of legislature broadcasts became significantly more interested in the legislature (Atkin & Greenberg, 1974). General political interest is related +.20 with TV public affairs viewing and +.20 with presidential debate exposure in a junior and senior high sample (Hawkins et al., 1979). In the Gollin and Anderson survey, newspaper reading is mildly related to interest in current events topics such as pollution, presidential activities, and inflation. Johnson (1973) found a correlation of +.42 between political interest and an index of exposure to broadcast and newspaper news, and Jackson-Beeck (1979) reported a modest correlation with newspaper reading. Finally, Atkin and Gantz (1978) found mild correlations between both adult- and child-oriented news viewing and national and international interest measures. It should be noted that the direction of causality is ambiguous in most of this research; although statistical controls have been employed in some studies, the reverse interest-to-exposure flow of influence may account for a portion of the relationship.

Other research has focused on attitudes toward political leaders and issues and attachment to the political system. Atkin (1977) discovered that liking for presidential candidates is moderately related to frequency of viewing campaign ads. Since these late elementary students have little partisan basis for selectively interpreting commercial claims, it appears that the mere exposure to repeatedly presented messages produces greater affect toward the attractively advertised candidates. The number of exposures to Carter ads correlates +.39 with liking Carter; the correlation is +.32 for frequency of Ford ad viewing and liking, and is +.26 in the case of Reagan. Furthermore, the closeness of attention devoted to each candidate's ads is much more strongly related to the liking ratings (+.65 for Carter, +.46 for Ford, and +.44 for Reagan). The relationships are stronger for the more impressionable younger children in the sample.

In a similar survey of elementary school children, sheer amount of exposure to TV newscasts correlates +.25 with liking for the various political figures often appearing in the news (Atkin & Neuendorf, Note 3).

A survey of adolescents by Berman and Stookey (1980) focused on support for government, as indexed by a feeling thermometer ranging from cool/unfavorable to warm/favorable. There is a negligible correlation between federal government support and both national news viewing (+.03) and public affairs TV viewing (-.03). On the other hand, watching the local late-evening news is negatively related to feelings toward the federal government (-.21), state government (-.14), and local government (-.15). All coefficients control for race, income, and political philosophy.

Hawkins et al. (1979) report that junior and senior high students who viewed the 1976 "Great Debate" tend to have greater bonding of partisan attitudes (that is, closer associations between voting preference and both candidate images and party affiliation). Debate viewers also have slightly greater levels of partisanship and political efficacy. Furthermore, political efficacy is slightly related to general TV news viewing but unrelated to newspaper reading.

Another survey of late elementary children indicates that TV news viewing is mildly associated with holding a party identification and expressing a candidate preference (Conway et al., 1975).

Rubin (1978) measured viewing of public affairs and news programming among elementary, junior high, and senior high school students. Exposure is slightly related to support for government, but negligibly associated with political efficacy, cynicism, and attitude toward the President. In a junior and senior high school sample, Byrne (1969) discovered that students exposed primarily to TV news rather than newspaper news tend to feel favorably toward government and to perceive that it is performing effectively.

In Chaffee's (1977) analysis of the Jennings and Niemi data for high school seniors, use of the print news media is mildly correlated with political efficacy and broadcast public affairs exposure is slightly negatively related to efficacy. Neither type of exposure is associated with either trust in the political system or strength of party identification.

A study conducted during the Watergate crisis shows that attending Watergate news is positively related to believing that Nixon was deeply involved in the scandal (Hawkins et al., 1975).

There is a small amount of self-report evidence relating to affective orientations. Chaffee et al. (1970) asked junior and senior high school students to rate
the importance of four sources of opinion on two current issues. On the
six-point scale, the media score highest (4.5), followed by parents (3.3), teachers
(3.2) and friends (2.5). Kraus and Lee (cited in Kraus & Davis, 1976) used a
self-report procedure to determine the relative influence of 18 possible sources
on political attitudes. High school seniors rank the mass media as most influential on 10 political topics on the list, and the media are rated second or third in
importance on the remaining 8 topics.

In a study examining trends in elementary students' orientations in 1974
versus 1962, Dennis and Webster (1975) found higher levels of cynicism, greater
rejection of political authority, more negative attitudes toward government, and
lower idealization of the President; the differences are sizable in each case. The
authors attribute the changes to the Vietnam war, civil rioting, and less heroic
presidents, all of which were transmitted vividly via the news media. In addition,
Hawkins et al. (1975) report that Nixon's image among elementary, junior, and
senior high students became severely tarnished between 1972 and 1973 as the
Watergate crisis unfolded; he was perceived as less wise, fair, good, strong, and
honest in the second wave of the panel survey.

Finally, the Atkin and Greenberg (1974) experiment where high school
students were shown programs about the legislature shows that significantly
more positive attitudes toward representatives developed but that political
efficacy remained unchanged.

In conclusion, this diverse collection of findings suggests that the mass media
significantly influence some affective orientations, although the impact is not as
great as for cognitive orientations. The variables most affected by news exposure
are interest, attitude toward leaders, and opinions about issues; more basic
dispositions such as political efficacy and party identification appear to be
resistant to change. The evaluative direction of impact seems to correspond to
the nature of media coverage of political affairs: Favorable news (or advertising)
leads to positive orientations, while unflattering messages produce negative
reactions. These studies have not explored processes of affective response,
although Tolley (1973) suggests that parents interpret informational inputs in
partisan terms for the child, and Bishop, Boersma, and Williams (1969) show
that some high school students in the late 1960s were skeptical of news media
credibility (and thus might be less influenced than more trusting youth).

Behavioral Effects

Children and adolescents have rather limited avenues for expressing overt
political behavior. The major opportunities are periodic participation around the
fringes of election campaigns and everyday discussions of political matters with
parents and friends.

Lewellen (1976) reports on a national survey of high school seniors that assessed various forms of political behavior. Public affairs exposure to the four major media is correlated +.21 with partisan political activities (for example, contributing money to candidates, working in campaigns, wearing buttons, or attending rallies), +.22 with political organization membership (such as involvement in NAACP or Young Democrats), and +.09 with expression of political opinion (for example, writing letters to newspapers or public officials). All of these coefficients control for demographic attributes, parental involvement in politics, and civics coursework.

Chaffee et al. (1970) found that public affairs media exposure is moderately correlated with active involvement in a presidential campaign; however, cross-lagged correlational analyses do not conclusively demonstrate that exposure is the causal agent in the relationship. Reporting data from a study of high school seniors, Chaffee (1977) shows that political activity is mildly associated with print media exposure but unrelated to broadcast exposure.

Six studies provide data relating news exposure to political discussions with parents. For both television news viewing and newspaper reading, there are mild to moderate positive correlations across all studies and age levels (Atkin & Greenberg, 1974; Roberts et al., 1975; Lewellen, 1976; Atkin & Gantz, 1978; Egan, 1978; Drew & Reeves, 1980a). Three studies also found positive relationships between news consumption and political conversations with friends (Atkin & Greenberg, 1974; Lewellen, 1976; Atkin & Gantz, 1978).

This small set of investigations indicates that the news media make a contribution to political behavior. Interpersonal discussions of politics appear to be stimulated by media exposure, and campaign participation is apparently prompted by exposure to newspapers and possibly TV news. However, the data are primarily correlational, and reverse or reciprocal causation may be operating to some extent.

Entertainment Media Effects

Young people spend several hours per day consuming the entertainment media, particularly television programs. In adolescence, they also listen to a great deal of radio and recorded music. During this exposure time, children and adolescents attend to dozens of advertisements each day.

Unlike news content, most young people do not approach entertainment for learning purposes (Schramm, Lyle, & Parker, 1961). Nevertheless, information acquisition or attitude formation may result from "incidental learning" through various processes, such as image cultivation (Gerbner, Gross, Signorielli, Morgan, & Jackson-Beeck, 1979) or observational modeling (Bandura, 1971). Thus, there may be significant political consequences from both general immersion in the fictional world portrayed in the entertainment media and specific exposure to certain role stereotypes or ideological themes (for example, TV programs dealing with law enforcement or racial relations or antiestablishment lyrics in songs). Furthermore, the sheer amount of time spent with entertainment may displace opportunities for direct learning from information sources, and enjoyment derived from entertainment may divert young people from political concerns; this may inhibit more serious forms of political learning.

In this section, some assorted examples of politically relevant consequences of entertainment exposure will be presented. One prominent type of television content deals with crime and the criminal justice system. In particular, police officers are highly overrepresented in dramas, and the portrayals are predominantly favorable (Dominick, 1973; Jeffries-Fox & Signorielli, 1979). Dominick (1974) found that crime show viewing is mildly correlated with the perception that police are more efficacious and with knowledge about a suspect's arrest rights, but not with attitude toward the police. Jeffries-Fox and Signorielli (1979) discovered that young people's images of lawyers and judges correspond to televised stereotypes of these roles (for example, judges are perceived as being fair and endangered by revengeful criminals). Meyer (1976) showed children an episode of a comedy program where the lead character tried to evade income taxes; most of the viewers accurately perceived the cheating behavior and some approved of tax evasion.

In the survey of adolescents' support for government, Berman and Stookey (1980) examined the relationship of this attitude with entertainment TV viewing. Averaging the coefficients for feelings toward federal, state, and local government, they report a negative correlation with viewing adult entertainment programs such as *M*A*S*H* or *Fantasy Island* (-.13), and with cartoon exposure (-.11). Police program viewing is negligibly associated with the support variable (+.04), while exposure to juvenile entertainment shows such as *Happy Days* or *Wonder Woman* is positively related (+.12). The authors are unable to interpret this mixed pattern of findings, but it does appear that the type of program viewed may have implications for affect toward government.

Since television presents such a great amount of crime, Gerbner et al. (1979) tested the perceptions of junior and senior high school students. Heavy TV viewers slightly overestimate the real-life crime rate and the frequency with which police use violence. In a study with the same age groups, Hawkins and Pingree (1980) found that the perceived prevalence of violence is mildly correlated with TV viewing, especially for exposure to crime-adventure shows and cartoons.

A number of investigations have explored linkages between broadcast entertainment programming and politically relevant attitudes and values, such as racial prejudice, ethnocentrism, and conventionality.

According to Volgy and Schwarz (1980), television programs featuring black characters typically portray society as free of racial bigotry or severe economic disadvantage. They found that frequency of viewing these programs is moderately associated with a lesser concern about racial problems.

Vidmar and Rokeach (1974) measured high school students' perceptions of the bigoted TV character Archie Bunker. Their findings suggest that this program reinforces racial prejudices, particularly among viewers with ethnocentric predispositions.

On the other hand, Roberts et al. (Note 4) reported significant decreases in ethnocentrism and more favorable attitudes toward foreigners after elementary children watched a series of programs stressing similarity among the world's people. Positive effects on racial and ethnic attitudes were also found by Goldberg and Gorn (1979) in an experimental study. Preschool white children were shown *Sesame Street* segments portraying Oriental and Indian children playing; children exposed to this treatment were twice as likely as the control group to select as playmates children from these backgrounds. In addition, Hur (1978) examined junior and senior high school students' responses to the *Roots* docudrama dealing sympathetically with slavery and racial prejudice. There is a very slight positive relationship between viewing *Roots* and holding a liberal opinion on the open-housing issue, especially for those who regarded the program as informative.

In a study of televised sports contests, Prisuta (1979b) examined several values relevant to politics. He argues that domestic sports such as football emphasize conservative values (such as competition, territoriality, ethnocentrism, nationalism, and strict regulation of activity by authority). Among high school students, sports viewing correlates moderately with national loyalty, mildly with authoritarianism (that is, accepting the legitimacy of those in power or opposition to dissent), and slightly with conservatism.

Weigel and Jessor (1973) explored TV's relation to conventionality, defined as a pattern of thought and action in conformity to established norms (for example, high conservatism, low political activism, negative attitude toward deviance). Among high school students, there is a moderately positive correlation between the conventionality syndrome and involvement with TV.

Musical recordings have long been considered a possible contributor to sociopolitical orientations. During the late 1960s, there was much concern about the effects of protest message themes, and rock music has frequently been a target of conservative critics. Two surveys have been conducted with primarily teenaged college students. Mashkin and Volgy (1975) found that students preferring rock or folk music had a much higher level of political alienation than fans of country music in 1972. However, this difference disappeared in a replication two years later as the political content of these musical genres became less differentiated. A 1973 survey found that record listening time is moderately related to political liberalism, but radio listening shows a moderately negative association (Fox & Williams, 1974). Preference for protest, blues, folk, or jazz music are all correlated with liberal attitudes, while pop hits and easy listening preferences are linked to conservatism.

Regarding tangentially political consequences of advertising, Atkin (in press) reviews evidence from four studies showing that advertising exposure is slightly correlated with materialism among adolescents. Speculation that ads produce dissatisfaction and alienation among economically disadvantaged subgroups has not been empirically examined.

Finally, there are some indications that entertainment media serve a displacement or diversion function with respect to political orientations. There is a mild to moderate negative association between television program viewing and political knowledge among adolescents (Chaffee et al., 1970; Rubin, 1976; Jackson-Beeck, 1979).

In conclusion, some of these findings provide a tentative indication that exposure to the entertainment media may directly or indirectly influence political socialization. More research is required to follow up on the notions explored in these initial studies.

INTERPERSONAL COMMUNICATION EFFECTS

Most early overviews of the political socialization literature conclude that the family environment plays the most important role in the development of the child's political orientations (Hyman, 1959; Greenstein, 1965; Davies, 1965; Dawson & Prewitt, 1969; Sigel, 1970). Nevertheless, recent research and reassessment of older research indicates that the potency of parental influence is overrated, particularly regarding direct transmission of partisan attitudes and opinions (Hess & Torney, 1967; Jennings & Niemi, 1968, 1974; Connell, 1972; Sears, 1975; Niemi & Sobieszek, 1977; Niemi, Ross, & Alexander, 1978).

Most of the political scientists have focused on affective variables. Theoretically, parents have an opportunity for considerable influence because of the unique physical and emotional dependency of the child (Davies, 1965). Parents can express ideas and values, and show verbal approval for conformity or disapproval for deviance, over a period of formative years. By providing modeling behavior, parents can be a source for the child's observational learning. Furthermore, the structural constraints in the family can indirectly shape the child's political development.

Despite such opportunities, political science research has not demonstrated substantial pairwise similarity in parent and child affect toward political affairs. Connell (1972) reexamined evidence from 20 studies that measured both parental and offspring attitudes and opinions. He showed that the parent-child correlations were mildly positive, with a median coefficient of +.20, although party preference was strongly related. Nevertheless, there was a close pooled correspondence in the distribution of attitudes and opinions between groups of parents and children in these studies. Connell proposed that older and younger generations develop affective orientations in a parallel rather than serial manner; political affect formation is shaped by common experiences (including the media), not processes within the family. Indeed, Sigel (1970) observed that the shared social status position, not teaching, may account for much parent-child correspondence.

In his review of the literature, Sears (1975) concluded that parent-child agreement is greatest for highly visible events (such as presidential candidates and wars), next highest for political party identification, and minimal for policy issues, regime norms, and general political dispositions (for example, efficacy, trust and support for government, interest).

One reason for the limited impact of parents may be lack of communication in the family about political matters. Several studies show that parent-child discussions occur infrequently (Jennings & Niemi, 1974; Hawkins et al., 1979; Gollin & Anderson, Note 1; Drew & Reeves, 1980a).

Thus, a more significant factor may be the structure rather than the content of family communication patterns. Chaffee et al. (1973) reconceptualized the traditional authoritarian-permissive continuum of family structure into an orthogonal two-dimension model involving socio- and concept-orientations. Bisecting the two dimensions, a fourfold typology was created and labeled as pluralistic, consensual, protective, and laissez-faire.

The conceptual differences among the four types have noteworthy implications for the political socialization process. In the pluralistic home, social constraints are minimal, while open discussion is emphasized. This should produce independent seeking and processing of political information and greater political competence. The child from a consensual background, where idea-orientation is encouraged but social disharmony is discouraged, would be expected to avoid conflictual aspects of politics while imitating parental orientations and gaining political competence. Laissez-faire children, who are exposed to little concept stimulation or social constraint, might be expected to have undirected patterns of socialization to politics. Children in the protective family see parents stressing obedience and harmony while deemphasizing conceptual matters; the consequence should be a lack of knowledge and greater persuasibility.

In two surveys of parent-adolescent pairs, Chaffee et al. (1973) showed that pluralistic youth have the highest political knowledge, campaign activity, system awareness, and political affect, and that both pluralistic and consensual youth score high in mass media public affairs usage. In each case, the children from protective family environments have the lowest levels.

Using this typology, Roberts et al. (1975) found that children from pluralistic families (and, to a lesser extent, those from consensual families) engage in more campaign public affairs exposure and have more conversations with parents about politics. Sheinkopf (1973) examined family communication patterns and anticipatory political socialization, the learning of social norms for adult citizenship obligations (for example, working in campaigns or attending meetings to support causes). The pluralistics score slightly higher than the consensuals, and both are slightly higher than the children from protective or laissez-faire families.

In conclusion, it appears that parents have a significant but limited persuasive influence on their children's attitudes and values. The structure of family communication also determines the manner in which young people approach the political system. More research is needed focusing on communication processes.

FUTURE RESEARCH PRIORITIES

Despite the outpouring of studies in the past few years, the body of knowledge about communication and political socialization is modest in scope and unimpressive in quality. This concluding section presents suggestions for future lines of inquiry, focusing on theoretical directions and methodological approaches for studying mass media effects on political orientations of young people.

Theoretical Directions

The learning theory perspectives implicit in most socialization research should continue to provide the basic framework for investigation of media effects. This should be combined with cognitive developmental and uses and gratifications concepts to account for individual differences in learning, along with a greater emphasis on the role of social influences that extend or mediate message impact. A blending of these perspectives yields an array of concepts, processes, and relationships that might profitably be pursued in future investigations. The primary thrusts should be to identify the conditions under which learning occurs and to elaborate the range of stimuli that may produce effects by examining content other than television news. Specifically, the following issues should be explored by researchers in the 1980s:

What antecedent factors govern exposure and response to politically relevant media content? The most critical variable for subsequent research is age (or stage of cognitive development), which determines the capacities for learning and the nature of information processing. Developmental concepts which have recently been applied to research on TV violence and advertising effects should be extended to political effects studies in a more sophisticated manner. In addition, social category variables such as socioeconomic status need more attention; for instance, investigators could assess whether a political knowledge gap develops among different strata of young people. A fuller examination is also needed for the social environment of the child, particularly the structure and substance of family communication regarding politics. Finally, more intensive efforts are necessary to understand the role of psychological factors such as basic affective predispositions and the proximate needs, interests, and tastes that motivate exposure and learning. For example, little is known about preadult selective exposure or the ways young people acquire the habit of following political affairs in the news media.

What processes intervene between message exposure and eventual changes in cognitive, affective, and behavioral orientations? One key factor is the role played by parents or peers in mediating responses to political content; for instance, parental interpretation of complex information may facilitate knowledge gain, and evaluative peer communication may shape the direction of attitudinal responses. A second factor is the motivational state of the young person while processing political messages; the implications of an incidental learning mode may be far different from instrumentally based consumption of political stimuli. In the psychological domain, it would also be interesting to explore processes such as information unitizing, counterarguing, emotional arousal, and selective perception. Little is known about the credibility young people attribute to the news media and the role this plays in their acceptance of the messages. Finally, the sequencing and patterning of relationships among transitory reactions and cognitive, affective, and behavioral changes needs considerable research attention.

What new dependent variables should be examined? Most of the research has focused on knowledge gain and certain affective orientations toward leaders and institutions. Beyond these obvious variables there is a need to assess the development of beliefs and perceptions about the political world (for example, the perceived levels of corruption, conflict, or crime in government and society, or the perceived state of the economy or foreign relations) and salience attached to issues, leaders, and institutions due to press agenda-setting. The structure of political cognitions should also be studied, focusing on complexity, rigidity, and bonding of various elements. Although behavioral outcomes have limited implications for prevoters, researchers can examine the acquisition of participatory norms during the adolescent years. Young people may be learning about the appropriate forms of participation and about how to make political decisions (such as the number of alternatives to consider, the relevant attributes to weigh, and early versus late decision-making).

What types of media content influence political orientations? Researchers have been preoccupied with television news programming as the critical independent variable in political socialization. More attention should be devoted to radio news (especially for teenagers, who are the most radio-oriented segment of the population), TV entertainment shows (especially contemporary portrayals of police, government, and the legal system in prime-time drama), commercial advertising, and public service messages. The role of the print media, particularly newspaper news and newsmagazines, has been largely ignored. Finally, more research should be conducted during political campaigns, when news coverage is richest and candidates are appearing in readily accessible spot advertisements and televised debates.

It should also be noted that researchers have ignored cross-national studies of political socialization; it would be useful to have comparative research across various types of countries in the rest of the world.

METHODOLOGICAL APPROACHES

The research methods employed by political socialization scholars have been largely restricted to simple bivariate survey designs or self-reported effects. More elaborate and sophisticated design and measurement approaches are needed to advance the research literature.

Researchers using conventional correlational surveys should focus on multivariate relationships among a broader set of variables beyond the basic association between media exposure and each political orientation. Regression and path-analytic techniques can be employed to represent the pattern of interrelationships among demographic characteristics, individual predispositions, motivations, and social influences as these predictor variables affect exposure and responses to politically relevant media content, and to assess the linkages among the various criterion variables. These techniques are also useful in isolating the contribution of media exposure controlling for contaminating influences. Contingent correlational analyses should be used to identify the specific conditions under which exposure is most strongly related to political orientations.

Longitudinal designs such as panel surveys should be utilized more extensively in the future. Short-term panels with measurement at two or more points across several weeks or months would provide time-order clarification of the direction of causality between exposure and orientations; there is considerable ambiguity regarding causal flow when variables such as TV news viewing and political knowledge are found to be associated in a static design. Long-term panels following young people over a period of years would be valuable in determining whether early socializing experiences influence adult political attitudes and behavior.

Although laboratory experimentation appears to have limited utility in studying political socialization, ecologically sensitive field experiments may be of value. While it is impossible to manipulate mass media content, it may be feasible to induce varying levels of exposure to these stimuli. This might be achieved by assigning school students to several conditions of at-home news reading or campaign program viewing, or by inducing parents to employ various types of interpersonal interpretation of political messages or to give the child encouragement to watch or read certain types of news. For youths living in institutional settings, access to TV programming could be manipulated in a manner similar to the TV violence field experiments.

Quasi-experimental designs can be devised to test the impact of specific media messages such as a debate, presidential address, or critical international news event. Using a staggered-sample design, researchers could measure randomized groups of young people either immediately before or after the content is disseminated in the media; assuming that no other historical contaminants occur over this short span, differences can be attributed to the mediated message.

One final suggestion for survey investigations involves the blending of content analysis with effects analysis. Researchers should explicitly measure the subject matter of current political media content to determine which types of knowledge or attitudes are likely to be acquired by youthful audiences. This is especially important for affective variables, which may be influenced in either a positive or negative direction depending on the tenor of content themes.

Regarding measurement, further work is particularly needed in measuring exposure to broadcast messages. Most studies have employed crude measures such as TV viewing time or amount of radio news listening. Precise measurement of the frequency of exposure and the degree of attention would provide a more sensitive indicator of the message inputs received by the audience. Survey researchers should use observational techniques and diary reports, along with an elaborated battery of generalized exposure and attention questionnaire items, in order to assess fully broadcast viewing and listening patterns.

In conclusion, the application of more advanced and detailed methodologies to theoretically based research investigations would provide an important contribution to illuminating many of the questions that remain concerning the role of communication in the political socialization process.

REFERENCE NOTES

1. Gollin, A., & Anderson, T. *America's children and the mass media.* New York: Newspaper Advertising Bureau, 1980.

2. McLeod, J., O'Keefe, G., & Wackman, D. *Communication and political socialization during the adolescent years.* Paper presented at the meeting of the Association for Education in Journalism, Berkeley, California, August 1969.

3. Atkin, C., & Neuendorf, K. *Television news exposure and children's knowledge about political figures.* Unpublished manuscript, 1980. (Available from Department of Communication, Michigan State University, East Lansing, Michigan 48824).

4. Roberts, D., Herold, C., Hornby, M., King, S., Sterne, D., Whitely, S., & Silverman, L. *Earth's a big blue marble: A report of the impact on children's opinions.* Unpublished manuscript, 1974. (Available from Institute for Communication Research, Stanford University, Stanford, California 94305).

REFERENCES

Almond, G., & Verba, S. *The civic culture*. Princeton: Princeton University Press, 1963.

Alper, S. W., & Leidy, T. The impact of information transmission through television. *Public Opinion Quarterly,* 1969, *33,* 556-562.

Atkin, C. Instrumental utilities and information-seeking. In P. Clarke (Ed.), *New models for communication research*. Beverly Hills, CA: Sage, 1973.

Atkin, C. Effects of campaign advertising and newscasts on children. *Journalism Quarterly,* 1977, *54,* 503-508.

Atkin, C. Broadcast news programming and the child audience. *Journal of Broadcasting,* 1978, *22,* 47-61.

Atkin, C. *Television advertising and consumer role socialization. In television and behavior: Ten years of scientific progress*. Washington, DC: Government Printing Office, in press.

Atkin, C., & Gantz, W. Television news and the child audience. *Public Opinion Quarterly,* 1978, *42,* 183-198.

Atkin, C., & Greenberg, B. Public television and political socialization. *Congress and mass communication (appendix to hearings before the Joint Committee on Congressional Operations)*. Washington, DC: Government Printing Office, 1974.

Bandura, A. *Social learning theory*. New York: General Learning Press, 1971.

Berman, D., & Stookey, J. Adolescents, television and support for government. *Public Opinion Quarterly,* 1980, *44,* 330-340.

Bishop, R., Boersma, M., & Williams, J. Teenagers and news media: Credibility canyon. *Journalism Quarterly,* 1969, *46,* 597-599.

Bittner, J., & Shamo, W. Readability of the "mini-page." *Journalism Quarterly,* 1976, *53,* 740-743.

Brim, O., & Wheeler, S. *Socialization after childhood: Two essays*. New York: John Wiley, 1966.

Byrne, G. Mass media and political socialization of children and preadults. *Journalism Quarterly,* 1969, *46,* 40-42.

Chaffee, S. Mass communication in political socialization. In S. Renshon (Ed.), *Handbook of political socialization*. New York: Free Press, 1977.

Chaffee, S., McLeod, J., & Wackman, D. Family communication patterns and adolescent political participation. In J. Dennis (Ed.), *Socialization to politics: A reader*. New York: John Wiley, 1973.

Chaffee, S., Ward, S., & Tipton, L. Mass communication and political socialization. *Journalism Quarterly,* 1970, *47,* 647-659.

Cohen, A., Wigand, R., & Harrison, R. The effects of emotion-arousing events on children's learning from TV news. *Journalism Quarterly,* 1976, *53,* 204-210.

Coldevin, G. Internationalism and mass communications. *Journalism Quarterly,* 1972, *49,* 365-368.

Comstock, G. et al. *Television and human behavior*. New York: Columbia University Press, 1978.

Connell, R. W. *The child's construction of politics*. Melbourne: University of Melbourne Press, 1971.

Connell, R. W. Political socialization in the American family: The evidence re-examined. *Public Opinion Quarterly,* 1972, *36,* 323-333.

Conway, M., Stevens, A., & Smith, R. The relation between media use and children's civic awareness. *Journalism Quarterly,* 1975, *52,* 531-538.

Cook, T., & Scioli, F. Political socialization research in the United States: A review. In D. Nimmo and C. Bonjean (Eds.), *Political attitudes and public opinion*. New York: David McKay, 1972.

Dawson, R., & Prewitt, K. *Political socialization*. Boston: Little, Brown, 1969.

Davies, J. The family's role in political socialization. *Annals,* 1965, *361,* 10-19.

Dennis, J., & Webster, C. Children's images of the president and of government in 1962 and 1974. *American Politics Quarterly,* 1975, *3,* 386-405.

Dominick, J. Television and political socialization. *Educational Broadcasting Review*, 1972, *6*, 48-55.

Dominick, J. Crime and law enforcement on prime-time television. *Public Opinion Quarterly*, 1973, *37*, 241-250.

Dominick, J. Children's viewing of crime shows and attitudes on law enforcement. *Journalism Quarterly*, 1974, *51*, 5-12.

Drew, D., & Reeves, B. Children and television news. *Journalism Quarterly*, 1980, *57*, 45-54. (a)

Drew, D., & Reeves, B. Learning from a television news story. *Communication Research*, 1980, *7*, 121-135. (b)

Easton, D., & Hess, R. The child's political world. *Midwest Journal of Political Science*, 1962, *16*, 229-246.

Egan, L. Children's viewing patterns for television news. *Journalism Quarterly*, 1978, *55*, 337-342.

Fox, W. S., & Williams, J. D. Political orientations and musical preferences among college students. *Public Opinion Quarterly*, 1974, *38*, 352-371.

Gerbner, G., Gross, L., Signorielli, N., Morgan, M., & Jackson-Beeck, M. The demonstration of power: Violence profile no. 10. *Journal of Communication*, 1979, 29, 177-196.

Goldberg, M., & Gorn, G. Television's impact on preferences for nonwhite playmates: Canadian "Sesame Street" inserts. *Journal of Broadcasting*, 1979, *23*, 27-32.

Greenstein, F. The benevolent leader: Children's images of political authority. *American Political Science Review*, 1960, *54*, 934-944.

Greenstein, F. *Children and politics*. New Haven, CT: Yale University Press, 1965.

Greenstein, F. Political socialization. *International Encyclopedia of the Social Sciences*. New York: Macmillan/Free Press, 1968.

Hawkins, R. *Children's acquisition of current events information in the context of family, peers, media use and pre-existing attitudes*. Unpublished doctoral dissertation, Stanford University, 1974.

Hawkins, R., & Pingree, S. Some processes in the cultivation effect. *Communication Research*, 1980, *7*, 193-226.

Hawkins, R., Pingree, S., & Roberts, D. Watergate and political socialization. *American Politics Quarterly*, 1975, *3*, 406-422.

Hawkins, R., Pingree, S., Smith, K., & Bechtolt, W. Adolescents' responses to issues and images. In S. Kraus (Ed.), *The great debates: Carter vs. Ford, 1976*. Bloomington: Indiana University Press, 1979.

Hess, R., & Torney, J. *The development of political attitudes in children*. Chicago: AVC, 1967.

Hirsch, H. *Poverty and politicization*. New York: Free Press, 1971.

Hollander, N. Adolescents and the war: The sources of socialization. *Journalism Quarterly*, 1971, *48*, 472-479.

Hur, K. Impact of "Roots" on black and white teenagers. *Journal of Broadcasting*, 1978, *22*, 289-298.

Hyman, H. *Political socialization*. New York: Free Press, 1959.

Jackson-Beeck, M. Interpersonal and mass communication in children's political socialization. *Journalism Quarterly*, 1979, *56*, 48-53.

Jeffries-Fox, S., & Signorielli, N. Television and children's conceptions of occupations. In H. Dordick (Ed.), *Proceedings of the sixth annual Telecommunications Policy Research Conference*. Lexington, MA: D. C. Heath, 1979.

Jennings, M. K., & Niemi, R. Transmission of political values from parent to child. *American Political Science Review*, 1968, *62*, 169-184.

Jennings, M. K., & Niemi, R. *The political character of adolescence*. Princeton: Princeton University Press, 1974.

Johnson, N. Television and politization: A test of competing models. *Journalism Quarterly*, 1973, *50*, 447-455.

Kohlberg, L. The cognitive-developmental approach to socialization. In D. Goslin (Ed.), *Handbook of socialization theory and research*. Chicago: Rand McNally, 1969.

Kraus, S., & Davis, D. *The effects of mass communication on political behavior.* University Park: Pennsylvania State University Press, 1976.

Lambert, W. E., & Klineberg, O. *Children's views of foreign people.* New York: Appleton-Century-Crofts, 1967.

Langton, K. *Political socialization.* New York: Oxford University Press, 1969.

Langton, K., & Jennings, M. K. Political socialization and the high school civics curriculum. *American Political Science Review,* 1968, *62,* 852-867.

Lewellen, J. Mass media and political participation. *Social Education,* 1976, *40,* 457-461.

Lyle, J., & Hoffman, H. Children's use of television and other media. In E. A. Rubinstein, G. A. Comstock, & J. P. Murray (Eds.), *Television and social behavior: Television in day-to-day life.* Washington, DC: Government Printing Office, 1972.

McIntyre, J., & Teevan, J. Television violence and deviant behavior. In G. Comstock & E. Rubinstein (Eds.), *Television and social behavior: Television and adolescent aggressiveness.* Washington, DC: Government Printing Office, 1972.

McLeod, J., Atkin, C., & Chaffee, S. Adolescents, parents, and television use. In G. Comstock & E. Rubinstein (Eds.), *Television and social behavior: Television and adolescent aggressiveness.* Washington, DC: Government Printing Office, 1972.

Mashkin, K. S., & Volgy, T. Socio-political attitudes and musical preferences. *Social Science Quarterly,* 1975, *21,* 450-459.

Meyer, T. The impact of "All in the Family" on children. *Journal of Broadcasting,* 1976, *20,* 25-33.

Mitchell, W. *The American polity.* New York: Free Press, 1962.

Niemi, R., Ross, R. D., & Alexander, J. The similarity of political values of parents and college-age youths. *Public Opinion Quarterly,* 1978, *42,* 503-520.

Niemi, R., & Sobieszek, B. Political socialization. *Annual Review of Sociology,* 1977, *3,* 209-233.

Prisuta, R. The adolescent and television news. *Journalism Quarterly,* 1979, *56,* 277-282. (a)

Prisuta, R. Televised sports and political values. *Journal of Communication,* 1979, *29,* 94-102. (b)

Roberts, D., Hawkins, R., & Pingree, S. Do the mass media play a role in political socialization? *Australian and New Zealand Journal of Sociology,* 1975, *11,* 37-43.

Rubin, A. Television in children's political socialization. *Journal of Broadcasting,* 1976, *20,* 51-60.

Rubin, A. Child and adolescent television use and political socialization. *Journalism Quarterly,* 1978, *55,* 125-129.

Schramm, W., Lyle, J., & Parker, E. *Television in the lives of our children.* Stanford: Stanford University Press, 1961.

Sears, D. Political socialization. In F. Greenstein & N. Polsby (Eds.), *Micropolitical theory.* Reading, MA: Addison-Wesley, 1975.

Sheinkopf, K. Family communication patterns and anticipatory socialization. *Journalism Quarterly,* 1973, *50,* 24-30.

Sigel, R. S. *Learning about politics: A reader in political socialization.* New York: Random House, 1970.

Tolley, H. *Children and war: Political socialization to international conflict.* New York: Teachers College Press, Columbia University, 1973.

Vidmar, N., & Rokeach, M. Archie Bunker's bigotry: A study in selective perception and exposure. *Journal of Communication,* 1974, *24,* 36-47.

Volgy, T., & Schwarz, J. TV entertainment programming and sociopolitical attitudes. *Journalism Quarterly,* 1980, *57,* 150-155.

Weigel, R., & Jessor, R. Television and adolescent conventionality: An exploratory study. *Public Opinion Quarterly,* 1973, *37,* 76-90.

CHAPTER 12

Communication and Election Campaigns

Garrett J. O'Keefe and L. Erwin Atwood

ELECTION CAMPAIGNS are at once fascinating theater featuring an immense variety of political communication activity and a ready-made field laboratory for testing provocative hypotheses and theories about what such communication means. In the following pages we shall present what we think recent campaigns have taught us about political communication.

Evidence gathered during the past decade has induced a substantially revised view of what people do with campaigns and how campaigns affect them. These revisions result in part from changes in the nature of the electorate and changes in the role of communication processes. The country appears in some ways less politically predictable now than in previous decades, as witnessed by the decline in political party affiliations and influence, the rise of independent and issue-based voting, and a greater tendency toward abstention (DeVries & Tarrance, 1972; Atwood & Sanders, 1975; Nie, Verba, & Petrocik, 1976; Barber, 1978; Ladd, 1978; Pierce & Sullivan, 1980). Accompanying these shifts has been the growth of mass media, particularly television, as agents of political information and influence, partially supplanting more informal channels of communication in party organizations (Graber, 1980; Meadow, 1980).

Small wonder that the findings of the classic campaign studies of the 1940s and 1950s have a seriously limited applicability in providing an understanding of campaigns and their effects today. Most seriously jeopardized are inferences from those investigations that (1) overwhelming numbers of voters make firm candidate decisions, based on party affiliations, early in campaigns; (2) mass media are used almost solely to reinforce those decisions; (3) the few voters deciding late in the campaign, being politically less involved, use the media only sparingly; and (4) when voter persuasion does occur, it is far more likely to result from interpersonal communications than from mass media (Lazarsfeld, Berelson, & Gaudet, 1944; Berelson, Lazarsfeld, & McPhee, 1954; Klapper, 1960). This limited political effects view of mass media was implicitly reinforced by other major election studies in their near exclusion of media-related analyses (Campbell, Gurin, & Miller, 1954; Campbell, Converse, Miller, & Stokes, 1960; Almond & Verba, 1963).

The role of media in political campaigns has undergone substantial change over the past 20 years, and the potential for media effects is now greater. Less apparent is the extent to which the media wield influence over the electorate, the processes by which this happens, and the ramifications of media effects for the political system.

A serious drawback in the more recent research has been the lack of consistent (or sometimes even visible) theoretic perspectives to guide problem development and provide a background for inference building and understanding. However, this condition may be a temporary and necessary consequence of rapidly changing perspectives in a multidisciplinary field.

What most present approaches to the understanding of communication and voter behavior seem to emphasize is a view of citizens actively making choices about how to use or not to use the campaign, as opposed to their passively letting the campaign impinge upon them. Effects of campaigns on voters therefore are seen as deriving primarily from interactions based on prior voter needs and dispositions and the ways in which media and other communication agents are used. This perspective can be seen in the uses and gratifications approach (Blumler & Katz, 1974; Chapter 2 in this volume), the various transactional approaches (McLeod & Becker, 1974; Kraus & Davis, 1976), and, to a lesser extent, in other of the opening chapters to this volume.

Another commonality is the recognition than any communication effects are unlikely to occur en masse or to be explained by any one set of factors. Rather, it is critical to examine the contingencies under which different messages result in different consequences for different people under different circumstances and at different points in time. It is important to take into account such variables as when in the campaign the voter finally chooses a candidate, the importance of the election to the voter, the amount and kind of information available, and the voter's preconceptions about what might be obtained from the campaign in the way of information and/or influence.

Our perspective in the following pages is necessarily an eclectic one, with a focus on binding together data and inferences from many viewpoints. We will first identify the campaign communication arena itself in terms of its outstanding content characteristics, patterns of audience exposure, and attention to those elements. Then we will examine some of the antecedents of the campaign communication behaviors of citizens, focusing on their underlying motives. The major portion of the chapter will be concerned with the effects of campaigns on voters, in terms of both learning and persuasive impact. Finally, some of the long-term consequences of campaigns will be considered. The research to be reported is derived primarily from the last decade. Extensive summaries of earlier research may be found elsewhere (Mendelsohn & Crespi, 1970; McCombs, 1972; Becker, McCombs, & McLeod, 1975; O'Keefe, 1975; Kraus & Davis, 1976; Graber, 1980; Meadow, 1980).

POLITICAL CONTENT IN THE MEDIA

Most people necessarily receive most of their political campaign information from the mass media, particularly television. But what voters can learn is probably less than conventional wisdom would suggest. As McClure and Patterson (1974) noted: "The quality and scope of media political content is overrated" (p. 9). Until recently, the analysis of campaign content focused on volume of coverage. At the same time, there has been the continuing question: Is the coverage biased? The question seems to reflect a long-term disbelief that the press will be fair to all candidates.

Bias in Political Content

Assessment of bias is a relative question usually focusing on whether or not equivalent space was given the major candidates, since only in rare instances is the distribution of events known. Major exceptions occur in the analysis of Agnew's speeches (Frye, Note 1) and of the 1960 and 1976 debates (Jackson-Beeck & Meadow, 1979; Bechtolt, Hilyard, & Bybee, 1977; Becker, Weaver, Graber, & McCombs, 1979).

Bias has been conceptualized most frequently in terms of the relative amounts of space (or time) devoted to each candidate (Kobre, 1953; Stempel, 1961, 1965, 1969; Becker & Fuchs, 1967; Meadow, 1973; Evarts & Stempel, 1974; Windhauser, 1976), and the outcomes vary widely for individual media. Meadow (1973) found the bulk of the space in 1972 was about the Democratic candidate. Evarts and Stempel (1974) reported that during the 1972 campaign the news magazines favored the Republicans while other media favored the Democrats. Stempel (1969) reported that the addition of a third-party candidate to the 1968 contest resulted in no additional space being allocated above the 1964 level, and there appeared to be a decline over time in the total amount of space the prestige press devoted to the campaigns. Neglect of third-party candidates was also documented by Einsiedel and Bibbee (1979) and Hofstetter and Zukin (1979).

Attempts to predict completeness of newspapers' campaign coverage have pointed to structural factors as the best predictors (Danielson & Adams, 1961; Arrendell, 1972; Fowler, 1979), including (1) size of news hole, (2) number of wires, (3) number of publishing days, (4) whether morning or evening edition, and (5) size of staff. These findings support others indicating that circumstances of coverage, production necessities, and travel schedules are more likely to create distorted campaign news than is outright political bias (Bailey, 1978; Hofstetter, 1978; Williams & Semlack, 1978; Arnston & Smith, 1978).

Malaney and Buss (1979) found news organizations structured so that reporting will tend to be negative toward candidates and parties. This also seems to reflect the journalistic emphasis that news is whatever is discordant—for example, the Eagleton affair in 1972 and President Ford's remarks during the 1976 debates about Soviet domination of Eastern Europe. While the news may be interpreted as negative vis-à-vis the political system, Einsiedel (1975) found that coverage was not necessarily negative toward the candidate involved.

The proportion of negative comment about candidates in the press has risen over the past three elections from a low of 41 percent about Humphrey in 1968 to a high of 58 percent for both Ford and Carter in 1976 (Graber, 1980). There also appeared to be a larger number of negative comments in newspapers (51 percent) than on television news (43 percent) in 1972. In 1976, 57 percent of the newspaper content was negative, while only 41 percent was so classified in 1968. What the long-term effects of negative comment about candidates and elections may be is unknown, but it may lead to distrust of government or to political malaise among the electorate.

Bias seems most likely to occur in a nonpresidential campaign where a newspaper has endorsed a candidate. Two studies by McCleneghan (1973, 1978) reported contradictory coverage outcomes. In the 1973 study the endorsed candidate received the greater news and editorial coverage, while in the 1978 study the unendorsed candidate received the greater space. However, in both studies the candidate placing the larger amount of advertising with these news-papers received the greater attention in the news.

News Content Characteristics

Election stories constitute only 13 percent of all newspaper and 15 percent of all television political news during a presidential election year (Graber, 1980). This seems less than might be expected given the normative emphasis placed on presidential elections. If the number of stories devoted to presidential politics is small, then the space allocated to congressional campaigns and other lower-level races is dismal. Converse (1962) reported abandoning an attempt to content-analyze congressional campaign news because of a lack of material.

The substance of campaign coverage is increasingly about the activities of the campaign itself rather than about traditional issues. The proportion of coverage devoted to campaign events increased in newspapers from 14 percent in 1968 to 51 percent in 1976 (Graber, 1980). Television coverage of nonissue materials increased from 26 percent of time devoted to the campaign in 1968 to 63 percent in 1976. Similar outcomes have been reported by others (Patterson, 1980; Russonello & Wolf, 1979; Hofstetter, 1978; Carey, 1976). Newspaper coverage of social problems during the campaign period declined from 22 percent in 1968 to 5 percent in 1976. Television coverage of these issues dropped from 30 percent in 1968 to 14 percent in 1976 (Graber, 1980).

Patterson and McClure (1976) reported that one-third of all network coverage of the 1972 presidential campaign was devoted to the campaign itself, and that only two issues—political corruption and the Vietnam war—were given greater coverage than was the campaign itself. Emphasis on coverage of rallies created day-to-day sameness on television news, since crowds look much the same regardless of the city. When issue statements of the candidates were reported between segments of campaign activities, voters tended to miss them, probably because of low levels of attention to the otherwise familiar campaign frenzy.

The press criticizes the candidates for not discussing the issues, and it downgraded the statements of Carter and Ford during the 1976 debates as "nothing new" and "dreary cliches" (Patterson, 1980, pp. 40-41). Yet, a review of the questions asked by the press corps representatives during the 1976 debates indicates they were the same old, dreary questions (Milic, 1979). Graber and Kim (1978) found nearly all topics in the debates had been covered earlier in the media. While the debates may have provided little more than repetition of previous campaign statements, the debate content has been issue-oriented (Ellsworth, 1965; Bechtolt et al., 1977; Jackson-Beeck & Meadow, 1979).

The press also seems to expect the candidates to be antagonistic to each other and seems disappointed when this does not occur. During the 1980 presidential primary campaign, newsman Howard K. Smith was reported to have said, following a debate between two Republican contenders,

> They did agree on some very important things but they didn't disagree as much as I wanted them to, which is very bad for show business but probably very good for the Republican Party [Note 2, p. A-3].

It appears that the news media thrive on a high level of motion, with or without substance. A number of writers have likened the campaign coverage to reporting a horse race (Barber, 1978; Broh, 1980; Patterson, 1980). Carey (1976) concluded that the media's treatment of the 1974 congressional campaigns as sporting events implicitly told the electorate: "Its a game, and good players make good public officials" (p. 57). At least good players can keep the game exciting for the press.

Advertising Content Characteristics

While the news is subject to the mechanics of travel schedules and the whims and policies of reporters and editors, the candidates can reach out directly to the voters through their advertising. Political advertising seems to serve at least two functions: It bolsters the morale of campaign workers (Sheinkopf, Atkin, &

Bowen, 1973), and it makes available information from candidates that has not filtered through the various value systems of the news business. This does not mean the information is of high quality or that it is particularly useful. It does mean that no one but the candidate or his representatives has altered it.

Most newspaper political advertising is run late in the campaign in an effort to create maximum popularity for the candidate just prior to election day (Mullen, 1963, 1968). Nor surprisingly, candidates tend to focus their advertising on issues thought to be most favorable to themselves (Patterson & McClure, 1976; Graber 1 80).

Descriptions of advertising content indicate that issue emphasis varies with the level of campaign. Bowers (1972) reported about 55 percent of the advertising content for congressional, senatorial, and gubernatorial candidates was about the candidates and their party affiliation, not about campaign issues. During the 1972 presidential campaign, up to 85 percent of the advertising contained some issue references (Hofstetter & Zukin, 1979). Patterson and McClure (1976) reported that the political commercials contained about five times as much issue information as did the network news programs, and that issue information in commercials was more coherent than that found in the news. Joslyn (1980) examined 156 political commercials used between 1960 and 1976 and found that while about 76 percent mentioned issues, only 20 percent contained specific issue positions.

CAMPAIGN COMMUNICATION BEHAVIORS

Given the massive amounts of campaign-related material the media provide, it is often naively assumed that a large proportion of the electorate is attending closely to a substantial portion of it. While the audiences' campaign "diet" obviously is critically dependent on the "menu" the media provide, a wide range of selective factors affect what the public acquires. For instance, even though television may be the main source of news for most Americans (Roper, 1977), the impact of telecasts in the campaign context can be easily overestimated. Most regular viewers of network television news follow newspapers closely as well, and newspapers appear to be the preferred source for more avid news followers (Patterson, 1980). Television news seems more favored by those who are casually or incidentally concerned with news. This is particularly true for the national network newscasts, which may only be viewed with any day-to-day consistency by well under a quarter of the adult population (Stevenson & White, 1980).

The ways in which people attend to political campaigns through the media do not seem to differ greatly from the ways in which they attend to the media in general. A fairly accurate view of attention to political news and commercials may be gained from studies of everyday news and advertising exposure (Roper,

1977; Robinson & Jeffries, 1979; Weaver, Wilhoit, & Riede, Note 3). There is ample evidence that those more dependent on television than on newspapers for political information are more likely to be from the lesser educated, lower income, and least politically involved segments of the populace (J. P. Robinson, 1976; Miller, Goldenberg, & Erbring, 1979; Becker & Whitney, 1980; O'Keefe, 1980; Stevenson & White, 1980). On the other hand, television can provide immediate and often intimate coverage of such campaign events as the nominating conventions, major speeches, and debates which often draw large audiences across a wide spectrum of the public (Mendelsohn & O'Keefe, 1976; Sears & Chaffee, 1979; Patterson, 1980). Televised campaign commercials have emerged as a key political communication device, potentially surpassing newscasts as sources of substantive information for many voters (Patterson and McClure, 1976). Often overlooked is the fact that people do talk about campaigns, sometimes with great frequency and impact (J. P. Robinson, 1976).

Selectivity Factors

The evidence is overwhelming that audiences attend selectively to political information in the mass media (Schramm & Carter, 1959; Blumler & McQuail, 1969; Rock, 1973; O'Keefe & Mendelsohn, 1974; Patterson & McClure, 1976; Roberts, 1979; Hofstetter, 1979; Patterson, 1980). They are more likely to attend to messages supporting or agreeing with their preferred positions or candidates. However, whether they purposely avoid opposing messages is much less clear. Selective attention also depends to a great degree on such factors as message availability, interest in the message topic, and the perceived utility of the message (Atkin, 1973).

The problem in selectivity research has become one of defining the conditions under which the selective processes operate, including attention to the message's form, content, and availability. For example, a politician who does not change his position on an issue will be likely to have that position reported in the news less often than if he changed his mind. Consistency is not "newsworthy" (Rock, 1973). Journalistic stories are likely to be chosen more on the basis of newsworthiness than information content (Graber, 1980). Campaign reporting at times may seem independent of the flow of events, and the same materials tend to be reported throughout the campaign at irregular intervals (Meadow, 1976; Graber, 1979). Consequently, information may not be available when needed. Patterson (1980) found news stories dealing with the "game" or contest aspects of the 1976 presidential campaign more likely to be recalled than were stories dealing with the substantive aspects of candidates and issues. This may reflect the relative emphasis given by the media to each story type. A similar pattern was found for the relative frequency of campaign topics voters discussed. Thus the degree of control voters have over what they watch, read, and hear during a campaign is often minimal.

Campaign Environment Factors

Changes in the political environment may also bring changes in media content and exposure patterns. Indeed, if changes occur in voting behavior from election to election, there is reason to suspect that changes are also taking place in voter communication behavior in different campaigns. For example, the same voters were found to change their information-seeking patterns from the 1972 to the 1974 national campaigns. In part, the change may have resulted partly from the more localized nature of the 1974 elections and partly from the intervening Watergate events (O'Keefe, Mendelsohn, & Lui, 1976). When these voters were reinterviewed in 1976, they appeared to be moving back to somewhat the same levels of media orientation found in 1972. Television again emerged as the most popular medium for following presidential campaigns, while newspapers were more important in statewide and local contests. The differences are not simply a matter of voter preference, but in large part result from the greater amount of drama-laden and entertaining journalistic coverage network television gives to presidential campaigns. Voters also appear to exhibit different media use patterns from primary to general election campaigns (Atwood & Sanders, 1976).

Overall, citizens are likely to enter each campaign with a considerable amount of stored knowledge shaped by years of political socialization. Most voters are likely to have learned the rudiments of campaign processes over the course of several elections, and they may be quite discerning in their use of campaign-relevant media. Voters may well approach various categories of elections with clear expectations as to the strategies they will use in making voting decisions or in buttressing choices made. They also may have developed tactics for seeking pertinent information and manipulating the campaign environment to their advantage.

MOTIVATION AND CAMPAIGN
COMMUNICATION BEHAVIOR

Some citizens clearly are more motivated than others to follow certain election campaigns. Differences in motivation depend on a host of social, psychological, and political contingencies. Important from a communication standpoint are the strength and nature of the motives and the ways in which they may affect communication behaviors and their possible consequences.

Interest in Campaigns

While public interest in a campaign can be expected to grow as election day approaches regardless of media inputs, the media do seem to play an important role in shaping the peaks and valleys of the interest, as well as in helping to determine its onset (Berelson et al., 1954; Mendelsohn & O'Keefe, 1976). Patterson (1980) found interest in the 1976 presidential election developing during the early spring primary races, apparently augmented by public exposure to television news more than to newspapers. Patterson lays the greater early impact of television on the relative inability of audiences to selectively avoid telecast content in which they may not initially be interested. Thus, such audiences are more likely to be inadvertently stimulated early in the campaign by television than by more easily avoided print media content. In the later stages of the campaign, exposure to televised conventions and the 1976 debates prompted higher short-term levels of interest. Newspaper exposure tended to have longer-range and more subtle impacts on voter interest over the course of the campaign. However, strong interest shifts were limited to well under half of the electorate, and the media seem to have accelerated interest primarily during the early primaries. Later in the campaign, heightened interest appeared to predict greater news exposure, rather than vice versa.

Greater potential for media-generated interest would appear most probably among less involved citizens with lower initial interest levels. Voters who decide on candidates early in the campaign typically have been found to have the highest interest levels, and voting abstainers the lowest (Berelson et al., 1954; Campbell et al., 1960; Mendelsohn & O'Keefe, 1976; O'Keefe & Mendelsohn, 1978). Events such as presidential debates may draw substantial numbers of the less involved citizens who have their interest in the campaign at least temporarily piqued (Sears & Chaffee, 1979; Patterson, 1980).

Patterson notes that in the pretelevision era the greater voter reliance on newspapers may have contributed to what appears to have been the rather steady and consistent levels of citizen political interest over the span of the campaign. Television, on the other hand, may well lend itself to sharper fluctuations in interest, particularly with its more immediate and dramatic coverage of such milestones as presidential debates and its emphasis on campaign activities. The extent to which volatility of interest may be related to increased change over time in other campaign orientations, such as the nature of media coverage, remains unclear. It may be that the earlier start-up times of contemporary campaigns, coupled with the increased emphasis of the media on the formative and often devisive candidate selection processes, have also added to voter instability.

Gratifications Sought from Campaigns

The reason underlying interest in campaigns (or the lack thereof) have been fruitfully developed under the uses and gratifications research approach discussed in Chapter 2 of this volume (Blumler & Katz, 1974; Swanson, 1977). Reasons for following campaigns, or gratifications sought from them, most emphasized by voters appear linked to needs for general surveillance of the political environment and for guidance in deciding for whom to vote. Several studies over the past two decades have found respondents giving high ratings to such surveillance-related reasons as "judging what the candidates are like" and wanting "to see what they would do if elected" (Blumler & McQuail, 1969; McLeod & Becker, 1974; Becker, 1979). Also highly rated have been vote-guidance-based motives, including wanting to help in "deciding about candidates" and "seeing where candidates stood on issues." Less highly regarded have been reasons associated with reinforcing existing decisions and enjoyment of the sometimes exciting "horse race" aspects of election contests. The low interest in the latter contrasts starkly with prevailing campaign news emphasis.

   The relative weight given such motivations does not seem to change much across varying levels of political involvement. While voters with the highest interest levels appear also to place the greatest weight on surveillance (McLeod & Becker, 1974), nonvoters also ranked it as their top reason for following the campaign, despite their diminished attendance to it. A national survey of citizens unlikely to vote in the 1976 election (O'Keefe & Mendelsohn, 1978) revealed that reasons associated with surveillance were rated most important, followed by vote guidance motives, including helping a person "make up my mind how to vote" and "to decide whether to vote or not." We suspect that undecided voters would be relatively more motivated by a need for vote guidance, but no direct evidence is available to support this proposition.

   Relatively unexplored have been motives for campaign-related interpersonal discussion. In the 1972 presidential campaign, most citizens in an Ohio sample said that learning about politics from others was their primary reason for talking about politics (O'Keefe, in press). Those who rarely discussed the campaign reported sociability as their main motive.

LEARNING FROM CAMPAIGNS

   Citizens' levels of information about candidates and issues are obviously dependent on media portrayals of the campaign and particularly on journalistic coverage of it.

Learning from News Coverage

   The amount of news coverage accorded the various candidates competing in the 1976 primaries was strongly correlated with gains in voter knowledge about them during that period (Patterson, 1980). Carter, who received the most coverage, jumped from being "known" by 20 percent of the public in February to recognition by 81 percent in June. It also seems clear that newspapers are generally superior to television news in conveying campaign-related information to the public. In Patterson's 1976 national sample panel study, regular exposure to newspapers had more impact on increases in voters' knowledge about candidates than did television news exposure. However, among the least interested members of the electorate, both media had about equal influence on such awareness. More politically concerned persons may gain more from the added depth of coverage newspapers afford.

Patterson also found newspaper reading was a primary factor in promoting citizens awareness of both the issues and candidates' positions on the issues. McLeod, Bybee, and Durall (1979) found similar effects in 1976 for newspapers on voters' knowledge of candidates' issue positions, as well as on involvement and participation in the campaign. The impact of television viewing on these variables was negligible. Quarles (1979) found that newspaper use among first-time voters predicted the accuracy of their knowledge about campaign issues. Television network news viewing was unrelated to accuracy. Among less interested voters, knowledge of party positions on issues was a better predictor of information gained about candidates' positions than was media exposure (Patterson, 1980).

While the media also appear to play a major role in the formation of voters' images or stylistic impressions of candidates' personal attributes, the process through which this occurs is not clear. Television is often assumed to be the most important component in transmitting "image information," but recent studies have found limits to its power (Hofstetter, Zukin, & Buss, 1978). Patterson (1980) found telecast viewing associated with image formation only during the early primaries, while newspaper readership was strongly and consistently related to image building over the campaign. However, he notes that television may be quite important in setting the perceptual stage, allowing newspaper exposure during the campaign to fill important gaps in candidate evaluations. This interplay between media may be particularly significant in cases where the candidate is relatively unknown early in the campaign, as was Carter in 1976. Newspaper exposure also appears to facilitate the ability of readers to offer reasons for supporting their preferred candidates, at least in senatorial races (Clarke & Fredin, 1978). The relationship was strongest in markets with competing daily newspapers. Television was negatively correlated with citizens' ability to give reasons for supporting their candidates.

Learning from Advertising and Media Events

In the 1972 presidential race, even campaign commercials surpassed television network newscasts in providing voters with knowledge of the candidates' issue stances (Patterson & McClure, 1976). In a 1972 Ohio sample, nearly a third of those voting reported the commercials of both candidates to be "informative" (Mendelsohn & O'Keefe, 1976), and individuals better able to recall campaign commercials were found to be more involved in the campaign (McLeod et al., 1979). Reports of substantial information gains from television commercials have been noted over a wide range of national and local campaigns (Atkin, Bowen, & Sheinkopf, 1973; O'Keefe & Sheinkopf, 1974; McClure & Patterson,

1974; Kaid, 1976). Learning from commercials seems most likely to occur when the voters' information needs are the greatest, including situations involving lesser political sophistication and/or greater difficulty in deciding on candidates (Annis & Meier, 1934; Atkin & Heald, 1976; Mendelsohn & O'Keefe, 1976). McClure and Patterson (1974) indicate that televised ad exposure resulted in the highest information gains among low interest voters, an outcome that may at least partly reflect a ceiling effect. While political ads can and do contain specific information about issues (Bowers, 1972; Patterson & McClure, 1976), there are, no doubt, severe limits to what any voter can learn from them.

Well-publicized candidate debates and other campaign spectaculars often succeed in bringing more extensive information to a broad spectrum of the public, including many persons ordinarily less attentive to mass mediated political stimuli (Sears & Chaffee, 1979; Bishop, Meadow, & Jackson-Beeck, 1978). Both debate and convention viewing were found associated with increased knowledge of candidates' issue stands among moderate and low interest voters in particular (Patterson, 1980). There is also some indication that while more politically interested persons spent more time watching the debates, less interested individuals learned about as much per unit of viewing time (McLeod, et al., 1979). This finding suggests that very little new information was presented in the debates, as we have already noted.

Two important areas of ambiguity in most research on what voters learn from campaigns are especially apparent in investigations of debate effects. One problem is that it is difficult to discern whether the audiences are gaining "new" information or simply being reminded of "old" information once forgotten (Miller & MacKuen, 1979). Another involves the possitiblity that the debates prompt citizens only to seek information from other sources, thus increasing their knowledge only indirectly. For example, the 1976 debates may have stimulated interpersonal discussion, with consequences for greater political information and involvement (McLeod, Durall, Ziemke, & Bybee, 1979).

Interpersonal Communication and Learning

There is also evidence that interpersonal communication may play a salient role in voter information-gathering processes during a campaign. A reanalysis of data from Kimsey (Note 4) suggests that many late-deciding voters may seek information first through interpersonal channels, probably quite informally, which then leads to information-seeking from media channels, perhaps for authentication of basic facts. Then it appears that further discussion results, possibly more for purposes of opinion-seeking. Tan (1980) found that interpersonal campaign discussion among voters led to increased newspaper readership, but that the relationship was not reciprocal. The recursiveness may be due to pooling of late deciders with the early ones who may have less reason for discussion contingent on newspaper use. Television viewing was unrelated to discussion.

The findings that late deciders are likely to seek information from interpersonal sources does not necessarily imply that the traditional model of opinion leadership is at work (Katz & Lazarsfeld, 1955). J. P. Robinson (1976) has shown that there is substantial discussion among members of the "opinion follower" group as well as among opinion leaders and between groups. His revised model of the two-step flow process suggests information acquisition from both the media and interpersonal sources among all segments of the public. Voters who decide early appear to discuss the campaign more (Chaffee & Choe, 1980; Lucas & Adams, 1978; Mendelsohn & O'Keefe, 1976) and are more likely to be opinion leaders than are late deciders (Andersen & Garrison, 1978). However, their communication during the campaign may be aimed more at surveillance, reinforcement, and/or contest excitement than at vote guidance-seeking. Patterson (1980) found most political discussions early in the campaign to be about the race itself, while talks closer to election day centered more on substantive issues. Atwood (1980) found that in the last eight weeks of a congressional campaign, voters talked primarily about what they disliked about the candidates.

Agenda-Setting

Increased interpersonal communication may affect another form of cognitive influence thought to stem from the media, that of agenda-setting. Audiences of the news media often appear to regard as more salient those issues which are given high priority in the news (McCombs & Shaw, 1972; Shaw & McCombs, 1977). However, an increasing body of evidence indicates that political agenda-setting may be largely absent in instances where audiences are also engaged in substantial discussion about politics, particularly if new information is at hand (Erbring, Goldenberg, & Miller, 1980). Similarly, membership in political interest groups appears to work against political agenda-setting, presumably since such organizations tend to supply their own agendas (Mullins, 1977).

The level of the campaign (Williams & Semlak, 1978; Tipton, Haney, & Basehart, 1975) and number and type of agenda items (Gormely, 1975) have been shown to interface with media agenda-setting. Although it has been one of the more heavily investigated communication hypotheses during the past eight years, clear-cut statements about agenda-setting seem to be more difficult to make today than they were when McCombs and Shaw (1972) published their seminal study. It appears that the fundamental generalizations to be made about agenda setting are that it arises (1) for some voters as a function of a need for information prior to making a decision, and (2) where there is a lack of commitment and interest in politics that might otherwise interfere with absorption of the media agenda.

Differences in Campaign Learning

Also important is the possible differential effort of media on learning by publics with varying levels of political sophistication. Recent evidence partly supports the "knowledge gap" hypothesis that mass media have stronger informational impacts on those already more informed about a particular topic (Tichenor, Donohue, & Olien, 1980). Thus, well-intentioned media campaigns aimed at providing information to bring the less knowledgeable up to the level of the more knowledgeable run the risk of having the plan backfire and actually increase the gap between the more informed and the less informed. In the political context, the 1976 debates may have functioned in a similar way with those viewers who were already more knowledgeable about the candidates gaining relatively more information than the previously less knowledgeable (Graber & Kim, 1978).

Debate-stimulated information gains appear to be higher for the better educated and more politically involved (Bishop, Oldendick, & Tuchfarber, 1978). The more educated may have an advantage in a greater ability to process politically relevant information, and may have a higher interest in such relatively abstract topics as politics (Wolfinger & Rosenstone, Note 5). However, caution must be used in interpreting such findings, in that differential levels of exposure based on prior political involvement may confound the differences found in learning and other effects. For example, while McLeod et al. (1979) found more debate viewing among highly involved citizens, no differences in information gain were discernable between more and less involved groups. Moreover, the less involved appeared to show gains on other indicies of campaign orientations about equal to those of the more involved, given the same amount of debate exposure.

For voters who are less informed and undecided early in a campaign, substantial information increases based on media content may be more the norm than the exception (Chaffee & Choe, 1980).   .

The traditional view of late-deciding voters as being less informed and less politically involved than early deciders does not seem to hold as well for recent elections as it did in prior decades. Mendelsohn and O'Keefe (1976) and Lucas and Adams (1978) both reported few differences in information-holding between early and late deciders in the 1972 and 1976 national contests, respectively. However, Lucas and Adams discovered early deciders were more likely to have discussed the candidates and to have attended more to televised network news programs. They suggest that these behaviors may have helped reinforce and authenticate information about candidates, thus permitting earlier cognitive closure and decision-making. This view helps partly to reconcile conflicting results from smaller sample studies in 1974 and 1976 which indicate lesser knowledge rates among campaign deciders (Atwood & Kuang, Note 6; Chaffee & Choe, 1980). In both of these investigations, the criteria for knowledge measurement included more specific indicies of the respondents' ability to discriminate between candidates than did the more "objective" knowledge items—for example, candidate names, used by Mendelsohn and O'Keefe (1976) and Lucas and Adams (1978). Presumably, politically knowledgeable but undecided voters making appropriate uses of campaign media in search of closure would be less able to discriminate between candidates. Early deciders also have been found to have more likes and dislikes about the candidates early in the campaign than do late deciders (Kimsey, Note 4).

PERSUASIVE EFFECTS OF CAMPAIGNS

While effects of campaigns can be established partly in terms of information gain by citizens, it is considerably more difficult to ascertain how such learning might combine with affective changes to impinge upon actual voting decisions. Most would agree with Davis (1979) that critical ingredients in any voting decision model include voters' perceptions of both how much they agree with candidates on key issues and how they evaluate more personal candidate attributes. A "rational" decision-making approach would hold that voters pick the candidate who comes the closest to agreeing with them on salient issues and who have more favorably regarded personal characteristics. These factors have become increasingly important with the decline in political party attachments and the rising importance of issue agreement in recent years (Nie, et al., 1976; Page & Jones, 1979; Hartwig, Jenkins, & Temchin, 1980). However, the relative predictive strengths of party versus issue position versus personality varies with election context. For instance, given the more clear-cut ideological differences between presidential candidates in 1964 and 1972, voters in those years appeared to base their choice more on issue stances (Shulman & Pomper, 1975). One assumes that similar shifts take place in local and statewide elections.

Influences of Persuasive Agents

Just how mass or interpersonal sources persuasively affect voters is a point of some contention. Certainly, the research on effects of campaign agents making overt efforts to persuade yields mixed findings. Despite the previously discussed potential of political advertising for stimulating learning, there is little evidence that ads have decisive effects on voters. There is no evidence to support some of the wild claims of a decade ago that clever marketing strategies applied by media campaign specialists were working manipulative magic on unsuspecting voters (MacNeil, 1968; McGinnis, 1969; Perry, 1968; Napolitan, 1972).

Current empirical research on this topic has centered on candidate television commercials, with the most comprehensive study dealing with the 1972 presidential campaign (Patterson & McClure, 1976). Commercials appeared to have practically no influence on voters' attitudes toward McGovern or Nixon, and only in very few instances could a claim be made that the commercials had "manipulative" effects on candidate choices. Voters' selective attention and recall patterns seemed to play a dominant role in inhibiting affective change. Mendelsohn and O'Keefe (1976) found that the 14 percent of the 1972 voters who were able to recall candidate commercials said that they had been influenced by them in some way. Reinforcement was the primary form of influence reported. Those deciding during the peak campaign period were most likely to report such influence. Among campaign deciders, voters having greater difficulty making a decision and those most dependent on television for political information tended to report more influence. Only slight changes in attitude toward local candidates have been attributable to televised ads (Atkin & Heald, 1976; Kaid, 1976). Of course, even relatively minor effects of ads on small segments of the electorate could be enough to sway a close election. The potential for this happening appears greatest among the less politically involved voters.

An intriguing model of advertising effects proposed by Rothschild and Ray (1974) suggests that among audiences least involved with the topic of an ad, repeated exposure to the ad may passively promote choosing of the object presented in the ad over other alternatives. More involved audiences confronted with the ad are more likely to go through a more formal response hierarchy in evaluating the ad and formulating a decision. While laboratory results reported by Rothschild and Ray support the model, it has yet to be tested in political campaigns.

Other overt forms of campaign persuasion appearing in the media also have been found to have discernible effects on voting decisions of at least small segments of the electorate. Newspaper editorial endorsements, for instance, were found to be associated with voting differentials of about three percent in a nationwide study of presidential voting (Robinson, 1974). Audiences of major, well-publicized televised candidate speeches appear to follow expected patterns of selective attention, with few prospective voters undergoing changes in candidate preferences (Mendelsohn & O'Keefe, 1976). On the other hand, a more important persuasive impact may result from direct candidate-to-voter interaction in local, less media-publicized campaigns (Kaid, 1977).

Candidate debates appear to have only a slight persuasive impact on voters, at least if the 1960 and 1976 presidential debates are any indication. While information gain undoubtedly takes place, consequential affective changes in candidate evaluation or voter conversion from one candidate to another seems rare (Kraus, 1962; Sears & Chaffee, 1979). However, exposure to media interpretations of who "won" or "lost" particular debates appears to have substantial influence on attitudes concerning which candidate was the better performer (Lang & Lang, 1978; Steeper, 1978).

Similar effects appear not to occur for reporting of general election polls, but the reporting of early East Coast election returns before West Coast voting is completed may induce small but disproportionate numbers of Republican and

Democratic partisans not to vote (Fuchs, 1965). Where polls appear to help and hurt is in the primary campaign by defining winners and losers in the early popular preferences (Becker & McCombs, 1978). Thus some candidates are defined as serious contenders, while others are labeled as not having long-term potential.

While it was noted earlier that interpersonal communication may serve as an important information source, in contemporary campaigns mass media appear clearly dominant over interpersonal agents as sources of influence on vote choices for most citizens (O'Keefe, in press). Persons seeking political advice from others, those giving advice to others, those sharing advice and opinions with others, and those Interactive in campaign discussionas all named media sources—especially television—as having more influence than did other people on their candidate choices in 1972.

Contextual and Situational Influences

It may be more profitable to further examine influences of various communications on voter decision-making by looking at some of the contextual and situational characteristics underlying the selection of candidates. Atkin (1980) has identified the importance of three factors: (1) definition, or the availability to the voter of attributes which adequately discriminate among candidates, (2) the degree of voter involvement in the particular contest, and (3) the decisional stage the voter is in at the time. Persuasive effects from mass media might be more likely under conditions of low definition, low involvement, and indecision. In addition, the stage of the campaign and the availability of information must be considered. The media would seem to play a more important role during peak campaign periods because of greater availability of stimuli, and thus have a greater liklihood of influencing undecided voters.

Such trends are found in Chaffee and Choe's (1980) panel study of Wisconsin voters' decision-making during the 1976 presidential campaign. Those reaching a final decision between late September and late October were more likely to base those decisions on candidate evaluations specific to the campaign than were other voters. This group, constituting 40 percent of the sample, was low in partisanship and had attended heavily to television and print media. Those who decided earlier appeared to base their choices more on partisanship considerations, were better educated, and had attended more to the early campaign. A third cohort included those deciding during the very last days of the campaign; and while they scored lowest on all measures of involvement with the campaign, they did vote. Their choices were based on latent political party ties. Thus early decisions based on partisanship seem to minimize the campaign's potential for effects, while lack of commitment and exposure to the campaign are necessary conditions for campaign influence.

Similarly, voters in 1972 who made up their minds from September on were more likely to report having their final choices for president influenced by media-depicted events (Mendelsohn & O'Keefe, 1976). Reanalysis of those data show partial support for the Chaffee and Choe (1980) inferences, in that party identification was less predictive of vote choices for the campaign deciders and that this group increased its attention to the campaign during its closing weeks.

The voters most likely to report being influenced during the campaign appeared more interested in the campaign, had greater difficulty choosing a candidate, and expected the campaign to have an influence on their vote decision. Exposure and attention to campaign media were weak predictors of influence, while precampaign anticipations (gratifications sought) were more important. Anticipation of influence also predicted changes in candidate perceptions attributable to the 1976 presidential debates (O'Keefe & Mendelsohn, 1979).

Gratifications sought from media in political campaigns have been linked to specific media effects and in some instances account for more of the explained variance in cognitive, affective, and behavioral changes than did amount of exposure (McLeod & Becker, 1974). Similarly, the relative strength of motivation for attending to the 1960 campaign in Britian interacted with campaign exposure to affect information gain and attitudinal changes (Blumler & McQuail, 1969).

The interplay between media use and time and difficulty of decision has been elaborated by Roberts (1979), who found that voters who followed the summer phases of the 1976 campaign through newspapers were better able to discriminate between the candidates early on. This ability appears to both facilitate their decision making and lead them to pay more attention to such later campaign events as the debates. On the other hand, greater difficulty in choosing a candidate was reported by those voters who spent less time with newspapers early in the campaign and who, as a consequence, were slower in making attitudinal discriminations.

Greater use of television news by voters early in the campaign had no impact on either candidate discrimination or decisional difficulty. Those experiencing decisional difficulty late in the campaign tended to use as decisional aids such brief forms of campaign communication as television spots. These voters usually avoided more substantive media content such as the debates. They also discussed the campaign more frequently as the campaign drew to a close, but they remained less interested in the election's outcome. Such low-involvement voters could be expected to be more open to incidental influence attempts and, in some cases, reinforcement of party leanings in the campaign's waning days, as Chaffee and Choe (1980) suggest. The degree of difficulty encountered and the communication tactics employed to alleviate difficulty seem to depend more on the context of the campaign than on voter personality attributes (O'Keefe et al., 1976).

While early deciders are often thought to have more of an air of informed rationality about them, they may in fact be more affectively than cognitively bound to their choices. Reanalysis of 1976 campaign data presented in Kimsey (Note 4) and Kimsey and Atwood (1979, Note 7) found little association between early deciders' cognitions concerning candidates and whom they favored. The impression is given that as long as there are no drastic changes in the information early deciders receive during the campaign, there is little reason for cognitive and affective orientations toward the candidates to be strongly linked. To some extent this squares with findings of Kinder (1978) and Markus and Converse (1979) that affective candidate evaluations can have a substantial effect on voters' perceptions of candidate issue positions. Candidates who were more positively evaluated were also seen as being more in agreement with voters' own issue stances, a finding replicated in analyses of the 1972 and 1976 national campaigns (Page & Jones, 1979).

A number of studies have shown that an assimilation-contrast effect (Sherif & Hovland, 1961) occurs in the assessment of issue positions held by both candidates and parties (Weisberg & Rusk, 1970; Sherrod, 1971; Granberg & Brent, 1974; King, 1977). Voters tend to assimilate the position of the preferred candidate or party (see it closer to their own than it actually is) on most issues. A contrast effect, a perception of increased distance between the position of the opposition candidate or party and the voter's own position, seems to occur only when the issue is one which polarizes the electorate—for example, Vietnam.

Patterson (1980) suggests that Carter's well-publicized success in the 1976 primaries put him in a favorable light among Democrats early in the campaign and prior to their knowing much about him and his policies. He began early with an image of a "winner" who had no strong drawbacks. A bandwagon effect of sorts may have gathered force, with the early, albeit superficial, positive effect toward Carter gaining momentum in part through the vogers' assimilation of his vague, early policy positions. Patterson found that in the early primaries Carter appeared to be gaining many votes on the basis of people knowing very little about him and even less about his competitors.

It seems quite clear that any adequate hypothesizing bearing on the capability of mass media and other communication agents to persuade voters must account for a wide range of variables in differing campaign situations and in voter orientations toward those situations.

LONG-TERM CONSEQUENCES OF
POLITICAL CAMPAIGNS

A central question concerning long-term influences of campaign media on political processes concerns the extent to which media have contributed to or accelerated the decline of party affiliation and the rise of greater instability or volatility among the electorate. Much of the current interest in changing political orientations has centered on the concept of volatility (Blumler, Note 8; McLeod Bybee, Luescher, & Garramone, Note 9). Western democracies in recent years have been characterized as becoming more volatile, in the sense that the political behaviors of their constituencies are becoming more difficult to predict from such traditional indicators as socialization variables, political party ties, and demographic characteristics. Increased volatility in the United States appears to have taken the form of increased abstention rates, reduced party affinities, split-ticket voting, and diminished citizens trust in political personages and organizations.

Given the increased emphasis the country has seen over the past 20 years or so on political campaigning per se, a logical consequence may be that voters become conditioned to expect such activity just prior to elections and thus tend to reserve final decisions until then, hence the rise in late-deciding voters. This may have occurred for the 1976 and 1980 presidential debates, both of which received massive amounts of publicity from the time of the nominating conventions. If, at the campaign's onset, such media spectaculars are "hyped" as providing voters with clear bases for decision-making, sizable numbers of voters might be expected to await these events before choosing a candidate. The risk in all this, of course, is that if the promoted events do not deliver the promised information, greater political disaffection may result, with increased nonvoting as one behavioral consequence.

If voters are indeed becoming more likely to base their votes on issue positions, the substantial decline in issue reporting noted earlier may contribute to such malaise. Not only might the mass media have a differential short-term impact on late-deciding voters, but the makeup of that group and the relative proportion of the electorate contained in it may be a long-term function of media campaign content. The increase in "horse race" coverage, coupled with the decline in issue coverage, may contribute to larger numbers of voters unable to discriminate between candidates for increasingly longer periods of time. These, combined with the increasingly negative tone of political campaign reporting, also may have contributed substantially to the decline in the proportion of eligible voters going to the polls since 1960.

Clear theoretical and empirical linkages between volatility and mass media use are still lacking. The prevalent line of reasoning concerning such a relationship is based on the observation that increased volatility has occurred concurrent with greater dependence on television as a source of political information and, presumably, of political influence. M. J. Robinson (1976) contended that the rise in political disaffection and malaise results from television news content and particular audience attributes. He argued that among the factors leading to this "videomalaise" are television's largely "inadvertent" news viewing audience; the relatively high credibility audiences attach to networks; the intepretive nature and negative emphasis in network reporting; and what Robinson sees as emphasis on violence, conflict, and antiinstitutional themes in television news.

While Robinson offers intriguing empirical support for his contentions, conflicting evidence has been presented by Becker and Whitney (1980). McLeod et al. (Note 9) were unable to find indications that any of their measures of behavioral and subjective political volatility were associated with either newspaper or television use during the 1976 presidential campaign. A related rationale for a media use-volatility linkage rests on the fact that increased volatility has paralleled the increasing proportion of young adults entering politically relevant life stages, and on some empirical support that the young are more susceptible to media influence (O'Keefe and Mendelsohn, 1978). However, key tests of the causal nature of this relationship remain to be executed. There is also evidence that, for many voters, campaigns serve a politically integrative function by increasing confidence in political institutions and processes (Miller et al., 1979; Dennis & Chaffee, 1978).

It is also likely that dependence of voters on mass media for campaign information varies with the political context of the times. Ball-Rokeach and DeFleur (1976) have argued that media dependency is likely to be heightened during periods of increased structural conflict and change within societies. They reason that since conflict and change typically challenge established social arrangements for coping with threats to societal norms and mores, greater dependence on media information as an aid in coping results. This increased dependence raises the potential for the media to effect cognitive, affective, and behavioral changes on audiences. Moreover, given the systematic relationships among the media, audiences, and structural stability within society, changes brought about by media within audiences may have a reciprocal impact on both media and the society. Sheingold (1973) averred that during times of political change and conflict, the more immediate kinds of information available to voters during political campaigns may have greater impact on electoral decision-making than do more traditional ideological considerations. For example, the extensive structural and psychological "filtering processes" outlined in the research of the 1940s and 1950s may well figure less prominently during such times, leaving political and social influence processes more focused on campaign stimuli and in greater flux; hence an increased potential for volatility as well as other perhaps even less subtle campaign effects.

The early research returns concerning the 1980 election, as of this writing, suggest few changes in the trends addressed above. More comprehensive and theory-based explanations of campaign communication behaviors and their long-term consequences would seem bound both in scholars' understanding of contemporary political contexts and in their development and use of appropriate research strategies.

A CONCLUDING NOTE

In many ways the dynamism that has marked political campaigns over recent years has been reflected in the research strategies and methods used to study them. Research reviewed in the previous pages has shown an increasing sophistication in approach and technique over the past decade. Yet, important deficiencies remain. Consider, for example, the expansion of political content analysis from simple measures of space or time devoted to topics to the incorporation of a wide range of manifest and latent content attributes found in both print and broadcast media. The results of such investigations provide a much more solid basis for inferences not only about the producers and purveyors of campaign-related content, but also about how audiences may interpret it. Still lacking, however, are reasonable assurances that the content characteristics and categories seen as meaningful by the researcher are viewed as similarly significant by audiences.

The studies reviewed here also include an extensive cataloging of voters' communication behaviors during campaigns. Yet, in many ways the measures of such key concepts as message exposure and attention seem needlessly crude, often deal with gross usage of one medium versus another, and fail to specify the content involved. Concern with simplistic attitudinal predispositions affecting selectivity has largely given way to the investigation of complex motivational bases underlying political communication behaviors. This is a healthy step regardless of whether the constructs used emerge from uses and gratifications approaches or others. Measurement problems still abound in this largely chartless realm of psychological endeavor, but continued efforts in this area are critical. Such research will surely increase in importance as new technologies develop. The surge of direct-mail campaign literature aimed at rather narrow target groups in recent years appears as only an early indication of much more selective (and less "mass" mediated) campaign techniques lying ahead as computer-based information systems make further inroads into both public and private sectors of society.

As campaigners become more adroit in targeting specific messages for specific audiences, persuasive efforts on the part of candidates will become more personalized and, thus, potentially more persuasive. The mass media, particularly television—if they continue the trend sketched above— will provide primarily the entertainment aspects of political campaigns, motion at the expense of substance. While not inevitable, such an outcome seems likely in view of the constraints described earlier.

The advantage of uses and gratifications and related paradigms is that they provide at least something of a roadmap for integrating what people want (or think they need) from communication with what they receive. Substantial advances are clear in the expanded range of campaign communication effects now under study. The greater emphasis on information gain in this regard has proven most productive, particularly as individual and situational constraints on communication behavior and learning are taken more into account. Suasive effects of campaign media remain troublesome to investigate, in part due to difficulty in identifying the processes of citizen attitude and behavior change per se and adequately specifying the communication behaviors associated with them. Yet, if definitive strides are to be made in the study of social influence processes, political campaigns seem an appropriate laboratory. Also productive has been the emphasis on denoting more adequately the kinds of factors which both impinge upon and interact with communication behaviors in campaign settings. Most heartening has been the greater attention given to the consequences of political communication for the social system, as well as to effects on individuals, and the potential interplay between the two.

The challenge remains for communication scholars to develop comprehensive and empirically based concepts and theories incorporating the above considerations as well as others. We realize this is hardly a novel appeal. Yet it takes on new relevance, and new promise, in light of the encouraging research thrusts noted above and the conceptual advances delineated in the early chapters of this volume.

REFERENCE NOTES

1. Frye, J. K. *Press mediation in the dissemination of Vice President Spiro T. Agnew's campaign speeches of October 19, 1969 to November 3, 1970.* Paper presented at the meeting of the International Communication Association, New Orleans, April 1974.
2. (UPI). Reagan-Bush debate "no contest." The Albuquerque *Tribune,* April 24, 1980.
3. Weaver, D. H., Wilhoit, G. C., & Riede, P. *Personal needs and media use.* Washington: American Newspaper Publisher Association, 1979.
4. Kimsey, W. D. *A path analysis of attitudes and cognitions in the 1976 presidential campaign.* Unpublished doctoral dissertation, Southern Illinois University, 1977.
5. Wolfinger, R. E., & Rosenstone, S. J. *Who votes?* Paper presented at the meeting of the American Political Science Association, Washington, D. C., August 1977.
6. Atwood, L. E., & Kuang, S. C. *Undecided voters, vote switchers, media use, and information holding in a congressional and a presidential campaign.* Paper presented at the meeting of the Association for Education in Journalism, Houston, Texas, August 1979.
7. Kimsey, W. D., & Atwood, L. E. *Decision time, attitudes, knowledge, and vote intentions: Two path models.* Paper presented at the meeting of the International Communication Association, Minneapolis, May 1981.
8. Blumier, J. E. *Electoral volatility: Examining communication and change among young voters.* Paper presented at the meeting of the World Association for Public Opinion Research, Montreux, Switzerland, May 1975.
9. McLeod, J. M., Bybee, C. R., Luetscher, W. D., & Garramone, G. M. *Mass communication and voter volatility.* Paper presented at the meeting of the Association for Education in Journalism, Seattle, August 1978.

REFERENCES

Almond, G., & Verba, S. *The civic culture.* Princeton: Princeton University Press, 1963.
Andersen, P. A., & Garrison, J. P. Media consumption and population characteristics of political opinion leaders. *Communication Quarterly,* 1978, *26,* 40-50.

Annis, A. D., & Meier, N. C. The induction of opinion through suggestion by means of planted content. *Journal of Social Psychology,* 1934, *18,* 65-81.

Arnston, P. H., & Smith, C. R. News distortion as a function of organizational communication. *Communication Monographs,* 1978, *45,* 371-381.

Arrendell, C. Predicting the completeness of newspaper election coverage. *Journalism Quarterly,* 1972, *49,* 290-295.

Atkin, C. K. Instrumental utilities and information seeking. In P. Clarke (Ed.), *New models for mass communication research.* Beverly Hills, CA: Sage, 1973.

Atkin, C. K. Political campaigns: Mass communication and persuasion. In M. E. Roloff & G. R. Miller (Eds.), *Persuasion: New directions in theory and research.* Beverly Hills, CA: Sage, 1980.

Atkin, C. K., Bowen, L., & Sheinkopf, K. Quality versus quantity in televised political ads. *Public Opinion Quarterly,* 1973, *37,* 209-244.

Atkin, C. K., & Heald, G. Effects of political advertising. *Public Opinion Quarterly,* 1976, *40,* 216-228.

Atwood, L. E. From press release to voting reasons: Tracing the agenda in a congressional campaign. In D. D. Nimmo, (Ed.), *Communication yearbook 4.* New Brunswick, NJ: Transaction Books, 1980.

Atwood, L. E., & Sanders, K. R. Perception of information sources and likelihood of split-ticket voting. *Journalism Quarterly,* 1975, *52,* 421-428.

Atwood, L. E., & Sanders, K. R. Information sources and voting in a primary and a general election. *Journal of Broadcasting,* 1976, *20,* 291-301.

Bailey, G. How newsmakers make the news: Covering the political campaign. *Journal of Communication,* 1978, *28,* 80-83.

Ball-Rokeach, S. J., & DeFleur, M. A dependency model of mass-media effects. *Communication Research,* 1976, *3,* 3-21.

Barber, J. D. (Ed.). *Race for the presidency: The media and the moninating process.* Englewood Cliffs, NJ: Prentice Hall, 1978.

Bechtolt, W. E., Jr., Hilyard, J., & Bybee, C. R. Agenda control in the 1976 debates: A content analysis. *Journalism Quarterly,* 1977, *54,* 674-681.

Becker, J., & Fuchs, D. A. How two major California dailies covered Reagan and Brown. *Journalism Quarterly,* 1967, *44,* 645-653.

Becker, L. B. Measurement of gratifications. *Communication Research,* 1979, *6,* 54-73.

Becker, L. B., & McCombs, M. E. The role of the press in determining voter reaction to presidential primaries. *Human Communication Research,* 1978, *4,* 301-307.

Becker, L. B., McCombs, M. E., & McLeod, J. M. The development of political cognitions. In S. H. Chaffee (Ed.), *Political communication: Issues and strategies for research.* Beverly Hills, CA: Sage, 1975.

Becker, L. B., Weaver, D. H., Graber, D. A., & McCombs, M. E. Influence on public agendas. In S. Kraus (Ed.), *The great debates: Carter vs. Ford, 1976.* Bloomington: Indiana University Press, 1979.

Becker, L. B., & Whitney, D. C. Effects of media dependencies: Audience assessment of government. *Communication Research,* 1980, *7,* 95-120.

Berelson, B., Lazarsfeld, P. F., & McPhee, W. N. *Voting.* Chicago: University of Chicago Press, 1954,

Bishop, G. F., Meadow, R. G., & Jackson-Beeck, M. (Eds.). *The presidential debates: Media, electoral, and policy perspectives.* New York: Praeger, 1978.

Bishop, G. F., Oldendick, R. W., & Tuchfarber, A. J. Debate watching and the acquisition of political knowledge. *Journal of Communication,* 1978, *28,* 99-113.

Blumler, J. G., & Katz, E. *The uses of mass communication: Current perspectives on gratifications research.* Beverly Hills, CA: Sage, 1974.

Blumler, J. G., & McQuail, D. *Television in politics: Its uses and influence.* Chicago: University of Chicago Press, 1969.

Bowers, T. A. Issue and personality information in newspaper political advertising. *Journalism Quarterly,* 1972, *49,* 446-452.

Broh, C. A. Horse race journalism: Reporting the polls in the 1976 presidential election. *Public Opinion Quarterly,* 1980, *44,* 514-529.

Campbell, A., Converse, P. E., Miller, W. E., & Stokes, D. *The American voter.* New York: John Wiley, 1960.

Campbell, A., Gurin, G., & Miller, W. E. *The voter decides.* Evanston, IL: Row, Peterson, 1954.

Carey, J. How media shape campaigns. *Journal of Communication,* 1976, *26,* 50-57.

Chaffee, S. H. (Ed.). *Political communication: Issues and strategies for research.* Beverly Hills, CA: Sage, 1975.

Chaffee, S. H., & Choe, S. Y. Time of decision and media use during the Ford-Carter campaign. *Public Opinion Quarterly,* 1980, *44,* 53-69.

Clarke, P., & Fredin, E. Newspapers, television, and political reasoning. *Public Opinion Quarterly,* 1978, *42,* 143-160.

Converse, P. E. Information flow and the stability of partisan attitudes. *Public Opinion Quarterly,* 1962, *26,* 578-599.

Danielson, W. A., & Adams, J. B. Completeness of press coverage of the 1960 campaign. *Journalism Quarterly,* 1961, *38,* 441-452.

Davis, D. Influence on vote decisions. In S. Kraus (Ed.), *The great debates: Carter vs. Ford 1976.* Bloomington: Indiana University Press, 1979.

Dennis, J., & Chaffee, S. H. Legitimation in the 1976 U.S. election campaign. *Communication Research,* 1978, *5,* 371-394.

DeVries, W., & Tarrance, V. L. *The ticket-splitter: A new force in American politics.* Grand Rapids, MI: Eerdmans, 1972.

Einsiedel, E. F. Television network news coverage of the Eagleton affair: A case study. *Journalism Quarterly,* 1975, *52,* 56-60.

Einsiedel, E. F., & Bibbee, M. J. The news magazines and minority candidates–Campaign '76. *Journalism Quarterly,* 1979, *56,* 102-105.

Ellsworth, J. W., Rationality and campaigning: A content analysis of the 1960 presidential debates. *Western Political Quarterly,* 1965, *18,* 794-802.

Erbring, L., Goldenberg, E. N., & Miller, A. H. Front-page news and real-world cues: A new look at agenda-setting by the media. *American Journal of Political Science,* 1980, *24,* 16-49.

Evarts, D., & Stempel, G. H. III. Coverage of the 1972 campaign by TV, news magazines, and major newspapers. *Journalism Quarterly,* 1974, *51,* 645-648.

Fowler, G. L. Predicting political news coverage by newspaper characteristics. *Journalism Quarterly,* 1979, *56,* 172-175.

Fuchs, D. Election day newscasts and their effects on western voter turnout. *Journalism Quarterly,* 1965, *42,* 22-28.

Gormley, W. J. Newspaper agendas and political elites. *Journalism Quarterly,* 1975, *52,* 304-308.

Graber, D. A. Media coverage and voter learning during the presidential primary season. *Georgia Journal of Political Science,* 1979, *7,* 19-48.

Graber, D. A. *Mass media and American politics.* Washington, DC: Congressional Quarterly Press, 1980.

Graber, D. A., & Kim, Y. Y. Why John Q. Voter did not learn very much from the 1976 presidential debates. In B. Ruben (Ed.), *Communication yearbook 2.* New Brunswick, NJ: Transaction Books, 1978.

Granberg, D., & Brent, E. E., Jr. Dove-hawk placements in the 1968 election: Application of social judgment and balance theories. *Journal of Personality and Social Psychology,* 1974, *29,* 111-146.

Hartwig, F., Jenkins, W. R., & Temchin, E. M. Variability in electoral behavior: The 1960, 1968, and 1976 elections. *American Journal of Political Science,* 1980, *4,* 553-558.

Hofstetter, C. R. News bias in the 1972 campaign: A cross-media analysis. *Journalism Monographs,* 1978, *58.*

Hofstetter, C. R. Perception of news bias in 1972 presidential campaign. *Journalism Quarterly,* 1979, *56,* 370-374.

Hofstetter, C. R., & Zukin, C. TV network news and advertising in the Nixon and McGovern campaigns. *Journalism Quarterly,* 1979, *56,* 106-115, 152.

Hofstetter, C. R., Zukin, C., & Buss, T. F. Political imagery and information in an age of television. *Journalism Quarterly,* 1978, *55,* 562-569.

Jackson-Beeck, M., & Meadow, R. G. Content analysis of televised communication events: The presidential debates. *Communication Research,* 1979, *6,* 321-344.

Joslyn, R. A. The content of political spot ads. *Journalism Quarterly,* 1980, *57,* 92-98.

Kaid, L. L. Measures of political advertising. *Journalism of Advertising Research,* 1976, *16,* 49-53.

Kaid, L. L. The neglected candidate: Interpersonal communication in political campaigns. *Western Journal of Speech Communication,* 1977, *4,* 245-252.

Katz, E., & Lazarsfeld, P. F. *Personal Influence.* New York; Free Press, 1955.

Kimsey, W. D., & Atwood, L. E. A path analysis of political cognitions and attitudes, communication, and voting in a congressional campaign. *Communication Monographs,* 1979, *46,* 219-230.

Kinder, D. R. Political person perception: The asymmetrical influence of sentiment and choice on perceptions of presidential candidates. *Journal of Personality and Social Psychology,* 1978, *36,* 859-871.

King, M. Assimilation and contrast of presidential candidates' issue positions, 1972. *Public Opinion Quarterly,* 1977, *41,* 515-522.

Klapper, J. *The effects of mass communication.* New York: Free Press, 1960.

Kobre, S. How Florida dailies handled the 1952 presidential campaign. *Journalism Quarterly,* 1953, *30,* 163-169.

Kraus, S. (Ed.). *The great debates.* Bloomington: Indiana University Press, 1962.

Kraus, S. (Ed.). *The great debates: Carter vs. Ford 1976.* Bloomington, Indiana University Press, 1979.

Kraus, S. & Davis, D. *The effects of mass communication on political behavior.* University Park: Pennsylvania State University Press, 1976.

Ladd, E. C., Jr. *Where have all the voters gone?* New York: Norton, 1978.

Lang, G., & Lang, K. Immediate and delayed responses to a Carter-Ford debate: Assessing public opinion. *Public Opinion Quarterly,* 1978, *42,* 322-341.

Lazarsfeld, P. F., Berelson, B., & Gaudet, H. *The people's choice.* New York: Duell, Sloan and Pearce, 1944.

Lucas, W. A., & Adams, W. C. Talking, television, and voter indecision. *Journal of Communication,* 1978, *28,* 120-131.

McCleneghan, J. S. Effect of endorsements in Texas local elections. *Journalism Quarterly,* 1973, *50,* 363-366.

McCleneghan, J. S. Effect of endorsements on newspaper space in Texas papers. *Journalism Quarterly,* 1978, *55,* 792-793.

McClure, R. D., & Patterson, R. E. Television news and political advertising. *Communication Research,* 1974, *1,* 3-31.

McCombs, M. E. Mass communication in political campaigns: Information, gratifications, and persuasion. In F. G. Kline & P. J. Tichenor (Eds.), *Current perspectives in mass communication research.* Beverly Hills, CA: Sage, 1972.

McCombs, M. E., & Shaw, D. L. The agenda-setting function of mass media. *Public Opinion Quarterly,* 1972, *36,* 176-187.

McGinnis, J. *The selling of the president 1968.* New York: Trident Press, 1969.

McLeod, J. M., & Becker, L. B. Testing the validity of gratification measures through political effects and analysis. In J. Blumler & E. Katz (Eds.), *The uses of mass communication: Current perspectives on gratifications research.* Beverly Hills, CA: 1974.

McLeod, J. M., Bybee, C. R., & Durall, J. A. Equivalence of informed participation: The 1976 presidential debates as a source of influence. *Communication Research,* 1979, *6,* 463-487.

McLeod, J. M., Durall, J. A., Ziemke, D. A., & Bybee, C. R. Expanding the context of effects. In S. Kraus (Ed.), *The great debates: Carter vs. Ford 1976.* Bloomington: Indiana University Press, 1979.

MacNeil, R. *The people machine*. New York: Harper & Row, 1968.

Malaney, G., & Buss, T. F. AP wire reports vs. CBS TV news coverage of a presidential campaign. *Journalism Quarterly, 1979, 56,* 602-610.

Markus, G. B., & Converse, P. E. A dynamic simultaneous equation model of electoral choice. *American Political Science Review, 1979, 73,* 1055-1070.

Meadow, R. C. Cross-media comparison of news coverage of the 1972 presidential campaign. *Journalism Quarterly, 1973, 50,* 482-488.

Meadow, R. C. Issue emphasis and public opinion: The media during the 1972 presidential campaign. *American Politics Quarterly, 1976, 4,* 177-192.

Meadow, R. C. *Politics as communication*. Norwood, NJ: Ablex, 1980.

Mendelsohn, H., & Crespi, I. *Polls, television and the new politics*. Scranton: Chandler, 1970.

Mendelsohn, H., & O'Keefe, G. J. *The people choose a president: Influences on voter decision making*. New York: Praeger, 1976.

Milic, L. T. Grilling the pols: Q & A at the debates. In S. Kraus, (Ed.), *The great debates: Carter vs. Ford 1976*. Bloomington: Indiana University Press, 1979.

Miller, A. H., Goldenberg, E. N., & Erbring, L. Type-set politics: Impact of newspapers on public confidence. *American Political Science Review, 1979, 73,* 67-78,

Miller, A. H., & MacKuen, M. Informing the electorate: A national study. In S. Kraus, (Ed.), *The great debates: Carter vs. Ford 1976*. Bloomington: Indiana University Press, 1979, 269-297.

Mullen, J. J. Newspaper advertising in the Kennedy-Nixon campaign. *Journalism Quarterly, 1963, 40,* 3-11.

Mullen, J. J. Newspaper advertising in the Johnson-Goldwater campaign. *Journalism Quarterly, 1968, 45,* 219-225.

Mullins, L. E. Agenda-setting and the young voter. In D. L. Shaw & M. E. McCombs (Eds.), *The emergence of American political issues: The agenda-setting function of the press*. St. Paul, MN: West Publishing, 1977.

Napolitan, J. *The election game and how to win it*. Garden City, NY: Doubleday, 1972.

Nie, N. H., Verba, S., & Petrocik, J. R. *The changing American voter*. Cambridge: Harvard University Press, 1976.

O'Keefe, G. J. Political campaigns and mass communication research. In S. H. Chaffee (Ed.), *Political communication: Issues and strategies for research*. Beverly Hills, CA: Sage, 1975.

O'Keefe, G. J. Political malaise and reliance on media. *Journalism Quarterly, 1980, 57,* 122-128.

O'Keefe, G. J. The changing context of interpersonal communication in political campaigns. In M. Burgoon (Ed.), *Communication yearbook 5*. New Brunswick, NJ: Transaction Books, in press.

O'Keefe, G. J., & Mendelsohn, H. Voter selectivity, partisanship, and the challenge of Watergate. *Communication Research, 1974, 1,* 345-367.

O'Keefe, G. J., & Mendelsohn, H. Nonvoting: The media's role. In C. Winick (Ed.), *Deviance and mass media*. Beverly Hills, CA: Sage, 1978.

O'Keefe, G. J., & Mendelsohn, H. Media influences and their anticipation. In S. Kraus (Ed.), *The great debates: Carter vs. Ford 1976*. Bloomington: Indiana University Press, 1979.

O'Keefe, G. J., Mendelsohn, H., & Lui, J. Voter decision making in 1972 and 1974. *Public Opinion Quarterly, 1976, 40,* 320-330.

O'Keefe, M. T., & Sheinkopf, K. The voter decides: Candidate images or campaign issues? *Journal of Broadcasting, 1974, 18,* 403-412.

Page, B. I., & Jones, C. C. Reciprocal effects of policy preferences, party loyalties, and the vote. *American Political Science Review, 1979, 73,* 1071-1089.

Patterson, T. E. *The mass media election: How Americans choose their president*. New York: Praeger, 1980.

Patterson, T. E., & McClure, R. D. *The unseeing eye: The myth of television power in national elections.* New York: Putnam, 1976.

Perry, J. M. *The new politics.* New York: Clarkson N. Potter, 1968.

Pierce, J. C., & Sullivan, J. L. (Eds.), *The electorate reconsidered.* Beverly Hills, CA: Sage, 1980.

Quarles, R. C. Mass media use and voting behavior: The accuracy of political perceptions among first-time and experienced voters. *Communication Research,* 1979, *6,* 407-436.

Roberts, C. L. Media use and difficulty of decision in the 1976 presidential campaign. *Journalism Quarterly,* 1979, *56,* 794-802.

Robinson, J. P. The press as king-maker: What surveys from last five campaigns show. *Journalism Quarterly,* 1974, *51,* 587-594, 606.

Robinson, J. P. Interpersonal influence in election campaigns: Two step-flow hypothesis. *Public Opinion Quarterly,* 1976, *40,* 304-319.

Robinson, J. P., & Jeffries, L. W. The changing role of newspapers in the age of television. *Journalism Monographs,* 1979, *63.*

Robinson, M. J. Public affairs television and the growth of political malaise: The case of "the selling of the pentagon." *American Political Science Review,* 1976, *70,* 409-432.

Rock, P. News as eternal recurrence. In S. Cohen & J. Young (Eds.), *The manufacture of news: A reader.* Beverly Hills, CA: Sage, 1973.

Roper Organization. *Changing public attitudes toward television and other mass media, 1959-1976.* New York: Television Information Office, 1977.

Rothschild, M., & Ray, M. Involvement and political advertising effect. *Communication Research,* 1974, *1,* 264-285.

Russonello, J. M., & Wolf, F. Newspaper coverage of the 1976 and 1968 presidential campaigns. *Journalism Quarterly,* 1979, *56,* 360-364, 432.

Schramm, W., & Carter, R. F. Effectiveness of a political telethon. *Public Opinion Quarterly,* 1959, *23,* 121-126.

Schulman, M., & Pomper, G. Variability in election behavior: Longitudinal perspectives from causal modeling. *American Journal of Political Science,* 1975, *19,* 1-18.

Sears, D. O., & Chaffee, S. H. Uses and effects of the 1976 debates: An overview of empirical studies. In S. Kraus (Ed.), *The great debates: Carter vs. Ford 1976.* Bloomington: Indiana University Press, 1979.

Shaw, D. L., & McCombs, M. E. (Eds.). *The emergence of American political issues: The agenda-setting function of the press.* St. Paul, MN: West Publishing, 1977.

Sheingold, C. A. Social networks and voting: The resurrection of a research agenda. *American Sociological Review,* 1973, *38,* 712-720.

Sheinkopf, K., Atkin, C. K., & Bowen, L. How political party workers respond to political advertising. *Journalism Quarterly,* 1973, *50,* 334-339.

Sherif, M., & Hovland, C. I. *Social judgment: Assimilation and contrast effects in communication and attitude change.* New Haven: Yale University Press, 1961.

Sherrod, D. Selective perception of political candidates. *Public Opinion Quarterly,* 1971, *35,* 554-562.

Steeper, F. T. Public response to Gerald Ford's statements on Eastern Europe in the second debate. In G. F. Bishop, R. G. Meadow, and M. Jackson-Beeck (Eds.), *The presidential debates: Media, electoral, and policy perspectives.* New York: Praeger, 1978.

Stempel, G. H. III. The prestige press covers the 1960 presidential campaign. *Journalism Quarterly,* 1961, *38,* 157-163.

Stempel, G. H. III. The prestige press in two presidential elections. *Journalism Quarterly,* 1965, *42,* 15-21.

Stempel, G. H. III. Prestige press meets the third party challenge. *Journalism Quarterly,* 1969, *46,* 699-706.

Stevenson, R. L., & White, K. P. The cumulative audience of television network news. *Journalism Quarterly,* 1980, *57,* 477-481.

Swanson, D. L. The uses and misuses of uses and gratifications. *Human Communication Research,* 1977, *3,* 214-221.

Tan, A. S. Mass media use, issue knowledge and political involvement. *Public Opinion Quarterly,* 1980, *44,* 241-248.

Tichenor, P. J., Donohue, G. A., & Olien, C. N. *Community conflict and the press.* Beverly Hills, CA: Sage, 1980.

Tipton, L. P., Haney, R. D., & Baseheart, R. J. Media agenda-setting in city and state election campaigns. *Journalism Quarterly,* 1975, *52,* 15-22.

Weisberg, J. F., & Rusk, J. G. Dimensions of candidate evaluation. *American Political Science Review,* 1970, *64,* 1167-1186.

Williams, W., Jr., & Semlak, W. D. Structural effects of TV coverage on political agendas. *Journal of Communication,* 1978, *28,* 114-119.

Windhauser, J. How the metropolitan press covered the 1970 general election campaign in Ohio. *Journalism Quarterly,* 1976, *53,* 264-270.

CHAPTER 13

Mass Communication and Public Opinion

Cliff Zukin

THE MASS MEDIA and public opinion are inextricably wed. The central role accorded the public in a liberal democracy requires at bare minimum information on which judgments about leadership may be made. A central question of democratic theory—how are public preferences transmitted to decision makers?—is a question about communication. At the other extreme, communication is inherent in such analytic tools as the "normal vote," where some information must penetrate the shield of every voter who defects from the long-term force of partisanship.

For this chapter, the term "communication" will refer to the mass media. The decline of the central city and with it the urban party organizations, coupled with the saturation by television, radio, and print, have reduced political dependency on interpersonal communications. It is primarily through media that citizens monitor their political process, gaining information and insights on the functioning of government, its leaders, and the problems confronting the nation in both international and domestic spheres. Officials monitor the media (and public opinion polls) as a microcosm or sampling of public concerns, searching for the elusive "mood" of the country and seeking the limits to which their actions shall be constrained by the scrutiny and parameters of public opinion.

While elections provide one linkage between public opinion and public policy, it is worth remembering that elections are quadrennial or biennial events. Issues on which citizens demand voice or information, or on which decision makers seek guidance, do not allow themselves to be so neatly scheduled. While political parties and pressure groups to some degree serve as opinion-to-policy linkage mechanisms, it is clear that the media also serve this function in contemporary politics.

Despite the centrality of the question, our knowledge of the media-opinion relationship is undernourished. Writing some 30 years ago, Bernard Berelson bemoaned the meager contribution social science had made in examining the role of the mass media in formulating and influencing public opinion. The role of the media, wrote Berelson (1960), "was not evident to a classical writer on public opinion twenty-five years ago [Walter Lippman], and it may be even less so today" (p. 527).

Much, of course, has happened since Berelson's gloomy assessment. Television has become the dominant medium of national politics. Even in 1952, when only one in two American households owned a receiver, more reported getting election information from television than from any other source (Campbell, 1962). Television has been a remarkable innovation, for both the speed and depth with which it penetrated the population (DeFleur & Ball-Rokeach, 1976).

Equally dramatic has been the growth and development of survey research, a primary investigative tool for assessing public opinion. George Gallup has been joined by a score of other national pollsters, including the three major commercial broadcast networks and various print outlets. No less than 21 academic polling organizations met at the University of Kentucky in January 1981 to coordinate studies of public opinion at the subnational level. At the present growth rate, it will not be long before pollsters outnumber respondents.

Yet, despite these trends, it is difficult to claim that we know a great deal more about the media-opinion linkage than we did 30 years ago. We know more about how people use the mass media and about the process by which private opinions form and change. However, we know relatively little about formation and change on any specific issue, and little about the long-term changes in public opinion that may be attributable to the mass media.

What we do know a great deal more about since the time of Berelson's writing are the *problems* in exploring the relationship between the mass media and public opinion. Indeed, it may be argued that we have learned more from research of the last two decades about how to study the relationship than about how the relationship works. It is easier—and, at this stage of the field's development, more useful—to offer generalizations about "problems of media research on public opinion" than generalizations about the "effects of the mass media on public opinion."

Much of the research conducted in the late 1960s and early 1970s is said to have contributed to the "minimal effects" view of the media. Many studies of this period, however, made significant contributions by raising conceptual and methodological difficulties involved in exploring the relationship between media usage and public opinion. Building on this body of knowledge, a host of studies conducted in the last half of the 1970s employing refined study designs and techniques discovered that the media play a more consequential role. The first section of this essay attempts to bring together many of these findings in a discussion of major problems relative to studying the mass media and public opinion.

The second section addresses selected topics bearing on the media and public opinion, principally opinion formation and change, the effects of nonelectoral information campaigns, citizen learning from the media, and the impact of the mass media on political institutions and the larger political culture. This, of course, leaves out many legitimate concerns in the domain of public opinion. The uses of political communication, the diffusion of political information, agenda-setting, socialization, electoral campaigns and debates, political propaganda, social movements and the use of political language—all separate contributions to this volume—are all subsets of "the mass media and public opinion." Their exclusion here is by no means a comment on their importance. Moreover, it may well be that we know more about these component parts than about the totality. In not all cases is the whole greater than the sum of the parts.

Also largely excluded from this essay is the effect of the mass media on *specific issues* of public opinion. A characteristic of public opinion, as Nimmo (1978) suggests, is that it is relatively persistent. Few concrete issues, such as the Vietnam war and Watergate, can be said to have totally captivated the public in the last 15 years, aside from general economic conditions. Thus, by definition, these issues constitute a somewhat atypical state of public opinion. The primary focus here is on more "normal times." Specific issues are treated when relevant to discussion of the general media-opinion process. While lack of space precludes a separate section on this topic, the point should be made that the relationship between the media and public opinion may have different modes—one set of relationships in what might be termed "normal" times, another in crisis situations, a third regarding highly salient issues, and so forth.

PROBLEMS IN THE STUDY OF
THE MASS MEDIA

The inability of social scientists to document clear-cut media effects, juxtaposed against the "conventional wisdom" crediting the media (principally television) with a massive reshaping of the political terrain, has been one of the great intrigues of behavioral research over the past two decades. It is time, however, to acknowledge that the doctrine of "minimal (or reinforcement) effects" is now only minimally accurate.

In addition to allowing us to build new knowledge regarding the role of the media, recent research also allows us to identify a number of barriers that impeded progress in this area. Three principal factors, which are not mutually exclusive, may be singled out for discussion: (1) The *timing* of early media studies militated against finding "effects." (2) The primary independent variable of "exposure" has suffered from parochial treatment in both conceptual and operational terms. (3) The scope of early media studies was primarily concerned with a search for direct, immediate, and deterministic "effects." This focus on a narrow set of dependent variables retarded other possible avenues of inquiry that are only now being developed. Each of these elements deserves further consideration.

The Timing of Studies

Early media research was largely conducted within the context of national elections. The growth of television in the early 1950s occurred simultaneously with movement from the Columbia single-site panel studies to the Michigan pretest-posttest design centering on national elections. This had the unfortunate consequence of focusing on the relationship between media and electoral behavior in the narrow time band immediately before and after national general elections. This is precisely the time at which media effects would be *least,* and reinforcement effects *most* likely to occur. As citizens had often formed opinions of the parties, candidates, and the dynamic issues of the campaign prior to this time, it is little wonder that reinforcement (or minimal) effects appeared so prominently in the literature.

If images of candidates and parties (the predominant questions of the time) are influenced by the media, it is far more likely to occur in the primary season when information levels are relatively low and nonincumbents relatively unknown. It is necessary to study the electorate at an earlier point in time and to again make use of the type of research design employed by the Columbia scholars. Recent studies employing this design have painted a clearer, and different, picture of media impact (Patterson, 1980; Mendelsohn & O'Keefe, 1976).

The reliance of political scientists on the national election studies of the University of Michigan Center for Political Studies has also been unfortunate in that the disproportionate attention given to impact of the mass media on electoral behavior has come at the expense of broader public opinion questions. Thus research directed toward media impact on other public opinion concerns has been slow to develop. Moreover, electoral research doubtlessly overstates the reinforcement effects of the media, as the strong mediating attitude of partisan identification has no consistently strong counterpart in nonelectoral situations.

What Is Exposure, and How Is it Measured?

The concept of "exposure" has proved to be particularly troubling, especially as it has been the principal independent variable employed to explain media "effects." In its more commonly used form, as a quantitative indicator of how much content a given individual attended, there are a number of grounds for criticism.

The first such criticism concerns the dominance of television and sounds somewhat paradoxical. Few effects have been found because television has a pervasive effect—a saturation effect. The medium is so dominant that everyone is touched by it, even that small percentage who do not own television receivers or watch much television. The frame of reference and common experiences provided by television reach us all, either through direct exposure or indirect exposure, through discussion with other people or the content of other media. A logical consequence of this is that studies attempting to attribute variation in attitudes or behavior to television exposure yield null findings, as there is little or no variation in the population to be explained. The common mode of study has consisted of correlating the extent to which some effect is present with the extent of exposure to the medium. This investigative strategy is futile because the key difference is not *how much* exposure an individual had to the medium, but whether the individual was exposed *at all.*

A growing number of studies have warned that exposure measures may obscure more than they reveal given saturation conditions, arguing that "more exposure" should not be expected to produce "more effects" (Iyengar, 1979; McLeod, Brown, Becker, & Ziemke, 1977; Zukin, 1977). Relying on the amount of media exposure to explain substantive effects is a risky strategy. It is tantamount to researching the relationship between pregnancy and sexual intercourse by comparing those who have sex five times a week with those who limit themselves to twice a week. Finding that pregnancy occurs in both groups hardly demonstrates that there is no relationship between the two variables.[1]

The work of Miller, Goldenberg, and Erbring (1979) raises a second issue and offers an important caution against equating media *exposure* measures with media *content* received. Reliance on a medium is not tantamount to exposure to a message; nor does exposure in general allow one to assume exposure to particular message content. Miller et al. argue that an interconnected data set of survey responses (including exposure measures) and media content is necessary to study media impact on public opinion. While their argument is clearly valid, the expense of collecting such information is a practical reality which scholars must confront. One should expect the equating of exposure and content to characterize much future research.

It must be borne in mind that such an assumption must necessarily increase error and depress, if not mask, relationships. Moreover, with substantial intra-medium variation in evaluative content on a given topic (in Miller's case, critical presentation of political issues and institutions) the risk in this assumption is considerably less justified in studies with evaluative or "affective" dependent variables. Variation in content on a topic would effect less what topics people thought about (cognitive elements) than what positions they took on the topic.

The recent proliferation of studies utilizing a "uses and gratifications" paradigm (see Chapter 2 of this volume) points to a third problem with the concept "exposure" and is also a welcome addition. This approach, focusing on individuals' motivations for exposure to media content, recognizes a *qualitative* dimension of exposure. Much as the early hypodermic needle model of mass communication was improved by recognizing the interposition of receiver predispositions between the message and effects (Klapper, 1960), including motivational predispositions will also enhance knowledge.

Much political science research has been characterized by the implicit assumption that individuals attend to the mass media for the sole purpose of acquiring information (Converse, 1966). Such an assumption is clearly untenable. The audience is active in the communication process and is goal-directed. Moreover, each audience member may have unique goals. One would not expect the same effects on a dependent variable of "knowledge" for one individual viewing political programming to acquire information as for another individual viewing "to pass the time," even though both could receive the same score on a quantiative "exposure" independent variable. Motivational variables may act as a powerful set of specifying conditions for media relationships. The explanatory power in qualitative definitions of exposure is at present largely untapped.

A strong case may also be made for substituting "dependency" measures for "exposure" measures (Becker, Sobowale, & Casey, 1979). By combining (a) reported reliance on a given medium for information on a particular topic, (b) the amount of attention paid to stories on the topic, and (c) the amount of exposure to a medium, Becker and Whitney (1980) find media *dependence* significantly related to various indicators of trust, comprehension, and knowledge. However, most of these same relationships were not significant when simple media *exposure* was used as the independent variable. Naked measures of exposure to a medium do not allow one to control for exposure to other sources of information, perceived utility of the information, or other concerns generally assumed to be embodied in the concept of "exposure."

The Scope of Early Studies

As noted earlier, the slow growth in knowledge of the media's impact on public opinion has roots in the early preoccupation with media influence on voting behavior—a special case of public opinion. Beyond being confined to the electoral arena, however, the questions asked focused on the direct and immediate effects of the media. Based largely on the excitement surrounding television's "presumed capacity to inform and stimulate the interests of the American electorate" (Campbell, 1962), studies of the 1950s and early 1960s were confined almost solely to straightforward electoral questions. The focus of studies was on how the media affected interest in the election, turnout, and partisan division of the vote. Left untouched by the rush to demonstrate "important" media effects were considerations of "indirect" and "long-term" effects.

In a model of "indirect effects," exposure to the media would impact on a variable X, which in turn would impact on variable Y. The notion of agenda-setting provides a ready example. Two candidates contesting an election may each have a natural advantage on different issues. The electorate prefers candidate Smith's position on abortion; candidate Jones's on energy. Should the media devote more time and space to abortion, telling people "what to think about," candidate Smith gains a relative advantage, even while correlations between media exposure and vote could well be close to zero. Indirect effects are much harder to unearth than direct effects but no less significant. Research strategies sophisticated enough to investigate these effects are only now emerging in full force (Erbing, Goldenberg, & Miller, 1980).

Only recently have we also seen attention turn to "long-term" effects of the media. The concern here is the impact of the media (as purveyors of information) on political institutions, the political culture, and the social fabric. Does daily, low-grade dosage of themes picturing political institutions in conflict on the nightly news lead over time to lower levels of efficacy and political trust? Does entertainment television, by picturing a violent society, cause paranoia and lower personal trust? As Key (1961, p. 402) stated the question two decades ago,

> Speculation about long-run effects of the media raises the question of whether the suggestions of the media, day after day, year after year, may not substantially affect people's opinions even on basic issues.

The difficulty in researching these questions is obvious. Media exposure over time is universal; there is no control group. It is now impossible to compare areas of high and low television density, as Simon and Stern (1955) did in the 1952 election. Any area that did not now have television would, *ipso facto,* be too atypical on other dimensions to use as a control. Moreover, in searching for effects over time, it is impossible to separate the contribution of the media from the variegated array of stimuli that make up the world we live in. Perhaps, as Key said, these questions "cannot be analyzed systematically in any satisfactory way" (1961, p. 402); however, investigations of the long-term effects of the media have clearly begun and constitute one of the most fascinating areas of current study.

The above discussion has not been an exhaustive treatment of problems in studying the media relative to public opinion. Researchers, for example, must be more responsible with the term "media." The mass media may refer either to a *channel* of communication or to the *source* of communication. Researchers investigating "what are the effects of the mass media" often fail to make this differentiation, which becomes critical when analyzing motivation or suggesting remedies. The failure of a channel of communication is quite different from the failure of a message, and there are ample opportunities for confusion. It is clear that research on the mass media, as it contributes to formulating and shaping public opinion, must overcome a number of hurdles in the coming decade if a solid body of knowledge is to emerge. The most important task appears to be in the clarification, refinement, and careful usage of the concept "exposure."

Problems in the Study of
Public Opinion

This essay was completed amid the aftermath of the 1980 presidential election. The election of a Republican "conservative" President and a Republican Senate are unarguable facts. The National Conservative Political Action Committee is flexing its self-reported (and media-reported) newly found muscles, claiming that conservatives arose in mass numbers to turn out the liberal vanguard—Senators McGovern, Bayh, Culver, Nelson, Javits, and Church, among others. Media commentary, as seen in newspaper columns and sources chosen as "newsmakers" by print and electronic journalists, appeared to have focused on the "new conservative mood" well in advance of the election (Entman & Paletz, 1980) and taken the election results as vindication of the shift in the climate of public opinion.[2]

Yet another measure of public opinion, survey results, finds no such change in climate. The ratio of self-identified conservatives to liberals actually dropped slightly between 1968 and 1978; analysis of NORC data fails to reveal increasing conservatism in public spending on a host of specific issues (Entman & Paletz, 1980). There is also a virtual consensus on the "liberal" position that government should guarantee jobs to all those who wish to work and aid in making low-cost health care available. Trends on various social issues (abortion, premarital sex, civil liberties, marijuana penalties, "womens" rights) have all been moving to the left (Ladd, 1978)—hardly evidence of a massive conservative backlash.

Herein rests a fundamental difficulty in relating the mass media to public opinion: What public opinion is rests largely in the hands of those organizing the discussion of it. Public opinion exists as much as a "true" message exists—the negotiation of stimuli between encoder and decoder. "To speak with precision of public opinion," as Key observed, "is a task not unlike coming to grips with the Holy Ghost" (1961, p. 8).

Nimmo (1978) has provided an excellent point of departure for a discussion of public opinion. In discussing the "opinion process" whereby the values, preferences, and beliefs of citizens are linked with policy choices of leadership, public expression may take three forms:

(1) The give-and-take of private opinions within social groups results in the expression of a *group opinion*. (2) When persons express views not through

organized groups but through the relative privacy of the voting booth, letters to congressmen, responses to an opinion pollster, etc., these choices made in isolation and separation from one another constitute *popular opinion*. (3) *Mass opinion* is the generally diffuse, unorganized expression of views frequently symbolized as culture, consensus, and what politicians glibly refer to as "public opinion" [p. 10].

Conceptualizing public opinion simultaneously on a variety of levels allows reconciliation of some of the apparent contradictions in opinion and allows us to speak with more precision about media effects. A *"mass opinion"* framework, for example, supports a neoconservative swing and ascribes to the media (through journalistic gatekeepers and communicators) tremendous impact (Entman & Paletz, 1980). By including and omitting information, "the media can play a large role in limiting the range of interpretation that audiences are able to make" (Ball-Rokeach & DeFleur, 1976, p. 13). Based on media discussion that shapes perceptions, Ladd (1978, p. 33) notes, "It must be acknowledged that many observers of the American scene *think* the country 'is moving right,' and more than a few political leaders are *acting* as though it were. This in itself is enormously consequential."

A *popular opinion* framework would most likely yield a minimal effects interpretation—that basic beliefs and evaluations have changed little; or come to a minor media effects interpretation (in the "liberal" direction) based on the axiomatic role of information in opinion change. As Key (1961, p. 235) noted, "Public opinion must be in substantial degree a product of the stimuli to which the public is subjected."[3]

The relationship between mass and popular opinion is little understood but enormously important for two reasons. First, leaders responding to their perception of mass opinion, and guided by the law of anticipated (electoral) consequences, may respond with policy actions. This response is inherent in Key's definition of public opinion: "Those opinions held by private persons which government finds it prudent to heed" (1961, p. 14). Policy thus is responsive to mass opinion but unresponsive to popular opinion. Second, given the greater media attention, the more mythical mass opinion may shape popular opinion, becoming a self-fulfilling prophecy of sorts (Noelle-Newmann, 1977). By this logic, television news' vivid portrayal of racial conflict in the late 1960s may be related to the tremendous gap between individuals' attitudes on racial matters and what individuals *believe* public attitudes to be. Numerous studies have documented that popular opinion is far more tolerant (or liberal) than the same public's perception of mass opinion (Fields & Schuman, 1976; O'Gorman & Garry, 1976; O'Gorman, 1979). Over time, as individuals come to believe that more conservative positions are socially acceptable, the lack of social constraints should make these positions easier to take. However, as noted above, we have not yet observed this occurrence in popular opinion.

The consideration of popular opinion, and problems associated with it, deserve special treatment. This is the predominant mode of opinion-expression considered by scholars searching for media effects. The reliance on survey research for information about popular opinion needs to be addressed, as it may be argued that this opinion has its birth in the survey research process.

The growth in sophistication and pervasiveness of surveys allows for a condition of "technological democracy." Surveys interacting with the mass media provide a fundamental link between leaders and the public: Polls transmit (both informed and uninformed) opinion to decision makers via the media. Leaders' actions are fed back to the public via the media, and the public's evaluations of leaders' actions are recorded by more opinion polls. Polls allow citizens to compete with interest groups by eliminating the costs of organizing. By organizing the voice of citizens and consumers, polls allow the public to compete in defining the issues (or setting the agenda) that government chooses to deal with. Thus, how polls measure and organize opinion is a fundamental question.

There are many possible sources of error in measuring public opinions. Most fundamental is the measurement of "nonattitudes" (Converse, 1970). In presenting respondents with a stimulus (a question), we infer the presence of an attitude from the response. While "attitude" may be defined in a variety of ways, most would agree that it is a relatively stable, enduring predisposition. Since only in panel studies can the same stimulus be presented to the same respondent to test for the same response, attitudinal research is largely inferential in cross-sectional designs. While evidence of change from time 1 to time 2 can be interpreted as either attitude change or initial measurement of a nonattitude, the latter interpretation now seems the most compelling (Converse, 1975).

Support is added to this interpretation by the excellent work of Bishop et al. (1980), who tested four forms of question wordings (with different introductions and knowledge filters) on a fictitious issue—"the 1975 Public Affairs Act." Their research concluded that the measurement of nonopinions is a substantial problem. With no introductory filter wording allowing respondents to state they were unfamiliar with the topic, as many as one in three ventured an opinion. While the authors argue that responses may reflect underlying social-psychological predispositions rather than random error, they concluded that "the distinction between what is a real topic and what is not may be irrelevant for much of the mass public" (Bishop et al., 1980, p. 210).

Even minor variations in question wording can affect responses tremendously. In October 1979, for example, the Eagleton Poll of Rutgers University conducted a statewide survey investigating New Jerseyans' opinions of the proposed SALT treaty. After 10 percent of the 1200 respondents who said they had heard or read nothing about SALT were filtered out, half were asked if they favored or opposed the U.S. and USSR "coming to a SALT agreement." The other half of the sample were asked if they favored or opposed the U.S. and the USSR "coming to an agreement to limit nuclear weapons." Responses to the first question found 48 percent in favor, 17 percent opposed, and 24 percent offering no opinion. Responses to the second question form found 73 percent in favor, 14 percent opposed, and only 7 percent undecided. The differences attributable to variation in question wording are striking, and it is worth remembering that they occurred *after* those without any information had been screened out. While there are technical procedures for asking *good* survey questions, there is no procedure for asking the *right* questions. It is possible to ask many good questions on the same topic, all of which will yield a different and valid reading of public opinion.

As Lippman (1922) noted over 50 years ago, the public is primarily concerned with direct experiences of life and has little time for public affairs. Put less gently by Converse (1975, p. 79) "popular levels of information about public affairs are, from the point of the informed observer, astonishingly low." The wide variance between the general public's level of information and the knowledge required to answer questions commonly asked by many survey organizations cannot be overly stressed. In 1978, for example, an Eagleton Poll found only one New Jerseyan in three able to spontaneously identify Clifford Case as one of the state's Senators, even though he had been in office 24 years. Even fewer could name 20-year incumbent Senator Harrison Williams. While this is only one indicator of knowledge—and admittedly a narrow one—the level of information observed cannot be reconciled with the information necessary to answer many of the questions researchers commonly pose to the mass public. The question reprinted below serves as a clear illustration of the problem. The difficulty of relating any independent media variable to responses should be self-evident.

> On the issue of a homeland for the Palestinian Arabs, would you favor having parts of the West Bank made into a Palestinian homeland under Jordanian rule, or making the West Bank an independent Palestinian state, or having the Palestininans live where they do now in Jordan, on the West Bank, in the Gaza Strip and in Lebanon? [Harris, Note 1].

Public opinion research has also been led astray by researchers posing "costless" questions to respondents. It is not unusual to see a sample overwhelmingly favoring both increased government services and lower taxes. However, most policy decisions are choices *among* values; too often questions put to the public do not indicate that the pie is not infinitely expandable.

The consequences of costless questions relative to identifying "true" public opinions are clear. While in 1978 76 percent adopted what could be termed a conservative position, feeling "the federal government is spending too much money" (Gallup, 1978, p. 14), roughly 90 percent took what could be termed a liberal position: They felt that spending was not excessive on environmental, health, crime, and educational programs. In addition, about three in four felt government spending was not excessive on urban problems or improving the conditions of blacks (Entman & Paletz, 1980).

Beyond often creating rather than measuring attitudes, and presenting artificial situations, we know only what we choose to ask about, clearly a small subset of potential public opinion (Edelstein, 1973). This entails organizing choices for others to make. The fact that alternatives must be structured and limited carries with it the price that often we do not know what we don't know. The idea that information conveyed by the media has changed something from time 1 to time 2 often does not occur to us until time 2. In many cases we simply have to be lucky to have a time 1 measurement of the phenomenon available.

A related concern is that it is often impossible to test for multiple dimensions of a problem, although almost all problems are multidimensional, and it is clearly true that different respondents structure different problems along unique dimensions. An example of the many dimensions of a given policy issue can be seen in the following data. After measuring general support (favor or oppose) for a process of initiative and referendum in New Jersey, a 1979 Eagleton Poll attempted to explore the cognitive underpinnings of opinion. Three statements about positive benefits of this process were presented to respondents for agreement, along with four statements posing negative costs. Between 62 and 82 percent agreed with *each* of the seven statements. For example, 78 percent agreed that "citizens ought to be able to vote directly on important issues and policies instead of their representatives voting for them," while 64 percent agreed that "the job of making laws should be left to elected representatives. If people don't like what they do they can vote them out of office."

The foregoing treatment of problems in public opinion is no more exhaustive than the earlier treatment of problems in studying the mass media. What should be clear from this discussion is that different worlds of public opinion coexist, each as valid as the next. Further, how public opinion is conceptualized and organized, and how observations about public opinion are collected, heavily influence—if not determine—what public opinion is thought to be. With no "true" measure of public opinion, the question of how the mass media relate to opinion is understandably thorny and complex. We cannot expect answers that are either quick or simple.

THE MASS MEDIA AS INFORMATION SOURCES

While it is difficult to pinpoint *what* effects the media have on public opinion, it is a far easier task to identify *how* they affect public opinion. The public is largely dependent on the mass media for its information about political issues, actors, and institutions. Windfall profits taxes, Abscams, seizures of hostages, and outbreaks of wars cannot be learned by personal experience. As a public we are quite dependent on the mass media to tell us about the shape and status of our political world. This is not to suggest that direct experience has little to do with how citizens view government and politics; supermarket prices and energy bills are confronted daily, accompanied by evaluations of government performance in these areas.

Early conceptualizations of media effects viewed the receipt of new information like a "hypodermic needle." An unwitting public exposed to new information would change attitudes (and behaviors) in line with the direction of the message. This model, of course did not square with the earliest empirical realities—information campaigns failed more often than they succeeded in changing attitudes. The audience could not be viewed as an inert element in the communication process. Rather, individuals were active members of this process, bringing stored information, predispositions, and different needs with them to the communication situation. As is still true today, "effects" of the mass media are largely perceiver-determined rather than content-determined.

In explaining why information campaigns failed, Hyman and Sheatsley (1947) set forth four general principles: (1) the reception of new information does not necessarily lead to attitude change; (2) people seek information congenial to their prior attitudes, which act as prisms in filtering and interpreting incoming information; (3) there exists a hard core of "chronic know-nothings"— a segment of the population lacking the motivation to become informed about political issues; and (4) it is the most interested who acquire the most new information.

For the most part, these generalizations remain true today, although not all may be argued with equal conviction. A slight restructuring of these basic principles organizes the questions to be addressed in this section: Under what conditions does information lead to attitude change? What is the role of motivation in learning? Are there information strata in the general public based largely on interest, and, if so, is there evidence of a widening "knowledge gap" between them?

Information and Attitude Change

We are bombarded daily with more information from our environment than we can process. The attitudes we have developed serve as informational gate-keepers by reducing these stimuli to manageable proportions. The information perceived as relevant is also organized and stored in accordance with existing predispositions. Thus, new information on a topic is largely recognized and interpreted on the basis of the information we already possess.

The amount of information held on a given topic is generally a measure of the salience of that topic, and salience is a critical variable for understanding the success or failure of information campaigns. On topics considered salient to an individual, belief systems generally contain a larger number of elements. There will be a greater number of beliefs (or cognitions) about the topic, and the evaluations attached to those beliefs (the affective component) will be relatively intense. Moreover, the elements in the belief system will be functionally inter-dependent, meaning that a change in one element gives rise to pressures for change or modification in other elements. Thus, as a general rule of attitude change, there is an inverse relationship between the impact of new information on a topic and the amount of stored information an individual holds on that topic.

Understanding the interaction between salience and perceptual mechanisms allows for a number of generalizations to be made regarding the effectiveness of information campaigns. Information campaigns directly confronting strongly held attitudes will be ineffective due to perceptual modifications of the incoming message (Grupp, 1970; & O'Keefe, 1971). Campaigns aimed at *activating* latent predispositions by trying to increase the perceived importance of the topic have a better chance of success than do campaigns aimed at *changing* predispositions (Jones & Saunders, 1977). Information campaigns are also more likely to be effective on "new" topics, about which the perceiver has little information (Mendelsohn, 1973). However, these same individuals are less likely to pay attention to communications on these topics, since they are not perceived to be salient.

The failure of many studies to incorporate measures of salience is a principal reason for the lack of demonstrable media effects. Simply put, different topics differ in their importance to different persons. One of the most fruitful lines of recent inquiry is in the area of "agenda-setting," which involves the manipulation of salience. The links between media attention to issues and the public's agenda is treated separately in this volume (see Chapter 4). But it is also essential to raise in this essay, as the general evidence is that the media affect more what topics people think about than what people specifically think about any given topic. In fact, this may be the media's most profound effect on public opinion.

> The mass media force attention to certain issues, they build up images of public figures. They are constantly presenting objects suggesting what individuals in the mass should think about, know about, have feelings about [Lang & Lang, 1966, p. 468].

One of the reasons agenda-setting research has built a significant history of findings in a relatively short period is that most researchers have approached the topic from the perspective of opinion *formation* rather than opinion *change*. The early concentrations on questions of opinion change has undoubtedly contrib-uted more strongly than is warranted to the minimal effects legacy. A focus on opinion formation reveals a more consequential role played by the mass media. Information conveyed through the mass media is more influential on new issues and new topics, where the inertia of predispositions does not need to be overcome; moreover, such information is relatively more efficacious in influencing cognitive than affective elements.

The resistance offered by prior attitudes has been a focal point in explaining the lack of media effects, or, more precisely, why exposure to attempts at persuasion generally lead to reinforcement rather than conversion. Individuals selectively expose themselves to information, selectively attend, perceive, and retain information in accordance with existing attitudes (Klapper, 1960). As Graber (1980) noted, much of the "minimal effects" legacy is rooted in cognitive consistency theories. While there are many variants of consistency theory (Inkso, 1967), all posit that inconsistency in attitude-elements produces an unpleasant psychological state of tension. Individuals are thus pressured or driven to restore harmony among cognitive and affective elements by modifying beliefs, evaluations, or the salience of elements.

The evidence of selectivity in exposure to information may be attacked on two fronts. Scars and Friedman (1967) noted that many studies fail to confirm a preference for supportive information. It may well be that persons can tolerate a larger amount of dissonance than is commonly assumed in consistency theories, or that some individuals strive to *optimize* rather than minimize tension. Moreover, with increasing use of the electronic media, selective exposure is exceedingly difficult. How does one avoid a 30-second advertisement placed between two of one's favorite prime-time programs? This means that information campaigns conducted through the broadcast media are more likely to circumvent barriers of exposure. Users of print media exercise far greater control over the content to which they are exposed. As will become evident, this fundamental difference in control over exposure has important consequences for citizen learning about politics.

Media Exposure, Motivation, and Citizen Learning

Television is the dominant medium of American politics, at least as far as national elections and events are concerned. More Americans reported getting their information about the 1952 election from television than from any other source, even though only about one of every two households owned a television receiver at the time. The superiority of television in providing information in presidential elections has been a static finding since 1952. The Roper studies (Note 2) commissioned by the Television Information Office show that television replaced newspapers as the main source of news "about what's going on in the world today" in 1963 (the year network news broadcasts were expanded to 30 minutes), and has gradually lengthened its lead ever since.

The preeminence of TV is grounded in a perceived ability to present not only more (or easier) information but "better" information as well. Various studies have found television perceived as less biased and more credible than other media, as well as more personal, dynamic, colorful, and even more *complete* than newspapers. The greater perceived credibility of TV is parly due to the personalized nature of the communicator. Through a process termed "para-social interaction," audience members come to feel they "know" the communicators in an illusion of face-to-face communication (Horton & Wohl, 1956). Television also allows viewers to use more sensory mechanisms (sight and sound) than does print, allowing the viewer to place greater trust in "what she has seen herself."

While television is the dominant medium for information about national politics among the general public, it shares this role with newspapers on state-wide issues and elections and gives way to newspapers as the most used information source for local politics. Newspapers are also the preferred source of information on more specific topics, such as science or health (Clarke & Ruggels, 1970; Wade & Schramm, 1969).

The difference in reliance on television for general political information versus information on specific policies is not surprising. Interest in specific policies is typically less than interest in general politics. And interest, as well as education, are strong correlates both of amount of exposure and preference for a medium. Both the better-educated and "opinion leaders," for example, rely more heavily on print than on the electronic media.

Television is very much a poor man's medium; the interest-poor, the educa-tion-poor and the information-poor. Indeed, it has been argued that television has created the "inadvertent audience." This audience which "will not *read* the news of the day but is willing to *listen* to or *watch* the news . . . receives its politically relevant information through a wholly passive process—one in which the viewer literally falls into the audience" (Robinson, 1975, p. 106).

While the learning process certainly cannot be "wholly passive," the evidence that people learn through "viewing-without-motivation" is compelling. Knowl-edge gain by simple exposure has been demonstrated in a wide range of political communication settings, including national elections (Blumler & McQuail, 1969), network news programs (Wamsley & Pride, 1972), television documentar-ies (Fitzsimmons & Osburn, 1968) and specific events such as the televised Watergate hearings (Robinson, 1974). The perceived remoteness of politics from peoples' day-to-day lives, coupled with increasing dependency on television, suggests that the passive learning process may be the dominant mode of citizen learning. Data attesting to the strength of passive learning and the inadvertent audience come from interviews conducted with a random sample of 1000 New Jerseyans in the fall of 1977.

While New Jersey is not typically described in glowing terms, it is heaven for media researchers. It is one of only two states in the country without an in-state commercial VHF television station; thus residents in the northern part of the state are served by stations located in New York City, and South Jerseyans are served by Philadelphia television. This unique media environment overcomes the "saturation" problem discussed earlier. With regard to local and state politics, the two regions receive very different messages.

Respondents were asked to name the candidates running for governor in New Jersey and for mayor of New York City. Interest in both races was also measured. Interviewing began in September, on the day following New York's primary, while the New Jersey candidates were selected in that state's primary the preceding June and had been campaigning in the three months before the study. Thus there was a far better chance for respondents to become informed about the election in their own state.

As expected, more New Jerseyans said they were "very interested" in their own gubernatorial election (41 percent) than in New York's mayoralty contest (14 percent). Yet, in the region of the state served by New York television, more could identify the Democratic candidate for mayor[4] than the Republican candidate for governor. The Democratic gubernatorial candidate, a four-year incumbent seeking reelection, was named by only six percent more than the mayoralty candidate. While there was no significant difference in the ability to name either New Jersey candidate by the region of the state, 63 percent of those served by New York television could identify the mayoralty candidate in contrast to only 15 percent of those served by Philadelphia television. The differences in identification by television area are striking and do not vanish with "interest" held constant.

Of particular relevance for the passive learning hypothesis is the comparison between respondents in each region who had no interest in the mayoralty election. Presumably this is a strong indicator of lack of motivation to acquire information. If motivation were a precondition of learning, we would expect little difference between TV markets. However, fully half of the uninterested living in the New York TV area knew the candidate's name compared to only nine percent of the uninterested served by Philadelphia TV.

Simultaneous controls for education, interest, and TV area in regression equations failed to compromise the strong evidence of passive learning. Table 13.1 presents the standardized regression coefficients for these three independent variables. While the amount of variation explained in knowledge is quite similar in each of the equations, the component variables have very different weights. Interest is the most powerful force behind knowledge of the New Jersey candidates. The lack of television coverage of the New Jersey election by both New York and Philadelphia stations meant a lack of easily available information. The region of the state where respondents live makes virtually no difference in the case of the New Jersey candidates.

In the case of the New York candidates, however, it is the part of the state in which respondents live that is the most significant factor. While interest and education are not unimportant, "TV area" is the most powerful variable in explaining knowledge. It is important to note that in this case *it was the*

TABLE 13.1   Knowledge of New York and New Jersey Candidates[a] as
Explained by Education, Interest, and TV Area

	New York	New Jersey
TV Area[b]	-.35	-.04
Education	.19	.14
Interest	.19	.41
R^2	.23	.20
Multiple R	.48	:45

Note: Cell entries are standardized regression coefficients (betas).
[a]The dependent variable of knowledge is the number of candidates (0, 1, or 2)
respondents were able to name in each election.
[b]Negative coefficient indicates New York TV area.

information environment, rather than the motivation to acquire information,
that proved to be the critical factor. Clearly, citizens learned passively, from the
simple availability of information.

The Knowledge Gap and Opinion Strata

But while television may have increased the information level of a portion of
the electorate, it is difficult to argue that it has been a "democratizing" medium.
One of the few iron laws in mass communication is that those who are already
better informed pay the most attention to the mass media and learn the most
from them. This is due both to greater interest (Genova & Greenberg, 1979),
which leads to increased exposure, and to the existence of better developed
belief structures. More sophisticated structures make it relatively cheaper, in
cognitive terms, to process, organize, and store new information. Thus the
expanded information environment may contribute to an increasing knowledge
gap between the informational haves and have-nots (Tichenor, Donohue, &
Olien, 1971).

There is clearly a segmentation in the American public in terms of media
reliance and learning from the media. The poorer educated rely more and more
on a medium that gives them little in the way of a framework in which to
understand politics. News stories confined to 60 to 90 seconds cannot provide a
context conducive to comprehension. Television-dependents are less knowledgeable about public affairs and more susceptible to persuasive messages. In a study
of "media reliance and political reasoning," Clarke and Fredin (1978) find
television reliers far less able than newspaper reliers to offer reasons for their
support of political candidates, with education and interest held constant. Their
conclusion, in fact, is that TV may actually *inhibit* learning. With a relatively
weaker informational base, the attitudes of television reliers are more susceptible

to change based on the receipt of new information. The increasing reliance on television is thus alarming to some who see increased volatility in public opinion as a residual consequence (Manheim, 1976).

Coupling concepts of the "inadvertent audience," "passive learning," and "knowledge gap" leads to a discussion of public opinion and the mass media in terms of strata and thresholds. We may conceptualize the public as existing in various layers with different levels, or intensities, of media coverage necessary to reach each layer. The notion of a public that may be grouped by interest and communicative behavior is certainly not a novel approach. Key (1961, p. 15) spoke of a top layer of "activitists" and a bottom layer of "apoliticals," but did not attempt to differentiate the public between these extremes. Distinctions between "attentive" and "nonattentive" publics are common to treatments of public opinion, and, of course, the "two-step flow" is based on the idea of segmentation. Nimmo (1978) found it useful to discuss the audience for political communication in terms of an attentive public and a general public comprised of "interesteds" and "indifferents."

What is suggested here is that there may now be a sufficient body of research for a preliminary attempt at labeling the middle layers of public opinion and providing some definition for them on the basis of communicative behavior. It appears that the mass public may be decomposed into four groupings, based largely on interest in politics. They may be tentatively labeled the "attentive," "latent," "inadvertent" and "apathetic" publics. The *attentives,* perhaps one-fifth of the public, are aware of candidates and issues when the media first devote attention to these subjects. Intense media coverage is not necessary for awareness, in that stories need not be on the front page or considered sufficiently important to be aired on the evening news. Attentives are more likely to be print-dependents and to use a multiplicity of media sources. They are more likely to use the mass media primarily for informational purposes and to engage in discussion of elections and current events. Attentives would presumably be disproportionately at the top of the sociodemographic ladder.

The *latent* public would lack the motivation to seek out information about politics. They would in essence be activated by events accorded prominence in the mass media, as indicated by front page stories in newspapers or heavy emphasis on national newscasts. Once activated, the latent public would behave very much like the attentive public in tracking information about the issue or event. Evidence of this group and pattern of behavior is suggested by Patterson's (1980) analysis of the 1976 election and Zukin and Keeter's (Note 3) analysis of the 1980 election, where a significant portion of the electorate became aware of candidates only after the heavy dosage of media attention surrounding a primary election victory. In both studies the evidence does not fit a pattern of gradual learning; rather, once a certain threshold of media attention was reached, an entire stratum of the public that was previously uninformed became knowledgeable. One would suspect that the latent public is exposed to both print and electronic media but relies mainly on television for its information. A mixture of social and informational motivations for exposure to political information would be expected in this group, perhaps a third of the public.

The *inadvertent* public, perhaps another third, is largely uninterested in the world of politics. This group would be largely, if not solely, dependent on television for information about political issues and events, learning passively. Moreover, they would not learn very well. Individuals in the advertent public would over time be expected to learn the "labels" of political debate but would have little or no content, or informational base, associated with those labels. For example, this group might be expected to recognize the term "SALT" but have only the vaguest idea of issues involved in the SALT treaty. Inadvertents may well engage in political behavior based on their beliefs, such as those who supported Carter in the 1976 primaries based on familiarity with the term "Carter," lack of negative information about Carter, and lack of information about other candidates (Patterson, 1980). Individuals in this group would be easily susceptible to opinion change, provided any new information could penetrate their lack of motivation and be cognized. As this group would engage in no interpersonal discussion of politics, it is suspected that they may be reached only through prominent and intense media coverage.

The *apathetic* public has no interest in politics and would make little use of the mass media for informational reasons. Relative reliance on the electronic media would be great but absolute exposure limited. If "chronic know-nothings" remain in an age of passive learning through television, they would certainly come from this stratum. Low sociodemographic status would characterize most members of this tier. While perhaps the most easily persuaded by new information, apathetics would be not only the hardest to reach but the least likely "targets," since they are also the least likely to participate in politics.

The tentative nature of this conceptualization is again stressed. Moreover, one should keep in mind that a single individual could fall into more than one stratum, depending on the issue. But there is sufficient evidence to suggest that incorporating "interest layers" of the public into research designs as an intervening variable would be rewarding. A first task would be to define the strata further in terms of social attributes, media behavior, and perceptions on basic political issues. In rough form, the questions to be addressed would include: Who relies to what extent on which media for what reasons and with what effects? One might also want to know who holds what opinions on what types of issues with what informational base. With strata more clearly identified, a second task would be to look within and between the groups on questions of opinion formation and change, susceptibility to information campaigns in shaping salience and responsiveness to persuasive appeals, and the level and nature of political activities.

THE MASS MEDIA AND POLITICAL CULTURE

The Impact of Informational Media

The effects of the mass media on the general context of public values and attitudes in which politics takes place is a relatively new area of study. Embodied in the political culture are beliefs about the legitimacy of political authority, beliefs about the political system and about the relationship of the governors to the governed, to name but a few.

The last decade and a half has witnessed a continual and dramatic erosion of the public's confidence in government, trust in political leaders, and sense of political efficacy (Miller, 1974). Between 1965 and 1978 the national election studies conducted by Michigan's Center for Political Studies have charted an increase of 31 to 74 percent in the belief that "government is run by few interests" rather than "for the benefit of all people." The feeling that the national government can be trusted "to do what is right" most or all of the time has declined from 76 to 30 percent;[5] the belief that "quite a few" of the people running the government "don't seem to know what they are doing" has almost doubled in the same period.

As popular opinion, values have changed markedly over the last 15 years to a point where a majority of the public now expresses fundamental doubts about the performance of governmental and other institutions.[6] Mass opinion also manifests a lack of self-confidence. In July 1979 a *New York Times*-CBS News survey (Note 5) found 86 percent agreeing that there "is a moral and spiritual crisis, that is, a crisis of confidence in the country today." It should be noted, however, that this survey was taken after President Carter's "crisis of confidence" speech, which certainly served to set the term on the public agenda. This survey may be saying less about "real confidence" than about the President striking a responsive chord.

A number of hypotheses have been advanced to explain this change in the political culture, including dissatisfaction with government performance in policy areas, social conflict associated with the Vietnam war, and the rising salience of a cluster of "social issues" in the 1960s. However, a theory that the mass media in some measure caused increased disaffection—"videomalaise"—has also been put forth to explain cultural changes. It is this last explanation that occupies attention here, for, if supported, it is evidence of a fundamental media effect of enormous consequences.

The "theory of videomalaise," articulated by Michael Robinson (1975, 1976, 1977) notes that the disaffection between the public and government began growing at the same time the networks' nightly news broadcasts expanded from 15 to 30 minutes and argues that the two occurrences are not simply coincidental. Television news, by picturing social and political institutions in a state of perpetual conflict, fosters cynicism, distrust of officials and institutions, inefficacy, and frustration.

The genesis of the theory come from controlled experiments Robinson conducted in 1971 with the CBS documentary "The Selling of the Pentagon." After 220 subjects from Columbus, Ohio were exposed to the documentary, a significant drop in efficacy occurred in the treatment groups, along with changes in cognitive beliefs about the military and Department of Defense. Robinson (1976) hypothesized that vivid images of direct conflict between institutions (Defense Department, CBS News, the Administration) "produced a psychological tension within subjects which they chose to reduce by questioning their own ability to cope with or comprehend politics" (p. 417).

The reliance of both local and national news on elements of conflict for its "news value," dramatic and visual properties, and need for balance has been well documented (Buckalew, 1969; Epstein, 1973; Hofstetter & Zukin, 1979; Lowry, 1970; Singer, 1970; Wamsley & Pride, 1972). Robinson argued that if the conflict in "The Selling of the Pentagon" is simply a concentrated version of images presented daily on the evening news, dependence on TV news should then be associated with political inefficacy and cynicism.[7] Robinson tested the predicted relationships with data from the 1968 Center for Political Studies' election survey and found confirming evidence. While the causal question of whether TV causes disaffection or those disaffected are most likely to rely on TV is not empirically addressed, Robinson (1975, p. 118) clearly prefers the former explanation.

Other authors have tested various forms and conditions of videomalaise, finding only mixed support for the theory. However, each study differs in design and measurement, and it is often difficult to interpret which factors account for how much of the differences in results. O'Keefe and Mendelsohn (1978) found increased attention (but not exposure) to TV news was not positively related to the malaise-related reasons for not voting (cynicism, distrust, efficacy). However, O'Keefe (1980), in analyzing data from the Summit County study, found only weak relationships between six indicators of malaise and independent variables of media reliance. But as he notes, his measure of media reliance is quite limited.[8] Berman and Stookey (1980), in a sample of adolescents 13 to 17, found small negative relationships between amount of TV news viewing and support for the government.

Becker et al. (1979) found television dependency to be related to distrust of local but not national government officials. Becker and Whitney (1980) found greater television dependency negatively related to trust and perceived complexity[9] of politics at the local level but not at the national level. Newspaper dependency was positively related to trust at both levels but only to comprehension at the national level. Moreover, in a strong argument for dependency measures, virtually all the relationships wash out when simple exposure is used as the independent variable.

The work of Miller et al. (1979) makes a valuable contribution to this question of study in a number of ways. Far more care is taken in conceptualizing the dependent variables of trust and efficacy. As noted earlier, their work raises serious criticisms of general exposure, as it masks intramedium differences in content. Matching 1974 CPS survey respondents with content analysis of the newspapers they reported reading, the study finds exposure to critical newspaper content negatively related to trust and efficacy. While Miller's work does not support Robinson's theory of videomalaise, it does confirm a central linkage: Critical media content is related to feelings of malaise.

It may well have been that the relationship between television dependency and malaise held in the 1960s but is no longer true today. The social dislocations of the '60s, along with the first televised war, certainly made the assumption equating exposure with negative content less problematic in 1968, when Robinson's survey data were collected, than in the 1970s. Or, as Robinson argued in commenting on the decreasing relevance of the theory (1977, p. 34), a ceiling effect has been reached. This would help explain why the correlation between dependency and malaise has declined while the absolute level of malaise remains constant.

In another context, the argument that the mass media have fostered malaise is unarguable. This contention would rest on the inherency of information in opinion change, realizing that the mass media are primary sources of political information and that cultural values have in fact changed. The question in this context is directed toward the "accuracy" of the information: How much of the growth in the belief that "government is too complex to understand" reflects that government has grown more complex, and how much is a function of the confusing or limited form in which information about government is presented? Are government institutions performing poorly? Or does the public receive a disproportionate amount of information about poor governmental performances as a function of journalistic values and organizational needs of broadcast journalism?

While there can be no satisfactory answer about what may rest on a value position about governmental performance, cases can be made for both sides. Government has become increasingly specialized and technologically oriented, and the problems it faces are more complex than in earlier times. It is not unreasonable that increasing numbers of persons would perceive government as complex, as Key predicted years ago (1961, p. 7). Yet, at the same time, the "formula coverage" adopted by broadcast journalism clearly militates against citizen understanding of the political process (Patterson, 1980). Ladd (1979) argued that the level of public confidence is "about right" given government performance, while Erbring et al. (1980) demonstrate public response to "real world cues." Yet welfare checks that *are* delivered on time are not generally considered newsworthy items. Even newspapers, which would expect to rely on conflict less than TV news, published a five-to-one ratio of critical to praise-worthy stories (Miller et al., 1979).

The question of whether the mass media contributed to the growth of political malaise over the last 15 years is one that probably will never be satisfactorily answered. The foregoing discussion does, however, illuminate some of the problems in determining long-term media effects and the broad scope of possible media effects. If the content of TV news is negative, for example, the entire public will be exposed to this information either directly or indirectly through interpersonal discussion and other media over a period of years. The message becomes part of the general culture, learned passively and perhaps existing in latent form, waiting for a crystallizing event or experience. As it becomes ingrained, it transcends measures of exposure or dependence; there is less and less variation to be explained. Moreover, it is for all intents and purposes impossible to partial out change attributable to the media versus all other sources and historical factors over a long period of time.

The Impact of Entertainment Media

The "political culture" focuses on values and attitudes that are in some way related to politics—a subset of social values. Politics does not take place within a vacuum; political values to a large degree are manifestations of social values. The political system coexists, influencing and being influenced by social and economic systems. The values people hold in social terms often frame the parameters of political activity. While political scientists have all but ignored the effects of the entertainment media on social values, researchers in "communication" have given attention to this relationship, and there is every reason to believe it may be more significant than more overtly "political" concerns.

Television viewing dwarfs all other leisure-time activities, and the amount of time spent viewing entertainment television dwarfs the amount of time spent viewing informational television. Based on time-budget diaries collected in 1965, Robinson concluded:

> Television has had a massive impact on American daily life, responsible for a greater rearrangement of time than usage of the automobile. Further-more, the time now devoted to television is of such magnitude that it has apparently not only unsurped time previously devoted to other mass media, but has eaten into substantial portions of time previously spent in various other forms of leisure [1969, p. 211].

While Robinson predicted a maintenance of the status quo for the future, television has come to dominate leisure time even more strongly. Diaries of 1975 reveal almost a 50 percent increase in TV viewing as a leisure-time activity from 1965 to 1975. Approximately 40 percent of all leisure time in 1975 was spent in front of the tube, up from 30 percent 10 years earlier (Robinson, 1979). A 1979 Roper survey pegs the median viewing time at slightly over three hours per day. Television has reduced the time spent with other media, in conversation, in social gatherings, on household tasks, and even sleeping (Comstock, 1978).

The most widely cited process by which television may affect persons is through "observational learning," where individuals may view the behavior of models and accept this as a guide for their own behavior. Learning is an experiential process, but we may learn through either direct or vicarious experiences (Bandura, 1978). Exposure to specific role models or even mythical situations and relationships may have meaning for the perceiver. While no hypodermic needle model of media effects is implied, the observation of behaviors may intermix with existing predispositions to enlarge the repertoire of behavioral responses individuals may draw from. The weight of evidence, for example, indicates that children exposed to aggressive models on television are more likely to exhibit aggressive behavior.[10]

Much of the empirical burden for investigating the values displayed on and effects of entertainment television has fallen on the shoulders of George Gerbner and colleagues at the Annenberg School of Communication. In a series of research reports on the Cultural Indicators Project (Gerbner & Gross, 1976; Gerbner et al. 1977, 1978, 1979, 1980) the argument is advanced that heavy exposure to cultural imagery as displayed on television shapes individuals' conceptions of reality—that "the dramatic pattern defines situations and cultivates premises about society, people and issues" (1976, p. 183).

In what the authors term "cultivation analysis," weekly samples of prime-time entertainment are content analyzed to indicate prevalent themes. This allows for deductions of "television answers" (answers "slanted in the direction of the world of television") to NORC survey questions. A greater proportion of "television answers" given by heavy than light viewers is taken to be evidence of media effects.[11]

The world of entertainment television is heavily populated by criminals, other evil-doers, and violence according to content studies. In general it appears from content analysis to be a "mean world." Gerbner et al. have found this TV reality reflected in response to a variety of survey questions in their series of published articles from 1976 to 1980.

Heavy viewers were relatively more likely than light viewers to:

> 1) overestimate their chances of being involved in violence and the proportion of people involved in law enforcement, 2) be less trustful of other people, 3) feel that others would take advantage of them given the opportunity, 4) believe that most others "look out for themselves rather than trying to be helpful, 5) are fearful of walking alone at night, 6) believe that public officials are not interested in the problems of the average citizen, and that the lot of the common man is getting worse, and 7) feel it is best for the U.S. to stay out of world affairs.

While many of the relationships are not strong, they hold through individual controls for education, race, and sex; and, taken as a whole, they provide evidence of television effects through vicarious learning. It does not take a large inferential leap to speculate on the political import of these findings. Should entertainment TV be contributing to anomie and felt loss of societal and individual control, evaluations of the institutions charged with the governance of society would be expected to decline. By this logic, it is entertainment TV rather than public affairs media that contributes to the loss of confidence in government.

However, studies published only recently have issued a fundamental challenge to the Annenberg analysis. In reexaminations of the NORC survey data used by the Annenberg researchers, both Hirsch (1980) and Hughes (1980) find that the relationships between exposure and a variety of dependent variables give way in the face of simultaneous controls for a variety of social status variables. In some cases the controlled relationships actually run counter to those stated by Gerbner and his colleagues.

Moreover, Hughes charged that the Annenberg researchers have ignored items where readily identifiable "television answers" can be determined in the General Social Survey data sets that do not support a cultivation interpretation. Hirsch rearranged the Annenberg independent variable, separating "nonviewers" from "light viewers" and "extreme viewers" from "heavy viewers." For many of the items reported by Gerbner, nonviewers were more likely to give the "television answer" than light viewers; extreme viewers were often less perturbed than heavy viewers. With these groups partialed out, few of the relationships are monotonic.

The Hirsch and Hughes studies surely represent the opening salvos in what will be a protracted discussion (Newcomb, 1978; Doob & Macdonald, 1979). At the time of this writing part 2 of Hirsch's work was not yet been published, and Gerbner and colleagues had only started to formulate a response (1980). Thus one area where a body of knowledge about media effects on public opinion has been developing must now again be considered a wide open question. The political consequences of social messages learned through exposure to entertainment television is an area in desperate need of more research. One issue on which public opinion has changed in the recent past is the greater support given to capital punishment. Can this be a consequence of the large amount of violence on entertainment television, the heavy local news emphasis on crime (Graber, 1979), or are these simply coincidental occurrences without causality?

Research investigating the impact of the entertainment media needs to become more sophisticated. As in the case of informational television, exposure has been equated with content. Again, this is a risky assumption. While the dominant thrust of entertainment fare may be "antisocial," pro-social messages are also present. It should also again be stressed that the message is more in the mind of the perceiver than in the content. Thus while the central tendency of entertainment television content may appear to reflect current cultural values and the social status quo (Greenberg, 1980; U.S. Commission on Civil Rights, 1977, 1979), there is a sufficient diversity of models presented so that those not predisposed to traditional roles and behaviors may also find guidance. A proper study of the effects of entertainment television would require knowledge of receiver predispositions, knowledge of specific programming viewed, and content analysis of those programs, all over time.

Entertainment television is quite possibly the greatest potential stimulus for change in social values. TV content may be a powerful shaper of social reality in areas where direct experience is limited. Northerners may learn about Southerners, suburbanites about urban life, adolescents about what "living together" entails. Opinions and stereotypes may form on the basis of such exposure, and while they are likely to give way when confronted with direct experience, not all members of the public will have direct experience in all areas treated by entertainment television.

Television, in both informational and entertainment modes, has doubtlessly contributed to a homogenization of American culture by standardizing the bulk of the information to which we are exposed. But to make us as a collectivity more similar, television must make each of us as individuals a little different from what we were.

A PROMISING FUTURE

The answer to the question of why we know so little about the relationship between the mass media and public opinion is twofold. First, we know less than we would like because the scientific process builds its knowledge slowly, and this field of study is only now maturing. Second, the problem under study is a conditional one. As Berelson (1948, p. 531) set forth the realities of media-opinion research:

> Some kinds of *communication* on some kinds of *issues*, brought to the attention of some kinds of *people* under some kinds of *conditions*, have some kinds of *effects*.

Given the series of conditional relationships inherent in the topic, it is probably the case that we know more than it might appear. The probabilistic nature of the question defies simple, straightforward answers and makes generalization difficult.

I suspect we have only recently moved from childhood to adolescence in the recent past—perhaps within the last decade. While as researchers we have long recognized that we were studying a communication *process*, it was first necessary to identify and investigate the separate elements of this process. Our childhood was spent determining relevant questions and concepts, designing appropriate measurement strategies, collecting evidence, and arguing about interpretations. This has necessarily been a slow process.

Nor has the process been speeded by the fact that researchers came from many diverse fields, principally from political science and communication (although communication itself is a youthful hybrid). However, there is no doubt that this interdisciplinary mixture is in the long run a source of strength. More communication researchers are now studying political dependent variables; more political scientists are studying communication independent variables. Political Communication is now becoming a recognized field, at least by those who are in it. New journals have emerged to facilitate communication, and there is increasing agreement on proper scope and methods.

What this has meant is that we are ready for adolescence, where our research is focused on the relationship between the mass media and public opinion as a process. Recent research clearly reflects this maturation in a number of ways. It is impossible not to notice the increasing sophistication of political communications research. Questions are being asked with probabilistic sensitivities, designs are paying greater attention to motivational states as intervening factors in the communication process, exposure variables are no longer equated with content without warning labels, and increasing attention is being given to long-term effects of the media. All the indicators point to a healthy and happy adolescence. After a sufficient period of studying the process *as a process,* we should be well equipped to confidently offer a mature set of generalizations on the relationship between the mass media and public opinion. In this wisdom will come the first evidence of adulthood.

Thus the prognosis is an optimistic one, and an exciting one. McLeod et al. (1977), after being forced to conclude that Watergate could not be described as a "communication event," turned their attention back to the larger process:

> [Instead] we have found interesting and diverse patterns of effects depending on the age of the person, which medium is used, and the motivational focus of media use. Such factors make the study of communication effects perplexing but fascinating [p. 19].

NOTES

[1]I am indebted to my colleague Gerald Pomper for suggesting this titillating analogy, a product of his fertile imagination.

[2]Polling results, of course, paint a very different picture of the election results. A *New York Times*-CBS postelection panel survey, coupled with data from exit polls, fails to demonstrate a groundswell of conservative voting. Moreover, the last-minute jump in Reagan support indicates people overcoming earlier reservations about wholeheartedly embracing him. The high level of agreement among various polls makes it extremely improbable that a clump of "hidden" conservatives was missed (see Clausen, Converse, & Miller, 1965). The

1980 election in time may not be remembered as "the year the polls were wrong" so much as the year when a substantial segment of the electorate decided to "take a risk."

[3]This interpretation would equate incoming stimuli with the mass media. While this assumption is not fully warranted, in that it excludes unmediated experience and interpersonal communication, the mass media are clearly the public's dominant source of political information.

[4]The Republican mayoralty primary was only minimally contested. The Democratic race, with Bella Abzug, Ed Koch, Mario Cuomo, and Abe Beame, received heavy media attention in the New York area.

[5]It should be noted that it is far from clear what this question is measuring. Disagreement with this question could indicate either that government leaders cannot be *trusted* or that they are not *competent* "to do what is right."

[6]A Louis Harris survey (Note 2) conducted a week after the November election, when one might expect confidence levels to be artificially buoyed momentarily by unfailed expectations, shows little change from the preceding year. The percentage expressing "a great deal of confidence" in societal institutions follows: higher education 36, medicine 34, TV news 29, the military 28, Supreme Court 27, organized religion 22, the press 19, Congress 18, the White House 18, executive branch 17, major companies 16, organized labor 14, law firms 13.

[7]Conflict is only one element, albeit the central one, in Robinson's (1975, p. 426) explanation of videomalaise. He speaks of six major interrelated factors: (1) the abnormal size and shape of the television news (an inadvertent) audience, (2) the high credibility of the networks, (3) the interpretive character of TV news coverage, (4) the "negativist emphasis" of TV news stories, (5) conflict, and (6) antiinstitutional themes of TV news programs.

[8]The question used asks the sample how much they rely on a medium "to help you make up your mind *about who to vote for.*" Respondents might have given different answers if some other specific use or general information was being asked about.

[9]One of the additional problems in reconciling various findings is that there is no uniformity of dependent variables. Even when the same concepts and labels are used, they are operationalized differently. The differences are too large to catalog here. Interested readers should consult the studies referenced.

[10]The relationship is by no means this simple. A tremendous number of studies have been done on the impact of televised violence, and many conditional relationships have been teased out. Summaries of a large number of studies may be found in Andison (1977) and Comstock (1975).

[11]For example, content analysis of both entertainment (Gerbner & Gross, 1976) and news programming (Graber, 1979) reveals high levels of crime and violence. To the NORC question, "During any given week, what are your chances of being involved in some type of violence—one in ten, or one in a hundred?" one in ten becomes the "television answer," which heavy viewers are expected to choose with more frequency than light viewers.

REFERENCE NOTES

1. Harris, L. *Differences persist in the Middle East.* New York: The Harris Survey. Press release of April 10, 1978.

2. Roper, B. *What people think of television and other mass media: 1959-1972.* New York: Television Information Office, May 1973.

3. Zukin, C. & Keeter, S. *The origin and development of voters' images of candidates during presidential primaries.* Paper presented at the meeting of the American Political Science Association, Washington, D.C., August 1980.

4. Harris, L. *Confidence in institutions.* New York: The Harris Survey. Press release of November 24, 1980.

5. *New York Times*-CBS News Poll. *Reaction to Carter's speech.* New York: *New York Times*-CBS News. Released CBS News, July 17, 1979; *New York Times,* July 18, 1979.

REFERENCES

Andison, F. S. TV violence and viewer aggression: A culmination of study results 1956-1976. *Public Opinion Quarterly,* 1977, *41,* 315-331.

Ball-Rokeach, S. G., & DeFleur, M. A dependency model of media effects. *Communication Research,* 1976, *3,* 3-21.

Bandura, A. Social learning theory of aggression. *Journal of Communication,* 1978, *28,* 12-19.

Becker, L., Sobowale, I., & Casey, W. Newspaper and television dependencies: Effects on evaluations of public officials. *Journal of Broadcasting,* 1979, *23,* 465-475.

Becker, L., & Whitney, D. C. Effects of media dependencies: Audience assessment of government. *Communication Research,* 1980, *7,* 95-120.

Berelson, B. Communication and public opinion. In W. Schramm (Ed.), *Mass communication* (2nd ed.). Chicago: University of Illinois Press, 1960.

Berman, D., & Stookey, J. Adolescents, television and support for government. *Public Opinion Quarterly,* 1980, *44,* 330-340.

Bishop, G., Oldendick, R., Tuchfarber, A., & Bennett, S. Pseudo-opinions on public affairs. *Public Opinion Quarterly,* 1980, *44,* 198-209.

Blumler, J. & McQuail, D. *Television in politics: Its uses and influences.* Chicago: University of Chicago Press, 1969.

Buckalew, J. News elements and selection by television news editors. *Journal of Broadcasting,* 1969, *14,* 47-53.

Campbell, A. Has television reshaped politics? *Columbia Journalism Review,* 1962, *6,* 10-13.

Clarke, P. & Fredin, F. Newspapers, television and political reasoning. *Public Opinion Quarterly,* 1978, *42,* 143-160.

Clarke, P. & Ruggels, L. Preferences among news media for coverage of public affairs. *Journalism Quarterly,* 1970, *47,* 464-471.

Clausen, A., Converse, P., & Miller, W. Electoral myth and reality: The 1964 election. *American Political Science Review,* 1965, *59,* 321-336.

Comstock, G. The effects of television on children and adolescents: The evidence so far. *Journal of Communication,* 1975, *25,* 25-34.

Comstock, G. The impact of television on American institutions. *Journal of Communication,* 1978, *28,* 12-28.

Converse, P. Information flow and the stability of partisan attitudes. In A. Campbell, P. Converse, W. Miller, & D. Stokes (Eds.), *Elections and the political order.* New York: John Wiley, 1966.

Converse, P. Attitudes and non-attitudes: Continuation of a dialogue. In E. Tufte (Ed.), *The quantitative analysis of social problems.* Reading, MA: Addison-Wesley, 1970.

Converse, P. Public opinion and voting behavior. In F. Greenstein & N. Polsby (Eds.), *Handbook of political science* (Vol. 4). Reading, MA: Addison-Wesley, 1975.

DeFleur, M., & Ball-Rokeach, S. *Theories of mass communication* (3rd ed.). New York: David McKay, 1976.

Doob, A., & Macdonald, G. Television viewing and fear of victimization: Is the relationship causal? *Journal of Personality and Social Psychology,* 1979, *37,* 170-179.

Edelstein, A. Decision making and mass communication. In P. Clarke (Ed.), *New models for mass communication research.* Beverly Hills, CA: Sage, 1973.

Entman, R., & Paletz, D. Media and the conservation myth. Journal of Communication, 1980, *30,* 154-165.

Epstein, E. *News from nowhere.* New York: Random House, 1973.

Erbring, L., Goldenberg, E., & Miller, A. Front page news and real-world cues: A new look at agenda-setting by the media. *American Journal of Political Science,* 1980, *24,* 16-49.

Ettema, J., & Kline, F. G. Deficits, differences and ceilings: Contingent conditions for understanding the knowledge gap. *Communication Research,* 1977, *4,* 179-202.

Fields, J., & Schuman, H. Public beliefs about the beliefs of the public. *Public Opinion Quarterly,* 1976, *40,* 427-448.

Fitzsimmons, S., & Osburn, H. The impact of social issues and public affairs television documentaries. *Public Opinion Quarterly*, 1968, *32*, 379-397.

Gallup, G. *Whither controls: A history of public attitudes toward wage-price restraints.* New York: Anerican Institute of Public Opinion, 1978.

Genova, B., & Greenberg, B. Interest in news and the knowledge gap. *Public Opinion Quarterly*, 1979, *43*, 79-91.

Gerbner, G., & Gross, L. Living with television: The violence profile. *Journal of Communication*, 1976, *26*, 173-199.

Gerbner, G., Gross, L., Eleey, M. F., Jackson-Beeck, M., Jeffries-Fox, S., & Signorielli, N. TV violence profile no. 8: Highlights. *Journal of Communication*, 1977, *27*, 171-180.

Gerbner, G., Gross, L., Jackson-Beeck, M., Jeffries-Fox, S., & Signorielli, N. Cultural indicators. Violence no. 9. *Journal of Communication*, 1978, *28*, 176-206.

Gerbner, G., Gross, L., Morgan, M., & Signorielli, N. The "mainstreaming" of America: Violence profile no. 11. *Journal of Communication*, 1980, *30*, 10-29.

Gerbner, G., Signorielli, N., Morgan, M., & Jackson-Beeck, M. The demonstration of power: Violence profile no. 10. *Journal of Communication*, 1979, *29*, 177-196.

Graber, D. Is crime news coverage excessive. *Journal of Communication*, 1979, *29*, 81-92.

Graber, D. *Mass media and American politics.* Washington: Congressional Quarterly Press, 1980.

Greenberg, B. (Ed.). *Life on television: Content analysis of U.S. TV drama.* Norwood, NJ: Ablex, 1980.

Grupp, F. Newscast avoidance among political activists. *Public Opinion*, 1970, *34*, 238-243.

Hirsch, P. The "scary world" of the nonviewer and other anamolies: A reanalysis of Gerbner et al.'s findings on cultivation analysis–Part 1. *Communication Research*, 1980, *7*, 403-456.

Hofstetter, C. R., & Zukin, C. TV network news and political advertising. *Journalism Quarterly*, 1979, *56*, 106-115, 152.

Horton, D., & Wohl, R. Mass communication and para-social interaction: Observations on intimacy at a distance. *Psychiatry*, 1956, *19*, 215-229.

Hughes, M. The fruits of cultivation analysis: A reexamination of some effects of television watching. *Public Opinion Quarterly*, 1980, *44*, 287-302.

Hyman, H., & Sheatsley, P. Some reasons why information campaigns fail. *Public Opinion Quarterly*, 1947, *11*, 412-423.

Inkso, C. *Theories of attitude change.* Englewood Cliffs, NJ: Prentice Hall, 1967.

Iyengar, G. Television news and issue salience. *American Politics Quarterly*, 1979, *7*, 395-416.

Jones, E., & Saunders, J. Persuading an urban public: The St. Louis privacy campaign. *Journalism Quarterly*, 1977, *54*, 669-673.

Key, V. O. *Public opinion and American democracy.* New York: Alfred A. Knopf, 1961.

Klapper, G. *The effects of mass communication.* New York: Free Press, 1960.

Ladd, E. Opinion roundup: Left, right or center–Which way are we going? *Public Opinion*, 1978, *1*, 33.

Ladd, E. Opinion roundup: A nation's trust. *Public Opinion*, 1979, *2*, 27.

Lang, K., & Lang, G. The mass media in voting. In B. Berelson & M. Janowitz (Eds.), *Reader in public and communication* (2nd ed.). New York: Free Press, 1966.

Lippman, W. *Public opinion.* New York: Free Press, 1922.

Lowry, D. Gresham's law and network TV news selection. *Journal of Broadcasting*, 1970, *15*, 397-407.

McLeod, J., Brown, J., Becker, L., & Ziemke, D. Decline and fall at the White House: A longitudinal analysis of communication effects. *Communication Research*, 1977, *4*, 3-22.

Manheim, G. Can democracy survive television. *Journal of Communication*, 1976, *26*, 84-90.

Mendelsohn, H. Some reasons why information campaigns can succeed. *Public Opinion Quarterly*, 1973, *37*, 50-61.

Mendelsohn, H., & O'Keefe, G. *The people choose a president.* New York: Praeger, 1976.

Miller, A. Political issues and trust in government: 1964-1970. *American Political Science Review,* 1974, *68,* 951-972.

Miller, A., Goldenberg, E., & Erbring, L. Type-set politics: Impact of newspapers on public confidence. *American Political Science Review,* 1979, *73,* 67-84.

Newcomb, H. Assessing the violence profile studies of Gerbner and Gross: A humanistic critique and suggestion. *Communication Research,* 1978, *5,* 264-282.

Nimmo, D. *Political communication and public opinion in America.* Santa Monica, CA: Goodyear, 1978.

Noelle-Neumann, E. Turbulences in the climate of opinion: Methodological applications of the spiral of silence theory. *Public Opinion Quarterly,* 1977, *41,* 143-158.

O'Gorman, G. Pluralistic ignorance and white estimates of white support for racial segregation. *Public Opinion Quarterly,* 1979, *39,* 311-330.

O'Gorman, H., with Garry, S. Pluralistic ignorance—A replication and extension. *Public Opinion Quarterly,* 1976, *40,* 449-458.

O'Keefe, G. Political malaise and reliance on media. *Journalism Quarterly,* 1980, *57,* 122-128.

O'Keefe, G., & Mendelsohn, H. Nonvoting and role of the media. In C. Winnick (Ed.), *Mass media and deviance.* Beverly Hills, CA: Sage, 1978.

O'Keefe, T. The anti-smoking commercials: A study of television's impact on behavior. *Public Opinion Quarterly,* 1971, *35,* 242-248.

Patterson, T. *The mass media election.* New York: Praeger/Eagleton, 1980.

Robinson, J. Toward a past-industrious society. *Public Opinion,* 1979, *2,* 41-46.

Robinson, J. Television and leisure time: Yesterday, today and (maybe) tomorrow. *Public Opinion Quarterly,* 1969, *33,* 210-222.

Robinson, M. The impact of the televised Watergate hearings. *Journal of Communication,* 1974, *24,* 17-30.

Robinson, M. American political legitimacy in an age of television. In D. Cater & R. Adler (Eds.), *Television as a social force.* New York: Praeger, 1975.

Robinson, M. Public affairs television and the growth of political malaise: The case of the selling of the Pentagon. *American Political Science Review,* 1976, *70,* 409-432.

Robinson, M. Television and American politics: 1956-1976. *The Public Interest,* 1977, *48,* 3-39.

Sears, D., & Freedman, J. Selective exposure to information: A critical review. *Public Opinion Quarterly,* 1967, *31,* 194-213.

Shafer, B., & Larson, R. Did TV create the "social issue?" *Columbia Journalism Review,* 1972, *72,* 10-17.

Simon, H., & Stern, F. The effect of television upon voting behavior in Iowa in the 1952 presidential election. *American Political Science Review,* 1955, *49,* 470-477.

Singer, B. Violence, protest and war in TV news: The U.S. and Canada compared. *Public Opinion Quarterly,* 1970, *34,* 611-616.

Tichenor, P., Donohue, G., & Olien, C. Mass media flow and differential growth of knowledge. *Public Opinion Quarterly,* 1971, *34,* 159-170.

U.S. Commission on Civil Rights. *Window dressing on the set: Women and minorities in television.* Washington, DC: Government Printing Office, 1977.

U.S. Commission on Civil Rights. *Window dressing on the set: An update.* Washington, DC: Government Printing Office, 1979.

Wade, S., & Schramm, W. The mass media as sources of public affairs knowledge. *Public Opinion Quarterly,* 1969, *33,* 197-209.

Wamsley, G., & Pride, R. Television network news: Rethinking the iceberg problem. *Western Political Quarterly,* 1972, *25,* 434-450.

Zukin, C. A reconsideration of the effects of information on partisan stability. *Public Opinion Quarterly,* 1977, *41,* 244-254.

CHAPTER 14

Communication and Public Policy

Roger W. Cobb and Charles D. Elder

THE STUDY OF PUBLIC POLICY is a broad field of inquiry aimed at understanding and informing the policy decisions of government. Policy itself is an abstraction, referring to the principles that govern the uses of political authority with respect to specific areas of social life. While policy is discerned from what governments say and do, it is not observed directly. Rather, it is inferred from the concrete actions and activities of government and the consequences that flow from them. To understand public policy, then, requires inquiry into the processes through which governmental decisions are made, implemented, and impact on society. In this sense, the study of public policy subsumes many of the traditional concerns of political analysis. It has been distinctive, however, in its emphasis on outputs and in its efforts to comprehend the overall process through which they are generated.

THREE CONCEPTIONS OF
THE ROLE OF COMMUNICATION

Although communication is obviously vital to the policy process, relatively little attention has been given to explicating its role. There would appear to be three rather different conceptions of that role. In perhaps the most common conception, communication is seen as more or less *incidental to the larger process*. Given this perspective, communication tends to be an explicit concern only to the extent that it may account for irregularities or performance failures. Thus, for example, in the study of implementation, lack of clarity, consistency, and fidelity in communication is commonly cited as a major obstacle to the faithful execution of policy mandates (Edwards, 1980, pp. 17-46).

A second conception of the role of communication in the policy process conceives that role largely in terms of a *specific set of actors;* namely, *the mass media.* The media participate in policy both as specialized interests with immediate stakes in the process and as active intermediaries in the general flow of policy communication. On matters such as broadcast regulation (Krasnow & Longley, 1978), freedom of the press (Graber, 1980, pp. 89-116), and general communications policy (Price, 1978), they act in much the same fashion as other interest groups. This aspect of their participation is distinctive only insofar as it affects and is affected by their more general activities as agencies of social intelligence and commentary. Through these activities, they help to structure the policy process and serve a number of important linkage functions. Three types of linkages relating to different phases in the process are particularly noteworthy.

The first involves the basic inputs of the policy process. By selectively directing attention to aspects of that environment, the media serve not only as conduits for demands but as active agents in stimulating, filtering, and structuring the inputs of the policy process. Of interest is the role of the media in defining both the systemic agenda of community concerns and the formal agenda of government (Cobb & Elder, 1975, pp. 14-15). Aspects of this gatekeeping and agenda-setting role are reviewed in detail elsewhere in this volume.

The second linkage relates to the internal dynamics of the formal aspects of policy-making. Here the media provide important channels for communication among policymakers and act as sources of readily usable, policy-relevant information. They allow the formal and often more restrictive channels of intragovernmental communications to be short-circuited or by-passed (Dunn, 1969, pp. 92-95; Nadel, 1971, p. 200); and reduce the often overwhelming information-processing tasks confronting policymakers (Kingdon, 1981, pp. 227-236).

The third linkage relates to the outputs of the policy process. It arises from the media's role as purveyors and interpreters of the public record (Nadel, 1971, p. 212). Vast amounts of information generated in the policy process are nominally matters of the public record. However, owing to the costs of accessing and digesting this information, that which is truly public tends to be limited to what is distilled by the media. Popular reactions to policy actions and actors are thus likely to hinge on what media choose to report and how. This may, in turn, affect the prospects of a policy being adopted or successfully implemented. It can also impact on popular confidence in government itself (Miller, Goldenberg, & Erbring, 1979).

The media's strategic location as intermediaries in the policy process inevitably means that their own biases will be projected into the process. These biases may be reflected in conspicuous advocacy, but they are also introduced in subtle ways through the criteria used by the media to allocate their necessarily limited attention and reporting capabilities. Recent research has fostered a growing appreciation of the media's participation in policy and of the potential biases they may introduce, intentionally or otherwise (Graber, 1980). However, we still know little of the scope, variability, and effects of their involvement. As Chaffee reminds us, the "media cannot be regarded as monolithic" (1975, p. 99); and, as Tichenor, Donahoe, and Olien (1980) show, the nature and consequences of their participation are likely to be contextually and situationally variable. Research on these and other questions relating to the mass media promises to add much to our understanding of the policy process. Implicit in these questions, however, is the presumption that it is not simply the media, but the structure and process of policy communication that is important. If this is so, inquiry on the role of the media can illuminate only a part of what we need to know. This brings us to the final conception of communication and public policy.

In this conception, communication is seen not as incidental or exogenous to the process, nor as confined to the role of the media. Rather, it is seen to be *the essence of policy,* as both a process and a product. Although the seeds of this perspective are to be found in a variety of research traditions, it represents a point of convergence that has only begun to be recognized and is yet to find expression in an integrated approach to the study of public policy. Its origins are found in the study of political communications and public opinion (Bennett, 1980; Nimmo, 1978) and in the study of cybernetics and organizational decision-making (Steinbrunner, 1974). However, it also emerges somewhat independently from process-oriented approaches to policy analysis (Wildavsky, 1979; Wilson, 1980). The perspective rests on the summary premise that public policy is part of an ongoing process of communication and feedback, the dynamics of which are structured and constrained by communications capabilities (Chaffee, 1975). It suggests that the process is not merely one of "the summation of fixed individual preferences but is the process of mutual modification of images both relational and evaluational" (Boulding, 1956, p. 102). It further suggests that the outputs of the process are not unitary or discrete but multidimensional and as continuous as the process itself. From this perspective, the Lasswellian questions of who communicates what to whom and how become the keys to understanding who gets what and why, the what in each case being "a complex universe in itself" (Edelman, 1964, p. 43).

Although the policy process has not generally been conceptualized in these terms, much of the literature might be interpreted as descriptive of or hypothetical about the communication process. As Bell (1975) has shown, the traditional concepts of power, influence, and authority which have structured much of the work on public policy can usefully be conceived as forms of communication. This is not to suggest that the perspective offers only new bottles for old wine. Rather, it is to suggest that there may be value in explicating and examining the assumptions implicit in various renderings of the policy process.

THE POLICY CYCLE

The policy process has generally been conceptualized in terms of a cycle or sequence composed of analytically distinct sets of activities. Although variously labeled (see, for example, Jones, 1977, pp. 11-12), most conceptions reduce to the following five components: problem identification, policy formulation, policy adoption, implementation, and evaluation. While this type of scheme suggests an orderly progression of activities, it is generally recognized that the logical sequence implied is frequently violated and that the various stages are seldom distinct empirically.

The first three stages correspond to the major elements of decision-making identified by Simon (1966)—that is, attention direction, alternative design, and choice. Collectively, they define what is sometimes called policy-making. However, these same elements are found in policy implementation, where the entire process may be reiterated over and over again. Although the policy adoption stages, where policies receive formal "legitimation," commonly commands the greatest attention, the overall process defines an ongoing decisional cycle with repetitions occurring within subphases. Important choices are made throughout. Each of these choices in some sense bears the imprimatur of government authority. Each serves not only to structure subsequent decisions but also to communicate important messages about the principles that govern the uses of political authority; that is, about policy. Although the structuring effect of these choices has generally been appreciated by students of public policy, what they communicate has not. For the most part, it has simply been assumed that the formally legitimated statements of policy and the material costs or benefits that flow from them are all that really counts. However, this view ignores significant outputs of the policy process and misses much of what public policy is about.

As Edelman (1964, 1975) has convincingly argued, the politics of policy are productive of significant symbolic as well as material costs and benefits. These symbolic products include status as well as reassurance. Claimants, as well as the general public, can find satisfaction and vindication in the mere attention officially accorded their concerns (Nadel, 1971, p. 62). Similarly, the failure of political authorities to attend (or to appear to attend) to matters of common concern communicates "information" from which policy inferences are drawn. As these inferences are what give policy its social meaning, they are ultimately what policy is.

In recognizing that policy is not simply a matter of what government says and does but of the inferences that are drawn from what is said and done, we are alerted to the diversity of stakes involved and the multiplicity of functions served by public policy. Perhaps the most obvious function is to coordinate the uses of collective resources in coping with, if not solving, specific substantive problems that fall within the competence of government. However, neither these problems nor the scope of governmental competence are a priori givens. They are politically defined and subject to continual redefinition. Because of this, policy inevitably and simultaneously serves other important social functions. These include the management of social conflict and the social construction or reconstruction of reality.

In addressing specific problems, policy is both an exercise in social control and an effort to alter or affirm relationships or circumstances that have socially constructed meanings. The stakes, then, are values and beliefs, as well as material interests and social status. Among these values and beliefs are the very ones that sustain political authority itself. Thus, to ignore the larger functions of public policy is to run the risk of undermining political authority and therein the utility of policy as an instrument of social problem-solving.

CONCEPTIONS OF POLICY DECISION-MAKING

Just as students of public policy have sometimes failed to appreciate the diversity of outputs and stakes involved in policy decision-making, so, too, have they failed to agree on the dynamics involved. These differences derive in part from different disciplinary traditions. They are important in that they tend to structure inquiry in different ways. As Allison (1971) has shown, they can result in markedly different interpretations of the same decisional events. Moreover, they can lead to sharply divergent prescriptive guidance. Not surprisingly, they tend to presuppose very different communication processes; and insofar as one perspective or another is accepted by policymakers themselves, they impact on the actual structure of policy communication. This impact is realized not only through the dispositions of policymakers but also through the decisional protocols regarding implementation that are frequently stipulated in legislation or in attendant regulation.

The decisional perspective that has tended to dominate formal policy analysis (Stokey & Zeckhauser, 1978) and which policymakers have seemingly found the most compelling prescriptively is the rational choice model, which derives largely from economics. From this perspective, policy decisions are—or ought to be—the product of goal-based, rational analytic and evaluative activity. Policy problems are identified largely on the basis of need as defined by market failures and so-called merit wants. These are discerned through analysis and needs assessment procedures that include surveys, public hearings, expert opinion, and the use of advisory groups. Policies are formulated on the basis of analysis and theory, with value tradeoffs reckoned in terms of economic efficiency and a presumed community preference function. Decisions are made on the same cost-benefit basis and largely amount to legitimation of the results of prior analysis. Implementation occurs through a carefully planned and well-organized administrative system. Evaluation is a matter of assessing effectiveness and involves the systematic comparison of goals and objectives with manifest results. Policy communications is primarily a matter of garnering and assuring the flow of relevant technical information to policy experts and administrators.

The second major decisional perspective is based on conceptions more common to political science, incorporating such traditional concerns as groups and institutional structures. While primarily descriptive in orientation, its prescriptive implications accord with Lindblom's well-known case for disjointed incrementalism as a decisional strategy (Braybrooke & Lindblom, 1963). From this perspective, the policy process is seen as one of mutual adjustment and accommodation of interests through the exercise of power and influence. Problems are identified on the basis of demands articulated through a variety of linkage structures to include parties, groups, and the media (Erikson, Luttbeg, & Tedin, 1980, pp. 12-15; Strouse, 1975, pp. 12-22). It is generally conceded that different groups or interests have differential access to policymakers, but analysts differ on how concentrated and stable this advantage is (Dye, 1979, pp. 3-16). In any case, policy formulation is a matter of interaction and mutual accommodation of organized interests, to include governmental agencies themselves. Decisions are generally the product of bargaining and logrolling but are colored by the anticipated reactions of constituents and other powerful interests. Implementation commonly involves a continuous process of negotiation between administrators and affected interests. Responsiveness in terms of the prevailing distribution of power and constituent preferences, both of which tend to be assessed impressionistically, provides the primary criterion for evaluation. In emphasizing interactions, this perspective implicitly places considerable premium on the structure of communication. However, it tends to assume fixed preferences based on self-interest and to see policy as simply the product of differential power and position, both of which are taken to be relatively stable.

A third conception of policy decision-making incorporates elements of the previous two but emphasizes the organizational dimensions of the process, particularly the importance of organizational routines and maintenance imperatives (Allison, 1971, pp. 67-96). This perspective suggests that government may be viewed as a complex organization wherein decisions are structured and made by subunits on the basis of standard operating procedures and in light of their own parochial concerns. Problems are identified through the projection of organizational interests onto the environment and the monitoring of the threats and opportunities it presents. Policy formulation and decision-making involve canvassing the organization's repertoire of routines and selecting the one that past experience suggests is appropriate to the exigencies of the current situation. Although some organizations may be anxious to exploit opportunities for expansion, most governmental organizations, it would seem, "are more risk averse than imperialistic" (Wilson, 1980, p. 376). Implementation is simply a matter of exercising organizational capabilities in a standard way. Evaluation consists of monitoring a rather narrow set of variables that the organization has learned are critical to controlling or adjusting to its environment. From this perspective, policy communication tends to be seen as routinized and rather narrowly circumscribed.

Each of these perspectives on policy decision-making undoubtedly captures aspects of the policy process. However, they all presuppose very different dynamics and are predicated on markedly different conceptions of the functions of policy. The economic model sees the policy process as simply an exercise in problem-solving, while the political model emphasizes the conflict management and social control functions of policy. The organizational process model suggests that policy is largely a matter of routine actions and reactions that serve to preserve established patterns of interaction and therein the interests and conceptions of social reality on which they are based.

While these models are generally regarded as competing alternatives, it is doubtful that any one is adequate to describe the variety found in the policy process. Allison (1971) suggests that all may be useful in describing the same decisional events, but it is unclear how different versions of the same facts serve to clarify the basic dynamics involved or facilitate the development of a coherent theoretical understanding of the policy process. Perhaps the various models are more appropriately regarded as variants, reflecting the variable forms that specific decisional processes may assume. If so, what is needed is a more all-embracing framework that can encompass the dynamics posited by existing models without presupposing them and that is sufficiently broad to capture the multiplicity of functions that policy serves.

THE NEED FOR A MORE FLEXIBLE VIEW
OF POLICY DECISION-MAKING

There have been a number of developments, both in the study of public policy and in the general literature on decision-making, that hold promise for the development of a more encompassing and flexible view of the policy process. Important substantive changes in the policy process have been observed in recent years that have called into question existing understanding of the process and fostered a growing appreciation of the need for a broader frame of reference and closer attention to communication processes. These changes include:

(a) enormous growth in the scope of governmental activity and in a blurring of traditional distinctions between what is public and private (Lowi, 1967) and among local, state, and national politics (Beer, 1976);

(b) the growing complexity of policy and policy-making resulting in, and stimulated by, increasing professionalization and bureaucratization of policy making and implementation (Heclo, 1978; Malbin, 1979; Meier, 1979);

(c) continuing "individualization" of American politics manifested by declining reliance on traditional intermediate institutions such as groups and parties to structure the relationships between policy-makers and the public (Ladd, 1978; Nie, Verba, & Petrocik, 1979) and the relationships among policymakers themselves (Fiorina, 1977);

(d) institutional changes that have served to further fragment and diffuse political authority; for example, the democratization of the operations of congressional committees (Dodd & Schott, 1979);

(e) the emergence of prominent new actors in the form of single-issue and ideologically oriented groups that seemingly defy the accepted logic of group politics and fail to abide by the norms of that politics (Berry, 1977; McFarland, 1976);

(f) continuing fragmentation and sectorization of policy and the policy process as a result of all of the above creating attendant problems of coordination, unanticipated spillovers, and stalemate (Wildavsky, 1979); and

(g) growing concern about the appropriateness, intrusiveness, costs, and effectiveness of public policy and governmental action generally (Aaron, 1978).

These changes are interrelated and appear to have been occasioned in part by changes in communication capabilities and the exploitation of communications technology. They have created a politics of policy that is more variable and less stably structured than traditionally understood (Heclo, 1978; Wilson, 1980). Actors within the political system have come to rely more on the mass media, mass mailings, selective targeting and mobilization techniques, direct individual contracting, and professional or issue-based channels as the principal means for policy-relevant communication. The apparent effects seem to vindicate Chaffee's hypotheses regarding how changes in the constraints on communication can affect "the intervening process through which the political system operates" (1975, p. 87). He suggests that modern communication capabilities

> serve to break down the factors that would foster nonrandomness and permit source-imposed or receiver-centered constraints on diffusion of information. . . . On the other hand, topic specific constraints—which imply that some kinds of information will not be diffused to any appreciable extent—become more likely [1975, p. 92].

While Chaffee attributes the hypothesized increase in topic-specific constraints to the control exercised by the mass media, they may also be understood as a product of the professionalization of policy issues and communication (Heclo, 1978).

A MORE ENCOMPASSING FRAMEWORK

If changes in the substantive character of the policy process are attributable to changes in the nature of policy communications, it follows that greater attention to this communication may hold the key to a fuller understanding of the nature and dynamics of public policy decision-making. Indeed, conceptual and theoretical developments in the study of decision-making are suggestive of such an analytic perspective. Within all of the major decision-making traditions, there have been rumblings of concern about the adequacy of prevailing paradigms and suggestions regarding the reconceptualization of the decisional process. To a remarkable extent, these suggestions converge toward the view that decision-making is highly contextually dependent, that the process is frequently pervaded by ambiguities, and that the "net of communicative activities in which the participants are embedded constitutes a critical part of the decision process" (Connolly, 1977, p. 209).

This view suggests that decisional phenomena will vary in structure from context to context. In well-established policy areas characterized by benign (low-conflict) environments, one would expect decision-making to be well structured and highly focused. In such areas, there will be well-established channels of formal and informal communications among a stable set of actors, although the substitution of one actor with another will not materially alter the process. Derthick (1979) suggests that this type of decisional process has tended, at least until recently, to characterize policy-making for social security. Even here, however, as Marmor (1973) shows in his analysis of the events surrounding the passage of Medicare, changes in the environmental context can disrupt the normal decision-making process with profound policy consequences. In this instance, the long-standing obstacles to medical assistance for the elderly were simply overwhelmed by a dramatic shift in the composition of Congress and the enhanced position of President Johnson as a result of the 1964 election.

In new or poorer-established areas of policy, or in areas characterized by hostile or conflictual environments, decision-making is likely to be more loosely structured and diffusely focused. The actors involved are likely to be unstable but highly consequential. Decisions are likely to be the product of who *happens* to communicate what to whom and how. Decisions may often be delayed, postponed, or not made at all. Price (1978) shows this to be the case in several areas of policy-making by the House Commerce Committee, to include communications and surface transportation. In stark contrast to Derthick's findings of a well-structured and stable pattern of decision-making with respect to social security, Sproull, Weiner, and Wolf (1978) find the history of the National Institute of Education characterized by a decisional process ill-defined in structure and purpose.

Although momentarily we will consider some of the contextual factors that may serve to constrain and structure policy decision-making, the essential point is that decisional phenomena can, at least theoreticaly, be classified along "a continuum from highly focused to highly diffused" (Connolly, 1977, p. 208). In effect, the rational analytic model defines one extreme and a yet-to-be-specified "diffuse decision" model defines the other extreme. The political and organizational process perspectives speak to points in between, the former tending toward and perhaps subsuming the diffuse end; the latter, toward the focused end of the continuum.

Connolly characterizes diffuse decisional processes as ones

> in which many participants, over an extended period of time, generate a decision in response to some decision problem, working with alternatives which may initially be unclear or unknown, with costs and benefits not reliably estimable, with unclear and/or conflicting preferences and with modifiable resources and constraints (1977, pp. 208-209)

In other words, it is a matter of decision-making under manifold uncertainties. Although Connolly seems to suggest that at least the decision problem may be taken as given, what is problematic or whether there is a "problem" may itself be uncertain. Drawing on Schattschneider (1960), Cobb and Elder (1975) argued that control over the definition of a problem is a major stake in the policy process. Because of the indeterminant nature of policy problems, Wildavsky (1979) advised would-be policy analysts that their role ought to be as much a matter of "creating" problems for which there are no solutions as of finding solutions to given problems.

Lindblom also noted that problems are often ill-defined and that definitions may be unstable as "what is desired itself continues to change under reconsideration" (1959, p. 86). Moreover, policymakers may agree on a "solution" without agreeing on what it is a solution to. Convergence on a policy without prior agreement on the focal problem or the policy's objectives, save perhaps in the vaguest terms, is particularly common in legislative decision-making.

March and Olsen (1976) argue that the uncertainties of decision-making may be even more pervasive than problem and solution uncertainty.

> Although we normally think of decision-making as a process for solving problems, that is often not what happens. Problems are worked upon in the context of some choice, but choices are made only when the shifting combinations of problems, solutions, and decision-makers happen to make action possible. Quite commonly this is after problems have left the choice arena or before they have been discovered [Cohen, March, & Olsen, in March & Olsen, 1976, p. 36].

Decision-making may be occasioned not only by problems in search of solutions and by solutions in search of problems but also by people in search of things to do or causes to champion and by choice opportunities in search of an agenda. The imperatives of decision may amount to little more than the need of presidents for programs, candidates for issues, senators for "specialties," and bureaucrats for work (Polsby, 1971, p. 304).

The ultimate in diffuse decision-making would seem to be "organized anarchy" (March & Olsen, 1976; Sproull et al., 1978). To capture the dynamics of this process, Cohen et al. (in March & Olsen, 1976) offer a framework in which decision-making is conceived as the confluence of four more or less independent streams of elements—people, problems, solutions, and choice opportunities. Although the flow of these elements may be structured by previous decisions momentarily frozen in the form of institutionalized roles and practices, decisions are simply the result of the chance intersection of these four elements. While this "garbage can" model of decision-making perhaps overstates the randomness to be found in the policy process, it is useful in highlighting its potential fluidity.

Policy decision-making often involves a changing cast of characters who come and go, differentially allocating their time in light of other things they want to do or must do. There are indeed problems that go unaddressed for want of solutions or opportunities to be considered, and there are always "solutions" floating around in search of problems and opportunities to be linked to them. Choice opportunities are limited by the press of competing claims and by obligations previously incurred that must be attended to. As a consequence, the particular coincidence of elements that yield a specific policy decision may be quite fortuitous; and even major policies can be made largely by accident. The prohibition against sex discrimination found in the 1964 Civil Rights Act is a notable example: It was the result of a ploy by opponents of the measure that failed (Orfield, 1975, pp. 299-300).

The point, however, is not that policy decision-making is necessarily so diffuse, but rather that the model allows us to define more fully the continuum along which policy decision-making may fall. It identifies the major elements that must be considered and suggests that it is the character and relative stability of the relationships within and among these elements that serve to distinguish different decisional processes.

These relationships define the structure of decision-making, a structure that is realized through the routinization or institutionalization of patterns of communication. While these patterns are likely to be taken for granted by participants, they will vary from one decisional context to another. Their essential function is to reduce the uncertainties of relevance to the decisional process. What is perceived as policy-relevant communication will vary with the scope of these residual uncertainties. In general, one would expect policymakers to endeavor to reduce the uncertainties attending their decisional roles by attempting to structure the process as much as possible. However, contextual factors may limit these possibilities; and contextual changes, to include those arising from policy decisions themselves, may cause previously structured patterns to break down.

CONTEXTUAL FACTORS AND
POLICY DECISION-MAKING

The constellation of contextual factors that bears on a particular policy decision is, in a sense, necessarily peculiar to that decision. However, following Kingdon (1981, pp. 289-292), policy decision-making may be viewed as a process occurring within a context of "successively narrow boundaries." While the details of this context may vary with the specific decision, its broader characteristics are likely to be a more stable function of historic practices and presumptions with respect to the general topic or area of policy. These characteristics define bounds that do not so much dictate choice as act as negative constraints on the range of possible choices. They serve to organize and channel the flow of people, problems, solutions, and choice opportunities. These contextual factors are economic, ideational, and structural in character.

Economic Constraints

Perhaps foremost among these contextual constraints are the needs and resources reflected by the economic character of the community. Political demographers have shown that a major portion of the variation in the material outputs of public policy among state and local governments can be accounted for by the economic characteristics of the jurisdictions they serve (Dye, 1966; Mazmanian & Sabatier, 1980). A similar pattern obtains across nations and holds largely without regard to the political characteristics of the systems involved (Collier & Messick, 1975; Heidenheimer, Heclo, & Adams, 1975). Although the governmental expenditure patterns often used to measure policy outputs in these studies are perhaps crude, they leave little doubt that both policy priorities and expenditure levels tend to be heavily dependent upon the economic character of the community. While the strength of the relations observed is striking, the dynamics involved are less clear.

Several hypotheses may help to account for the similarities in the way policies develop as economic resources expand. Economic development may itself create a fairly uniform set of problems that require public solutions (Sharkansky, 1975). Imitation or diffusion may also partly account for the convergent patterns (Collier & Messick, 1975; Gray, 1973; Walker, 1969). Inglehart (1977) suggests that economic development alters that basic need priorities of people in predictable ways, giving rise to a common progression of demands on and expectations of government. Economic growth also occasions changing patterns of interdependence that may result in characteristic forms of social organization with attendant biases toward certain types of policy.

Ideational Constraints

Of course, assumptions about economic resources and their distribution are also important. "Poverty," for example, can be a problem only in the presence of relative affluence, but how that "problem" and its "solutions" are conceived depend heavily upon beliefs regarding the prospects and limits of economic growth and accepted standards of distributive justice. Thus, ideas and ideology represent a second important source of constraint on policy decision-making.

Culture. The commonly shared beliefs, values, and attitudes that define the culture circumscribe not only what will be considered permissible but, even more fundamentally, what is seen as problematic. The atomistic individualism, materialism, and suspicion of political authority that are the hallmarks of the American political culture have very much colored public policy in the United States in comparison to other nations at all levels of government (Heidenheimer et al., 1975; James, 1972). Significant patterns of subcultural variation have also been identified that impact on expectations of government and participation in the policy process (Elazar, 1972).

The culture gives definition to the standards of procedural and substantive legitimacy by which policy decision-making will be judged. These standards are reflected in the legitimacy accorded various demands and in the prevailing "public philosophy" that serves to rationalize and justify the exercise of political power (Lowi, 1967). They serve to guide media surveillance of the policy process by giving procedural and substantive meanings to the "public interest" that the media presume to guard (Blanchard, 1974, pp. 192-200; Dunn, 1969, pp. 60-62; Nadel, 1971, pp. 212-214). They also provide criteria that help policymakers separate the politically feasible from the unfeasible through the dynamics of "anticipated reaction" (for a striking example, see Cavala & Wildavsky, 1970). Because these standards are generally shared by both policy elites and the public, they ensure a modicum of virtual, if not active, representation in the policy process (Erikson et al., 1980, pp. 238-267).

The bounds imposed by the culture, of course, are not immutable. Elements of the culture are constantly being renegotiated in light of new experiences and understandings. In fact, that is partly what public policy is all about. Nonetheless, cultural change tends to be a slow process with all but minor changes normally requiring generations. Even then change is likely to be successfully negotiated only through effective leadership that is sensitive to the prevailing ideational climate. Lamb's analysis (1974, pp. 179-190) of the sharply different popular responses to the cognate forms of welfare reform proposed by Nixon in his Family Assistance Plan and by McGovern in his 1972 presidential campaign shows vividly how important cultural constraints can be. It also suggests how they may be altered or circumvented through communication that respects the limits and appreciates the possibilities of political persuasion (Nimmo, 1978, pp. 98-130; Sears & Whitney, 1973).

Knowledge. More specific ideational constraints on the flow of people, problems, solutions, and choice opportunities in the policy process arise from the knowledge base of society and how that knowledge is distributed. As Wildavsky (1979, pp. 62-67) observed, a problem without a conceivable solution is simply a fact of life. While what is problematic in this sense is in part a matter of resources, it is also a matter of available technologies and the state of accepted "knowledge." Abortion, for example, was neither a major problem nor a "solution" in search of a "problem" prior to the development of the technology that made it a relatively safe and inexpensive procedure. Similarly, environmental pollution was an annoyance and smoking merely a bad habit prior to the development of knowledge and perspectives that made them community problems. By the same token, through new "knowledge" old solutions become problems themselves. Thus, with respect to the mentally handicapped, institutionalization becomes the problem; "deinstitutionalization," the solution.

As knowledge expands and changes, new uncertainties and conflicts are created. The policy process thus becomes an arena for competition over what will be accepted as knowledge and whose "expertise" will be valued (Aaron, 1978). The terms of such debates tend to be abstruse; and command of the specialized language of the area, an implicit criterion for participation in the process (Heclo, 1978). Policy problems tend to become self-generating as experts and policy professionals (both in and outside of government) assume an increasingly prominent role. As areas of policy become more exclusively the province of knowledge communities, or what Heclo (1978) calls "issue networks" and Walker (Note 1) refers to as "communities of policy professionals," the overall policy process becomes increasingly differentiated and fragmented. This further compounds the general problems of coordination and consistency.

Policy professionalization contributes to growing "knowledge gaps" that not only limit participation but also render the policy process less intelligible to those not immediately involved. These knowledge gaps are not so much the product of strictures on the flow of information as the diversity of communications. They "widen as the flow of information appealing to concerns of specialized groups increases" (Tichenor et al., 1980, p. 188). Thus, while policy professionalization comports with and is sustained by culturally based preferences for rational problem-solving, it biases participation in ways that are both predictable and contrary to other tenets of the political culture. In emphasizing problem-solving, it ignores the other functions of public policy.

Knowledge constraints on policy, of course, arise not only from the presence of putative knowledge but also from the lack thereof. In the absence of substantive "knowledge" and/or a recognized community of experts, the ideational constraints that derive from historic practices and past precedents in a policy area tend to be singularly dominant. That which has been done before or marginal modifications of the same will circumscribe the range of what is considered both possible and appropriate. History, rather than theory and explanation, becomes the justification for a course of action; and policy tends to develop in an incremental and remedial but nondirectional and non-goal-oriented way (Braybrooke & Lindblom, 1963). Given the inherent uncertainties of all knowledge, policymakers are likely to gravitate toward this approach. This impulse may act as a check on the influence of would-be "knowledge" brokers and represents a challenge that they are likely to have to labor long to overcome.

Climate of the Times. A final source of ideational constraint on decision-making deserves brief mention. Although somewhat amorphous, it is potentially important. For want of a better term, we will call it the "climate of the times." As Aaron (1978, p. 147) observes, "Each era is the temporal meeting place of attitudes, political and social movements, and intellectual developments, all shaped by demographic trends and historic events deeply rooted in the past." Sundquist (1968) argues that there are cycles in the life of the polity characterized by periods of activism and change followed by periods of consolidation and immobilization. Although the periodicity and specific causes of these cycles are unclear, Bennett (1980) suggests that they are related to the shifting emphasis placed on the conflicting cultural themes of equality and achievement as a result of changing social and economic conditions. In any case, periods of activism tend to be sustained by popular expectations of action aroused through aggressive advocacy and guided by some vague concept of theme legitimated through the electoral process—for example, the "War on Poverty" and "supply side economics." In effect, these periods afford choice opportunities for problems and solutions that may have floated around for some time.

Structural Constraints

In addition to economic and ideational constraints, policy decision-making is further constrained by structural properties of the social, political, and institutional context in which it occurs.

Social Structure. At the local level, numerous studies have shown that participation in the policy process and its problem-solution content tend to vary with the social structure of the community (Tichenor et al., 1980; Verba & Nie, 1972). Similar contextual factors are revealed through the study of groups and organizations operating at the state and national levels (Dye, 1979; Wilson, 1973). Traditionally, this group structure has tended to be organized around particularized interests. It has been sustained largely by the individual and group exclusive benefits that accrue from membership. However, the development of truly national press and communications technologies that allow members of the general public to be reached both directly and selectively has facilitated the emergence of potent new groups organized around issues and ideas rather than private interests. These groups are sustained by a common ideology or a shared conception of the "public interest" or common good (McFarland, 1976, pp. 1-43; Nadel, 1971, pp. 191-247). This has altered the "mobilization of bias" in terms of participation in politics and injected new problems and solutions into the choice arena.

Because of their peculiar character, these groups tend not to honor many of the traditional norms of interest group politics (Berry, 1977; McFarland, 1976) and are often quite uncompromising in their views. Like mass movements, their base is potentially very fragile. The latitude of the political entrepreneurs who create and lead them is likely to be severely limited by the imperatives of keeping the faith in order to keep the faithful. Environmental advocates, for example, are not likely to eschew direct regulation in favor of the auctioning of "pollution rights" as a means of pollution control, even though a compelling case can be made that the latter is a more efficient and effective "solution." Even given this sensitivity, it may be difficult to sustain the group, since expressive needs are generally more easily satisfied than instrumental ones (Edelman, 1964, pp. 22-43; Zurcher & Kirkpatrick, 1976, pp. 332-333).

The presence of such groups in a policy arena predictably means policy decision-making will tend to be more conflictual and command greater public visibility. Although these groups will often involve policy professionals, their power is heavily dependent upon the press and the public credibility of their leaders. Thus, like political parties, they tend to simplify issues and act to reduce the information costs of popular involvement. Because their political capital rests on beliefs and values, they may serve as an effective counterforce to traditional economic interests. By the same token, however, because the people they mobilize tend to be atypical in the intensity and extremity of their views, their very effectiveness can skew governmental policy away from the modal preferences of the general public, reducing overall governmental responsiveness (Verba & Nie, 1972, pp. 341-342).

Political Context. Parties and elections are, of course, the major means through which the political context of policy decision-making has traditionally been structured. Political scientists have long emphasized the importance of parties as "linkage" institutions for aggregating and distilling popular preferences and for organizing government so as to provide a modicum of accountability (Ladd, 1978). Parties define alternatives for political leadership and policy choice. Although not always perceived by the electorate, these choices bear significantly on policy decision-making (Bunce, 1980; Erikson et al., 1980, pp. 276-279). However, at the subnational level, party competition is often lacking; and local officials in most communities are elected in nonpartisan elections. In the absence of parties, social structure tends to assume a much more prominent role in structuring the policy process; and electoral participation, which Verba and Nie (1972, pp. 322-327) find vital to responsiveness, declines.

Parties are among America's least esteemed inventions; their role in guiding voting behavior and organizing policy decision-making has diminished over the past two decades. This decline has many sources to include numerous "reforms" aimed at further democraticizing both parties and the policy process. Most important, however, the decline is attributable to the development of communication and campaign technology that has obviated many of the traditional functions of parties and enabled candidates to become something of parties unto themselves. As a consequence, elections have become more of a vehicle for reflecting diversity rather than aggregating it. This militates against the development and maintenance of the types of policy coalitions necessary to exercise political authority in a consistent way. Moreover, since policy is a collective endeavor, the pursuit of policy individualism by elected officials, while perhaps serving their electoral interests, makes it difficult to hold anyone accountable for what government does and does not do.

Institutional Structure. The formal institutional context of policy decision-making varies across the traditional three levels of government, with countless regional and subregional layers interposed. The familiar separation and sharing of powers found at the federal level is mirrored at the state level and to some extent at the local level as well. Although policy decision-making has tended to be viewed primarily in terms of executive, bureaucratic, and legislative decision-making, the courts have assumed an increasingly prominent role in the process, providing an alternative choice arena that is distinctive in its structure and biases (Shapiro, 1978).

That variation in institutional structure can profoundly affect policy decision-making is well documented at all levels of government. Dodd and Schott (1979), for example, show in detail how changes in the institutional structure of Congress have altered and generally tended to fragment policy decision-making, enhancing the relative power of the bureaucracy and interest groups. As the role of the federal government has expanded to include many of the traditional concerns of state and local government, the latter have become increasingly dependent upon and structured around federal programs. As a consequence, state and local government has become more a matter of participation in a nationally defined and vertically segmented policy process (Beer, 1976). Within this process, state and local governments are both implementing agencies and interested parties that assume a role similar to that of other interest groups. Because they retain a distinct claim to political authority, they find the problems of intergovernmental coordination central concerns; and implementation becomes as much a process of continuous policy-making as it is execution (Edwards, 1980). To cope with these problems, a variety of new institutional structures have been created that tend to further bureaucratize the policy process and constrain the flow of people, problems, solutions, and choice opportunities.

COMMUNICATIONS AND THE DYNAMICS
OF POLICY DECISION-MAKING

Much of the work on public policy has taken the form of case-analytic studies aimed at illuminating the politics of decision-making in specific areas of policy (see, for example, Davidson, 1974, on manpower policy; Thomas, 1975, on education; and Krasnow & Longley, 1978, on broadcast regulation). The burden of much of this literature has been to suggest that many areas of policy tend to be dominated by a limited and rather stable set of actors operating within a relatively closed communications network. At the national level, these subsystems or subgovernments are typically comprised of an executive agency, members of relevant congressional committees and subcommittees, and representatives of major organized interests (Ripley & Franklin, 1980). Because of this pattern, they are often referred to as "iron triangles." Such subsystems have developed historically as a result of specialization and differentiation occasioned by the growing scope and complexity of public policy decision-making. They have the effect of not only structuring opportunities for participation in crucial phases of the policy process but also institutionalizing sectors or domains of policy in forms reflecting historical conceptions of "problems" warranting attention and their "solution" possibilities.

The presence of such subsystems suggest that the overall policy process is largely decomposable into more or less independent policy sectors. Moreover, it suggests that much of policy decision-making may occur toward the more structured end of the decisional process continuum. However, a number of recent observers have noted that policy subsystems may vary substantially in structure and penetrability, belying the conventional "iron triangle" conception. They further suggest that even in well-established areas of policy, the process is often characterized by considerable instability and conflict (Heclo, 1978; Wilson, 1980).

Although the existence of policy subsystems has long been recognized, neither the variation among them nor the dynamics through which they are created, sustained, and change are well understood. It seems clear, however, that these subsystem dynamics derive largely from three basic facts. First, substantial consensus is required for policy decisions to be made. There are a myriad of institutional obstacles that can be overcome only through the agreement, or at least the acquiescence, of a large number of people. As continuing bodies, policy-making institutions operate on the basis of a large number of formal and informal arrangements that cannot be ignored with respect to any given decision without imperiling the viability of the ongoing process and the standing of individual participants and the roles they occupy.

Second, the stakes involved in policy decisions are multiple and diverse. The motivations that prompt a decision are likely to be as variable as the parties involved, directly and indirectly, in making it. The range of potential participants and interested parties is large. There are elected officials with reputations and careers to protect and with personal as well as constituent interests to promote. These officials may be interested in making "good" policy, but reelection and/or higher office are likely to be prominent concerns. There are also staff members, bureaucrats, and outside policy experts who have jobs to do, reputations to build, careers to promote, and professional commitments to honor. There are specific groups and organized interests which, along with the general public, may have both material and symbolic stakes involved. And, of course, there are the media and their representatives who may have their own interests to serve and axes to grind. Reconciling this diversity or finding points of common convergence sufficient to afford that modicum of consensus necessary for a policy decision is no mean task.

Third, the attention capabilities of both policymakers and policy-making institutions are necessarily limited. Time is a scarce resource, and the agenda of government is always crowded. The number of policy issues that can actively be considered and acted upon constitute a small portion of the range of possible issues demanding attention. Policy subsystems serve to structure the agenda of government and to focus the attention of policymakers through a routinized division of labor. As products of past decisions, they represent legitimated formulae for accommodating established interests. By structuring participation and by providing preexisting decisional premises, subsystems serve to limit the conflicts and uncertainties that must be dealt with at any one time, therein facilitating the development of the type of consensus necessary for decision.

Policy Innovation and Subsystem Formation

While established policy subsystems may account for much of public policy, they represent a routinization of decision-making that is not likely to account for major shifts in policy or major policy innovations. Since policy decisions require substantial consensus and are not likely without the acquiescence of those most immediately affected by them, major policy innovation is likely to occur only when an issue is broadly salient and the mobilization of bias is distinctly one-sided. These conditions are most likely to obtain in the face of a recognized crisis or a scandal. The latter may effectively compel the acquiescence of interests that stand to be affected adversely. Neither a crisis nor a scandal will be sufficient by itself, however. What is also required is effective exploitation of the situation. The policy implications of a crisis or scandal are matters of definition. Indeed, whether a particular situation constitutes a crisis or scandal as opposed to being merely a dramatic event or a regrettable set of circumstances depends on how it is defined. The impetus of events is important, but what ultimately counts is the interpretations given to them.

Even when a situation is recognized as problematic, a lack of clarity regarding what is at issue can prevent or delay any major policy action. The situation may not even command active governmental attention unless it is effectively defined as an appropriate matter of governmental concern, a test that is likely to be a continuing obstacle to policy innovation. Moreover, for an issue to be broadly salient, it must be readily understandable. Complex or technical definitions create confusion and uncertainty that are not conducive to the mobilization of the support required for major policy innovation.

Public salience will also vary with the scope and distribution of the perceived stakes involved in a policy issue. These stakes are themselves matters of definition and are subject to redefinition. Both Lowi (1964) and Wilson (1973, 1980) argued that the politics of policy varies with the costs and benefits involved. Although Lowi's conception of these dynamics has perhaps commended greater attention (see, for example, Ripley & Franklin, 1980), Wilson's argument (1980) serves to clarify and extend the basic idea. He identifies four types of politics: (a) majoritarian, where both the benefits and costs are widely distributed; (b) interest group politics, where both the costs and benefits are concentrated; (c) client politics, where the benefits are concentrated, but not the costs; and (d) entrepreneurial politics, where the benefits are diffuse but the costs are concentrated.

Wilson suggests that the fate of policy proposals of these various types will hinge not only on who is to get what but also on general beliefs regarding what constitutes an equitable distribution of costs and benefits. The standards of equity established in one policy can prompt the demand that it be applied elsewhere. Wildavsky (1979) similarly noted the spillover effects of one policy or another and the important role conceptions of equity play in the policy process. In fact, he argues that a concern with equity accounts for much of the sharp increase in social welfare expenditures over the past decade.

In terms of his fourfold scheme, Wilson (1980) finds that modern communication capabilities have greatly facilitated the development of what he calls "entrepreneurial politics" and have undermined the cozy security that once characterized client politics. Because of the diffuse benefits in the former and the diffuse costs in the latter, these types of politics traditionally have not been conducive to the mobilization of public concern. However, by making it feasible for policy entrepreneurs to reach the mass public and direct their attention, modern communication capabilities have made these areas of policy accessible to the public, altering the prevailing mobilization of bias.

Policy Entrepreneurs. We have repeatedly seen that policy innovation or major policy changes hinge on control over the definition of what is at issue. Given this and the multiplicity of obstacles that must be overcome in the policy process, the success or failure of a new policy proposal is likely to depend heavily on its effective advocacy by a policy entrepreneur and on his ability to orchestrate the flow of people, problems, solutions, and choice opportunities. Eyestone (1978) distinguishes two types of entrepreneurial roles: the initiator and the broker. The first is responsible for shepherding an idea to the point that it commands the active attention of decisionmakers; the second, for building the coalitions of policymakers necessary to assure its passage through the intricate institutional processes necessary for its adoption as policy. Both roles may be played by the same person but often are not. Both, however, involve what Bardach (1972) called the "skill factor" in politics; namely, the ability to assemble a hetero- geneous coalition of support through persistence, persuasion, sensitivity, and anticipated reaction.

Policy entrepreneurs are found both inside and outside of government. Walker (1977) notes that senators frequently play this role on matters that are perceived to be publicly salient and are simple to explain. On more technical issues and on brokerage matters, members of the House of Representatives often play prominent entrepreneurial roles. Wilbur Mills's deft handling of the Medi- care issue in the mid-1960s provides a particularly well-documented example (Marmor, 1973). The President and presidential appointees, of course, fre- quently assume entrepreneurial roles. A striking illustration is found in Francis Keppel's ingenious engineering of the passage of the 1965 Elementary and Secondary Education Act (Murphy, 1973).

Nonelected officials may also act as prime movers in policy innovation (Fritschler, 1975). Wilbur Cohen's exploits in this regard are legendary. For years, he has been a remarkably successful advocate and broker on issues relating to social security (Derthick, 1979). Malbin (1979) finds that congressional staff members have also come to play a much more active role as initiators and brokers in the policy process. Although there would appear to be no shortage of policy entrepreneurs in government, Congress, in legislation such as the Older Americans Act, has actually mandated that program administrators play this role, in effect formally institutionalizing policy advocacy.

The exploits of prominent policy entrepreneurs outside government, people like Ralph Nader and John Gardner, are well known (McFarland, 1976). There are, however, countless others, who, though perhaps less visible, have been instrumental in bringing about major policy changes. Mary Lasker, for example, was perhaps the person singularly most responsible for the creation of the National Institute on Cancer (Rettig, 1977). Policy entrepreneurship, of course, need not be directed at bringing about policy change, but can be oriented toward preventing it. Phyllis Schlafly's crusade against the Equal Rights Amend- ment is but one notable case in point (Boles, 1979).

Public advocacy that is sensitive to the operational needs and reportorial practices of the press and to the necessity of making issues intelligible and relevant to the public can overcome the inertia inherent in the policy process and bring major policy change. Jones (1974) shows how perceived public concern prompted major policy innovation with respect to air pollution, despite the resistance of powerful organized interests and the uncertain feasibility of the solution adopted. Popular mobilization, however, is difficult to sustain and seems to follow an "issue attention cycle," as suggested by Downs (1972). As public attention and concern diminish, policy decision-making, particularly during the implementation stage, is likely to assume or revert to traditional patterns of subsystem dominance. In the absence of "watchdog" groups or the continuing attention of policy entrepreneurs and the press, a policy may be redefined to produce effects quite different from those initially intended.

Subsystem Maintenance and Change

The flow of people, problems, solutions, and choice opportunities in stable policy subsystems contrasts sharply with the loosely structured and uncertain processes of major policy innovation. Participatory rights will be defined in terms of a stable set of roles characterized by a high degree of specialization. This role structure will reflect and be sustained by a well-understood "problem-solution" paradigm. This paradigm establishes the premises and defines the parameters of decision, to include the focal problems, the variables of uncertainty, and the range of admissible solutions. This commonality of perspective will be manifested in a shared and often arcane language that serves to insulate and promote the autonomy of the subsystem (see, for example, Derthick, 1979, pp. 58-59). Choice opportunities will tend to be regularized by institutional practice.

The problem-solution paradigm may be highly articulated, reflecting a putatively advanced state of knowledge. It may resemble or perhaps involve a "scientific paradigm," with decision-making taking on the character of "normal science" in an applied guise (Kuhn, 1970; Walker, Note 1). In the absence of such a recognized body of knowledge, historical practice and patterns of successful adaption may serve as an effective substitute. Steinbrunner (1974) notes, for example, that decisional systems may persist and thrive in the face of unfathomed complexity through the processes of feedback and adaption. Essentially all that is involved is learning through experience what variables are critical, structuring attention capabilities to monitor these variables, and developing through trial and error a viable response repertoire. Wilson (1980, p. 377) observed that government agencies "quickly learn what forces in their environment can [threaten them] and work hard to minimize the chance that they will be vulnerable."

The potential threats to a policy subsystem can include the charge of "doing nothing." In the absence of clear and predictably favorable performance criteria or a well-articulated and widely accepted policy paradigm, the subsystem is likely to need the support of a well-defined constituency that can attest to the merits of its product or provide a rationale for its existence (Sproull et al., 1978, pp. 92-98). In any case, performance gaps in the form of manifest failures or the chronic inability to keep critical variables within an acceptable range may occasion "state changes" (Steinbrunner, 1974, pp. 80-81) involving a fundamental shift in the problem-solution paradigm in a fashion analogous to "scientific revolutions" (Kuhn, 1970). However, this presupposes at least some relatively unambiguous performance expectations and the availability of a compelling alternative. Even then, there is likely to be prolonged resistance that may require generational changes in subsystem participants or effective external advocacy to overcome. Walker (Note 1) finds striking examples of such paradigm shifts in the areas of forest management and highway safety.

Save for "grand opportunities" afforded by the coincidence of environmental changes and the presence of aggressive policy entrepreneurs, policy-making in highly structured sectors is likely to be incremental. The reason may be not so much a lack of "knowledge" as a desire to avoid upsetting existing environmental arrangements. This incrementalism, however, may be goal-oriented and involve successive serial adjustments that have substantial cumulative effect. Derthick (1979) suggests, for example, that the enormous growth in social security is attributable to the fact that members of that subsystem have been both sensitive to the opportunities and limitations imposed by their environment and steadfast in their commitment to the expansion of their "social insurance" paradigm. She also suggests that policy-making in this area has suffered critically from the restrictive nature of the communication network involved.

CONCLUSIONS

None of the patterns we have described is well understood, and none has been the subject of much systematic research. It is clear, however, that communication plays a vital role in the policy process, and that, by mapping the patterns of communication involved, we can gain a better understanding of the diversity and dynamics of the process. It is also clear that changes in communication capabilities and the exploitation of those capabilities have altered the policy process in ways that are only dimly understood. On one hand, these changes have sharply increased the amount of information available to the public and facilitated the emergence of prominent new actors in the policy process. This has altered the prevailing mobilization of bias, although it has not necessarily made the process more responsive to the general public. On the other hand, changes in communication capabilities have contributed to the continuing fragmentation of the policy process, making it more difficult to fathom by citizen and analyst alike. They have undermined intermediate structures that have traditionally served to make the process comprehensible and meaningful to the average citizen. These changes have also contributed to a growing "knowledge gap" that is likely to put the disadvantaged at greater disadvantage and frustrate the many for whom participation is a civic duty but not a full-time commitment.

There are, then, a host of important questions relating not only to the nature and dynamics of public policy but also to its multivarious impacts that warrant the attention of communication-oriented researchers. By surveying some of the dimensions of public policy as it is currently understood, it is our hope that we may have stimulated greater interest in exploring these questions.

REFERENCE NOTE

1. Walker, J. *The diffusion of knowledge and policy change.* Paper presented at the meeting of the American Political Science Association, Chicago, August 29-September 2, 1978.

REFERENCES

Aaron, D. *Politics and the professors.* Washington, DC: Brookings Institution, 1978.

Allison, G. *Essence of decision.* Boston: Little, Brown, 1971.

Bardach, E. *The skill factor in politics.* Berkeley: University of California Press, 1972.

Beer, S. The adoption of general revenue sharing. *Public Policy,* 1976, *24,* 127-198.

Bell, D. *Power, influence and authority.* New York: Oxford University Press, 1975.

Bennett, W. *Public opinion in American politics.* New York: Harcourt Brace Jovanovich, 1980.

Berry, J. *Lobbying for the people.* Princeton: Princeton University Press, 1977.

Blanchard, R. The Congressional correspondents and their world. In R. Blanchard (Ed.), *Congress and the news media.* New York: Hastings House, 1974.

Boles, J. *The politics of the equal rights amendment.* New York: Longman, 1979.

Boulding, K. *The image.* Ann Arbor: University of Michigan Press, 1956.

Braybrooke, D., & Lindblom, C. *A strategy of decision.* New York: Free Press, 1963.

Bunce, V. Changing leaders and changing policies. *American Journal of Political Science,* 1980, *24,* 373-395.

Cavala, B., & Wildavsky, A. The political feasibility of income by right. *Public Policy,* 1970, *17,* 321-354.

Chaffee, S. The diffusion of information. In S. Chaffee (Ed.), *Political communication.* Beverly Hills, CA: Sage, 1975.

Cobb, R., & Elder, C. *Participation in American politics: The dynamics of agenda-building.* Baltimore: Johns Hopkins University Press, 1975.

Collier, D., & Messick, R. Prerequisites versus diffusion: Testing alternative explanations of social security adaptation. *American Political Science Review,* 1975, *69,* 1299-1315.

Connolly, T. Information processing and decision making in organizations. In B. Starr & E. Salancik (Eds.), *New directions in organization behavior.* Chicago: St. Clair Press, 1977.

Davidson, R. Policy making in the manpower subgovernment. In M. Smith (Ed.), *Politics in America: Studies in policy analysis.* New York: Random House, 1974.

Derthick, M. *Policymaking for social security.* Washington, DC: Brookings Institution, 1979.

Dodd, L., & Schott, R. *Congress and the administrative state.* New York: John Wiley, 1979.

Downs, A. Up and down with ecology—The "issue attention cycle." *Public Interest,* 1972, *12,* 38-50.

Dunn, D. *Public officials and the press.* Reading, MA: Addison-Wesley, 1969.

Dye, T. *Politics, economics and the public.* Englewood Cliffs, NJ: Prentice-Hall, 1966.

Dye, T. *Who's running America?* Englewood Cliffs, NJ: Prentice-Hall, 1979.

Edelman, M. *The symbolic uses of politics.* Urbana: University of Illinois Press, 1964.

Edelman, M. *Political language.* New York: Academic Press, 1975.

Edwards, G. *Implementing public policy.* Washington, DC: Congressional Quarterly Press, 1980.

Elazar, E. *American federalism.* New York: Crowell, 1972.

Erikson, R., Luttbeg, N., & Tedin, K. *American public opinion.* New York: John Wiley, 1980.

Eyestone, R. *From social issues to public policy.* New York: John Wiley, 1978.

Fiorina, M. *Congress: Keystone of the Washington establishment.* New Haven, CT: Yale University Press, 1977.

Fritschler, A. *Smoking and politics.* Englewood Cliffs, NJ: Prentice-Hall, 1975.

Graber, D. *Mass media and American politics.* Washington, DC: Congressional Quarterly Press, 1980.

Gray, V. Innovation in the states. *American Political Science Review,* 1973, *67,* 1174-1185.

Heclo, H. Issue networks and the executive establishment. In A. King (Ed.), *The new American political system.* Washington, DC: American Enterprise Institute, 1978.

Heidenheimer, A., Heclo, H., & Adams, C. *Comparative public policy.* New York: St. Martin's Press, 1975.

Inglehart, R. *The silent revolution.* Princeton: Princeton University Press, 1977.

James, D. *Poverty, politics and change.* Englewood Cliffs, NJ: Prentice-Hall, 1972.

Jones, C. Speculative augmentation in federal air pollution policy making. *Journal of Politics,* 1974, *36,* 438-464.

Jones, C. *An introduction to the study of public policy.* North Scituate, MA: Duxbury Press, 1977.

Kingdon, J. *Congressmen's voting behavior.* New York: Harper & Row, 1981.

Krasnow, E., & Longley, L. *The politics of broadcast regulation.* New York: St. Martin's Press, 1978.

Kuhn, T. *The structure of scientific revolutions.* Chicago: University of Chicago Press, 1970.

Ladd, E. *Where have all the voters gone?* New York: Norton, 1978.

Lamb, K. *As Orange goes.* New York: Norton, 1974.

Lindblom, C. The science of "muddling through." *Public Administration Review,* 1959, *19,* 79-88.

Lowi, T. American business, public policy, case studies, and political theory. *World Politics,* 1964, *16,* 677-715.

Lowi, T. The public philosophy: Interest-group liberalism. *American Political Science Review,* 1967, *61,* 5-24.

McFarland, A. *Public interest lobbies.* Washington, DC: American Enterprise Institute, 1976.

Malbin, M. *Unelected representatives.* New York: Basic Books, 1979.

March, J., & Olsen, J. *Ambiguity and choice in organizations.* Bergen: Universitetforlaget, 1976.

Marmor, T. *The politics of medicare.* Chicago: AVC, 1973.

Mazmanian, D., & Sabatier, P. A multivariate model of public policy making. *American Journal of Political Science,* 1980, *24,* 439-468.

Meier, K. *Politics and the bureaucracy.* North Scituate, MA: Duxbury Press, 1979.

Miller, A., Goldenberg, E., & Erbring, L. Type-set politics: Impact of newspapers on public confidence. *American Political Science Review,* 1979, *73,* 67-84.

Murphy, J. The educational bureaucracies implement novel policy. In A. Sindler (Ed.), *Policy and politics in America.* Boston: Little, Brown, 1973.

Nadel, M. *The politics of consumer protection.* Indianapolis: Bobbs-Merrill, 1971.

Nie, N., Verba, S., & Petrocik, J. *The changing American voter.* Cambridge: Harvard University Press, 1979.

Nimmo, D. *Political communication and public opinion in America.* Santa Monica, CA: Goodyear, 1978.

Orfield, G. *Congressional power: Congress and social change.* New York: Harcourt Brace Jovanovich, 1975.

Polsby, N. Policy initiation in the American political system. In I. Horowitz (Ed.), *The use and abuse of social science*. New Brunswick, NJ: Transaction Books, 1971.

Price, D. Policy making in Congressional committees. *American Political Science Review, 1978, 72*, 548-574.

Rettig, R. *Cancer crusade*. Princeton: Princeton University Press, 1977.

Ripley, R., & Franklin, G. *Congress, the bureaucracy and public policy*. Homewood, IL: Dorsey Press, 1980.

Schattschneider, E. *The semi-sovereign people*. Hinsdale, IL: Dryden Press, 1975.

Sears, D., & Whitney, R. *Political persuasion*. Morristown, NJ: General Learning Press, 1973.

Shapiro, M. The Supreme Court. In A. King (Ed.), *The new American political system*. Washington, DC: American Enterprise Institute, 1978.

Sharkansky, I. *The United States: A study of a developing country*. New York: David McKay, 1975.

Simon, H. Political research: The decision making framework. In D. Easton (Ed.), *Varieties of political theory*. Englewood Cliffs, NJ: Prentice-Hall, 1966.

Sproull, L., Weiner, S., & Wolf, D. *Organizing an anarchy*. Chicago: University of Chicago Press, 1978.

Steinbrunner, J. *The cybernetic theory of decision*. Princeton: Princeton University Press, 1974.

Stokey, E., & Zeckhauser, R. *A primer on policy analysis*. Cambridge: MIT Press, 1978.

Strouse, J. *The mass media, public opinion, and public policy analysis*. Columbus, OH: Charles Merrill, 1975.

Sundquist, J. *Politics and policy*. Washington, DC: Brookings Institution, 1968.

Thomas, N. *Education in national politics*. New York: David McKay, 1975.

Tichenor, P., Donohoe, C., & Olien, C. *Community conflict and the press*. Beverly Hills, CA: Sage, 1980.

Verba, S., & Nie, N. *Participation in America*. New York: Harper & Row, 1972.

Walker, J. The diffusion of innovations among the American states. *American Political Science Review, 1969, 63*, 880-899.

Walker, J. Setting the agenda for the U.S. Senate. *British Journal of Political Science, 1977, 7*, 432-445.

Wildavsky, A. *Speaking truth to power*. Boston: Little, Brown, 1979.

Wilson, J. *Political organization*. New York: Basic Books, 1973.

Wilson, J. The politics of regulation. In J. Wilson (Ed.), *The politics of regulation*. New York: Basic Books, 1980.

Zurcher, L., & Kirkpatrick, R. *Citizens for decency*. Austin: University of Texas Press, 1976.

CHAPTER 15

The Rhetoric of Political Movements

Herbert W. Simons and Elizabeth W. Mechling

TO READERS with a strong preference for tidy data sets, value-free research generalizations, and clearly bounded theoretical domains, the subject of this chapter comes highly unrecommended. Political movements are massive, impassioned, and ineluctable. Their sheer size and duration make them difficult to comprehend; their deviant ideologies often evoke polemical commentary in place of detached scholarship; their amorphousness and diversity render them resistant to coherent theoretical accounts.

With these caveats we offer a review and commentary on what political movements are, how they attempt to secure their ends, and what might be done to make sense of the frequently paradoxical rhetoric generated by them. To be featured in the chapter are theory and research bearing on patterns of movement rhetoric and explanations for those patterns. Covered briefly are objectivist and interactionist accounts of the relationship between rhetoric and situation, collective behavior theories and resource management theories, and our own "Requirements-Problems-Strategies" (RPS) approach. Although the theories deal with patterns generic to movements as a whole or to broad classes of movements, we believe they can also guide analyses of the rhetoric of particular movements. No theory of rhetoric can as yet be applied predictively to particular cases or tested rigorously through an analysis of such cases. But theory can at least provide a rough guide to the rhetorical terrain and a clearer conception of the factors impelling and constraining the rhetorical choices of movement leaders.

WHAT ARE POLITICAL MOVEMENTS?

Just what groupings and activities qualify as political movements is a matter of some debate. Coined as a term in social theory during the great wave of optimism following the overthrow of the *Ancien Régime*, the term "movement" initially evoked images of those *dans le mouvement* participating in an inevitable and progressive tide of history (McGee, 1980). Contemporary scholars no longer assume that movements march to Destiny's mandate, but they have retained the sense of movements as long-term, collective efforts in behalf of a cause.

A distinction is frequently drawn between historical movement and social or political movements. The former are longer and more amorphous cultural trends; the latter involve an identifiable, more time-restricted collectivity—that is, an organization or grouping of organizations whose members operate together to promote or resist social change. Women's suffrage and women's liberation may be viewed as social or political movements. Both are part of a centuries-long historical movement for female-male equality. The typical social (or political) movement is a loosely coordinated collectivity consisting of one or more core organizations such as SNCC, SCLC, NAACP, and CORE for the civil rights movement of the 1960s as well as a large number of persons who identify with the movement but are formally unaffiliated (Lang & Lang, 1961). The core organizations are largely voluntary associations which operate as much in competition as in cooperation with other groups within the same movement (McCarthy & Zald, 1977). Likewise, movements as a whole simultaneously compete and cooperate with each other. For example, although the civil rights and antiwar movements of the sixties were aligned against common enemies, they had to compete for financial support and media attention (Zald & McCarthy, 1975).

The terms "social movement" and "political movement" will be used more or less interchangeably in this chapter. "Social movement" might be considered the broader term, in that it includes efforts at changing individuals, not just institutions (Aberle, 1966), as well as efforts at altering nonpolitical institutions. Hence, political movements might be viewed as social movements with a political agenda. However, virtually all social movements are political to some degree. Wilson (1973) observed:

> [While] the formation of religious movements as a response to social unrest may still be common in modern times, in general, the likelihood of social movements occurring with strong religious imagery and symbolism is declining and discontent is becoming secularized. The state has usurped the churches' role as the institution of ultimate responsibility [p. 143].

It should be added that those social movements which do not initially conceive their missions in political terms are frequently politicized by encounters with authorities or redefine their goals to include political influence (Turner & Killian, 1972).

More important, in our judgment, than the distinction between political and social movements is the distinction, commonly drawn by sociologically oriented movement theorists, between institutionalized and non-institutionalized collectivities (Blumer, 1939; Smelser, 1962; Turner & Killian, 1972; Wilkinson, 1971; Wilson, 1973). Movements are noninstitutionalized in the sense that the larger society has not yet conferred legitimacy upon them. On this basis they may be distinguished from the official actions of government agencies, business organizations, interest groups, lobbies, established religious denominations, entrenched political parties, publicly sanctioned labor unions, and the like. Movements often take place within institutions: For example, maverick Roman Catholic groups instigated many of the changes that were formalized by Vatican II, and reform-minded Democrats have pressed for changes in the Democratic Party. But these actions are not those of the institutions themselves. Not infrequently, a movement's efforts are supported by institutional authorities, but the latter's influence in these cases is informal rather than official (Gamson, 1968).

The distinction between movements and institutions would appear to be of immense theoretical significance, in that it calls attention to the disadvantaged position of movements and their ideas relative to mainstream organizations within the larger society. Most specialized theories of communication are of the "top-down" variety or at best assume the existence of symmetrical power/status relationships. Thus, we have "top-down" theories of management, child-rearing, and health communication, and we have symmetry-assuming theories of legal conflict, labor-management relations, and small group interaction. But, as Rogers (1973) observed, we have far fewer theories about how those in low-power/status positions exercise influence.

Illustrative of the differences between institutionalized and noninstitutionalized status is the history of the American labor movement. Well into the Depression era, collective bargaining was resisted by most corporations, strikes were considered illegal, and any but the most timorous labor organizations were viewed as illegitimate by political authorities and by the society at large. Although New Deal legislation conferred legitimacy on union organizations and on such practices as dues checkoffs, strikes, and formal grievance procedures, the militant ideologies and pressure tactics of large segments of organized labor remained unrespectable well into the 1940s and '50s. Today, only a few maverick labor organizations remain uninstitutionalized. The process of legitimation has taken place in large measure through tacit rather than formal bargaining (Schelling, 1963). Labor has moderated its tone, and other established institutions within society have accommodated to them.

No sharp dividing line distinguishes movements and nonmovements on the institutionalization dimension. First, while some movements are grass-roots undertakings, others are highly professionalized, and most require third-party support, including support from elites (Jenkins & Perrow, 1977; Turner & Killian, 1972; Zald & McCarthy, 1975). Interest groups such as Common Cause and the National Rifle Association might best be viewed as quasi-movements.

Second, a movement's ideas, modes of action, and core organizations may become institutionalized at different points in time. Once unpopular ideas may become acceptable within the larger society, but the organizations which promoted them may not. Or a movement that once operated outside approved channels of influence may discover that while its methods are now tolerated, its ideas are not. There is also the familiar case of movement organizations that acquire sufficient resources to engage their antagonists as power equals and that may even seize the reins of power (as Allende did in Chile) but nevertheless find that while the organization has been institutionalized, its more radical programs for change are still considered illegitimate. Although this chapter will focus on collectivities which remain uninstitutionalized on all three dimensions, it will also deal with the foregoing types of borderline cases.

That legitimacy may be conferred differentially upon a movement's ideas, modes of action, and core organizations is but one factor complicating the task of charting the course of political movements, and even of assigning them a name and a place in history. Complicating matters further is the fact that changes in ideas, modes of action, and core organizations within a movement may occur independently of each other. The same ideas may be promoted by a succession of movement organizations; the same organization may shift modes of action or add new goals. And movements may also have effects on the forms of rhetoric used by later groups (Lucas, 1976; Turner & Killian, 1972). Depending upon whether scholars are primarily interested in a movement's ideas, rhetoric, or social structure, they may chart its course very differently and even disagree as to how to divide the history of movements into "chunks." This, we believe, has been a major source of quarrels over labels and definitions by scholars (for example, Cathcart, 1972; McGee, 1980; Riches & Sillars, 1980; Sillars, 1980; Zarefsky, 1977). To Zarefsky, for example, the "War on Poverty" remained a movement even as the cause was officially taken up by the government. To sociologists wedded to the notion of movements as noninstitutionalized collectivities, the movement existed outside government in groups such as the Urban League and the National Welfare Rights Organization. To historians of ideas, the struggle to end poverty might well be regarded as a centuries-long political movement, not tied to any one organization within or outside government. So long as we can recognize the sources of ambiguity in the sociological conception of political movement and can provide reasonable grounds for distinguishing between prototypical cases and borderline cases, the construct should remain manageable enough. The distinction between institutionalized and noninstitutionalized status appears to us to remain particularly useful for purposes of rhetorical analysis, despite its complexities and ambiguities.

FUNCTIONS AND PATTERNS OF
MOVEMENT RHETORIC

The many uses of the term "rhetoric" in vogue in our culture reflect a controversy spanning two millenia over its place in social and academic pursuits

(Burke, 1969). In its noblest sense, rhetoric is the provision of good reasons, ably stated, in behalf of a cause considered just. Among its more pejorative senses are those of flattery, exhibitionism, deception, and exploitation. More neutrally, rhetoric is attempted persuasion, the use of symbols to influence beliefs and attitudes. That sense of the term encompasses its eulogistic and dyslogistic conceptions. Rhetoric is a vehicle for inducing cooperation and for giving effectiveness to truth. But its province is also, in Burke's (1969) words, "the region of the Scramble, of insult and injury, bickering, squabbling, malice and the lie" (p. 19).

Movements employ rhetoric in a variety of ways. Issued by or in the name of any good-sized movement are ideological documents, ranging from guiding manifestos to position papers on matters of transitory concern. The movement and its cause are also celebrated in action—through in-group rituals and ceremonies and by means of collective displays of power and purpose to outsiders. Leaders, too, strike a variety of postures and poses in interviews with the press, in small group meetings, in speeches to mass audiences. All of these communications—the verbal statements and the paralinguistic displays—may be considered rhetorical insofar as they are not purely expressive or purely coercive (Simons, 1976; Simons, Mechling, & Schreier, in press). The messages may at once be expressive of shared principles *and* be staged for maximum audience effect. They may combine appeals and arguments with threats of punishment or promises of reward, or simply be used to establish the credibility of a threat or promise. They may involve implicit appeals, as in acts of civil disobedience (Doolittle, 1976; Zinn, 1968). They may be designed to influence targets indirectly, as when movements attempt to convince masses of people that X is desirable so as to get them to constrain political authorities into performing Y action.

Among objectivist social scientists and historians (for example, Oberschall, 1973; Shorter & Tilly, 1974) there has been a tendency to trivialize the role of ideological rhetoric in the movement-making process: to regard it as relatively inconsequential by comparison to situational determinants, or as a mere consequence of these "out-there" factors. The dismissal of what some critics refer to derisively as the "hearts and minds" approach derives, in part, from the materialist strain in Marxian theory (Marx & Engels, 1930), from theories stressing the unplanned aspects of social change (see Sorokin, 1937-1941), from Parsonian structuralism (Parsons, 1937), and, more recently, from dissatisfaction with collective behavior theories with their implicit put-down of movements and of movement rhetoric (to be discussed). Objectivists are hardly a unified group, but they would be more prone, for example, to point to shifts in the distribution of power and wealth within French society in accounting for the French revolution than, say, to Rousseau's writings or to Danton's agitations. Similarly, the objectivist might claim that the early rhetoric of the women's liberation movement was a predictable consequence of the pill, the dishwasher, and the need for female labor during World War II.

To those who adhere to the objectivist view, the principal determinants of political movements include the following: (a) structural factors such as competition between elites, the existence of communication networks, democratization (Barnhart, 1925; Boisen, 1939; Brinton, 1952; Hobsbawm, 1952; Marshall, 1927; Parsons, 1960); (b) inadequate social control mechanisms (Smelser, 1962); (c) precipitating events such as assassinations or visible incidents of police violence (Lang & Lang, 1961; Johnson, 1966; Smelser, 1962); and, most important, (d) "strain" on the equilibrium of the social system. Depending on the theorist, "strain" is either the result of real deprivation, of relative deprivation (Dahrendorf, 1959; Oberschall, 1973; Rudé, 1962, 1964), of relative deprivation (Brinton, 1952; Gurr, 1970; Pettigrew, 1971), of status inconsistency (Lipset & Raab, 1970; Snyder & Tilly, 1972), or of abrupt reversals following prolonged periods of rising expectations and gratifications (Davies, 1962, 1969, 1974; Williams, 1957).

Most theorists assign some credence to the objectivist view, but they tend to qualify it in various ways. First, it is argued that situational factors are necessary but not sufficient to account for the rise of political movements or for the fates of the causes they advance. It is pointed out, for example, that even Marx saw movement leaders as capable of hastening or inhibiting the inevitable demise of capitalism (Wilkie, 1976); that is, they have freedom within the realm of situational necessity (Marcuse, 1964).

Second, it is argued that situational factors include not just impersonal, "scenic" events but also man-made events. Furthermore, "out-there" phenomena have meaning and take on significance only as they are perceived by a society, culture, or segment thereof (Hayes, 1976; Nesbitt, 1972).

At the other extreme from the objectivist view is an array of perspectives which, for simplicity's sake, we shall label the "interactionist position" (Blumer, 1939, 1966; Bormann, 1972, 1977; Brown & Goldin, 1973; Farrell, 1976; McGee, 1975; Mauss, 1975; Skolnick, 1969; Turner & Killian, 1972). Rather than treat situational forces as objective determinants of movements and their rhetoric, interactionists assert that the "out-there" is, itself, socially constructed by dialectical processes of labeling, issue articulation, opposition, and affirmation. In all of these activities movement rhetoric is said to play a decisive role. Hence, movements create their contexts as significantly as they are shaped by those contexts.

Turner and Killian (1972) have developed an "emergent norm" theory to explain how it is that injustices seem so self-evident after movements have helped to define them but are so difficult to identify beforehand. They also ask why some apparent problems (such as job discrimination against the physically unattractive) do not occasion collective action. In their view, the role of the outside intellectual is crucial. Emergence of a movement requires someone who is sufficiently alienated and independent-minded to perceive as problems what an aggrieved but dependent and thoroughly socialized group cannot identify. Prerequisite to success is a movement's confidence that it will be able to prevail; and here, again, outside groups are important to provide legitimation and support to the emerging movement.

In a similar way, Blumer (1971) maintains that social problems are collectively defined, not discovered. Mauss (1975), following Blumer, argued that the sociological study of social problems can be best accomplished via study of social movements. Bormann (1972, 1977) likewise suggested that perceptions of problems and their solutions begin as "fantasy themes" and "chain out" to larger and larger publics. In addition to the importance of agitation, including violence, in calling attention to social problems, Blumer (1951) pointed to the role of third parties who foresee gains for themselves by elevating the apparent importance of a problem, to the influence of adventitious happenings that shock public sensitivities, and to the willingness of "establishments" to grant a problem legitimacy.

Skolnick (1969), Edelman (1967, 1971), Simons (1972, 1976), Turner (1969), and others have asserted that processes of social construction are also at work in the development of culturally legitimated meanings for such politically sensitive terms as "order," "violence," "repression," "deviance," "protest," "persuasion," "coercion," and "symbolic speech." McGee (1975, 1977, 1980) has probably gone farthest in rejecting the objectivist position. He maintains that history has always been "executed within a rhetorical matrix" (1977). All so-called "out-there" phenomena—problems, movements, even "the people" in whose name causes are advanced—are rhetorical fictions that become "real" only insofar as believing audiences grant them that status; and they retain that status "so long as the rhetoric which defined them has force" (1975, p. 243). McGee argues, for example, that "a kind of rhetoric defines 'the people' at each stage in a 'collectivization process' of coming-to-be, being, and ceasing-to-be an objectively real entity" (1975, p. 243). Says McGee:

> "The people" may be defined rhetorically from four distinct perspectives. The seeds of collectivization stay dormant in the popular reasonings. Such dormant arguments do not define "the people" at a specific moment, but they do represent the parameters of what "the people" of that culture could possibly become. From time to time advocates organize dissociated ideological commitments into incipient political myths, visions of the collective life dangled before individuals in hope of creating a real "people." Regardless of its actual effects, such a myth contains "the people" of a particular time more surely than general ideological commitments, for it focuses on specific problems in specific situations. A third kind of rhetoric emerges when masses of persons begin to *respond* to a myth, not only by exhibiting collective behavior, but also by publicly ratifying the transaction wherein they give up control over their individual destinies for sake of a dream. At this state, a "people" actually exists in a

specific, objective way. As rhetoric defines each of the first three stages of collectivization, so there is a rhetoric of decay as society becomes quiescent and ideological commitments are once again dissociated [p. 243].

Is interactionism incompatible with situationalist explanations for observed patterns of rhetoric? McGee (1977, 1980) would have us believe that it is, but we are convinced that his objections apply only to the objectivist variant of the situationalist perspective. One need not demean the importance of rhetoric in order to assume that situation shapes rhetoric; one need only assert that rhetoric is not fully determined by situation. Even assuming that one must look to "speaker/speech/audience" relationships for evidence of situation," as McGee (1977) suggests, one must also look to situational factors (however constructed) for an understanding of the bases for rhetorical invention. Indeed, we know of few interactionists who, while emphasizing the influence of rhetoric on situation, do not also assume that situational factors impel and constrain rhetorical choice.

We will present our view of how situation shapes rhetoric later in this chapter. The important point for our purposes here, however, is that objectivists unduly minimize the influence of ideological rhetoric on the emergence and long-term success or failure of political movements.

Ideological messages set forth diagnoses (what is wrong), prognoses (what is to be done), and rationales (who should do it) (see Wilson, 1973). In Griffin's (1969) colorful language, they "identify *what equals what, what opposes what, what follows what*. [They] identify the 'heaven' of the movement as well as its 'hell'; its god or gods as well as its devils" (p. 463). Ideologies are expressed in the person as of symbolic leaders, in symbolic acts of protest and defiance, and in legends and myths about founding fathers, martyrs and sages, and cowards and traitors (Benson, 1969; Boss, 1976; Feuer, 1969; Klapp, 1964; Lane, 1962; Lanternari, 1965; McGuire, 1977; Turner & Killian, 1972; Weber, 1949; Windt, 1973). Some statements of ideology are highly elaborated (for example, *Das Kapital;* others are simplified for mass consumption (such as *The Communist Manifesto*); some are reduced to catchwords in leaflets, posters, chants, and songs (Denisoff, 1968; Rush & Denisoff, 1971). Full-blown ideological statements imply an epistemology, an ethic, and a theory of the nature of man (Lane, 1962). They also contain a revisionist history, a morally toned interpretation of present conditions, and an account of the future in which the movement is said to play an important role (Turner & Killian, 1972).

Statements of ideology are used to mold and reinforce the views of constituents, to influence "outsiders," and to protect the movement against attack (Gurr, 1970; Heberle, 1951; Lang & Lang, 1961; Smelser, 1962; Toch, 1965; Turner & Killian, 1972). Ideological messages perform these rhetorical functions by providing rationales for movements' goals and tactics; by offering "correct" and understandable interpretations of past, present, and future; by delegitimizing competing ideologies; by offering defenses against counterarguments; and by providing "immunizing" rationales for potentially embarrassing situations. For some movements ideological statements translate self-interest into an ideal, equating the movement's interests with the interests of the larger society. For other movements promotion of the collectivity's ideology is an end in itself.

Pressure tactics also occupy an important role in the affairs of political movements. At any given time and place, movement activists select from a *repertoire* of collective actions that is relatively small compared to the total number of options theoretically available (Tilly, 1979). Guiding the selection of pressure tactics, apparently, are the world views of the activists, including their theories about what "works" (Bormann, 1969, 1972, 1977); patterns of repression in the world to which the actor belongs (Tilly, 1979); and traditions and customs about appropriate action within the larger culture (Jamieson, 1973, 1975; Tilly, 1979). Repertoires are flexible, as Tilly (1979) observed from his study of contentious events in England and the United States:

> The idea of a repertoire implies that the standard forms are learned, limited in number and scope, slowly changing and peculiarly adapted to their settings. Pressed by a grievance, interest or aspiration and confronted with an opportunity to act, groups of people who have the capacity to act collectively choose among the forms of action in their limited repertoire. The choice is not always cool or premeditated; vigilantes sometimes grab their guns and march off on the spur of the moment, while angry women make food riots. Nor are the performances necessarily frozen, regimented and stereotypical; demonstrators against the Stamp Act and the arrival of dutied tea often invented new ways of broadcasting their message and regularly responded to unanticipated contingencies by improvising. The repertoire is the repertoire of jazz or commedia dell-arte rather than of grand opera or Shakespearean drama. Nevertheless, a limited repertoire sets serious constraints on when, where and how effectively a group of actors can act [p. 9].

Patterns of movement rhetoric may be identified at varying levels of abstraction. Among studies of patterns spanning particular movements, Fireman and Gamson (1979) identified four stock arguments for movement participation common to all movements: necessity, opportunity, solidarity, and responsibility. Shubs (Note 1) content analyzed some 2000 speeches, pamphlets, and other documents issued just prior to the American Revolution (1760-1776) and to the achievement of independence in India (1925-1945). He found that frequent and increasing use was made by both movements of group inclusion symbols such as "fraternity" and "comrade"; "noble affiliation" symbols such as "nation" and "Gandhi" that linked the movement to strongly held norms; and goal symbols such as "peaceful assembly" and "unity." Kanter (1968) identified commitment mechanisms differentiating 9 long-lasting and 21 short-lived utopian communities. They included sacrifice and investment mechanisms, renunciation of outside ties, regularized group contact, communistic sharing, surrender of individualized prerogatives, and self-mortification. Lasky (1976) found structural and metaphoric similarities in the prophetic writings of modern-day utopian revolutionaries and early millenarians. Leahy and Mazur (1978) found great similarities in use of expert testimony, statistical interpretations, and recruitment appeals among movements opposed to fluoridation, abortion, and nuclear power.

Numerous efforts have been made to classify the rhetoric of protest movements on a continuum from moderate to militant (Bowers & Ochs, 1971; Cathcart, 1980; Deutsch, 1969; Lipsky, 1968; Oppenheimer & Lakey, 1964; Specht, 1969). Classifications of this kind tend to confound verbal and nonverbal behaviors, however. Clarity is gained, we believe, by conceiving of the moderate-to-militant continuum as having *ideological* and *behavioral* subdimensions. These dimensions, it is assumed, are usually correlated.

Simons (1976) distinguished between moderate and militants on the ideological subdimension as follows:

> In general, the militant tends to express greater degrees of dissatisfaction. Whereas the moderate tends to ask "how" questions, the militant asks "whether" questions. Whereas the moderate sees "inefficiencies" in existing practices, the militant sees "inequities." Whereas the moderate might regard authority figures as "misguided" though "legitimate," the militant would tend to regard these figures as "willfully self-serving" and "illegitimate." Whereas both may pay homage to law, the militant is more apt to derogate man-made laws in the name of "higher" laws. Moreover, militants may extend the scope of their "devil" to ordinary citizens, whereas the moderate tends to soft-pedal any differences with the citizenry [pp. 279-280].

The behavioral subdimension concerns tactics used to exert pressure on adversaries. Moderate tactics are coactive or institutionally legitimized (Simons, 1976). They include litigation, lobbying, petitioning, marching, and peaceful picketing. At the other extreme are politically motivated acts of violence such as hijackings, kidnappings, rioting, assassinations, and armed insurrections. Between these behavioral extremes are nonviolent forms of agitation that vary in degree of militancy depending on the manner in which they are played out. They include acts of noncooperation such as boycotts, strikes, and tax refusals and acts of harassment and obstruction such as sit-ins, traffic tie-ups, and building occupations.

The clearest instances of militant movements are those which combine extreme dissatisfaction with the existing system with a vision of a perfect order and a commitment to armed struggle. The clearest instances of moderate movements are those which employ pure persuasion for the attainment of reformist goals. Each is, of course, indictable by the logic of the other. Lasky (1976) has drawn the contrast well:

> Men believe they are making the history that history has made for them. The reformer, in the eyes of the militant, is the despicable betrayer of the true cause. He plasters and refuses to pull down. He tinkers and patches. He trims instead of cutting to the roots. He reconsiders when he should revolt. He compromises. He concedes. He hesitates and temporizes. He prefers prudence to passion, and caution to audacity. He feels safe with the old and uneasy with the new.
>
> The revolutionary, in the eyes of the moderate, is the crazed subverter of a fragile social order. He comes to destroy. He adores the fire and longs for the ashes. He hears the sky thundering and the rumble of the earth. His demands can never be fulfilled, and he presses on ruthlessly for the next radical phase. There is never an end. His extremism is in permanence [p. 86].

Not all movement organizations are demonstrably moderate or militant. Of the civil rights groups of the 1960s, some, like Martin Luther King's Southern Christian Leadership Conference, manifested ideologies and pressure tactics *intermediate* between those of the clearly moderate NAACP and the decidedly militant Black Panther Party. Though King and his followers questioned the legitimacy of "Jim Crow" laws, they did so in a spirit of agapé love. And though they repeatedly violated these laws, they practiced civil disobedience in the "classic" manner by acceding to the judgments of the courts (Scott & Brockriede, 1969; Zinn, 1968). Other groups, such as Andrew Young's Urban League, were goaded by "Black Power" activists into becoming more strident in their ideological pronouncements, but they remained behaviorally moderate. Still other civil rights groups employed a wide range of pressure tactics or were ideologically factionalized.

The moderate-militant continuum with its two subdimensions appears to capture well the dominant qualities of rhetoric associated with a great many change-oriented movements. There are, however, some movement activists for whom the militancy continuum is less salient. We label them "expressivist."

By contrast to militants and moderates, expressivists tend to see "the devil" as residing within all of us. Like militants, they reject many of society's institutionalized structures and mores. But, whereas militants seek to change institutions directly, expressivists believe that, just as institutions are people-created, so they can only be changed by changes in people (Simons, 1976). Common in the ideologies of movements for personal transformation are the themes of primitive man as "noble savage," of sin and personal responsibility, and of possible self-improvement and enlightenment (Turner & Killian, 1972).

Moreover, whereas militants and moderates are not averse to employing manipulative strategems, expressivists reject manipulation as contrary to their values. All movement groups "shoot from the hip" at times, but for expressivists naturalness and directness are matters of principle. Indeed, some feminists have characterized both moderate and militant approaches as "masculinized" forms of manipulation which are antithetical to everything they believe in. Hence, says Campbell (1973), they are led oxymoronically to employ "anti-rhetorical" forms of rhetoric in an effort to blend the personal and the political. These include personal testaments in consciousness-raising groups and displays of alternative lifestyles.

As with moderates and militants, one may expect of expressivists that their behaviors will generally correspond with their ideologies. In some cases they may perceive themselves ideologically compelled to lash out at society through modes of expression which, by most standards, would be viewed as offensive and counterproductive. Thus, as Windt (1972) noted, both the Yippies of the 1960s and the Cynics of ancient Greece were driven to the use of the diatribe. Like the Jerry Rubins and Abbie Hoffmans of the sixties, the Cynics "were critics of convention, gadflies of popular culture, censors of men who did not act on their beliefs" (p. 6). Rejecting laws, civil authorities, political institutions, and social mores, the Cynics refused to engage in conventional modes of dialogue or debate lest their moral principles be compromised. Hence they engaged in the diatribe as a last resort.

EXPLAINING PATTERNS OF RHETORIC: THE QUESTION OF RATIONALITY

The foregoing classification of general patterns of movement rhetoric masks the disorder and complexity one finds on examining the day-to-day rhetoric of particular movements. Indeed, the rhetoric of particular movements often appears anomalous and sometimes self-defeating. Some movements seem excessively violent; others fall victim to opposing interests by speaking loudly and carrying a small stick. Often, too, movements project an air of unreality. Leaders are deified and the cause sanctified. History is bent to the needs of ideology. Evils are oversimplified and personalized. The very authorities movement leaders ultimately seek to influence are labeled as devils or fools or puppets. And generalized "if-only" beliefs are used to justify magical solutions to political problems (Smelser, 1962). Having foisted deceptions on the general public, movement enthusiasts frequently come to believe their own rhetoric, and the movement is torn asunder when members come to realize that their leaders are not saints, or that not all outsiders are bad or mad, or that evils cannot be wished away by strident symbolic acts or empty threats.

The Collective Behavior Tradition

To the "old" school of collective behavior theorists such as Neil Smelser (1962) and Eric Hoffer (1951), these anomalous characteristics of movement rhetoric were prima facie evidence of irrationality. They were fortified in their view by system-oriented assumptions about conflict and social change (Simons, 1972). Although a long activist tradition had existed within sociology, by the mid-twentieth century most theorists tended to identify with the interests of existing social systems rather than with insurgents seeking collectively to effect basic changes in those systems (Friedrichs, 1970). By the pluralist interpretation, orderly change in Western democracies was assumed to take place within the system and by noncoercive means (Dahl, 1967). Conflicts in general were seen as unhealthy deviations from an otherwise normal state of equilibrium (Parsons, 1937). Thus, from this perspective, movements were unnecessary and dysfunctional. Smelser (1962) linked movements with crazes, hostile outbursts, and other such forms of irrational collective behavior. Accented by the perspective were crowd polarization, the lure of empty slogans and meaningless rituals, the magic of social contagion, and the unthinking, self-destructive impulsiveness of gullible masses. In the writings of Eric Hoffer (1951), protest leaders were depicted as demagogues, their followers dismissed as mesmerized fools, and their causes psychologized out of existence. Both leaders and followers were assumed to suffer from characterological defects.

To rhetoricians rooted in the Greco-Roman rhetorical tradition, the system-oriented perspectives of writers such as Smelser seemed highly compatible. Black (1980) noted that Greek society scarcely knew the concept of ideology, let alone the concept of fanatical belief. Nor, as he pointed out, could it comprehend—let alone approve—agitation, rebellion, or other forms of uninstitutionalized conflict as we know them today. As Booth (1971) observed, Aristotle's *Rhetoric*, while appropriate for "insiders" with shared values, was considerably less applicable to those seeking to penetrate "totally hostile circles." Well into the sixties, rhetoricians displayed an anticonflict, pro-"establishment" bias—manifested, for example, in the assumption that friendly, coactive forms of persuasion, useful in academic discussions or legislative debates, were equally appropriate in conflicts with repressive, recalcitrant elites (Simons, 1972).

Problem-Centered Perspectives

Within the past two decades collective behavior theory has been subjected to attack on several fronts. To many observers the causes advanced by the protestors of the sixties seemed warranted enough, and their actions likewise seemed justified in terms of their ends and circumstances. Thus, for example, Scott and Smith (1969) questioned whether the traditionally prescribed ethic of reason, civility, and decorum did not serve Establishments rather than justice.

Their arguments were reinforced by numerous "violence" studies which challenged pluralist images of democratic politics in America (Gamson, 1975; Skolnick, 1969; U.S. Riot Commission, 1968; Walker, 1968).

Also called into question by the protests of the period were stereotypes about the demographic characteristics of movement activists and about the dynamics of movement participation. Were the protestors drawn from the rabble of society, as Hoffer had suggested? Numerous studies of white and black activists provided evidence that they tended to be more affluent, better educated, and less anomic than their nonactivist counterparts (Fogelson & Hill, 1968; Hundley, 1970; Laue, 1965; Lipset & Raab, 1970). Were they mesmerized by their leaders or caught up by social contagion? Aerial photographs showed few protestors even listening to their leaders at mass rallies; most were clustered in small groups (Milgram & Toch, 1969). Were they maladjusted? Once more, clinical evidence seemed to undermine this stereotype (Keniston, 1968).

Nor were these findings limited to left-oriented activists of the sixties and early seventies. Contrary to what had previously been thought, for example, the rank and file of leading far-right groups were found to include large members of professionals, small businessmen, and other relatively affluent persons (Crain, 1969; Rogin, 1967; Wolfinger, 1964). Leaders of the American, French, and Russian revolutions have also been disproportionately affluent and well educated (Brinton, 1952; Oberschall, 1973; Palmer, 1959). Most "successful" revolutionary leaders, according to another study, have also demonstrated considerable flexibility and cognitive complexity (Suedfeld & Rank, 1976).

Since the mid-sixties, movement theorists have tended to be more problem-centered and actor-oriented; that is, they have focused on the problems of movement leaders rather than on the problems of society in coping with them (Simons, 1972). Rather than seeking to explain anomalous patterns of movement rhetoric in terms of the aberrant personality traits or characterological defects of movement activists, they have emphasized in their accounts the perils of movement-made constraints and the extraordinary dilemmas which movement leaders confront. Thus, they have suggested, if movements spoke loudly, it might be because that was the only way they could be heard. If they carried a small stick, perhaps this was because they generally lacked the resources to carry a big stick. If movement activists deceived others, perhaps it was because these others were not only hostile to the cause but immensely more powerful. If they sometimes believed their own deceptions, it might be because the myths they accepted were necessary to secure some degree of organizational discipline and social cohesion.

Particularly prominent in recent years has been the resource management (RM) perspective (Coleman, 1957; Fireman & Gamson, 1979; Gamson, 1975; Jenkins & Perrow, 1977; Lipsky, 1968; McCarthy & Zald, 1973, 1977; Oberschall, 1973; Snyder & Kelly, 1979; Tilly, 1973, 1975, 1979; Tilly, Tilly, & Tilly, 1975; Wilson, 1973). RM theorists tend to stress continuities between movement-making and the management of institutionalized collectivities (Marx & Wood, 1975). Of central importance to both is the acquisition and effective deployment of resources; that is, of that which has value or utility. While acknowledging that some movement activists behave self-destructively, RM theorists remind us that movements own no patent on rhetorical incompetence. Most movement leaders are alleged to be rational—or at least no less rational than the heads of business organizations or government agencies. The differences in their behavior lie essentially in the situations they confront. Indeed, some RM theorists so emphasize rationality as to minimize the importance to movements of ideological concerns (Oberschall, 1973). Like the heads of institutionalized collectivities, movement leaders are assumed to base resource allocation decisions on calculations of risk-reward ratios. As Oberschall (1973) argued:

> The very real theoretical gain achieved is that a theory of mobilization of opposition and conflict groups, social and mass movements, of protest behavior and collective political action, is essentially the same as the theory of mobilization for economic interest groups, and that the simple assumption of rationality in economic theory is sufficient in this theoretical effort. Thus, one need not make assumptions about individual motivation based on alienation or psychopathology, and a single theory spans the entire range of political and social movements, regardless of whether they are designated as extremist, leftist, rightist, centrist, or mass movements by their supporters and detractors [p. 118].

Finally, RM theorists address themselves to many of the practical concerns of movement activists (McCarthy & Zald, 1977). Parsonian structural-functionalism has been turned inward from a concern with how society could manage the problems of goal-attainment, integration, adaptation, and pattern maintenance to a concern with how movements wrestled with these same problems (Wilson, 1973). Thus, for example, McCarthy and Zald (1977) addressed the question of how movements might best integrate "conscience constituents" and "beneficiary constituents." Lipsky (1968) concerned himself with the problem of simultaneous adaptation to insiders, the mass media, elite representatives, opposition groups, and the general public. Gamson (1975) compared strategies of influence by 53 protest organizations, selected on an equal probability basis from a larger list of 467 such groups that were operative in the United States from 1800 to 1945.

THE REQUIREMENTS-PROBLEMS-
STRATEGIES APPROACH

Elsewhere we have attempted to identify and account for patterns of movement rhetoric in terms of a "requirements-problems-strategies" (RPS) approach (Simons, 1970; 1976; Simons et al., in press). Ours is a framework for analysis rather than a formal theory, one designed to accommodate the diverse perspec-

tives offered by objectivists and interactionists, while at the same time incorporating the research findings and insights provided by problem-centered theorists. With RM theorists we assume that most activists are rhetorically competent
in the sense of adapting their rhetoric appropriately to their ends and circumstances. As indicated earlier, however, we depart from those RM theorists who
minimize the importance of ideology. Indeed, we regard as a vital resource such
legitimacy as might be achieved through ideological rhetoric.

The broad outlines of our approach are as follows. At a macroscopic level we
identify general rhetorical requirements incumbent upon leaders of all collectivities, general problems stemming from predictable cross-pressures and constraints,
and general patterns of rhetoric (that is, strategies) designed to fulfill requirements in the face of cross-pressures and constraints. At a microscopic level, at
which we seek to understand patterns peculiar to a given movement or to an
event in the life of a movement, we again focus on problems. Any given
situation, we argue, will present itself as a configuration of conflicting rhetorical
requirements constituting competing demands on the leader. The tactics
employed to resolve or reduce problems will at best reflect tradeoffs among
competing demands, and they will thus generate new problems. The situation at
any given point will not fully determine rhetorical choice, but it will restrict the
strategically appropriate options available to the leader. Hence, while the rhetoric of the movement will not be fully predictable from a knowledge of
situation, a "reading" of the situation should render it more explicable.

General Requirements

Regardless of their purpose, membership, or structure, all human collectivities
must attract, maintain, and mold personnel and other resources; all must secure
adoption of their product or service; all must react to responses by the larger
structures of which they are a part (Barnard, 1938; Merton, 1968). Political
movements are in no way exempt from these requirements (Oberschall, 1973;
Turner & Killian, 1972). Although the agendas of political movements range
widely from change (or resistance to change) in authorities, laws, or law
enforcement to sweeping restructurings of political values and institutional
arrangements (Gamson, 1968), all are required to (a) mobilize human and
material resources from within the movement, (b) exert influence on outsiders,
and (c) resist efforts at counterinfluence. The survival and effectiveness of any
movement are dependent upon adherence to its program, loyalty to its leadership, a collective willingness and capacity to work, energy mobilization, and
member satisfaction. Movement organizations must also generate support from
those outside the movement who can provide funds, information, media access,
or direct pressure on authorities. Finally, efforts must be made to counter or
contain opposition groups or others who may be hostile to the movement's
cause.

Political movements face particular complications in regard to these requirements. As a consequence, the management of movement organizations is uniquely complex. Simons (1970) argued:

> Movements are severely restricted from fulfilling these requirements by dint of their informal compositions and their positions in relation to the larger society. By comparison to the heads of most formal organizations, the leaders of movements can expect minimal internal control and maximal external resistance. Whereas business corporations may induce productivity through tangible rewards and punishments, movements as voluntary collectivities must rely on ideological and social commitments from their members. Existing outside the larger society's conceptions of justice and reality, moreover, movements threaten and are threatened by the society's sanctions and taboos: its laws, its maxims, its customs governing manners, decorum, and taste, its insignia of authority, etc.
>
> Although organizational efficiency and adaptation to pressures from the external system are clearly prerequisite to promotion of a movement's ideology, in other respects the various internal and external requirements of a movement are incompatible. *Shorn of the controls that characterize formal organizations, yet required to perform the same internal functions, harassed from without, yet obligated to adapt to the external system, the leader of a movement must constantly balance inherently conflicting demands on his position and on the movement he represents* [p. 4].

Cross-Pressures

Although internal mobilization, external influence, and adaptation to counterinfluences are clearly prerequisite to accomplishment of a movement's goals, in other respects the various internal and external requirements of a movement are incompatible. As a consequence, movement leaders must cope rhetorically with a predictable set of problems.

1. *The moral versus the political.* Movements must balance the need for power against the need for value purity. To deal with pressures from the external system, movements may lose sight of their values and become preoccupied with power for its own sake. Careful, by contrast, to remain consistent with their values, they may foresake those pressure tactics which are necessary to secure implementation of programmatic goals (Griffin, 1969; Turner & Killian, 1972).

2. *Reality versus myth.* Movements must assess realistically the problems they confront as well as their resources available for overcoming them. Yet movements are also dependent on myths of purity, power, and solidarity which may be quite at variance with realistic assessments.

3. *Genuineness versus manipulativeness.* Leaders of political movements face discrepancies between role expectations and role definitions. Expected to be

sincere and spontaneous, they must nevertheless handle dilemmas with consummate manipulative skill.

4. *Membership needs versus organizational cohesion.* An energized membership is the strength of any movement and its *esprit de corps* is essential to goal implementation. Yet morale cannot be secured through abdications of leadership. Members may feel the need to participate in decision-making, to undertake pet projects on their own initiatives, to put down leaders or other followers; to obstruct meetings by socializing, or to disobey directives. The leadership cannot ignore these needs; yet it cannot accede to all of them, either.

5. *Coherence versus flexibility.* The various pronouncements and activities of the movement must appear to form a coherent whole. What is said to insiders must dovetail with what is said to outsiders. What is said must square with what is done. Yet movements must also adapt their rhetoric to different audiences, shift positions opportunistically, and engage in actions that may be at variance with their earlier pronouncements.

6. *Cooperativeness versus combativeness.* As suggested earlier, movement leaders have interests in common with other leaders, with third parties capable of providing resource support, and even with most antagonists. Yet there is reason to be suspicious of these others as well and to exploit divisions among them.

Strategies

The RPS approach uses as the "test" of a movement leader his or her capacity to devise strategies that will resolve rhetorical problems and thus fulfill rhetorical requirements. It is a test on which we expect few movement leaders will receive perfect grades.

Earlier in this chapter we described a continuum of rhetorical strategies bounded by moderate rhetoric on the one hand and militant rhetoric on the other. Each strategy offers unique advantages and disadvantages. Militant tactics confer visibility on a movement; moderate tactics gain entry into decision centers. Militant supporters are more easily energized; moderate supporters are more easily controlled. Militants tend to be more effective at pressuring "power vulnerables," those who have power/status/wealth to lose, who cannot run, and who cannot easily retaliate. Militants tend to be more effective with "power invulnerables," those at the opposite extremes on these three variables. Finally, for different reasons, militants and moderates must both be ambivalent about successes and failures (Simons, 1970).

Based on our assumption of rationality, we predict that most movement leaders will deploy their resources appropriately in threading their way through the web of conflicting demands on their positions. The prediction is by no means confirmed in all studies (Simons et al., in press). But there is evidence that most movements seek a balance between militancy and moderateness. Consistent with prescriptions offered by theorists and practitioners, they tend to eschew violence or to combine it with reasoned appeals (Gamson, 1975). More or less consciously, a hierarchy of goals is articulated, from the easily attainable to the unattainable, and from the concrete to the ambiguous (Ash, 1972; Greer, 1949; Turner & Killian, 1972). There tends, too, to be some degree of synchronization among the militant and moderate organizations or factions within many movements (Ash, 1972). Most movements apply varied pressure on adversaries, especially capitalizing on gaffes or hypocritical acts by the opposition (see Gamson, 1975). Divisions among elite groups are exploited, and antagonism toward personalized targets by mass publics is promoted (Ash, 1972; Lucas, 1976). At the same time, movements seek support from third parties (Gamson, 1975), though not always with the degree of consistency recommended by practical theorists (Deutsch, 1969; McCarthy & Zald, 1973).

Yet rhetorical competency by no means assures long-term success. Compelled as they are to adapt and justify tactics both internally and externally, movement leaders often find that their rhetoric compounds old problems or introduces new ones. Not uncommonly, for example, pressure tactics employed as a result of the problem of illegitimacy reinforce images of illegitimacy held by political authorities and the general public. Moreover, the often desperate need for resources may require that they forge unholy alliances, stoop to ethically questionable tactics that alienate even their own followers, or sacrifice long-term objectives for short-term gains.

The nearly insoluble nature of some dilemmas is illustrated in two movement case studies of recent vintage, Bromley and Shupe's (1979) on the "Moonies," and Gitlin's (1980) study of SDS and the mass media. Both SDS in the late sixties and the "Moonies" in the early seventies suddenly found themselves the objects of considerable publicity by the mass media. Both movements welcomed the attention they initially received. Indeed, they would have found it nearly impossible to promote their goals without media publicity, yet both were ultimately damaged by adverse publicity. As Gitlin (1980) observed, the celebrity status accorded movement leaders often becomes transformed into notoriety; movements become overly dependent on the media to carry their message; and, worse still, movements come to define themselves almost exclusively in terms of images of them provided by the media. Not uncommonly, as in the SDS case, they are projected into the limelight before they have developed a sufficiently broad social base, allow the media to define their goals and determine their leaders, commit themselves prematurely to specific society-wide goals, and spout revolutionary rhetoric in nonrevolutionary situations. By most standards the SDS leadership was rhetorically sophisticated (Bowers & Ochs, 1971; Griffin, 1964); yet they were unable to reconcile the contradictions attendant upon the need for publicity and the need to define their goals and mobilize support on their own terms.

If the constraints and cross-pressures confronting movement leaders are extraordinary, so, too, is the potential for rhetorical invention in the face of problems. Movement leaders are forever inventing rhetorical rationales for structures already in place, as when leaders of the Unification Church endowed their serendipitously discovered tactic of street solicitations with theological significance after it had proved financially successful (Bromley & Shupe, 1979).

Several studies utilizing the RPS framework have focused on justificatory rhetoric of this kind. Simons, Chesebro, and Orr (1973) assessed the rhetorical alternatives available to left-oriented movement leaders in the wake of the McGovern candidacy in 1972. Shive (Note 2) examined the means by which Mao Tse-tung presented a congruent image of his movement to multiple audiences at a time when he was forced to align with the Kuomintang in a United Front against the Japanese invaders. Reynolds (Note 3) investigated efforts by "liberation" theologists in Latin America to reconcile radical Marxism with their own positions in the Church. Jablonski (1980) examined pastoral letters by American bishops following Vatican II to determine how they reconciled conflicting rhetorical requirements.

SUMMARY AND CONCLUSIONS

The concern of this review has been with patterns of rhetoric by political movements and explanations for those patterns. Covered, if only briefly, have been objectivist and interactionist perspectives on the relationship between rhetoric and situation, collective behavior theories, resource management theories, and our own RPS approach. Excluded or barely mentioned, unfortunately, have been life-cycle theories (for example, Griffin, 1969), social theories in the Marxist tradition (see Habermas, 1975; Debray, 1967), critical methods (see Bormann, 1972), comparative studies of effects (for example, Gamson, 1975), important essays on the ethics of movement rhetoric (such as Haiman, 1967), and all but a few of the hundreds of case studies of movement rhetoric that have been contributed by rhetoricians and social scientists. A more comprehensive synthesis and commentary is provided in Simons et al. (in press).

Amid recent controversies over definitional issues among rhetoricians (for example, Sillars, 1980), we have argued for preserving the widely employed sociological conception of movements (whether labeled "social" or "political") as sustained efforts in behalf of a cause by noninstitutionalized collectivities. Political movements were defined as social movements with a political agenda, a definition which, admittedly, excludes very few social movements.

Three questions about the ideological rhetoric of political movements have surfaced periodically in this review: whether it is consequential or unimportant, whether it is generally rational or irrational, whether it is creative or merely reflective of situational influences. In their well-evidenced critiques of system-oriented collective behavior theories, resource management theorists such as Oberschall (1973) have tended to minimize the importance of ideological rhetoric and to portray movement leaders almost as though they were businessmen in disguise. We have sought a synthesis between the thesis of collective behavior theory and the antithesis of resource management theory. Movement leaders may be presumed to be no less rational than leaders of established institutions. But the situations they confront, as well as their strong commitments to principles, fairly dictate heavy reliance on ideological appeals and accounts. They have, after all, few material selective incentives to offer potential recruits, and few chips with which to bargain with political authorities.

Moreover, ideological rhetoric need not be viewed as irrational. Admittedly, there are ambiguities in conventional conceptions of the notion of ideology, and there is considerable variation in ideological rhetorics. On one hand, there is the sense of ideologists as influenced by passions, cognitively simple, unrealistic, perhaps unscientific. On the other hand, there is the sense of ideologists as principled, altruistic, and at least clever in their constructions of integrated systems of belief. Our own view regards ideological *messages* by movement leaders (as opposed to the belief systems themselves) as both expressive *and* rhetorical, largely reflective of genuine commitments and strategically adapted to audiences (that is, rational in the means-ends sense of the term). With the interactionists reviewed here, we see ideological rhetoric as performing indispensable functions for movements in helping activists to interpret the situations they confront and to justify their use of pressure tactics.

Our position in the debate over the relationship between rhetoric and situation follows from the foregoing comments. As a way of preserving and dialectically encompassing the partial truths offered by objectivists and interactionists, we have argued that movement leaders are impelled and constrained by situational factors—some factors more determinative of choice than others—but that they are free to innovate within the limits imposed by situational constraints.

The view of political movements as largely voluntary, noninstitutionalized collectivities operating at a resource disadvantage relative to those they oppose figures prominently in our own RPS approach. But for the "expressivist" alternative (reviewed briefly here), movement leaders display patterns of verbal and nonverbal rhetoric ranging on a continuum from moderate to militant. The strategies and tactics they employ are designed to fulfill rhetorical requirements not unlike those incumbent upon the leaders of established institutions. However, they can expect minimal internal control and maximal external resistance. Moreover, the choices they make in light of these problems inevitably create new problems in a never-ending cycle.

We began this review by suggesting that the study of movements was not everyone's cup of borscht. For those undeterred by the "warning on the package," we urge that they immerse themselves in case studies of movement rhetoric that will at once contribute significantly to the historical record and also serve as exemplars of theoretically interesting types of movement rhetoric. Studies of this kind might properly be called "socio-rhetorical" (Mechling, Note 4). They draw on social-scientific theory and research in constructing categories and in identifying situational influences while employing rhetorical constructs and methods in analyzing discourse and symbolic actions of the movements under investigation.

There is precious little that can be said reliably about political movements as a whole; they are simply too diverse. But distinct genres of movement rhetoric can emerge from studies of particular types of movements. Generalizations can be on the order of middle-level propositions of the kind suggested by Merton (1968).

An example of what we mean is provided by Mechling's (Note 4) study of the free clinic organizations which emerged from the counterculture of the 1960s. Mechling recognized the free clinics as representative of a type of movement organization which she called the "Counter-Institutional Movement Organization" (CIMO). Other examples of CIMOs include alternative schools, gay churches, and the early food cooperatives. CIMOs differ from most protest organizations in providing a tangible service to a group perceived to be wrongfully denied those services by the institutions which the movement opposes. The provision of services is intended partly as a model of reformation of the offending institution.

As in all of the studies utilizing the RPS approach, Mechling focused on patterns of rhetoric following from conflicting rhetorical requirements. Inherent in all CIMOs, she contended, is a conflict between their ideological requirements and their service requirements. In the face of this conflict, she maintained, CIMOs will institutionalize and deradicalize at a faster pace than most protest movement organizations. First, the service function requires resources incompatible with being "counter to." Once resources have been invested in services, there is considerable and quite visible loss should these investments be abandoned. By contrast, antiinstitutional stances are relatively easy to "write off." Second, the services rendered may be valued by established sectors of the external system. The CIMO may thus be positively reinforced for provision of these services. Third, the immediacy of the service gives it a sense of preeminence. The service function is adopted as a response to a felt need. To cease meeting that need is counter to the ideological core of the collectivity. Thus, while the service function is a component of the antiinstitutional stance, the antiinstitutional stance is not necessary to the service function.

Of interest to Mechling was the relationship between patterns of rhetoric and degree of institutionalization for any given free clinic organization. An index was developed for distinguishing among noninstitutionalized, partially institutionalized, and fully institutionalized stages of development. Onto these stages she charted rhetorics of Division, Amelioration, and Respectability. These correspond, in Burkean (1945, 1959, 1969) terms, to frames of rejection, transition, and acceptance.

Particularly interesting was the rhetoric of the partially institutionalized stage, for it was at this stage that the conflicts between the CIMO's antiinstitutional stance and its service commitments were most visible. Mechling hypothesized that the rhetoric at this stage would be marked by highly ambiguous figures of speech, deniable messages, suppressed premises, qualified generalizations, messages highly tailored to particular audiences, and rationalizations for uncertainty and apparent inconsistency. While her data did not permit tests of all these hypotheses, in general it appeared that the rhetoric of the free clinic organizations matched their degree of institutionalization.

Whatever the political consequences of the movements of the sixties and seventies, it seems clear from the foregoing review that they have generated a great deal of useful theory and research. We think it especially important that scholars have challenged irrationalist stereotypes of movement activists and their rhetoric that had been forged from an earlier generation's representative exemplars. Could it be, however, that movement scholars were simply shifting with the political winds? Will they change their tune once again as they examine the movements of the 1980s, many of them reflective (thus far, at least) of conservative, antiintellectual doctrines? It will be interesting to survey the scholarly literature a decade hence.

REFERENCE NOTES

1. Shubs, P. *Revolutionary symbology: Comparative case studies of American and Indian independence movements.* Paper presented at the American Political Science Association annual meeting, New York, 1968.
2. Shive, G. *Mao tse-tung and the anti-Japanese united front: A rhetorical analysis of a mixed-motive conflict.* Unpublished Ph.D. dissertation, Temple University, 1978.
3. Reynolds, K. *Rhetorical requirements, problems and strategies of Catholic clerical revolutionaries in Latin America.* Unpublished paper, Temple University, 1980.
4. Mechling, E. W. *From paradox to parody: A socio-rhetorical theory of counter-institutional movement organizations, applied to the free clinic movement.* Unpublished Ph.D. dissertation, Temple University, 1979.

REFERENCES

Aberle, D. *The peyote religion among the Navaho.* Chicago: AVC, 1966.
Ash, R. *Social movements in America.* Chicago: Markham, 1972.
Barnard, C. *The functions of the executive.* Cambridge: Harvard University Press, 1938.
Barnhart, J. D. Rainfall and the populist party in Nebraska. *American Political Science Review,* 1925, *19,* 527-540.
Benson, J. A. James Otis and the "Writs of Assistance" speech—Fact and fiction. *Southern Speech Journal,* 1969, *34,* 256-263.
Black, E. The mutability of rhetoric. In E. E. White (Ed.), *Rhetoric in transition: Studies in the nature and uses of rhetoric.* University Park: Pennsylvania State University Press, 1980.

Blumer, H. Collective behavior. In R. E. Parks (Ed.), *An outline of the principles of sociology.* New York: Barnes and Noble, 1939.

Blumer, H. Sociological implications of the thought of George Herbert Mead. *American Journal of Sociology,* 1966, *71,* 535-544.

Blumer, H. Social problems as collective behavior. *Social Problems,* 1971, *18,* 298-305.

Boisen, A. T. Economic distress and religious experience: A study of the Holy Rollers. *Psychiatry,* 1939, *2,* 185-194.

Booth, W. C. The scope of rhetoric today: A polemical excursion. In L. F. Bitzer & E. Black (Eds.), *The prospect of rhetoric.* Englewood Cliffs, NJ: Prentice-Hall, 1971.

Bormann, E. G. *Discussion and group methods: Theory and practice.* New York: Harper & Row, 1969.

Bormann, E. G. Fantasy and rhetorical vision: The rhetorical criticism of social reality. *Quarterly Journal of Speech,* 1972, *58,* 396-407.

Bormann, E. G. Fetching good out of evil: A rhetorical use of calamity. *Quarterly Journal of Speech,* 1977, *63,* 130-139.

Boss, G. P. Essential attributes of the concept of charisma. *Southern Speech Communication Journal,* 1976, *41,* 300-313.

Bowers, J. W., & Ochs, D. J. *The rhetoric of agitation and control.* Reading, MA: Addison-Wesley, 1971.

Brinton, C. C. *The anatomy of revolution.* New York: Vintage, 1952.

Bromley, D. G., & Shupe, A. D. *"Moonies" in America: Cult, church and crusade.* Beverly Hills, CA: Sage, 1979.

Brown, M., & Goldin, A. *Collective behavior: A review and reinterpretation of the literature.* Santa Monica, CA: Goodyear, 1973.

Burke, K. *A grammar of motives.* New York: Prentice-Hall, 1945.

Burke, K. *Attitudes toward history.* Los Altos, CA: Hermes, 1959.

Burke, K. *A rhetoric of motives.* Berkeley: University of California Press, 1969.

Campbell, K. K. The rhetoric of women's liberation: An oxymoron. *Quarterly Journal of Speech,* 1973, *59,* 74-86.

Cathcart, R. S. New approaches to the study of movements: Defining movements rhetorically. *Western Speech,* 1972, *36,* 82-88.

Cathcart, R. S. Defining social movements by their rhetorical form. *Central States Speech Journal,* 1980, *31.*

Coleman, J. S. *Community conflict.* New York: Free Press, 1957.

Crain, R. *The politics of community conflict.* Indianapolis: Bobbs-Merrill, 1969.

Dahl, R. A. *Pluralist democracy in the United States: Conflict and consent.* Chicago: Rand McNally, 1967.

Dahrendorf, R. *Class and class conflict in industrial society.* Stanford: Stanford University Press, 1959.

Davies, J. C. Toward a theory of revolution. *American Sociological Review,* 1962, *27,* 5-19.

Davies, J. C. The J curve of rising and declining satisfaction as a cause of some great revolutions and a contained rebellion. In H. D. Graham & T. Gurr (Eds.), *The history of violence in America.* New York: Praeger, 1969.

Davies, J. C. The J curve and power struggle theories of collective violence. *American Sociological Review,* 1974, *39,* 607-610.

Debray, R. *Revolution in the revolution* (B. Ortiz, trans.). New York: Grove Press, 1967.

Denisoff, R. S. Protest movements: Class consciousness and the propaganda song. *Sociological Quarterly,* 1968, *9,* 228-247.

Deutsch, M. Conflicts: Productive and destructive. *Journal of Social Issues,* 1969, *25,* 7-41.

Doolittle, R. J. Riots as symbolic: A criticism and approach. *Central States Speech Journal,* 1976, *27,* 310-317.

Edelman, M. *Symbolic uses of politics.* Urbana: University of Illinois Press, 1967.

Edelman, M. *Politics as symbolic action.* Chicago: Markham, 1971.

Farrell, T. B. Knowledge, consensus, and rhetorical theory. *Quarterly Journal of Speech,* 1976, *62,* 1-14.
Feuer, L. S. *The conflict of generations.* New York: Basic Books, 1969.
Fireman, B., & Gamson, W. Utilitarian logic in the resource mobilization perspective. In J. D. McCarthy & M. N. Zald (Eds.), *The dynamics of social movements: Resource mobilization, tactics and social control.* Cambridge, MA: Winthrop, 1979.
Fogelson, R., & Hill, R. Who riots, a study of participation in the 1967 riots. In *Supplemental studies for the National Advisory Commission on Civil Disorders.* Washington, DC: Government Printing Office, 1968.
Friedrichs, R. W. *A sociology of sociology.* New York: Free Press, 1970.
Gamson, W. *Power and discontent.* Homewood, IL: Dorsey Press, 1968.
Gamson, W. *The strategy of social protest.* Homewood, IL: Dorsey Press, 1975.
Gitlin, T. *The whole world is watching: Mass media in the making and unmaking of the new left.* Berkeley: University of California Press, 1980.
Greer, T. H. *American social reform movements: Their pattern since 1865.* Englewood Cliffs, NJ: Prentice-Hall, 1949.
Griffin, L. M. The rhetorical structure of the "New Left" movement: Part I. *Quarterly Journal of Speech,* 1964, *50,* 113-135.
Griffin, L. M. A dramatistic theory of the rhetoric of movements. In W. H. Rueckert (Ed.), *Critical responses to Kenneth Burke.* Minneapolis: University of Minnesota Press, 1969.
Gurr, T. R. *Why men rebel.* Princeton: Princeton University Press, 1970.
Habermas, J. *Legitimation Crisis* (T. McCarthy, trans). Boston: Beacon, 1975.
Haiman, F. S. The rhetoric of the streets: Some legal and ethical considerations. *Quarterly Journal of Speech,* 1967, *53,* 99-114.
Hayes, J. J. Gayspeak. *Quarterly Journal of Speech,* 1976, *62,* 256-266.
Heberle, R. *Social movements.* New York: Appleton-Century-Crofts, 1951.
Hobsbawm, E. Economic fluctuations and some social movements since 1800. *Economic History Review,* 1952, *5,* 1-25.
Hoffer, E. *The true believer: Thoughts on the nature of mass movements.* New York: Harper & Row, 1951.
Hundley, J. R. The dynamics of recent ghetto riots. In R. A. Chikota & M. C. Moran (Eds.), *Riot in the cities.* Rutherford, NJ: Fairleigh Dickinson University Press, 1970.
Jablonski, C. Promoting radical change in the Roman Catholic Church: Rhetorical requirements, problems and strategies of the American bishops. *Central States Speech Journal,* 1980, *31.*
Jamieson, K. M. Generic constraints and the rhetorical situation. *Philosophy & Rhetoric,* 1973, *6,* 162-170.
Jamieson, K. M. Antecedent genre as rhetorical constraint. *Quarterly Journal of Speech,* 1975, *61,* 406-415.
Jenkins, C., & Perrow, C. Insurgency of the powerless: Farm workers movements (1946-1972). *American Sociological Review,* 1977, *42,* 249-268.
Johnson, C. *Revolutionary change.* Boston: Little, Brown, 1966.
Kanter, R. M. Commitment and social organization: A study of commitment mechanisms in utopian communities. *American Sociological Review,* 1968, *33,* 499-517.
Keniston, K. *Young radicals.* New York: Harcourt Brace Jovanovich, 1968.
Klapp, O. E. *Symbolic leaders: Public dramas and public men.* Chicago: AVC, 1964.
Lane, R. *Political ideology.* New York: Free Press, 1962.
Lang, K., & Lang, G. *Collective dynamics.* New York: Crowell, 1961.
Lanternari, V. *The religion of the oppressed.* New York: Mentor Books, 1965.
Lasky, M. J. *Utopia and revolution.* Chicago: University of Chicago Press, 1976.
Laue, J. H. Changing character of Negro protest. *Annals of American Academy of Political and Social Science,* 1965, *357,* 119-126.

Leahy, P., & Mazur, A. A comparison of movements opposed to nuclear power, fluoridation, and abortion. In L. Kriesberg (Ed.), *Research in social movements, conflicts and
social change* (Vol. I). Greenwich, CT: JAI Press, 1978.

Lipset, S. M., & Raab, E. *The politics of unreason: Right wing extremism in America,
1790-1970.* New York: Harper & Row, 1970.

Lipsky, M. Protest as a political resource. *American Political Science Review,* 1968, *62,*
1144-1158.

Lucas, S. E. *Portents of rebellion: Rhetoric and revolution in Philadelphia, 1765-76.*
Philadelphia: Temple University Press, 1976.

McCarthy, J. D., & Zald, M. N. *The trends of social movements in America: Professionalization and resource mobilization.* Morristown, NJ: General Learning Press, 1973.

McCarthy, J. D., & Zald, M. N. Resource mobilization and social movements: A partial
theory. *American Journal of Sociology,* 1977, *32,* 1212-1241.

McGee, M. C. In search of "the people": A rhetorical alternative. *Quarterly Journal of
Speech,* 1975, *61,* 235-249.

McGee, M. C. The Fall of Wellington: A case study of the relationship between theory,
practice, and rhetoric in history. *Quarterly Journal of Speech,* 1977, *63,* 28-42.

McGee, M. C. "Social Movement": Phenomenon or meaning? *Central States Speech Journal,*
1980, *31.*

McGuire, M. Mythic rhetoric in *Mein Kampf:* A structuralist critique. *Quarterly Journal of
Speech,* 1977, *63,* 1-13.

Marcuse, H. *One-dimensional man.* Boston: Beacon, 1964.

Marshall, R. Precipitation and presidents. *The Nation,* 1927, *124,* 315-316.

Marx, G. T., & Wood, J. L. Strands of theory and research in collective behavior. In A.
Inkeles (Ed.), *Annual review of sociology* (Vol. 1). Palo Alto, CA: Annual Reviews Inc.,
1975.

Marx, K., & Engels, F. *The communist manifesto.* New York: International Publishers,
1930.

Mauss, A. L. *Social problems as social movements.* Philadelphia: J. B. Lippincott, 1975.

Merton, R. K. *Social theory and social structure.* New York: Free Press, 1968.

Milgram, S., & Toch, H. Collective behavior: Crowds and social movements. In G. Lindzey &
E. Aronson (Eds.), *Handbook of social psychology.* Reading, MA: Addison-Wesley,
1969.

Nesbitt, R. Conflict and the Black Panther party. *Sociological Focus,* 1972, *5,* 105-119.

Oberschall, A. *Social conflict and social movements.* Englewood Cliffs, NJ: Prentice-Hall,
1973.

Oppenheimer, M., & Lakey, G. *A manual for direct action.* Chicago: Quadrangle Books,
1964.

Palmer, R. R. Sur la composition de la gauche à la constituante. *Annales Historiques de la
Revolution Française,* 1959, *31.*

Parsons, T. *The structure of social action.* New York: McGraw-Hill, 1937.

Parsons, T. Social strains in America. In T. Parsons (Ed.), *Structure and process in modern
societies.* New York: Free Press, 1960.

Pettigrew, T. F. *Racially separate or together?* New York: McGraw-Hill, 1971.

Riches, S. V., & Sillars, M. O. The status of movement criticism. *Western Journal of Speech
Communication,* 1980, *44,* 275-287.

Rogers, E. M. Social structure and social change. In G. Zaltman (Ed.), *Processes and
phenomena of social change.* New York: John Wiley, 1973.

Rogin, M. P. *The intellectuals and McCarthy: The radical specter.* Cambridge: MIT Press,
1967.

Rudé, G. *Wilkes and liberty.* Oxford: Clarendon, 1962.

Rudé, G. *The crowd in history.* New York: John Wiley, 1964.

Rush, G. B., & Denisoff, R. S. *Social and political movements.* New York: Appleton-Century-Crofts, 1971.

Schelling, T. *The strategy of conflict*. New York: Galaxy Books, 1963.

Scott, R. L., & Brockriede, W. *The rhetoric of black power*. New York: Harper & Row, 1969.

Scott, R. L., & Smith, D. The rhetoric of confrontation. *Quarterly Journal of Speech*, 1969, *55*, 1-8.

Shorter, E., & Tilly, C. *Strikes in France, 1830-1968*. Cambridge: Cambridge University Press, 1974.

Sillars, M. O. Defining movements rhetorically: Casting the widest net. *Southern Speech Communication Journal*, 1980, *46*, 17-32.

Simons, H. W. Requirements, problems, and strategies: A theory of persuasion for social movements. *Quarterly Journal of Speech*, 1970, *56*, 1-11.

Simons, H. W. Persuasion in social conflicts: A critique of prevailing conceptions and a framework for future research. *Speech Monographs*, 1972, *39*, 229-247.

Simons, H. W. *Persuasion: Understanding, practice, and analysis*. Reading, MA: Addison-Wesley, 1976.

Simons, H. W., Chesebro, J. W., & Orr, C. J. A movement perspective on the 1972 presidential campaign. *Quarterly Journal of Speech*, 1973, *59*, 168-179.

Simons, H. W., Mechling, E. W., & Schreier, H. Functions of communication in mobilizing for collective action from the bottom up: The rhetoric of social movements. In C. Arnold & J. Bowers (Eds.), *Handbook of rhetorical and communication theory*. Boston: Allyn & Bacon, in press.

Skolnick, J. *The politics of protest*. New York: Ballantine, 1969.

Smelser, N. *Theory of collective behavior*. New York: Free Press, 1962.

Snyder, D., & Kelly, W. R. Strategies for investigating violence and social change: Illustrations for analysis of racial disorders and implications for mobilization research. In J. D. McCarthy & M. N. Zald (Eds.), *The dynamics of social movements: Resource mobilization, tactics and social control*. Cambridge, MA: Winthrop, 1979.

Snyder, D. R., & Tilly, C. H. Hardship and collective violence in France 1830-1960. *American Sociological Review*, 1972, *37*, 520-532.

Sorokin, P. A. *Social and cultural dynamics* (4 vols.). New York: American Book Co., 1937-1941.

Specht, H. Disruptive tactics. *Social Work*, 1969, *14*, 5-15.

Suedfeld, P., & Rank, A. D. Revolutionary leaders: Long-term success as a function of changes in conceptual complexity. *Journal of Personality and Social Psychology*, 1976, *34*, 169-178.

Tilly, C. Does modernization breed revolution? *Comparative Politics*, 1973, *5*, 425-447.

Tilly, C. Revolution and collective violence. In F. Greenstein & N. Polsky (Eds.), *Handbook of political science*. Reading, MA: Addison-Wesley, 1975.

Tilly, C. Repertoires of contention in America and Britain. In M. Zald & J. D. McCarthy (Eds.), *The dynamics of social movements: Resource mobilization, social control and tactics*. Cambridge, MA: Winthrop, 1979.

Tilly, C., Tilly, L., & Tilly, R. *The rebellious century: 1830-1930*. Cambridge: Harvard University Press, 1975.

Toch, H. *The social psychology of social movements*. Indianapolis: Bobbs-Merrill, 1965.

Turner, R. The public perception of protest. *American Sociological Review*, 1969, *34*, 815-831.

Turner, R., & Killian, L. *Collective behavior*. Englewood Cliffs, NJ: Prentice-Hall, 1972.

U.S. Riot Commission. *Report of the national advisory commission on civil disorders*. New York: Bantam, 1968.

Walker, J. L. *Rights in conflict*. New York: Grosset & Dunlap, 1968.

Weber, M. Objectivity in social science and social policy. In E. A. Shils & H. A. Finch (Eds.), *Max Weber—On the methodology of the social sciences*. New York: Free Press, 1949.

Wilkie, R. W. Karl Marx on rhetoric. *Philosophy & Rhetoric*, 1976, *9*, 232-246.

Wilkinson, P. *Social movement*. London: Pall Mall, 1971.

Williams, R. Racial and cultural relations. In J. Gittler (Ed.), *Review of sociology.* New York: John Wiley, 1957.

Wilson, J. *Introduction to social movements.* New York: Basic Books, 1973.

Windt, T. O. The rhetoric of charismatic leaders. *Pennsylvania Speech Communication Annual,* 1973, *29,* 30-38.

Wolfinger, R. America's radical right. In D. Apter (Ed.), *Ideology and discontent.* New York: Free Press, 1964.

Zald, M. N., & McCarthy, J. D. Organizational intellectuals and the criticism of society. *Social Service Review,* 1975, *49,* 344-362.

Zarefsky, D. President Johnson's war on poverty: The rhetoric of three "establishment" movements. *Communication Monographs,* 1977, *44,* 352-373.

Zinn, H. *Disobedience and democracy.* New York: Vintage, 1968.

CHAPTER 16

Government and the News Media

L. John Martin

GOVERNMENT AND MASS MEDIA in modern society are linked to the public in a classic triangle of interrelationships. Each acts and is dependent on the other two to the extent that a two-way analysis of relationships is merely a sterile exercise. When Rivers, Miller, and Gandy (1975) recently reviewed the literature on the topic, they were disheartened—not by the paucity of studies but by the lack of effort to "bring together studies of the government with studies of the media." Consequently, they conclude, "there is relatively little research that can give us a better understanding of the relationship between these institutions" (p. 217).

One reason for the apparent gaps in our efforts to study this nexus of our social essence is that the trichotomy of media-public-government is laced with normative problems that we would rather leave to lawyers and philosophers than tackle empirically. Social scientists and communication specialists who have focused on the problem in the context of communication and national development, where the three elements converge, have arrived at an impasse (see Golding, 1974). Some have skirted the issue by using an "index approach," which segments society into measurable compartments, then tries to come up with a causal model of development that includes beta weights for a variety of available indices. Other researchers have approached communication and development a priori, positing their own system as the norm or ideal against which they measure how far from grace the developing country happens to be.

The way out of the impasse, of course, is not to do more unidimensional or two-dimensional studies, as Rivers et al. propose (1975, pp. 229-233), but to study the interaction among the three variables, from the viewpoint of each of the variables in turn. Thus, numerous agenda-setting studies focus on what the media do to people about government. More studies are needed on how government actions in regard to media affect people, or how people's use of the media affects government, or how people's views of government affect media, and so forth.

This overview first touches on the role of the press vis-à-vis the government, which underlies any study of the place of the press and government in society. Few empirical studies have been done on this subject, other than opinion surveys that focus on what the various elements of society think this role ought to be. In all probability—and there is evidence to support this (see Shaw, 1972)—the role assigned to the press depends on the socialization process one has been through.

The interrelationships between the government and the press have been studied somewhat more fully—mainly descriptively, however. Thus, access to news can be and has been studied normatively (that is, what is the law?) and positively (what is the practice?). How government informs the press about its activities and, as a corollary, how the press informs itself about government have been the topics of many master's theses. Finally, how these two adversaries see each other is the subject of numerous surveys—albeit with minuscule samples.

Two essential approaches to the study of mass media and government are the impact of government on the press and the impact of the press on government. These two sections are based on a very few empirical studies because very few exist. One aspect of government impact on the press is the effort made at various levels by various branches of government to get into the headlines. There are more studies on this topic than on others, especially in the realm of congressional visibility. Congress thrives on publicity to a greater degree than do other branches of the government (in fact, the judiciary is notorious for its diffidence); and congressmen, senators, and their staffs are more willing to cooperate in studies than are other government employees.

Finally, a short section is devoted to the public view of the media as intermediaries between itself (that is, the public) and the government. Here, again, the number of available studies is large. But far too little has been done to link the three elements in a "transactional" model.

ROLE OF THE PRESS

Unlike the totalitarian press, mass media in the United States function as watchdogs over government, scrutinizing its activities in an effort to keep its authority within appropriate bounds. "Nothing," says Alan Barth (quoted in Hachten, 1963), "expresses more clearly the essential differences between a totalitarian society and a free society than the relationship in each of the press to the government."

The role of the press vis-à-vis the government varies from country to country, but in all cases the relationship is symbiotic and depends on the country's political ideology. In the United States, journalists and public officials see the functions of the mass media somewhat differently, while the general public has yet another viewpoint about their role.

Reporters, according to a number of studies (Nimmo, 1964; Dunn, 1969; Sigal, 1973), see as one of their primary roles the collection and presentation of "objective" information. Most scholars no longer believe that reporters—or anyone else for that matter—can write about an event from any but a subjective viewpoint (Merrill & Lowenstein, 1971, pp. 228-241), although some journalists still insist they do (see *Editor & Publisher*, Sept. 2, 1972, p. 7). The aim is to present the news as impartially and with as little bias as possible.

A second role of the press is to interpret the news so that those readers who are unfamiliar with the workings of government can understand the relevance of the facts they read. In the past two decades, "advocacy journalism" has been very much in vogue. The advocacy journalist "defines his bias and casts his analysis of the news in that context" (Dennis, 1971). Advocacy journalism is a form of interpretation, although some profess to see a difference between advocacy and interpretation, in that one can explain the meaning of facts (interpretation) without necessarily advocating a particular viewpoint, a distinction others reject.

A third role, and one that is considered by many reporters as the key responsibility of the press in a democracy, assigns to the mass media the function of being the representative of the public vis-à-vis the government. This is the role that sets the press up as a watchdog over the government for the public. It is because of this putative role, implicit in the First Amendment, that the mass media demand access to government records, now written into law under the 1966 Freedom of Information Act.

A fourth function of the press is identified by Nimmo (1964) as a responsibility to determine public opinion and to inform the public and the government about the climate of opinion. One reporter, according to Nimmo (p. 36), termed this "an essential ingredient of a democratic process." In effect, it is more than that. It is this particular function of the mass media that creates a mass society—more correctly, a public—that is bonded together into a social system through a common fund of knowledge, a common *Weltanschauung*.

Finally, many reporters also see themselves as participants in the governmental process (Sigal, 1973, p. 76; Dunn, 1969, pp. 11-18). In this role, they may precipitate action by focusing attention on an issue. The press has been eminently successful in influencing policy by the way it presents its facts and through the proponents and opponents it chooses to quote. Another way in which reporters believe they participate in government is by influencing public officials to consider the impact of their behavior when it is reported in the press (Dunn, 1969, pp. 15-16).

Owners of the mass media in the United States probably subscribe to all these roles of the press but would add one of their own. A major function of the press, in their view, is to remain solvent and to make a profit for the shareholders. In this respect, their view differs radically from the prevalent view in the Communist bloc and the Third World. News, in the eyes of the West, is and should be a commodity as free as the air we breathe, saleable when processed by a reporter and editor. Both Communist countries and the Third World, on the other hand, look upon news as an instrument of national control and development, subject to governmental manipulation and use (see Sussman, 1979).

While government officials in the United States, according to the studies mentioned above, agree that the role of the press is to inform, to interpret, and to serve as a watchdog over the actions of government, state officials in Wisconsin, for example, also consider the press to be responsible for bringing problems to the attention of the government (Dunn, 1969, pp. 62-63). In Los Angeles County, according to Lyle (1965, p. 128), public officials consider as part of the surveillance function of the press the responsibility of bringing government information to the attention of the public. They see this as a constant need of local government.

The public view of the role of the press parallels that of the reporter and of the public official, according to Lyle. But Berelson (1949), in a seminal study of what missing the newspaper means to the New York public, found that while "almost everyone" agreed it was "very important that people read the newspaper" to keep abreast of public affairs, only a third of the public "had any notion of what in the world they wanted more information about." Other uses of the press (apart from providing information about and interpreting public affairs) included, among its most missed functions, serving as a tool for daily living by providing radio logs and advertisements. These were missed by fully half of the public. The remaining four reasons given for needing the newspaper were completely unrelated to government news.

GOVERNMENT-PRESS RELATIONS

Scholars have examined the relationship between the press and the government in terms of access to government news by the press, the production and use of press releases, other sources of news, and evaluation of the press by government officials and of public information officers by reporters.

Reporters, according to a model developed by Jackson-Beeck and Kraus (1980), are a captive audience of three elements: editors, politicians and government agencies, and the public. Only editors are free in this model. The public and politicians/government agencies are dependent on mass communications to maintain their power. Miller (1978, p. 23) likewise concludes in a case study of the relationship between reporters and Congress that "politicians are, to some extent, at the mercy of reporters; however," she adds, "they have their own ways of getting back at people who break the rules." In another sense, of course, editors depend on their reporters' view of the world for whatever control they exercise, thus placing reporters in a more central, interactive role than in the Jackson-Beeck/Kraus model.

One way in which government agencies and politicians exercise control over the activities of the press is by giving or withholding access to news and news sources. Cohen (1967, p. 209) found that one State Department office would talk freely to reporters while others talked to no one. At the state level, a majority (87 percent) of the capitol press corps in Albany, New York found variations in ease of access to news, and about three-fourths of the press corps attributed this to the personality of the leader rather than to the substance of the news (Morgan, 1978, pp. 107, 114). However, only some 22 percent of reporters felt that access to political news was hard in Albany. On the other hand, better than two-thirds of the reporters said state agencies restricted the flow of news by deliberately issuing vague or incomprehensible press releases. All legislators, and 85 percent of civil servants in Albany, thought that reporters were generally given enough access to news and newsmakers (p. 94). Incidentally, all states except Mississippi and the District of Columbia today have laws giving reporters free access to "public records" (Gillmor & Barron, 1979), although there are wide differences in definitions of "records" from state to state.

As for sources of government news, reporters have a variety of options available to them. They can use or rewrite the many press releases that emanate from government public information offices in most departments, or they can follow up on stories prompted by the press releases. Follow-ups normally involve interviewing government officials to whom they can get access. Nimmo (1964) found that lower-tier officials are more accessible in Washington than are agency heads, even to reporters with long experience and many contacts. Those reporters who consider themselves expositors or interpreters of the news generally turn equally to middle-level officials and to public information officers (PIOs); while for the reporter who is a mere recorder of the news, the public information officer tends to be his or her most common source.

The value of government press releases is often underrated by reporters who are unwilling to admit their dependence on them (see Glick, 1966; Hale, 1978; however, compare Keir, 1966). But content analysis shows (Glick, 1966, p. 53) that reporters depend on them much more than they claim. True, reporters do not often use a press release as received; Kaid (1976) found that only 8 percent of state senate candidates' releases were published. But, at the same time, her study showed that only 31 percent of their releases were completely ignored. In a study of information officers of the federal government, Nimmo reports that 41 percent of their press releases were used (Nimmo, 1964, p. 146). Government agencies, on the other hand, tend to overrate the usefulness of their handouts (Glick, 1966).

Court press releases were found by Hale (1978) to increase the chances of a case being reported by the California press. Of the 88 decisions that were the subject of court releases, 58 (66 percent) were picked up by at least one newspaper, as against only four (8 percent) of the 51 cases not covered by press releases that were written up by the press.

Communication scholars believe the press should write more interpretive articles to explain judicial proceedings. Very few of the smaller newspapers in Minnesota were found to do this, according to one study. Drechsel, Netteburg, and Aborisade (1980) report that in 80 county seat newspapers in Minnesota during one month in 1978, only 14 stories appeared on local court activities that could not be categorized as spot news. The remaining 317 items of court news were straight, factual news stories of one type or another, 244 of them based on the public records or the reporter's observation, and presenting only one side of the case.

The weight given to different types of news in a political campaign is shown in a 1972 Illinois study by Kaid (1976). She found that all releases dealing with campaign announcements were published by the press, as were 67 percent of releases dealing with personal information about the candidate. But only 56 percent of press releases that discussed issues were carried by at least one paper. Graber (1971) found a similar emphasis on the personalities of the candidates in a nationwide study of 20 newspapers covering the 1968 presidential election. Little information was provided about the candidates' political philosophies or executive abilities (p. 181), and the issues mentioned were mainly those raised by the candidates themselves, with little substantive discussion of them.

Understandably, government PIOs prefer to dispense information through the press release, which can be cleared by higher levels of authority; while reporters, Nimmo discovered (p. 146), prefer to gather their own information through the interview. The news conference is the reporter's second preference, according to that study.

Sigal, in a content analysis of news stories appearing in the *New York Times* and the *Washington Post* (1973), breaks down the reporter's sources according to whether they are routine, informal, or enterprise. Routine sources account for some 58 percent of items in the study. Informal channels, by which he means background briefings, leaks, nongovernment and newspaper sources, provided about 16 percent of the papers' contents, while close to 26 percent of the stories depended on the reporter's own enterprise. Among routine sources, Sigal found that the press conference was the most commonly used, providing around one-fourth of all news items. Background briefings were the best informal source, accounting for 8 percent, and close to 24 percent of the enterprise-based items were gathered through interviews.

Nimmo (1964, p. 89), classifying newsmen's channels of information some-what differently—under the headings of government, professional, and other

TABLE 16.1   Sources of Washington Correspondents

Idea Source	Percentage
Government sources:	
Scheduled functions	56%
PIO releases	40
Congressional tip	25
Secondary officials	43
Top level officials	15
Professional sources:	
Personal curiosity	38
Colleagues	10
Assignment	43
Topical (rewrite)	48
Other:	
Friends	25
Special interest associates	3

sources—found that press conferences and a variety of scheduled functions were mentioned by more reporters as a major source than any other (Table 16.1).

The consensus of reporters and government officials (but not including government public information officers) is that reporters are more enterprising in seeking their sources than government employees are in contacting the press (Glick, 1967). Government information officers believe they are just as active in seeking the press as vice versa.

Most studies show that, in the opinion of reporters and bureau chiefs in Washington, it is hard to beat the President and the White House press conference as a news source (Sigal, 1973, p. 70; Glick, 1967, p. 55; Miller, 1977, p. 464). If publicity is being sought, "the way to get covered is to become the best and most complete source of information about a topic already being covered," Miller (1977) determined in a study of news coverage of Congress.

Government officials in Washington are satisfied with the performance of the press on the whole (Nimmo, 1964, p. 136; Cohen, 1976); not so the officials in state capitals, such as Madison, Wisconsin and Albany, New York, who "spend a good bit of their time criticizing the press" (Dunn, 1969; see also Morgan, 1978, p. 83). Texas legislators rate television news coverage of their legislature higher than newspaper coverage (Merwin, 1971). Glick (1967) found that DHEW officials tended to rate the quality of reporting and the objectivity of reporters higher than did respondents at the State Department. Both departments, however, felt that wire service reporters generally did a better job than correspondents of out-of-town newspapers. The latter tend to be very selective in their news interests, focusing on developments that concern the readers in their circulation area.

Reporters, in turn, are less satisfied with the performance of public information officers than vice versa (65 percent expressed satisfaction with PIOs in the Nimmo Washington study, as against 86 percent of the PIOs who were satisfied with the performance of newsmen). Two-thirds or more of the journalists and public information officers interviewed in Washington by Nimmo considered government officials as having the primary responsibility for leadership (1964, p. 184). About a third of each group believed that the press, as the representative of the public, had this responsibility, or that the responsibility was shared with government officials.

GOVERNMENT IMPACT ON THE PRESS

The American press, as we have said, views news as a saleable commodity, but one to which it has a constitutional right of free access. The U.S. government does not question this right most of the time and, indeed, welcomes the free publicity, unless it happens to be negative. The question of who benefits more—the press or the government—from this symbiotic relationship has not been resolved. The issue is more apparent when the question is posed in terms of the right of access by the press to information of a nongovernmental nature, such as news about an individual. Controversies, for example, raged over whether the mass media (for example, television) should pay some of the principals in the Watergate incident for the right to interview them and get their story. Many felt that the public had a right to know what went on. The Watergate cast of characters, on the other hand, said they owned the rights to their story and could dispose of them for profit.

As far as government news is concerned, there is no doubt it is a most important staple of the national and international desks of the *New York Times* and the *Washington Post,* as Sigal (1973, p. 60) points out. The benefit, at least to metropolitan newspapers, is both direct—in that the news can be sold—and indirect, in that government departments "dig out" much of the news for reporters and give it to them free (Glick, 1967, p. 28). Reporters are not always willing to admit their reliance on press releases, Glick determined (p. 31), but acknowledge that they often use such handouts as a starting point for their own digging.

There is no doubt that reporters must pay a price for access to government news. Reporters become reluctant to bite the hand that feeds them or to ask their sources to take responsibility for the information if they print it. "Reinforcing the pressure to get news, the pressure to get it first makes reporters reluctant to reject information provided through routine channels, lest they jeopardize their access through less formal channels," Sigal concludes (1973, p. 54).

There are other ways in which government can control news, including harassment of correspondents, denying them special benefits (such as accreditation and the right to travel on government aircraft), and playing favorites in leaking news.

On the judicial side, the Warren Commission, which made recommendations following the national trauma over the Kennedy assassination, called on the press and law enforcement establishments voluntarily to curb pretrial news that might prejudice the rights of defendants in criminal cases. The press appears to have cooperated, and Gerald (1970) found that few metropolitan newspaper editors reported any serious difficulties from law enforcement officers denying them access to information, except in regard to seeing evidence, such as loot.

The executive branch of the federal government has always held that, in the words of Assistant Secretary for Public Affairs Arthur Sylvester, "news generated by actions of the government as to content and timing are part of the arsenal of weaponry that the President has in the application of military sources and related forces to the solution of political pressure" (quoted in Glick, 1967, pp. 17-18). This is a view widely held among foreign service officers (Chittick, 1970). In fact, policy officers, to a larger extent than PIOs, would be willing to withhold information for such reasons as that it might embarrass friendly governments or that it might expose differences of opinion within the State Department. While the Freedom of Information Committee of the American Society of Newspaper Editors has attacked such invasions of First Amendment doctrine, Glick (1967) reports that 23 of 40 reporters interviewed felt that a valid case could be made for withholding certain types of information from the press in the name of executive privilege. Only 25 percent said that such a case could not be made. Glick's sample included officers in the Department of Health, Education and Welfare. In a broader study conducted by Nimmo (1964), only 40 percent (as against Glick's 58 percent) of information officers said they believed that even the timing of news releases should be purposely manipulated by the government.

At the state level, Morgan (1978) found both legislators and civil servants (and especially the former—87 versus 71 percent) categorically opposed to trying to influence political news coverage by releasing vague or contradictory news items. However, some 24 percent of bureaucrats thought it might sometimes be good policy. Journalists, in this same study, overwhelmingly (86 percent) agreed that legislators and bureaucrats could become too cozy at the expense of the public, but only 64 percent thought that newsmen themselves might become involved in a triangular relationship at the expense of the public.

The most notorious case of an effort by a government official in recent times to intimidate the press was, of course, the series of speeches by Vice President Spiro Agnew attacking the news media in general and particularly network television. He accused a "little group of men" of wielding "a free hand in selecting, presenting and interpreting the great issues of our nation," exercising "a form of censorship" each night with responsibility "only to their corporate employers." Many journalists believed these speeches could have a chilling effect on the press. But the only effect they seem to have had, according to a small amount of empirical evidence available (Lowry, 1971), is that network news attributed 9 percent more of its facts (significant at the .001 level) to named sources.

The other overt effort on the part of government to control the content of the news media is in broadcasting. Under the Fairness Doctrine, which had its origins in the 1949 FCC report, "In the Matter of Editorializing by Broadcast Licensees," interpreting the 1934 Communications Act, a station must devote a reasonable amount of time to public issues and must present contrasting viewpoints on all topics. News programming was excluded from these requirements in 1959 (Pember, 1977, pp. 418-419). Some 78 percent of television news personnel in a study by Buss and Malaney (1978) said they thought there was too much government control of broadcasting; 21 percent said the control was about right under the Fairness Doctrine.

MAKING THE HEADLINES

The President of the United States has no peer in his ability to command the attention of the press and, through it, that of the public. Except in 1949, presidential news measured in column inches exceeded congressional news and also joint presidential/congressional news (most of the time even a combination of the latter two) on the front pages of the *New York Times* between 1922 and 1957, according to a study by Cornwell (1959). A follow-up study by Balutis (1976) found a similar pattern of emphasis between 1958 and 1974. Both authors concluded that Congress has been declining in power vis-à-vis the President.

Balutis showed that presidential news, as a proportion of the total amount of news about the national government, rose from 61.9 percent in the 1958-1963 period, to 68.7 percent in 1964-1969, and to 73.1 percent in 1970-1974. Congressional news (not counting news in which both President and Congress are mentioned) declined at the same time from 33 percent in 1958-1963 to 23.7 percent in 1964-1969 and to 17.8 percent in 1970-1974. To demonstrate the leverage presidents have in manipulating the press, Balutis quotes a researcher who found that during a 10-year period of the Johnson, Nixon, and Ford administrations, they had sought coverage of their public speeches 45 times and were granted all but one. The Democratic leadership in Congress, meanwhile, asked for coverage 11 times in seven years but received it only three times.

"Television," says Seymour-Ure (1974, p. 85) "has shifted the balance of power towards the President. The President has a direct link with the people: he needs no sympathetic journalists or party organizations as intermediaries." Of course, he needs the cooperation of the networks; but, as we have seen, he has little trouble getting that. At the same time, congressional opportunities to exploit television are limited; hence the frequent efforts to hold sensationalistic hearings.

Presidents since Roosevelt have used the press conference to increase their visibility. Roosevelt held two a week and Truman said he would hold one each week but only if he had news to impart. Presidents Harding, Coolidge, and Hoover held press conferences, but the questions had to be submitted in writing. Truman refused to make his press conferences "for background only," as he was advised to do (Lorenz, 1966). Kennedy introduced live telecasts. He had more news coverage than either Eisenhower or Truman (Pollard, 1964), and he opened up the White House to reporters so that they could have direct access to presidential staff. Johnson's main contribution to presidential visibility was the televised announcement, often on the spur of the moment (Cornwell, 1966). Nixon and Ford continued traditions set by their predecessors, while Carter attempted to revert to, but soon gave up, the informal (this time televised) fireside chat.

Presidents attain their visibility because they are almost unique in their breadth of control over the social and economic lives of the public. Johnson's press secretary, George Reedy (1970), pointed out that presidents have front-page news materials that they can trade for their visibility. They have also been known to generate news to draw attention away from undesirable events, such as the major anti-Johnson speech Senator Robert Kennedy was purportedly preparing one day in 1967 (Seymour-Ure, 1974). Similarly, Nixon and Ford were able to turn the focus away from Watergate with statements on the economy, the energy crisis, and so forth (Miller, 1977).[1]

At the lower levels of the executive branch of government—at least in Washington—the press is influenced by the knowledge that its most significant audience is the federal bureaucracy. As the *Washington Post's* own promotional advertising put it (quoted in Bagdikian, 1967),

> No rule says that U.S.I.A. appointees must read this newspaper (but they all do). When one newspaper enjoys 100% readership among the key officials of a government department—such as the U.S. Information Agency—you might think reading it was a rule. It isn't—but reading the Washington Post certainly is the rule throughout official Washington. It is read by 95% of all top appointees, and virtually every Congressman.

Dunn (1969) found in Wisconsin that the press release was favored by most bureaucrats as the most convenient and fastest way to reach the public. The governor's office and Wisconsin legislators also add to their visibility by making speeches and attending meetings. Press conferences are used somewhat less frequently, and then mostly by the governor's office. About a third of Dunn's sample of Wisconsin bureaucrats use the technique of cultivating close personal relations with reporters and discovering their special interests to achieve press visibility. One in five increase their visibility by providing tips, background information, and suggestions. This latter method is used more frequently by the Wisconsin governor and legislators than by other bureaucrats (1969, p. 143).

In Washington, the Pentagon discovered it could promote itself very successfully by assisting Hollywood in the production of war movies. Shain (1972) shows that war pictures for which the Pentagon provided assistance are more likely to emphasize military professionalism than films made without Pentagon help. While unassisted movies also portrayed the American military favorably, generals and admirals in assisted films received particular praise. Orwant and Ullmann (1974) found that Army officers in the Pentagon generally were even more willing than civilian employees to let the media publish whatever they wished about the military. They were dubious, however, about press coverage of the war in Vietnam or about life in the Army, and less willing than civilians to concede that the press truthfully reported on military drug and racial problems.

Miller (1977) concluded that press coverage of Congress can be explained largely in terms of the workload of the reporter: To make the daily headlines and to come up with the stories most likely to be used by the editors, the reporter must seek out the "ultimate spokesman." For national news, this is, of course, the President of the United States, who represents the largest constituency of any elected official. Miller's advice to congressional staff is that "the way to get covered is to become the best and most complete source of information about a topic already being covered" (p. 464).

Based on a 1973-1974 study of the content of four major newspapers, Miller speculates that the reason certain senators, bills, and committees receive greater coverage in the press than others is that fewer people need to be contacted to get a major, newsworthy story. This saves time and effort and gives the reporter a better chance of being printed than if he or she tried some less foolproof source. "Conceiving of press coverage as the search for the ultimate spokesman helps explain why the Democratic Party received almost twice as much coverage in Congress as did the GOP," she explains (p. 464).

This is inspired analysis, since research going back to Matthews's 1960 study of U.S. senators has focused on such factors as the seniority of senators, their committee assignment, the size of the state from which they come, their ideology, and the security of their seat. Wilhoit and Sherrill (1968), for example, found that state size, seniority, and committee assignment were significantly related to wire service coverage of senators. But the correlation was higher for Republican senators than for Democrats. Weaver and Wilhoit (1974) determined that state size and committee assignment were correlated with the visibility of senators in news magazines. But this was true only for Republican senators, and Republican senators were mentioned only 9.9 times on the average, while

Democrats were mentioned an average of 11.9 times. Seniority failed to correlate significantly with visibility. Furthermore, those senators who were mentioned the most often were the party leaders—Robert F. Kennedy and Everett Dirksen. Kennedy was mentioned almost twice as often as Dirksen.

In a more recent study (Weaver & Wilhoit, 1980), path analysis showed that—at least in the 91st (1969-1970) and 93rd (1973-1974) Congresses—a senator's activity was the best predictor of his visibility (path coefficients were .48 and .59, respectively). But in the 89th Congress (1965-1966), staff size with a path coefficient of .44 was clearly the best predictor (the coefficient for activity was .10). The most active senators tended to be from the most populous states and had the largest staffs. Since a large staff is necessary for a senator to be active and since it is based on state size and committee assignment, it is understandable that senators from large states would tend to be active. But since it is quite conceivable that a senator from a large state may have a smaller staff than one from a small state, because of his less important committee assignment, activity cannot be measured solely by the size of the state.

Seniority alone may not secure a prestigious committee assignment for a senator, although it helps. Since Weaver and Wilhoit measured power in terms of seniority and prestige committee leadership, their conclusion that staff size and power are sometimes negatively related is understandable. A senator from a small state might conceivably have a more important committee assignment than one from a large state, giving him a larger staff, and he may also be less senior than the senator from the large state.

Miller's finding (1977) that the primary factor determining committee coverage is jurisdiction over a newsworthy topic explains why, in a Democrat-dominated Senate, state size and the prestige of a committee assignment should correlate much more consistently with the visibility of Republican senators than with the visibility of Democrats. For Democrats, who were wooed by reporters if they presided over a newsmaking committee, state size alone or committee assignment alone would not have played as important a role in competition with their fellow Democrats who had access to news of importance to the press. Otherwise, however, as Miller showed in her study, senators with the largest constituencies or those who are involved in some scandal or official misconduct have the best chance of coverage.

The kind of coverage a legislator will get depends on the attitude of the chairman of the committee, Miller found (1978). Both Congress and the reporter must play by the rules (Davison, 1975), if the former desires visibility and the latter access to exclusive items of information. The price of a leak is good coverage, credit for the committee, and mention of the congressman or senator as high in the story as possible (Miller, 1978, pp. 660-661).

Occasionally, leaks are used by diplomats as a kind of "trial balloon" in order to test reactions of the public or a foreign government (Davison, 1975). The

White House, too, has been known to use the "trial balloon" by releasing information at a lower echelon to test reactions.

PRESS IMPACT ON GOVERNMENT

While every branch of the government attempts to get the best possible press coverage for itself, if necessary by "controlling" or "managing" the output or access to news, the press does not deny serving as a "gatekeeper," determining what the public will read. Few government releases reach the public the way they are written; many, if used at all, merely serve as a "tickler" for a story (Glick, 1967, p. 37). News is also "managed" when the editor decides how much of it to print, when to print it and where, what headline to give it and what to put in the lead paragraph, whether to use a picture with it, and, of course, whether to comment on it in an editorial. Thus, Glick (1966) discovered in a 1963 flow of news study that a substantial amount of governmental news about health and welfare did not reach the public.

Davison (1975) and Cohen (1967) consider the small number of foreign correspondents who cover the world for the American reader as another form of news management. There are some 50 to 200 diplomatic correspondents who interpret the world for fairly small American audiences, and these reporters have a relatively free hand in deciding what they will cover, according to Davison. Since they tend to be concentrated in Western European capitals, the American public is better informed about them and especially those aspects of European news the correspondents happen to be personally interested in (Cohen, 1967). Furthermore, because foreign news audiences are small and specialized, editors tend to use different standards in both selection and editing than they do for domestic news items (1967). Cutlip (1954) reports that foreign news stories are cut more drastically at every stage in the writing and editing process than is local news. Thus, the press exercises a strong gatekeeping function not only over what the public is told about world events but also what government officials themselves know about the world, especially those parts of the world for which they have no direct responsibility.

Do publishers, too, attempt to manage or control what goes into their newspapers? Of some 613 managing editors who replied to a questionnaire in 1967 (Bowers), almost two-thirds said their publishers had, at one time or another, directed the use or nonuse, display, or content of the news in the paper. Almost one-third said they at least occasionally intervened on local news. Intervention was inversely related to the distance of the event from the newspaper (Table 16.2).

A majority of legislators (66 percent) and a plurality of civil servants (43 percent) in Albany, New York felt that the press, in one way or another, was biased in its coverage or handling of the news (Morgan, 1978). Legislators mostly

TABLE 16.2   Proportion of Publishers Making Editorial Decisions

Story Origin	Percent Ever Intervene	Percent at Least Occasionally Intervene
Local Stories	65	31
State, Regional Stories	48	17
National Stories	39	11
International Stories	34	9

said bias resulted from either disregarding news or overconcentrating on certain individuals. Civil servants said bias stemmed from disregarding news or concentrating on unfavorable publicity. These are forms of control or news management that the government generally feels helpless to counteract. Lyle (1965), however, found in a California study that the major problem of local governments is not in reaching the media but in getting the attention of the public.

This being the case, how can one say that the press plays an important role as a rallying agent of the public? Brzezinski and Huntington (1963) claim that political pressure is funneled upward by the press in the United States, in contrast to the Soviet Union, where pressure is in the reverse direction. In the field of energy policy, Lambeth (1978) saw little evidence of press influence. In fact, the press was ranked lowest in influence by six of eight groups interviewed, including trade and news media reporters, economic and public interest group leaders, presidential appointees, lawmakers, and legislative staff.

There are two areas, however, where most studies show that people believe the press plays an important role or where there is definite evidence of it. One is that of setting an issue agenda for the public on political issues (Shaw & McCombs, 1977). This includes the agenda that is set for public officials (Rivers et al., 1975, pp. 224-225). The other is in local public affairs. City managers in 45 council-manager cities, ranging in population from 100,000 to 790,000, felt the media—especially newspapers—were highly influential in determining the policies and issues of municipal government in their communities (Boynton & Wright, 1970). Similarly, only three percent of legislators, ten percent of civil servants, and four percent of journalists felt the press plays a small role in New York State politics (Morgan, 1978). Close to eight out of ten civil servants and nearly nine in ten legislators thought the press plays a large role.

Another important role played by the press is to provide feedback to government officials often isolated from large segments of the public. The President, especially, is surrounded by people who are anxious to please him; the press provides a truer reflection of his performance as seen through the eyes of others (Reedy, 1970). Cohen (1963, p. 213), too, found that the narrower an official's specialization in the State Department, the greater his "dependence on the press for his larger view of the world."

The view that is provided serves another controlling function. Since most government leaders at their various levels tend to be exposed to the same newspapers, magazines, and television programs, they tend to develop common cognitive structures that create a socializing bond among them. Thus, Weiss (1974) shows what American leaders read, and what they read tends to be extremely similar. Sigal (1973, p. 133) contrasts the administrative levels in the British and American civil service. Whereas in Britain these levels "link up formally through an extensive network of interdepartmental committees and informally through the 'old boy net,' the clubs, the luncheon, the weekend in the country," senior officers in the U.S., who number 50 times as many as the British civil service, must lean on the press to keep them informed about one another.

THE PUBLIC VIEW

How much knowledge about the government does the public get from the press? The question might be posed differently: What sources other than the mass media does the public have for information about government? Personal experience is one such source. But personal experience is necessarily limited. Some individuals may have a great amount of information about certain aspects of government but not about others. Friends and neighbors may be another source. But here, again, most people's interactions with others are few, and much of the information thus gained originated with the mass media in the first place.

In view of this dependence on the media, three questions arise: What media do people depend on? How much of an impact do they have on people in matters pertaining to their relationship with the government? How dependable are the media?

First, as among newspapers, television, and the other mass media, many studies indicate that television today plays an important role in political socialization (Atkin & Gantz, 1978; Chaffee, Ward, & Tipton, 1970; Clarke & Fredin, 1978; Comstock, 1975; Conway, Stevens, & Smith, 1975; Dominick, 1972; Hollander, 1971; Johnson, 1973; Robinson, 1976; Rubin, 1976, 1978). Swanson (1973) reports that 69 percent of the public in southern Illinois claimed to have received most of their political information about the 1972 presidential elections from the mass media, and, of these, 54 percent named television as their major source as against 23 percent who listed newspapers. Only 8 percent said their political information had come through interpersonal communication.

Newspaper readership goes up with education and income and peaks at 35 to 49 years of age (Bagdikian, 1971, pp. 49-51). Political and other leaders, as we have seen (Weiss, 1974), tend to read the same types of publications. How does reliance on newspapers versus reliance on television for information about government and politics affect one's political outlook?

Studies indicate that those who tend to rely heavily on television for political news tend more readily to become cynical about the usefulness of voting and to distrust government more (O'Keefe & Mendelsohn, 1978). Evidence also exists that those who are dependent on television are less knowledgeable about public affairs than are those who rely on newspapers (O'Keefe, 1980). On the other hand, Rubin found that while television was linked with lower levels of knowledge among adolescents, those who had a high level of exposure to television displayed less political cynicism than those who did not (Rubin, 1978). Berman and Stookey (1980) concluded from a study of 600 13- to 17-year-olds that while only a small amount of the variance regarding the affective orientation of adolescents toward government can be explained on the basis of their television viewing, their viewing habits explain more than other variables that had been considered important, such as race, family income, and political ideology.

Although people have few alternatives to the mass media for obtaining information about government and an interpretation of what all the information means, fewer than four in ten (39 percent) said in 1973 that they had a great deal or quite a lot of confidence in newspapers as an institution, according to a Gallup poll (quoted in McCombs & Becker, 1979). About the same proportion (38 percent) expressed confidence in television news. Congress (at 42 percent) and the Supreme Court (at 44 percent) were only a notch higher in the confidence of the public. Confidence in the "people running these institutions" is even lower, according to surveys of the National Opinion Research Center (NORC, 1979). The most recent data show people who run the military ahead of other institutional leaders in the public esteem (see Table 16.3), with people running television news, the executive branch of the government, and Congress bringing up the rear. A 1975 Louis Harris poll indicated that while 90 percent of the population believed in the institution of local government, only 14 percent had confidence in its leadership, as compared with 51 percent who said they had confidence in garbage collectors (quoted in Kraus & Davis, 1976, p. 6).

Among blacks, confidence in television is much higher than it is in government, according to a study by Greenberg and Dervin (1970). Miller et al. (quoted in Kraus & Davis, 1976), in fact, found that between 1968 and 1972, the confidence of blacks in government dropped four times as fast as that of whites. There is evidence, however, according to Kraus and Davis, that the dependence of blacks on television for information about politics decreases with education.

The power of the press to persuade people to take a particular stand in political matters has never been demonstrated. Mott (1944) calculated that in 35 presidential election campaigns between 1796 and 1940, the majority of Ameri-

TABLE 16.3   Confidence in Institutions and in People Running Them
              (in percentages)

Institution	1966	1971	1973	1976	1979
Military	62	27	40	23	31
Newspapers	29	18	30	20	21
TV News	25	––	41	28	14
Executive Branch	41	23	19	11	13
Congress	42	19	29	9	13

can newspapers gave their support to the winning candidate 18 times and to the losing candidate 17 times. Nor does the modern soothsayer—the pollster—speaking through the mass media carry overwhelming weight with the public, as we have seen in numerous elections, most recently in the 1980 election campaign. The *ménage à trois* of media, government, and the public is a classic example of a cyclic love-hate relationship in which the bonds are indissoluble.

NOTE

[1]Of course, publicity-conscious politicians have been known to use this tactic in reverse, as when Senator Edward Kennedy announced his impending divorce from his wife Joan during the Reagan inaugural celebrations and the press euphoria over the return of the U.S. hostages from Iran.

REFERENCE NOTE

1. Cohen, S. J. *Perceptions of the performance of Washington media reporters by press secretaries of federal executive and legislative office holders receiving frequent national media exposure.* Unpublished M.A. thesis, University of Maryland, College Park, Maryland, 1976.

REFERENCES

Atkin, C. K., & Gantz, W. Television news and political socialization. *Public Opinion Quarterly,* 1978, *42*, 183-198.

Bagdikian, B. H. What makes a newspaper nearly great? *Columbia Journalism Review,* 1967, *6*, 35.

Bagdikian, B. H. *The information machines: Their impact on men and the media.* New York: Harper & Row, 1971.

Balutis, A. P. Congress, the President and the press. *Journalism Quarterly,* 1976, *53*, 509-515.

Berelson, B. What "missing the newspaper" means. In P. F. Lazarsfeld & F. N. Stanton (Eds.), *Communications research, 1948-49.* New York: Harper & Row, 1949.

Berman, D. R., & Stookey, J. A. Adolescents, television, and support for government. *Public Opinion Quarterly,* 1980, *44*, 330-340.

Bowers, D. R. A report on activity by publishers in directing newsroom decisions. *Journalism Quarterly,* 1967, *44*, 43-52.

Boynton, R. P., & Wright, D. S. The media, the masses and urban management. *Journalism Quarterly*, 1970, *47*, 12-19.

Brzezinski, Z., & Huntington, S. *Political power USA/USSR*. London: Chatto & Windus, 1963.

Buss, T. F., & Malaney, G. D. How broadcasters feel about the fairness doctrine. *Journalism Quarterly*, 1978, *55*, 793-797.

Chaffee, S. H. *Political communication: Issues and strategies for research*. Beverly Hills, CA: Sage, 1975.

Chaffee, S. H., Ward, L. S., & Tipton, L. P. Mass communication and political socialization, *Journalism Quarterly*, 1970, *47*, 647-659, 666.

Chittick, W. C. American foreign policy elites: Attitudes toward secrecy and publicity. *Journalism Quarterly*, 1970, *47*, 689-698.

Clarke, P., & Fredin, E. Newspapers, television and political reasoning. *Public Opinion Quarterly*, 1978, *42*, 143-160.

Cohen, B. C. *The press and foreign policy*. Princeton: Princeton University Press, 1963.

Cohen, B. C. Mass communication and foreign policy. In J. N. Rosenau (Ed.), *Domestic sources of foreign policy*. New York: Free Press, 1967.

Comstock, G. The effects of television on children and adolescents: The evidence so far. *Journal of Communication*, 1975, *25*, 25-34.

Conway, M. M., Stevens, A. J., & Smith, R. The relation between media use and children's civic awareness. *Journalism Quarterly*, 1975, *52*, 531-538.

Cornwell, E. E., Jr. Presidential news: The expanding public image. *Journalism Quarterly*, 1959, *36*, 275-283.

Cornwell, E. E., Jr. The Johnson press relations style. *Journalism Quarterly*, 1966, *43*, 3-9.

Cutlip, S. M. Content and flow of AP news—From trunk to TTS reader. *Journalism Quarterly*, 1954, *31*, 434-446.

Davison, W. P. Diplomatic reporting: Rules of the game. *Journal of Communication*, 1975, *25*, 138-146.

Dennis, E. E. *The magic writing machine*. Eugene: School of Journalism, University of Oregon, 1971.

Dominick, J. R. Television and political socialization. *Educational Broadcasting Review*, 1972, *6*, 48-56.

Drechsel, R., Netteburg, K., & Aborisade, B. Community size and newspaper reporting of local courts. *Journalism Quarterly*, 1980, *57*, 71-78.

Dunn, D. D. *Public officials and the press*. Reading, MA: Addison-Wesley, 1969.

Gerald, J. E. Press-bar relationships: Progress since Sheppard and Reardon. *Journalism Quarterly*, 1970, *47*, 223-232.

Gillmor, D. M., & Barron, J. A. *Mass communication law: Cases and comment* (3rd ed.). St. Paul, MN: West Publishing, 1979.

Glick, E. M. Press-government relationships: State and H.E.W. departments. *Journalism Quarterly*, 1966, *43*, 49-56, 66.

Glick, E. M. *The federal government-daily press relationship*. Washington, DC: American Institute for Political Communication, 1967.

Golding, P. Media role in national development: Critique of a theoretical orthodoxy. *Journal of Communication*, 1974, *24*, 39-53.

Graber, D. The press as opinion resource during the 1968 presidential campaign. *Public Opinion Quarterly*, 1971, *35*, 168-182.

Greenberg, B. S., & Dervin, B. *Use of the mass media by the urban poor*. New York: Praeger, 1970.

Hachten, W. A. The press as reporter and critic of government. *Journalism Quarterly*, 1963, *40*, 12-18.

Hale, F. D. Press releases vs. newspaper coverage of California supreme court decisions. *Journalism Quarterly*, 1978, *55*, 696-702, 710.

Hollander, N. Adolescents and the war: The sources of socialization. *Journalism Quarterly*, 1971, *48*, 472-479.

Jackson-Beeck, M., & Kraus, S. Political communication theory and research: An overview 1978-1979. In D. Nimmo (Ed.), *Communication yearbook 4.* New Brunswick, NJ: Transaction-International Communication Association, 1980.

Johnson, N. R. Television and politicization: A test of competing models. *Journalism Quarterly,* 1973, *50,* 447-455, 474.

Kaid, L. L. Newspaper treatment of a candidate's news releases. *Journalism Quarterly,* 1976, *53,* 135-137.

Keir, G. J. Government public relations and the press in Michigan. *Journalism Quarterly,* 1966, *43,* 551-552.

Kraus, S., & Davis, D. *The effects of mass communication on political behavior.* University Park: Pennsylvania State University Press, 1976.

Lambeth, E. B. Perceived influence of the press on energy policy making. *Journalism Quarterly,* 1978, *55,* 11-18, 72.

Lorenz, A. L., Jr. Truman and the press conference. *Journalism Quarterly,* 1966, *43,* 671-679, 708.

Lowry, D. T. Agnew and the network TV news: A before/after content analysis. *Journalism Quarterly,* 1971, *48,* 205-210.

Lyle, J. *The news in megalopolis.* San Francisco: Chandler, 1965.

Matthews, D. R. *U.S. senators and their world.* Chapel Hill: University of North Carolina Press, 1960.

McCombs, M. E., & Becker, L. B. *Using mass communication theory.* Englewood Cliffs, NJ: Prentice-Hall, 1979.

Merrill, J. C., & Lowenstein, R. L. *Media, messages and men: New perspectives in communication.* New York: David McKay, 1971.

Merwin, J. How Texas legislators view news coverage of their work. *Journalism Quarterly,* 1971, *48,* 269-274.

Miller, S. H. News coverage of Congress: The search for the ultimate spokesman. *Journalism Quarterly,* 1977, *54,* 459-465.

Miller, S. H. Reporters and congressmen: Living in symbiosis. *Journalism Monographs, 53,* January, 1978.

Miller, S. H. Congressional committee hearings and the media: Rules of the game. *Journalism Quarterly,* 1978, *55,* 657-663.

Morgan, D. *The capitol press corps: Newsmen and the governing of New York state.* Westport, CT: Greenwood Press, 1978.

Mott, F. L. Newspapers in presidential campaigns. *Public Opinion Quarterly,* 1944, *8,* 348-367.

Nimmo, D. D. *Newsgathering in Washington: A study in political communication.* New York: Atherton Press, 1964.

NORC (National Opinion Research Center). General social survey. *Public Opinion,* October/ November 1979, *2,* 32.

O'Keefe, G. J. Political malaise and reliance on media. *Journalism Quarterly,* 1980, *57,* 122-128.

O'Keefe, G. J., & Mendelsohn, H. Nonvoting and the role of media. In C. Winick (Ed.), *Mass media and deviance.* Beverly Hills, CA: Sage, 1978.

Orwant, J. E., & Ullmann, J. Pentagon officers' attitudes on reporting of military news. *Journalism Quarterly,* 1974, *51,* 463-469.

Pember, D. R. *Mass media law.* Dubuque, IA: William C. Brown, 1977.

Pollard, J. E. The Kennedy administration and the press. *Journalism Quarterly,* 1964, *41,* 3-14.

Reddy, G. *The twilight of the presidency.* New York: World, 1970.

Rivers, W. L., Miller, S. H., & Gandy, O. Government and the media. In S. H. Chaffee (Ed.), *Political communication: Issues and strategies for research.* Beverly Hills, CA: Sage, 1975.

Robinson, M. J. Public affairs television and the growth of political malaise: The case of the selling of the president. *American Political Science Review,* 1976, *70,* 409-432.

Rubin, A. M. Television in children's political socialization. *Journal of Broadcasting,* 1976, *20,* 51-60.

Rubin, A. M. Children and adolescent television use and political socialization. *Journalism Quarterly,* 1978, *55,* 125-129.

Shain, R. E. Effects of Pentagon influence on war movies, 1948-70. *Journalism Quarterly,* 1972, *49,* 641-647.

Seymour-Ure, C. *The political impact of mass media.* Beverly Hills, CA: Sage, 1974.

Shaw, E. F. The press and its freedom: A pilot study of an American stereotype. *Journalism Quarterly,* 1972, *49,* 31-42, 60.

Shaw, D. L., & McCombs, M. E. *The emergence of American political issues: The agenda-setting function of the press.* St. Paul, MN: West Publishing, 1977

Sigal, L. V. *Reporters and officials: The organization and politics of newsmaking.* Lexington, MA: D. C. Heath, 1973.

Sussman, L. R. Mass news media and the Third World challenge. In D. B. Fascell (Ed.), *International news: Freedom under attack.* Beverly Hills, CA: Sage, 1979.

Swanson, D. L. Political information, influence and judgment in the 1972 presidential campaign. *Quarterly Journal of Speech,* 1973, *59,* 130-142.

Weaver, D. H., & Wilhoit, G. C. News magazine visibility of senators. *Journalism Quarterly,* 1974, *51,* 67-72.

Weaver, D. H., & Wilhoit, G. C. News media coverage of U.S. senators in four congresses, 1953-1974. *Journalism Monographs,* April 1980, *67.*

Weiss, C. H. What America's leaders read. *Public Opinion Quarterly,* 1974, *38,* 1-22.

Wilhoit, G. C., & Sherrill, K. S. Wire service visibility of U.S. senators. *Journalism Quarterly,* 1968, *45,* 42-48.

CHAPTER 17

Politicians and the Press:
An Essay on Role Relationships

Jay G. Blumler and Michael Gurevitch

THIS ESSAY probes our ability conceptually to interpret the relationship between mass media personnel and politicians in competitive democracies. It accordingly focuses on the "political" subarea of the much wider field of mass media-source interactions in a certain form of society—one that is "liberal-democratic." In such a society, the relations of media men to would-be communication and information sources are (1) problematic, (2) pivotal, and (3) exceptionally difficult to analyze.

They are *problematic* because they are not authoritatively prescribed in advance. Acceptance of the norm of editorial independence, plus the rarity of overt state control over media content, initially leaves the choice of sources in the hands of media employees. Even otherwise politically accountable public service broadcasting organizations are entitled to such discretion. According to the British Annan Committee on the Future of Broadcasting (1977), for example, "the evidence we received reverberated with the plea that the Government, politicians and indeed quasi-political organisations should not be permitted to control broadcasting directly." In a liberal-democratic state, then—closely defined exceptions apart—journalists are free to make their own arrangements with sources. As a result, they also zealously safeguard the near-sacred principle of confidentiality toward sources.

Media-source relations are *pivotal* in at least two senses. First, biography and observation confirm that such contacts typically absorb much of the energy, time, and thought journalists devote to their work. Even though reporters are obliged by their essentially intermediate situation to face many ways at once—

relating to such diverse reference groups as superiors, colleagues, and audience images—among these, reliable and well-placed sources are particularly preoccupying and formative. This is because "the news is rooted not merely in organizational process and professional norms but in the action, inaction and talk of the elites who are the sources and subjects of most political stories" (Entman & Paletz, 1980). In Gans's (1979) view, although "there is no single or simple explanation of the news," out of a "handful of explanatory factors . . . those governing the choice of sources are of prime significance." Sigal (1973) has also noted that "newsmen, by adhering to routine channels of news-gathering, leave much of the task of selection of news to its sources."

Second, divergent interpretations of the media-source power balance lie at the heart of diametrically opposed views of the sociopolitical functions of mass communications. In this controversy we seemingly confront the equally plausible claims of Marx (or rather his latter-day disciples) and McLuhan. According to one paradigm, the mass media (even when formally independent and neutral) are essentially subordinate to society's institutionally dominant power holders, treated as accredited witnesses whose opinions are regularly sought and whose interests and ideologies are systematically reinforced. In Hall, Connell, and Curti's (1976) version, "the media *accurately* reflect and represent the prevailing structure . . . of power" in society. According to a quite contrary thesis, however, the mass media are themselves power bastions, reality definers, and sites of professional cultures, with which other institutions must then come to terms. Exponents of the first perspective tend to deploy a terminology of source "control and management of information," involving "direct and indirect control and manipulation of the media" (Chibnall, 1977). Holders of the second view use a language of source adaptation instead, such that "media . . . are the dominant institutions of contemporary society . . . to which other institutions [must] conform" (Altheide & Snow, 1979). The same clash runs through the specifically political communication literature. Tracey (1978), for example, alleged that "linkages between the broadcasting organisation and the government of the day promote programme output which is compatible with the views of the dominant political institutions and in particular with government." But Smith (1981) reckons that "politicians have had to endure a more complete change of social role and professional *mores* as a result of television than almost any other group."

Media-source relations are *difficult to analyze* because their constituent elements are not easily isolated or disentangled. As Nimmo (1978) pointed out:

> Journalists do not gather news like a child plucking pansies from the meadow. Political news is the joint creation of the journalists who assemble and report events and other political communicators—politicians, professionals and spokespersons—who promote them.

Such a fusion occurs because each communicator is amply motivated to "study" the other when pursuing his or her interests. Politicians are highly salient to reporters as staples of running stories; information resources for background insight; and even audiences for their output, providing knowledgeable feedback. At times they may also serve as validators of ambiguous political situations, the news status of which would otherwise be uncertain. As a news executive of a British television company told one of us when interviewed during the 1979 campaign for elections to the European Parliament:

> There's a buzz in the air to which we react. If, for example, we were receiving a lot of complaints about our coverage of economic affairs or industrial relations or the trade unions, if people from certain sectors of society were complaining a lot, were giving us trips to show us round places, were taking us out to lunch—one would take note of that, and the fact that they were doing it would be an indication that they were taking it very seriously and also that there's something there, I suppose.

But politicians must also tailor their activities to news media workways so as to make themselves more widely known; build up and sustain opinion constituencies; cultivate policy awareness and support; test public reactions to likely initiatives; and counter rivals' publicity efforts as well as damaging critical fire from other quarters.

Thus, the process whereby media constructions of political issues are shaped and produced is subtle and complex. It involves a close interaction between political advocates and media professionals, in the course of which the two sides may virtually be said to constitute a subtly composite unity. This is not to say that they merge to form a new unified whole in which their separate identities are lost. On the contrary, each side to some extent retains its separate purposes, its distance from the other, and occasionally even its oppositional stance toward the other. Nevertheless, the political messages which emanate from the dominant patterns of interaction between both sides are in a sense traceable to a composite source. In fact, it would be extremely difficult to detect, within any given political message, the specific contribution to its shaping that was uniquely made by either side. They are inextricably intertwined.

The need to hone the conceptual tools we can apply to such relationships stems from policy concerns and theoretical puzzles alike. In the case of policy, the feasibility of promoting any desired political communication goal—whether it be building a more enlightened citizenry, reducing knowledge gaps, satisfying audience needs and expectations, or variegating the media issue-agenda—must largely depend on openings available in the predominant interaction patterns forged between prominent political actors and journalists. Similarly, the construction of adequate explanations of the production of political messages should be promising for the advancement of theory, the complexities of the process offering a useful testing ground on which rival approaches can demonstrate the sharpness of their analytical teeth. Moreover, identification of the main forces and mechanisms of interaction controlling these relationships should facilitate comparative political communication analysis, both across different societies and across different political situations and time periods within the same society.

THE AVAILABLE PARADIGMS

Analysis of the relationship between politicians as communicators and media personnel as observers of the political scene is in some conceptual disarray at present. Confusion arises because the models that are most often applied to it, the adversarial and exchange perspectives, share two fundamental defects. First, each is irretrievably partial in focus. Seeking to hit off its essence in some central flash of insight, neither can do justice to the inherent complexity of the relationship. Second, these views misleadingly pose as rivals in contention over the same ground—as if politician-journalist relations were most suitably to be treated as *either* adversarial *or* exchange-driven. Yet, at their most plausible, they are really applicable to *different* phenomena (instead of offering alternative interpretations of the *same* behaviors). Such a lack of comparability is further exacerbated by the fact that one of these positions, the adversarial, is permeated with prescriptive norms, for which there is no counterpart in the other.

The Adversary Model

The adversarial viewpoint is primarily ideological, prescribing how journalists should regard leading politicians and government figures. The relationship should pivot on an assumed-to-be-abiding conflict of interest between themselves and politicians. Journalists should never be "in the pockets" of the latter. They should warily scrutinize their conduct and rhetoric, supposing that the "real story" could lie hidden below the source-constructed surface. How far journalists in different societies actually accept such a creed (which may reflect an American cultural bias) has not often been empirically examined, but most accounts support de Sola Pool's (1973) conclusion that "it has a powerful pull on the journalist's imagination." If so, its appeal springs from two roots: a view of political power and a sense of responsibility to audiences.

Thus, the adversarial ethic stems partly from the presupposition in liberal-democratic theory of the self-serving propensities and potential fallibility of wielders of power. It follows that they should be carefully watched lest they abuse their powers, exceed their mandates, commit blunders they would prefer to conceal, and elevate themselves to positions of nonaccountable authority. From this standpoint, it is natural to ascribe to the mass media the role of watchdog, protecting the public from the power of rulers, digging out evidence of abuse and error, and treating official information sources like Greeks bearing gifts. So far as members of the audience are concerned, they have needs and interests which, according to liberal theory, may well diverge from those of rulers. To pursue their goals effectively, they need access to trustworthy sources of information, which can tell them about developments in the wider political environment that may impinge on their fate. Such a surveillance service is then assigned to the mass media, which are expected independently to interpret environmental events according to their own lights and not just take on trust what interested parties *say* their policies are designed to achieve.

Once this is accepted as a legitimate stance for the mass media to adopt toward ruling elites, it would not be surprising if it bred in turn an adversarial attitude to the media among holders of and contenders for political power. For one thing, a view of the media as adversaries might simply be a way in which power contenders reciprocate the perceived antagonism of the media toward themselves. The American literature frequently cites the Johnson and Nixon regimes as periods when both sides were caught up in a vicious circle of mutual suspicion and hostility. Politicians may also resent their dependency on the mass media for access to the electorate, sometimes seeing them as blocking or severely limiting channels for explaining themselves properly to the public (Crossman, Note 1). They may also regard some reporters as hypocritical in their approaches to affairs of state—proclaiming their devotion to serious informational service, on the one hand, while continually unleashing floods of sensational and trivial stores, on the other.

Presumably all this explains why, as Sanders and Kaid (1978) have concluded, "the adversary model remains predominant in the minds of academics and practitioners." Despite its absorption into the professional ideology of many journalists, however, and the periodic eruption of stormy rows between politicians and reporters that appear to give it empirical credence, this perspective is open to serious objection on three grounds.

First, the adversarial ethic is extremely narrow; it cannot provide a comprehensive normative guide to journalists' behavior toward their political sources and contacts. In itself, it includes, for example, no principles about the access rights of government spokesmen and critics; judiciousness; fairness; provision of an informed view of the problems and difficulties of government; or a readiness to give credit where it is due, as well as to publicize mistakes and wrongdoing. Even William Rivers (1970), the most wholehearted academic exponent of "the notion that there is an ideal relationship for government officials and journalists everywhere, and that . . . relationship should be that of adversaries," was obliged, when developing that viewpoint in detail, to hedge it about with a whole host of qualifications: asking, for example, "How much adversarity is enough?"; seeking to "define the limits of adversarity"; and declaring that an adversarial stance is not to be equated with a "knownothing belligerence towards government," with treatment of the President like "public property" rather than as a "public servant," with an indiscriminate "manufacturing" of conflict in pursuit of "adversarity with a vengeance," or with an "escalation" of adversarity to such a pitch that "the two institutions are driven to polar positions," ensuring that "heat exceeds light." The cumulative buildup of all these qualifications vividly demonstrates the impossibility of taking the adversarial ethic to its logical conclusion.

Second, regarded as an empirical account, the adversarial model is blind to certain essential features of journalists' daily relations with politicians. As Grossman and Rourke (1976) argued, it "provides no mechanism for understanding the enormous amount of cooperation and even collaboration that takes place in the interaction between the press . . . and the government." But it is not only to be faulted for its inherently limited explanatory power. When coupled with its normative stance, forms of mutual assistance that may be indispensable to keep political messages flowing to the public in tolerably full supply are liable to be castigated as "croneyism."

Third, if it is true that the production of political messages is a *joint* enterprise, involving both sides in some degree of interaction (whether collaborative or complementary), mutually adversarial positions cannot be sustained for any length of time (except in a limited way and within clearly defined and mutually respected boundaries) without eroding the very basis of the relationship. Perpetual war, hostility, and obstruction would only impede each side from the effective pursuit of any constructive political communication task.

The Exchange Model

It is mainly in contrast to the adversary model that portrayals of interaction between political spokesmen and media representatives in terms of social exchange appear refreshingly realistic. For example, drawing on other investigators' studies of congressional press relations, Weaver and Wilhoit (1980) noted:

> In accepting and providing tips and leads, in willingness to float "trial balloons" and accept leaks and in various arrangements of quid pro quo, reporters and Congressmen are often tacit, if not intentional, partners in the news. . . . "You scratch my back and I'll scratch yours."

In place of idealized visions of the journalistic St. George tracking down the political dragon, then, this injects into the analysis the dimension of self-interest (implying the presence of "purposive actors, who know their interests and have certain resources by which they can act to realize those interests"; Coleman, 1980). Thus, exchange theory provides a plausible explanation of how the relationship is sustained through the many tensions and vicissitudes to which it is prone. A relationship persists, it implies, so long as its continuity and outcomes are perceived by the actors involved to serve their separate or joint interests. It thus overcomes a major weakness of the adversary model.

A closely argued application of the exchange model to the relationship between the American press and presidency has been provided by Grossman and Rourke (1976). This hinges on the idea that "reporters and officials have reason and resources to trade with each other, and that this interdependence is the key to understanding their interaction." Or, as Tunstall (1970) succinctly states, political communication "can be seen as an exchange of information for publicity." What politicians and reporters will agree to in striking bargains with each other, then, will depend on their respective calculations of advantage and disadvantage, including impressions "of the resources, needs and likely actions of the other side," while from time to time they will also strive to alter the previous terms of trade in their favor. Grossman and Rourke also itemize the assets the American President brings to the publicity bargain—his lofty place on the media's news agenda, his entitlement to secrecy in certain issue domains, his ability to manipulate certain forums of exchange such as press conferences—as well as the strategies that are open to media men when trying to shift the relationship in their favor—contacting *other* information sources, undertaking investigative reporting, and activating outside pressures to compel the President to release information.

The strengths of this approach are evident. First, it captures well the flavor of many moments when politicians and reporters decide to deal with each other. Though it suggests that much political reporting takes place because each side benefits from it, it need not imply that this is typically a matter of either actor being in the pocket of the other. It is compatible with the preservation of a certain distance and even an oppositional mentality in the relationship. The politician who survives an apparently tough encounter with an aggressive television interviewer may expect to gain more public credit than one who submits himself only to less challenging tests. And, as Grossman and Rourke point out, each side is free, in advance of the exchange, to deploy whatever power resources it can command in order to strengthen its hand with the other.

Second, this model seems more sensitive to the fluid nuances of the political advocate-professional communicator relationship than the adversarial view. Indeed, it has a built-in explanation for such fluctuations. When more cooperation between the two sides is observed, the reason must lie in the enlarged area of benefit that each expects to enjoy through collaboration with the other. If, on the other hand, cooperation declines and conflict increases, this is because the perceived benefits of withholding collaboration now outweigh the previous advantages of going along with what the other had proposed or was prepared to accept. Whichever way the relationship turns, the exchange model is capable of explaining it.

Third, as already pointed out, an exchange view explains how the relationship can be sustained amid the many tensions that inhere in it and disputes that punctuate it. This is precisely the issue on which the adversary model failed. It posits the relationship to be adversarial without suggesting a mechanism for sustaining it through all the built-in conflicts. But such a mechanism lies at the heart of the exchange model.

Despite these advantages, the exchange perspective also suffers from two defects which limit its explanatory power. First, it overly stresses the more personal, immediate, and nonformalized calculations made and bargains struck. In Grossman and Rourke's (1976) words:

> If we look at the process of exchange between executive officials and media representatives . . . most striking is the informality of the relationship, the fact that it is based on unwritten rules, unnegotiated exchanges of commodities and mutual understandings.

But this begs the question of how the relationship is rendered *predictable.* The theory is vulnerable to the charge of being more concerned with ad hoc variations in the relationship than with its enduring regularities and structure. There is a more or less stable background of patterned assumptions and practices, within which journalist-politician exchanges take place, that are not themselves entirely derivable from this version of exchange theory.

Second, the exchange model fails to mention those norms that regulate the behavior of individuals working in institutional settings, which define what is permissible or impermissible in the terms of exchange they may offer or accept. Such norms may sometimes seem vague or porous, but they do exist and affect behavior. For example, the self-images of media professionals include ideals of service to the audience, which set bounds to the forms of political coverage that they could even contemplate providing (Blumler, 1969). Political commitments will similarly guide or limit officials' dealings with media representatives. Such normative influences on the chief producers of political communication may be taken for granted by exchange theory, but they cannot be explained by it.

A Power Variant

When examining the publicity strategies pursued by the Jimmy Carter organization in the 1976 race for the Democratic presidential nomination, F. Christopher Arterton (1978) used language taken "from the analysis of power relations," focusing "attention upon the political aspects of campaign-media interactions." Arterton particularly noticed that each side took account of the other partly through influences that were *external* to their actual exchanges. "Campaigners recognize," he claimed, "that the reported news is a result of many factors, most of which lie beyond their ability to affect." But each side could still strive to structure the situation in such a way as to narrow the other side's range of options to ones optimally favorable to themselves. Such an approach sliced both ways. The power of the media inhered in certain "values which journalists bring to campaign reporting: the need to simplify and condense, their preference for the novel or unexpected, the attractiveness of conflict or a dramatic element, and the fascination with the 'horse race' aspects to the election," to which publicity-seeking campaigners had to adapt. Politicians' rhetorical options were thus narrowed. Contrariwise, as candidates became more newsworthy, they enjoyed more power to influence reports about themselves, partly through skilfully exploiting competitive pressures between rival news organizations and individual correspondents. The key mechanism here was not so much a bargain or an exchange, then, as a convergence, propelled by fields of power forces to which the principal actors both contributed and reacted.

An important feature of this diagnosis, to be reckoned with in our own search for a more serviceable conceptual framework, is the indication that in political reporting media professionals may be guided by factors lying outside the field of direct interactions with politicians—and vice versa for the strategies of publicity-seeking candidates and officials. Arterton acknowledges the influence of such "external" factors without attending fully to their conceptual elaboration, confining himself to power relations at that level while ignoring normative ones. Yet he also describes the "press crises" that at some stage afflicted all major campaigns (Carter's fuzziness on the issues; Ford's East European gaffe), stemming (in his opinion) from journalists' hostile reactions to the overly orchestrated publicity successes which the candidates concerned had hitherto managed to score. In noting the normatively fueled source of such a journalistic about-face, Arterton thus takes us to the brink of analyzing the interaction of political communicators with each other in terms of role relationships without actually embarking on such an analysis.

Analytical Dilemmas

It is as if the field of mutual interaction and influence between politicians and journalists has been illuminated from time to time by various uncoordinated searchlights, each exposing a certain portion of the terrain to view without individually or jointly lighting up its entirety. Evidently we lack a more over-arching framework that could transcend, while incorporating, the leading conceptual offerings so far favored by outstanding analysts. The need for such an approach can be outlined from two standpoints.

First, there is the difficulty of meaningfully juxtaposing the available perspectives. Through what questions could they possibly be harnessed to each other? Should we ask how much exchange or how much adversariness a given relationship exhibits? Should we try to specify the conditions under which relationships might become more adversarial or more exchange-oriented? The project is futile—like enquiring when a certain tree might bear apples rather than oranges.

A second source of difficulty is the inescapable tension between the normative and operational levels of the relationships reviewed. On the one hand, the normative implications of liberal-democratic press theory prescribe an adversarial role for the media vis-à-vis the ruling institutions of society. But no lasting relationship can be built on such a basis in practice. On the other hand, theories which focus exclusively on operational interactions, attempting to explain how they work in practice, tend to ignore or minimize the role of normative ideologies and prescriptions in the outlook and conduct of those involved.

What seems to be required, then, is an approach that can take account of the complex cross-pressures which play on both parties to the relationship. On the normative plane, it would recognize the pull of norms and ideologies on actual behavior. On the operational plane, it would start from the proposition that both sets of actors have a stake in maintaining the political communication process itself, which is patterned by both norms and behavioral regularities, though it is also the target of periodic jockeying designed to change the prevailing ground rules; and that they typically appreciate the need to maintain a working relationship, to which each can settle and in light of which make their respective "battle plans."

Recognition of the tension between the normative and operational levels also sheds light on another characteristic feature of the relationship—its instability and vulnerability. Sensitive observers of the media-government dance in liberal-democratic societies often comment on the "delicacy" of the relationship, its fragility and proneness in moments of conflict to escalate into unanticipated mini-confrontations. This reflects the fact that both sides are simultaneously exposed, on the one hand to the pull of ideologies which are often incompatible because they stem from different sources, and on the other hand to pressures to maintain in some repair the tissues of continuing interaction. At one level, then, the two sides are pulled apart in divergent directions. At another level they are hauled back together toward a joint or parallel course.

The inherently precarious and potentially conflict-laden strains generated by such cross-pressures cannot provide a smooth basis for continually working together. What such a relationship requires is a measure of predictability and shared understandings, by recourse to which each side may reasonably try to anticipate the other's actions and reactions. To facilitate its continuity, that is, the relationship must, to some extent, be regularized and institutionalized.

AN EXPANDED FRAMEWORK

The production of political communications is inherently complex. When approached unilaterally, essential features tend to be distorted or ignored. Both in order to overcome the resulting theoretical problems and to structure empirical data derived from many observations of political communicators at work in Britain (Blumler, 1969, 1979; Blumler, Gurevitch, and Ives, 1978), we have developed an alternative analytical framework couched in the following summary terms: Media-disseminated political communications derive from interactions between (1) two sets of mutually dependent and mutually adaptive actors, pursuing divergent (though overlapping) purposes, whose relationships with each other are typically (2) role-regulated, giving rise to (3) an emergent shared culture, specifying how they should behave toward each other, the ground rules of which are (4) open to contention and conflicting interpretation, entailing a potential for disruption, which is often (5) controlled by informal and/or formal mechanisms of conflict management. The following sections outline some implications of each of these elements in turn.

Dependence and Adaptation

Political communication originates in mutual dependence within a framework of divergent though overlapping purposes. Each side of the politician-media professional partnership is striving to realize certain goals vis-à-vis the audience; yet it cannot pursue them without securing in some form the cooperation of the other side. Sometimes they share certain goals—for example, addressing, and sustaining credibility with, a large audience. As Fant (1980) pointed out, in televizing American presidential nominating conventions, "the networks and the parties have a common desire to attract as many television viewers as possible." Usually the actors' purposes are in some tension as well: Journalists are primarily aiming to hold the attention of a target audience through some mixture of alerting, informing, and entertaining them. Politicians are primarily trying to persuade audience members to adopt a certain view of themselves, or of their parties or factions, and of what they are trying to achieve in politics.

Whatever the exact mixture of goals, each side needs the other and must adapt its ways to theirs. Politicians need access to the communication channels that are controlled by the mass media, including the hopefully credible contexts of audience reception they offer. Consequently, they must adapt their messages to the demands of formats and genres devised inside such organizations and to their associated speech styles, story models, and audience images. As a verbal example of such adaptation, it is striking to note that it was a British politician, dedicated to his party's social reform program (and not a TV newsman), who told us (Blumler et al., 1978):

> Voters formulate their impressions in rather vague terms and the most they can take in is some sort of a nutshell, namely something that some leader has said or done that he has seen on TV. That is about as much as they can take and about as much as they will get. Some of them will even be sick of that. They will be getting much more than they really want. That is because the ordinary person isn't really interested in politics. . . . The ordinary person comes home tired out from work, and all he wants to do is to put his feet up and watch the telly. He has done his stint of hard work from 9 to 6, and after that he wants to forget about the world's problems and does not want to have to exercise his mind.

Likewise, journalists cannot perform their task of political scrutiny without access to politicians for information, news, interviews, action, and comment: "To be convincing purveyors of reality . . . journalists must get as close as they can to the sources of events" (Polsby, 1980). And as a verbal example of the resulting adaptation, it is striking to note that it was a British broadcasting executive, firmly devoted to the independence of his organization (and not a politician), who extolled the virtues of the party handout to us (Blumler et al., 1978) in these terms:

> There is no great merit in taking a subject, talking to it and then letting some sub-editor get it down to the essentials for you, rather than doing that job yourself. If we were a newspaper with endless columns of print, he might not have to bother. In the case of broadcasting, however, a man who can prepare this kind of comment pithily and concretely will get the coverage he is seeking.

Thus, each side to the prospective transaction is in a position to offer the other access to a resource it values. The mass media offer politicians access to an audience through a credible outlet, while politicians offer journalists information about a theater of presumed relevance, significance, impact, and spectacle for audience consumption. Because such resources are finite, however, rivals inside each camp compete more or less keenly for them, further strengthening the pressures promoting a mutual adaptation. The scope and terms of politicians' access to the media depend not only on conventional limitations of time and space (a 30-minute news bulletin; a 10-minute interview) but also on the "threshold of tolerance" a given organ's audience is assumed to exhibit toward political messages. So in competing for favorable attention in the preferred "slots," politicians adjust to perceived media values and requirements, a process that is illustrated by British campaigners' conviction that at election time "the essential requirement . . . was to keep the news initiative from one's rivals" by fashioning more catchy "golden phrases" for newsmen to headline and circulate (Blumler et al., 1978). But politicians also command scarce resources. Not only is the amount of informational raw material they can supply limited; it may also vary in quality—for example, a strong leak on a headline development is worth more than a speculative rumor about a more technical issue from a lower-placed source. Politicians are therefore in a position, especially when newsworthy, to "ration the goodies," use them as bargaining counters, and direct reporters' attention to their pet themes. "Pack journalism," which stems from a subtle mixture of (1) uncertainty about what really counts as political news and (2) anxiety not to miss something the competition will be carrying, intensifies the ensuing adaptations. As Polsby (1980) pointed out:

> Nobody who intends to supply the masses with their daily ration of news can afford to be out on a limb too often, peddling what may come to be viewed as an ideosyncratic version of reality. . . . Competitiveness thus entails snuggling up to news sources.

Of course, many of these factors operate as variables, not constants. Politicians vary in their need for media publicity. Local radio station managers, interviewed in Britain about the broadcasting of Parliament, for example, often equated MPs' efforts to get their debate contributions heard by listeners with the narrowness of their majorities over opponents at the previous General Election. Similarly, journalists will be more anxious to cover certain politicians and events than others. As recent American studies have suggested (Ostroff, 1980; Clarke & Evans, 1980), the pressure on them to follow the top politicians and uncritically pass on their initiatives is greater in presidential campaigns than in state-level races. But despite such sources of variation, the forces of mutual dependence, competition, and adaptation will tend most formatively to shape political communication about precisely those personalities and situations that receive the heaviest and most regular coverage in political news.

Role Relationships

The recurrent interactions that result in political communication for public consumption are negotiated, not by unsocialized individuals, but by individuals-in-roles—whose working relationships are consequently affected by normative and institutional commitments. In Chittick's (1970) definition:

> The term "role" refers . . . to the socially prescribed behavior of a position holder. . . . Role theory posits that position holders will behave in accordance with both their own role expectations and those of counter position holders.

What theoretical advantages flow from treating political communicators as occupants of roles, the terms of which guide their own behavior and shape their relationships with and expectations of their counterparts in the message production process? These may be outlined from three perspectives.

First, such an approach explains the behavior of political communicators by locating them in their respective organizational settings, where their roles are chiefly defined and performed. In the case of political journalists, role-anchored guidelines serve many functions. They provide models of conduct to be observed when contacting politicians or appearing before the public as "representatives" of their organizations, whose standards they are supposed to display (Kumar, 1975). They steer activity in countless daily routines. In an observation study of BBC current affairs producers at work during the British General Election of 1966, for example, certain initiatives taken to improve their campaign coverage were traced to "the internal role-definitions of their positions to which television journalists subscribe," including responsibilities "to serve the audience adequately" and "to the standards of their own profession" (Blumler, 1969). They are a source of support when conflict erupts. When, during the British General

Election of 1979, a BBC news executive dealt with various party complaints about unfairness, for example, he was observed to handle them confidently partly *because* he was an institutional figure. He could draw on corporation policy, professional standards, and past precedents both to justify what had been done and to suggest solutions to difficulties. So long as he was true to his role, he was protected (Gurevitch & Blumler, in press). Professional roles may also dictate journalists' reactions to proposed innovations. Changes which are interpreted as enhancing or extending their established roles (such as the broadcasting of Parliament) will tend to be welcomed. Those which are perceived as challenging or denying their roles (such as the Blumler et al. [1978] recommendation that election reporting in daily news bulletins be drastically reduced) will tend to be rejected.

In contrast to professional journalists, many practicing politicians are only part-time communicators. Even so, their media arrangements are often tended by full-time specialists with corresponding roles to match—press officers, publicity aides, campaign managers, speech writers, and so on. And when functioning as communicators, politicians also act out certain role prescriptions themselves: "representing" the interests of a party, government, or department of state; responding to the expectations of political colleagues, with whom their reputations can be strengthened or weakened by the quality of their public appearances; and addressing the electoral audience in a certain style. In fact, there may often be a close connection between a politician's public image and his internal communication-role definition. Certainly impressions of politicians' qualities as communicators have become increasingly important features of their public images in recent years—and so, presumably, of their internalized communication roles as well.

Second, a focus on roles as shapers and regulators of behavior also connects the interactions of media professionals and partisan advocates to the surrounding sociopolitical culture of the society concerned. This helps to explain their patterned continuity over time and their variety across diverse societies. A noteworthy example recently came to light in the formation of broadcasting policy for coverage of the 1979 elections to the European Parliament in the nine member states of the European Community. A team of comparative investigators of the role of broadcasting in those elections concluded: "In most countries the point of departure for organising how television would present the campaign to viewers was a set of past principles, conventions, programme formats and practices of *General Election* coverage" (Blumler, Note 2). In each political communication system, cultural influences ensured that politicians' and broadcasters' European election roles would correspond closely to previously formed national election patterns. In toto they therefore amounted to nine more or less distinct campaigns instead of a single uniform one. In other words, mass media structures, their organizational and professional ideologies, and their specific work practices are in every society specific to and shaped by its culture. Likewise, the structure and operations of the political institutions of society are products of the same cultural forces. It is not surprising, therefore, that a high degree of fit should be found between those institutions, which is reflected, at the interface between media and political institutions, in a fit between the role-regulated behaviors of the interacting communicators.

Several general features of such interaction are underlined by the considerations spelled out above. For one thing, communication behavior is *normatively prescribed*, involving *legitimated* expectations and actions. This suggests that the capacity of the participants to exchange resources or exercise influence is constrained by the guidelines pertaining to the roles they perform. Thus, political reporters cannot, without great risk, offer politicians any type of news treatment that lies outside the authority of their roles. Likewise, politicians will tend to avoid behavior vis-à-vis media personnel (such as blatant favors or explicit sanctions) that would be construed to breach their role prescriptions. Exchange and the tussles of mutual influence are normatively bounded. In addition, behavior on both sides is conditioned by expectations of how each will, because they should, behave toward the other. This has important consequences for the structure of the interaction. It underlies and explains the *predictability* of the behavior patterns involved and the ability of each side to count on much that the other will do so long as *its* expectations are met. It also helps to explain the note of outrage that is sometimes sounded during adversarial episodes—reflecting the injured party's conviction, not merely that its interests were damaged, but that supposedly accepted moral boundaries had been overstepped. And it explains the relative *stability of structure* of those many joint activities out of which political communication daily emerges.

Third, a reference to role conceptualization clarifies the partial plausibility of the adversary and exchange models and helps to reconcile their apparent opposition. On the one hand, exchange mechanisms are set in motion when performance of role obligations on either side requires the enlisting of cooperation from the other. On the other hand, adversarial relations are triggered when the role obligations of the two sides are such as to bring them into collision course with each other.

An Emergent Shared Culture

Many British television journalists and party publicists, when interviewed by the authors afterwards about their roles in the country's General Elections of February and October 1974, often emphasised the need for *mutual trust* in their relations with each other. A party press officer said: "If I gave the media a bum steer over the significance of a speech about to be made by my Leader, they would no longer take my guidance so seriously in the future." Another concluded a lengthy account of campaign exchanges by baldly asserting: "Both sides are operating on the basis of news values." Broadcasters also mentioned special efforts they had made to convince politicians they could be trusted to respect and apply shared norms. A 50-minute discussion program focused one of its three campaign editions on an issue the parties expected Labour to prefer, another on one plugged by the Conservatives, and yet another on one that both could agree was important. Vox pop interviews with floating voters in a magazine item had to be balanced in respect of their likely eventual leanings. And the senior political correspondent of an evening news bulletin said:

> If Labour material led the election news on the previous night and again on the current night, by golly the next night it would have to be Conservative led.

This was not to imply that uncertainty could be eliminated from the relationship. It was as if the communicators were playing a game with more or less agreed-upon rules, in which one or another participant would sometimes make an unexpected move—or even campaign for revised rules. Several party officials pictured their publicity initiatives as pieces of bait dangled before newsmen. The journalistic fish *might* not bite, but if the anglers chose the right bait for the conditions, and the political weather did not suddenly change, they stood a good chance of making a catch. In the process, however, each side needed to count on the other's observance of certain rules of conduct to an extent sufficient (1) to allow campaigners to frame publicity strategies that could be coherently unfolded and (2) to enable news executives to give assignments to reporters, camera crews, and OB units without risking a waste of precious resources.

All this reflects an underlying sociological imperative. In any continuing relationship based on mutual dependence and need, a culture, structuring all the areas of behavior in which both sides regularly interact, tends to emerge. The norms of that culture then (1) regulate the relationship, (2) get embedded in behavioral routines which often assume the status of precedents to be followed in the future, (3) are points of reference when disputes arise over alleged failures to respect existing ground rules or demands to change them, and (4) revert back to and become absorbed into the internal role definitions of the respective actors. This does not mean that all participants will embrace the operative norms equally enthusiastically or without reservation. Cultural differences will persist and be voiced as well. But a shared culture is continually reestablished, even in the face of disagreement, because it is indispensable to undergird the relationship.

Such norms of mutual working can govern a wide range of matters. For example, the emergent culture normally includes shared criteria of *fairness*. In a British election campaign, the two major parties are usually reckoned to deserve equal amounts of air time and the Liberals 60 percent of their share, while minor and new parties merit one five-minute broadcast so long as they put up candidates in a specified minimum number of constituencies. In other countries, quite different principles of fairness are applied—for example, absolutely equal treatment for all political parties regardless of size in Denmark. The Anderson candidacy in the American presidential campaign of 1980 was interesting from this point of view, because there was so little precedent to follow in arranging coverage of his peculiar appeal. An emergent culture had to be hastily cobbled together, and Anderson's attempt to prize a regular stream of stories from the media may have suffered from his lack of enduring organization (which undermined the expectation of continuing interaction after the election was over).

The shared culture may also include certain criteria of *objectivity*. The many distancing devices, described by Tuchman (1972) as "strategic ritual protecting newspapermen from the risks of their trade . . . including critics," owe much of their defensive efficacy to their acceptance by politicians and other news sources as valid marks of an objective approach.

Role relationships are also regulated by criteria of *behavioral propriety in interaction*. Respect for embargoes, the anonymity of sources, and the confidences of "off-the-record" disclosures come to mind here. In addition, certain boundaries distinguishing acceptable from impermissible areas of questioning may be well defined in one national news culture while following different lines in another. For example, the state of health of politicians is more searchingly probed by reporters in the United States than in Britain. Harold Wilson's belief that his sources of private income were off-limits to a questioning interviewer triggered a fierce row between the Labour Party and the BBC in 1971, obliging the latter to take many steps to mend the rift—even though Mr. Wilson's reaction was widely regarded at the time as overly extreme (Briggs, 1979).

In addition, and perhaps most significantly, interaction is regulated by a to some extent shared framework of *news values,* indicating both *who* and *what* will tend to be treated as newsworthy. As Elliott (1977) pointed out, "Accepting some sources as official and reliable while questioning or ignoring others is an important part of journalistic routine," and those inside the charmed circle of access will expect its existing boundaries to be maintained more or less intact. Shared substantive definitions of news make it possible for each side to try to manipulate the situation to its own advantage. Politicians, for example, needing exposure but lacking control over it can then so adjust their behavior to strengthen their chance of winning the most favorable coverage possible in the prevailing news-based definition of the situation.

In all these spheres complex processes and calculations play on the emergence, entrenchment, and revision of the ground rules. First, for each side there is often a mixture of benefit and cost in conforming to the prevailing pattern. Despite their highly privileged access rights, for example, top politicians may occasionally be on the receiving end of extremely unfavorable treatment, due to the access of journalists to other news sources, a pile-up of incidents casting doubt on their competence and power to control events, or even the impact of a "hoist-with-his-own-petard" syndrome, when a statesman's verbal blunders are flung back into his face. The fact that politicians rarely object to such treatment suggests either that they accept the ruling news-value system or realize that complaining would be counterproductive. Likewise, during the British General Election of 1979, some television journalists criticized their own overly receptive response to visual events stage-managed by the party Leaders. Yet they continued to present them, even after questioning their newsworthiness, partly because they could not aford unilaterally to suspend a shared convention. Instead, they occasionally salved their reportorial consciences by clothing them in a skeptically toned commentary.

Second, the existing fabric of news values is not solely a media product, which is then imposed on and accepted by politicians as a fait accompli. Politicians' definitions of situations may not only differ from those of journalists; at times they may also contribute to what counts as political news. The recent history of election coverage in Britain includes several episodes of attempted news creativity by politicians. The first use of the walkabout as a regular campaign device in the 1970 General Election is a case in point. It originated in the need of the Labour Leader for a source of daily appearances in a campaign that he wished to play in low-key vein, stirring up no enlivening issues. Yet during the 1979 campaign Leader walkabouts were screened almost daily in TV news (Pilsworth, 1980); broadcasters had come to accept them as a routine feature of their election coverage.

Third, an ever-evolving shared culture emerges from an ever tactically shifting process in which the principal actors strive to influence each other for their own benefit. As Polsby (1980) pointed out, journalistic professionalism demands that "news media élites establish their own account of day-to-day reality, independent of that propounded by the politicians whom they cover." In response, politicians can try either to exploit the dominant story lines or challenge their legitimacy. Rather more frequent recourse to the latter strategy has been encouraged in recent years by a growing awareness of the ultimate subjectivity of news judgments, which are relative to certain values and can only be universal in application of there is agreement on such underlying values (Gans, 1979). Barring such an agreement, more and more groups may come to regard the news as it applies to their affairs as wittingly or unwittingly politicized and therefore fit to be pressurized. Hence, the mass media have latterly been urged to assign more understanding reporters to racial beats, to be less strike-fixated in their coverage of industrial relations, and to look differently at feminist concerns. At a given time, then, the dominant system of news values will in part reflect the outcomes of previous tugs of war between journalists and representatives of numerous sectional groups, including politicians.

Fourth, despite much argument and tactical struggle, the influence of certain forces promoting normative integration can be detected in modern political communication systems as well. One is the presence inside media and political institutions of boundary roles, whose occupants are closely familiar with the values and practices of the other camp. The publicity advisors of politicians may convey to their masters an impression of the current news-value system as part of the natural order of things. Likewise, media organizations often appoint to their executive teams one or more individuals who are particularly sensitive to and au fait with leading politicians and their publicity problems. Both sides also seem to feel the need to be in a position, when engaged in or anticipating disputes, convincingly to appeal to principles that transcend their purely sectional interests. This strengthens the elements of shared culture by emphasizing their overarching standing. In the previously mentioned observation study of the British General Election of 1966, for example, it was noted that "the appeal of a political party to a principle of fairness which the producers themselves regarded as legitimate . . . helped to remind the broadcasters of considerations that had been overlooked in the hectic conditions of election programming" (Blumler, 1969). For their part, media men also seem motivated to enter potentially tense situations with "clean hands"—able to say, if a row was to erupt, that they at least had behaved quite properly and responsibly.

Underlying Sources of Conflict

However tightly woven, the web of mutual need and shared understandings cannot eliminate conflict. In foregoing pages we have characterized politicians and journalists as locked into a complex set of transactions which, though mutually beneficial, also include potentials for disagreement and struggle. Underlying the resulting disputes are certain *role-related,* and therefore *abiding,* sources of conflict—ones that continually arise because they are part and parcel of a system of interacting role partners whose purposes to some extent diverge.

First, the participants' differing organizational and professional role commitments give rise to the "cui bono" question of political communication: Who is supposed to be its main beneficiary? All commonly recognized that multiple purposes will be served, but their priorities are inevitably different. Politicians tend to regard the political communication process predominantly as an agency of persuasion, available to themselves (and their competitors) for mobilizing public support for their own causes and views, rather than as a channel for more detachedly educating and enlightening the electorate. When in power, they naturally tend to regard promotion of the national interest, as defined by their policies, as more important than the incessant search for their Achilles' heels and "criticism for the sake of criticism." For media professionals, the scales of ultimate aims are differently balanced. It is true that they often acknowledge politicians' special access rights, particularly at election time. Indeed, radical critics of mass communication have little difficulty in marshaling evidence intended to document media subservience and deference to those in power. Yet the principle of service to the audience is an integral part of the professional ideology of media personnel in liberal-democratic societies and is supposed to override the service proffered other interests. Though in interaction they are often pulled very close to politicians' needs, journalists can never entirely forget their audience clients. The following musings by a BBC commentator on the coverage by British television of a recent round of political party conferences exemplify such a spirit (Dimbleby, 1980):

> Perhaps television has become too much at the service of the parties and their Conferences. . . . The broadcaster is there, after all, at the service of the viewer, not the party. It would be a pity to confuse what the former wants with what the latter may choose to provide.

Second, different perceptions of the division of labor in the production of political messages generate the "agenda-setting" question of political communication: Who should determine which definitions of political problems citizens will think and talk about most often? This arises because the reality-structuring role of the mass media is at one and the same time formative, ambiguous, and doubtfully legitimate. That is, it often obliges politicians to discuss issues in terms they find irrelevant or repugnant; it is not always admitted that this is happening; and nobody "elected" media men to play such a part. It is therefore sometimes perceived as an "intervention" in the political arena itself, distorting its natural parameters, which presupposes in turn that the proper role of the media is one of reflecting and transmitting the statements, decisions, and comings and goings of the "primary" political actors. Intriguingly, such assumptions may be voiced on both sides of the media-political institutional divide. Of course, some politicians would prefer the active role of the media in politics to be reduced. Some reporters, though, not only defend themselves from criticism by claiming to do no more than reflect the world as it is: One professional version of the essence of the journalistic role *defines* it in gatekeeping rather than advocacy terms (Janowitz, 1975). But this, then, gives credence to the politicians' expectations of a mirroring rather than a framing of their activities and utterances by journalists; and stokes up resentment over the "usurpation" of their rightful position as setters of the political agenda. As Weaver (1972) pointed out, the problem is "insoluble" when posed in these terms:

> *Any* body of knowledge possesses its biases. The only way to ensure that every citizen truly is master of his own opinions is to ban *all* media. . . . But such an imposition of ignorance would exercise its own tyranny.

Of course, the combatants could try to transcend this conflict, accept the inevitability of "biases" in media portrayals of politics, and raise for discussion instead the question of *which* biases should be propagated by journalism (and in what variety). But that would only transfer abiding conflict to another plane.

Third, different ways of interpreting each other's roles give rise to a "fixing-of-responsibility" question about political communication: Who is to blame when it goes wrong and proves unsatisfactory? Post mortems after uninspiring election campaigns, for example, often show each side disclaiming responsibility and pointing the finger of censure at the other: Journalists decry the politicians' evasive rhetoric; politicians deplore the journalists' reduction of their rivalry to a horse race. The origins of such a process are deep-seated and involve contradictions between three perceptual tendencies:

(1) *When presenting itself to others,* each side depicts its role as in some sense sacred. The politician cloaks himself in a representative capacity. The journalist claims to enshrine freedom of expression and the public's right to know.

(2) *When reflexively contemplating its own role,* each side takes full account of certain constraints that limit its ability to realize its more idealized goals. Indeed, each side often treats imperfections in the electoral audience—its ignorance, indulgence in fixed stereotypes, and lack of commitment to sustained intellectual effort—as explaining and justifying the compromises it must make when addressing ordinary people.

(3) But *when regarding the contributions to political communication of its counterpart,* each side lacks charity and is quick to point to the gap between its role performance and its role professions, interpreting this as evidence of inadequacy—or even hypocrisy.

Since the defects of political communication are plausibly and regularly blamed on the failures of the *other* partner to the process, neither assumes responsibility for putting them right, inadequacies persist without correction, and so the cycle of mutual criticism is perpetuated as well.

Conflict Management

The preceding discussion has identified certain built-in sources of recurrent conflict. If our argument about the need to sustain the relationship is valid, then in any liberal-democratic society the political communication system will also include some mechanisms for managing conflict. In form, these will differ from one society to another, and their workings will not always be visible or openly discussed. In a sense they are delicate, for the cooperation required to smooth out conflict may seem at odds with the principle of media independence and its implication that political forces should not be in a position to dictate how journalists comment on political affairs. British arrangements are quite interesting in this connection, since they have moved quite far in the direction of institutionalizing conflict management. Consideration of some of the procedures that have been developed there highlights several functions that mechanisms of conflict management can perform for political communication systems.

First, there are numerous procedures for airing and dealing with complaints about the violation of ground rules. These may be hierarchically structured. In the case of the BBC, for example, aggrieved politicians with quite specific complaints may directly approach the editor of the offending program. Complaints with broader implications may be channeled through a political party's broadcasting officer at national headquarters, or its Chief Whip in Parliament, to the chief assistant to the director general of the BBC. However, specially serious causes of concern might be personally raised by senior politicians with the corporation's director general himself or with the chairman of its board of governors. The loftier the channel through which the complaint flows, the more likely it is to trigger a semiformal investigation and delivery of a verdict and reply in writing. But in all such exchanges the personalities and temperaments of the individuals handling the complaints are crucial. Those with a grievance to put like to feel that they are dealing with someone who is fair and sympathetic. Those receiving protests like to feel that they are dealing with a person of reason and common sense. A high valuation is often placed by those who are regularly involved in such transactions on attitudes that facilitate calm and accommodation: moderation, avoidance of single-minded assertions of principle, readiness to compromise, sensitivity to the other side's flash points. Ambiguities of stance often result—as these thoughts, conveyed to one of the authors by a highly placed party spokesman, amply show:

> The more you try as a political party to bind the broadcasters to things you want, the more you get into a jam about it. If, however, the broadcasters are to enjoy a greater freedom in political coverage, then it is correspondingly necessary for them to pay attention to strong party feeling and not deliberately to flout such feelings, as perhaps some of them are inclined to do.

Second, forums may be created to review existing ground rules and consider proposals for modifying them. For example, the Committee on Political Broadcasting, representing the main political parties, the BBC, and ITV, meets annually and in advance of every General Election campaign to discuss the number, lengths, distribution and scheduling of party political broadcasts. In fact, suggested changes are usually aired first in informal soundings of everybody's views, aiming to hammer out disagreements well before any proposals are tabled for finalization at a formal committee meeting.

Third, institutions may be established to socialize the members of one side to the needs and demands of the other side as a precondition of access to its resources. An example is the Lobby Committee in the precincts of Parliament, which, though staffed by journalists, ensures the conformity of their accredited colleagues to certain rules of behavior that are regarded as quid pro quos for privileged access to ministers and MPs.

Fourth, forums of consultation may be created to secure the continuing cooperation of one of the sides in a joint task. One example is the D-Notice Committee, which involves newspaper editors in a voluntary censorship of specified forms of security-sensitive information. Another is the aforementioned Committee on Political Broadcasting, at the preelection meetings of which broadcasters outline their campaign programming plans, both as a courtesy to the politicians who will be affected by them and to allow objections to be raised in advance that could be highly disruptive if they were to erupt while the campaign was already in hectic flood.

THE SYSTEMATIZATION OF
POLITICAL COMMUNICATION:
CONSEQUENCES AND POLICY IMPLICATIONS

This essay has outlined some unfamiliar ways of approaching the communication elites whose joint activities yield political news and comment for the masses. It interprets their relationship as one that typically develops through patterned interactions, which are shaped and constrained in turn by requirements seated in their roles as political advocates and mass media professionals. "Married 'til death us do part," they badly need each other's services and dependability; but as a result of their conflicting purposes, roles, and definitions of politics, they are periodically buffeted by upsets and strains. Yet even such conflicts often bind as well as divide them, since key figures inside each camp tend to acquire stakes in workable conflict management.

What principal consequences flow from such a system for the production of political messages in competitive democracies? When we try briefly to itemize them (as in the paragraphs below), we do not find all our answers reassuring.

(1) The system gives a rather privileged position in political communication output to the views of already established power holders. Of course, many others get a say as well, but only the activities and statements of those in well-entrenched positions tend regularly to be relayed to electoral audiences as a matter of course. Sometimes the news-value justification for such near automatic access is not easy to spot: It is as if the comments of the most highly accredited witnesses are worth transmitting, not for what they have said but for what they are. That is why, when commenting in a recent report on the British assumption "that at election time a party Leader is always news," we agreed that "this is true when a fresh statement of policy is being made, but we wonder if it is true when a Leader buys a new raincoat . . . [or] when his hovercraft is late for an engagement" (Blumler et al., 1978). Occasionally the beneficiaries of such treatment also resist the proposed extension of more ample communication access to other groups. In the British system, for example, Scottish and Welsh National parties had to fight hard to win even limited party broadcasting rights;

and at the time of writing there are signs that the newly formed Social Democratic Party could face a similar struggle.

(2) The other side of the coin is that leading politicians get their say almost entirely through formats devised and controlled by journalists. Such a "subordination" is the price they pay for their privileged access position. This *is* a price, because it denies them direct access to the mass audience, except in circumscribed ghettoes (party broadcasts) or paid advertisements. Thus, the system has more or less settled for the reduction of political messages to the demands of journalism, with its emphasis on the dramatic, the concrete, the personalizable, and the arresting—and with its turbulent and episodic view of the flow of time (Bensman & Lilienfeld, 1971). Perhaps the main reason for this is the assumption, by now largely shared by all orthodox communicators in partisan and professional circles, that audience tolerance for unmediated political communications is lower than for mediated ones, and that journalistic mediation enhances message credibility and acceptability. As a result, "the political order is liable to be exposed to faster flowing, though sometimes ephemeral, cross-currents of change" (Blumler, 1977a)—with whatever threats these may pose to the stability and cohesion of democratic accountability processes.

(3) Meanwhile, the needs of the audience may be relegated to a back seat in the political communication bus. This is because, in their preoccupation with a complex of conflicting interests, mutual dependencies, and problems of second-guessing each other, the two main sets of communicators may well lose sight of the ordinary voter's concerns and come to behave largely in those ways that seem likely to forge the most convenient accommodation to the other side's behavior available at the time (Blumler, 1977b). Fortunately, potentially strong antidotes to such a tendency can be found in the journalistic ethnic of audience service. Yet even this may be impoverished in application by the hold of sharply stereotypical impressions of what the average audience member is like as a news-processing animal. And if prevailing audience images fail to do justice to genuine kernels of concern among members of the public to make some sense of their political environment, then communication dictated by them could ultimately prove frustrating to its would-be receivers because of not seeming to them to provide anything worth heeding.

(4) Finally, much of a society's political news "conveys an impression of eternal recurrence" (paraphrasing Rock, 1973). Although a strain toward the ritualization of political communication (such that "new political situations . . . fall quickly into old symbolic molds"; Bennett, 1980) has many sources, one of its roots may be traceable to the inherent caution of interdependent communicators. It is as if political communication systems can vibrate overresonantly to the principle of "Better the Devil you know than the one you don't know." This is not to imply that innovatory impulses are often stifled at birth; but that they

may have to fight a steep uphill battle even to stand a chance of being tried. This is essentially because pressures to maintain the stability of the working relationship between "partisans" and "professionals" militate against the purposive introduction of new political communication forms. Indeed, our own observations suggest that innovatory communication proposals often start life with three strikes against them. First, a new departure may not get off the ground because it is in somebody's interest not to cooperate—as with the fate of numerous attempts to stage party Leader debates on British television at election time. Second, an innovation may be risky because of the uncertainty it would generate. The authors believe that this explains why certain changes in British party broadcasting formats they recommended a few years ago were not adopted in the end, despite an initially favorable reception; when it came to the crunch the political parties were unwilling to court the risks of fashioning propaganda in unfamiliar contexts. Third, some innovations may offend, because they seem to violate shared cultural norms and established precedents. That is the lesson which Tracey (1977) drew from Harold Wilson's furious rejection of the BBC's *Yesterday's Men* broadcast in 1971:

> What one can say, then, is that programmes which stray from forms and practices that normally govern the coverage of politicians—that is, the formal interviews, studio discussions, reportage of speeches, information about parliamentary affairs, etc.—is [sic] likely to provoke a sharp reaction.

Such formidable blockages to innovation are worrying, not because novelty should be valued for its own sake, but because freshness of approach is indispensable when tackling the inherently difficult tasks of making political information palatable and political argument comprehensible to large masses of voters.

REFERENCE NOTES

1. Crossman, R. H. S. *The politics of television.* Granada Guildhall Lecture, London, October, 1968.
2. Blumler, J. G. *Comparative analysis of broadcasting organization policy for the European elections.* Paper presented to Conference on the Role of Broadcasting in the European Elections, Brussels, September, 1980.

REFERENCES

Altheide, D. L., & Snow, R. P. *Media logic.* Beverly Hills, CA: Sage, 1979.
Arterton, F. C. The media politics of presidential campaigns: A study of the Carter nomination drive. In J. D. Barber (Ed.), *Race for the presidency: The media and the nominating process.* Englewood Cliffs, NJ: Prentice-Hall, 1978.
Bennett, W. L. Myth, ritual, and political control. *Journal of Communication,* 1980, *30,* 166-179.
Bensman, J., & Lilienfeld, R. The journalistic attitude. In B. Rosenberg & D. M. White (Eds.), *Mass culture revisited.* New York: Van Nostrand Reinhold, 1971.

Blumler, J. G. Producers' attitudes towards television coverage of an election campaign: A case study. In P. Halmos (Ed.), *The sociology of mass-media communicators.* Keele: University of Keele, 1969.

Blumler, J. G. The intervention of television in British politics. In *Report of the Committee on the Future of Broadcasting.* Cmnd 6753-I. London: Her Majesty's Stationery Office, 1977. (a)

Blumler, J. G. The election audience: An unknown quantity? In RAI/Prix Italia *TV and elections.* Torino: Edizioni Rai Radiotelevisione Italiana, 1977. (b)

Blumler, J. G. Communication in the European elections: The case of British broadcasting. *Government and Opposition,* 1979, *14,* 508-530.

Blumler, J. G., Gurevitch, M., & Ives, J. *The challenge of election broadcasting: A role analysis.* Leeds: Leeds University Press, 1978.

Briggs, A. *Governing the BBC.* London: BBC, 1979.

Chibnall, S. *Law-and-order news: An analysis of crime reporting in the British press.* London: Tavistock, 1977.

Chittick, W. O. *State Department, press, and pressure groups.* New York: John Wiley, 1970.

Clarke, P., & Evans, S. H. "All in a day's work": Reporters covering congressional campaigns. *Journal of Communication,* 1980, *30,* 112-121.

Coleman, J. Authority systems. *Public Opinion Quarterly,* 1980, *44,* 143-162.

de Sola Pool, I. Newsmen and statesmen: Adversaries or cronies? In W. Rivers & M. J. Nyham (Eds.), *Aspen notewook of government and the media.* New York: Praeger, 1973.

Dimbleby, D. Conference television: Serving the viewer or the party? *The Listener,* 1980, *104,* 536.

Elliott, P. Media organizations and occupations: An overview. In J. Curran, M. Gurevitch, & J. Woollacott (Eds.), *Mass communication and society.* London: Edward Arnold in association with The Open University Press, 1977.

Entman, R. M., & Paletz, D. L. Media and the conservative myth. *Journal of Communication,* 1980, *30,* 154-165.

Fant, C. H. Televising presidential conventions, 1952-1980. *Journal of Communication,* 1980, *30,* 130-139.

Gans, H. J. *Deciding what's news: A study of CBS evening news, NBC nightly news, Newsweek and Time.* New York: Pantheon, 1979.

Grossman, M. B., & Rourke, F. E. The media and the presidency: An exchange analysis. *Political Science Quarterly,* 1976, *91,* 455-470.

Gurevitch, M., & Blumler, J. G. The construction of election news at the BBC: An observation study. In J. S. Ettema & C. D. Whitney (Eds.), *Communicators in context: Current research on mass communicators.* Beverly Hills, CA: Sage, in press.

Hall, S., Connell, I., & Curti, L. The 'unity' of current affairs television. In *Cultural studies 9.* Birmingham: Centre for Contemporary Cultural Studies, University of Birmingham, 1976.

Janowitz, M. Professional models in journalism: The gatekeeper and the advocate. *Journalism Quarterly,* 1975, *52,* 618-626, 662.

Kumar, K. Holding the middle ground: The BBC, the public and the professional broadcaster. *Sociology,* 1975, *9,* 67-88.

Nimmo, D. *Political communication and public opinion in America.* Santa Monica, CA: Goodyear, 1978.

Ostroff, D. H. A participant-observer study of TV campaign coverage. *Journalism Quarterly,* 1980, *57,* 415-419.

Pilsworth, M. Balanced broadcasting. In D. Butler & D. Kavanagh (Eds.), *The British General Election of 1979.* London: Macmillan, 1980.

Polsby, N. W. The news media as an alternative to party in the presidential selection process. In R. A. Goldwin (Ed.), *Political parties in the eighties.* Washington: American Enterprise Institute for Public Policy Research and Kenyon College, Gambier, Ohio, 1980.

Report of the Committee on the Future of Broadcasting. Cmnd 6753. London: Her Majesty's Stationery Office, 1977.

Rivers, W. *The adversaries: Politics and the press.* Boston: Beacon, 1970.

Rock, P. News as eternal recurrence. In S. Cohen & J. Young (Eds.), *The manufacture of news: Social problems, deviance and the mass media.* London: Constable, 1973.

Roeth, I., Katz, E., Cohen, A. A., & Zelizer, B. *Almost midnight: Reforming the late night news.* Beverly Hills: Sage, 1980.

Sanders, K. R., & Kaid, L. L. Political communication theory and research: An overview 1976-77. In B. D. Ruben (Ed.), *Communication yearbook II.* New Brunswick, NJ: Transaction Books, 1978.

Sigal, L. V. *Reporters and officials.* Lexington, MA: D. C. Heath, 1973.

Smith, A. TV and the politician. *Irish Broadcasting Review,* 1981, *10,* 7-10.

Tracey, M. 'Yesterday's men'—a case study in political communication. In J. Curran, M. Gurevitch, & J. Woollacott (Eds.), *Mass communication and society.* London: Edward Arnold in association with The Open University Press, 1977.

Tracey, M. *The production of political television.* London: Routledge & Kegan Paul, 1978.

Tuchman, G. Objectivity as strategic ritual: An examination of newsmen's notions of objectivity. *American Journal of Sociology,* 1972, *77,* 660-679.

Tunstall, J. *The Westminister lobby correspondents: A sociological study of national political journalism.* London: Routledge & Kegan Paul, 1970.

Weaver, D. H., & Wilhoit, G. C. News media coverage of US Senators in four congresses, 1953-1974. In *Journalism Monographs* No. 67. Minnesota: Association for Education in Journalism, 1980.

Weaver, P. H. Is television news biased? *The Public Interest,* 1972, *26,* 57-74.

PART IV

Methods of Study

CHAPTER 18

Cultural Criticism

Philip Wander

Cultural criticism . . . is often able to state little more than the obvious:
that television, and other media, is dominated by various forms of capitalist ideology. Such an approach yields analyses of particular cultural pro-
ductions that are banal and repetitive, and provides no way of taking
seriously the rebellious, oppositional, and subversive moments in almost all
forms of popular culture.

—Douglas Kellner (1979)

I believe a crucial element "the critical faculties of the best minds"—
ought to re-examine this program, scrutinize the future ones, and begin
resisting television's glib and cynical assumptions.

David Eisenhower (1977)

Cultural criticism, developed and refined during revolutionary periods in the
eighteenth and nineteenth centuries, is the practice of interpreting cultural
products in the context of ideological struggles. It examines the world view
conveyed by such products, facts they do or do not acknowledge, and consequences and alternatives they do or do not ignore in light of moral, social,
economic, and political issues. Criticism, working out of this tradition, refuses to
look on culture as an isolated, refined, or politically innocent activity. However
aesthetically pleasing, whatever the professed aims, it insists on asking the
question: What does the product have to say in context? It is a question more
likely to be asked during periods of conflict. It can be raised by any party to the
conflict. This question can be and has been raised not only about a particular
product but also about the medium through which it is communicated. While
the media and the products they convey have changed over the centuries in quite

497

dramatic ways, arguments over their impact on society or their potential dangers, over what we now call "popular culture"—have not. The issues raised in English literary journals in the nineteenth century are virtually the same as those debated today (Lowenthal, 1964).

However important the questions raised by cultural criticism, there exist a number of obstacles to pursuing such a critique. In academic fields of study, specialization sometimes declares that social, political, economic, and moral implications of cultural products are not appropriate to a given area of research or criticism. Among the students of the arts, the use of aesthetic criteria to determine the critical object filters out not only some of the most influential cultural products but also some of the most popular of the mass media. Humanistic criticism, still fighting the "two cultures" battle identified a quarter of a century ago by C. P. Snow, often ignores the best scientific work on the effects of a given medium or the content of popular culture. Taken together, however, these barriers do not muddle cultural criticism half so much as does the conventional view of the mass audience. I cannot stress strongly enough the problems which the "mass audience" stereotype introduces into serious, informed, and otherwise enlightened critique (Ben-Horin, 1977).

The dance-crazed, commercially dominated, TV-addicted teenager; the nothing-better-to-do housewife hooked on soap operas and pulp magazines; the beer-drinking, pot-bellied oaf watching his football game; the addled elderly viewer who writes a letter to an actor asking for medical advice or insults a popular "villain" in public; the blank-faced, anesthetized, stupified "videot"— each of these characters has entered into that "museum" of received opinion called "common sense." Criticism, even that which is ordinarily embarrassed by any association with common sense, nevertheless plays off these stereotypes. Indeed, these stereotypes—the teenager, housewife, blue-collar sports fanatic, and the gullible older viewer or child who assumes that an actor is the character he depicts on film—are frequently accepted as real and representative by critics, who avoid arguments by joining them together under the label "isolated, alienated, apathetic spectators." The generic term is the same, however—the "mass audience."

The Mass Audience and Public Opinion
in the Twentieth Century

For one sensitive to political issues associated with such stereotypes (and they are quite profound), the question, phrased in historical terms, becomes: How did the public or publics, so crucial to political debates in the eighteenth and nineteenth centuries, become the mass? How did the media become implicated in the creation of hundreds of millions of isolated, mindless, and quiescent individuals? There are similar themes embedded in the arguments over popular culture going back to the eighteenth century. But why are certain of these themes no longer the subject of argument, no longer conceived of as even potential issues? Confining our analysis to the pessimistic, often cynical view of the "mass audience," there have been, I think, a number of events which have occurred in the twentieth century that, taken together, so far incline us to a bleak and pessimistic view of the world that similar claims made about the masses and the impact of media in earlier periods take on wholly different meanings. The signal event in this great transformation was World War I.

Our sensibilities, informed by Dada, surrealism, and despair grounded in the reality of human slaughter and the seeming inevitability of war, are not in sympathy with the generation that fought "The Great War." They seem childlike and quaint; their experience a prelude; their past lost in the dark varnish and gilt edges of Victorianism. The "front generation" had been taught that the object of life was to reach out to beauty and love, and that mankind was on the way to perfection (Fussell, 1975). The horrors of colonialism had been confined to people of color in other parts of the world. Poetry, art, philosophy, and religion in prewar Europe conveyed not the vapors of idealism but its palpability. Wrote Francis Thompson, just before the Great War:

> O world invisible, we view thee,
> O world intangible, we touch thee,
> O world unknowable, we know thee,
> Incomprehensible, we clutch thee!

For the survivors, those who remembered the smell of rum and blood, bodies putrifying on the barbed wire, the staff officers who never saw a trench, there could be only disillusion. Truth, Hope, Progress, Human Perfection became lies whispered by the ignorant and hypocritical to the young and naive. Of the Common Man,

> With the other masquerades
> That time resumes,
> One thinks of all the hands
> That are raising dingy shades
> In a thousand furnished rooms.

The old Ideals not only failed to prevent the slaughter; they had enlisted in its justification and died in uniform.

Part of the disillusionment was occasioned by official attempts to control and direct public opinion. Propaganda ministries operated at home to bolster morale and abroad to demoralize the enemy. The power exercised by governments over their citizens during the course of the war, the dictatorships arising out of the war, and the savage experience of the front generation had their effects on political theory, especially on the belief in popular government. In America, for example, objections raised during the 1880s over the participation of immigrants and anarchists in political affairs were greatly intensified, after the war, by fears of a coming Bolshevik revolution, runaway prices, business depression, revolutions in Europe, and widespread strikes. Early in 1920 Attorney General Palmer's agents rounded up over 6000 "aliens" for deportation and were prepared to arrest thousands more (Coben, 1964).

In the aftermath of this social, economic, and political instability, a young Harold Lasswell wrote about the techniques of persuasion employed by the allies during World War I. "Propaganda," he declared in 1927,

> is a concession to the wilfulness of the age. The bonds of personal loyalty and affection which bound a man to his chief have long since dissolved. Monarchy and class privilege have gone the way of all flesh, and the idolatry of the individual passes for the official religion of democracy. It is an atomised world, in which individual whims have wider play than ever before, and it requires more strenuous exertions to co-ordinate and unify them formerly [Lasswell, 1927/1971].

What is society to be based on; what will hold it together in the modern age? Lasswell's answer remains instructive, conveying as it does both despair over the loss of ideals and a vision of the future in which the mass media play a central role. "The new antidote to wilfulness," he concluded, "is propaganda. If the mass will be free of chains of iron, it must accept chains of silver. If it will not love, honour and obey, it must not expect to escape seduction" (Lasswell, 1927/1971, p. 222).

Lasswell's silver chains and atomized individuals seduced into proper behavior reflects not only the impress of the war but also a fundamental economic transformation, not unrelated to the war effort with its centralizing tendencies and its planning for national markets. This was the shift away from a prewar economy involving heavy industry and vast public projects—railway construction, shipbuilding, street lighting, and so on—toward the mass production and mass distribution of goods for individual consumption. "Consumer capitalism," we now call it, an orientation that, in America, came to be equated with owning one's home and stocking it with manufactured products variously called "labor-saving devices," "modern appliances," "new fashions,' 'and "modern miracles" (Williams, 1975).

The relationship between national efforts to propagandize the public during the war and the growth of consumer capitalism is symbolized in the title of a book written by George Creel, head of the committee in this country which had the responsibility for distributing government information during the war. The book, *How We Advertised America,* appeared in 1920. Public opinion became problematic during this period. In 1923, E. L. Bernay's seminal book on commercial advertising, *Crystallizing Public Opinion,* was published. Walter Lippman's classic, *Public Opinion,* and John Dewey's *The Public and Its Problems* appeared in 1927, the same year as the first of a series of monographs—L. L. Thurstone's, "The Method of Paired Comparisons for Social Values," *Journal of Abnormal and Social Psychology*—which led directly to the development of public opinion polling.

Centralized government, the growth of a new type of economy, the rise of the modern corporation, consumer credit, and new communications technology—propaganda—these were the dynamos of the modern world, or what we are beginning to call "modernism," a particular socioeconomic configuration generating its own world view. William Grahm Sumner, in "The Forgotten Man," noted the impact of modernism on a being nurtured in another world: the individual delving away in patient industry, supporting his family, paying taxes, casting his vote, supporting the church and the school, cheering for the politician of his admiration. There was, Sumner thought in 1911, no provision made for this sort of individual in the "great scramble" (cited in Schneider, 1963, p. 356). John Dewey drew on the sense of community he experienced as a young boy growing up in rural Vermont. For generations, students had found solace in Thoreau's "Walden" and Emerson's verdant prose, but this was the world, the "myth" vanquished by modernism. The economics, technology, and culture personified in modernism had danced their way into the limelight. Radio insinuated the ideology of consumerism into every home, and movies modeled new fashions, modern sensibilities ("sophistication"), and the latest products for millions of people weekly all over the country.

Public Opinion and the Authoritarian State

Europe, materially and spiritually destroyed by the war, had become a garrison state, with authority vested in central governments and communicated through mass media. This provided a mechanism for accomplishing two things: controlling the internal world of the individual experiencing confusion and fear, and controlling the external world of civil conflict, inflation, and joblessness. This mechanism, joined with an official willingness to use whatever force was necessary to maintain order, is what we now refer to as the "totalitarian state." Disastrous and terrifying in retrospect, it provided a real alternative for coping with social and psychological chaos during and after the war.

Its willingness to employ force in order to preserve order made it seem all the more viable to the front generation which considered pain and cruelty as authentic experiences in contrast to the ideals smashed during the war. Within this historical context emerges what Hannah Arendt, in her study of the origins of totalitarianism, called "mass man"—an isolated, apathetic figure filled with despair and self-loathing. It was this sort of person through whom the potential of a political party demanding absolute allegiance and a leader with whom to identify, to live, and to find meaning in the creation of a society a thousand years into the future could be realized (Arendt, 1958).

The collapse of democratic political theory in cultural criticism in our time, through the stereotype of the "mass audience," finds its origins in a historical configuration which included World War I, the collapse and disillusionment following it, the rise of a new kind of economy with its use of new communications technology to shape public opinion, and the emergence of the totalitarian state. It also included the popularity of fascism in Italy and Germany, as well as the ability of National Socialists to execute millions of innocent men, women, and children with little or no opposition. These facts are the burden of political theory in the twentieth century. As a pivotal element in the creation of these facts, the media became a symbolic arena over which various social, political, and economic views continued to struggle.

With the collapse of the Weimar Republic and the rise of a mass-based fascist movement in Germany, some critics simply abandoned the concept of "popularity." It was no longer relevant when the masses were being manipulated by the media. Max Horkheimer, writing in 1941 (four years after the "War of the Worlds" broadcast in the United States), declared that response to artistic products no longer depended on their truth content. In democratic societies, the "amusement industry" decides what will be popular; in totalitarian states "propaganda ministries" have a similar function. Horkheimer struggled with the pessimism inherent in his diagnosis. "One day," he mused,

> we may learn that in the depths of their hearts, the masses, even in the fascist countries, secretly knew the truth and disbelieved the lie, like catatonic patients who make known only at the end of their trance that nothing has escaped them [Horkheimer, 1941/1972, p. 290].

World War II began. Two years later, the leader through whom the masses found new life proceeded with the final solution.

Like the "Great War," World War II involved a state-controlled economy, total involvement of the civilian population, and a media which was reliable, patriotic, and firmly under government jurisdiction. For those of us born during or after World War II, all this takes on the shape of a dream, a collage of history books, film documentaries, and stories told to us by our fathers—that is, except for what occurred in the media. Television, exploiting all available cultural content, replays old films and kiddie cartoons from that era. Each of us is in a position to "recall" popular culture during the 1940s. Leering, sadistic, cowardly enemies; courageous friends and allies; victorious American soldiers, endangering their lives in the service of their country. Movies, cartoons, newsreels, newspapers, magazines, advertising—everything blends together in awesome, strange, and fascinating uniformity.

A garrison state, even when formed as a temporary response to external crisis, does not automatically release its hold when the crisis is past. Nor can the transformation erase the power and authority it had been able to exercise. There is a decisive difference between a ruling group achieving and maintaining control through terror and an elected government acting on the basis of voluntary and temporary submission. In both instances, however, the success of centrally directed and unquestioned activity poses problems for theories based on public participation. A society nominally democratic, with a crisis ideology calling for an eventual return to a government guided by public opinion, overcomes one crisis—winning the war—only to face another—transforming a garrison state into an open society.

The difficulty lies not only in deconstructing institutional arrangements built during the war (a centralized economy and a large state bureaucracy, for example), but also in making the transition with citizens who have been, for the duration, systematically misinformed on almost every important issue. Sigmund Freud wrote about psychoses associated with World War I. Exacting a high degree of obedience and sacrifice from its citizens, the state governments, through secrecy and censorship, treated citizens like children. This, argued Freud, left them psychologically defenseless against every unfavorable turn of events and every sinister rumor (Freud, 1915/1963, p. 112). Machinery set up in this country during World War II to ensure that documents of "national interest" did not become public continues to operate into the 1980s. The "news," in modern societies, tends to be constructed from handouts authorized by government officials, agency bureaucrats, and corporate executives.

However much in the national interest and however circumspect, government misinformation during the war was deliberate, systematic, and successful. Richard Crossman, director of political warfare in England, later member of the Joint Anglo-American Psychological Warfare Section of General Eisenhower's Staff, wrote about his activities:

> Freed from the limitations imposed by democracy, we were able to experiment with any and every black magic in the use of words which might help to "save lives": and we were provided—at least, toward the end of the war—with funds, staff, and material far beyond the means of any newspaper, advertising agency or political party. Here was a unique chance for what seemed to be a supremely interesting scientific experiment [Lerner, 1949/1971, p. 324].

Initial experiments in "black magic" were abandoned not because they proved ineffective but because short-term successes were offset by long-term loss of credibility brought on by the discovery, on the part of the target audience, of distortion, half-truths, and outright lies. Thus the allies, early on, altered their propaganda efforts in the interests of accuracy and truth. "Our German newscasts were," he writes, "more objective and sober in their treatment of the news than any British or American newspaper" (Lerner, 1949/1971, p. 342).

This situation, however, created a tactical problem. Since information transmitted to the enemy was different and, if we are to believe Crossman, more accurate, the government had to ensure that it did not fall into the hands of the home audience. Not sure that the British had made the right decision about dealing with this problem—marking leaflets distributed in enemy territory "top secret," Crossman considered the thinking behind it to be sound enough: preventing "ill-informed" public opinion from mauling and mutilating the weapon of psychological warfare.

Two world wars, the emergence of consumer capitalism and the modern corporation, the triumph of "modernism" over traditional, rural-based culture, and the development of the totalitarian state—it is in this context that fears about the disintegration of the individual and with him the will to resist bureaucratically directed thought control become real. These fears found expression in two novels whose titles have become part of the language: *Brave New World* by Aldous Huxley, published in 1932, and *1984* by George Orwell, appearing in 1949. Both novels have been made into films, the most recent being a television mini-series of "Brave New World" first aired in 1980.

Apart from individual characters and their fortunes, what these works and many others which followed (such as *Farenheit 451, THX 1138,* and *Day of the Locust*) portray is "mass society," the kind of society Arendt saw giving rise to fascism. In her analysis of mass society in Germany, the crucial feature was the party structure achieved by the National Socialists. More important than the impact of mass media in Nazi Germany (though this, too, was a contributing factor) was, in Arendt's opinion, the absolute allegiance by the membership and the deliberate and unrestrained use of terror which was a major factor in government policy. Other critics, however, placed much more emphasis on the role of the media.

Public Opinion and Mass Media

In their book *The Dialectic of the Enlightenment* written in 1944 and published in German in 1947, Max Horkheimer and Theodore Adorno stressed the role of the mass media in creating and sustaining mass society. The authors were members of the Frankfurt Institute for Social Research. This school included among its members Leo Lowenthal, Eric Fromm, and Herbert Marcuse. It has had a considerable intellectual influence on the postwar period in Europe and the United States. Horkheimer edited and Adorno wrote a major portion of *The Authoritarian Personality* (1950), an influential study of the psychological roots of antisemitism and fascism in America. Marcuse, during the 1960s, advanced and popularized the school's diagnosis of modern society and the threat of mass media in *One Dimensional Man* (1964), a seminal work in the orientation of the New Left during the late 1960s and early '70s. Fromm's work, *Beyond the Chains of Illusion* (1962), the *Sane Society* (1955), and *The*

Anatomy of Human Destructiveness (1973), continued to address issues raised by other members of the school in the 1930s and 40s.

The school's analysis of the role of mass media in the modern world, first articulated in the *Dialectic,* takes on meaning in two historical contexts. One was the Weimar Republic, its collapse and the growing popularity of fascism in Germany; the other was the movie industry and life in Hollywood, California, where the school was relocated for the duration of the war. In their chapter on "The Culture Industry: Enlightenment as Mass Deception," (1944/1972), Horkheimer and Adorno fashioned a critique which anticipates (when it does not actually guide) the debate over the media up to the present day. Reflecting not only the realities of Nazi Germany and the quality of art produced by commercial interests (the "culture industry") in the United States but also, one assumes, the shock of cultural dislocation in the move from Germany to the United States, they wrote:

> Real life is becoming indistinguishable from the movies. The sound film, far surpassing the theater of illusion, leaves no room for imagination or reflection on the part of the audience, who is unable to respond with the structure of the film, yet deviate from its precise detail without losing the thread of the story; hence the film forces its victims to equate it directly with reality. The stunting of the mass-media consumer's powers of imagination and spontaneity does not have to be traced back to any psychological mechanisms; he must ascribe the loss of those attributes to the objective nature of the products themselves, especially to the most characteristic of them, the sound film [Horkheimer & Adorno, 1944/1972, p. 126].

The loss of a sense of reality, an inability or unwillingness to distinguish fact from image, reality from fiction, and the blunting of the imagination by electronic mass media—these by now have become familiar themes.

About radio, they argue that its entry into the private space and the simultaneity of its reception are more important than what it has to say:

> The metaphysical charisma of the Fuhrer invented by the sociology of religion has finally turned out to be no more than the omnipresence of his speeches on the radio, which are a demoniacal parody of the omnipresence of the divine spirit. The gigantic fact that the speech penetrates everywhere replaces its content [1944/1972, p. 159].

Regarding television, the authors, aware of its potential in the 1940s, thought its consequence would be

> enormous and promise to intensify the impoverishment of aesthetic matter so drastically, that by tomorrow the thinly veiled identity of all industrial culture products can come triumphantly out into the open, derisively

fulfilling the Wagnerian drama of the *Gesamtkunstwerk*—the fusion of all the arts into one work [1944/1972, p. 124].

In a society populated by alienated, isolated individuals, the "insane pace of 'modern' life," compassing the disintegration of family ties and religious faith, class interest, and the meaninglessness of work, the culture industry exploits the time away from work to commend existing conditions or to divert people's concerns away from them.

Through electronic mass media, the culture industry not only diminishes human potential and, through advertising and "entertainment" programming, celebrates the institutional arrangements bringing about "mass society," but it also absorbs the time available to the individual to experience his or her potential to create, nurture, love, and enjoy authentic relationships as well as to join with others in efforts to bring about social, economic, and political change. Thus the culture industry finds, reinforces, and further isolates "mass man." This I take to be the burden of the Frankfurt critique of the culture industry, mass media, and modern society developed during the 1930s and 40s. It remains a dominant theme in cultural criticism today.

What made this critique so immediately relevant in the 1960s, through Marcuse, was that it did not restrict itself to Germany or to the Soviet Union, but located the impulse toward totalitarianism in capitalist democracies as well, a possibility historically realized in the collapse of the Weimar Republic. But while it may have gained some credence in the late 1960s, one would not have expected it to find much support in this country just after World War II. Having won the war against fascism, the United States was going about the business of getting things back to normal. The suggestion that the seeds of totalitarianism were germinating in America would not have seemed to most people to be all that plausible. Though a critic of the status quo, the leading American social theorist of the period, C. Wright Mills, in an essay entitled "The Sociology of Mass Media and Public Opinion" (1950/1967—intended for publication in a State Department Russian language journal, *Amerika*), dismissed social analysis failing to distinguish between radically different political systems.

On the question of mass media, Mills wrote that no view of American life could be considered realistic which assumed public opinion to be wholly controlled or entirely manipulated by the media. He grounded his argument in recent history, political theory, and social science research. Totalitarianism in Germany (and, by implication, in Stalinist Russia), he noted, included the deliberate, unchecked, and systematic use of terror to secure compliance. The execution of dissidents was only the most vivid exercise of force. Civilian spies, sudden searches without legal recourse, official and unofficial harassment, public inquisitions with no opportunity for response, arbitrary and capricious internment, the threat of death—through these factors totalitarianism is a political system within which terror becomes policy and isolation, fear, and apathy on the part of the individual became a way of life.

Under such conditions, participation by individuals in informal groups, discussions over public issues exploring diverse points of view, and the emergence of informal leaders of opinion becomes impossible. Such groups, or "publics" in democratic political theory, cease to exist in totalitarian states. The public or "publics" (Mills used the plural to distinguish groups of informed and interested citizens talking about public issues from "mass opinion" manufactured by opinion surveys), in Mills's view, constituted the shield against an uncritical response to mass media. For "publics" not only weighed the issues but they also interpreted relevant information, including information provided by the media.

When media are not totally monopolized, when citizens can measure content against personal experience or direct knowledge of events, and, most importantly, when citizens can secure, through face-to-face communication, points of resistance, the impact of the cultural industry can be mediated, limited, and overcome. In American society, Mills argued, radio, newspapers, magazines, and movies are but one force. They may express but they cannot create "public" opinion. The actual strength of mass media lies in its acceptability to a number of juries—circles of opinion and their unofficial leaders.

The elections of 1948 offered, Mills thought, proof of the independence and unpredictability of public opinion and the ability of labor unions to hold their own against a Republican-owned press (between 1945 and 1948 Mills had published a dozen articles on unions and public opinion; see, for example, Mills, 1945, 1946, 1947, 1948). This combined with his theory of publics, a "two-step" flow of information mediated through such groups and the leaders of opinion existing within them (a theory suggested in Lazarsfeld et al.'s [1948] study of voting patterns in Erie County, Pennsylvania in 1940). Such thought sums up Mills's case for the continued vitality of democratic politics in the United States.

Public Opinion and "McCarthyism"

Four years after "The Sociology of Mass Media and Public Opinion," Mills published a pamphlet entitled "Mass Society and Liberal Education" (1954/1967). In this work he completely reversed himself. The nature of the reversal and the historical context in which it took place provide an insight into why cultural criticism in this country abandoned publics as mediators and adopted a position akin to the Frankfurt School in its view of the mass media and its effects on the mass audience. In 1954 Mills saw a structural trend transforming what was once a society guided by publics into a "mass society," a situation leading to many of the psychological and political problems Americans now confront. The media markets had not yet achieved ascendance over primary groups, but the danger was clear, for we see the "success of the demagogue in exploiting these media, and the decreased chance to answer back" (Mills, 1954/1967, p. 358). In just four years, the United States had traveled a consider-able distance down the road to mass society; at the end of that road lies "totalitarianism," as in Nazi Germany and Communist Russia. Alienation from work, disintegration of personal relationships, and the domination of leisure time by the entertainment industry, Mills concluded, were eroding the soil necessary to nurture a representative democracy.

What caused this sudden about-face? The answer, Mills made clear, was what we now call "McCarthyism," but which at the time, and especially for left-wing intellectuals, looked like the beginnings of totalitarianism in the United States. From 1952 on, very little stood between Senator McCarthy and the mass movement named after him except the Eisenhower-Nixon administration and a Republican press. Purges of leftists—"Communists," "com-symps," "pinkos," "fellow travelers," and the like—had begun under the auspices of the House Un-American Activities Committee (HUAC). The "Hollywood Ten" were tried in 1948. The Eisenhower administration, in its first four months in office, fired over a thousand federal employees under its "security program" (Democrats responded that they had fired even more "risks" under President Truman's loyalty program; see LaFeber, 1972, p. 138). Purges were occurring in education and in the culture industry. Writers, actors, radio announcers, movie directors, television performers—anyone considered to be guilty of "un-American" tendencies—could be working one day and out of a job the next, with little possibility of future employment in the industry. This situation was dramatized during the 1970s in Streisand and Redford's *The Way We Were,* and in Woody Allen's *The Front.*

Two world wars, consumer capitalism, the growth of the corporate state, new media technologies, and their exploitation by totalitarian states provide the historical context within which the debate over mass media and popular culture has been conducted in the Western world. The attack on the "omnipotence of mass media" initiated by liberal social scientists in the 1940s and '50s (Bauer & Bauer, 1966), its roots in democratic political theory, did not and, in the studied neutrality of the sciences, could not give much assistance in the struggle against what left-wing critics were calling the "radical right," mass society, and public support (one-third of the population looked favorably on McCarthy and his tactics) for McCarthyism.

There was some evidence available at the time that McCarthyism might have been less an expression of totalitarian tendencies than a symptom of alienation from impersonal, bureaucratic political and economic institutions (Trow, 1959), along with anxieties prompted by foreign policy reversals and a loss of a monopoly on nuclear arms (Heilbruner, 1959). It also became apparent that these fears were being exploited by established groups interested in increased military spending, a consortium formed during the war and including the military, the armaments industry, and their allies in government (liberal pump-primers as well as representatives from districts enriched by defense contracts). This structural analysis and the importance of revitalizing democratic society informed Mills' book, *The Causes of World War Three* (1958).

Without passing judgment on the efforts made at the time to fight McCarthyism, the media theory and the stereotype of the mass audience on which it was based now appear to have

(1) underestimated the degree to which American publics, during World War II, had been conditioned to accept censorship, loyalty tests, and the like as a part of being a citizen;

(2) underestimated the degree to which American publics, by the mid-twentieth century, had grown to resent centralized control of the economy, government, and jobs through the corporate state;

(3) overestimated the similarities among fascism, Stalinism, and McCarthyism—failed, in other words, to appreciate the distinctions between unemployment, insecurity, and public humiliation, and the deportation and executions of millions of people, distinctions lost in the elasticity of terms such as "purge"; and

(4) overlooked the political importance and social implications of popular movements protesting the regional hearings of HUAC, the Rosenberg executions, and civil rights violations.

The underlying error in critical theory developed during the 1930s, '40s, and '50s, an error which animates cultural criticism up to the present time, lies in its inability to account for change. Unable to predict or explain changes in a manipulated "mass audience," it falls silent in the face of it; when the relevant events pass, it contains no recollection of them. Thus the real indictment to be made against the stereotypical mass audience in our time does not lie in its failure to interpret the historical events (or the data) out of which it emerged, but rather in its inability to anticipate, account, or even provide for the rise of popular-based, voluntary sociopolitical movements in America and Europe during the 1960s and '70s: the civil rights movement in the United States during the late 1950s and early '60s; the antiwar movements in Europe and America in the mid-1960s and early '70s; the feminist and antinuclear movements of the 1970s and early '80s; the opposition to nuclear arms throughout the period; revolutionary movements in East Germany, Czechoslovakia, Hungary, and Afghanistan, and national strikes in Poland; actions opposed by the established order and, where the media was an important force, ignored or opposed by it.

The Rise of "Publics" and the Role of the Mass Media

What part the media played in these events is difficult to say. There is no way to reduce it to a formula, conduct a controlled experiment, or render it into statistics. Some critics claimed, during the 1960s, that national coverage of local movements caused them to become nationwide. A radical critic recently argued that the publicity accorded Students for a Democratic Society (SDS) during the 1960s and '70s effectively destroyed its long-term political effectiveness (Gitlin, 1980). It is, therefore, easier to talk about the role the media did *not* play. They did not, over the last quarter-century and despite the spectacular rise of television, prevent opposition to official policies, even where the media were state-controlled, from forming and expressing itself on a number of issues.

Beyond this, there is the analysis of Wladislaw Markiewicz, secretary of the social sciences branch of the Polish Academy of Science, linking political action and mass media:

> The infantilism, boorishness and ritual schematism of political mass propaganda . . . led to results which were the exact opposite of what had been intended. What this propaganda was to popularize, in point of fact, aroused spontaneous aversion, whereas what it was intended to render repulsive became almost pleasing [cited in Smith, 1980].

Early attempts at settlement included promises by the government to ease its grip on the press and broadcast media. Meanwhile, an important leader of the Solidarity Movement, Bogdan Lis, was calling for the reintroduction of criticism and dialogue as a normal and lasting element in day-to-day living.

The ability of groups of people to meet face to face, talk over public matters without fear, to publish leaflets, newspapers, and radio programs providing alternatives to state-controlled or commercially dominated mass media is crucial in the creation of popular mass movements. They are not likely to occur in a society organized along the lines laid down by the National Socialists in the 1930s. Nevertheless, their absence, under such conditions, cannot be taken as evidence that the masses have, through modern technology and the entertainment it can provide, been rendered apathetic and quiescent. At the same time, cataloguing popular movements over the last few years does not prove that democratic political structures actually exist, or that, when improvised, they prove politically viable. The long-term success of publics, when measured in structural changes or a redistribution of political or economic power, hardly suggests that the need for radical economic, social, and political change is past. Moreover, the rise of publics opposed to such changes or for changes enhancing the power of established authority provides little ground on which to restore the old beliefs in human perfectability and representative democracy. What it does supply is considerably more modest, realistic, and hopeful, and that is a historical critique of theory rooted in isolated, alienated, passive masses, a vantage point from which to anticipate, understand, and even describe movements for change in modern society rooted in the willingness and ability of individuals to join together for the purpose of influencing public policy.

The inadequacy of the "mass audience" to fathom individual or group potential to engage in meaningful political activity shows up in its inability to explain the popularity of certain kinds of cultural content—content which, given the stereotype, the mass audience ought to have rejected, ignored, or, at the very least, distorted. Given the "cold war" mentality officially endorsed during the 1950s and '60s, films like *Dr. Strangelove, Fail Safe,* and *The Spy Who Came in From the Cold,* and TV series like *Get Smart* should have played only to small audiences in college towns. In the early 1970s, the most popular shows on American television—*All in the Family, Maude, The Jeffersons,* and *M*A*S*H* —regularly raised the most controversial issues: racism, sexism, the war in Vietnam (or Korea), and so on. In the late 1970s, a news documentary, muckraking *60 Minutes* and its imitators became top-rated shows. Even more dramatically, the success of miniseries like *Roots, Holocaust,* and *Shogun* (the last episode of which attracted an audience of over a hundred million people for a series in which most of the dialogue was in Japanese), led, at least in the commercial world, to a reconsideration about what the mass audience might or might not entertain in the way of social, political, and cultural content.

Recent history reveals far more potential for voluntary, collective, and informed political activity than either the popular stereotype of the mass audience or traditional cultural criticism find possible. This is also true when the question has to do with the "taste" or the capacity of this audience to seek out, understand, or appreciate certain kinds of cultural content. Two world wars, the rise of consumer capitalism and the corporate state, the ongoing threat of totalitarianism—this configuration does not become any less real when our assumptions about the impact of the media and the mass audience are considered in light of things which have occurred during the past quarter-century. Mass media are part of and necessary to what we call "modern" life. But they have not, in the absence of official terror and in spite of rampant alienation, isolation, and insecurity built into modern life, transformed the "masses" into apathetic, apolitical, and passive individuals.

Revising the Theory and Practice of Cultural Criticism

Reformulation of our assumptions about the media, popular culture, and the mass audience to focus on important issues and allow for the emergence of publics will alter the practice of criticism. Out of necessity, it will take us beyond the facile condemnation of the media, the culture it provides, and the audiences it assembles. For the critic, the choice will no longer lie between silence and sarcasm or despair. Today it lies between silence and serious critical analysis. This follows from a change not only in the concept of the audience for mass media but also in the audience for media criticism. From a small group of people for whom popular culture is at best offensive, the audience for criticism expands to include those who are exposed to, participate in, and perhaps even enjoy some of the products of the culture industry.

If rejection is no longer automatic, if analysis is no longer equated with ridicule, and if the audience for cultural criticism is no longer a small, literary elite, then not only will we have to reconsider what to say about cultural products but also how to say it. For an audience which enjoys popular culture and which is interested in its analysis, the language of academics and literary professionals (the convoluted phrasing, esoteric terms, learned allusions to Stendahl, Art Deco, and the "Potemkin") becomes an obstacle. Reviews in the popular press sometimes achieve a fresh and supple mode of expression, but usually only with reference to the immediate object, the work taken in isolation. The solution is difficult, but the problem is simple enough to state: how to say something worthwhile about cultural products, popular culture, or the media without assuming that one's audience possesses an intimate knowledge of methodologies fashionable in academic circles, the works of art treasured by literary professionals, or the canonical texts of Marxism.

The problems posed by reformulating the theory underlying cultural criticism are real, and they are bound to be reflected in critical practice. Not that current practice is free of problems. The absence of a substantial body of first-rate criticism dealing with mass media or popular culture could, I suppose, be attributed to the inadequacy of the subject matter. But the causes go much deeper. They reach down, as I have tried to argue, to its fundamental theoretical assumptions about the individual and society. From the point of view of the reader, the problem may be stated this way: Writing about the media had better not be dull, or it will be overwhelmed by its object. Despite some brilliant methodological strategies (Barthes's work comes to mind), I do not believe that good criticism will come from enlisting in a cult (Barthian, Burkean, Althusarian, or Freudian). Mass media pervade modern life. As a source of shared images, information, and experience, they offer a common language (Gouldner, 1976). Criticism which fails to grasp this fact—which is unable to integrate the imagery, information, misinformation, and personal experience into the critical narrative—will have little to say to the people most involved in and influenced by popular culture.

Under the assumption that getting at the "meaning" of cultural products in a historical context is potentially interesting to the "mass audience," or at least to a significant portion of it, cultural criticism places itself in the position of adding another dimension to whatever pleasures and consolations are to be had from listening to popular music, going to the movies, and watching TV. It is the ability to talk about them, to argue over their meaning, their relationship to moral, social, political, and economic issues of public import. To this end, we will examine the "what" in which "facts" about cultural content may play a part in exploring the world of popular culture, the significance of "negation" in the face of this world, and the relevance of "potential consciousness" in understanding this world. We will also be considering the historical context in which the exploration is to take place, along with the people for whom it is to take on meaning.

The Place of "Fact" in Cultural Criticism

The symbolic environment made possible by mass media—what we have been referring to as the "world of popular culture"—is external to the thought that posits it. Cultural products exist in time and space. We can make statements about them which other people can check for themselves. In modern society, everyone is an expert on the media. Statements about content which can be verified we will call "facts." With a given product, such facts *refer* to a moment in the process of creation—the end result as we have been given to see it. In the case of popular culture, such facts refer to products as they appear at a certain time and place for a certain audience. Since the critic, scientist, viewer, one who makes out the facts, must do so in the face of an infinitude of potential facts—every object being infinitely divisible—the "facts" found necessarily *reflect* the interests of the searcher and the finder, the one who declared a given piece of the whole of popular culture to be somehow relevant. This holds true whether the relevant piece is part of a given product, one product out of a number of products, or popular culture out of the totality of human experience and creations. The "this" to which our facts refer can only be distinguished in relation to something else which is "not this." Thus facts reflect the interests of the fact finders by virtue of their articulation, their having been called to our attention instead of multitudes of other facts which might have been called to our attention. Facts *invite* interpretation according to the context in which they are placed. To talk about one episode compared with another places criticism in the context of a series. To talk about one series in relation to another places criticism in the context of prime time. To talk about an episode, a series, or prime time in a historical context is to draw popular culture into the context of moral, social, economic, and political issues.

Culture, therefore, is politically neutral only when the decision has been made to detach it from its historical context. The decision about whether or not to place cultural products or the medium through which they are communicated into an historical context is not determined by, nor does it depend upon, the intent of the creator (writer, actor, producer, newspaper owner, or network executive). It is determined by the degree to which the juxtaposition of products with objective conditions or existing conflicts raises important issues. The question is not nearly as abstract as it may appear. Thus writes Meredith Tax:

> Cultural products which present foreign wars as the heroic effort of a master race to ennoble mankind are, to the degree that they are successful as art, objectively in the interests of imperialists, who are people who make foreign wars against other races for profit. Cultural products that present people who have no money or power as innately stupid or

depraved, and thus unworthy of money or power, are in the interests of the ruling class and the power structure as it stands. Cultural products which present women who do not want to be household slaves or universal mothers or sex objects as bitches or sexual failures objectively aid male supremacy [Tax, 1973, pp. 15-16].

This is not to say that critics with a different ideological bent might be inclined to present facts with different political implications or "meanings" in a given historical context, only that such facts, because the stuff they refer to is available to everyone, provide a *basis* for analysis, debate, and even agreement at a given time and place.

This is easily enough illustrated. Consider the facts about prime-time television produced by a content analysis of prime time sponsored by a labor union. In September 1979, the International Association of Machinists and Aerospace Workers undertook a nationwide media project involving 1500 of their members, who were trained to watch TV programming and evaluate the content (I.A.M., 1980). During the month of February 1980, they monitored network and local news coverage and network entertainment programming. Using content analysis, a method whereby program themes, characters, or other aspects of content are defined and counted, they classified characters on prime time as incumbents of either unionized or nonunionized jobs.

The following facts appeared: prostitues outnumbered machinists; there were more butlers than government workers; more witch doctors than welfare workers; more private detectives than production line workers. Another set of facts emerged out of monitoring news programming for the side that took on labor-management issues involving inflation, energy, foreign trade, health, and tax reform. Using definitions of what constituted a labor and management view on these matters, and comparing network performance, the machinists found that, although the three networks differed slightly, corporate views were much more likely to be shown than were union views on crucial issues.

Beyond questions of definition—whether labor and corporate positions were adequately spelled out, accurate (they were provided in the final report), fairly applied, and properly quantified—there is a point at which anyone watching TV can keep track of the "image" of people portrayed in a labor role and determine for oneself how many appeared and how they were treated. Armed with knowledge about union and corporate views on issues, there is a point at which anyone can note the "themes" developed in the news and assess their ideological bend. Beyond what anyone wants to believe or expects to see, the results are "facts."

Why the machinists were interested in such facts was neither ignored nor masked under the assertion that they were found. The image of American labor has declined over the years. Shown during major strikes or exposes of corruption on the news; characterized as criminals, victims, and bigoted buffoons on entertainment programming; rarely if ever shown as bright, thoughtful, capable citizens, the media, argue the machinists, have contributed to this decline. The machinists' critique, therefore, issues out of authentic concerns. Whatever we may think about unions in general or the machinists in particular, these concerns point to a context in which the facts take on more than merely statistical significance.

Other facts reflect different interests. Research done by teams of social scientists, under the direction of Professor Greenberg at Michigan State University, found that characters on prime time TV differed from the general population in several ways over the period 1975-1978 (Greenberg, 1980, pp. 39-46):

(1) Males outnumber females by a ratio of 3-1.
(2) Whites outnumbered Blacks by a ratio of 9-1, reflecting the general population, but Blacks were confined to only a few shows.
(3) "Hispanic" Americans were under-represented by a ratio of 5-1.
(4) The young were over-represented by a ratio of 6-1; characters between 20 and 49 years of age were over-represented by a ratio of 2-1; characters 65 years and older were under-represented by a ratio of 5-1.
(5) Professional and Managerial occupations were over-represented by a ratio of 2-1, while laborers were under-represented 3-1.
(6) Males held 70% and females 30% of the professional positions, consistent with the general population; females held 15% and males 85% of the managerial positions, leaving females under-represented; and males held 81%, females 19% of the service positions, leaving females under-represented.
(7) Whites held a 20-1 ratio over Blacks in managerial and professional jobs, leaving Blacks under-represented.
(8) The number of characters who were lawbreakers exceeded the percentage in the general population by a ratio of 20-1.

These statistics indicate that prime-time television is a preserve for white, middle- to upper-middle-class males, and for the young, with Blacks confined to a programmatic ghetto, women barely approaching the status accorded them by a society discriminating against them; while laborers, Mexican-Americans, and senior citizens have all but disappeared. It is, moreover, a world riven with crime. Although the ratios would be difficult to validate, anyone can, through observation and recollection, verify the general claims underlying the ratios and frequencies.

The meaning of the preceding facts was not made clear in the research reported in *Life on Television* (1980). The funds for the work came from a grant made in 1975 by the Office of Child Development in the Department of Health, Education and Welfare to support a project focusing on parental influence on what children learn from TV. Subsequent grants, in 1976 and 1977, expanded the research to include actual learning through TV. There was, however, no effort on the part of the authors to explain why DHEW was interested in such data, or, in fact, why the project or its findings took on any meaning beyond the statistical tables it yielded, except to say, " 'Hey, that's what television is saying and showing' " (Greenberg, 1980, xi). Either through political naivete or through professional reluctance, the research threatened to become meaningless.

But of course it was not and is not meaningless. Its ideological content announces itself in the context of social issues, the demographics taking on meaning in a social order employing gradations based on age, race, sex, and vocation. Facts about cultural content were not situated in a historical context, and yet to one who has remained alive to public matters over the last 25 years, they can only be interpreted in light of movements for civil rights and an end to racism; equality for women and an end to sexism; for economic, social, and political justice for senior citizens and an end to agism. It is in this context that the facts reported by Professor Greenberg confront an established order in which discrimination has become second nature, though the author masks this inter-pretation as much as he can by suggesting that the results are of "special interest" in the context of the culture industry and its critics, and that they provide "systematic evidence" for both sides (Greenberg, 1980, p. 46).

Criticism refusing to detach data about the content of prime time from conditions existing outside life on TV must find the fact that prostitutes outnumber machinists, witch doctors outnumber welfare workers, men out-number women, and whites outnumber minorities in the good paying jobs, and that senior citizens have nearly disappeared on prime time important for under-standing social relations in real life. Except where, in real life, each office building is a mystery for those who do not work in it, and each setback in hiring, pay increase, and promotion is felt in isolation by often silent individuals, discrimination in popular culture is available to everyone. Issues raised through what is commonly available can be referred back to discrimination in the everyday world which is based on information much less widely known.

The Place of Negation in Cultural Criticism

As important as the manifest content of mass media can be, criticism must not confine itself to that which is prominent, emphatic, and seldom contradicted in such content. While this restriction may prove useful in research on the part culture plays in conditioning people, with the unambiguous existence and repetition of certain images or themes operating as "reinforcement," the meaning of cultural content goes beyond the boundaries imposed by behavioral research. In an historical context with real issues, what does not appear in the media may be more important than what does. An interesting counterapproach to content analysis, writes Greenberg, lies in the notion that if something is absent from TV, that absence stamps the "thing" as lacking in value, given the influence of TV on public opinion (1980, p. xxii). Such an approach is more than a counter to content analysis; it is its complement.

A full understanding not only of the content of a given product, medium, or of all popular culture includes not only what in fact appears, but also what in fact does not appear. The theoretical significance of this becomes obvious when popular culture is placed in a historical context. From this view, it is apparent that:

(1) Manifest content may mask significant *facts* about the real world (the potential of women in managerial positions, for example).

(2) Manifest content may ignore important *possibilities* for change in the real world (reducing crime through other than augmented police forces).

(3) Manifest content may be influenced by *socioeconomic and political interests* operating in the real world (the likelihood of major advertisers becoming the subject of an expose).

The preceding statements form the basis for critical realism and, in the case of popular culture, pretty much exhaust what it can say that is worth reading.

The effort at finding discrepancies between cultural content and personal experience, scientific fact, or ideological truths, embracing reality while denouncing distortion, however, overlooks the possibility that:

(4) Manifest content may communicate significant "facts" about the real world (that the President has committed illegal acts).

(5) Manifest content may communicate significant possibilities for change in the real world (that women can hold professional positions).

(6) Manifest content may mask and/or unmask potential in the real world (that the ordinary individual can be quite intelligent and resourceful).

If the media can reveal as well as conceal important "facts" about the established order; if it can open up as well as close down important possibilities for individual and collective action, then pointing out discrepancies between fact and fiction does not exhaust the critical effort. In order to assess the significance of what appears, we must be able to imagine alternatives—what might have or should have but did not, in fact, appear.

But how do we go about discovering what does not appear in popular culture without losing ourselves in the maze of the totality? For what does not appear is everything else, a world of nearly infinite possibility. The question can be rephrased: Is there anything important that does not show up? Or, are there limits on what can show up that might lead to important omissions? Growing out of the realization that the way the process of cultural production is organized will affect the final product, cultural criticism can focus on what a given product, medium, or popular culture in general is not likely to include as a result of vested interest. For example, because sponsors on commercial TV want to reach a young audience, we would predict a disproportionate number of characters on prime time falling into the age group of the target audience (the link being that the audience has an easier time identifying with characters their own age or with their own interests). In commercial terms, the advertisers want to reach the audience nearing the peak of the buying curve—a combination of earning power and readiness to consume commercial products. This curve falls off dramatically in the late 30s, a fact translating itself visually into shows with relatively few (compared with the general population) characters over 50, fewer still who are main characters or happy or admirable people. As a matter of historical fact, when sponsors, a little over ten years ago, included qualitative along with quantitative measures in assessing the "quality" of the audience assembled by the networks, shows attracting children and senior citizens were canceled, even though they attracted large audiences (Brown, 1971). A more refined analysis of the role of vested interest in the production of popular culture might suggest a number of hypotheses about what is and what is not likely to appear.

Is there information, are there important "facts" originating in the world outside popular culture that are not showing up on the "news," "advertising," "prime-time"—the "media"? Comparing crime on prime time with FBI statistics reveals that while most thefts on TV are solved and the thief apprehended, the ratio in real life runs about ten to one in favor of the criminal. Similarly, while most murders on prime time are plotted by people unknown to the victim, murders in real life tend to be committed by family members and close friends. Even more startling, the percentage of characters involved in violent crimes on prime time is 20 times greater than the percentage of people in real life, a distortion which has led to research into whether or not "heavy" viewers tend to be more fearful about the likelihood of a crime being committed than are "light" viewers (Gerbner et al., 1980). Academic research, government publications, personal experience, and other mass media suggest possibilities for determining what does and does not appear, what is or is not representative in popular culture.

Based on knowledge about what in fact appears, what are we able to infer about what does not or only rarely appears in popular culture? For example:

(a) Most characters on prime time conform to conventional standards of beauty—they tend to be white or near white, fine-featured, young, well proportioned, and of average height.

There is room for greater specificity and quantifiable comparisons, but given that this is roughly the case, the negation can be phrased in the following way:

(a[1]) Few characters appear on prime time who are fat. Not many have scars, limps, or protruding lips. Few adult characters are under five feet or over six feet, four inches tall. Not many characters appear to be over 65.

(a²) When physically "deviant" characters do appear, they tend not to be cast as intelligent, strong, or virtuous.

In the same way that we can make claims about the type of characters who do and do not populate the world of prime time, we can also make some observations about the type of consciousness they do and do not display:

(b) Most characters on prime time are self-interested (personal safety, personal gain, personal happiness).

Again, putting the matter in the form of a negation:

(b¹) Characters on prime time tend not to be interested in social problems, political action, or cooperative activity of any sort which does not relate to family or vocational responsibilities.

But the type of characters or potential agents who show up in the media represent only one aspect of the drama. What actions do they or do they not tend to engage in?

(c) Action tends to be directed at controlling "deviant" behavior (capturing criminals or correcting children, in-laws, or parents who have become troublesome, dangerous, or eccentric).

Again reversed:

(c¹) Action on prime time tends not to involve trying to reform major institutions—corporations, schools, or government; it rarely encourages behavior inconsistent with the interests of established authority.

The people and actions on prime time tend to take place in certain predictable locations:

(d) Action tends to take place in living rooms, office buildings, and in automobiles carrying people from one such place to another.

Once we realize the locations which tend to appear and check the validity of the claim, we are in a position to talk about the locations which, for whatever reason, do not occur.

(d¹) Prime time rarely takes us inside factories, the corporate boardrooms, the cloakroom of the Senate, shacks lived in by sharecroppers, or slum tenements in metropolitan areas.

The instruments available to people on prime time to assist them in solving their problems also reveal something about our "reality":

(e)   The instruments used to solve problems on prime time tend to be lethal weapons, pleasing personalities, money, and expertise.

Phrased as a negation:

(e^1)   The instruments used by people on prime time to solve their problems tend not to involve collective or cooperative activity (that is, union organizing, voter registration, and the like), the acquisition of greater knowledge, or developing new ways of acting.

The purposes manifest in the characters, actions, locations, and instrumentalities appearing in the media are also describable:

(f)   The purposes manifest in the drama of prime time tend to be securing one's place in or moving up the social ladder, protecting oneself from those who would take one's life or property or good name, and finding and keeping love and happiness.

Again the negation:

(f^1)   The purposes manifest on prime time tend not to involve an assessment of the future and the possibilities it presents; they tend to locate a sense of obligation in officially sanctioned codes of conduct (moral, vocational, and legal), and not in rational deliberation or utopian vision.

(f^2)   Action based on purely rational deliberation and utopian vision tends to be associated with illegal, immoral, or pathological ends.

As the facts change, the inference made from them also changes. But both claims—one having to do with what appears and the other about what does not or only infrequently appears—are verifiable; and because the content of popular culture is available to everyone, such claims may be examined, modified, or denied by the critic's audience.

The facts about popular culture relevant to a historical context have to do with human action, the drama taking place in the social, economic, and political spheres. Factual statements made about the manifest content of popular culture take on meaning within a dramatic event. In 1975, the most common character on prime time was a young, good-looking, white male employed by a law enforcement agency. Putting this together with observations about scenes, actions, instruments for problem-solving, and purposes common to prime time, we arrive at a not uncommon dramatic event: handsome, young, white police detective apprehends older, white male suspect after violent struggle. Filled out in more detail, Detective X traps Executive Y in his office trying to destroy evidence linking him to the murder of Z (killed to prevent his turning evidence of Y's embezzlement over to the board of directors). Defending himself from attack, X scuffles, shoots, and subdues Y. The sequence is crime, investigation, complication, chase, struggle, and capture. Translated into political terms, the event reads: The established order, acting through its officially designated agent, discovers and punishes deviant behavior.

Having identified a dramatic formula, we can talk about what it does not contain and what sort of variations rarely show up. In the matter of officially proscribed or "deviant" behavior, we rarely get to see morally and contextually justifiable deviance—like stealing food in order to feed hungry children— suggesting structural reforms or radical changes in the established order. "Criminal conduct" tends to be both illegal and immoral, with the suspect already positively identified (we often witness the crime and can identify the "criminal"), so that whatever happens to the suspect in the course of apprehension, including his death, has already been unambiguously justified.

From knowledge about the common elements in dramatic action and recurring formulas, we are in a position to talk about the kinds of dramatic action which do not appear. I do not recall ever having seen an elderly, black woman employed by a labor union lead a boycott against a company attempting to relocate in an area or part of the world—Hong Kong would provide an exotic backdrop—where there are no unions. The sequence involving corporate decision, discovery, collective response, legal maneuver, social consequence (threatened unemployment), and alternative solutions (government regulation, worker ownership, retooling) is unfamiliar as a dramatic event on prime time. Few union executives have ever appeared, fewer still who were black or female. Of those who have appeared, they have tended to be middle-class, white males engaged in criminal activities. While it is true that many corporate executives are shown as being involved in criminal activities, few have been portrayed carrying out company policies violating the interests of the surrounding community (such as relocating, dumping chemicals in local sewers, streams, or lakes, or refusing to release information about radiation leaks), even though such behavior most certainly occurs and periodically makes its way into the news. However the absence of such content is explained—corporate interest forbids it, the audience is neither interested in nor prepared for it, or the action is not sufficiently dramatic—the question remains: Have we ever seen such a story or anything like it on prime time, in mass magazines, in the movies? Are such stories important for us to consider?

We may talk about what vested interest is likely to discourage, what one medium covers that another does not, and what may be inferred from what in fact appears about what in fact does not appear, but this is not the same as saying certain kinds of content *cannot* appear. Cultural criticism that does not begin and end in a condemnation proceeding or a vast, monolithic commercial conspiracy to control content is not obliged to overlook exceptions or changes in content. In 1975 there were 41 crime shows on prime time; by 1978 the number of shows had dropped to 23. This change in programmatic content is relevant to a critique of violence, the rise of a police state, and the nature of problems shown on TV. Cultural criticism, in my view, does not have to ignore news content about corporate lobbying or violations of law and the public interest. It does not have to dismiss images of successful and vigorous senior citizens, blacks, women, and union members when they do, in fact, appear. What this means for criticism is that it is free to affirm certain images, themes, and types of dramatic action appearing on commercial TV or in popular culture in general, when it ought to be affirmed. There is no law that says, or historical evidence to deny the claim, that popular culture cannot play a critical role by periodically floodlighting society with important social, moral, economic, and political alternatives. The debates which took place on *All in the Family* in the early 1970s no doubt "distorted" the actual willingness to argue real issues in the average American family, in state legislatures, or in Congress, for that matter; but the distortion lay in favor of open and informed dialogue, not away from it.

At the same time, when popular culture does not offer alternatives, when it ignores important "facts," when it sticks to conventional and unenlightening dramatic events, there is no question but that criticism should be prepared to point this out. How long are we going to assume that American society is so open to merit that all the buffoons are located in the lower classes? TV has always been populated with wealthy criminals, but the first wealthy, professional fool I ever remember seeing on a popular TV series was Arthur, the doctor who lived next door to Maude Findlay. The first intelligent, powerful, and sensitive working man I can recall was Arthur Fonzarelli, the "Fonz," of *Happy Days,* and even he had to be shored up by layers upon layers of mesmerized young women.

The Concept of Potential Consciousness in Cultural Criticism

One of the failures of public opinion polling is that its descriptive methods capture only what people already think. The problem, politically speaking, is not to focus on what a group thinks, but to discover the changes in consciousness it can tolerate without having to change its basic nature. In this way, works of art have a contribution to make, beyond formal excellence and aesthetic pleasures. Great works of art, argues French sociologist Lucien Goldman (1971) indicate the maximum potential consciousness of these privileged social groups with enough time and interest to try to make sense of the world or develop a world view.

Because they issue out of the culture industry seeking to maximize profits by catering to the mass audience, the media do not play a part in Goldman's analysis. He confines himself to high culture. Still, I think there is an application to make. The culture industry must, whatever the medium, avoid offending large portions of the mass audience, including large or potentially influential groups which are also part of the mass. Because of this condition, popular culture is often accused of being predictable, bland, and dull. Yet given what ordinarily appears, a product unique in light of the way in which certain public issues are usually treated represents potential consciousness designed to embrace the mass, including the groups or "publics" which make up a portion of the mass. Not only are the products of the culture industry intended to be inclusive; there is also built into the system a mechanism for monitoring the results, a feedback mechanism known as "audience response." Products failing to secure adequate popular support (and this varies from medium to medium), or which actually offend and turn off a significant portion of the audience (significant in terms of numbers or "ratings," or in terms of power such as corporate sponsors or the administration) are not likely to be produced, or, if produced, shown, or if shown, not likely to continue or to be imitated.

What all this creates is a system in search of successful formulas for attracting mass audiences, willing to repeat such formulas until they fail, and interested in "public relations" campaigns to create audiences and audience ratings to determine worth. The machinery is not designed to produce great art or innovative work. When unique work does appear, when vast changes in content occur, they occur *in spite of* the tendencies of the system. And changes, even in prime time, do take place: the shift from westerns to law-and-order shows to situation comedies from the 1950s to the 1980s being a case in point. Because of the way the system is constructed, the shifts can only take place with significant popular support for a new and different kind of product. From *Gunsmoke* to *Kojak* to *All in the Family* to *Happy Days* to *60 Minutes,* one encounters more than changes in fashion. One encounters different kinds of world views or potential consciousnesses in the whole society.

Rather than arguing over whether or not such shows represent worthwhile art or whether their writers, producers, and actors sought to universalize their world views, I suggest we focus on the historically relevant and unique products in popular culture that manage to gain the attention of a mass audience. We should ask ourselves: What are the ideological implications of this product? Once this is worked out (and all this depends on our knowledge of existing problems and the world views of the publics trying to deal with them), we are in a position to talk about the horizon of consciousness within which a mass audience can tolerably, if not comfortably, function.

To be sure, the culture industry has certain biases that influence dramatic programming, and the mass audience's tolerance, even delight, in bizarre entertainment may greatly exceed its willingness to entertain the historical projects implied. Then there is the fact that, during a given period, shows embodying quite different world views may be equally popular. With all these limitations (and they are not less relevant to analyzing the products of high culture) there is cause to pursue a critique which, beyond recurring, familiar, or influential products, examines unique, unfamiliar, and potentially influential work. This reason has to do with what the mass audience or particular groups within it might tolerate as a different way of looking at the world.

In the film *Saturday Night Fever,* a commercially successful film whose music, costuming, and dance all became enormously popular, one unique feature was its focus on the problems of working-class teenagers at the moment just before their entry into an adult world of jobs, parenthood, and making ends meet. For Tony Manero, a model of success in teen fashions and a hero on the dance floor, the question is how to find a life as exciting as the one he must inevitably leave. Traditional beliefs about the rewards of hard work fall flat in the face of Tony's meaningless, dead-end job in a paint store, and in his father's layoff after years of being a company man. The lack of economic support subverts family life. Tony and his young disciple dimly understand that the only chance they have of making it lies in not getting married and having children. This is a working-class "reality" the girl who loves Tony cannot grasp. Her pathetic attempts to get him to play the traditional roles—lover, husband, father—fail, not because she schemes; she tells him what she's doing. Making love in the back seat of a car, Tony asks her what she's using. "Nothing," she murmurs; "it's alright. I love you." She does not fail because she is unattractive or because she would make a bad wife and mother, or because her parents interfere or because Tony cannot be tamed. She is doomed because traditional roles have become meaningless, an economic trap, a dead end.

The boy whose girlfriend is pregnant becomes despondent. He leaps off the bridge. The symbol of the bridge leading out of the ghetto into Manhattan includes a history of the number of people killed in building it and who were trampled to death on the day it first opened. Tony's only hope to make it out of Brooklyn, out of the dingy, bleak life that is suffocating his family and everyone he knows, is to leave and enter into the world of his woman friend, a secretary in Manhattan, who, we discover, had to barter her body for a survival course in the corporate jungle.

In the context of economic and social problems, *Saturday Night Fever* explored the human realities of unemployment, insecurity, and the destruction of ethnic culture, family, and the threat to girls brought up to be like their mothers, to play roles no longer functional and the exploitation they face when they try to escape. The film is about human potential blunted and distorted in a society geared to meaningless work and periodic unemployment. Disillusion, alienation, the failure of capitalism with its reserve army of the unemployed, the sacrifice of communal relationships—these are the themes dramatized in *Saturday Night Fever.* Dramatizing a social critique of economic and social conditions, it symbolizes an alliance between leftist intellectuals (for whom "alienation" has become an article of faith), the working class, and the feminist movement. Just as Tony's growing awareness is pitted against the brutal accommodation of his companions to existing conditions, so the ideological coalition, in the film, of the working class and a middle-class feminist movement stand against popular culture, like the jiggle shows on prime time, which exploit what ought to be issues.

The realism in *Saturday Night Fever* is neither forced nor programmatic. That its deeper sociopolitical structure and implications were lost on reviewers and ignored by social critics—presumably put off by the Hollywood ballyhoo of bright lights, disco, and bikini underwear—accentuates the subtlety of its art. Once seen, its critique is, I think, unmistakable and convincing. But did the audience who flocked to the film or who watched it on TV understand its political message? Wasn't the real response to imitate Travolta, carry a comb, seek out a disco—duplicate, in other words, what the film was saying was ultimately a futile lifestyle? Beyond the fact that the actual response is not the question but rather the response made possible by the film lies the observation that the film did not condemn popular music and dance. What it did was contrast the excitement and vitality of the dance floor, where Tony transcended his everyday world, with the unacceptable alternatives offered him by the adult world.

The enigmatic ending, with Tony resolved to do whatever is necessary to escape his family, home, neighborhood, and friends, to overcome his impulse to see women as playthings, merely hints at fulfillment, and then mostly with the possibilities for growth with an authentic "relationship." It does not suggest that the real world, even in Manhattan, is anything but a jungle. It is here that the political coalition between organized labor and the feminist movement also founders. Going beyond the observation that most people cannot make it the way things are, to lay out concrete alternatives would require the groups involved to consider essential, structural change in society. This is the point where *Saturday Night Fever* risked losing its audience; this is where leftists, middle-class feminists, and organized labor have not been able to forge an alliance. It is one thing to protest existing conditions and quite another to envision, agree, and act on an alternative.

Saturday Night Fever, therefore, drew back from the social critique giving it both thematic and historical coherence into a window seat with two individuals drawn together in their struggle to find a better life than the one they were born into; and if they look back, it is not to reflect on the casualties, the people they grew up with, but on the burst of vitality they once felt on the dance floor. And if we look back on the way the film ended, there is no clear trajectory into a bright and inviting future, only the declaration that the couple in the window seat are committed to making it and will try not to savage each other in the attempt.

Summary

Criticism traditionally calls on some form of determinism to deal with mass media. Hypnotized, addicted, blank-faced, the audience becomes the "mass," an aggregate of isolated, apathetic, alienated, and potentially dangerous spectators. Linked with "electronic" media, the same arguments, fears, and stereotypes involving the impact of popular culture appear in the eighteenth and nineteenth centuries. But while the case against the media should have been greatly strengthened by the addition of film, radio, and TV and by the rise of the culture industry manufacturing cultural products, recent history does not support the thesis that the media stifle talk about public issues or movements critical of the established order. From an intellectual consensus, during the 1930s, that the state and private enterprise could, through mass media, control the masses and through leftwing fears, during the 1950s, that it could create public apathy, we moved into a period, during the 1960s and '70s, when popular sociopolitical movements set the agenda for the "news," so much so that right-wing critics began to talk about a "fourth estate," a liberal-dominated media able to foment rebellion.

Out of this historical development and a growing body of research, including uses and gratifications theory and a modified effects approach (Real, 1980), cultural criticism is in a position to develop a theory which

(1) takes seriously the potential of the mass audience and the groups or "publics" within it, while at the same time identifies obstacles to realizing that potential;

(2) treats popular culture as an important and consequential source of personal experience and social "reality," and not merely as a preserve of nonart;

(3) strives to understand cultural products in the context of social, political, moral, and economic or "public" issues, while not ignoring the non- or even antipolitical function that the media can serve;

(4) moves beyond academic and literary jargon to find a language comprehensible to those who consume cultural products and might like to learn more about what they mean;

(5) focuses both on what appears in the content of mass media or popular culture, and also on what does not appear or what is "negated";

(6) studies not only the uniformities in media content but also the unusual, the contrary, the unique for the "potential consciousness" they offer; and

(7) specifies the content of popular culture and its meaning in a social, moral, economic, and political context, and considers organizational structures making certain kinds of content more or less likely to appear.

The debate over the media and the culture they communicate, pitting them against great art and personal experience, has become moot. If only for economic reasons, high culture is no longer competitive for the vast majority of people, and personal experience, in the modern world, includes experiencing the products of mass media. A society becomes "modern," writes Susan Sontag in her book on photography, when one of its chief activities is

> producing and consuming images, when images that have extraordinary powers to determine our demands upon reality and are themselves coveted substitutes for firsthand experience become indispensable to the health of the economy, the stability of the polity, and the pursuit of private happiness [Sontag, 1977, p. 153].

To the extent to which the products of popular culture are, in their origin, transmission, or reception, implicated in public issues, even the pursuit of private happiness may be enriched by criticism. The extent to which this pursuit diverts masses of people away from public issues, thwarts personal relationships and participation in movements for change becomes politically significant. The extent to which popular culture, through news or entertainment, conveys information about or provokes debate over public issues becomes a basis for personal interaction crossing the barriers of age, sex, race, and class. It again takes on political significance, becoming an ally in the critical act. In either case, the media, through what they do and do not show, provides us with a language with which to talk about important issues. If there is a requiem to be said for the media, it is to be said for an alien being grown monstrous, absorbing tens of millions of people into its mass. Media, in the modern world, have become moments in the lives of real people.

REFERENCES

Adorno, T. W., Frenkel-Brunswick, E., Levinson, D. F., & Sanford, S. N. *The authoritarian personality.* New York: Harper & Row, 1950.

Arendt, H. *The origins of totalitarianism.* New York: Meridian Books, 1958.

Bauer, R. A., & Bauer, A. America, "mass society" and mass media. In C. S. Steinberg (Ed.), *Mass media and communication.* New York: Hastings House, 1966.

Ben-Horin, D. Television without tears. *Socialist Review, 1977,* 7-35.

Brown, L. *Television: The business behind the box.* New York: Harvest Book, 1971.

Coben, S. A study in nativism: The American red scare of 1919-20. *Political Science Quarterly, 1964, 79,* 52-75.

Crossman, R. H. Supplementary essay. In D. Lerner (Ed.), *Psychological warfare against Nazi Germany.* Cambridge: MIT Press, 1971. (Originally published, 1949)

Eisenhower, D. Sins of "Washington." *Newsweek, 1977,* 104.

Fromm, E. *The sane society.* New York: Holt, Rinehart & Winston, 1955.

Fromm, E. *Beyond the chains of illusion.* New York: Simmon & Schuster, 1962.

Fromm, E. *The anatomy of human destructiveness.* New York: Holt, Rinehart & Winston, 1973.

Freud, S. Reflections upon war and death. In P. Rieff (Ed.), *Freud: Character and culture.* New York: Collier Books, 1963. (Originally published, 1915)

Fussell, P. *The great war and modern memory.* New York: Oxford University Press, 1975.

Gerbner, G., & Gross, L. Living with television: The violence profile. *Journal of Communication,* 1976, *26,* 173-200.

Gerbner, G., Gross, L., Morgan, M., & Signorielli, N. The "mainstreaming" of America: Violence profile no. 11. *Journal of Communication,* 1980, *30,* 10-29.

Gitlin, T. *The whole world is watching: Mass media in the making and unmaking of the new left.* Berkeley: University of California Press, 1980.

Goldman, L. The importance of the concept of potential consciousness for communication. In *Cultural creation in modern society* (B. Grahl, trans.). Saint Louis: Telos Press, 1971.

Gouldner, A. *The dialectic of ideology and technology.* New York: Seabury Press, 1976.

Greenberg, B. *Life on television: Content analyses of U.S. TV drama.* Norwood, NJ: Ablex, 1980.

Heilbruner, R. *The future as history.* New York: Grove Press, 1959.

Horkheimer, M. Art and mass culture. In *Critical theory: Selected essays.* New York: Seabury Press, 1972. (Originally published, 1941)

Horkheimer, M., & Adorno, T. The culture industry: Enlightenment as mass deception. In *Dialectic of the enlightenment.* New York: Seabury Press, 1972. (Originally published, 1944)

I.A.M. Media Project. 1300 Connecticut Ave. NW, Suite 909, Washington, D.C. 20036, 1980. (Publication available on request.)

Kellner, D. TV, ideology, and emancipatory popular culture. *Socialist Review,* 1979, *9,* 13-53.

LaFeber, W. *America, Russia, and the cold war, 1945-1971.* New York: John Wiley, 1972.

Lasswell, H. *Propaganda technique in World War I.* Cambridge: MIT Press, 1971. (Originally published, 1927)

Lazarsfeld, P., Berelson, B., & Gaudet, H. *The people's choice.* New York, Columbia University Press, 1948.

Lerner, D. *Psychological warfare against Nazi Germany.* Cambridge: MIT Press, 1971. (Originally published, 1949)

Lowenthal, L. An historical preface to the popular culture debate. In N. Jacobs (Ed.), *Culture for the millions? Mass media in modern society.* Boston: Beacon, 1964.

Marcuse, H. *One dimensional man.* Boston: Beacon, 1964.

Mills, C. The trade union leader: A collective portrait. *Public Opinion Quarterly,* 1945, *9,* 158-175.

Mills, C. What research can do for labor. *Labor and Nation,* 1945, *1,* 17-20.

Mills, C. Five publics the polls don't catch. *Labor and Nation,* 1947, *3,* 17-19.

Mills, C. Grass-roots union with ideas: The auto workers—Something new in American labor. *Commentary,* 1948, *20,* 240-247.

Mills, C. Mass media and public opinion. In I. L. Horowitz, *Power, politics & people: The collected essays of C. Wright Mills.* New York: Oxford University Press, 1967. (Originally published, 1950)

Mills, C. Mass society and liberal education. In I. L. Horowitz, *Power, politics & people: The collected essays of C. Wright Mills.* New York: Oxford University Press, 1967. (Originally published, 1954)

Mills, C. *The causes of World War Three.* New York: Simon and Schuster, 1958.

Real, M. The channels of American culture: Mass media and American studies. *American Quarterly,* 1980, *32,* 238-258.

Schneider, H. *A history of American philosophy* (2nd ed.). New York: Columbia University Press, 1963.

Smith, J. Rebirth of critical thought in Poland. Santa Cruz *Sentinel,* October 6, 1980.

Sontag, S. *Photography.* New York: Farrar, Straus and Giroux, 1977.

Tax, M. Culture is not neutral, whom does it serve? In L. Baxendall (Ed.), *Radical perspective in the arts.* Baltimore: Pelican Books, 1973.

Trow, M. Small businessmen, political tolerance, and support for McCarthy. *American Journal of Sociology,* 1959, *64,* 270-281.

Williams, R. *Television: Technology and cultural form.* New York: Schocken Books, 1975.

CHAPTER 19

Content Analysis

C. Richard Hofstetter

CONTENT ANALYSIS has been defined in a variety of ways and utilized for diverse purposes. Its techniques have been associated with the generation of indicators from virtually every element in the communications process. Primarily, however, observations of content have been used as indicators of the "what," or message, involved in communication. Content analysis techniques comprise measurement models; the assumptions involved connect concepts to observations.

In one sense, content analysis has been around as long as individuals have tried to make sense out of written or spoken messages. But this view is too broad. It does little to aid understanding of the scientific uses which have been made of analysis techniques in political communication research. It may be useful to look at a few explicit definitions. According to several of these, content analysis is a research technique for or involving

> the objective, systematic and quantitative description of the manifest content of communication [Berelson, 1952, p. 18].

> multipurpose research method developed specifically for investigating a broad spectrum of problems in which content of communication serves as the basis of inference [Holsti, 1968, p. 597].

> making replicable and valid inferences from data to their context [Krippendorff, 1980, pp. 16-18].

Historically, what we recognize as content analysis developed along with modern social science immediately prior to and after World War II. The above-mentioned definitions reflect emphasis on the scientific, on developing empirical indicators, making generalizations for purposes of description and theory-building, and quantification of results. Emphasis on quantitative description of material has waned to some extent in relation to emphasis on hypothesis-testing and in relation to theoretical concerns of a more sophisticated social science during recent years (George, 1959, 1969; Holsti, 1970; Shneidman, 1963; Walker, 1977).

Most content analyses in political communication research have focused on the visual and/or oral products of mass media. Some analyses have been based on messages conveyed via interpersonal communication. The messages which are analyzed typically are originated for purposes other than content analysis so that the techniques are unobtrusive in character. The messages assume quite diverse forms. As we shall see, content analysis in political communication research as utilized various units of analysis, measurement models, substantive materials, and has been developed in the service of many objectives. It has been limited only by the imagination of persons using it.

This essay focuses on a few examples of recent content analysis in which inferences about political phenomena have been made. Particular attention is devoted to alternative modes of analysis and applications of techniques; no pretention is made of reviewing exhaustively even the subset of content analysis literature in political communications. I have found the superb works of Holsti (1968) and Krippendorff (1980) helpful in these tasks, and their guidance is clear throughout. Literature presented as illustrative is organized in the simplistic fashion of inferences about sources, messages, and effects.

SOME METHODOLOGICAL PARAMETERS

It is useful to organize the discussion of content analysis in political research around several methodological as well as substantive parameters. These include the nature of sampling, unitizing content, and measurement. Unitizing involves the formation of units functionally defined, for purposes of sampling, measurement, aggregation, and generalization. The types of units commonly employed are sampling units, recording units, and context units.

Sampling Units

Most sampling problems arise in relation to the way in which various units in content analysis are formed as well as the nature and availability of material. Once a set of units for an analysis has been determined, sampling proceeds in much the same way that it does in research using other techniques of measurement. Sampling in political communication research commonly involves simple random or serial techniques widely employed in the social sciences. Occasionally, multistage sampling is employed, and saturation sampling is often used. Indeed, the frequency of saturation sampling and the simplicity of sampling designs distinguishes content analysis from other social science techniques. I assume readers are familiar with both practical and theoretical aspects of sampling or can review sources such as Budd (1967, pp. 16-30).

Sampling units define the basis for selecting material (Krippendorff, 1980, pp. 72-80), and are determined by decisions about how material being studied is to be divided for purposes of generalization. In studies of television news content, for instance, the news story is quite commonly selected as a sampling unit (Hofstetter, 1976; Frank, 1973). Either all or some stories are selected by sampling, and analysis of data subsequently are generalized to the universe of stories being sampled. Sampling units in political communication research are generally messages that have a "stand alone" quality to them. Such units represent "bundled" messages which convey a complete segment of information and can be understood without further elaboration. News stories and editorials comprise complete messages in this sense. Single words or paragraphs from news stories do not.

Recording Units

Recording units are the symbols from a message which are counted or evaluated during coding of content in relation to each variable. It defines what is observed in a narrow sense (Holsti, 1968, pp. 647-648). Functionally speaking, recording units are portions of sampling units which are scrutinized during the coding process.

Recording units are more varied than sampling units in political communication research. Symbols, words, themes and phrases, full-face televised shots, sentences, paragraphs, action film, and location settings (within sampling units) are all commonly employed as recording units. Entire sampling units are sometimes used as recording units, as when overall evaluations about the extent to which a news story favors a controversial issue is made; but recording units usually involve smaller amounts of content than sampling units. In general, the smaller the recording unit, the more reliable and precise a measurement or observation is likely to be. On the other hand, larger recording units, more closely approximating complete, bundled messages, may be more theoretically meaningful and consequently more valid measures. Thus, a paradox may arise between validity and reliability in content analysis research.

Context Units

Krippendorff (1980, pp. 81-82) defines a context unit as a portion of material which is examined to locate the recording unit. If, for instance, an analyst is counting the number of times the symbol "democracy" is used in a series of speeches (the sampling unit), then sentences within selected speeches might be used as the basis for searching for symbols. Content coders would read selected speeches sentence by sentence, counting the number of sentences in which the recording unit (the word "democracy") appears.

Definition of Units

Krippendorff (1980, pp. 83-87) outlines five ways in which units for sampling, recording, and providing context are frequently defined. Physical units, or bodies of material, commonly appear as units in political communication research. A newspaper story is a physical unit which can be delineated easily from other stories and other physical units. Some television news stories can be delineated from others on the basis of content or changes in video characteristics, although distinguishing stories can sometimes be difficult.

Syntactically, units are derived from the grammar in which a text is written. Symbols, words, sentences, and paragraphs may all be defined grammatically. Themes as recording units, for instance, are sometimes defined in terms of "complete thoughts or sentences" about something which is grammatically correct. Referential units are defined by some object, character, or event to which a concept refers. Instances of international terrorism, for example, appearing in editorials in the *New York Times* might comprise definitions of the concept "terrorism."

Propositional units and kernels require recording units to assume certain structures. Evaluation-assertion-analysis, a form of analysis based on actors, objects, and actions (Holsti, 1968, pp. 651-653), for instance, forms a unit by linking combinations of objects by verbal connectors and then scores the unit according to a predetermined set of rules. Finally, thematic units are defined in more abstract terms as units which include a broader, more general theme or meaning. Analyses of the concepts "freedom" or "democracy" in combination with other concepts may involve abstract notions and appear frequently in less quantitative thematic analyses.

SOME EARLY AND LINGERING TRADITIONS

Berelson provides an excellent summary of the state of the art of content analysis by the early 1950s in his classic survey (1952). Having developed an interest in the quality of public affairs reporting, the earliest content analysis studies described newspaper content of the day in terms of the frequency of simple subject-matter categories of content. Samples were haphazard and recording units frequently ill-defined.

Much of the impetus to the development of modern content analysis came in the wake of World War I and interest in foreign propaganda Harold D. Lasswell contributed to the development of scientific content analysis techniques and popularized them in academic communities through a combination of scholarly publication, government service relating to the analysis of communication, and instruction during the 1930s, '40s, and '50s. Among other areas,

Lasswell pioneered what we may loosely refer to as "propaganda analysis." I use some of Lasswell's work and that of his students and co-workers to illustrate the tradition.

Propaganda Analysis

Lasswell (1971) executed one of the best-known early studies of propaganda uses during World War I and published his study as a book in 1927. The study involved traditional methods of literary review to a greater extent than later content analyses he conducted and was devoid of quantitative indicators and statistical analysis.

Focusing primary interest on the techniques of propaganda employed by the contending powers in the war, Lasswell reviewed vast bodies of literature, including many items of propaganda, as well as studies about propaganda in World War I, and concluded that the propaganda had four main objectives (1971, p. 195):

1. To mobilize hatred of the enemy;
2. To preserve friendship of allies;
3. To preserve friendship and gain cooperation of neutral powers; and
4. To demoralize the enemy.

World War I propaganda was also summarized by several tactical objectives (1971, p. 200):

1. To arouse the interest of specific targeted groups;
2. To nullify certain ideas which could not be suppressed effectively; and
3. To avoid falsehoods which were likely to be contradicted before goals were attained.

Based on his evaluation of propaganda produced by major powers during the war, Lasswell concluded that the strategic and tactical objectives were executed with differing degrees of success by the major powers involved in the war. The Germans were assumed to have been less effective in reaching their general goals than were the Allies, and Britain was assumed to have conducted a particularly effective propaganda effort.

Lasswell later argued for the use of systematic quantitative indicators in studying World War II enemy propaganda in one set of essays subsequently published in book form (Lasswell, 1965, pp. 47-51). He argued that "describing the structure of attention in quantitative terms" would be useful for:

1. Anticipating enemy action;
2. Detecting enemy propaganda and aiding legal prosecution;
3. Contributing to the most economical means of controlling propaganda (created by the enemy); and

4. Improving understanding of attitudes in order to facilitate a more humane politics.

Propaganda was defined largely in terms of persuasive communication being sent to mass audiences for the purposes of manipulation without general knowledge of the source or purpose of the material. Exposure was important so that people would be in a better position to evaluate the messages completely. Faith in the benefits of freely flowing information was based on the not unreasonable assumption that information about the sources and nature of information would further enlighten the public.

Several of the essays published in the volume are particularly instructive concerning the nature of propaganda analysis at the time. Leites and de Sola Pool (1965) investigated the conditions under which Comintern (the internationalist communist organization between 1919 and 1943) defeats were reported by its own press. Focusing on electoral and strike defeats of communist groups, the analysis was based on English-language newspapers which carried commentary concerning current affairs under the auspices of the Comintern.

Leites and de Sola Pool first established a longitudinal sample of strike and electoral defeats for Communist Party organizations. Up to three instances of each kind of defeat were drawn for each year, 1919-1943, from reports in *Inprecorr,* the Comintern English-language weekly, and also reports in the *New York Times.* A saturation sample of all articles reporting an event included in the sample of defeats was then drawn from *Inprecorr.* Articles were required to include at least one mention of a defeat and to have been published within three months of the event. All statements in the article were then coded for the presence of any of a set of themes related to a general typology, including severity of the setback, repression, violence, magnitude of the event, frankness, and other items.

Leites and de Sola Pool discerned a trend toward decreasing "realism" during the period, in that news stories increasingly presented events in entirely favorable or unfavorable ways without much effort to strike a balance. Sometimes events reported in the *Times* were overlooked entirely. As the Party line shifted from "Left" to "Right" periods, radical shifts in published material occurred, with less measured self-indulgence during "Left" periods and more favorable symbols during "Right" periods.

News articles with at least one mention of a targeted defeat published within three months of the defeat comprised the sampling units in the study, and saturation sampling was conducted. Note that purposive sampling of events, assumed to represent a universe of certain kinds of events, was also conducted prior to sampling of printed content. News articles also formed the contextual unit for more general judgmental variables, while sentences (and possibly paragraphs in some instances) composed the contextual unit for thematic analysis.

Statements, and sometimes themes or symbols within statements, were the recording unit in the study, while measurement generally involved simple classification of statements, themes, or symbols according to predefined categories. Several intensity scales, based on judgments concerning the extremity of statements within articles, were also developed.

During World War II, Lasswell (1965) prepared evidence for the prosecution of several cases involving publication of material by persons alleged to be working for enemy powers without registering as such (a McCormack Act violation at the time). The analysis involved demonstrating how material disseminated in the United States was associated with material known to have been produced by the foreign power in question and thereby contributed circumstantial evidence of the person's association with the power.

In one of the cases, statements from 11 issues of *The Gallilean* were shown to contain themes consistent with themes broadcast by German shortwave radio into the United States during the same period. Among the 1240 statements from *The Gallilean* analyzed, 1195 were judged to be parallel to and consistent with themes in Nazi broadcasts. Changes in the Nazi line which appeared in the broadcasts during the period of study, moreover, were reflected by subsequent changes in themes in *The Gallilean*.

In another case, Lasswell also demonstrated high levels of thematic consistency between known Nazi propaganda themes and themes in a limited number of issues of *Today's Challenge* and *The Forum Observer,* distributed by F. E. Auhagen. Thematic content in the *Reader's Digest* and *Saturday Evening Post* published during the same period was also analyzed for purposes of comparison. Frequency analyses of data showed high levels of consistency between material in the periodicals distributed by Auhagen and official Nazi strategic aims and low levels of consistency between material in the two mass publications and Nazi strategic aims.

It is interesting to note that the illustration focuses on differences in the way scientific and legal evidence can be interpreted. Lasswell's analysis provides quite strong scientific evidence for his hypotheses involving foreign influence: a large number of tests are formulated, and the evidence is supportive in each instance. The data constitute circumstantial evidence from a legal viewpoint.

Almond (1954) based a portion of his study of the appeals of communism on differences in media portrayal of communist roles, or an "esoteric model" (internally publicized) and an "exoteric model" (externally publicized) of the ideal Party member. Intensive analysis of themes in classical communist works by Lenin and Stalin, and editorials in a Cominform publication and in the *Daily Worker* in 1948, provided the basis of the content analysis. Saturation sampling of shorter works, serial sampling of every other page of the longer works, and serial sampling of every fourth editorial during 1948 were conducted. Pages and editorials, thus, constituted the sampling units.

The recording units were made up of themes, defined as traits, characteristics, or roles, while sentences or groups of sentences appear to have made up contextual units. Data were classified according to a typology developed from an initial reading of the books, and cross-tabulations were prepared for two segments of the material: material from the *Daily Worker* which was assumed to be an exoteric publication and material from the other periodical, which was assumed to be an esoteric publication.

The portrait of the "ideal communist" painted by the publications of Lenin and Stalin involved 11 themes. Most important of these were a group of tactical concerns oriented toward gaining and maintaining power. Rationality, in terms of single-minded commitment toward this goal, was the most frequently mentioned theme; militance, organization, and discipline were also frequently mentioned. More abstract goals, such as peace, brotherhood, and cooperation, were rarely mentioned in esoteric material.

While the above were designed primarily for internal communication, thematic material in the *Daily Worker,* designed for external communication, contrasted markedly. An overriding emphasis was placed on antagonistic actors in the exoteric material, while esoteric material stressed discussion of communist organization. Style differences were also apparent, with a greater use of cliche modifiers in esoteric and a straight news style without cliches in exoteric material. Exoteric material maintained a much greater emphasis on long-range goals, such as peace, while esoteric material emphasized tactical, power-oriented goals. Almond concluded that the differences between exoteric and esoteric material constituted the major vulnerability to communist organizations.

In his study of World War II propaganda analysis, George (1959) discussed a considerably more sophisticated set of techniques for analyzing enemy propaganda than those which had been used in published research. Content analysis is used as one portion of propaganda analysis which infers the purpose or goals and objectives of propaganda from manifest content. Analysis also is useful in identifying the structural, syntactical, and linguistic features of material; but analysts must also specify situational and historical contexts (who produces the propaganda for whom under what circumstances) and the behavior context (what instrumental implications the propaganda may have for a range of other behaviors).

George distinguishes a direct model of analysis, as employed in several of the preceding studies, from an indirect model. The direct model is based on the assumption that intentions, expectations, and situational factors can be inferred directly from the manifest content of propaganda. The indirect model is based on the assumption that a more complex chain of reasoning is required concerning what intervenes between manifest content, as measured by techniques of content analysis, and situational factors and elite behaviors.

A "logic-of-the-situation" approach is required in drawing inferences from propaganda. It assumes that alternatives are selected based on the logic of the immediate situation. Analysts try to reconstruct what the initial conditions were which would account for messages and then evaluate, based on all the various kinds of information which can be garnered, whether the reconstruction is adequate. If it is inadequate, the analyst searches for additional factors which link all of the pertinent variables in reasonable ways. The basis of activity in the indirect approach is theory-building and is analogous to what social scientists do in constructing an explanation sketch about some new area of research which is devoid of elaborated theories. George also advocates a nonquantitative approach to analysis which is not based on the presence or absence of specific, predefined indicators. Propaganda, according to this view, is highly instrumental and dynamic, generating a stream of activity and information in which policies, situations, and even goals may be subject to rapid change. Moreover, manipulation of audiences, including enemy propaganda analysts, is of prime significance, and the same indicators may mean different things from one datum to the next.

In a massive study bridging World War II propaganda studies and later substantive and methodological developments in content analysis, de Sola Pool (1951, 1952, 1970) and co-workers coded the presence of 416 symbols (words appearing on specially constructed symbol lists) for appearances in texts of editorials from "prestige papers" in the United States, Great Britain, France, Russia, and Germany. Lead editorials from the newspapers had been serially sampled from the first and fifteenth days of each month during a period generally from 1890 to 1949. The larger project, termed RADIR, was designed to develop new ways of describing trends in political history, basing inferences about attitudes and behaviors on elite communication.

Conclusions from the RADIR project are too numerous to summarize, but illustrations from several specific studies can be drawn. The analysts found, for instance, that the five nations studied tended to develop reciprocity in the way favorable and unfavorable judgments were made about each other following World War I (de Sola Pool, 1951, pp. 11-15). Two trends were marked in editorial content, the trend toward highly nationalistic symbolic content in USSR communication since World War II. In relation to democratic symbols, the analysts found that component symbols associated with democracy shifted considerably and differently in various nations during the period of study, and that an expected increase in hostility toward democracy appeared in German texts during the 1930s.

Propaganda studies provided a useful stimulus to demonstrate what could be done with content analysis techniques. Extremely imaginative, policy-relevant indicators were derived and numerous applications made in generally applied research settings. These trends reached a zenith, perhaps, in George's analysis of propaganda studies and methodology.

But the early propaganda work was constrained by a variety of factors, some of which were to be rectified in later research. First of all, modern computing and data processing capabilities were not generally available and made many thematic and symbol analyses impractical and other such work very costly and labor-intensive. The results may have been to divert analysts from varieties of analyses, especially those involving the use of complex indicators derived from large numbers of other indicators, which could not be performed.

Much analysis was limited by its applied nature and was frequently based on theoretical models in which very simple isomorphism between words and meanings was assumed. The work, moreover, was limited by the underdeveloped state of theory in allied disciplines, especially in the areas of interpersonal communication, the psychology of attitudes and attitudinal change, and political socialization. The studies are frequently cited for their imaginative qualities in the area of measurement rather than for theoretical insights about society.

INFERENCES ABOUT COMMUNICATION SOURCES

As documented by Berelson, content analysis studies grew exponentially during the first portion of the century (Berelson, 1952), and there is no evidence that the pace has slowed since 1952 or that the rate of growth of studies in political communication research based on content analysis has been any slower. Although it is possible to sketch a large number of discrete uses of content analysis (Berelson, 1952), I use a simplified method of dividing studies into a more limited number of dimensions. In this section, a limited number of studies illustrate the range of inferences made about sources of communication. Content is analyzed so that something about the origin of messages, often quite distant and distinct from any purpose of the messages involved, can be inferred. And political communication researchers have been quite innovative in the vast array of inferences made on the basis of content.

Authorship

One of the more widely cited content analysis studies involves analysis of the characteristics of language in order to identify the authorship of 12 of the Federalist Papers. Written in 1787-1788 in an attempt to bolster support for the U.S. Constitution among inhabitants of New York, the Federalist Papers were written by Hamilton, Madison, and Jay. But 12 remain of disputed authorship.

Mosteller and Wallace (1963) compared the differential frequency of words in texts known to have been written by Hamilton and by Madison with frequencies of the same words in the disputed texts. Care was taken to select words relatively free of context so that variation would not be contingent on particular substance discussed. Samples of blocks of text were selected for analysis and frequencies tabulated for pools of words known to discriminate in texts of known authorship. A form of Bayesian inference was then used to conclude that Madison had written all 12 disputed texts.

Inaccessible Sources

Content analysis has been employed widely to draw inferences about individuals, groups, and institutions which otherwise would have been inaccessible. The behavior of public officials, key actors, historical groups, and others long since dead or appearing in contexts which disallow access have been studied due to creative applications of the method.

Soviet Union. Milton Lodge (1968) based a study of elite attitudes about participation in policy-making and decision-making on analysis of messages published in representative periodicals. A quota sample of 600 lead articles for each of five different elites was selected in serial fashion for 1952 and for each odd year from 1953 to 1965. Samples were drawn from the top one or two national periodicals published for the Central Party (CPSU) elite and for the more specialized economic, military, literary, and legal elites.

Themes relating to participation were then coded (once) for each paragraph in sampled articles, and rates for the entire article were calculated. Lodge concluded that increases in participation occurred as the USSR moved away from the Stalinist period. Specialist elites increased participation in policy-making, increasingly pressed the Party elite for more participation, portrayed themselves as participants to a greater extent, and tended to justify their actions in increasingly more instrumental, less ideological ways.

In a more extensive study of Soviet elite perceptions, Stewart (Note 1) content analyzed all publicly available documents attributed to any current Politburo member or candidate during January 1972-July 1979. Texts from journal and newspaper articles, radio and television addresses, interviews, books, and other recorded written communications were included. Coding data thematically on a sentence-by-sentence basis, Stewart measured issue salience by tabulating the relative frequency with which an issue was mentioned in texts by a person. He defined issues inductively according to clusters of issue identifiers which occurred among texts. A modified form of assertion-evaluation-analysis was also developed by scaling issues according to weights assigned to adjectives and adverbs associated with issues. This analysis focused on evaluations of issues.

Stewart concluded that rhetoric relating to "the ideological struggle" was the most salient issue and that this issue elicited the most favorable evaluations from the Politburo collectively and individually. Although the leadership of the Politburo was more extreme (in either positive or negative directions, depending on specific issues) than others and thereby was assumed to play a leadership role, Brezhnev tended to be more centrist on issues. Positive correlations, moreover, were found among indicators of support for the ideological struggle, détente, and arms control despite the logically contradictory nature of such relationships. Stewart speculated that these correlations may mean that Politburo members believe they can continue both the ideological struggle and also have détente and arms control.

Angell (1964) described basic values of Soviet and American elites in a comparative analysis. Drawing a serial sample of issues from major periodicals assumed to represent each of six elites (cultural, military, scientific, labor, and government/Party and economic in the USSR, or cosmopolitan and provincial in the United States), Angell tabulated mention of 40 predefined value categories among economic, social-political, and external relations dimensions in material published from May 1, 1957 to April 30, 1960, a period judged to exemplify stable U.S.-USSR relations. Among many other findings, Angell concluded that the labor elite was given much more attention in the United States than in the USSR, and that planning was emphasized more by USSR elites than by U.S. elites. This was particularly true of military and scientific elites in the two societies.

China. Political support for various factions were evaluated in a content analysis of printed obituary notices from national and regional groups in the Peoples' Republic of China following the death of Mao (Chai, 1977). Classifying words and phrases in relation to the Cultural Revolution, the permanent revolution, in relation to moderates and to the repression of moderates, Chai constructed a "verbal attack" index based on the percentage of the total symbols which were anti-rightist among different groups. He concluded that military leaders did not prefer moderates over radicals strongly and that municipal elites were more favorable to radicals than were provincial elites.

The White House. Donley and Winter (1970) conducted an analysis of motivation of several Presidents based on a content analysis of inaugural addresses. Complete texts of addresses between 1905 and 1965 were coded for achievement and power motivation according to procedures developed from techniques used in scoring Thematic Apperception Tests. Sentences were used as recording units in coding, and final scores were calculated by dividing the number of instances of each motive found in texts by the number of words in the text and then multiplying by a constant.

Results of the analysis support commonsense expectations. Johnson, Nixon, Kennedy, and T. Roosevelt were high on achievement, while Taft, Coolidge, Eisenhower, and Harding were low. T. Roosevelt, Truman, Kennedy, and Johnson were also high on power motivation, while Taft, Harding, Coolidge, and Hoover were low on this motive.

Miller and Sigelman (1978) concluded that President Johnson varied the content of his speeches substantially to fit his audience in a study of statements about Vietnam. Copying all 497 paragraphs which contained a reference to

Vietnam from public statements of President Johnson made from July 1, 1967 to January 20, 1969, Miller and Sigelman rated each theme in the sample along a five-point scale from "very dovish" to "very hawkish." Audiences were coded as "hawkish" or not based on the analysts' judgments. Statistical analysis showed that the content of statements varied with the type of audience so that it appeared that statements were "tailored" for particular audiences.

Wilson and Williams (1977) took advantage of the transcripts of recorded conversations in the Oval Office (concerning Watergate) to compare differences between face-to-face and telephone communication. Using a purposive sample of eight conversations of each type between President Nixon and top aids, the analysts segmented conversations into a series of "acts," constituting the coding units, based on Bales Interaction Process Analysis. Acts were coded in terms of three function categories—opinion or information, direction or metastatements, and acknowledgment or phatic—and three activity categories—add or agree, disagree or request, and anticipate. Analysis revealed, as hypothesized, that uncertainty was greater in telephone conversations (more questions and shorter utterances) and that telephone conversations were probably less pleasant (more disagreements and shorter in total duration) than face-to-face conversations.

The operational code is a concept defined in terms of ten beliefs. Five involve general beliefs about the nature of man and five involve beliefs about instrumental ways of attaining political ends. Developed by Leites (1951, 1953) in studies of Bolshevik behavior, the code is not viewed as deterministic in proscribing behavior but is assumed to act as a prism in influencing actors' perceptions of political events (George, 1969; Holsti, 1970). Thematic content analysis is used to define the ten belief dimensions in studies using the concept.

Holsti concluded from a careful study of John Foster Dulles's basic writing, for instance, that the former Secretary of State viewed the cold war as a moral rather than political conflict, that the cold war was assumed to form a zero-sum contest in politics, that the short-run is full of danger but the long-run prospects of victory for the United States are good and that change is ubiquitous. The code included such instrumental beliefs as the view that political goals should be based on moral principles rather than on expediency, risk of conflict should be minimized when the adversary is strong, and one should negotiate when the adversary is strong.

In another study, Walker (1977) concluded that former Secretary of State Kissinger's negotiating behaviors coincided generally with his operational code revealed in content analysis of his basic scholarly writings. Walker conducted a thorough thematic analysis of Kissinger's work on European diplomatic history. He then analyzed the texts of speeches and interviews in the State Department *Bulletin*, along with several "insider" books by respected journalists, in order to specify Kissinger's negotiating behaviors in relation to Vietnam peace talks in Paris. Walker discerned correspondence between behaviors and principles in the

operation code and, more generally, that statesmen, in contrast to revolutionaries, follow a strategy which minimizes the risk of loss and focuses on
relative gain. Johnson (1977) added interview data and personal materials to
published texts in operationalizing former Senator Frank Church's code in a
study of the senator's leadership behavior.

Sigelman and McNeil (1980) studied President Johnson's daily diary in order
to test hypotheses about the effects of organizational stress on interaction in
White House decision-making. All presidential contacts with Vietnam advisers
between October 10, 1967 and June 30, 1968 were coded in terms of who saw
the President, how the interaction occurred, and the duration of the interaction.
Data for 15 key advisers were then tabulated into three time periods—pre-Tet,
Tet, and post-Tet, coinciding with periods of low, high, and diminishing stress,
respectively.

Contrary to the hypothesis, the number of persons seeing the President was
greatest (not least) during Tet, the period of greatest stress. A greater concentration of advisers, moreover, was present in the pre-Tet period, and inferred levels
of activation were greatest during the post-Tet period.

Congressional Behavior. Content analysis has also been employed to measure
variables associated with behavior of elites to whom access is difficult but not
impossible. Hermann, for example, used a carefully selected set of texts from the
Congressional Record as the basis for relating personal characteristics of congressmen to foreign policy voting (1977). The most pro- and anti-foreign aid
congressmen in the 81st Congress (1949-1950) were selected based on recorded
roll-call votes. All statements appearing in the *Congressional Record* by sampled
persons were then selected, and statements over 900 words, labeled as speeches,
and those which had been revised were eliminated so that as close to spontaneous text as possible was included.

A total of 40 units of 120 words each were then selected from the sample of
statements purposively so that approximately equal numbers of units were
drawn from the beginning, middle, and end of statements for each congressman
in the sample. For each unit, optimism, cognitive complexity, "humanitarian"
ideology, and international involvement were measured by thematic analysis of
statements. Optimism, for instance, was measured by judging whether statements in a unit were generally positive or negative, cognitive complexity by
judging whether or not statements indicated flexibility and ambiguity, humanitarian ideology by judging whether statements indicated concern for the welfare
of people and a desire to help others, and international involvement by judging
whether statements indicated desire for a more or less active role in the
international arena.

Care was taken to mask the identity of congressmen when coding, and all
texts were randomly coded. Each dimension, moreover, was coded separately.

As hypothesized, those favoring foreign involvement were more likely to vote in favor of foreign aid. Those favoring foreign aid were also more optimistic, held more cognitively complex views, and were higher in humanitarian ideology than others (Hermann, 1977, pp. 328-330).

Indicators of Other Behaviors. Techniques of content analysis have been used often to develop indicators of historical processes, action and interaction which is tied into the communication process more or less directly. Besides interest in the communication process itself, analysts also frequently focus attention on the development of a variety of other indicators which are related to yet other processes.

Historical Studies. Democratic and Republican (or, at times, Whig) Party platforms were the basis for Ginsberg's (1972) study of the nature of party conflict and change. He tabulated the presence or absence of favorable and unfavorable assertions concerning seven general dimensions of study in each paragraph of the platforms. Themes relating to capitalism, internal sovereignty, redistribution, international cooperation, universalism, labor, and ruralism were then analyzed with respect to time and party.

High levels of salience (defined as frequent mentions) were found in party platforms for internal sovereignty during 1852-1868, for capitalism during 1872-1940, and for international cooperation during 1944-1964. Considerable interparty conflict (extent to which party platforms diverged on a dimension) appeared in relation to internal sovereignty during 1848-1880, capitalism during 1888-1932, and international cooperation during 1944-1968. Finally, Ginsberg reported that periods of most intense conflict between parties coincided with electoral realignments, when issues in conflict were extremely salient to one party and apparently were being effectively communicated to mass publics by that party. The implications were extended in a second study in which thematic analysis of over 60,000 U.S. public laws suggested that major changes in public policy emphasis corresponded to periods of major electoral realignment, and that popular choice, based on platforms, had generally been transformed into public policy (Ginsberg, 1976).

Content analysis has also been used to reconstruct characteristics of interaction among nations. Holsti (1965), for instance, tested hypotheses about the relation of stress among decision makers to perceptions of time, alternatives, and communication flows. Verbatim texts of most documents sent by key decision makers in Britain, France, Russia, Germany, and Austria-Hungary from June 27, 1914 to August 4, 1914 were analyzed using the perception (units defined in terms of identifiable perceiver, perceived or agent, action or attitude, and target) as the recording unit (N = 4883). Stress was defined thematically as the perception of a threat to high-priority values.

Holsti found support for hypotheses relating stress to increasing concern about time, shifts in attention from the distant to a more immediate future, perception of decreased numbers of alternatives, and rapid increases in communication loads. Increasing stress was also related to increased stereotypy in documents, use of extraordinary communication channels, and enhanced intra-coalition communication at the cost of intercoalition communication.

Both human coders and computer analysis were employed in a study of the Cuban missile crisis (Holsti, Brody, & North, 1965). Using a "two-step mediated stimulus-response" model as a theoretical structure, Holsti and co-workers measured a series of perceptual variables by content analyzing messages by key decision makers. All relevant publicly available documents by major actors were analyzed using the General Inquirer computer program and a special dictionary designed for perceptual data. Perceptual units were defined in terms of perceiver, perceived agent of action, action or attitude, and target of action on the general dimensions of potency, activity, and evaluation. Levels of violence were assessed by three judges.

The analysts concluded that after an initial, highly stressful period of crisis, rigidly negative-strong-active perceptions were somewhat modified, evaluations became more neutral, and perceptions became more passive as reflected in message content. Unlike the World War I crisis, moreover, each side perceived the nature of its adversary's actions accurately.

International Action. A burgeoning body of literature concerning the way nations behave has developed in relation to the "event" during the last two decades. Some aspects of international behavior deal with communication processes, although much of the data are garnered from content analyses of press accounts of what has transpired within and between various countries (Hermann, East, Hermann, Salmore, & Salmore, 1973; Burgess & Lawton, 1972).

McGowan and Rood (1975) concluded, in a study of alliance formation and change, that a decline in the rate of alliance formation precedes a change of the international system in a balance of power situation. Employing the alliance as a recording unit (as indicated by citation of a treaty among the major European powers), the analysts content analyzed nine "authoritative and representative" diplomatic histories covering the 1814-1914 period. Multiple sources were used in discerning 55 alliances during the period.

Political Campaigning. Content analysis has been used traditionally to describe and evaluate media coverage of political campaigns. Yet the amount of such analysis has increased sharply with the rise of television as a key medium in American campaigns. Scholars have become increasingly interested, for instance, in the manifest content of televised campaign coverage and in paid commercials. Content analysis has been used much less to describe campaigns and campaign communication processes as objects of analysis. The two concerns are separated for analytical reasons here.

In a study of 14 candidate speeches and 11 newscasts, Ellsworth (Note 2) used a version of the General Inquirer and a special campaign dictionary to describe the preelection period during October and November 1968. Measuring content related to economic discussion, group appeals, foreign affairs, partisan politics, and other categories, he found Wallace to be most partisan in that Wallace made most references to parties. Humphrey, in contrast, stressed the campaign more than public policy, and Nixon was more partisan and Humphrey less partisan than the distribution of party loyalists among the electorate would suggest. Ellsworth also reported that news coverage stressed the competitive character of the campaign through use of party labels and candidate references disproportionately.

Jackson-Beeck and Meadow (1979) concluded that several agenda were present in the presidential debates of 1960 and 1976, and that the contenders were far from fully responsive to questions and to rebuttals. But, questions posed by journalists were not very representative of what concerned the more general public. Using 13 broad issue categories (such as housing, urban problems, health care, social welfare, and defense) as units of analysis, and then more specific substantive concerns within the issue categories (among these, inflation, public spending, size and scope of government, and morality in government), the authors coded verbatim texts of the debates. More general judgments of the extent to which candidates responded to questions and rebuttals and the extent to which verbiage was germane to issues were made on the basis of examination of the two kinds of responses. Survey data were used to indicate what popular concerns were at the time.

Between one-third and two-thirds of the contenders' words were directed to questions or rebuttals, although responses were generally cohesive and addressed to a chosen broad issue. Candidates exercised latitude in using responses to state their own concerns. And, while both journalist interrogators and candidates discussed qualifications for office, candidates injected a number of topics in their responses which were unrelated to questions asked.

Shneidman (1963, 1969) developed an innovative method for studying the ways of thinking evident in Nixon and Kennedy's commentary during the first two debates in the 1960 campaign. He developed categories of idio-logic, or style of thinking, contra-logic, or private notions of causality and purpose, psycho-logic, or aspects of personality related to thinking, and pedago-logic, or practical ways of instructing others. Many specific instances of each general category were then coded from textual material, using the instance as the recording unit.

Analysis of simple frequency tabulations were employed to contrast Kennedy and Nixon. Based on a top-heavy predicate structure and balanced term structure, for instance, Kennedy was characterized as employing an idio-logic described as meandering and loose-knit. Use of irrelevant premises and conclusions and mixing forms of assertions suggested an impulsive character in his rhetoric. Nixon, in contrast, was described as having an idio-logic which was more cohesive, balanced, and univocal. Shneidman found it to be more cerebral, controlled, and deliberate.

Buss and Hofstetter (1976) applied Shneidman's analytic framework to a sample of televised campaign advertising used by Nixon and McGovern during the 1972 campaign. McGovern's advertising was characterized by somewhat greater amounts of *ad populum* appeals than Nixon's. Nixon's advertising was characterized by more *ad hominem* appeals than McGovern's.

Using time segments as a recording unit, Davis (1978) analyzed the nature of eye-to-camera exposure by Ford and Carter during the 1976 debates. Time spent looking directly at the camera and time spent looking elsewhere were measured. Each candidate maintained more direct eye contact with the camera when responding to the other person's points and when making closing statements than at other times. Although Davis hypothesized that eye-to-camera contact would favor candidates differently, both Carter and Ford kept similar amounts of contact.

Pomper (1967) analyzed major party platforms during the 1944-1964 period in order to study the role of platforms in campaigns. All sentences were coded into three major categories on the basis of thematic content, statements of rhetoric or fact, evaluations of past party record and performance, and statements of future policy. Evaluations were then coded as general or policy approval or criticism, future policy statements were coded in six thematically defined subcategories, and pledges or action were coded in nine specific topical areas.

Pomper concluded that party platforms constituted an information resource for voters by including discussion of policy, with some specific assertions about past records, especially about the incumbent party. Platforms also laid out future policy objectives, but were most specific in the area of distributive benefits. A tendency to emphasize issues in the area of a party's strength and to ignore issues in areas of the opponent's strength was discerned. Platforms also linked a party's own loyal constituents explicitly to policies which would benefit them as groups. In an analysis of 3194 pledges from the same data set, Pomper and Lederman (1980) also found that pledges were fulfilled to a large extent, which implies that platforms may be more important as vehicles of communication to mass electorates than more cynical analysts have suggested.

Graber (1976) concluded that the information environment surrounding the 1968 and 1972 campaigns as contributed by the press and television news was dominated by personal rather than professional qualities of candidates, and that issues coverage was oriented to excitement and "horse race" aspects of the campaign. These conclusions were based on a thematic analysis of an extensive sample of U.S. daily newspapers and network evening news coverage during the last four weeks of each campaign. A more detailed discussion of methods is presented below.

Hofstetter and Zukin (1979) concluded that production rather than purposive, reformist principles characterized the content of news and advertising materials during the McGovern-Nixon campaign. Based on a thematic analysis of 1037 news stories about either or both candidates and 136 "topics" (largely coterminous with what would be paragraphs in textual material) in nearly all paid advertising by the campaigns, the authors concluded that television news failed to present content that facilitated voters being able to compare candidate issue positions, that television focused on the major candidates to the exclusion of much else of significance, and that Nixon was covered in terms of his status as President rather than in a candidate role similar to the way McGovern was covered. Paid political advertising emphasized the strengths of a condidate's issue positions but failed to contrast them with the opposition. Neither presented an image of competing programs, and the content of advertising largely coincided with news, although visual material was in somewhat sharper relief in advertising.

Nonverbal and paralinguistic behavior of Hubert Humphrey and George McGovern were studied during the first California Democratic Party Primary debate which was broadcast on television in June 1972. Coding all responses (nods, blinks, gross body movements as instances of nonverbal behaviors and speech disturbances and frequencies of nonimmediate terms as instances of paralinguistic behavior) during the videotaped debate and also evaluating issues associated with each behavior in terms of stress, Frank (1977) concluded that nods and blinks differentiated between the least and most stressful topics for candidate Humphrey, while each of the paralinguistic and nonverbal behavior indices distinguished high and low stress issues for candidate McGovern.

INFERENCES ABOUT THE MEDIA

Many of the studies based on content analysis linked to political communication have focused on descriptions of messages about politics. Many of the studies have characterized the way some political event, actor, institution, or process has been portrayed, and some of the analysis has contained a substantial evaluational component.

News Coverage. Mass media play a central role in the diffusion of politically relevant information throughout American society. Scholarly attention to the content of these media has paralleled growing attention to public opinion and the impact the media have had on public opinion in electoral campaigns. Thematic analysis appears to have been the modal unit of analysis (as well as sampling, recording, and contextual unit) in much of this research.

A series of studies executed by Graber (1971) provides an extensive description of the kinds of information about candidates which are available to the public in the popular press. Graber analyzed campaign news stories in 20 newspapers selected in a purposive sample to represent major regions of the nation, communities of different sizes, varying partisan contexts, and varying ownership patterns. A total of 3163 news stories printed during the last four weeks of the 1968 presidential campaign were coded for electoral thematic content, candidate qualities, issues, and comments about candidates.

A reflected in the press, the 1968 campaign coverage included more about the Republican candidate (Nixon) but used sources more favorable to the Democratic candidate (Humphrey). No relationship was found between editorial endorsements and news coverage of the campaigns. Graber reported, however, that the bulk of coverage (77 percent) emphasized personal qualities of the candidates, including attention to personal attributes, style, and image. Much less attention was devoted to such professional capabilities as skill or ability. The press gave a uniform picture of issues as well as candidates much of the time for information about issues. The press tended to discuss issues in relation to the campaign facing the candidates rather than evaluate the issues independently of the campaign.

Graber (1976) reported similar findings when she enlarged the study to include the 1972 campaign and television coverage of both campaigns. Similar categories were used to extend analysis of the same sample of newspapers to include the last four weeks of the 1972 campaign. Videotapes of the 1972 period and logs of television stories for the 1968 period were analyzed. Thematic television content was coded in similar ways to press content, although not all dimensions of content could be coded from the 1968 logs.

Content in 1972 was similar to that in 1968, Graber concluded, in terms of heavy emphasis on personal qualities, and this was no less true of television than of newspaper coverage. Excitement of the campaign and various "horse race" aspects of the race served as a focus for issues coverage. The press tended to portray candidates in negative, rather than positive, ways. Television coverage was very similar but considerably more constrained in terms of time.

The assertion, defined as "one complete thought" about an actor linked to an object, served as the recording unit in a study of network evening news coverage of Thomas Eagleton, July 25-August 1, 1972 (Einsiedel, 1975). All assertions mentioning Eagleton were coded as positive or negative from transcripts of 20 news stories and five commentaries broadcast during the period of study. Einseidel concluded that significant differences among networks appeared, with only NBC presenting Eagleton news negatively and Eagleton commentary very negatively. ABC and CBS were more benign and similar in coverage.

Adams (1978) coded thematic content in news stories from a random sample of 95 early and late evening news programs broadcast by ten TV stations in Western Pennsylvania, August 17-September 8, 1976. Duration, levels of sensationalism, and degree of human interest were also coded for each story. Nonsensational local news dominated other types of coverage in evening news. Human interest stories consumed only about two minutes of each broadcast. Similar coverage was found when hour-long broadcasts were analyzed.

Belkaoui (1978) found a moderate shift in the direction of favorable coverage of Arabs in the "prestige press." Sampling 442 articles in 110 issues of *Time, Newsweek, US News and World Report,* and Sunday editions of the New York *Times* during 1967-1973, he measured images of Arabs and Israelis by coding relevant phrases as positive, neutral, or negative based on adjectives used in stories. According to a thematic analysis of texts, images of Arabs were more polarized than images of Israelis.

Funkhouser (1973) described trends in public affairs news reporting in news magazines during the 1960s. All articles during 1960-1970 in *Time, Newsweek,* and *US News and World Report* were coded according to major issue addressed. The frequency of specific events occurring during the period was then compared to instances of media coverage, and the two were found not to coincide closely. Public opinion data demonstrated, however, that public concern corresponded to media coverage, suggesting that agenda-setting may have been occurring.

Accuracy. The New York *Times* has been generally regarded as the "paper of record" concerning foreign affairs. Smith (1971) based an evaluation of its accuracy in coverage of a Sino-Indian conflict by comparing items about the conflict in the *Times* with three Indian *White Papers.* The "event interaction," defined as an interaction between national actors, constituted the recording unit, and 21 variables were recorded from the *Times* and the *White Papers* during November 1961-January 1963. Notes, memoranda, and officials' letters were also coded to supplement the other data.

Smith's analysis revealed that the *Times* provided information about event interactions by year accurately, when distributions from the two sources were compared. Closer analysis revealed, however, that the chronology of specific events, including protests, complaints, and border violations, were inaccurately reported in the *Times.*

In another study, Arrendell (1972) concluded that such factors as number of days published and size of newshole were related to completeness of coverage. Arrendell employed seven national criterion newspapers in establishing 292 campaign events so that five Republican and five Democratic events were selected each week during the 1968 campaign. He then sampled 109 Texas newspapers and checked to see whether an event from the criterion sample had been included.

Biased Coverage. Few aspects of political communication have raised tempers as much as assertions that press coverage is biased politically in some way. Several ironies have appeared in studies about the issue. Few situations allow bias to be measured independently from the media being studied, since the facts surrounding a number of events are rarely discernible solely from media accounts. Nonpolitical biases, whatever their political implications may be, are rarely appreciated despite the overwhelming significance of such concerns as structural bias and situational bias. Another irony is the failure of studies to demonstrate clearly that political biases make much difference as far as American society is concerned. Only some of the more serious, less polemical studies are mentioned here.

Lefever (1974) conducted a thematic analysis of texts of CBS coverage of the U.S. military during 1972-1973 network news programming. Based on his findings that coverage of the American military was less favorable than coverage of the Russian military, and that CBS carried more unfavorable than favorable material about the U.S. military, Lefever concluded that CBS's coverage of the military was biased. But no baseline was used, and there is no reason to believe that coverage of U.S. military items should indeed have been even less favorable than Lefever reported. More bad than good coverage does not make a case for bias any more than more good than bad coverage. Clearly, unfavorable coverage does not necessarily imply hostile, biased coverage.

The overwhelming significance of characteristics of the media (structural factors) and of the campaigns involved (situational factors) rather than political prejudices were demonstrated to be most important in accounting for political news during the 1972 campaign (Hofstetter, 1976). Using a cross-media, multi-method approach which incorporated analysis of network television news, newspaper and AP wire coverage, paid advertising, and a series of national surveys of voters, campaign workers and activists, and local television station news personnel, attention was focused on differences in coverage between newspapers in comparison to differences between television and print media. A necessary condition to establish political bias, as distinct from other forms, was for differences in coverage to appear between networks within the television medium, since differences between types of media might well be due to characteristics of the medium (size of newshole, economic incentives, ratings, and so on) which have nothing to do with partisan prejudices (Hofstetter, 1978).

Videotapes and machine-readable texts of news stories from July 10, 1972 to November 6, 1972 were analyzed using stories, themes with sentences, and logical attributes as recording units. The analysis was replicated for paid political advertising, the Washington *Post* and Chicago *Tribune,* and AP wire coverage. An amazing degree of parallelism was found in the manifest content of news coverage in the 4349 television stories about the campaign. McGovern, Nixon, and various issues received very similar coverage, with only minor and unsystematic exceptions on a large number of indicators of exposure, quality of exposure and coverage, linkages of campaigns and parties, and issue linkages. Similar findings emerged from an extensive analysis of themes (assertions) within each medium and evaluative ratings based on the stories (Hofstetter, 1976). Thus, content was influenced more by the nature of the media and the political situation. Political bias had little discernible impact.

Some differences in the use of logical attributes between networks were discovered when the Shneidman scheme of logical analysis was applied to subject-object linkages (Buss & Hofstetter, 1977), but differences failed to give one side or the other any clear advantage. Cross-media differences clearly appeared in news coverage (Hofstetter, 1978). Newspapers were more clearly critical than the networks; wire coverage fell between print and video news in this regard. But evidence from the analysis revealed that candidates were treated in parallel terms by each medium and that a combination of structural and situational biases, but not political biases, were present. Finally, whatever the nature of coverage, survey data revealed that fair proportions of the electorate perceived bias in TV and print news but that negative connotations were not associated with the presence of bias (Hofstetter, 1979). Political bias did not exist, despite perceptions of it. However, perceptions of bias made little difference in behaviors.

Meadow (1973) reported similar findings in his study of network news and three Philadelphia newspapers in a cross-media comparison of 1972 coverage. Coding such indicators as length of items, location of items, and editorial comment, he concluded that a striking uniformity of coverage among the media appeared. McGovern received somewhat greater coverage, but Nixon was presumably favored by greater coverage once presidential news was included along with candidate news.

Selecting 25 days between Labor Day and election eve, 1972 at random, Evarts and Stempel (1974) focused their analysis on political news by the networks, three weekly news magazines, and six major newspapers in a bias study of the Nixon-McGovern campaign. Sentences were drawn from texts in selected issues, and symbols associated with Nixon, Agnew, Republican and Democratic Parties, McGovern, and Shriver were coded directionally (favorable, neutral, and unfavorable) according to evaluative, activity, and potency dimensions. Symbols were also coded according to whether they appeared in attributed or unattributed contexts. News magazines were found to be slightly more favorable to the Republicans than other media, but evidence was not clear-cut. No evidence of a liberal bias, moreover, was discerned in the analysis.

Friedman, Mertz, and DiMatteo (1980) compared evaluations of facial expressions among anchors during the 1976 network evening broadcasts in another novel approach to studying an aspect of bias. Videotaped news programs were divided into 2.5-second segments in which a major party candidate's name was mentioned by an anchor (Cronkite, Chancellor, Walters, Brinkley, and Reasoner). The 227 segments were then played without audio to a panel of 40 students, who rated each segment on a 21-point scale from extremely negative to extremely positive. Verbal content was evaluated separately. Analysis showed Cronkite, Brinkley, and Reasoner to be more favorable to Carter and Chancellor and Walters to be more favorable to Ford in facial expressions. Corresponding verbal content was quite neutral, so that facial expressions were not simply a reflection of what was being said in the news. Frank (1973) coded a large number of similarly innovative and novel dimensions from the 1972 campaign, and concluded that little bias existed.

Influences on Coverage. Lowery (1971) concluded that former Vice-President Agnew's attacks on television news coverage had some effects. Sampling 45 news stories about the administration before and 45 after the attacks, Lowery coded sentences spoken by network reporters in terms of reports (verifiable), labeled or unlabeled inferences, and favorable and unfavorable judgments. Although very few judgments appeared and no before-after differences in unlabeled inferences were found, an increase of nine percent in attributed report sentences and a decrease in labeled inferences was discerned. Lowery concluded that news personnel were "playing it safe" by using attribution.

Historical and content analysis techniques were combined in a study of the impact of Pentagon sponsorship of war movies produced during 1948-1970 (Shain, 1972). Types of heroes were coded for Pentagon-sponsored and other-sponsored movies based on screening of 40.5 percent of the films and reading an average of 5.8 reviews of the remaining films. Heroes during the early part of the period were more likely to be cast as "professional warriors," while heroes during the latter part were more likely to be cast as "self-indulgent." Pentagon sponsorship was associated with casting of heroes as "professional warriors."

Collating Content Analysis with Effects Research

Content analysis has been used in conjunction with public opinion surveys in efforts to assess the influences of mass media. Most of the designs are fairly simple. Thematic analysis of a specific set of messages in selected media is conducted, and individuals' views, attitudes, and behaviors are measured through survey research about issues, candidates for public office, or some other policy concern.

Fairly simple thematic analysis of local media was employed, for instance, in the Elmira study in order to gauge informational context for behavior, and then to compare interest and attention with this context (Berelson, Lazarsfeld, & McPhee, 1966). In a far more sophisticated analysis, Patterson (1980) concluded that exposure to newspapers was associated with perception of the prevailing topics of news as being significant, and that television is less likely than newspapers to impress messages on audiences. Basing analysis on content analyses of nine news outlets, including network news, *Time* and *Newsweek*, and four daily newspapers, Patterson made an extensive analysis of the interrelationship between thematic content of the media and numerous dimensions of voter response in Erie, Pennsylvania, and Los Angeles, California.

In a more limited content analysis, Miller, Goldenberg, and Erbring (1979) concluded that media style in reporting, especially media critical content, was associated with enhanced public cynicism and diminished levels of political efficacy; although the strength of many relationships between exposure levels and dependent variables was not found to be strong. Based on a national study of voting behavior in the 1974 congressional election, Miller et al. performed a thematic analysis of all front-page articles in the 94 newspapers for ten noncontiguous days during the three weeks preceding personal interviews which were reported as having been read by seven or more survey respondents in drawing these conclusions.

COMPUTER-AUGMENTED APPLICATIONS

Krippendorff (1980) describes the potential of advances in computer technology during the last several decades for revolutionizing content analysis techniques. Computers are able to read large volumes of data (in the form of numbers, characters of other kinds, or strings of characters) sequentially, perform logical operations at extremely high speed, and allow analysts to specify any series of operations by programming. Programs then are able to execute instructions with perfect reliability. But computer-augmented content analysis requires programming in order to function, and programming which is sensitive to contexts of material and which allows analysis of relatively unstructured material is by no means simple or straightforward to create. Moreover, although computers are currently capable of performing many millions of complex operations each second, the number of operations required to "understand" an ordinary language like colloquial English is very large.

In general, the full potential of computer-augmented content analysis has not been realized in political communication research. In addition to standard statistical analysis of numerical data for which generalized statistical packages are employed nearly universally, some utilization of computers has appeared in information retrieval and the analysis of textual data. Information retrieval programs involve sets of search and locate operations, and may, for instance, retrieve a specific list of symbols and text associated with the symbols which appears in the immediate proximity, as in the KWIC (Key Word In Context) system. A pioneer in computer applications in political science, Janda (1968), provides a discussion of several alternative computer-linked systems used for a variety of functions. Traditional content analysis may be performed on the texts retrieved, but the computer programs work more to format data for subsequent noncomputer operations than to perform what most see as content analysis.

A number of studies illustrate computer analysis of textual material, the second class of computer-augmented content analysis. Studies in political communication research have utilized some combination of manual precoding of text according to grammatical structure, kernellization of sentences, and the like. The General Inquirer system has been most broadly used in the area, although other systems, such as VIA, have also been used in political communication studies.

The VIA program functions to replace a larger number of words with fewer, more general words based on similarities in roots. Kessel (1977), for example, used the VIA system in a study of electoral politics. Keypunched texts for the 1972 party platforms and acceptance speeches, campaign speeches, and the 1973 Inaugural Address and State of the Union Address were analyzed in stages. First, function words (prepositions, conjunctions, and articles) were screened out and root word groups established from the remainder of the text. Infrequent root groups were eliminated. Second, a number of variables from sentences in which words appeared were then coded in association with words and the resulting data were factor analyzed (Kessel, 1977).

Kessel found that about one-fifth of the words analyzed for each party's text were associated with social benefits. Concern for bureaucracy also emerged in nomination materials for both Republicans and Democrats (that is, in platforms and acceptance speeches). On the basis of these and other findings, Kessel concluded that a clear distinction exists between the electoral "season," or phase, and other phases in terms of the types of appeals used.

The General Inquirer programs also base analysis on word-out-of-context and with-manual coding. The inquirer is composed of a system of programs using substantively developed dictionaries used in tagging textual material, usually words, and then counting and indexing tags, locating and retrieving contexts associated with tags, and coding thematic material (Holsti, 1968). Concluding that Soviet and Chinese attitudes about the United States were influenced by the level of East-West tension, Holsti (1966) based an illustrative General Inquirer content analysis on 38 Soviet and 44 Chinese documents published during seven periods of low and high conflict between 1950 and 1963. Verbatim texts, amounting to 150,000 words, were keypunched after three manual coding operations had been completed. Complex sentences were coded into one or more themes, the syntactical positions of key words in the text were identified by numeric codes, and each of them was also coded by time and mode of expression. The Stanford Dictionary, a specially constructed set of tags defining the substance and intensity of attitudes along the dimensions of affect (evaluation), strength, and activity, was then employed in the analysis of themes for which the United States appeared as agent. When East-West conflict was high, both Chinese and Russian attitudes about the United States were very similar; when conflict ebbed, Chinese and Russian attitudes were found to diverge.

Using the General Inquirer with a special value dictionary, Namenwirth (1969) found a relationship between unemployment levels in the United States and the ways in which Democratic and Republican Party platforms treated wealth-related values for the period 1844-1964. A dictionary of 76 general value terms, mostly subcategories of the Lasswellian value scheme, was constructed.

Then, focusing the study on a single value category, "wealth-other" (wealth references to participants and transactions were excluded) which included 195 words, the analyst used the Inquirer to tabulate frequencies of the wealth-other value in platforms by party and year. During periods of high unemployment, further increases in unemployment had smaller effects on references to wealth in GOP than in Democratic platforms, suggesting that Republicans were less sensitive in communicating and formulating public policy about unemployment than their opponents in the same environment.

Krippendorff (1980) discusses the development of other computer programs focusing on the individual word in the genre of VIA and the General Inquirer, such as Words, a program which inductively develops more general thematic content categories from root forms appearing in texts. He also describes possible applications of artificial intelligence to content analysis problems. Involving both syntactic and semantic analyses, artificial intelligence approaches transform outputs from the analyses into a logic of discourse which permits interpretation of information within its parameters. Although the potential is high, artificial intelligence applications are not generally present in political communication literature at this time. At the same time, word-based computer content analysis studies have become increasingly common, even if they have not proliferated as rapidly as studies based on manual forms of analysis. Krippendorff (1980) concludes that computer-augmented content analysis is most likely to be successful when texts being studied are limited in vocabulary, syntax, and semantics; when the logic of the texts is represented computationally (rather than being computed); and when additional knowledge (such as hypotheses and theory independent of the particular text being analyzed) contributes to inferences made from texts.

DISCUSSION

Content analysis in political communication research during the last several decades can be characterized in terms of proliferation on a series of dimensions, including objectives of studies, sampling, recording, contextual units used, and other aspects of measurement. Although common theoretical underpinnings, beyond many of the assumptions required for measurement, have not constrained or guided research to any great extent, the number and variety of studies have continued to expand in geometric progression. Innovation and creativity have also grown rapidly as analysts have sought new materials and adapted new techniques in analysis.

Content analysis is now entrenched as a set of measurement techniques in nearly every area of political communication research. Indeed, clear distinctions of the field may well have blurred due to the adoption of content analysis as a data-making technique and to communication materials generated by political processes being used as bases for making inferences about a panalopy of behaviors. The net of inclusion has been cast wide in this review in order to incorporate examples so that the breadth of research could be appreciated. And concomitant with increases in innovation and creativity has arisen increased attention to rigor in such matters as reliability and validity and in terms of explicit commitment to theory- and model-building in analysis.

One way of conceptualizing the research is to outline general dimensions along which change has occurred. Not only has the number and quality of studies increased, but the range of content sources, the historical and longitudinal dimensions of design, the kinds of inferences made, and attention to consequences of behaviors studied have expanded markedly. The studies used as illustrations in this essay suggest the range of sampling, recording, and contextual units which have appeared in recent analyses. Words, symbols, sentences, themes, pictures, paragraphs, pages, segments, word-blocks, stories, passages, persons, issues, setting events, and a host of others have all served as one or more units. Theoretical models have ranged from theories of thinking and interaction to theories of alliances and their behaviors. Increasingly, research has utilized multiple units and levels of analysis simultaneously as the sophistication and complexity of theory has increased.

Research has also increasingly used data from content analysis along with other data to address cross-level types of research problems, as in the innovative study by Haight and Brody (1977), which combines quantitative analysis of news content with survey and other kinds of data in modeling presidential popularity. Further elaboration and development of strategies which combine different types of data with content analysis data and different levels of analysis should prove to be no less fruitful in explaining political communication variables.

Explicit concern for reliability and validity are present in much research. Indeed, reliability data are reported quite routinely and properly as a prerequisite to publication. Ample room exists in many studies, however, to enhance evidence of the validity of indicators. In one study, for instance, Strand and Hofstetter (1977) reported a successful multitrait, multimethod validation of content indicators designed to evaluate news reporting. More attention should be devoted to validating indicators, and emphasis on validity should increase in direct proportion to increasing indirectness of measurement (or the tenuousness of conceptual-operational coordination) in studies. This is particularly true as esoteric indicators occasionally based on theories with little support and of questionable face validity are introduced in the absence of other, complementary measures. Research should flourish as multiple measures and multiple content analysis strategies are developed.

Capabilities in the area of computer-augmented content analysis continue to expand with enhancements in hardware and software technologies. Although content analysis studies in political communication using computer-augmented procedures have become more numerous, such studies have failed to increase in number and in technical sophistication at the same rate as computer capabilities have increased. Most published studies are based on computer analysis of words-out-of-context in the mode of the General Inquirer and similar systems. And analysts have used increasing volumes of machine-readable data (present in burgeoning amounts since computers have become incorporated in printing and other information diffusion processes) only to a limited extent. It is reasonable to expect very rapid progress once researchers effectively begin to access machine-readable data resources and are able to employ new software advances developing in the area of artificial intelligence.

I anticipate that future research in the area of political communication will continue to develop as it has during the last 30 years. Substantive theories will increasingly use content analysis techniques to measure an increasing diversity of concepts with ever-increasing levels of sophistication. But several caveats are clearly suggested by the preceding discussion.

First, scarce resources will be conserved to the extent that computer augmentation is engaged in the actual coding of content as distinct from statistical analysis applications. Developments in hardware technologies are making computing very inexpensive. Attention to the concomitant development of software will make machine-augmented analysis more practical. It is likely that interdisciplinary work, combining political communication research with models developed in linguistics, psychology, and computer science, should prove particularly fruitful. This may also be true of increased utilization of artificial intelligence approaches.

Second, greater attention to developing content analysis techniques explicitly as measurement devices will prove fruitful and should be emphasized in all work, relatively applied or not. Attention to such concerns which enhance rigor as multimethod, multitrait approaches, alternative strategies of combining units of measurement for purposes of contextual and structural analyses, and similar strategies are essential. Research will also improve as work becomes more oriented to theory-building strategies and moves away from applications without explicit theoretical concern.

REFERENCE NOTES

1. Stewart, P. D. *Elite perceptions and the study of Soviet decision-making.* Unpublished manuscript, 1980.
2. Ellsworth, J. W. *Political campaign rhetoric and news media coverage: Some inferences from automated content analysis.* Unpublished manuscript, 1971.

REFERENCES

Adams, W. C. Local public affairs content of TV news. *Journalism Quarterly*, 1978, *55*, 690-695.
Almond, G. Q. *The appeals of communism.* Princeton: Princeton University Press, 1954.

Angell, R. C. Social values of Soviet and American elites: Content analysis of elite media. *Journal of Conflict Resolution,* 1964, *8,* 330-420.

Arrendell, C. Predicting the completeness of newspaper election coverage. *Journalism Quarterly,* 1972, *49,* 290-295.

Belkaoui, J. M. Images of Arabs and Israelis in the prestige press, 1966-74. *Journalism Quarterly,* 1978, *55,* 732-738, 799.

Berelson, B. R. *Content analysis in communication research.* New York: Free Press, 1952.

Berelson, B. R., Lazarsfeld, P. F., & McPhee, W. N. *Voting: A study of opinion formation in a presidential campaign.* Chicago: University of Chicago Press, 1966.

Budd, R. W. *Content analysis of communications.* New York: Macmillan, 1967.

Burgess, P. M., & Lawton, R. W. *Indicators of international behavior: An assessment of events data research.* Beverly Hills, CA: Sage, 1972.

Buss, T. F., & Hofstetter, C. R. An analysis of the logic of televised campaign advertisements: The 1972 presidential campaign. *Communication Research,* 1976, *3,* 367-392.

Buss, T. F., & Hofstetter, C. R. The logic of televised news coverage of political campaign information. *Journalism Quarterly,* 1977, *54,* 341-349.

Chai, R. A content analysis of the obituary notices of Mao Tse-tung. *Public Opinion Quarterly,* 1977, *41,* 475-487.

Davis, L. K. Camera-eye contact by the candidates in the presidential debates of 1976. *Journalism Quarterly,* 1978, *55,* 431-437, 455.

de Sola Pool, I. *Symbols of internationalism.* Stanford: Stanford University Press, 1951.

de Sola Pool, I. *Symbols of democracy.* Stanford: Stanford University Press, 1952.

de Sola Pool, I. *The prestige press.* Cambridge: MIT Press, 1970.

Donley, R. E., & Winter, D. G. Measuring the motives of public officials at a distance: An exploratory study of American presidents. *Behavioral Science,* 1970, *15,* 227-236.

Einsiedel, E. F. Television network news coverage of the Eagleton affair: A case study. *Journalism Quarterly,* 1975, *52,* 56-60.

Evarts, D., & Stempel, G. H. III. Coverage of the 1972 campaign by TV, news magazines, and major newspapers. *Journalism Quarterly,* 1974, *51,* 645-648, 676.

Frank, R. S. *Message dimension of television news.* Lexington, MA: D. C. Heath, 1973.

Frank, R. S. Nonverbal and paralinguistic analysis of political behavior: The first McGovern-Humphrey California primary debate. In M. G. Hermann (Ed.), *A psychological examination of political leaders.* New York: Free Press, 1977.

Friedman, H. S., Mertz, T. I., & DiMatteo, M. R. Perceived bias in the facial expressions of television news broadcasters. *Journal of Communication,* 1980, *30,* 103-111.

Funkhouser, G. R. Trends in media coverage of the issues of the 60's. *Journalism Quarterly,* 1973, *50,* 533-538.

George, A. L. *Propaganda analysis: A study of inferences made from Nazi propaganda in World War II.* Westport, CT: Greenwood Press, 1959.

George, A. L. The "operational code." A neglected approach to the study of political leaders and decision making. *International Studies Quarterly,* 1969, *13,* 190-222.

Ginsberg, B. Critical elections and the substance of party conflict: 1844-1968. *Midwest Journal of Political Science,* 1972, *16,* 603-625.

Ginsberg, B. Elections and public policy. *American Political Science Review,* 1976, *70,* 41-49.

Graber, D. A. The press as opinion resource during the 1968 presidential campaign. *Public Opinion Quarterly,* 1971, *35,* 168-182.

Graber, D. A. Press and TV as opinion resources in presidential campaigns. *Public Opinion Quarterly,* 1976, *40,* 285-303.

Haight, T. R., & Brody, R. A. The mass media and presidential popularity: Presidential broadcasting and news in the Nixon administration. *Communication Research,* 1977, *4,* 41-60.

Hermann, C. F., East, M. E., Hermann, M. G., Salmore, B. G., & Salmore, S. A. *CREON: A foreign events data set.* Beverly Hills, CA: Sage, 1973.

Hermann, M. G. Some personal characteristics related to foreign aid voting of congressmen. In M. G. Hermann (Ed.), *A psychological examination of political leaders.* New York: Free Press, 1977.

Hofstetter, C. R. *Bias in the news: Network television news coverage of the 1972 election campaign.* Columbus: Ohio State University Press, 1976.

Hofstetter, C. R. News bias in the 1972 campaign: A cross-media comparison. *Journalism Monographs,* 1978, No. 58.

Hofstetter, C. R. Perception of news bias in the 1972 presidential campaign. *Journalism Quarterly,* 1979, *56,* 370-374.

Hofstetter, C. R., & Zukin, C. TV network news and advertising in the Nixon and McGovern campaigns. *Journalism Quarterly,* 1979, *56,* 106-115, 152.

Holsti, O. R. The 1914 case. *American Political Science Review,* 1965, *59,* 365-378.

Holsti, O. R. External conflict and internal consensus: The Sino-Soviet case. In P. J. Stone, D. C. Dunphy, M. S. Smith, & D. M. Ogilvie (Eds.), *The general inquirer: A computer approach to content analysis.* Cambridge: MIT Press, 1966.

Holsti, O. R. Content analysis. In G. Lindzey & E. Aronson (Eds.), *Research methods, 2: The handbook of social psychology.* Reading: Addison-Wesley, 1968.

Holsti, O. R. The operational code approach to the study of political leaders: John Foster Dulles' philosophical and instrumental beliefs. *Canadian Journal of Political Science,* 1970, *3,* 123-157.

Holsti, O. R., Brody, R. A., & North, R. C. Measuring affect and action in international reaction models: Empirical materials from the 1962 Cuban crisis. *Peace Research Society Papers,* 1965, *2,* 170-190.

Jackson-Beeck, M., & Meadow, R. C. The triple agenda of presidential debates. *Public Opinion Quarterly,* 1979, *43,* 173-180.

Janda, K. *Information retrieval: Applications to political science.* Indianapolis: Bobbs-Merrill, 1968.

Johnson, L. K. Operational code and the prediction of leadership behavior: Senator Frank Church at mid-career. In M. G. Hermann (Ed.), *A psychological examination of political leaders.* New York: Free Press, 1977.

Kessel, J. H. The seasons of presidential politics. *Social Science Quarterly,* 1977, *58,* 418-435.

Krippendorff, K. *Content analysis: An introduction to its methodology.* Beverly Hills, CA: Sage, 1980.

Lasswell, H. D. Detection: Propaganda detection and the courts. In H. D. Lasswell & N. Leites (Eds.), *Language of politics: Studies in quantitative semantics.* Cambridge: MIT Press, 1965.

Lasswell, H. D. Why be quantitative? In H. D. Lasswell & N. Leites (Eds.), *Language of politics: Studies in quantitative semantics.* Cambridge: MIT Press, 1965.

Lasswell, H. D. *Propaganda technique in World War I.* Cambridge: MIT Press, 1971.

Lefever, E. W. *TV and national defense: An analysis of CBS news.* Boston: American Strategy Press, 1974.

Leites, N. *The operational code of the Politburo.* New York: McGraw-Hill, 1951.

Leites, N. *A study of Bolshevism.* New York: Free Press, 1953.

Leites, N., & de Sola Pool, I. Interaction: The response of communist propaganda to frustration. In H. D. Lasswell & N. Leites (Eds.), *Language of politics: Studies in quantitative semantics.* Cambridge: MIT Press, 1965.

Lodge, M. Soviet elite participatory attitudes in the post-Stalin period. *American Political Science Review,* 1968, *62,* 827-839.

Lowery, D. T. Agnew and the network TV news: A before/after content analysis. *Journalism Quarterly,* 1971, *48,* 205-210.

McGowan, P. J., & Rood, R. M. Alliance behavior in balance of power systems: Applying a poisson model to nineteenth-century Europe. *American Political Science Review,* 1975, *64,* 859-870.

Meadow, R. G. Cross-media comparison of coverage of the 1972 presidential campaign. *Journalism Quarterly,* 1973, *50,* 482-488.

Miller, A. H., Goldenberg, E. N., & Erbring, L. Type-set politics: Impact of newspapers on public confidence. *American Political Science Review,* 1979, *73,* 67-84.

Miller, L. R., & Sigelman, L. Is the audience the message? A note on LBJ's Vietnam statements. *Public Opinion Quarterly,* 1978, *42,* 71-80.

Mosteller, F., & Wallace, D. L. Inferences in an authorship problem. *Journal of the American Statistical Association,* 1963, *58,* 275-309.

Namenwirth, J. Z. Some long- and short-term trends in one American political value: A computer analysis of concern with wealth in 62 party platforms. In G. Gerbner, O. R. Holsti, K. Krippendorff, W. J. Paisley, & P. J. Stone (Eds.), *The analysis of communication content: Developments in scientific theories and computer techniques.* New York: John Wiley, 1969.

Patterson, T. E. *The mass media election: How Americans choose their president.* New York: Praeger, 1980.

Pomper, G. "If elected, I promise": American party platforms. *Midwest Journal of Political Science,* 1967, *11,* 318-352.

Pomper, G. M., with Lederman, S. E. *Elections in America:* Control and influence in democratic politics (2nd ed.). New York: Longman, 1980.

Shain, R. E. Effects of Pentagon influence on war movies, 1948-70. *Journalism Quarterly,* 1972, *49,* 641-647.

Schneidman, E. S. The logic of politics. In L. Arons & M. A. May (Eds.), *Television and human behavior: Tomorrow's research in mass communication.* New York: Appleton-Century-Crofts, 1963.

Shneidman, E. S. The logic of politics. In L. Arons & M. A. May (Eds.), *Television and* G. Gerbner, O. R. Holsti, K. Krippendorff, W. J. Paisley, & P. J. Stone (Eds.), *The analysis of communication content: Developments in scientific theories and computer techniques.* New York: John Wiley, 1969.

Sigelman, L., & McNeil, M. White House decision-making under stress: A case analysis. *American Journal of Political Science,* 1980, *24,* 652-673.

Smith, R. F. U.S. News and Sino-Indian relations: An extra-media study. *Journalism Quarterly,* 1971, *48,* 447-501.

Strand, P. J., & Hofstetter, C. R. Television news coverage of the 1972 election: A convergent and discriminant validation of some selected indicators. *Political Methodology,* 1977, *4,* 507-522.

Walker, S. G. The interface between beliefs and behavior: Henry Kissinger's operational code and the Vietnam War. *Journal of Conflict Resolution,* 1977, *21,* 129-168.

Wilson, C., & Williams, E. Watergate words: A naturalistic study of media and communication. *Communication Research,* 1977, *4,* 169-178.

CHAPTER 20

Experimental Studies

Roy E. Miller

IN ORDER to understand better the role of experimentation in political communication research, it is useful to have at one's command a summary conceptualization of the vast research which concerns political communication. One such organizing schema which has withstood the test of time was offered by Harold Lasswell as a set of questions whose answers could be used to describe any act of communication: "Who says what in which channel to whom with what effect?" (Lasswell, 1948, 1971, p. 37). If one adds to Lasswell's classic set of questions that of "in what context," and if one assumes some working definition of "political," then one has a functional means by which to classify conceptually the great bulk of political communication research. However, as Nimmo (1978) indicated, when using Lasswell's pentad one should keep in mind that political communication is really a transactional process that may take place over numerous channels and may have multiple effects.

Viewed within this organizing formula, political communication studies may accentuate source variables, message variables, channel variables, audience variables, contextual variables, or some combination of these. Beyond that, studies may be primarily descriptive in their orientation, or they may be more analytical and explicitly concerned with the questions focusing on causes and effects in the communication process (Selltiz, Wrightsman, & Cook, 1976). For reasons which will be discussed below, experimental studies in political communication research invariably fall into the category of "effects" research; that is, their principal concern is with elucidating the cause and effect dynamics of the political communication process. Accordingly, the general objectives of this chapter are

(1) to acquaint the reader with the logic of experimental research;

(2) to discuss the strengths and weakness of experimental research, and in so doing point out the reasons why the experimental approach is a superior research strategy for dealing with questions of cause and effect;

(3) to illustrate the use of experimentation in political communication research by briefly reviewing selected studies which emphasize various components of Lasswell's conceptual schema; and

(4) to offer some suggestions regarding future experimental studies in political communication research.

LOGIC OF EXPERIMENTAL RESEARCH

All research efforts can basically be dichotomized into those which rely on "passive-observational strategies" and those which use "experimental strategies" (Cook & Campbell, 1979). While the passive-observational strategies are perhaps most commonly referred to as "ex post facto" (Kerlinger, 1973), the use of that term is undesirable because it unnecessarily suggests that the research effort and observation are taking place only "after" the event of interest has occurred. While this may be true for historical research based on content analysis of written documents, film, or videotape (for example, Hofstetter, 1976), and while indeed much survey research involves interviewing that is done exclusively after the event of interest has occurred (see Glaser, 1965), other nonexperimental studies use measures which are collected during (rather than after) the event of interest—such as studies based on nonparticipant observation (see White, 1961, 1964) as well as those based on participant observation (for example, Napolitan, 1972). Accordingly, the term "passive-observational" seems more appropriate when referring to nonexperimental studies in general.

What is common to passive-observational studies is the absence of any preplanned and active manipulation of one or more of the independent variables for the primary purpose of evaluating the causal effects of such variables. Accordingly, what are often referred to as "natural experiments" are in fact passive-observational studies, given that in such studies the researcher does not actively manipulate any independent variables but rather merely observes results of naturally occurring phenomena. Then too, participant observation studies generally are instances of passive-observational research even though they may contain elements of attempted active manipulation by the researcher. This is so because generally the attempted manipulations are impromptu rather than preplanned; their purpose is often to ingratiate the researcher with the individuals who are being observed, and the success of the attempted manipulations is usually totally beyond the control of the researcher.

On the other hand, experimental studies are ones in which the researcher engages in preplanned and active manipulation of one or more independent variables for the purpose of facilitating causal inferences. These actively manipulated independent variables are called "treatment" variables. In order to make causal inferences, however, one needs some basis of comparison. For example, if a researcher allowed a group of subjects one minute to read a particular newspaper story and then measured the amount of cognitive information which was retained from the story, obviously one could easily calculate the average amount of information retained. However, we would not know whether or not a change in the amount of message exposure would cause a change in the amount of information retained. For example, would giving our subjects more exposure to the message result in their retaining more information? In order to address this causal question we must make some type of comparison.

There are many different ways in which a comparison could be made. For example, we might compare the information retained from this particular story by these subjects to that retained by the same subjects after a much longer reading of a different newspaper story. Or we might compare the amount of information retained by these subjects from a one-minute exposure to that retained by a different group of subjects from a much longer exposure to the same story. In either of these cases, however, the results of the comparison may be suspect. In the former instance, the results of the comparison may be drastically affected by various aspects of the two stories other than the amount of exposure to the two stories—for example, by the difference in the complexity of the two stories, by the difference in the style with which the stories are written, by differences in the size of the type in which the stories are printed, and so forth. In the latter instance, on the other hand, any observed differences in results may be strictly a function of preexperimental differences in the two groups of subjects, for example, in their degree of interest in the story, in the degree to which their vision may be impaired, in their relative ability to store and retrieve information from short-term memory, and so forth. While the necessary uncertainties surrounding the first type of comparison make it of extremely dubious value, the potential lack of preexperimental equivalence in the second instance has historically been dealt with by means of "matching," "random assignment," or some combination of both.

One of the great breakthroughs in the history of experimental design was the realization that random assignment of subjects (units) to treatment groups would give the researcher a probability basis for assuming preexperimental equivalence of all treatment groups on all independent variables other than those being actively manipulated (McCall, 1923; Fisher, 1925). This, of course, does not mean that all treatment groups will be empirically exactly alike prior to the experiment; rather, it means that whatever differences exist before the onset of the experimental manipulations will be the result of chance alone. The rules of probability then allow us to specify the extent of the differences between the treatment groups that would be expected by chance alone in the long run—that is, if the experiment were repeated an infinitely large number of times. Then, if after the introduction of the experimental treatment the groups are found to differ by an amount significantly greater than that which would be expected by chance alone, one may infer that the experimental treatment caused the difference.

In contrast to the use of random assignment, at times the principle of matching is used as a means of increasing preexperimental group equivalence (Selltiz, Jahoda, Deutsch, & Cook, 1959). Unfortunately, for pragmatic reasons one can never match on more than a few variables, and therefore matching is a totally inadequate method of establishing preexperimental group equivalence. On the other hand, matching is more appropriately viewed as a way of increasing the efficiency of one's design. In other words, matching on variables that are strongly related to the dependent variable will result in those variables being made statistically unrelated to the dependent variable, and thus the experimental treatment variable will explain more of the variance in the dependent variable than it otherwise would have done. Perhaps an oversimplified hypothetical example would help make this point clear.

Let's assume that our experimental study of the effect of the length of exposure (treatment variable) to a newspaper story on the cognitive information retained (dependent variable) was done using eight naturally occurring intact university classes rather than individual students as the experimental units. Furthermore, let's assume that the classes had been randomly assigned to one of two treatment conditions, one which allowed a one-minute exposure to the message and another which had a two-minute exposure. In addition to obtaining a measure of the average amount of information retained by each of our classes, we also obtain a dichotomous measure of the degree of interest in the story for each of the classes. Table 20.1 presents the hypothetical data results from this experiment.

In this example, as one would expect, the average information score for classes with a "high" amount of interest in the message was much higher (77.5) than that for classes with a "low" degree of interest in the message (62.5). On the other hand, the data indicates that our treatment variable had no effect—that is, the average information score of the classes getting the two-minute exposure to the message (mean = 70) was exactly the same as that for the classes getting the shorter exposure (mean = 70). This is the case even though an inspection of the table clearly indicates that the long-exposure, high-interest class did better (mean = 85) than the short-exposure, high-interest classes (mean = 75), and that the long-exposure, low-interest classes did better (mean = 65) than the short-exposure, low-interest class (mean = 55). In this case, the causal effects of the treatment variable have been totally obscured by the confounding effects of another variable. The effects of increased exposure have been suppressed by the fact that three out of the four long-exposure classes were also low-interest classes—a pure chance artifact of the random assignment procedure.

TABLE 20.1   Hypothetical Experimental Results without Matching

Class	Length Of Message Exposure	Amount Of Message Interest	Mean Information Score
1	2 minutes	High	85
2	1 minute	High	75
3	2 minutes	Low	65
4	1 minute	High	75
5	2 minutes	Low	65
6	1 minute	Low	55
7	2 minutes	Low	65
8	1 minute	High	75

Now let's assume that the data pertaining to "interest levels" had been obtained earlier, that pairs of classes had been matched in terms of their interest levels, and that these matched pairs had then been randomly assigned to treatment groups. This matching procedure would necessarily have resulted in the same number of high- and low-interest classes in each of the treatment conditions. Now, making the same assumptions as in Table 20.1 regarding the joint effects of interest and exposure, the data might look like that presented in Table 20.2.

Now the mean information score of the classes having the longer exposure to the message is 75, whereas that of the classes with the shorter exposure is only 65. In other words, by equating the treatment groups in terms of one confounding variable (interest), the effects of the treatment variable (length of exposure) have now appeared. The experiment has been made more "sensitive" to the effects of the treatment variable.

Mention should be made of the two different ways in which matching is sometimes done; namely, the "matched-pairs technique" versus the "matched-group technique" (Townsend, 1953). These two methods have been otherwise referred to as "precision" matching versus "frequency distribution" matching (Selltiz et al., 1959). When using the matched-pairs technique, sets of individual subjects are matched in terms of one or more characteristics, and then the individuals are assigned to the various treatment conditions. For example, the use of this technique would ensure that for every 22-year-old white Catholic male in one treatment group there was a 22-year-old white Catholic male in every other treatment group. Actually, the term "matched individuals" would often be more appropriate than "matched-pairs" given that there will be as many individuals in each matched set of individuals as there are treatment groups, and experiments often have more than just two treatment groups. The matched-

TABLE 20.2 Hypothetical Experimental Results with Matching

Class	Length Of Message Exposure	Amount Of Message Interest	Mean Information Score
3	2 minutes	Low	65
1	2 minutes	High	85
5	2 minutes	Low	65
9[a]	2 minutes	High	85
6	1 minute	Low	55
2	1 minute	High	75
10[a]	1 minute	Low	55
4	1 minute	High	75

[a]These two classes replace classes 7 and 8 in Table 20.1 in order to accomplish the required matching.

group technique, on the other hand, attempts to match treatment groups in terms of the overall distribution of a given variable or variables within the groups—rather than on a paired case-by-case basis. For example, a researcher using this technique might attempt to ensure only that the mean age, percentage white, percentage Catholic, and percentage male was the same for all of the treatment groups, regardless of whether or not there were subjects in each of the treatment groups with exactly the same combination of characteristics.

When attempting to match individual subjects, the task is made more burdensome for a couple of reasons. First and foremost, if one attempts to match on more than just a couple of variables, then one quickly encounters the need to have a very large subject pool from which to draw matched sets of individuals. Second, this problem is aggravated by the fact that the researcher often needs the resources to measure a large number of cases in the subject pool with respect to the matching variables, even though only a few of those cases will actually be used in the experiment. Accordingly, one can say that the matched-pairs technique, at the very best, is at times quite costly and time-consuming and, at the very worst, that it is almost impossible to match on very many variables simultaneously.

Because of the problems associated with the need for a large subject pool when using the matched-pairs technique, the matched-group technique is often used as a substitute. Though the use of this technique usually results in the loss of many fewer individuals from the starting subject pool, there are still a couple of problems specifically associated with this technique. First, it should be remembered that just because the distributions for a given variable across treatment groups are identical with respect to some measure of central tendency

TABLE 20.3   Hypothetical Matched-Group Distributional Results

Subject	Treatment Group	Sex	Age
1	A	Male	Old
2	A	Male	Old
3	A	Female	Young
4	A	Female	Young
5	B	Male	Young
6	B	Male	Young
7	B	Female	Old
8	B	Female	Old

(such as the mean), they are not necessarily similar with respect to other characteristics, such as their standard deviations, skewness, and kurtosis. Second, it should be remembered that although treatment groups may be equated with respect to the distributional characteristics of single variables, they may be badly mismatched with respect to the multivariate distributions of these same variables. For example, let's consider the distributional data in Table 20.3.

It is the case that the two treatment groups in Table 20.3 are identical in terms of the univariate distributions of the two matching variables; that is, both groups are 50 percent male and 50 percent female, and both groups have 50 percent elderly subjects and 50 percent young subjects. However, when one looks at the bivariate distribution, the picture is drastically different. While Group A is composed of all elderly males and young females, Group B is composed of all young males and elderly females. In terms of multivariate considerations, the two groups are not at all similar.

Before leaving the subject of matching, it should again be emphasized that matching increases the sensitivity of an experiment to treatment effects only when the matching variables are moderately or strongly related to the dependent variable in the experiment. Accordingly, therefore, the utility of one's matching efforts depends primarily on the adequacy of one's preexperimental theoretical and empirical information. Even with good information concerning which variables to use as matching variables, the researcher may often find that it is costly and difficult to obtain preexperimental measures of these "most useful" matching variables. For example, in our hypothetical experiment concerning exposure and information retention, it might be useful to match our subjects with respect to any physiological impairment in their short-term memory capabilities. To do so, however, might require that all of our potential subjects undergo a series of costly, time-consuming, and perhaps even painful physiological diagnostic tests—most of which would not generally be available to the ordinary political communication researcher (such as, for example, the brain scan or electroencephalogram). Thus, because of the sometimes prohibitive nature of obtaining measures on these "most useful" matching variables, the researcher all too often is left with little more than easily ascertainable demographic variables to use as matching variables, such as age, sex, and race—variables which often are not very helpful in increasing the sensitivity of the experiment.

It should also be pointed out that matching procedures should never be used in lieu of random assignment. Rather, any matching procedure which is chosen should necessarily include random assignment in its final step (see Stanley & Beeman, 1958; Thorndike, 1942). For example, if one were using a matched-pairs procedure, then once the matched sets of individuals had been selected, random procedures should be used to assign the individuals to treatment groups. This random assignment feature should be an integral part of any matching procedure in order to justify the assumption of statistical prexperimental group equivalence on all independent variables other than the matching variables.

The random assignment of subjects and treatments to experimental conditions is the *sine qua non* of what is termed the "completely randomized," "true," or "pure" experiment. On the other hand, studies which involve the active manipulation of treatment variables but which do not employ random assignments of subjects and/or treatments are referred to as "quasi-experiments." As it is often more difficult to assign individuals or larger social groups to treatments at random than it is to randomly assign rats, amoebas, agricultural plots, geological specimens, plants or monkeys, we see a greater use of quasi-experiments in the social and communication sciences than in the other so-called harder sciences.

We have seen that in the completely randomized experiment we are able to infer treatment effects because random assignment justifies our assumption of preexperimental statistical or probabilistic equivalence between our groups. On the other hand, the interpretation of results from quasi-experiments usually involves the comparison of nonequivalent groups which differ from each other in many ways beyond the presence of the treatment whose effects are being tested. The task of the quasi-experimental researcher, therefore, is basically that of separating the effects of the treatment variables from those due to the initial noncomparability of the treatment groups. The difficulty of this task necessarily results in the researcher having less confidence in the causal inferences drawn from quasi-experiments than in those generated on the basis of completely randomized experiments.

In addition, as Cook and Campbell (1979, p. 342) pointed out, the use of a completely randomized design

> creates the conditions for which the best known statistical models were created. Tests of differences between randomly formed groups are less

biased and more powerful than tests with nonequivalent groups. We therefore have greater faith both in magnitude estimates of effects and in inferences about rejecting the null hypothesis.

It is clear that empirical research studies can be arrayed from passive-observational studies to quasi-experiments to completely randomized experiments. Furthermore, which category a particular study falls in depends on how much active "control" is exercised by the researcher.

As an aid to a summary understanding of the logic of control in experimental research, it is probably worthwhile to consider four types of variables discussed by Kish (1959), all of which are theoretically capable of causing changes in one's dependent variables. First, there are the particular independent variables with which the researcher is directly concerned. In experimental research these treatment variables are controlled by the researcher through active, intrusive, physical manipulation. Second, there may be a number of independent variables that are potential causes of the dependent variable but that are prevented from producing any effects in a given experiment because they do not vary. That is, these variables are controlled by being physically held constant during the experiment. For example, in our hypothetical experiment concerning exposure and information retention, the possible effects of independent variables such as type size, amount of light in the room, reading ability of our subjects, and level of noise in the room could all be controlled by holding them constant. One objective of experimental design is to bring as many independent variables as possible into this second category.

In addition to these two types of variables, however, there are two additional types of independent variables that must be considered. The third type consists of all those variables which do produce changes in the dependent variable during the course of the experiment but whose effects are unrelated to those of the treatment variables. For example, in our earlier hypothetical experiment outlined in Table 20.2, whereas interest level obviously affected information retention, it was made into a type 3 variable by using it as a matching variable and thus making its effects unrelated to those of the treatment variable. The fourth type consists of all those variables that also produce changes in the dependent variable during the course of the experiment but whose effects are in some way systematically related to those of the treatment variables. These type 4 variables are referred to as "confounding" variables. For example and again considering the hypothetical experiment of Table 20.2–if all of the classes with a two-minute message exposure were held during evening hours when people are getting tired, but the one-minute classes were all held during the midmorning hours when people are fresh and alert, then the hour the class was held would probably be affecting the information levels of our subjects, and, given that it was systematically related to our treatment variable it would be a type 4 confounding variable. In the ideal experiment there would be no type 3 or 4 variables—everything except the treatment variables would be physically held constant. This, of course, is an unattainable ideal. In real-world experiments we can usually hold only a small, finite number of variables physically constant. Accordingly, type 3 and type 4 variables are always present. We control type 4 variables by changing them into type 3 variables through the procedures of matching and random assignment. Exclusive reliance on matching would always leave the researcher with a large number of unknown type 4 variables, but through the use of random assignment (either alone or in conjunction with matching) we enable ourselves to make use of the probabilistic assumption that all type 4 variables have been transformed into type 3 variables (see Blalock, 1972, p. 25, for an exception to this general assumption). Finally, the experimenter makes use of statistical significance tests in order to make inferences concerning the effects of the treatment variables as compared with the effects of other type 3 variables (Kish, 1959, p. 331).

In sum, in experimental research one controls treatment variables by active physical manipulation. One then controls as many possible confounding variables as is practical by physically holding them constant during the course of the experiment. The effects of other confounding variables are controlled by making them statistically independent of the effects of the treatment variables; this is done through the use of matching and random assignment. And, finally, significance tests are used to assess the probability that the observed differences between treatment groups could be a chance artifact due to the influence of other type 3 random variables. In other words, the significance tests tell us whether or not the treatment group differences are large enough to need explaining at all, or if they should instead be dismissed as being nothing more than random or chance occurrences.

CONSIDERATIONS IN THE SELECTION OF
A RESEARCH DESIGN STRATEGY

As we have seen, empirical research design strategies fall into one of three general classes: (a) passive-observation, (b) quasi-experiment, or (c) randomized experiment. However desirable the use of multidesign strategies might be, the fact remains that most research projects are carried out using a single strategy. Accordingly, let us now turn our attention to some of the broad considerations that come into play in the selection of a research design strategy.

Internal Validity

In order to have confidence in our causal inferences, it is generally agreed that at least three types of evidence are required:

1. Covariation between the presumed cause and presumed effect.
2. Proper time order, with the cause preceding the effect.

3. Elimination of plausible alternative explanations for the observed relationship. [Selltiz et al., 1976, p. 115]

In a given piece of research, how certain we are that the evidentiary requirements have been met is in part a function of our research design; in particular, it
is a function of the "internal validity" of the design. In the words of Campbell
and Stanley (1966, p. 5), internal validity is the *"sine qua non"* of causal
research; it is the "basic minimum without which any experiment is uninterpretable." In other words, internal validity is the extent to which our research
design allows us to feel confident that our inference that "X caused Y" is a valid
one—at least in the immediate research setting.

In terms of the types of evidence required to best support our causal
inferences, it is the case that any of the three design strategies can be used to
establish the fact of covariation between variables. In other words, any design
strategy can indicate whether or not two variables are related—that is, vary
together, are correlated, or have changes in the values of one accompanied by
changes in the values of the other. On the other hand, whereas experimental
designs can with certainty always provide evidence of the proper time order
among variables, this is not so for all passive-observational designs, such as
cross-sectional surveys. And, finally, it is clearly the case that the randomized
experiment is the most powerful strategy for the elimination of plausible
alternative explanations. Its great strength in this area comes from the fact that
through random assignment of subjects type 4 confounding variables are transformed into type 3 randomized variables.

For example, in their classic study of the 1948 presidential campaign
Berelson, Lazarsfeld, and McPhee (1966, p. 244) concluded that "the more
attention to the mass media in general, the more exposure to political materials
in particular." Furthermore, they indicated that this finding holds even with a
control for political interest. However, the conclusion is based on data gathered
using a passive-observational design, and the authors did not exercise simultaneous statistical controls for any number of potentially relevant variables.
Accordingly, the reader is left with a variety of alternative explanations which
may be more valid than the causal connection asserted by the authors. More
specifically, it may be that highly educated persons manifest both a higher
degree of attention to the mass media in general as well as a greater exposure to
political materials in particular; or that political partisanship causes both general
media attention and specific exposure to political content; or that both variables
are influenced by such characteristics of individuals as their income, sex, occupa-
tion, or social class. While it is possible that these explanations could have been
investigated by the authors, other viable explanations depend on variables that
probably were not even thought of by the researchers when the survey questions
were being constructed. For instance, perhaps both general media attention and

specific exposure to political content are caused by the amount of "stake" one has in one's community, or by the extent to which one has a social psychological "need to structure and understand reality," or perhaps by the level of "cognitive complexity" one uses in integrating social phenomena. In any case, there are relatively narrow limits within which such potentially confounding variables can be dealt with using passive-observational designs. However, randomized experiments transform all of these potentially confounding variables (even ones the researcher hasn't thought about) to randomized variables which are statistically independent of any treatment variable effects. Accordingly, for the researcher whose primary pupose is making causal inferences, randomized experiments provide the greatest degree of internal validity, while passive-observational studies generally are the least internally valid.

External Validity

While internal validity concerns the degree of confidence we have in our causal inferences for the immediate research setting, external validity is concerned with the question of generalizability. As Campbell and Stanley (1966, p. 5) again so succinctly put it, given evidence that X causes Y in a particular research setting, the question is: To what "populations, settings, treatment variables, and measurement variables can this effect be generalized?" These four areas of external validity need some amplification.

The first of these areas, sample representativeness, is concerned with the question of to what broader empirical and theoretical populations we are justified in inferring the results of a particular piece of research. For example, are the conclusions of *The People's Choice* (Lazarsfeld, Berelson, & Gaudet, 1944), the classic study of the 1940 presidential campaign, generalizable only to the voters of Erie County, Ohio, or to all of the voters in Ohio, or to all of the voters in the midwestern United States, or to all of the voters in the entire United States, or only to voters in counties with a population of approximately 43,000, or only to voters who live on the shores of Lake Erie, or to whom? Quite obviously, the populations of theoretical interest to political communication researchers are seldom the same as the populations from which we actually derive our data. Indeed, we often seem obsessed with the desire to generalize beyond the logical boundaries permitted by our samples.

Passive-observational studies often rely on the use of probability sampling (Kish, 1965) to enhance their sample generalizability. On the other hand, historically, experimental studies have relied largely on replication of experimental findings with various subject pools as a means of increasing their generalizability. Although the extensive use of volunteer subjects (especially college freshmen) in experimental research has appropriately led to the criticism that they are often greatly lacking in their sample representativeness (Rosenthal & Rosnow, 1975), it should be emphasized that in any particular research instance an experimental study may be stronger, weaker, or equally as strong in its sample representativeness as a given passive-observational study. For example, in a randomized field experiment (Kerlinger, 1973, p. 401) using subjects selected from an identifiable population through random sampling procedures, the sample representativeness would be as great as any passive-observational study of the same population.

The second area, ecological or contextual generalizability, is concerned with the question of to what physical, mental, spatial, and temporal settings or environments we are justified in inferring the results of a particular piece of research. For example, are findings which are based partly on subjects viewing the 1976 presidential debates in large lecture halls on a university campus (Lang & Lang, 1978) applicable to the vast audience that watched those debates in the privacy of their own homes? Are findings regarding communication processes during a time of perceived crisis (Greenberg & Parker, 1965) equally descriptive of such processes during "normal" times? Are conclusions regarding the political effects of the mass media which are based primarily on data from one political culture (Seymour-Ure, 1974) equally applicable to other cultures? Are conclusions regarding the impact of television in political campaigns which are based on data gathered during one particular presidential campaign (Patterson & McClure, 1976) generalizable to campaigns in other historical epochs?

In most instances, laboratory experiments suffer from a relative lack of contextual representativeness due to the highly controlled artificial environment within which they are carried out. However, in general, again, we find that with respect to contextual representativeness field experiments may attain parity with the best designed and executed passive-observational studies.

The last two areas of consideration in discussing external validity concern how representative our treatment variables and all other measured variables are of the total pool of possible operationalized indicators of our theoretical concepts. For example, with respect to our independent variables, are conclusions derived from studies of either the 1960 presidential debates (Kraus, 1968) or the 1976 presidential debates (Kraus, 1979) theoretically generalizable to the effects of "presidential debates" in the abstract? Or, with respect to dependent variable representativeness, are conclusions from studies of the agenda-setting power of the media which are based on measuring personal agendas in terms of the relative importance of a set of seven issues chosen by the researcher (Shaw & McCombs, 1977) theoretically generalizable to the effects of the media on people's "agendas" in the abstract? In both of the above instances we have many possible indicators of the theoretical concepts in question, and as researchers we should always be concerned with whether or not the operationalized indicators we use are representative of the many possible indicators of our theoretical concepts.

Obviously, the desire for variable generalizability leads to a prescription for the use of multiple indicators—multiple measures of the same variable—in any research effort. While laboratory experiments are probably the most facilitative of the use of multiple indicators, field experiments and passive-observational studies generally entail many more constraints on the nature and number of indicators which may be used.

Ethical Acceptability

According to some, an additional consideration in the selection of a research design strategy is the ethical acceptability of the alternative strategies. However, it would seem to be the case that no given degree of ethical acceptability adheres in principle to the different design strategies. Rather, the implementation of any strategy may involve ethical questions (Hobbs, 1968), and those questions at best seem resolvable only on a case-by-case basis. For example, while field experiments in some circumstances may utilize covert observational data collection techniques and thus be ethically questioned because they involve subjects in research without their knowledge or consent, the same is true of many passive-observational studies which rely on either participant or nonparticipant observation. In addition, many experiments may at times be ethically questioned because the researcher fails to give potential subjects a complete, explicit, and accurate account of the nature of the research in order to aid them in deciding whether or not to participate. Rather, they are told some cover story usually involving only half-truths. Even more serious is the practice of actively deceiving or lying to subjects regarding the nature of the research. Again, however, these practices are not applicable only to experimental studies. Deception is often practiced in passive-observational studies of various social groups. The study by Festinger, Riecken, and Schachter (1956) of an unorthodox religious cult, and that of Humphreys (1970) concerning males who engage in homosexual practices in public restrooms, are but two examples of such studies. And, of course, the question of obtaining "informed consent" is not only relevant to experiments but is equally applicable to most passive-observational studies. One must also realize, however, that by far the great majority of experiments do not involve any deception whatsoever. For instance, Stricker (1967) found in his review of 457 studies reported in four psychology journals for 1964 that only 19.3 percent used any form of deception. Obviously, the use of deception is not a necessary feature of experimental studies.

Accordingly, it seems most reasonable to take the position that different degrees of ethical acceptability do not in principle adhere to the alternative research design strategies. Rather, the implementation of any design strategy in a given circumstance may involve the researcher in any number of ethical concerns. Those might possibly include such things as involving people in research without their knowledge or consent, withholding the true nature of the research from potential participants, actively deceiving research participants, leading research participants to commit acts which diminish their self-respect, exposing research participants to physical or psychological stress, invading participants' right to privacy, withholding presumed benefits from participants in control groups, or violating a guarantee of confidentiality. In any case, given the unique aspects of any particular research situation, a primary requisite for the researcher should be the ethically acceptable implementation of whatever design strategy is chosen.

Theoretical Needs

Beyond the considerations discussed thus far, there are additional factors the researcher should take into account when selecting a research design strategy. Several of these can be grouped together for discussion, given that they relate to the general theoretical needs of the researcher.

To begin with, we must recognize that some political communication research is basically atheoretical. Its concern is primarily for the detailed and accurate description of some social phenomenon, as illustrated, for example, by the work of Seltz and Yoakam (1968) detailing the production diary of the 1960 presidential debates; the piece by Alexander and Margolis (1978) outling the events which went into the making of the 1976 presidential debates; almost all of Porter's (1976) book, which describes the many efforts of the Nixon administration to intimidate, harass, and regulate the news media; and the effort by Brown and Hain (1978) to delineate the role of the News Election Service in assembling and reporting the vote on election night. Certainly descriptive research is vitally important in any discipline, but its research design requirements are not nearly the same as those of research whose object is to elucidate causal explanations generated from some theoretical perspective.

Given the present concern with theoretically based causal analysis, one of the distinct advantages of laboratory experiments is that they generally provide the researcher with the greatest capability for physically holding things constant. This ability often allows the researcher to approximate more closely the theoretical parameters within which the causal relationships of concern are expected to manifest themselves. Furthermore, this ability to experimentally approximate theoretical *ceteris paribus* conditions generally facilitates any research effort whose goal is to unravel multivariate causal relationships. In other words, reducing the amount of "noise" in data by holding various conditions constant often makes it easier for the researcher to render valid causal inferences in those circumstances which represent a complex of contingent theoretical conditions.

Measurement Concerns

A couple of measurement concerns at times may affect our choice of a research design strategy. First, laboratory experiments often have an advantage over studies that are done in natural settings because they frequently allow for more specific and unambiguous operationalized indicators of our theoretical concepts. For example, in field studies concerning the effects of the televised presidential debates, "exposure" might typically be measured by the use of diary records, metered readings, or simply verbal self-reports to interview questions like "Did you watch the televised presidential debate held last evening?" Certainly these indicators are nowhere near isomorphic with our theoretical concept of exposure. Persons may have their TV sets turned on and to the right channel, yet be asleep on the sofa. Other persons may indeed be sitting in front of the television set, yet paying no attention to it but instead working their favorite crossword puzzle. Others may make a serious attempt to watch and listen to the debate, but the distractions of such things as children wrestling on the floor, teakettles boiling over on the stove, neighbors calling on the phone, salesmen knocking on the door, and family members beginning conversations unrelated to the debate drastically impinge on their viewing efforts. In other words, measures used in field settings may be more ambiguous and nonspecific than we would like—with respect to the debates, we may not know whether a person watched and listened, or mostly just listened, or missed the 13 minutes in the middle, or slept through the whole thing even though the television set was turned on and to the right channel. However, the use of a controlled laboratory environment and observational measurement techniques would eliminate most of these sources of ambiguity.

Beyond the question of ambiguity of our measures, it is sometimes the case that field research necessarily introduces systematic sources of error (or bias) into our measures. For example, all of the factors previously discussed which might affect the measure of debate "exposure" as typically operationalized in field studies tend to contribute to overestimates of exposure. Accordingly, in this particular instance, studying the effects of the debates by means of a laboratory experiment would not only provide for the elimination of much of the ambiguity of our exposure measure, but would also eliminate much of the systematic measurement error in that variable.

A word should also be said here regarding the use of the laboratory as a means for potentially reducing the random error component of our measures. Unlike systematic errors, random errors tend to result from idiosyncratic, unpredictable, accidental, or transient personal factors of either the measurer, the person being measured, or the interaction of the two. Accordingly, random errors do not vary in any systematic way across all subjects but are self-compensating and thus introduce to net bias in our measures. This random noise, however, necessarily decreases the confidence we have in any statements we make about relationships among our research variables (Namboodiri, Carter, & Blalock, 1975, chap. 12). In studies done in natural settings, particularly surveys which use either telephone or face-to-face interviews, the sources of random error increase with each increase in the size of the field staff. For example, different interviewers may read questions differently; persons with different accents may articulate words differently; the more people involved, the more random transcription errors are made in both recording and coding responses; the more interviewers, the greater variation generally in the extent and quality of their question probes; and so forth (Moser & Kalton, 1972, pp. 378-409). In the execution of laboratory experiments, however, the researcher is at times able to eliminate some of the sources of random measurement error by, for example, a greater reliance on contextual standardization, a greater application of minimal variance presentation techniques through the use of mechanical devices such as tape recorders and closed-circuit television, and a greater use of technological and observational measurement procedures.

Finally, we should make explicit mention of the need in passive-observational and quasi-experimental studies for variables to be measured in order for their potential confounding effects to be accounted for in analysis. This, of course, necessitates that the researcher have a priori information that the variables may be potentially relevant and, therefore, that they need to be measured. At times, hoever, the researcher may not have very good information about all of the variables that may be theoretically relevant. In this circumstance, it will be remembered that randomized experiments have the unique advantage of setting all these type 4 variables to type 3 variables via the process of random assignment; accordingly, they need not even be known to the researcher, let alone measured.

Other Pragmatic Concerns

Beyond all the considerations discussed thus far there are three other concerns which may affect one's selection of a research design strategy and which will be mentioned here: feasibility, convenience, and cost-effectiveness. First, it is obvious that not all design strategies are equally feasible in any given circumstance. For example, disregarding simulation possibilities, it is unlikely that any political communication researcher could do an experimental study that involved active manipulation of the content of an address delivered by the President of the United States; nor would it be feasible to manipulate experimentally the race or gender of the Chief Justice of the Supreme Court in order to investigate the effects of these ascriptive characteristics on the persuasive impact of, for example, a school busing or abortion decision. Likewise, it would probably be very unlikely that any Western scholar would be able to do a survey of the members of the Soviet Central Committee; nor is it feasible to do a nonparticipant-observational study of the communication networks in meetings of the President's cabinet. However, in general it is probably the case that passive-observational studies are the most feasible in most circumstances, laboratory experiments (be they randomized or quasi-experiments) are the next most feasible, quasi-experiments done in natural settings come next, and completely randomized field experiments are probably the least feasible—given the social, economic, and political constraints of the real world.

With respect to convenience, it should be pointed out that experiments often have an advantage over passive-observational studies in that experiments can be executed almost totally at the convenience of the researcher. In passive-observational studies, however, the stimulus events are naturally occurring rather than researcher induced. Accordingly, with passive-observational studies the researcher is sometimes in a bind from both ends. First, one must wait around for a natural event to occur before one can study it. For example, it would be pretty hard to do an information diffusion study relating to people's knowledge of the Mount St. Helens eruption using a passive-observational strategy unless the mountain had already erupted. And once an event has occurred in the natural world which is deemed worthy of study, the use of a passive-observational strategy often puts pressure on the researcher to get into the field as quickly as possible in order to minimize the problems associated with the frailties of the human memory.

Of course, a basic consideration in all research is cost. Cost alone, however, does little to aid us in the selection of a research design strategy, given that we can do almost any type of study either very expensively or relatively cheaply. Accordingly, the more important consideration should be cost-effectiveness. However, the use of any such criterion necessitates a measure of the effectiveness of a research design. Admittedly, there is no measure which has received the unqualified endorsement of the majority of researchers. However, it is here suggested that when doing research the primary object of which is to render explanations of cause and effect, it is certainly reasonable to define the effectiveness of a design in terms of the degree of confidence one can have in the causal statements which are made on the basis of that design. Accordingly, given that the greater the internal validity of the design, the greater our confidence in our causal statements, the greater the internal validity, the greater the effectiveness of the design. Proceeding from this perspective, a couple of suggestions can be offered. In general, it would seem that field experiments should cost only slightly more than sample surveys having the same N-size, given that there will be some additional cost for the field delivery of the treatments. However, the much greater internal validity of randomized field experiments would tend to make them more cost-effective than surveys. On the other hand, because of the often higher costs of doing field research, it would seem that randomized field experiments would often not be quite as cost-effective as laboratory experiments.

In conclusion, in our discussion of various considerations that might enter into the selection of a research design strategy we have delineated many of the relative strengths and weaknesses of the alternative strategies. In general, we have found the strength of passive-observational studies to lie in their greater external validity and feasibility. However, it is clear that the use of field experiments and the random selection of subject pools would do much toward equating the alternative design strategies in terms of their external validity. On the other hand, experimental studies tend to be superior in terms of their greater internal validity, utility in theory development and testing, measurement advantages of various types, convenience, and cost-effectiveness. Given their numerous advantages—especially their greater internal validity—it would seem that, where feasible, the use of experimental designs constitutes the optimum research design strategy for the causal analysis of the effects of political communications. It is suggested, therefore, that experimental designs deserve much greater consideration and use by the community of political communication scholars.

AN ILLUSTRATIVE LOOK AT THE USE OF EXPERIMENTATION IN POLITICAL COMMUNICATION RESEARCH

Experimental research in the area of political communication has been around for over 50 years, dating back to the seminal study by Harold Gosnell (1927) of the effectiveness of nonpartisan-sponsored mailed postcards in stimulating voter turnout during a series of voter registration drives conducted in Chicago in the 1920s. However, for the most part such experimental work has been concentrated in the years since World War II. In general, this research consists of two types of studies—those which are explicitly concerned with the communication process in the political arena, and those many more studies whose concern is with the communication process but with little or no particular cognizance of its political ramifications. While the primary focus here will be on the former, an occasional reference will be made to the latter, including mention of a few passive-observational studies which are related to experimental works.

Source

The question of what differential effects, if any, various source characteristics have on the acceptability of persuasive communications has been of concern to a variety of communication researchers. For example, Lorge (1936) found that people interpreted the same statements differently when they were ascribed to such different sources as Abraham Lincoln and then-current labor leaders. A locus of interest on the role of the communicator spawned what, without a doubt, is one of the best-known research programs in the history of communication studies: the Yale Communication Research Program. In a series of experiments, Hovland and his associates clearly demonstrated that when the sources were considered highly "credible," persuasive communication and short-term opinion change were facilitated (Hovland & Weiss, 1951; Hovland, Janis, & Kelley, 1953; Kelman & Hovland, 1953). Bettleheim and Janowitz (1950) found that anti-Semitic propaganda was more likely to be effective when ascribed to a known Jew in contrast to various other sources. And Dantico (1977) found in a study of simulated juror decisions that the credibility of the information source (plaintiff, defendant, or witness) affected both the verdict rendered by the juror as well as the severity of the sentence recommended by the juror.

Over the years this initial concern with source "credibility" has been conceptually broadened to include "attraction" (Mills & Aronson, 1965; Kiesler & Goldberg, 1968; Berscheid & Walster, 1969; McCroskey & McCain, 1974), "homophily" (Brock, 1965; Berscheid, 1966; McCroskey, Richmond, & Daly, 1975; Andersen & Todd de Mancillas, 1978), and the multidimensional generic concept of source "valence" (Andersen & Kibler, 1978). While there have been occasional attempts to investigate the role of more objective source characteristics, such as sex, race, and marital status (Adams, 1975), it would be fair to say that the dominant strain of source-related experimental research has concerned the role of source credibility and its conceptual extensions. In general, the common finding of this strain of research is that the more credible, liked, or homophilous source is advantaged in producing persuasive communication effects.

Message

The relative effectiveness of differential message characteristics has been the subject of extensive experimental communications research. This research has concerned questions such as whether persuasive communications are more effective when they present only one side of an argument or when they also cite opposing arguments (Hovland, Lumsdaine, & Sheffield, 1949; Lumsdaine & Janis, 1953; Thistlewaite & Kamenetzky, 1955), whether attempted persuasion is likely to be more effective if the communication draws explicit conclusions rather than allowing audience members to draw the conclusions themselves (Mandell & Hovland, 1952), whether persuasive communications which employ threat appeals are likely to become more or less effective as the threats become more extreme (Janis & Feshbach, 1953; Janis & Milholland, 1954), what is the effect of repetition or cumulative exposure to persuasive messages (Peterson & Thurstone, 1933; Hovland et al., 1949), and what difference, if any, the "order" of persuasive presentations makes (Lund, 1925; Hovland et al., 1957).

In a more explicitly political vein, some of the experimental literature concerning message content has dealt with differential effects from the use of "emotional" versus "rational" political leaflets (Hartmann, 1936), the use of demagogic appeals versus partisan information by political candidates (Jaros & Mason, 1969), the role of multiple contacts in political campaigns (Baer, Bositis, & Miller, in press; Miller, Bositis, & Baer, in press), the role of the length of a candidate's name (Nanda, 1975), the role of ballot position (Bain & Hecock, 1957; Kamin, 1958; Coombs, Peters, & Strom, 1974), the effects of political commentary or "instant analysis" on major political phenomena (Robinson, 1975, 1976; Davis, Kaid, & Singleton, 1977), and the influence of type and content of political commercials on candidate image and voter intentions (Kaid & Sanders, 1978). In general, it is the case that there have been a great many experimental investigations into numerous aspects of the role of message content; and while the studies in some areas have produced notably inconsistent findings (such as the literature dealing with the "recency" versus "primacy" question), it is clear that the many facets of the message content itself must necessarily be of concern to the political communication scholar.

Channel

For some time scholars have shown a concern for the relative effectiveness of different channels of communications. For example, the early work of Wilkie (1934) suggested that face-to-face contact was the most effective for persuasive communication, and that radio was next most effective, with print being the least effective of the three. The greater effectiveness of face-to-face contact over print (direct mail) was further supported in studies of attempted voter activation in a local charter revision referendum (Eldersveld & Dodge, 1954) and in an investigation of persons with a history of never voting in local elections (Eldersveld, 1956).

This line of research concerning channel differences has continued to the present with some studies further supporting the superiority of face-to-face contacts (Croft, Stimpson, Ross, Bray, & Breglio, 1968; Baer et al., in press), other studies suggesting that written materials are preferable to oral presentation (Wall & Boyd, 1971; Garey & Sacco, 1977), other studies finding little or no difference in the effectiveness of various channels (Tannenbaum & Kerrick, 1954; Sawyer, 1955; Frandsen, 1963; Sanders & Atwood, 1979), and still other studies suggesting that channel effectiveness varies with audience characteristics, such as age (Miller et al., in press). In general, the dominant theme of this research would seem to be that in many circumstances there are no differences in channel effectiveness, but when differences are found they tend to favor the superiority of the interpersonal (face-to-face) channel.

Audience

By far the vast majority of experimental communications research concerning audience characteristics has revolved around the role of selection biases in the communication process; namely, selective exposure, selective perception, and selective retention. Selective exposure refers to the tendency of people to expose themselves to messages which are congruent with their existing opinions and to avoid information or persuasive appeals which are dissonant with their existing beliefs and attitudes. On the other hand, selective perception refers to the tendency of individuals to incorrectly perceive or interpret messages in terms of what they want to perceive, habitually perceive, or expect some form of social or physical reward for perceiving. Selective retention involves the selective retaining or forgetting of message content. Over the years the literature on the role of selection biases in the communication process has grown voluminous (see Klapper, 1960; Sears & Freedman, 1967), and no attempt will be made here to itemize studies in this area. It should be noted, however, that such studies owe an important intellectual debt to the classic investigations of Sherif (1936), Asch (1952), and Levine and Murphy (1943).

Beyond the work dealing with the role of selection biases, mention should also be made of the research dealing with "persuasibility." This literature strongly indicates that some people are in general more persuasible than others—regardless of the topic (Janis et al., 1959)—and that feelings of inadequacy or low self-esteem seem to be the principal personality correlate of this general persuasibility (Janis, 1954).

Before leaving this brief discussion of experimental communications research related to audience characteristics, mention should be made of a relatively new strain of literature in this area. With a small but growing interest in "biopolitics," a body of literature is developing which focuses on biological/physiological influences on political behavior, and those biological characteristics are of course audience characteristics (Somit, 1968, 1976; Somit, Peterson, & Richardson, 1978). Whereas to date the biological focus has not yet noticeably been brought into the investigation of the political communication process, with an exception in the work of Jaros (1972), it would seem very likely that in the future we will see a growing concern with the question of how biological characteristics affect that process.

Context

Explicit concern for contextual variables has received less concern in the political communications literature than it deserves. If one views the object of political communication research primarily to be that of developing empirically validated theoretical explanations, then certainly one of the areas justifying increased attention is that of specifying contingent conditions which constrain known facets of the communication process. In other words, there needs to be greater concern for explicating the boundaries or parameters of our theoretical knowledge—specifying contextual constraints.

One area in political communications in which there has been some concern for the role of a central contextual variable involves studies of the "bandwagon" effect. In particular, the question has been investigated as to whether or not voters respond differently to simulated political campaigns in the presence of varied polling information concerning the relative support of the candidates. In this area there are mixed findings; studies by Laponce (1966) and Fleitas (1971) suggest that the presence of polling information favors net voting shifts in support of the underdog, while Coombs et al. (1974) suggest that the net shifts generally favor the front-runner.

An additional contextual area that has received some consideration is the impact of the level of election on the outcomes of campaign communications. For example, it has been shown (Adams, 1975) that minority political candidates (female, Chinese, black) are more successful in winning elections at the local level than at the national level. In addition, there is evidence (Miller, Note 1) that "drops" of campaign brochures are effective means of increasing voters' cognitive information levels concerning local political candidates, regardless of the office being sought (state's attorney, circuit judge, or county coroner).

In conclusion, the object of this section has been to illustrate the variety of substantive political communication concerns which have been addressed by scholars using experimental methods. Those various concerns generally come under what has been called "effects" research; that is, the effects of various source, message, channel, audience, and contextual variables on the outcomes of the political communication process. Given that the experimental tradition in political communication research is over a half-century old and has provided many theoretical insights into the nature of the communication process, it is abundantly clear that this research tradition will continue into the foreseeable future. Accordingly, attention is now turned to some closing thoughts and suggestions regarding that future.

SUGGESTIONS FOR FUTURE EXPERIMENTAL STUDY

Having detailed the logic of experimental research, discussed the strengths and weaknesses of experimental research, and illustrated the use of experimentation in political communication research, it would now seem appropriate to offer some suggestions regarding the future. These suggestions will take two forms—prescriptive and predictive. Let's consider first some prescriptive thoughts regarding a few things which ought to receive greater attention in future experimental studies of political communication.

In order to increase the external validity of our studies, with only minimal costs in terms of internal validity, there should be greater emphasis on the creative use of field experiments. Furthermore, as an additional means of increasing the external generalizability of our findings at little or no noticeable cost, we should make greater use of post hoc blocking variables in our analyses. Post hoc blocking variables are those measured variables which may be used to assign subjects to fairly homogeneous analytical groups (blocks) after the experiment is completed—such as age, sex, race, income, and religion. Each of these analytical groups can then be expected to contain subjects in each of the treatment conditions, thus transforming a simple single-factor experiment into a Treatment X Block design. This would enable us, for example, to indicate specifically whether or not our experimental findings held regardless of the sex, age, race, or religion of the subject. In other words, the increased use of such blocking variables would allow us to have greater confidence that our experimental findings were not artifacts of what are often obviously unrepresentative subject pools. The greater use of post hoc blocking variables would have additional benefits in that they would likely increase the precision of our experiments (Keppel, 1973, chap. 23) as well as force us to give greater attention to contextual variables. This would result in our giving increased attention to the necessary and desirable task of specifying the contextual boundaries for our findings. In general, we should make every effort to utilize factorial designs. The use of such designs would result in increased attention to and analysis and discussion of interaction effects—thus adding to the richness of our theoretical understanding of the communication process.

We should also make greater use of experiments as a tool for testing explicit theoretical predictions concerning communication outcomes. All too often our studies take the form of efforts that are guided by little more than educated common sense, a modicum of literature, and the question of "Did X make any difference?" In this same vein, we should make greater use of the various causal modeling techniques in our analysis of experimentally generated data, such as the Simon-Blalock techniques (Blalock, 1972) or the use of structural equation models (Duncan, 1975). All too often our analytic procedures consist of little more than analysis of variance. We should remember, however, that an F-test is a significance test, and as such it does nothing more than indicate to us that we have a difference large enough to need explaining—it does not help us explain the difference. On the other hand, the object of causal modeling techniques is to develop a theoretically sound and empirically justified model of the causal dynamics of the process under investigation—in this instance, the communication process. Merely knowing that an independent variable has some effect is only a part of the intellectual ball game. The more important part is to understand and be able to explain the causal dynamics of the process by which the effect is produced.

Now for some predictions about areas of likely future growth in experimental studies of political communication. First, as indicated earlier, it would seem certain that increased attention will be given to the role played by the biological characteristics of audiences in communication outcomes. When one couples with this the idea that information processing theory will play a greater role in our theoretical explanations, it becomes likely that the biological characteristics of principal concern will be neurological states. This, of course, implies the likelihood of a massive importation of measurement technology from the medical sciences.

With respect to message sources, it seems certain that more attention will be given to the softer concept of "image" in contrast to objective source characteristics. The relatively uncharted area concerning a political candidate's "video-style" would seem to be a natural for future growth. Similarly, it is likely that the softer aspects of message content will play a growing role in our studies. That is, we will probably see more concern given to the nonverbal component of political messages. Every new communications technology will stimulate a rash of studies investigating whether or not it produces any unique channel effects. Accordingly, we are certain to see in the near future some studies which compare interactive cable TV and, for example, newspapers with regard to their information dissemination effectiveness. Finally, given the growing number of persons who consider themselves to be independents, and given the seeming contraction in the role of political parties in our system, it would seem likely that increased attention will be given to nonpartisan elections by political communication scholars. Similarly, given their likely greater usage and perhaps importance, it seems probable that elections on referenda will receive increasing attention in political communication studies.

In many ways the likely concerns of political communication scholars for the next decade will be both tremendously interesting and extremely challenging. The sources of interest inhere in the new questions which will be addressed. The sources of challenge, on the other hand, are not new. Devising appropriate measurement technologies is an old problem. Then too, scholars have always been faced with the difficulty of choosing a research strategy which will reliably provide answers to their questions. In this chapter an attempt has been made to describe the logic, strengths, and weaknesses of one such strategy—experimentation. In addition, various uses of the experimental strategy in past political communication research have been illustrated. It is hoped that the discussion has shown that the use of experimentation in political communication studies has been profitable in the past and that it is the optimal strategy for dealing with questions of cause and effect in future political communication research.

REFERENCE NOTE

1. Miller, R. E. *Literature drops in county-level political campaigns: What do they accomplish?* Paper presented at the annual meeting of the Southwestern Political Science Association, Dallas, March 1981.

REFERENCES

Adams, W. C. Candidate characteristics, office of election, and voter responses. *Experimental Study of Politics*, 1975, *4*, 76-91.

Alexander, H. E., & Margolis, J. The making of the debates. In G. F. Bishop, R. G. Meadow, & M. Jackson-Beeck (Eds.), *The presidential debates: Media, electoral, and policy perspectives*. New York: Praeger, 1978.

Andersen, P. A., & Todd de Mancillas, W. R. Scales for the measurement of homophily with public figures. *Southern Speech Communication Journal*, 1978, *43*, 169-179.

Andersen, P. A., & Kibler, R. J. Candidate valence as a predictor of voter preference. *Human Communication Research*, 1978, *5*, 4-14.

Asch, S. E. *Social psychology*. Englewood Cliffs, NJ: Prentice-Hall, 1952.

Baer, D., Bositis, D. A., & Miller, R. E. A field experimental study of a precinct committee-man's canvassing efforts in a primary election: Cognitive effects. In M. Burgoon (Ed.), *Communication yearbook 5,* in press.

Bain, H. M., & Hecock, D. S. *Ballot position and voter's choice.* Detroit: Wayne State University Press, 1957.

Berelson, B. R., Lazarsfeld, P. F., & McPhee, W. N. *Voting: A study of opinion formation in a presidential campaign.* Chicago: University of Chicago Press, 1966.

Berscheid, E. Opinion change and communicator-communicatee similarity and dissimilarity. *Journal of Personality and Social Psychology,* 1966, *4,* 670-680.

Berscheid, E., & Wolster, E. H. *Interpersonal attraction.* Reading, MA: Addison-Wesley, 1969.

Bettleheim, B., & Janowitz, M. Reactions to fascist propaganda: A pilot study. *Public Opinion Quarterly,* 1950, *14,* 53-60.

Bishop, G. F., Meadow, R. G., & Jackson-Beeck, M. (Eds.). *The presidential debates: Media, electoral and policy perspectives.* New York: Praeger, 1978.

Blalock, H. M., Jr. *Causal inferences in nonexperimental research.* New York: Norton, 1972.

Brock, T. C. Communicator-recipient similarity and decision change. *Journal of Personality and Social Psychology,* 1965, *1,* 650-653.

Brown, J., & Hain, P. L. Reporting the vote on election night. *Journal of Communication,* 1978, *4,* 132-138.

Campbell, D. T., & Stanley, J. C. *Experimental and quasi-experimental designs for research.* Chicago: Rand McNally, 1966.

Cook, T. D., & Campbell, D. T. *Quasi-experimentation: Design and analysis issues for field settings.* Chicago: Rand McNally, 1979.

Coombs, F. S., Peters, J. G., & Strom, G. S. Bandwagon, ballot position, and party effects: An experiment in voting choice. *Experimental Study of Politics,* 1974, *3,* 31-57.

Croft, R. G., Stimpson, S. V., Ross, W. L., Bray, R. M., & Breglio, V. J. Comparison of attitude change elicited by live and videotaped classroom presentations. *AV Communications Review,* 1968, *17,* 315-321.

Dantico, M. Individual decision-making: An experimental investigation of the bases for choice. *Experimental Study of Politics,* 1977, *6,* 1-30.

Davis, D. F., Kaid, L. L., & Singleton, D. L. Information effects of political commentary. *Experimental Study of Politics,* 1977, *6,* 45-68.

Duncan, O. D. *Introduction to structural equation models.* New York: Academic Press, 1975.

Eldersveld, S. J. Experimental propaganda techniques and voting behavior. *American Political Science Review,* 1956, *50,* 154-165.

Eldersveld, S. J., & Dodge, R. W. Personal contact or mail propaganda? In D. Katz (Ed.), *Public opinion and propaganda.* New York: Holt, Rinehart & Winston, 1954.

Festinger, L., Riecken, H. W., & Schachter, S. *When prophecy fails.* Minneapolis: University of Minnesota Press, 1965.

Fisher, R. A. *Statistical methods for research workers.* London: Oliver & Boyd, 1925.

Fleitas, D. W. Bandwagaon and underdog effects in minimal-information elections. *American Political Science Review,* 1971, *65,* 434-438.

Frandsen, K. D. Effects of threat appeals and media transmission. *Speech Monographs,* 1963, *30,* 101-104.

Garey, R. B., & Sacco, J. F. Major energy institutions and conversation messages: Effects on attitude and information. *Experimental Study of Politics,* 1977, *6,* 25-44.

Glaser, W. A. Television and voting turnout. *Public Opinion Quarterly,* 1965, *65,* 71-86.

Gosnell, H. F. *Getting out the vote: An experiment in the stimulation of voting.* Chicago: University of Chicago Press, 1927.

Greenberg, B. S., & Parker, E. B. *The Kennedy assassination and the American public: Social communication in crisis.* Stanford: Stanford University Press, 1965.

Hartmann, G. W. A field experiment on the comparative effectiveness of "emotional" and "rational" political leaflets in determining election results. *Journal of Abnormal and*

Social Psychology, 1936, *31,* 99-114.

Hobbs, N. Ethical issues in the social sciences. *International Encyclopedia of the Social Sciences,* 1968, *5,* 160-166.

Hofstetter, C. R. *Bias in the news: Network television coverage of the 1972 campaign.* Columbus: Ohio State University Press, 1976.

Hovland, C. I., Janis, I., & Kelley, H. H. *Communication and persuasion.* New Haven, CT: Yale University Press, 1953.

Hovland, C. I., Lumsdaine, A. A., & Sheffield, F. D. Studies in social psychology in World War II. *Experiments on Mass Communication* (Vol. 3). Princeton: Princeton University Press, 1949.

Hovland, C. I. et al. *The order of presentation in persuasion.* New Haven, CT: Yale University Press, 1957.

Hovland, C. I., & Weiss, W. The influence of source credibility on communication effectiveness. *Public Opinion Quarterly,* 1951, *15,* 635-650.

Humphreys, L. *Tearoom trade: Impersonal sex in public places.* Chicago: AVC, 1970.

Janis, I. L. Personality correlates of susceptibility to persuasion. *Journal of Personality,* 1954, *22,* 504-518.

Janis, I. L., & Feshbach, S. Effects of fear-arousing communications. *Journal of Abnormal and Social Psychology,* 1953, *48,* 78-92.

Janis, I. L., & Milholland, H. C. The influence of threat appeals on selective learning of the content of a persuasive appeal. Journal of Psychology, 1954, *37,* 75-80.

Janis, I. L. et al. *Personality and persuasibility.* New Haven, CT: Yale University Press, 1959.

Jaros, D. Biochemical desocialization: Depressants and political behavior. *Midwest Journal of Political Science,* 1972, *16,* 1-28.

Jaros, D., & Mason, G. L. Party choice and support for demogogues: An experimental examination. *American Political Science Review,* 1969, *63,* 100-110.

Kaid, L. L. & Sanders, K. R. Political television commercials: An experimental study of type and length. *Communication Research,* 1978, *5,* 57-70.

Kamin, L. J. Ethnic and party affiliations of candidates as determinants of voting. *Canadian Journal of Psychology,* 1958, *12,* 205-212.

Kelman, H. C., & Hovland, C. I. Reinstatement of the communicator in delayed measurement of opinion change. *Journal of Abnormal and Social Psychology,* 1953, *48,* 327-335.

Keppel, G. *Design and analysis: A researcher's handbook.* Englewood Cliffs, NJ: Prentice-Hall, 1973.

Kerlinger, F. N. *Foundation of behavioral research* (2nd ed.). New York: Holt, Rinehart & Winston, 1973.

Kiesler, C. A., & Goldberg, G. N. Multidimensional approach to the experimental study of interpersonal attraction: Effect of a blunder on the attractiveness of a competent other. *Psychological Reports,* 1968, *22,* 693-705.

Kish, L. Some statistical problems in research design. *American Sociological Review,* 1959, *24,* 328-338.

Kish, L. *Survey sampling.* New York: John Wiley, 1965.

Klapper, J. T. *The effects of mass communication.* New York: Free Press, 1960.

Kraus, S. (Ed.). *The great debates: Background-perspective-effects.* Gloucester, MA: Peter Smith, 1968.

Kraus, S. (Ed.). *The great debates: Carter vs. Ford 1976.* Bloomington: Indiana University Press, 1979.

Lang, G. E., & Lang, K. The formation of public opinion: Direct and mediated effects of the first debate. In G. F. Bishop, R. G. Meadow & M. Jackson-Beeck (Eds.), *The presidential debates: Media, electoral and policy perspectives.* New York: Praeger, 1978.

Laponce, J. An experimental method to measure the tendency to equibalance in a political system. *American Political Science Review,* 1966, *62,* 982-993.

Lasswell, H. D. The structure and function of communication in society. In L. Bryson (Ed.), *The communication of ideas.* In W. Schramm & D. F. Roberts (Ed.), *The Process and Effects of Mass-Communication* (rev. ed.). Urbana: University of Illinois Press, 1971. (Originally published, 1948)

Lazarsfeld, P. F., Berelson, B., & Gaudet, H. *The people's choice.* New York: Duell, Sloan and Pearce, 1944.

Levine, J. M., & Murphy, G. The learning and forgetting of controversial material. *Journal of Abnormal and Social Psychology,* 1943, *38,* 507-517.

Lorge, I. Prestige, suggestion, attitudes. *Journal of Social Psychology,* 1936, *7,* 386-402.

Lumsdaine, A. A., & Janis, I. L. Resistance to counter propaganda produced by one-sided and two-sided "propaganda" presentations. *Public Opinion Quarterly,* 1953, *17,* 311-318.

Lund, F. H. The psychology of belief: IV. The law of primacy in persuasion. *Journal of Abnormal and Social Psychology,* 1925, *20,* 183-191.

McCall, W. A. *How to experiment in education.* New York: Macmillan, 1923.

McCroskey, J. C., & McCain, T. A. The measurement of interpersonal attraction. *Speech Monographs,* 1974, *41,* 261-266.

McCroskey, J. C., Richmond, V. P., & Daly, J. A. The development of a measure of perceived homophily in interpersonal communication. *Human Communication Research,* 1975, *1,* 323-332.

Mandell, W., & Hovland, C. I. Is there a law of primacy in persuasion? *American Psychologist,* 1952, *7,* 538.

Miller, R. E., Bositis, D. A., & Baer, D. L. A field experimental study of a precinct committeeman's efforts at stimulating voter turnout in a primary election: Telephone vs. mail vs. face-to-face appeals. *International Political Science Review,* in press.

Mills, J., & Aronson, E. Opinion change as a function of the communicator's attractiveness and desire to influence. *Journal of Personality and Social Psychology,* 1965, *1,* 173-177.

Moser, C. A., & Kalton, G. *Survey methods in social investigation* (2nd ed.). New York: Basic Books, 1972.

Namboodiri, N. K., Carter, L. F., & Blalock, H. M., Jr. *Applied multivariate analysis and experimental design.* New York: McGraw-Hill, 1975.

Nanda, K. An experiment in voting choice: Who gets the "blind" vote? *Experimental Study of Politics,* 1975, *4,* 20-35.

Napolitan, J. *The election game and how to win it.* Garden City, NY: Doubleday, 1972.

Nimmo, D. *Political communication and public opinion in America.* Santa Monica, CA: Goodyear, 1978.

Patterson, T. E., & McClure, R. D. *The unseeing eye: The myth of television power in national elections.* New York: Putnam, 1976.

Peterson, R. C., & Thurstone, L. L. *Motion pictures and the social attitudes of children.* New York: Macmillan, 1933.

Porter, W. E. *Assault on the media: The Nixon years.* Ann Arbor: University of Michigan Press, 1976.

Robinson, M. J. Understanding television's effects—Experimentalism and survey research: An offer one shouldn't refuse. *Experimental Study of Politics,* 1975, *4,* 99-133.

Robinson, M. J. Public affairs television and the growth of political malaise: The case of "The Selling of the Pentagon." *American Political Science Review,* 1976, *70,* 409-432.

Robinson, M. J. The impact of "instant analysis." *Journal of Communication,* 1977, *27,* 17-23.

Rosenthal, R., & Rosnow, R. L. *The volunteer subject.* New York: John Wiley, 1975.

Sanders, K. R., & Atwood, L. E. Value change initiated by the mass media. In M. Rokeach (Ed.), *Understanding human values.* New York: Free Press, 1979.

Sawyer, T. M. Shift of attitude following persuasion as related to estimate of majority attitude. *Speech Monographs,* 1955, *22,* 68-78.

Sears, D. O., & Freedman, J. L. Selective exposure to information: A critical review. *Public Opinion Quarterly,* 1967, *31,* 194-213.

Selltiz, C., Jahoda, M., Deutsch, M., & Cook, S. W. *Research methods in social relations* (revised one-volume edition). New York: Holt, Rinehart & Winston, 1959.

Selltiz, C., Wrightsman, L. S., & Cook, S. W. *Research methods in social relations* (3rd ed.). New York: Holt, Rinehart & Winston, 1976.

Seltz, H. A., & Yoakam, R. D. Production diary of the debates. In S. Kraus (Ed.), *The great debates: Background-perspective-effects.* Gloucester, MA: Peter Smith, 1968.

Seymour-Ure, C. *The political impact of mass media.* Beverly Hills, CA: Sage, 1974.

Shaw, D. L., & McCombs, M. E. *The emergence of American political issues.* St. Paul, MN: West Publishing, 1977.

Sherif, M. *The psychology of social norms.* New York: Harper & Row, 1936.

Somit, A. Towards a more biologically oriented political science: Ethology and psychopharmacology. *Midwest Journal of Political Science,* 1968, *12,* 550-567.

Somit, A. (Ed.). *Biology and politics.* The Hauge: Mouton, 1976.

Somit, A., Peterson, S. A., and Richardson, W. D. *The literature of biopolitics.* Dekalb: Northern Illinois University, Center for Biopolitical Research, 1978.

Stanley, J. C., & Beeman, E. Y. Restricted generalization, bias, and loss of power that may result from matching groups. *Psychological Newsletter,* 1958, *9,* 88-102.

Stricker, L. J. The true deceiver. *Psychological Bulletin,* 1967, *68,* 13-20.

Tannenbaum, D. A., & Kerrick, J. Effects of newscast items upon listener interpretation. *Journalism Quarterly,* 1954, *31,* 33-37.

Thistlewaite, D. L., & Kamenetzky, J. Attitude change through refutation and elaboration of audience counterarguments. *Journal of Abnormal and Social Psychology,* 1955, *51,* 3-12.

Thorndike, R. L. Regression fallacies in the matched groups experiment. *Psychometrika,* 1942, *7,* 85-102.

Townsend, J. C. *Introduction to experimental method.* New York: McGraw-Hill, 1953.

Wall, V. D., & Boyd, J. A. Channel variation and attitude change. *Journal of Communication,* 1971, *21,* 363-367.

White, T. H. *The making of the President 1960.* New York: Atheneum, 1961.

White, T. H. *The making of the President 1964.* New York: Atheneum, 1965.

Wilke, W. H. An experimental comparison of the speech, the radio, and the printed page, as propaganda devices. *Archives of Psychology,* 1934, *169.*

CHAPTER 21

Survey Research

George F. Bishop

THERE SHOULD BE no need here to document the discipline's excessive dependence on survey research as a methodological strategy for generating and testing theory, or to discuss its neglect of feasible alternatives (see Rothschild, 1975; Sinaiko & Broedling, 1976). One has only to be reminded of the extraordinary frequency with which that exemplar of political communication research—studies of the presidential debates—continues to be approached by questionnaires and interviews in assorted survey designs to realize how deep the addiction has become (see Bishop, Meadow, & Jackson-Beeck, 1978; Katz & Feldman, 1962; Sears & Chaffee, 1979). Much of this practice stems, no doubt, from the success of the Inter-University Consortium for Political and Social Research and the Survey Research Center at the University of Michigan in diffusing survey skills and techniques to several generations of scholars through their annual summer training programs. This, along with the increasing acceptance of telephone interviewing methods as a cost-effective, quality alternative to personal interviewing, and the widespread availability of computer software packages for processing and analyzing large-scale data sets, has made it much easier—indeed, too easy, some might say—to do survey research. So that we now have a coterie of researchers in political communication and public opinion scattered across numerous colleges and universities with the requisite skills, if not always adequate resources, to mount at least local surveys which approximate, in varying degrees, the sophistication of that parental model in political research: the biennial American National Election Studies. Nor, in this writer's judgment, is it an accident that communication researchers, in trying to correct the "limited effects" hypothesis handed down to them through the Columbia and Michigan voting studies, have themselves been coopted into adopting the

591

dominant survey-based paradigm as the principal means for testing it. One, it seems, must often do as the established do to gain acceptability. And doing political communication research almost exclusively via surveys for roughly two decades now gives ample testimony to our uncritical imitation of, and need for approval from, such imprimaturs.

There should be no need here, either, to review the voluminous technical literature that has accumulated over the years on the sundry aspects of survey methodology. That task is presently being performed comprehensively in a forthcoming *Handbook of Survey Research,* edited by Peter H. Rossi and James D. Wright. The writer assumes, moreover, that the reader has read, or is at least aware of, previous treatments related to this chapter's topic by Hyman (1973) in the *Handbook of Political Psychology* and by Boyd with Hyman (1975) in the *Handbook of Political Science.* I also presume a passing acquaintance with such basic reference books as Kish's (1965) *Survey Sampling,* Kahn and Cannell's (1967) *The Dynamics of Interviewing,* Rosenberg's (1968) *The Logic of Survey Analysis,* and Hyman's (1972) *Secondary Analysis of Sample Surveys.* Since the publication of these classic volumes, a number of other useful sourcebooks on survey research have also come out which should be part of one's professional library, among them: Dillman's (1978) *Mail and Telephone Surveys,* Sudman's (1976) *Applied Sampling,* and Sonquist and Dunkelberg's (1977) *Survey and Opinion Research: Procedures for Processing and Analysis.* In addition, countless textbooks and monographs on multivariate analysis, such as those in the Sage series on *Quantitative Applications in the Social Sciences,* have appeared in the last decade or so, many of which are directly relevant to the special problems associated with survey data. Among the more accessible and valuable sources here are Fienberg's (1980) *The Analysis of Cross-Classified Categorical Data,* Reynold's (1977) *The Analysis of Cross-Classifications,* and Sheth's (1977) *Multivariate Methods for Market and Survey Research.*

For those with even more specialized interests in survey methodology, there are several advanced monographs and edited collections worth knowing about: Alwin's (1977) *Survey Design and Analysis*; Bailar and Lanphier's (1978) *Development of Survey Methods to Assess Survey Practices*; Bradburn, Sudman, and associates' (1979) *Improving Interview Method and Questionnaire Design*; Cannell et al.'s (1980) *Experiments in Interviewing Techniques*; Groves and Kahn's (1979) *Surveys by Telephone: A National Comparison with Personal Interviews*; Namboodiri's (1978) *Survey Sampling and Measurement*; Sudman and Bradburn's (1974) *Response Effects in Surveys*; and a forthcoming volume by Schuman and his associates at Michigan in which they report on their experiments in survey question wording. For even more up-to-date developments the reader should see the quarterly newsletter, *Survey Research,* which is available, gratis, from the Survey Research Laboratory at the University of Illinois in Urbana (61801). Each issue contains a list of new methodological publications in the field, as well as brief summaries of current research at just about all of the academic survey centers in the United States, plus a growing number of entries for various nonacademic and foreign-based research organizations. Specialized bibliographies and searches on nearly every nonsampling aspect of survey design and practice—for example, randomized response techniques, interviewer recruitment and training, and nonresponse bias—can also be obtained, free of charge, through the Survey Methodology Information System (SMIS) maintained by the Statistical Research Division of the U.S. Bureau of the Census. Finally, of course, there are the traditional journals and annuals as sources for the latest wrinkles in survey methodology: *Public Opinion Quarterly, Journal of Marketing Research, Political Methodology, Sociological Methodology, Sociological Methods and Research,* and the *Journal of the American Statistical Association*—not to mention several new ones that have cropped up in the last several years. Should all these sources fail the earnest scholar, one can always call or write for the name of a specialist from any of the major professional associations, in particular the American Association for Public Opinion Research (Princeton, New Jersey), the American Marketing Association (Chicago, Illinois), and the survey research division of the American Statistical Association (Washington, D.C.).[1]

PROBLEMS AND POTENTIALS

With these preliminaries out of the way, we can now address the special problems and potentials of surveys in political communication and public opinion research. Almost all of the methodological issues that will be discussed in the following pages do, of course, cut across disciplinary boundaries in the social and behavioral sciences. But as I shall try to show, there is a unique perspective that political communication researchers can bring to bear on some fundamental difficulties with the survey-based paradigm. Indeed, as I shall argue later, the problems that afflict survey research in political communication and related fields often appear, superficially, to be "methodological"; that the real difficulty facing us is essentially a theoretical one: *a lack of any explanatory model of the cognitive processes which underlie the verbal self-reports of our survey respondents.*

Let me begin, however, by phrasing the problem in more conventional terms, so that the later theoretical translations in the chapter will not come so abruptly: The primary obstacle to improving survey research in political communication is not one of reducing the magnitude of random error in our studies, but rather that of eliminating those systematic sources of extraneous variation arising from the interaction between interviewer and respondent, and the immediate context of the interview. There is certainly no lack of theory and techniques for dealing with the *random* error components in our surveys. Generations of mathematical statisticians and social scientists have worked out numerous adjustments to sample designs, measurement procedures, quantitative analyses, and the like to save most of us from sinking into the abyss of chance results. And there is no shortage of "methodologists" around to bail us out if we should forget some of the basics. But there is precious little guidance on how to control or minimize the unknown systematic biases introduced by such sources as refusals; variations in survey question wording, format, and context; "don't knows" and other nonresponses; response styles; interviewer variability; and so forth. In my judgment, the magnitude of error contributed to our surveys by these kinds of extraneous factors greatly exceeds that stemming from random sampling and measurement error and, in some cases, may well surpass that created by our principal experimental or independent variables.

Before opening with an astonishing illustration of the enormity of the systematic error problem in public opinion surveys, let me briefly outline the topics to be covered in the balance of the chapter. First, I take up the basic issue of whether some respondents should even be asked certain questions on politics without a "filter" for interest or information, citing recent demonstrations of the pitfalls awaiting the unwary researcher. Next I consider the thorny decisions that must be made about the wording, format, and sequencing of survey items, traditional assumptions about which are now the subject of increasing research. Following that I plunge into the murkier pool of issues which arise from variations among survey respondents in the *meaning* of identically worded items at a given point in time, and from changes in *meaning* of those items within the same general population over time. It is here that we begin to see the truly theoretical character of our present obstacles in survey research, in particular the role of the mass media in altering the connotations of the key symbols in our survey items. And it is there that I propose a program of research for political communication which would link the concerns of agenda-setting studies with the problem of monitoring and explaining changes in the *meaning* of public opinion indicators.

Having exposed the weak theoretical underpinnings of our survey measurement practices, I then review some current work in cognitive social psychology which has profound implications for how we design our survey instruments. Examples from some of my recent experiments on question form effects are used to illustrate the application of an information-processing approach to survey measurement. There the chapter concludes with still another proposal for a program of research, one which would investigate survey response effects from the perspective of contemporary cognitive-response approaches to communication and persuasion.

SELECTED EXAMPLES OF SYSTEMATIC ERROR

No attempt will be made here to cover the rapidly accumulating literature on what Sudman and Bradburn (1974) have labeled generically, "response effects" in surveys. The reader is referred to their encyclopedic review of the pre-1974 work on this topic and to Bradburn's chapter on the same subject in the forthcoming *Handbook of Survey Research.* What I will do here is examine some selected illustrations of the magnitude and scope of the problem, beginning with a rather fundamental one: the extent to which survey respondents are providing us with "informed" opinions as opposed to what have been called elsewhere "pseudo-opinions" (Bishop, Oldenick, Tuchfarber, & Bennett, 1980).

Opinion-Giving in Survey Interviews

There are few among us who have not wondered about how often respondents give what we would call "top-of-the-head" reactions to our survey questions. It is well known that the level of political knowledge in the general population tends to be rather low (see, for example, Converse, 1975; Hyman, Wright, & Reed, 1975), so there is little reason to expect that respondents will have given much thought to the typical issues and topics constituting most surveys in political communication. Yet, until fairly recently, one could find virtually no systematic investigations of these widespread assumptions. That empirical gap has been filled at least partly, however, in a series of experiments by me and my colleagues at the Behavioral Sciences Laboratory of the University of Cincinnati (Bishop, Oldenick, & Tuchfarber, in press) and by Howard Schuman and his associates at the University of Michigan's Survey Research Center (Schuman & Presser, 1980).

In the Cincinnati experiments, all of which were carried out as part of a larger project on question form effects in surveys, we tested the notion that respondents frequently give opinions on topics they know little or nothing about by asking them for their opinions on a nonexistent issue: "The 1975 Public Affairs Act." Embedded in a series of other items concerning current public affairs issues (such as national health insurance, diplomatic relations with Cuba, and SALT), we found that roughly one-third of our adult (18 and over) respondents in the Cincinnati metropolitan area would volunteer that they either agreed or disagreed with the idea of repealing this fictitious statute—that is, in the absence of any explicit attempt to filer them out with a screening question such as "Do you have an opinion on this or not?" When such a screener was used, most respondents acknowledged that they didn't have an opinion, but about 5-10 percent would persist nevertheless and tell us that they did and go on to say that they either agreed or disagreed with the proposition. And lest the reader get the idea that this finding might not replicate or generalize to other settings, let me mention that we have replicated it in several independent surveys in the Cincinnati area. At the same time, Schuman and Presser (1980) reported data from two separate national studies, showing that about 25-30 percent of the U.S. public will volunteer an opinion on highly obscure legislative bills—"the Agricultural Trade Act of 1978" and "the Monetary Control Bill of 1979"—which, while technically not fictional, are very unlikely to be familiar to even the best-informed among us. There is thus convincing evidence that the magnitude of this response tendency is indeed substantial.

Even more significant is that all of these analyses indicate that such respondents are not merely giving random reactions when they express an opinion, as Converse (1964, 1970) postulated, but basing their answers instead on more enduring social-psychological dispositions toward the political world. My colleagues and I discovered, for instance, that giving opinions on the fictitious 1975 Public Affairs Act was significantly associated with lower levels of education, race (blacks were about twice as likely as whites to do so), and low trust in other people. Schuman and Presser (1980) also found similar associations between low levels of education and opinion-giving on the obscure pieces of legislation in their surveys and—interestingly—between a construct generically related to trust (confidence in government) and the direction of respondents' opinions on such issues.

Although the cognitive processes underlying this response tendency are somewhat elusive, it appears that respondents are not deliberately trying to decieve interviewers (see Bishop, Oldenick, Tuchfarber, & Bennett, 1980), but rather are attempting to protect their self-esteem against being thought stupid or uninformed because they have *no opinion.* Hence, they search for cues in the content of the item—for example, it's about "public affairs"—and from the context provided by immediately preceding items (in this instance, other questions about government and politics) to make attributions about its *meaning,* and then fall back on basic response dispositions such as trust/mistrust in answering it. In the case of our question about the fictitious Public Affairs Act, for example, it seems that respondents who felt the need to protect their esteem by giving an opinion assumed the question had something to do with "the government," however ambiguously, and therefore responded to it in terms of their basic tendency to trust or mistrust the government in general. For we found among respondents who answered the question that those with low trust in other people (as measured by the SRC modification of Rosenberg's Misanthropy Index) tended to *favor* repealing the Public Affairs Act, whereas those with higher levels of faith in others tended to *oppose* its repeal. In this respect our fictitious issue may have functioned somewhat like a Rorschach ink blot, into which respondents could project whatever meaning came to mind and then respond to it accordingly.

The evidence from our experiments also indicates that respondents who volunteer opinions on the fictitious Public Affairs Act tend to be more likely to give opinions on other issues that are "real" and more likely to have "liberal" opinions on those topics. While there is as yet no apparently feasible way to accurately estimate the magnitude of this systematic error, which may be present in many of our public opinion polls and surveys, I would venture that it is rather large, especially on the more complex domestic and foreign policy issues which make up much of the content in political communication studies. Given these concerns, what can be said about the practical implications for the average researcher? Quite simply, it is this: One must use filter or screening questions with *all* or nearly all political content. This has become the standard practice for many, if not most, of the public policy items which appear in the American National Election Studies at the Michigan Center for Political Studies. And there are increasing indications that the practice is diffusing to other academic survey centers and to commercial organizations such as the CBS/New York *Times* and NBC/AP polls.

But political communication researchers have not—at least not at the time of this writing—begun to make significant use of filter questions in their work (see the various studies of the 1976 presidential debates). One reason for this may be the understandable reluctance of those who must frequently work with limited funds for small-scale local surveys to ask extra (filter) questions which not only increase costs but also reduce the number of cases available for analysis (20-25 percent is the modal range of cases removed by filters on many SRC/CPS issue questions.). The more critical barrier to adopting filter questions, however, seems to be the substantive one—namely the lack of knowledge until fairly recently of how large the potential may be for systematic error in surveys without them. That is no longer excusable, and one should consider constructing filter questions to screen out the uninformed or uninterested on all but the most familiar political topics. Where feasible, it would also be desirable to supplement this practice with items that measure respondents' *objective* knowledge of specific topics (see Graber, 1978), since filters will tend to remove those with ambivalent feelings on an issue along with the apathetic or uninformed. In fact, there is little guidance on how one should actually word a filter question. There is evidence, moreover, that identically worded filters may not mean the same thing to all respondents (Bishop, Oldenick, & Tuchfarber, in press). The best advice under these circumstances is probably to follow in the tradition of "multiple indicators" and use different versions of filters, such as those that have appeared in the SRC/CPS election surveys over the years.

A Note on Effects of Filter Questions

Despite the evident advantages of removing respondents who have given little or no thought to a topic, one should be aware that the use of a filter may itself introduce systematic error of another kind. The research to date, in fact, indicates that while using a filter may have relatively modest (but statistically significant) effects on the *marginal* distribution of responses to survey items, it may create dramatic variations in the magnitude of association between items, especially those of the attitudinal variety (see Bishop, Tuchfarber, Oldenick, & Bennett, 1979; Schuman & Presser 1978b). Even more disconcerting, such effects can occur in completely opposite directions. That is, in some instances, filtering significantly increases the amount of association between items, but in other situations it produces equally significant decreases, and in still other circumstances, no effect at all. Schuman and Presser (1978b) speculated that certain types of respondents, whom they call "opinion floaters," may be responsible for some of these perplexing findings. Such individuals are said to lack opinions on the specifics of a given issue but respond, instead, in terms of a generalized disposition to evaluate others positively or negatively, or as trustworthy or untrustworthy (a disposition that bears striking similarities to the one previously identified in the discussion of factors determining responses to the fictitious 1975 Public Affairs Act). So when one does not employ a filter, these respondents will tend to inflate the degree of correlation between items insofar as those items contain cues that elicit this underlying disposition (for example, "Russian leaders" or "Arab nations"). Yet, as I indicated, the data from our experiments and those by Schuman and Presser also show that filtering will often increase, rather than decrease, the size of interitem correlations, presumably because it takes out those people with what Converse (1970) called "non-attitudes." Theoretically, then, this emerging literature is still very much in flux. Yet the only sensible advice that can be given is to read it, whether one uses filter questions or not. In either case there are likely to be unintended consequences for the conclusions one reaches about assorted political communication effects.

Decisions About Question Wording and Format

Those looking for explicit guidance on what question form or arrangement is "best" for studying this or that topic in political communication will find no comfort here either. As I shall try to demonstrate later, there are no best or correct ways of constructing questions outside the context of a particular theory of respondents' verbal self-reports in the survey interview. What seems to happen in practice is that most of us contruct items on the basis of largely semiconscious prejudices favoring one kind of format or another. The agree/disagree or Likert-type format is probably the most common, one that has been wittingly or unwittingly inculcated into generations of young researchers. The diffusion of the American National Election studies through the ICPSR, usually with the original interview schedules included, also seems to have stimulated a fair amount of imitation and sheer replication of various "standard" measures (for example, party identification and interest in politics). Replication is, of course, essential if one wants to make comparisons with the national norms provided by such studies as those at SRC/CPS. And if one is contemplating adding another point to the time-series that are available from these sources, replication of wording, context, sampling procedures, and so forth are obviously in order. But it appears that much of the research that is done not only in political communication but also in nearly all allied fields today blindly imitates the wording, formats, and structures that have been made available by the SRCs, the NORCs, the Gallups, and others. And while I am sure that many readers could offer good theoretical rationales (or rationalizations?) for why they have used this or that SRC/CPS question form, my hunch is that they do it more for reasons of convenience and, perhaps, for stamping one's work with some sign of sophistication and acceptability.

Whatever the reason for current practices, it is time we seriously reevaluate them, for empirical evidence is now beginning to accumulate on the sizable substantive consequences which may ensue as a result of using one question form rather than another (see Bennett, Tuchfarber, & Oldenick, Note 1; Kalton, Collins, & Brook, 1978; Presser & Schuman, 1980; Schuman & Presser, 1977, 1978a). I want to emphasize, however, that the literature on this topic thus far does not contain any firm generalizations. What exists are mostly low-level empirical demonstrations of various form effects, many of which are modest in magnitude. There is, moreover, little theoretical insight into why such effects occur or do not occur under different conditions. Nevertheless, I shall give an illustration of a question form effect from a current project at the Behavioral Sciences Laboratory which I think will convince even the most reluctant or indifferent among us that we face truly formidable difficulties in deciding how to word or select our survey questions.[2]

A key choice that must frequently be made in framing a question is whether to present one or two sides of an issue. In the former mode respondents are typically asked to approve or disapprove, favor or oppose, or agree or disagree with some single statement of opinion—for example, "the government ought to see to it that everybody who wants to work can find a job" (see Miller, Miller, & Schneider, 1980, p. 172). On the other hand, one can, in the interest of "fairness" or "balance," offer respondents a second *substantive* alternative, as in the well-known revision of this item which took place at the time of the SRC 1964 American National Election Study:

> "Do you think that the government should see to it that every person has a job and a good standard of living, or should it let each person get ahead on his own?"

In a series of split-ballot experiments conducted over the last couple of years in an omnibus vehicle known as the Greater Cincinnati Survey, we have pitted these two basic question formats against one another to determine their relative impact on item distributions and interrelationships (see Bishop et al., Note 1). Table 21.1 shows one of the more striking examples of form effects from those experiments. In this particular case we had randomly assigned respondents to receive one of three question forms: (a) an agree/disagree version of a question on the issue of school desegregation that had been asked originally in the SRC

TABLE 21.1: Percentage of Respondents Giving a "Liberal" Response to the School Desegregation Issue by Race by Question Format

QUESTION FORMAT	Black	White
A. "Do you agree or disagree with the idea that the government should stay out of the question of whether white and black children go to the same schools?"	41.8% (122)	24.8% (602)
	$X^2 = 13.91, p < .001 \ (Q = .37)$	
B. "Do you think the government should see to it that white and black children go to the same schools, or stay out of this area as it is none of its business?"	71.2% (156)	21.0% (814)
	$X^2 = 157.23, p < .0001 \ (Q = .81)$	
C. "Do you agree or disagree with the idea that the government should see to it that white and black children go to the same schools?"	61.1% (36)	31.5% (200)
	$X^2 = 10.36, p < .01 \ (Q = .55)$	

Response by Question Format $X^2 = 6.13, p < .05$

Response by Race by Question Format: $X^2 = 27.27, p < .001$

Note: Entries in parentheses are Yule's Q-coefficients.

1956-1960 election surveys, (b) a substantive choice form SRC instituted in the 1964 national election study, and (c) a second agree/disagree version, which we constructed with the first substantive alternative of Form B (see Table 21.1) specifically to create a "positive" counterpart of the "negative" proposition in Form A, thus allowing us to assess more adequately any possible acquiescence response style effects.

As the reader can see from Table 21.1, the interactive influence of question form on racial differences in attitudes toward this fundamental issue in American politics borders on the amazing. Using the original SRC form on this topic (A), in which respondents had to *disagree* with the proposition that "the government should stay out of the question of whether white and black children go to the same schools," in order to be classified as "liberal," we find a statistically significant but modest discrepancy (17%) between black and white respondents. But with the substantive choice form (B) the difference in the percentage supporting government-enforced school desegregation becomes almost three times as large (50.2 percent). Form C, in which one had to *agree* with the idea that "the government should see to it that white and black children go to the same schools" to be categorized as "liberal," also generated fairly sizable racial differences (29.6 percent), though not nearly as large as those produced by Form B. Not surprisingly, then, the chi-squared value at the bottom of Table 21.1 for the interaction of question form with response to this issue by race is statistically significant well beyond the .001 level.

Other analyses we have done (data not shown here) show equally striking variations by question form in the magnitude of association between responses to the school desegregation issue and conceptually related items (such as government-guaranteed employment and fair treatment for blacks in jobs and housing). Nor are these effects limited to interactions involving race and race-related issues. More generally, we have found that such form effects on topics of all kinds tend to be greatest among those respondents with lower levels of education or, more precisely, among those with the least amount of interest in, or information about, politics (Bishop, Oldenick, & Tuchfarber, in press; see also Schuman & Presser, 1977).

It is not my intent to multiply more such examples of question form effects. The one I have just given should be sufficient to sensitize the reader to the nature and scope of this increasingly significant problem in survey research. Many of us have always claimed to know that how we word our questions can make an important difference in the results, and so one should be rather careful about this matter. But we are now beginning to find out, empirically, just how important that old admonition about question wording really is. To paraphrase an old cliche, we ignore it now at our empirical peril.

Let me conclude this section by encouraging the reader to acquaint himself or herself with other recent reexaminations of some classic concerns in the construction of survey questions: whether one should use open-ended or closed items (Schuman & Presser, 1979); whether one should offer respondents a middle alternative in forced-choice questions (Kalton, Roberts, & Holt, 1980; Presser & Schuman, 1980); and whether one should ask a set of items in a particular order (Smith Note 2; Turner & Krauss, 1978). And if one should still need a convincing case history of the relevance of this methodological excursion to "substantive" problems in the literature, I can think of no better illustration than the theoretical controversy about the sources of change in the American electorate between this author's research team (Bishop, Oldenick, & Tuchfarber, 1978; Bishop, Oldenick, Tuchfarber, & Bennett, 1978, 1979; Bishop, Tuchfarber, Oldenick, & Bennett, 1979) and that of Sullivan's (Sullivan, Piereson, & Marcus, 1978, 1979b) on the one hand versus that of Nie and his colleagues on the other (Nie with Anderson, 1974; Nie, Verba, & Petrocik, 1976; Nie &

Rabjohn, 1979). Let me add, in reviving this controversy, that it is a particularly good example of how researchers can easily be drawn into all manner of post hoc theorizing about the causes of *apparent* political change—much of which, incidentally, was attributed to mass media coverage of the political events of the 1960s and early 1970s (see Nie et al., 1976)—when in fact it was most likely due to a simple methodological artifact: changes in question wording and format.

But I have encountered an even more fundamental problem in public opinion and political communication research, one that has received very little attention and yet holds considerable promise for advancing the theoretical foundations of the discipline: *differences in the meaning of identically worded questions,* not only among various types of respondents but also over time in the same general population. Let me here give the problem the attention it deserves and, in the process, recommend an agenda of research for the 1980s.

THE MEANING OF SURVEY QUESTIONS

Probably the most crucial assumption all of us make as we design our surveys is that the items will have the same meaning for the respondents as they do for us. In the language of the laboratory experiment, they should all be exposed to an identical "stimulus." This, after all, is why we concern ourselves so much with things like keeping the wording (and context) of questions constant and standardizing, as much as possible, the probing and feedback techniques of the interviewer. For if these things vary across respondents, we have that much more extraneous variation to contend with in making inferences about the causal structure of the data. Let us examine more closely this nearly unquestioned assumption in the practice of survey research.

Variations in Meaning Among Respondents

Although many researchers have long recognized the problems that can be created by variations in survey question wording and interviewer behavior, there appears to be much less sensitivity to the difficulties that can arise from fluctuations in the meaning of an identically worded item, either across time or among different types of individuals. One of the very few empirical investigations of this issue can be found in the methodological classic, *Gauging Public Opinion,* by Hadley Cantril and his associates (1944, chap. 1). There they demonstrated with the limited analytical tools of their time that respondents frequently misconstrued the intent or implications of questions drawn from national surveys during that era. While the items they selected were chosen to illustrate the consequences of such things as vague terminology and stereotyped statements, they were not that atypical at the time and, as we shall see, still representative of question wording practices today.

For reasons that are not clear, however, the problem of question meaning dropped from the research agenda following the publication of the Cantril volume, though it fortunately had diffused into textbooks like Stanley Payne's *The Art of Asking Questions* (1951). Not until 1966 did the problem receive any serious empirical attention in an article by Howard Schuman entitled, "The Random Probe: A Technique for Evaluating the Validity of Closed Questions." This technique, which involves probing a given item among a randomly selected subset of respondents (for example, "Can you tell me a little more about what you mean when you say you 'disagree'?") provides researchers a quantitative method for determining what survey questions mean to individual respondents. Using this procedure in a cross-national study, for example, Schuman found that a number of respondents—especially those with less education—frequently misinterpreted the purpose of survey questions. In another application of the technique some years later, Schuman and Hatchett (1974, chap. 2) found that, while the great majority of (black) respondents had correctly understood the general intent of most of the questions about current racial issues, there were striking exceptions (see Schuman & Hatchett, 1974, chap. 6). But despite its clear utility, the random probe technique has not, to my knowledge, diffused beyond these basic studies by Schuman and his colleagues.

Among the handful of other inquiries that could be located on this same problem is one by Belson (1968), in which respondents were interviewed in-depth about their perceptions of television programs in Great Britain. Intensive probing by a team of highly trained interviewers showed that there was considerable misinterpretation of many questions, most of which concerned relatively concrete aspects of television viewing. Moreover, as Belson observes, such misinterpretations, involving as they did subtle shifts in meaning and the respondent's frame of reference, were not likely to be detected by ordinary pretesting; therefore, he recommends a more concentrated form of pilot study which queries respondents in great detail about the meaning of their answers and about the process by which they arrive at them.

Another instructive example comes from an analysis by Graber (1978) of problems she encountered in trying to measure audience effects of the 1976 presidential debates. One of the central difficulties, she writes,

> concerns the latitude of meanings that are embedded in many questions, including amply pretested ones. Failure to specify the intended meaning may yield answers that are useless because the analyst does not know which meaning particular respondents had in mind. For instance, a question asking respondents to express agreement or disagreement on a seven-point scale with the statement that "Ford, as president, would reduce unemployment" produced three different ratings from one respondent. Ford's desire to reduce unemployment was given the highest positive rating; his ability to do so, given an obstreperous congress and economic realities, was evaluated at the midpoint; and his anticipated performance, compared to Carter, was rated at the most negative end of the scale.

Without specifying which meaning was desired, it would have been impossible to produce comparable scoring for the respondents in our study
[p. 116].

She also gives an example of how a simple rating question—asking respondents to indicate whether the debate performance of each candidate was good,
bad, or indifferent—came across as highly ambiguous (pp. 116-117):

Respondents inquired, among other things, whether the ratings were to be
made 1) in comparison with other, unspecified, political debates that they
had witnessed; 2) in comparison with the Kennedy-Nixon debates; 3) by
comparing the candidates with each other; or 4) by measuring the candidates against the respondent's pre-debate expectations. When asked to
respond to all four options, one respondent stated that performance had
been good for both candidates, compared to most other debates; bad for
both, compared to the Kennedy-Nixon debates; good for Carter, compared
to Ford and indifferent for Ford, compared to Carter; and good for Ford
and indifferent for Carter, when compared to the respondent's expectations.

The meaning of "performance" also caused some consternation. Did this
mean style, substance, poise, "presidential" demeanor, or what? Some
respondents found it difficult to make a combined judgment, claiming that
the imaginary scores on the various dimensions were so wide apart that
averaging them out seemed inappropriate.

Though they were based on interviews with a small panel of voters, Graber's
observations confirm the suspicions many of us frequently have about possible
discrepancies in respondents' frames of reference as they answer even our most
carefully pretested items. But without doing the kind of intensive interviewing
and probing that she, Belson, and researchers of another era have called for (see,
for example, Lazarsfeld, 1944), we must simply assume away this unwanted
variation in much the same way we often sweep interactions and other nuisances
under the table.

Question Meaning as a Variable
in Survey Analysis

Only recently have some researchers begun to incorporate differences in
respondent interpretations of survey questions as an independent or intervening
variable in their analyses. One such investigation by Bradburn and Miles (1979)
quantified *how often* (how many times a day or week) respondents meant when
they chose an answer category like "very often" or "not too often" to describe
positive and negative feelings. Not unexpectedly, the authors discovered significant disparities in the meaning of these commonly used adverbial quantifiers, as
well as some evidence for the notion that their meaning may shift as a function

of the overall contextual frequency of the event (see also Hakel, 1969). With this information they were also able to make some modest improvements in the predictive power of their affect scales—enough, in fact, to warrant further exploration.

Faced with a similar problem of pinning down respondents' understanding of broad political concepts such as "liberal/conservative," "Democrat/Republican," and "big government," Fee (Note 3) turned to a technique dating back to Lazarsfeld's early methodological work: the use of open-ended questions in a pilot study to develop the closed-ended items required for the subsequent survey. In this case, she did it to get the respondents' definitions of the type of political symbols just described; she then classified these definitions into a fixed number of response categories, thus creating a closed item for assessing the meaning of each symbol. In the follow-up survey respondents were asked to indicate how closely each of the definitional categories came to their own interpretation of the concept; they were also asked to express their attitude toward the same symbol, independently, in the usual rating scale manner. Doing this, Fee found, for example, that the symbol of *big government* elicited four distinct connotations—"welfare-statism," "corporatism," "federal control," and "bureaucracy," each of which related somewhat differently to the respondent's attitude toward the symbol as expressed on the separate rating scale. What she was able to do, in other words, was make use of respondent variations in item meaning as another control or explanatory factor.

Both studies reveal the facile assumptions most of us make when we construct new questions or rely on already available measures in such archives as Roper and ICPSR. One need think here of how many of our indicators of media exposure and attention are based on such ambiguous adverbial quantifiers as "regularly," "somewhat often," "once in a while," and so on (see Patterson, 1980, chaps. 6 and 7) to appreciate how vulnerable they are to systematic error arising from differences in respondents' interpretations. But this problem, as we will now see, becomes even greater when we ponder variations in meaning over time.

Changes in Question Meaning Over Time

I was unable to locate a single study which dealt with the crucial issue of changes in the meaning of survey items over time. About all that can be offered, therefore, are suggestive illustrations. But the few studies that are available should leave little doubt as to the reality of the problem and its theoretical implications for political communication research.

A good example comes from a trend analysis I and my co-workers performed on a question having to do with the issue of whether "the U.S. should keep soldiers overseas where they can help countries that are against communism" (Bishop, Bennett, Tuchfarber, & Oldenick, Note 4, pp. 129-131). When this item was first used in the SRC 1956-60 election studies, a substantial majority of Americans agreed with the policy, a finding which probably reflected the dominant cold war, anticommunist thinking of that period. But when it was replicated in a national survey by NORC in December 1973, the American public had become much less supportive of such a military posture—in fact, it was almost evenly divided on its wisdom.

What had happened? My speculation is that this item had acquired many of the negative connotations associated with the divisive Vietnam era, which was just then drawing to a close (late 1973)—that is, keeping soldiers overseas meant places like Vietnam. I also suspect that the symbol "communism" no longer elicited anywhere near the degree of unfavorable evaluation that it had in the Eisenhower years. Because of these shifts in the item's *meaning* and *implications*, I would argue, public support for the policy of containment declined. Similarly, one might hypothesize about how recent events in Afghanistan may have again altered Americans' associative reactions to the issue of stationing U.S. troops overseas in noncommunist countries, thus restoring some of the item's previous cold war connotations. None of these propositions can be directly tested, of course, with the existing data sets. For merely replicating such items, without the kind of systematic probing I shall propose later, cannot reveal these social-psychological modifications in the semantic structure of the issue.

Another illustration of the same theoretical difficulty appears in the controversial analysis of change in the American electorate by Norman Nie and his associates (1976). The reader may recall that these investigators discovered a curious reversal of the general trend of increasing "ideological" sophistication in the American public, involving a question on whether the government in Washington was "getting too powerful for the good of the country and the individual person." Responses to this item, when it was first introduced in the SRC 1964 election, correlated substantially with those given to many other policy issues, especially those of the New Deal (social welfare) variety; they also showed a strong connection, in the expected direction, with respondents' attitudes toward "liberals" and "conservatives." The item, in other words, seemed to behave as though it were tapping much of the traditional *meaning* associated with the role of the federal government in domestic affairs.

In the SRC 1968 election study, however, the magnitude of these interitem associations began to decline, and by the time of the CPS 1972 survey they had fallen precipitously, to a point in many instances where there was virtually no relationship at all between perceptions of the appropriate size of the federal establishment and its involvement in such matters as employment, health care, and racial integration (Nie et al., 1976: 125-138). How had this come about? Though their evidence is indirect, Nie and his co-workers made a persuasive case that this issue had taken on a host of new connotations in the late 1960s, revolving around the protests against the Vietnam war, among other things (for example, the power of the government to control dissent); thus it could not be expected to differentiate among conventional groupings within the electorate in the way it once did. Both "liberals" and "conservatives," to put it another way, had now become almost equally concerned with the growing power of the government, albeit for different reasons. Bennett and Oldendick (Note 5) reached similar conclusions about the factors responsible for trends on this indicator. And while the support for their inferences is likewise indirect, they, along with Nie and his colleagues, may have struck on a major, and perhaps obvious, impediment to monitoring political change with "subjective" indicators: event-based differences in respondent interpretations of survey questions.

My final example is drawn from recent analyses of a well-documented shift in U.S. public opinion: the growth of tolerance for politically and socially deviant groups. I am referring to the studies by Davis (1975) and Nunn and his associates (1978), both of which have demonstrated some rather remarkable increases in the apparent willingness of Americans to extend fundamental civil liberties to such groups as atheists, communists, and socialists. This trend, together with similar data on racial attitudes and other social issues (Taylor, Sheatsley, & Greeley, 1978), has been interpreted as an indicator of a broad movement in the direction of "cultural liberalism." There is little question about the magnitude or direction of these changes, at least as of the early 1970s. Disagreement exists, however, as to the causal origins of these trends, and there is reason to think once more that they are rooted in subtle alterations of the meaning of such key symbols as "atheist," "communist," and "socialist."

My suspicions are based on a reconceptualization and reanalysis of the growth-of-tolerance thesis by Sullivan and his colleagues (1979a). Recognizing that the concept of tolerance presumes opposition or disagreement, they develop a strong argument for viewing most, if not all, of the apparent growth of "liberal" attitudes toward communists, socialist, and atheists as an illusion due to the decreasing threat value of these groups in American society today. Even more convincing, they show that when one does control for the degree to which a respondent dislikes a certain outgroup of his or her own choosing, there is no evidence that Americans are any more tolerant now than they were 25 years ago! That is, when the researchers held constant what Osgood and his followers (Osgood, 1957; Snider & Osgood, 1969; Osgood, May, & Hiron, 1975) would call the "evaluative" meaning of such social stimuli, differences in tolerance disappeared.

Sullivan et al.'s findings also suggest that the apparently higher levels of tolerance for atheists, socialist, and communists that have frequently been observed among better-educated respondents are equally illusory. This occurs because such groups are not, for various sociohistorical reasons, as threatening to those with greater educational attainments. Thus tolerating freedom of expression by them is not particularly difficult, as compared to, for example, approving of marches or demonstrations by members of the Ku Klux Klan, the American Nazi Party, or—to take a more current example—Iranian students or PLO sympathizers in the United States. Any relationship between education and tolerance, then, would seem due largely to the types of outgroups that have been selected in previous investigations.

Their model, moreover, provides a more satisfying "psychological" explanation of why Davis (1975), Nunn et al. (1978), and other researchers find that factors like cohort replacement and rising levels of educational attainment account for significant portions of the observed increase in tolerance of "left" political and social groups—namely, because the less-educated, older cohorts for whom such groups are more threatening are being succeeded by better-educated, younger cohorts for whom this is much less true. Yet we also know that much of the change in tolerance over the past couple of decades remains unexplained; for it has increased in *all* segments of the population, indicating that groups such as atheists, communists, and socialists have become less threatening to almost everyone. Similar patterns turn up in the trends toward liberalization of racial, sexual, and related social attitudes (Taylor et al., 1978). Nearly all of the indicators move in the same general "left" direction throughout the population, though the movement has sometimes been more rapid in some subgroups than in others. Indeed, on a wide variety of public opinion indicators, one sees again and again a generalized linear trend of everything with time (see, for example, the SRC/CPS series on trust in government and the Harris and Gallup questions on confidence in U.S. institutions), as though there was some common homogenizing social force pushing all groups now this way, now that way, sometimes with remarkable suddenness. This means that the typical models of political change, consisting of sociodemographic variables—most of which shift fairly slowly over time—cannot possibly offer an adequate explanation for what looks like an unusually dynamic process.

There are more appropriate conceptual models available, however, and I suspect that many of the existing difficulties in modeling political trends lies in the failure to link the shifts that occur over time in the connotations of the key symbols contained in our survey questions with a very likely causal factor: *changes in the frequency and evaluative context of these symbols in the mass media*. It is this symbolic environment, then, that needs to be monitored and disaggregated systematically if we are to get hold of the frequently inexplicable trends in survey-based indicators of public opinion. Let me make a somewhat lengthy theoretical digression now to lay the foundation for a strategy that may potentially solve the problem, with special emphasis on the role of political communication in the process.

CONCEPTUAL MODELS OF CHANGE
IN SURVEY ITEMS

A review of the rapidly growing literature on the agenda-setting function of mass communications (see Chapter 4 in this volume) leads one to the firm conclusion that the media, through their selective emphasis on various public affairs content, can create substantial alterations in the salience of political issues and symbols in the consciousness of the mass public (see McCombs, 1981; McCombs & Shaw, 1972; McCombs & Stone, Note 6; McLeod, Becker, & Byrnes, 1974; Tipton, Haney, & Basehart, 1975; Shaw & McCombs, 1977) Many studies, moreover, suggest that trends in public opinion may often bear a stronger relationship with media coverage than with more "objective" real-world conditions, particularly for issues that are more remote from personal experience (see Beniger, 1978; Beniger, Watkins, & Ruz, 1978; Funkhouser, 1973; Rosengren, Note 7; Zucker, 1978). There is now convincing evidence, for example, that a good deal of the "crisis of confidence" in U.S. government can be traced to the critical character of the mass media in American politics (Miller et al., 1980; McLeod, Brown, Becker, & Ziemke, 1977; M. Robinson, 1976). One would also expect that extensions of these investigations would show that a similar media-induced "malaise" has produced the related decline of confidence in U.S. institutions more generally.

It is interesting to note here the frequent observation of the striking discrepancy between the negativism Americans have increasingly expressed toward institutions in general and the overall positive outlook they have evinced toward their personal lives, as well as their *own* congressman, doctor, or lawyer, (see Ladd & Lipset, 1980). In the latter case they have, of course, more direct experience and familiarity, and thus media effects are greatly attenuated. But in responding to institutions in general, they are clearly more dependent on mass media information, most of which tends to be critical, and apparently more so in the last decade or two. Such media effects are, to anticipate the discussion below, "contingent" on the personal experience of the respondent.

Audience-Contingent Effects Model

Research on mass media effects has also begun to display signs of significant theoretical progress. Whereas much of the previous research on agenda-setting relied on a "mirror image" model, which predicts a relatively direct transfer of the salience of issues in the media to the public's agenda of priorities (see McCombs et al., Note 6), recent analyses at the Center for Political Studies (Erbring et al., 1980) have created compelling reasons for replacing it with a better-fitting "Audience-Contingent Effects Model." The key proposition in this theoretical framework, as its label would suggest, is that the salience of any given public affairs issue depends on the personal attributes of respondents which may make them more or less sensitive to its emphasis and implications in the media. Being unemployed, for instance, heightens one's attention to that topic as it appears in the news. So, too, do other personal experiences, such as being victimized by a crime or waiting in long lines at gasoline stations, act as "modulators" of one's reactions to media coverage of relevant content. On the other hand, where respondents have little direct experience with an issue, media effects are more closely linked with the degree of exposure to news and with one's general interest in public affairs (see Patterson, 1980, chap. 13). The heart of the model, in other words, is that media stimulation interacts with the audience's nonmedia experience, including real-world "contextual" conditions in the respondent's community, to generate differences in the salience of particular political cognitions.

Using data from several sources—a content analysis of front page stories in the local newspapers reportedly read by respondents, statistics on "real" events in their communities (crime, unemployment), and their responses to the standard CPS question on the "most important national problem"—Erbring and his associates produced evidence which is generally consistent with the contingent effects model. Furthermore, they demonstrated that informal communication about political events with friends, relatives, and co-workers can either dilute or enhance the impact of media coverage, depending on the nature of the issue and its path of diffusion in the community over time. In particular, they show that the influence of the mass media tends to be quite powerful for people who are *not* integrated into everyday networks of informal communication about public affairs, but that it is virtually negligible for those who are integrated.

I seriously question, however, whether these effects truly reflect being exposed to the specific content of interpersonal interactions, on which Erbring and his colleagues have no *direct* measures as in the case of media content. In fact, the relevant literature here would indicate that people who engage in political conversations tend to be more involved in public affairs in the first place (see Converse, 1966), and that political opinion givers and receivers are generally the same people (Robinson, 1976). So informal political communication, which Erbring and his associates have found to be the most powerful modulator of media impact, represents the weakest link in their causal analysis. We have, in any case, no practical way of directly monitoring the actual public affairs content to which people are exposed in their personal networks on a day-to-day basis (that is, in a nonexperimental design). Such self-reports of political interaction are therefore probably best regarded as alternative indicators of the more general factor of political motivation.

Though the audience-contingent effects model represents a distinct improvement on its theoretical predecessors, it has focused largely on explaining variations in only one of the dimensions of media effects with which we are concerned: the relative *salience* of political and social issues. But we are also interested in accounting for the differences media coverage can create in the polarity and associative connotations of the various symbols used in the wording of public opinion indicators. By and large, I am talking about changes in the basic "good/bad" or evaluative dimension of meaning identified by Charles Osgood (1957), or what social psychologists would normally refer to as an *attitude*. There are, of course, numerous models of attitude change in the experimental literature, and I will certainly not try to review them here (see, for example, Fishbein & Ajzen, 1975). I shall, instead, briefly highlight one which, in my judgment, best fits the processing of media communications on public affairs: information integration theory (Anderson, 1971, 1978).

Information Integration Theory

Developed originally in the context of experimental work on impression formation, the theory has shown considerable utility in accounting for attitude change within the traditional communication and persuasion paradigm. Essentially, the model postulates that attitude (or opinion) change follows a general principle of information integration, in which one's opinion toward an object or topic reflects a weighted average of relevant information stimuli. More formally, the model can be represented by:

$$R = \Sigma \, W_i \, S_i$$

where R is the overt response to an item or scale;

S is the scale value or location of the informational stimulus on a dimension of judgment (such as the evaluative dimension of the semantic differential); and

W is the relevance or psychological importance of the stimulus, and the sum is over all relevant information stimuli.

These parameters will, of course, differ depending on the dimension of judgment as well as the individual. Note, too, that the first term in the equation, $W_o S_o$, ordinarily represents the person's initial opinion—that is, prior to receiving any external communication. The evidence to date suggests that this initial internal state is simply "averaged" in with (as opposed to "added" to) other relevant information in the process of attitude change (see Anderson, 1978, pp. 11-19).

To take a concrete illustration of what I have in mind, consider the trends during recent years in public support for nuclear power. Prior to the accident at Three Mile Island, almost all U.S. surveys showed consistent majorities of Americans in favor of constructing nuclear power plants. In the aftermath of the massive media publicity of that incident, however, the pollsters unanimously reported a substantial decline in public support for continuing nuclear development (see *The Gallup Report,* July 1979), one which cut across all sociodemographic groups and which would therefore be unexplainable with the usual partitions of the data. It also took place in a very brief period of time, which means that the source of the change must have been fairly instantaneous. While there is no direct evidence, I would argue that the nature and intensity of the media's coverage of the Three Mile Island episode induced a sudden (negative) shift in the *evaluative* connotations of the symbol, "nuclear power," and, in turn, the drop in public support for nuclear development. One can also view this in terms of the *associative* connections that the media established in the minds of many—that is, "nuclear power" elicits "Three Mile Island" as a first-order association. And as such associations faded from short-term memory, or became less "salient," public support tended to return to its previous level.

Using the information integration model, we would predict that a respondent's opinion on a specific question concerning nuclear power would be the result of a simple weighted average of his or her initial opinion and the scale values of the relevant media content on Three Mile Island (TMI). The weight for the respondent's initial opinion in this instance (W_o) would be represented by the *personal importance* of the issue to him or her which would subsume the audience contingency construct in Erbring et al.'s (1980) model. The weight for the scaled dimension(s) of media content, on the other hand ($W_i S_i$), would be indicated by the frequency (and density) with which a respondent had actually been exposed to the messages about TMI. Since the weights in an averaging model must sum to 1.00, attitude change on TMI would be inversely proportional to the personal relevance of the topic, or what Erbring et al. have called "issue sensitivity."

More generally, one would expect that the effects of exposure to media content would be greatest among those respondents for whom an issue is least important. Previous research shows that these are usually the very people for whom public affairs is of relatively low salience and who, in other words, are least likely to be exposed to any type of political communication in the mass media or in their interpersonal networks. But when they are exposed to such information, they tend to be significantly more susceptible to changes in attitude (see Miller & Mackuen, 1978; Patterson & McClure, 1976; Patterson, 1980). This proposition bears a striking resemblance to Philip Converse's "floating" voters hypothesis in his seminal article on "Information Flow and the Stability of Partisan Attitudes" (1966). Indeed, his proposition—that "the probability that any given voter will be sufficiently deflected in his partisan momentum to cross party lines in a specified election varies directly as a function of the strength of short-term forces toward the opposing party and varies inversely as a function of the mass of stored information about politics" (p. 141)—can be seen as a special case of the more general *principle of information integration,* in which the "mass" of stored information represents the weighted value of a respondent's initial internal state, and the strength of the "short-term" forces (with their associated partisan valences) stand for the weighted scale values of the information from the campaign environment. Theoretically, moreover, all of the variables identified thus far can be profitably viewed as determinants of either the weight or scale value parameters in the basic equation of the integration model. This includes even fundamental demographics, such as age and education, which in this framework become *indicators* of the magnitude and character of information about public affairs issues that one has either already been exposed to or is likely to be exposed to in the future.

Let me summarize by saying that what appeared at first glance to be merely a "methodological" problem—that is, the changing meaning of survey items—turns out, after closer analysis, to be a central theoretical one: namely, how to link changes in the structure of public affairs content in the mass media with changes in the distribution and structure of public opinion. That is the reason for this apparent detour through the substantive literature and for the statement in the opening section of the chapter about the often superficial "methodological" character of our problems in survey research. Political communication researchers can, moreover, make a unique contribution in the years ahead toward solving the difficulties associated here with the changing meaning of survey items.

One way to tackle this would be to construct "random probes" of closed-ended items, such as the Gallup presidential approval question or the Harris confidence in institutions series, and then link the open-ended responses volunteered to such probes with a content analysis of public affairs stories in the mass media during the same general period. One would, for example, expect respondents during a foreign affairs crisis like those that occurred recently in Afghanistan and Iran to be likely to volunteer something about these episodes in response to a probe about *why* they approve or disapprove of the president's performance in office. That is, such randomly probed closed-ended items should behave much like the open-ended questions that are typically used in agenda-setting research, reflecting the topical emphasis of the mass media. Thus, if the president's handling of some foreign affairs situation is what is front page news, that is what respondents are likely to volunteer as "reasons" for their approval or disapproval. The task, then, for political communication researchers in the coming years is to devise better ways of linking such changes in the connotative meaning of survey items with ongoing content analyses of the mass media along the lines proposed by Deweese (1977) and McCombs (Note 8). One must, in other words, begin to think of a program of research consisting of both a *continuous survey* of the general public and a *continuous monitoring* of public affairs content in the mass media. Only in this way are we likely to be able to model adequately the dynamic changes that take place in the public opinion indicators we use to measure the impact of political communications.

AN INFORMATION-PROCESSING APPROACH
TO SURVEY RESPONSES

At this point it should be evident that the lack of even a rudimentary model of how respondents arrive at their answers or opinions in response to our questions presents the greatest obstacle to improving the practice of survey research in political communication and allied fields. Here I would like to offer an approach which I believe has considerable heuristic value for remedying this atheoretical state of affairs and which has the potential of radically altering the entire survey-based paradigm: the information-processing models of cognitive psychology (see, for example, Lachman, Lachman, & Butterfield, 1979). This theoretical perspective has already begun to sweep through much of the traditional cognitive and attitudinal literature in social psychology, and by the time this chapter is in print, it may well have become the dominant paradigm in that field. In the next few pages I shall try to give the reader a rough overview of this approach as it bears on the measurement of respondents' attitudes, interests, and other self-reported states in the survey interview (see Becker, 1979).

Probably the most significant generalization that has emerged from this vast literature is that people, when asked to make a judgment or verbal report of any kind, will tend to give the answer that is most immediately *available* to them in memory (see Nisbett & Ross, 1980; Wyer & Carlston, 1979). What this means in the context of the survey interview is that when we ask respondents to give their opinion on some political object or issue, they do not make an exhaustive search of their long-term memories for a representative sample of relevant experiences or information, but respond instead in terms of whatever seemingly *relevant* piece of information is most "salient" at the moment. This indeed would seem to be the principle which underlies the agenda-setting effect of the mass media with which so many of us have been preoccupied. Thus, when we ask people, "What is the most important problem facing the country?" we tend to get responses reflecting the topics that have been made most "salient" or *available* to them by the front pages of the newspaper and the headlines of the evening network news broadcasts. So this phenomenon is relatively familiar to us in another guise.

But its full implications are not, for the research I have cited in cognitive social psychology demonstrates that people's judgments about themselves and others in various domains may often be affected by quite fortuitous events or occurrences which "prime" one or another cognition to be *accessible* to them at the time they make the judgment (see Wyer & Srull, in press). To take a familiar example, consider what happens when we ask respondents a question about their interest in politics, such as the standard one utilized by SRC/CPS:

> "Some people seem to follow what's going on in government and public affairs most of the time, whether there's an election going on or not.

Others aren't that interested. Would you say that you follow what's going on in government and public affairs most of the time, some of the time, only now and then, or hardly at all?"

One would like to believe that what respondents do when they hear this question is search their memory for all or nearly all relevant instances of where and when they have paid attention to, or participated in, politics and then give the generalized response, "I follow it most of the time." This is very unlikely, however, and the evidence I have been exposed to would suggest that, again, what happens is that respondents answer such questions largely in terms of whatever information is most *available* to them in memory about *recent* instances of their having paid attention to politics in one form or another.

A good illustration comes from a set of omnibus surveys my research organization has carried out in the metropolitan Cincinnati area over the last couple of years, in which the standard SRC/CPS question on political interest has been asked several times.[3] In May-June of 1979, when this question was asked near the beginning of the interview schedule (its location is a crucial factor, as I note below), about 49 percent of our telephone survey sample (N = 1152) claimed to follow "what's going on in government and public affairs" *most of the time.* But in late fall of that year (November-December), when it was asked in roughly the same location, the figure for following politics *most of the time* jumped to 57 percent. Six months later, however (May-June, 1980), the figure dropped back to the previous level of 49 percent.

What explains these fluctuations? In the absence of an experimental design, one can only speculate, but it appears that it was the onset of the hostage crisis in Iran, which occurred exactly during the field period of our November-early December 1979 survey, that temporarily inflated respondents' self-perceptions of how often they followed politics. A corroborating piece of evidence for this interpretation can be found in the Nielsen ratings, which showed a 13 percent increase in viewing audiences for the 6:30 p.m. network news during the same period, an increase evidently attributable to Americans' sudden interest in the hostage-taking episode.[4] And, to cite another supportive instance from an entirely different data base, one can look at the well-known trends in reported interest in following the political campaign from the SRC/CPS election series and discover that interest has always been higher in presidential than in off-year election campaigns. This familiar and, perhaps, obvious datum indicates, however, that respondents do tend to answer such items in terms of the information that is most readily *accessible* to them. In the examples I have given, it seems as though they are basing their responses on the most *recent* instances of their having paid attention to politics—for example, watching the evening news lately to follow the Iran episode—and much less, if at all, on any previous information in memory about their attention to public affairs, or the lack of it. This is not exactly what many of us assume when we use such indicators of political involvement to represent *enduring* dispositions of our respondents as key variables in analysis (see Patterson, 1980, chaps. 7 and 8).

If this was all one had to worry about, some way to cope could surely be found, for example, by multiplying measures of such volatile phenomena as reports of interest. As usual, things are not so easy. There is even more convincing evidence accumulating in the same social-psychological literature that the behavior itself of answering questions may act as a "primer" which makes some cognitions more *accessible* or salient than others. When people are later asked other related items, they will often respond in terms of the cognitions that have just been made available to them from their answers to the previous questions, particularly if they have direct implications (see Salancik & Conway, 1975).

To continue with the earlier example of self-perceived interest in politics, let me cite a relevant finding from a current project in which we had varied the *location* of the standard SRC/CPS question so that it appeared either immediately before or after a series of questions on various public policy issues. Specifically, we asked respondents for their opinions on seven policy issues (including national health insurance, diplomatic relations with Cuba, and the SALT negotiations), in addition to the fictitious 1975 Public Affairs Act discussed previously. On each of these topics, however, we also used a preliminary filter question with some respondents but not with others; that is, we randomly assigned some respondents to receive a filter question, such as "Do you have an opinion on this or not?" or "Have you thought much about this or not?" to screen out the uninformed or uninterested. The remaining respondents (also randomly assigned) received no filter question, so that they had to volunteer that they did not have an opinion, or respond "don't know," if that was the case (see Bishop, Oldenick, & Tuchfarber, in press). Table 21.1 shows the relationships between giving or not giving an opinion on one of the issues in that experiment—the SALT negotiations—and respondents' self-perceived interest in government and public affairs, controlling for the presence or absence of a filter question and the location of the interest question. In this case, the interest question was asked either immediately after the SALT item or just before the beginning of the seven issue items. In other words, the question on SALT was asked *last* in all conditions, so that it occurred just before the interest question in the after-location condition, whereas in the before-location condition it is not asked until seven questions later in the sequence.

As we see in Table 21.2, respondents who gave an opinion on the SALT issue were much more likely to report that they followed politics *most of the time* than those who had not given an opinion on the issue. Although this relationship was statistically significant in all conditions, it was especially strong in one key group: among those respondents who were exposed to a filter which explicitly

TABLE 21.2: Percentage of Respondents Saying They Follow What's Going On in Government and Public Affairs *Most of the Time*, by Opinion-Giving on the SALT Issue by Filter/No Filter by Location of the Question about Interest in Government and Public Affairs

	Interest Question Asked Before the SALT Issue				Interest Question Asked After the SALT Issue			
	–FILTER–		–NO FILTER–		–FILTER–		–NO FILTER–	
	Opinion on SALT	No Opinion on SALT	Opinion on SALT	No Opinion on SALT	Opinion on SALT	No Opinion on SALT	Opinion on SALT	No Opinion on SALT
	65	39	61	38	65	28	58	36
	(Q = .48)*		(Q = .44)*		(Q = .66)*		(Q = .43)*	
	(N = 764)		(N = 388)		(N = 788)		(N = 371)	

*p < .001

617

asked them if they had an opinion on the SALT issue—just before they were asked about how interested they were in politics (Q = .66). Here we find that the level of self-perceived interest is lowest for those who just told the interviewer they had "no opinion" on the SALT issue in response to the filter (28 percent). This figure is noticeably lower than the one for respondents in the nonfilter condition who had *volunteered* that they had no opinion on or didn't know about the SALT issue (36 percent), also just before answering the question on political interest. To put it in theoretical terms, those respondents who said they had no opinion on the SALT issue in answer to an explicit filter to that effect were responding to the interest question in terms of the information that was most available to them—namely, the information in short-term memory that they had or had not just given an opinion on an issue that is a *relevant* instance of one's interest in politics. At the same time, it appears that merely volunteering that one has no opinion, or doesn't know, as in the nonfilter condition, is not as memorially vivid or salient as just having answered an explicit filter. That is why respondents in this condition tended to report a higher level of interest (36 percent) than their counterparts in the filter condition (28 percent).

Consider now the situation where the interest question was asked before the various issue items—in fact, seven items before the SALT issue. Whatever information was available to respondents about their interest in politics when they answered it in this location would have to be drawn from recent memories about their attention to politics outside the interview. The most likely external source for inferring one's interest in politics under such circumstances would be mass media events such as those that took place during the Iran episode, which, as I noted earlier, probably accounted for the significant increase in political interest at the time of our metropolitan Cincinnati survey in November-December 1979. Other evidence that would seem to confirm this interpretation is that we have generally found reported interest in public affairs to be higher when the question is asked at the beginning of the interview schedule just *before* questions on respondents' political opinions than when it is asked after such items, particularly among those respondents with lower levels of education (see Bishop, Oldenick, & Tuchfarber, in press). But the critical point is that respondents who are asked the question about their interest in politics beforehand simply do not have the same information available to them in memory as those who are asked to respond to a series of political opinion items in the presence or absence of a filter. It is that difference in the nature of the information available which shapes the differences in self-perceptions of interest in politics.

Relations to Self-Perception Theory

These data are also congruent with Bem's (1978) self-perception theory of how people infer their internal states (for example, beliefs, attitudes, or interests) from observations of their own behavior. Indeed, Bem's proposition can be viewed as a special case of the more general principle of information availability; as he puts it (1978, p. 222):

> Individuals come to "know" their own attitudes, emotions, and other internal states partially by inferring them from observations of their own overt behavior and/or the circumstances in which this behavior occurs. Thus to the extent that internal cues are weak, ambiguous, or uninterpretable, the individual is functionally in the same position as an outside observer, an observer who must necessarily rely upon those same external cues to infer the individual's inner states.

Strictly speaking, in the theoretical framework being developed here, it is not one's behavior per se that is the crucial cue, but rather the information that one has encoded in memory (Wyer & Srull, in press) that contains the implications for any judgments about one's internal states. Even more important to the present formulation is Bem's second proposition, which is another way of saying that those respondents whose internal cues are weakest, ambiguous, or uninterpretable in a given domain (such as politics) will be most likely to rely on the information that is immediately available to them from observations of their own behavior in making inferences about their internal states. We would expect such respondents, for example, to be more likely to infer their interest in politics, or the lack of it, from observing their own behavior of giving or not giving an opinion on an issue like SALT. And what types of people are most likely to have weak or ambiguous internal cues about politics? Answer: the same people who have been shown time and again to be most susceptible to political campaign communications, variations in question wording on public affairs issues, and the like—the less educated and politically uninvolved.

Let me give one more example of how this information-processing approach can be applied to another problem in question construction that we considered earlier: whether to offer respondents one or two sides of an issue. As I noted in discussing that problem, the general finding has been that less-educated respondents tend to be most susceptible to the *availability* of a second substantive alternative on an item; that is, they are more likely to choose it if one is offered. Conversely, they are also more likely to agree with or, as we say, "acquiesce to" single-sided opinion statements. The intriguing theoretical question, of course, is what accounts for these superficially different response effects. I have already hinted at it with my emphasis on the word *availability*. That is, other things being equal, we may ask: What kinds of respondents are most likely to have available to them counterarguments or cognitions for opposing or disagreeing with a given statement of political opinion? Clearly, it would be the better-educated, politically involved respondents who *pay* more *attention to* and "think about" public affairs issues and events. Conversely, it is the less-educated respondents who are least likely to have a reason or counterargument available to them in memory for opposing or disagreeing with a particular proposition in a Likert-type format, for example. This is why so many researchers over the years have found a significant and consistent relationship between education and the acquiescence response style (see Jackman, 1973). The availability principle would also account for the tendency of the less educated to be more influenced by the presentation of a second substantive alternative in survey questions—namely, because it makes *available* to them a counterargument or cognition that is normally more accessible to their better-educated counterparts (see Bishop et al., Note 1).[5]

But before letting the reader get away with the idea that all this psychological theory is perhaps important, but tangential, to concerns in political communication research, I want to locate the problem in a framework that is more familiar: the persuasion research paradigm. It may be quite fruitful, for instance, to think of the survey interview as a microcosmic communication and persuasion experiment, in which the interviewer is presenting statements of political belief or opinion that are more or less *persuasive communications* with which a respondent is asked to agree or disagree, for instance. Much like respondents in a standard persuasion experiment, they try to relate such opinion statements to their existing repertoire of information about a given domain—for example, foreign policy (see Perloff & Brock, 1980). In doing so, they will generate cognitions or arguments which will lead them to either agree or disagree with whatever position is being advocated in the opinion statement. And analogous to what has been found in persuasion research, as a respondent's *involvement* in a particular domain increases, the likelihood of generating relevant cognitions or arguments increases, which is another way of saying that such cognitions are more likely to be *available* to the better-educated, more politically involved individuals.

To carry the conceptualization a bit further (see Perloff & Brock, 1980), one would predict:

(a) that highly involved respondents will tend to *disagree* with an opinion statement if it is incongruent with their previous position (that is, because of the *availability* of counterarguments);
(b) but if it is congruent, they will tend to agree (because of the *availability* of supportive cognitions);
(c) less involved respondents will tend to agree, or "acquiesce" (because of the lack of *available* counterarguments).

Further refinements could be introduced here, but I think the reader has enough information *available* to him or her now to digest the implications of the information-processing paradigm that I am fostering for future survey studies in political communication research. Because of its greater familiarity, many may prefer to use the perspective of persuasion research as a handle. That will do as an initiation to making the paradigmatic shift that is now under way, since it will get one to think more often about what is truly important in designing our survey questions: what relevant cognitions, if any, are stimulated by the wording, format and location of the survey items we present to respondents in our interviews, including the way they are presented by our interviewers. For it is those evoked, *available* cognitions that form the basis of respondent reactions as much, if not more than, the literal content of the items themselves.

This concludes a somewhat unorthodox journey to a heretofore familiar paradigm: the survey-based study of political communication and public opinion. The traditional assumptions underlying that paradigm, however, have only recently become exposed to theoretical scrutiny. As I have tried to communicate here, we must begin to think of building a theory of the survey instrument itself and of the larger symbolic context in which it is embedded before we can make further progress on the "substantive" problems of the discipline. Indeed, we may begin by thinking of the survey interview as a microcosm of political communication research, in which one wittingly or unwittingly manipulates the information available for "processing," an analogue to the computer that I find hard to resist.

NOTES

[1] A subcommittee of the American Statistical Association's Section on Survey Research Methods has recently published an informative, nontechnical brochure entitled, "What Is A Survey?" (Ferber, Sheatsley, Turner, & Waksberg, 1980) that is available free upon request for single copies and with a small per-copy charge for multiple copies. It is especially useful for informing undergraduate students and educated members of the general public about what is involved in conducting a quality survey. Those interested may write to the American Statistical Association, 806 Fifteenth Street, N.W., Washington, D.C. 20005.

[2] The research cited here was supported by a grant from the National Science Foundation (SOC 78-07407) to me and my colleagues at the University of Cincinnati, Robert W. Oldendick and Alfred J. Tuchfarber.

[3] Copies of the technical reports for the Greater Cincinnati Surveys referred to here are available from the author at the Behavioral Sciences Laboratory (132), University of Cincinnati, Cincinnati, Ohio 45221.

[4] See *The Nielsen National TV Ratings,* 2nd November and 1st December, 1979 Reports. Northbrook, IL: A. C. Nielsen Company.

[5] An experiment is currently under way to test this proposition, by manipulating the cognitions that are available to respondents just before they answer a typical agree/disagree item—for example, by having them answer an open-ended question on a topic with direct implications for a subsequent agree/disagree item. In this way, we may be able to increase or decrease acquiescence systematically thereby demonstrating its contextual specificity.

REFERENCE NOTES

1. Bishop, G. F., Bennett, S. E., Tuchfarber, A. J., & Oldendick, R. W. *Effects of presenting one vs. two sides of an issue in survey questions.* (Available from Behavioral Sciences Laboratory, University of Cincinnati) Unpublished manuscript.

2. Smith, T. W. *Can we have confidence in confidence?* Revisited. (GSS Tech. Rep. No. 11). Chicago: University of Chicago, National Opinion Research Center, April 1979.

3. Fee, J. F. *Symbols in survey questions: solving the problem of multiple word meanings.* Unpublished manuscript, National Opinion Research Center, University of Chicago, 1978.

4. Bishop, G. F., Bennett, S. E., Tuchfarber, A. J., & Oldendick, R. W. *Trends in the structure of American political behavior: A secondary analysis of methodological artifacts* (Tech. Rep. to the National Science Foundation on Project SOC 77-10509). Cincinnati, Ohio: Behavioral Sciences Laboratory, University of Cincinnati, 1979.

5. Bennett, S. E., & Oldendick, R. W. *The power of the federal government: the case of the changing issue.* Paper presented at the annual conference of the Midwest Political Science Association, Chicago, Illinois, April 1977. (Available from Department of Political Science, University of Cincinnati)

6. McCombs, M. E., & Stone, G. (Eds.). Studies in agenda-setting. Syracuse, NY: S. I. Newhouse School of Public Communication, Syracuse University, 1976.

7. Rosengren, K. E. *Mass media content, political opinions, and social change.* Paper presented at the Nordic Symposium on Content Analysis, Rattvik, Sweden, March 1979.

8. McCombs, M. E. *Computerized content analysis of newspapers on a continuing basis.* Paper presented at the annual conference of the Southern Association for Public Opinion Research, Chapel Hill, North Carolina, March 1979.

REFERENCES

Alwin, D. F. (Ed.). *Survey design and analysis: Current issues.* Beverly Hills, CA: Sage, 1978.

Anderson, N. H. Integration theory and attitude change. *Psychological Review,* 1971, *78,* 171-206.

Anderson, N. H. Cognitive algebra: Integration theory applied to social attribution. In L. Berkowitz (Ed.), *Cognitive theories in social psychology.* New York: Academic Press, 1978.

Bailar, B. A., & Lanphier, C. M. *Development of survey methods to assess survey practices.* Washington, DC: American Statistical Association, 1978.

Belson, W. A. Respondent understanding of survey questions. *Polls,* 1968, *3,* 1-13.

Becker, L. B. Measurement of gratifications. *Communication Research,* 1979, 6, 54-73.

Bem, D. J. Self-perception theory. In L. Berkowitz (Ed.), *Cognitive theories in social psychology.* New York: Academic Press, 1978.

Beniger, J. R. Media content as social indicators: The Greenfield Index of agenda-setting. *Communication Research,* 1978, *5,* 437-453.

Beniger, J. R., Watkins, S., & Ruz, J. E. Trends in the abortion issue as measured by events, media coverage and public opinion indicators. *Proceedings of the Annual Conference of the American Statistical Association,* Social Statistics Section, 1978, *21,* 118-123.

Bishop, G. F., Meadow, R. G., & Jackson-Beeck, M. (Eds.). *The presidential debates: Media electoral and policy perspectives.* New York: Praeger, 1978.

Bishop, G. F., Oldendick, R. W., & Tuchfarber, A. J. Effects of question wording and format on political attitude consistency. *Public Opinion Quarterly,* 1978, *42,* 81-92.

Bishop, G. F., Oldendick, R. W., & Tuchfarber, A. J. Experiments in filtering political opinions. *Political Behavior,* in press.

Bishop, G. F., Oldendick, R. W., Tuchfarber, A. J., & Bennett, S. E. The changing structure of mass belief systems: Fact or artifact? *Journal of Politics,* 1978, *40,* 781-787.

Bishop, G. F., Oldendick, R. W., Tuchfarber, A. J., & Bennett, S. E. Effects of opinion filtering and opinion floating: Evidence from a secondary analysis. *Political Methodology,* 1979, *6,* 293-309.

Bishop, G. F., Oldendick, R. W., Tuchfarber, A. J., & Bennett, S. E. Pseudo-opinions on public affairs. *Public Opinion Quarterly,* 1980, *44,* 198-209.

Bishop, G. F., Tuchfarber, A. J., & Oldendick, R. W. Change in the structure of American political attitudes: The nagging question of question wording. *American Journal of Political Science,* 1978, *22,* 250-269.

Bishop, G. F., Tuchfarber, A. J., Oldendick, R. W., & Bennett, S. E. Questions about question wording: A rejoinder to revisiting mass belief systems revisited. *American Journal of Political Science, 1979, 23,* 187-192.

Boyd, R. A., & Hyman, H. H. Survey research. In F. I. Greenstein & N. W. Polsby (Eds.), *Handbook of political science* (Vol. 7). Reading, MA: Addison-Wesley, 1975.

Bradburn, N. M. Response effects. In P. H. Rossi & J. D. Wright (Eds.), *Handbook of survey research.* New York: Academic Press, in press.

Bradburn, N. M., & Miles, C. Vague quantifiers. *Public Opinion Quarterly, 1979, 43,* 92-101.

Bradburn, N. M., Sudman, S., & associates. *Improving interview method and questionnaire design.* San Francisco: Jossey-Bass, 1979.

Cannell, C. F., Oksenburg, L., & Converse, J. M. *Experiments in interviewing techniques: Field experiments in health reporting, 1971-1977.* Ann Arbor: Institute for Social Research, University of Michigan, 1980.

Cantril, H., & Research Associates. *Gauging public opinion.* Princeton: Princeton University Press, 1944.

Converse, P. E. The nature of belief systems in mass publics. In D. E. Apter (Ed.), *Ideology and discontent.* New York: Free Press, 1964.

Converse, P. E. Information flow and the stability of partisan attitudes. In A. Campbell et al. (Eds.), *Elections and the political order.* New York: John Wiley, 1966.

Converse, P. E. Attitudes and non-attitudes: Continuation of a dialogue. In E. R. Tufte (Ed.), *The quantitative analysis of social problems.* Reading, MA: Addison-Wesley, 1970.

Converse, P. E. Public opinion and voting behavior. In F. I. Greenstein & N. W. Polsby (Eds.), *Handbook of political science* (Vol. 4). Reading, MA: Addison-Wesley, 1975.

Davis, J. A. Communism, conformity, cohorts, and categories: American tolerance in 1954 and 1972-73. *American Journal of Sociology, 1975, 81,* 491-513.

Deweese, L. C, Computer content analysis of "day-old" newspapers: A feasibility study. *Public Opinion Quarterly, 1977, 41,* 91-94.

Dillman, D. A. *Mail and telephone surveys.* New York: John Wiley, 1978.

Erbring, L., Goldenberg, E. N., & Miller, A. H. Front-page news and real-world cues: A new look at agenda-setting by the media. *American Journal of Political Science, 1980, 24,* 16-49.

Ferber, R., Sheatsley, P., Turner, A., & Waksberg, J. *What is a survey?* Washington, DC: American Statistical Association, 1980.

Fienberg, S. E. The analysis of cross-classified categorical data (2nd ed.). Cambridge: MIT Press, 1980.

Fishbein, M., & Ajzen, I. *Belief, attitude, intention, and behavior.* Reading, MA: Addison-Wesley, 1975.

Funkhouser, G. R. The issues of the sixties: An exploratory study in the dynamics of public opinion. *Public Opinion Quarterly, 1973, 37,* 62-75.

Gallup Organization, Inc. Public opinion about nuclear power issues. *The Gallup Report, 1979, 3,* 8-9.

Graber, D. A. Problems in measuring audience effects. In G. F. Bishop, R. G. Meadow, & M. Jackson-Beeck (Eds.), *The presidential debates: Media, electoral, and policy perspectives.* New York: Praeger, 1978.

Groves, R. M., & Kahn, R. L. *Surveys by telephone: A national comparison with personal interviews.* New York: Academic Press, 1979.

Hakel, M. D. How often is often? *American Psychologist, 1969, 23,* 533-34.

Hyman, H. H. *Secondary analysis of sample surveys.* New York: John Wiley, 1972.

Hyman, H. H. Surveys in the study of political psychology. In J. N. Knutson (Ed.), *Handbook of political psychology.* San Francisco: Jossey-Bass, 1973.

Hyman, H. H., Wright, C. R., & Reed, J. S. *The enduring effects of education.* Chicago: University of Chicago Press, 1975.

Jackman, M. Education and prejudice or education and response set? *American Sociological Review, 1973, 38,* 327-339.

Kalton, G., Collins, M., & Brook, L. Experiments in wording opinion questions. *Applied Statistics, 1978, 38,* 327-329.

Kalton, G., Roberts, J., & Holt, D. The effects of offering a middle response option with opinion questions. *The Statistician*, 1980, *29*, 65-78.

Kahn, R. L., & Cannell, C. F. *The dynamics of interviewing*. New York: John Wiley, 1967.

Katz, E., & Feldman, J. J. The debates in the light of research: A survey of surveys. In S. Kraus (Ed.), *The great debates: Kennedy vs. Nixon, 1960*. Bloomington: Indiana University Press, 1962.

Kish, L. *Survey sampling*. New York: John Wiley, 1965.

Lachman, R., Lachman, J., & Butterfield, E. C. *Cognitive psychology and information processing*. Hillsdale, NJ: Lawrence Erlbaum, 1979.

Ladd, E. C., & Lipset, S. M. Anatomy of a decade. *Public Opinion*, 1980, *3*, 2-9.

Lazarsfeld, P. E. Controversy over detailed interviews—An offer for negotiation. *Public Opinion Quarterly*, 1944, *8*, 38-60.

McCombs, M. E. Setting the agenda for agenda-setting research: An assessment of the priority ideas and problems. In G. C. Wilhoit & H. de Bock (Eds.), *Mass communication review yearbook* (Vol. 2). Beverly Hills, CA: Sage, 1981.

McCombs, M. E., & Shaw, D. L. The agenda-setting function of the mass media. *Public Opinion Quarterly*, 1972, *36*, 176-187.

McLeod, J. M., Becker, L. B., & Byrnes, J. E. Another look at the agenda-setting function of the press. *Communication Research*, 1974, *2*, 137-165.

McLeod, J. M., Brown, J. P., Becker, L. B., & Ziemke, D. A. Decline and fall at the White House: A longitudinal analysis of communication effects. *Communication Research*, 1977, *4*, 3-22.

Miller, A. H., Goldenberg, E. N., & Erbring, L. Type-set politics: The impact of newspapers on public confidence. *American Political Science Review*, 1979, *73*, 67-84.

Miller, A. H., & Mackuen, M. Informing the electorate: A national study. In S. Kraus (Ed.), *The great debates: Carter vs. Ford 1976*. Bloomington: Indiana University Press, 1979.

Miller, W. E., Miller, A. H., & Schneider, E. J. *American national election studies data sourcebook, 1952-1978*. Cambridge: Harvard University Press, 1980.

Namboodiri, K. (Ed.). *Survey sampling and measurement*. New York: Academic Press, 1978.

Nie, N., with Anderson, K. Mass belief systems revisited: Political change and attitude structure. *Journal of Politics*, 1974, *36*, 540-591.

Nie, N., & Rabjohn, J. R. Revisiting mass belief systems revisited. *American Journal of Political Science*, 1979, *23*, 139-175.

Nie, N., Verba, S., & Petrocik, J. R. *The changing American voter*. Cambridge, MA: Harvard University Press, 1976.

Nisbett, R., & Ross, L. *Human inference: Strategies and shortcomings of social judgment*. Englewood Cliffs, NJ: Prentice-Hall, 1980.

Nunn, C. Z., Crockett, H. J., Jr., & Williams, J. A., Jr. *Tolerance for nonconformity*. San Francisco: Jossey-Bass, 1978.

Osgood, C. E. *The measurement of meaning*. Urbana: University of Illinois Press, 1957.

Osgood, C. E., May, W. H., & Miron, M. S. *Cross-cultural universals of affective meaning*. Urbana: University of Illinois Press, 1975.

Patterson, T. E. *The mass media election: How Americans choose their president*. New York: Praeger, 1980.

Patterson, T. E., & McClure, R. D. *The unseeing eye: The myth of television power in national elections*. New York: Putnam, 1976.

Payne, S. L. *The art of answering questions*. Princeton: Princeton University Press, 1951.

Perloff, R. M., & Brock, T. C. . . . and thinking makes it so: Cognitive responses to persuasion. In M. E. Roloff & G. R. Miller (Eds.), *Persuasion: New directions in theory and research*. Beverly Hills, CA: Sage, 1980.

Presser, S., & Schuman, H. The measurement of a middle position in attitude surveys. *Public Opinion Quarterly*, 1980, *44*, 70-85.

Reynolds, H. T. *The analysis of cross-classifications*. New York: Free Press, 1977.

Robinson, M. J. Public affairs television and the growth of political malaise: The case of "the selling of the Pentagon." *American Political Science Review*, 1976, *40*, 409-432.

Robinson, J. P. Interpersonal influence in election campaigns: Two step-flow hypotheses. *Public Opinion Quarterly*, 1976, *40*, 304-319.

Rosenberg, M. *The logic of survey analysis*. New York: Basic Books, 1968.

Rossi, P. H., & Wright, J. D. (Eds.). *Handbook of survey research*. New York: Academic Press, in press.

Rothschild, M. L. On the use of multiple methods and multiple situations in political communication research. In S. H. Chaffee (Ed.), *Political communication: Issues and strategies for research*. Beverly Hills, CA: Sage, 1975.

Salancik, G. R., & Conway, M. Attitude inferences from salient and relevant cognitive content about behavior. *Journal of Personality and Social Psychology*, 1975, *32*, 829-840.

Schuman, H. The random probe: A technique for evaluating the validity of closed questions. *American Sociological Review*, 1966, *31*, 218-222.

Schuman, H., & Hatchett, S. *Black racial attitudes: Trends and complexities*. Ann Arbor: Institute for Social Research, University of Michigan, 1974.

Schuman, H., & Presser, S. Question wording as an independent variable in survey analysis. *Sociological Methods and Research*, 1977, *6*, 151-170.

Schuman, H., & Presser, S. Attitude measurement and the gun control paradox. *Public Opinion Quarterly*, 1978, *41*, 427-438. (a)

Schuman, H., & Presser, S. The assessment of "no opinion" in attitude surveys. In K. F. Schuessler (Ed.), *Sociological methodology 1979*. San Francisco: Jossey-Bass, 1978. (b)

Schuman, H., & Presser, S. The open and closed questions. *American Sociological Review*, 1979, *44*, 692-712.

Schuman, H., & Presser, S. Public opinion and public ignorance: The fine line between attitudes and non-attitudes. *American Journal of Sociology*, 1980, *85*, 1214-1225.

Sears, D. O., & Chaffee, S. H. Uses and effects of the 1976 debates: An overview of empirical studies. In S. Kraus (Ed.), *The great debates: Carter vs. Ford, 1976*. Bloomington: Indiana University Press, 1979.

Shaw, D. L., & McCombs, M. E. (Eds.). *The emergence of American political issues: The agenda-setting function of the press*. St. Paul, MN: West Publishing, 1977.

Sheth, J. N. (Ed.). *Multivariate methods for market and survey research*. Chicago: American Marketing Association, 1977.

Sinaiko, H. W., & Broedling, L. A. (Eds.). *Perspectives on attitude assessment: Surveys and their alternatives*. Fort Worth, TX: Pendleton Publications, 1976.

Sinaiko, H. W., & Broedling, L. A. In search of house effects: A comparison of responses to various questions by different survey organizations. *Public Opinion Quarterly*, 1978, *42*, 443-463.

Snider, J., & Osgood, C. E. *The semantic differential: A sourcebook*. Chicago: AVC, 1969.

Sonquist, J. A., & Dunkelberg, W. C. *Survey and opinion research: Procedures for processing and analysis*. Englewood Cliffs, NJ: Prentice-Hall, 1977.

Sudman, S. *Applied sampling*. New York: Academic Press, 1976.

Sudman, S., & Bradburn, N. M. *Response effects in surveys*. Chicago: AVC, 1974.

Sullivan, J. L., Piereson, J., & Marcus, G. E. Ideological constraint in the mass public: A methodological critique and some new findings. *American Journal of Political Science*, 1978, *22*, 233-249.

Sullivan, J. L., Piereson, J., & Marcus, G. E. An alternative conceptualization of political tolerance: Illusory increases 1950s-1970s. *American Political Science Review*, 1979, *73*, 781-794. (a)

Sullivan, J. L., Piereson, J., Marcus, G. E., & Feldman, S. The more things change, the more they stay the same: The stability of mass belief systems. *American Journal of Political Science*, 1979, *23*, 176-186. (b)

Taylor, D. G., Sheatsley, P. B., & Greeley, A. M. Attitudes toward racial integration. *Scientific American*, 1978, *238*, 42-49.

Tipton, L. P., Haney, R. D., & Basehart, J. R. Media agenda-setting in city and state election campaigns. *Journalism Quarterly,* 1975, *52,* 15-22.

Turner, C. F., & Krauss, E. Fallible indicators of the subjective state of the nation. *American Psychologist,* 1978, *33,* 456-470.

Wyer, R. S., Jr., & Carlston, D. E. *Social cognition, inference and attribution.* Hillsdale, NJ: Lawrence Erlbaum, 1979.

Wyer, R. S., Jr., & Srull, T. K. Category accessibility: Some theoretical and empirical issues concerning the processing of social stimulus information. In E. T. Higgins, C. P. Herman, & M. P. Zanna (Eds.), *Social cognition: The Ontario symposium on personality and social psychology.* Hillsdale, NJ: Lawrence Erlbaum, in press.

Zucker, H. G. The variable nature of news media influence. In B. D. Ruben (Ed.), *Communication yearbook II.* New Brunswick, NJ: Transaction Books, 1978.

CHAPTER 22

Intensive Analysis

Steven R. Brown

JUST A FEW short years ago, the intensive study of single cases was referred to as one of those "dusty relics stashed away in the attic of human knowledge" (Brown, 1974, p. 1), and at the time there seemed to be little likelihood that the situation would change markedly. A brief bibliography which accompanied the paper noted above, for example, contained only a few references to intensive studies which had appeared from 1970 onward. Since that time, however, there has been a rush of activity in certain quarters—a second edition of Chassan's (1979) important work, Stephenson's (1974) seminal statement, the volumes by Hersen and Barlow (1976) and Kratochwill (1978), and Eckstein's (1975) summary chapter, plus numerous illustrative studies and special panels on the case approach at meetings of the International Society of Political Psychology (New York, 1978), the Midwest Political Science Association (Chicago, 1978), and perhaps elsewhere. It cannot be said that interest has as yet reached dangerous levels, but it does seem to be on the rise.

The term *intensive analysis* grew out of the personality-culture literature (Lasswell, 1938) and usually refers to a strategy of inquiry in which attention is focused on a single individual or small number of them over a relatively prolonged period, as epitomized by the depth interview of psychoanalysis. The large-sample opinion poll is paradigmatic of the *extensive* end of the continuum inasmuch as the contact between observer and observed is relatively brief and

Author's Note: Thanks are due to Tom Bacher, Raymond Brown, James Carlton, Peter Haas, Lisa Handley, David Kotting, Seo-Hang Lee, and Betty Yelverton, members of the graduate seminar in which the explorations reported here were undertaken; and special appreciation to Seo-Hang Lee for the opportunity to utilize results from the single case study for which he was primarily responsible.

the responses obtained are comparatively simple (often "yes" or "no" to a series of standardized questions).

Behavioral scientists have become well versed in the statistical procedures which have been developed and refined for summarizing and rendering precise the relationships among group and aggregate responses emanating from the extensive standpoint, and a limitation of intensive methods has often been said to be their inability to approximate similar standards of precision. Many of the problems associated with the quantification of performances at the individual level have been overcome, however, so to earlier efforts (for example, Payne & Jones, 1957) can now be added the more recent advances of Edgington (1975), Huber (1977), and Kratochwill and Brody (1978), among others. With respect to the design as opposed to the analysis of intensive studies, reference is increasingly made to multiple baseline, reversal, withdrawal, and other schemes of systematic inquiry as summarized, for example, by Kazdin (1978). Students interested in the systematic study of single cases therefore seem well on their way to regaining the kind of scientific acceptability they enjoyed before the outbreak of actuarial procedures. We have come a long way, indeed, since Meyer (1926, p. 271) remarked: "A description of one individual without reference to others may be a piece of literature, a biography or novel. But science? No."

Yet despite this praiseworthy refocusing on the individual, there are still reasons for doubting whether all is well. In the first place, most social scientists outside psychology—and, increasingly, psychologists as well—study phenomena in nonexperimental settings and are in the unenviable position of having to go to the data rather than wait for the data to come to them. Consequently, they are not in the position to exercise control over contingencies which permit the application of those intensive designs which are currently in favor.

But even more important is the issue of *subjectivity*; that is, the methodological position that the individual's own standpoint is of importance in understanding his behavior, and that only he can give us a noninferential version of what that standpoint is. Virtually all case studies perpetrated by contemporary N = 1 practitioners deal with manipulable effects which are objective about the person—reduction in objectively scorable symptoms, increases in the number of words spelled correctly, improvements in language facility, and the like. There are exceptions, of course: Morris (1979), for example, wishes to involve one's imaginative "future history" as a way of incorporating Kierkegaardian subjectivity; and Wolf (1978), after devoting a lifetime to the paradigm of objective psychology, now acknowledges the importance of measuring subjective matters so long as they do not implicate internal causal variables. However, the balance of effort currently favors the manipulation and counting of objective traits and characteristics, the existence and importance of which are taken as axiomatic.

The methodological principles and procedures outlined below wend their way into this picture via the dictionary distinction which is made between two meanings of *intensive*. The first, which is objective, refers to quantitative increases or decreases in degree or amount, as in the intensification of heat, light, color, emotion, and reinforcing consequences: To add more or to increase frequency is to intensify in a quantitative sense. But to intensify can also refer to vividness, which is qualitative in nature, as when an idea or concept is sharpened in such a way as to produce enrichment of appreciation or understanding (Brown, in press-a). The objective mode produces facts useful for prediction and control; the subjective mode also produces facts, but facts which include the standpoint of the self, hence leading to improved understandings about the person whose self is included. Science requires both, ultimately, but current single-case strategies are concerned almost exclusively with prediction. A strategy for the intensive analysis of single cases should also be at hand for those situations in which we require more vivid understandings.

AN EXEMPLIFICATION:
SOURCES OF POLITICAL CHARISMA

We could begin almost anywhere, really, and with virtually any subject matter, for subjectivity abounds in all places in which individuals are engaged in communication, whether that communicability is with themselves (as in daydreaming) or with others in the conversing, arguing, and bantering of everyday life. Charisma is selected as a focus of inquiry because of its intrinsic importance in contemporary affairs and because it deserves elucidation, since it is one of those catch-all terms which behavioral scientists and political pundits often call upon to provide an explanation of political events in order to avoid admitting they really don't have the foggiest notion what's going on. Wilson (1975) says that charisma and leadership have become somewhat disjoined over the years, and that at present *"charisma . . .* connotes appeal more than it connotes authority" (p. 1). We would like to be able to show, then, how the intensive study of single cases might help dissipate some of our foggy notions and improve our understanding of the nature of the appeal which some political and other public figures have for members of the public.

The concept of charisma was popularized by Max Weber (Eisenstadt, 1968), who delineated three factors of domination, two of which were external in nature: *Coercive power* (of sword and purse) referred to imposed domination of strong over weak, whereas *mutual interest* (for example, utilitarian associations) referred to self-imposed limitations for the purpose of cooperative gain. The third, *legitimacy,* is an internal constraint which refers to a belief in the leader's commands as rightful and moral, and to obedience as morally obligatory. Legitimacy, in turn, is of three kinds: Traditional, charismatic, and rational. Traditional authority demands submission and, according to Weber, evolved from religion, which in turn evolved from magic and, before that, animistic and preanimistic thinking. In Freudian terminology, it is a remnant of preoedipal psychology (McIntosh, 1970) and provides emotional support for the monarchy and church. Domination can also be experienced as legitimate because of its inherent rationality (postoedipal), as in a bureaucracy which operates according to an impersonal rule of law.

Charismatic authority lies somewhere between traditional and rational authority and refers to a situation in which followers believe the leader (toward whom they are compellingly drawn) to be divinely chosen or anoited, or at any rate as endowed with extraordinary powers. Charisma is therefore not a trait of the leader's personality, but an experience in the minds of the followers; hence, it expresses an interactional or transactional, if not a directly interpersonal, relationship. Charisma is also prophetic in nature and inherently threatening to the established order ("It is written . . . but I say unto you . . ."), and conse- quently lends itself to psychoanalytic interpretation as an evolutionary advance to the oedipal stage of psychosocial development (see, for example, Downton, 1973, pp. 221-230; Hummel, 1975; Schiffer, 1973), although more primitive preoedipal features associated with borderline and narcissistic personality organi- zation are often present as well (see Kernberg, 1979; Volkan, 1980). As a result, oedipal phenomena such as conscience, guilt, and "the return of the repressed" are often in abundance, as are such defenses as projection and identification which are associated with this stage.

These theoretical conjectures are highly speculative, of course, as much of psychoanalytic theory still is; nevertheless, they provide an adequate staging area for launching an intensive study and indicate where to look for promising leads. Our intent, therefore, is not in any sense to *prove* the psychodynamic theory of political charisma, but to take it along with us (so to speak) like a hunting dog, to point out interesting directions that might otherwise pass unnoticed.

Symbols of Identification

An intensive analysis can begin with virtually any person, in principle, for we are all representatives of the social order by virtue, not of genetic inheritance, but of our participation in it (Frazier, 1978, p. 132). We stand to sharpen our understanding, however, to the extent that we can specify the location in social space of those representative personalities we select for more detailed inspection. In short, it is often fruitful to discern the major contours and segments of an audience before selecting a smaller number of persons as subjects.

In the immediate case, a list was comprised of several hundred names of persons living or dead who could be considered to be charismatic in one way or another, either positively or negatively, by virtue of commanding or having commanded a following. The population of names generated was then divided as best as possible into Lasswell's eight value categories (Lasswell & Kaplan,

1950)—for example, enlightenment (Albert Einstein, Walter Cronkite), skill (Donna Summer, Mikhail Baryshnikov), wealth (Howard Hughes, Baron Philippe de Rothschild), well-being (Dr. Jonas Salk, General Douglas McArthur), affection (Rod McKuen, Mother Theresa), power (Richard Nixon Jimmy Carter), respect (Alex Haley, Gloria Steinem), and rectitude (Billy Graham, Pope John Paul II). As usual, questions could be raised concerning whether this or that figure belongs in this or that category (Is Ayatollah Khomeini, for example, a religious figure [rectitude] or a political one [power]?), but the main purpose of this exercise was to effect a primitive categorization as a basis for dimensional sampling.

Ultimately, a sample of 56 names was selected, with efforts being made to include (although not in equal measure) representatives from all the value sectors. The names were then typed, one to a card, and presented to a sample of persons who were instructed to provide a Q sort by distributing the names from "those persons who I find most appealing and toward whom I feel drawn" down to "those I find most unappealing, or am most repulsed by." The scoring continuum ranged from +5 to −5 in typical Q-technique fashion, as has been outlined in greater detail elsewhere (Brown, 1980; Stephenson, 1953). Only 36 persons participated in this particular study, but similar studies using other sets of names of public figures and other subjects have been carried out in recent years and have produced virtually identical results.

The 36 Q sorts were intercorrelated, providing a 36 x 36 correlation matrix which was factor analyzed. Two significant factors were indicated, and these are shown graphically in Figure 22.1, along with a table of representative loadings (for example, Q sort no. 1 is saturated 0.77 on factor I, and 0.02 on II). In this instance, the unrotated loadings lend themselves to the simplest interpretation, and it is on the basis of the unrotated loadings that estimations were made of the factor scores associated with each of the 56 names of public figures.

As can be gathered from Figure 22.1, factor I expresses a tendency among all respondents to rank-order the 56 names in the same general way—that is, all 36 subjects have a significant positive loading on factor I. Consequently, we will refer to it as the *consensus* factor. Factor II, on the other hand, represents sociopolitical *conflict* insofar as some subjects (such as nos. 24 and 28) are at one end of the factor, whereas others (nos. 13 and 18, for example) are at the other end. Subject 1 is therefore prototypical of what is consensual in her culture by virtue of the fact that the symbols of identification with which she is absorbed are shared with all others on factor I: She has no significant loading on II. Subjects 13 and 24 also participate in this consensus, but unlike subject 1 they are not totally absorbed by it: In addition to the identifications they have in common, 13 and 24 also identify and counteridentify with certain public figures which put them into conflict with one another.

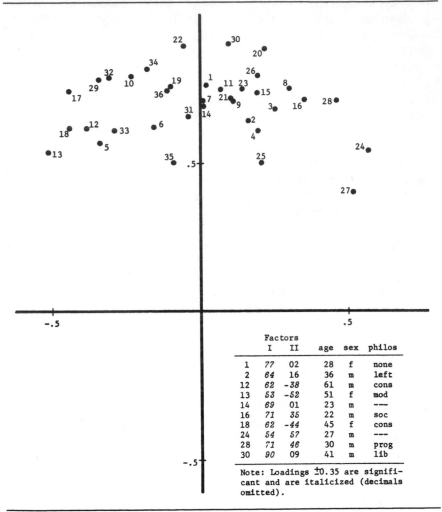

Figure 22.1: Patterns of Identification with Public Figures, Represented in Two-Factor Space

We get a glimpse of the social consensus by examining the names of those public figures located (in terms of their factor scores) at the positive and negative poles of factor I:

Factor I, score +5 +4: Albert Einstein, Jesus Christ, Martin Luther King, Jr., Mother Theresa, Charles Darwin, John F. Kennedy, Mahatma Gandhi

Factor I, score −5 −4: Idi Amin, Adolf Hitler, The Reverend Jim Jones, Richard Nixon, Charles Manson, Joseph McCarthy, Ayatollah Khomeini

Those with high positive scores in factor I are generally understood as having made positive contributions to humanity, whereas those assigned high negative scores are (in America at least) widely regarded as villains. It is noteworthy that the positive pole of the factor is dominated by persons who are dead, four of the seven having died by violent means. The importance of martyrdom and collective guilt in the establishment of consensus vis-à-vis social and political heroes and heroines is thereby suggested.

Factor II is orthogonal to the consensus of factor I and represents the major polarity which divides the citizenry of any political society—namely, the ideology utopia dimension (Lasswell & Kaplan, 1950), the former comprised of persons viewed as aligned with the status quo, and the latter as aligned with alternatives to the established order. Public figures representing the extremes of this factor are as follows:

Factor II, +5 +4 (utopia): Mao Tse-tung, Yasser Arafat, Karl Marx, Ayatollah Khomeini, Marquis de Sade, Mahatma Gandhi, Fidel Castro

Factor II, -5 -4 (ideology): General Douglas McArthur, Billy Graham, Gerald Ford, Ronald Reagan, Richard Nixon, Jesus Christ, General George Patton

Hence, persons in the upper righthand quadrant of Figure 22.1 (such as nos. 24 and 28) not only give high scores to consensus figures such as Einstein and Christ, but also tend to favor such anti-Establishment figures as Mao and Marx. By the same token, persons in the upper lefthand quadrant (for example, nos. 13 and 18) favor both consensual figures and figures who have come to symbolize the Establishment, such as Nixon and Ford. Respondents such as no. 1, however, represent relatively pure expressions of the consensus, with little of the conflict (ideological or utopian) apparent in their identifications with public figures.

Szymanski (1977) distinguishes between *celebrities* (public figures who are liked) from *heroes* (public figures who are respected), the former being "for the moment" and appealing to our pleasure principle and the latter being "for all time" and appealing to our perfection principle (superego, ego ideal). Factors I and II, including both poles of the latter, give prominence to heroes rather than celebrities, although the heroes of factor II (like Cherubim to Seraphim) are of a lesser order compared to those of I. Additionally, the ideology-utopia polarity of factor II is confounded by an inner versus outer dimension: Except for Christ, the figures at the ideology pole of factor II are all Americans, whereas the utopian figures are all non-Americans.

It almost goes without saying that the media are of considerable importance in bringing specific symbols to the collective focus of attention. Charles Darwin, for example, was the subject of biographical treatment aired on the Public Broadcasting System near the time of this study (early 1980), and Mother

Theresa had just received a Nobel Prize, which helps account for their high positive scores on the consensus factor. Similarly, American diplomatic personnel were being held hostage in Iran, which explains Khomeini's high negative score. In the same way, the telecasting in late 1975 of *Franklin and Eleanor* served to boost both Roosevelts to scores of +4 on the consensual factor which emerged in a similar study completed in early 1976; at the same time, presidential candidate Jimmy Carter had not yet won the New Hampshire primary, and consequently his score of 0 on all three 1976 factors was an accurate reflection of the public's lack of feeling about him.[1]

Ellens (1979) suggests that life is increasingly an adjunct of communication processes and that the "dominance of culture by communication is an inescapable and pervasive reality of our time" (p. 192). It would be overstating the case, however, to say that factors I and II are merely creatures of the media. Milton's *Paradise Lost* (1674) is a tribute to the same theme of Saints-and-Sinners of which factor I is a modern-day continuation (complete with some of the same *dramatis personae*). The media may to a greater or lesser extent influence the *content* of these categories for each generation or era, and they undoubtedly perform the task of reinforcement, but the factors themselves are likely historical inheritances that have come to us and will be transmitted in roughly the same structural form as shown in Figure 22.1. Nor is appeal to archetypes completely satisfying if by that term a biological metaphor is implied.

More acceptable is Boulding's (1979) concept of deep structure: a "repeatedly experienced social patterning, which was given a few initial 'kicks' in a certain direction in the early days of human settlement and continued in that direction through social drift—and is now perceived as in some way basic to the structuring of human relationships" (p. 70). This explanation at least has the virtue of implicating direct experience and hence paves the way for more detailed studies of individual lives.

Ingredients of Charisma

Factors I and II above provide a degree of insight into the patterns of identification which are involved structurally in the appeal public figures have for segments of the mass public. The value of an intensive analysis is that it permits deeper probes into a phenomenon, but a set of guidelines is required to point the way and to indicate what we should be looking for. Although various schemes exist, Schiffer (1973, chap. 2) provides a convenient list of eight "ingredients of charisma" which can serve as a starting point.

1. Foreignness. According to the old adage, familiarity breeds contempt; its corollary, according to Schiffer, is that something foreign (yet familiar) breeds charisma. Hence, we are mysteriously drawn, like moth to flame, to something or someone who is out of the ordinary—the exceptionally tall or short (Napoleon), the espouser of novel ideas, and the speaker who sounds somewhat unusual (the Kennedys, Jimmy Carter, Henry Kissinger) all benefit from their slight differences. Subjects located at the positive pole of factor II appear especially vulnerable to the appeal of foreignness inasmuch as all +5 and +4 scores were assigned to non-Americans. This first ingredient relates to some degree to the idea of "distance from me." As a surrogate for this ingredient, a number of subjects from the first study (see Table 22.1) were instructed to rank-order the same 56 names of public figures from "most like me" (+5) to "most unlike me" (-5).

2. Imperfection. According to Schiffer, "A leader with charisma is of necessity perceived as someone, not only to a degree foreign, but to a degree *subtly* defective." The defect cannot be too great—more like Eisenhower's weak heart, John Kennedy's bad back, or Carter's faintness during a running marathon than George Wallace's more thorough incapacity—for otherwise the gap is too wide for our identifications to bridge: It must stimulate our empathy, not our disgust. The patch-covered eye of Moshe Dyan, the significant but not overwhelming mental distress of Senator Eagleton, the neuroses of the characters in the television soap operas (such as *Dallas*)—all these minor stigmata enhance the fantasy that "the leader or central figure needs me" and render possible the followers' projections of their selves into the drama: What the leader is or is doing "is something attainable by all of us" (Schiffer, 1973, p. 30), at least potentially so. The key idea is *attainability*. In an effort to draw near to this complicated feeling, which is related to the first ingredient, subjects were instructed to provide a second Q sort under the following condition: Rank-order the 56 names from "those whose achievements could possibly have been my own" (+5) to "those whose achievements could not have been my own, i.e., whose achievements were (or are) beyond my capability" (-5).

3. Calling. The condition of performance representing this ingredient involved Q sorting the 56 names from "those who seem to be responding to a higher calling, i.e., who appear to have a special 'rendezvous with destiny' " (+5) to "those who appear to have no special calling" (-5). The Gandhis, Hitlers, Mother Theresas, and even Ralph Naders of the world seem not to be motivated by material gain but by some higher calling, and their actions remind us of the discrepancy between our own ideals and how we actually behave. By allying ourselves with such figures, we give ourselves the opportunity to recover our own sense of mission, our own conscience.

4. Fighting Stance. Rank-order the names from "those who take (or have taken) a heroic stand against other persons, groups, or overwhelming odds" (+5) to "those who have not taken a heroic stand" (-5). This ingredient, which, along with the sixth, Schiffer regards as the most important, gives due recognition to the polarized aggression of preoedipal sibling rivalry and of the oedipal rivalry between child and parent which have been repressed (according to psycho-analytic theory) and which are restimulated in the charismatic relationship. Each of us struggled against overwhelming odds during childhood, and each gave in reluctantly (or so the story goes) and identified with the aggressor; we harbor resentment, however, and under some conditions may welcome the opportunity for another round.

5. Social Station. Our first experience with aristocracy also occurs in child-hood, during which time we exaggerate the importance and perfection of our parents and take pleasure in being noticed and accepted by them. Despite the fact that we later develop a more realistic attitude vis-à-vis parents, the need for hierarchy appears to persist even within the most avowedly egalitarian societies and groups, protestations to the contrary notwithstanding—hence the instruction to rank the 56 names from "those for whom society at large has the highest respect" (+5) to "those who society disrespects" (-5).

6. Sexuality. According to Schiffer (1973), "Man's universal curiosities and explorations with the earliest sexual activities of his parents is the setting that first inspires the mystique which the adult seeks desperately to recapture as a familiar yet mysterious complex lurking within the projected image of his 'adopted' charismatic object" (p. 46). To direct attention toward this ingredient, subjects were instructed to Q sort the 56 names from "those who are the most sensual in a nontrivial sense, i.e., who have a mystique about them" (+5) to "those who are the most 'unsensual,' not just lacking in sensuality, but its very opposite" (-5).

7. Hoax. This ingredient has proved to be the one most difficult for subjects, at least on a conscious level, since it implies a certain acceptance of the idea that one's heroes and heroines are not really totally serious about what they are doing. The appeal of hoax is presumably related to our own theatrics as projected onto the charismatic figure—as when the morally indignant support a crusade against pornography while at the same time secretly enjoying all the naughtiness that their puritanical archaeology has unearthed. The closest we dare come, therefore, is to request that the Q sort be performed in light of "those who temper their behavior with humor, who do not take themselves or their roles completely seriously" (+5) to "those who are completely serious about what they are doing" (-5).

8. Lifestyle. "Those who lead (or have led) innovative lifestyles, full of newness and excitement" (+5) to "those whose lifestyles seem stale, boring, and uninter-esting" (-5). This condition of experimentation is self-evident, and relates to the continuing desire to recapture the delights of childhood and to escape boredom. The New Frontier, a society governed by the principle "to each according to need," and the opportunity to be "born again" are therefore appealing due to the fresh behavioral routines they suggest, and leaders who appear to act on these fantasies gain in charismatic stature by virtue of the opportunities they provide the rest of us for vicarious indulgences of one kind or another.

Three additional conditions of performance were included to supplement Schiffer's eight ingredients:

9. Impulse. "Those who act impulsively, on the spur of the moment, on the basis of their feelings" (+5) to "those who are constrained, who do not act on impulse" (-5).

10. Reason. "Those who are most realistic, who act on the basis of reason and rationality" (+5) to "those who act unrealistically, irrationally" (-5).

11. Morality. "Those who are moral, i.e., whose behavior is rooted in morality" (+5) to "those who are immoral, i.e., whose behavior runs counter to moral principles" (-5).

These latter three Q sorts were designed to focus more explicitly on the tripartite division of the personality (Lasswell, 1932)—id (impulse), ego (reason), and superego (morality). Finally, each subject's original Q sort (*Appeal*) was added as the twelfth condition, yielding a 12 x 12 correlation matrix for each of the individuals selected for more intensive investigation. The factor matrices which resulted are shown in Table 22.1.

Before turning to the data, it bears repeating that our business is not to document the existence or nonexistence of oedipal conflicts, archetypes, or other psychodynamic mechanisms as such, but to examine behavior and, where it appears to be shy or recalcitrant, provide means whereby it can be coaxed into the open for closer inspection.[2] The 12 conditions of instruction above were designed to be inducements of this kind—that is, were designed to reveal at least some of the principles of subjective categorization utilized by individuals chosen for intensive scrutiny. In this connection, Schiffer's ingredients of charisma (supplemented by Lasswell's triple-appeal formulation) lay claim to a certain "representativeness" in a methodological sense (Baas & Brown, 1973), and their utilization as behavioral probes facilitates the expectation that the reactions which they produce will bring into prominence as *operant factors* the outlines of already-existing schemata. Consequently, it is not even assumed that individuals under investigation will necessarily understand the instructions in the same way: Subject A, for example, may interpret the *hoax* condition as something akin to "persons with a sense of humor," whereas B might think more in terms of shysters who try to pull the wool over your eyes." It might be said that such an individualistic strategy virtually precludes predictability, but theoretical physics at the level of quanta is also indeterminant, and so science is not thereby precluded.

The eight individuals represented in Table 22.1 (nos. 2, 7, 9, 13, 16, 21, 22, and 28) are the same as those with matching numbers in Figure 22.1—hence, 16

TABLE 22.1 Operant Factor Structures for Selected Single Cases

| | Subjects From Figure 22.1 | | | | | | | | | | | | | | | | | |
| | 2 | | 7 | | 9 | | 13 | | 16 | | | 21 | | 22 | | 28 | | |
	A	B	C	D	E	F	G	H	I	J	K	L	M	N	O	P	Q	R
1 foreignness	X		X		X		X		(66)	27	14	X		X		X		
2 imperfection	X	-X	X	-X	X			X	(55)	-10	-28	X			X	-X	X	
3 calling		X		X		X		-X	-01	(82)	20		X	X			X	
4 fighting stance		X		X		X	X		15	(82)	09		X	X	-X	X	X	
5 social station	X		X		X		X		16	06	(-55)	X		X				-X
6 sexuality	X		X			X	X	X	(62)	06	31		X	X	X	X		
7 hoax	X	-X	X	-X		-X		X	(72)	-23	-08			X	X	X	-X	
8 lifestyle	X	X	X	X		X	X		21	-01	(77)	X	X	X	X		X	
9 impulse	X	X	X	X	-X	-X		X	-13	00	(94)	-X			X			X
10 reason	X		X		X		X		00	-02	(-94)	X		X		X		
11 morality	X		X		X		X		(45)	(40)	(-44)	X		X		X		
12 appeal	X		X		X		X		(71)	(35)	-29	X		X		X		

X and ( ) = significant loadings; all others insignificant (decimals omitted).

and 28 tend significantly toward the utopian pole of factor II (which favored figures inimical to the American status quo), whereas no. 13 is inclined to a significant degree toward the ideological pole (and is consequently in identification with pro-Establishment figures); the other five subjects are clustered more closely around the consensus factor. These eight were chosen to a large extent on the basis of their accessibility and willingness to participate in more depth, although efforts were also made to select subjects "regarded as more instructive for theory-building than others" (Eckstein, 1975, p. 106)—that is, subjects who were spatially dispersed in terms of Figure 22.1 as a function of the diversity of their patterns of identification. In accord with the principle of specificity (Kantor, 1978), each subject's 12 x 12 correlation matrix was separately factor analyzed, and examination of Table 22.1 indicates that most produced two factors; subjects 16 and 28, who were farthest out on the utopian factor, produced three factors each, suggesting more complex identificatory systems.

The most readily discernible commonality involves instructional conditions 1, 10, 11, and 12: In virtually every instance, the *appeal* ingredient ("persons toward whom I feel drawn") is on the same factor with *foreignness* ("those most like me"), *reason* ("those who are rational"), and *morality* ("those who are moral"). This might be referred to as the *autocentric principle*, the tendency "to confound outer stimuli with the reactions that they evoked in the interior self," and to create a psychosocial blend in which "there is relatively little separation of the personal from the social, of the objective from the subjective" (Gutmann, 1973, p. 573)—a kind of narcissism in which public figures who are judged appealing are also judged to be rational and moral—and, incidentally, like the self. It is to be noted in addition that *social station* ("those for whom society at large has the highest respect") is also on the *appeal* factor for all but utopian subjects 16 and 28, who might have been expected to disengage their identification from widely respected social and political figures.

The factor matrix for subject 16 is complete with factor loadings for more detailed inspection. As can be seen, factor I is defined by self-identifications (*foreignness*, "most like me," loading 0.66) as well as by *appeal*, although the latter is mixed (has a significant loading on factor J as well). Public figures with the highest factor scores on factor I include Sigmund Freud, Indira Gandhi, activist Jane Fonda, and comedian Steve Martin—all of whom this subject characterizes as brilliant and open-minded—as well as Mahatma Gandhi, former Connecticut Governor Ella Grasso, and scientist Carl Sagan. (The negative pole of the factor is populated by such figures as Idi Amin, Joseph McCarthy, Richard Nixon, Adolf Hitler, and Generals McArthur, Patton, and De Gaulle.) It is noteworthy that those public figures at the top of the factor are perceived as having a "mystique" about them (*sexuality*) and a sense of humor (*hoax*); the Amins and Nixons, by way of contrast, are austere and unappealing.

Subject 16's self (*foreignness*) is not significantly associated with factor J, but the factor still represents a dimension which is appealing to him (*appeal* loading = 0.35), although in lesser amount than factor I. Factor J is also the recipient of a segment of this subject's multiplex conception of morality, which is significantly associated with all three factors. Figures at the positive pole of factor J include Christ, Mao, Castro, Mother Theresa, Ayatollah Khomeini, Hitler, and Mahatma Gandhi, and so we see that it is this aspect of appeal (the factor J portion) which accounts most for this subject's association with the positive pole of factor II in the first study (see Figure 22.1). And, as Table 22.1 indicates, this segment of appeal is dominated by conditions of response to a higher *calling* and the aggressiveness of a *fighting stance*.

William James (1890, p. 291) distinguishes between "what a man calls *me* and what he simply calls *mine*," and with respect to subject 16, it can be said that factor I (and to a lesser extent J) is *him* whereas K is merely *his*—that is, K represents certain images which he has but which are not manifestly connected to his self. (Specifically, *foreignness, imperfection,* and *appeal* are not significant on factor K.) K is of great interest, nonetheless, inasmuch as it represents a sharp conflict between impulsiveness and reason—psychoanalytically speaking, between id and ego—with *impulse* being joined by innovative *lifestyle,* and *reason* being joined by *social station* and yet another manifestation of *morality.* Representing the impulsive pole of this dichotomy are Charles Manson, Idi Amin, Yasser Arafat, singer Donna Summer, actor Marlon Brando, the Reverend Jim Jones, and Fidel Castro. At the other end, representing rationality and social respect, are Harry Truman, Justice William O. Douglas, General George Patton, Margaret Thatcher, Walter Cronkite, Mahatma Gandhi, and millionaire J. Paul Getty.

Table 22.2 displays the names and factor scores associated with public figures who have varying degrees of association with this subject's three factors. With respect to factor I, Freud, Indira Gandhi, and Joseph McCarthy might serve best as "political Rorschachs" were we to invite this subject into a conversation designed to clarify the nature of factor I; Manson and Douglas would serve the same function for factor K. Christ or Mao might have been the best selections for factor J, with Ford representing the negative pole; however, Marx was chosen, despite his comparatively low score, on the basis of comments the subject made during interviews with him. The general strategy, as the factor scores indicate, was to select public figures who were highly associated (positively and negatively) with one factor but not the other two. Mahatma Gandhi would not have been appropriate according to this criterion, since he is highly representative of all three of this subject's dimensions—I, J, and K-negative; Fidel Castro would have been an ill-advised choice for similar reasons. Phyllis Schlafley, opponent of the Equal Rights Amendment, received a score of zero on all the factors indicating her overall lack of importance to subject 16 for all the

TABLE 22.2   Factor Scores Associated with Public Figures (Subject 16)

| | Factor Scores | | |
| | Self-Appeal | Aggressive Appeal | Impulse vs. Rationality |
Public Figures	Factor I	Factor J	Factor K
Sigmund Freud	(+5)	+2	+1
Indira Gandhi	(+5)	0	0
Joseph McCarthy	(-5)	-2	+1
Karl Marx	0	(+2)	0
Charles Manson	-2	+2	(+5)
William O. Douglas	-1	0	(-5)
Jesus Christ	+1	+5	+1
Mao Tse-tung	-1	+5	-2
Gerald Ford	0	-5	-1
Mahatma Gandhi	+4	+4	-4
Fidel Castro	+3	+5	+4
Phyllis Schlafley	0	0	0

(   ) = distinguishing factor scores for public figures selected for further examination.

conditions examined here; she, too, would be of little interest unless we wished to examine how the subject responded to a stimulus object of low saliency, in which case she would be the best choice.

The Fertile Soil of Political Imagery

In previous studies using this same general approach to charisma, subjects were asked why they found certain public figures appealing and others unappealing, in response to which a large number of attributed characteristics were advanced. Of Richard Nixon, for example, one respondent said: "He seems to feel threatened, as if expecting to be taken advantage of." Of Jane Fonda, another respondent said: "She's spunky. She really stands up for what she believes in." Attributed characteristics such as these are the ingredients of images.

As is conventional in Q-technique studies, this verbal outpouring of attributions, called a concourse (Stephenson, 1978), was provided with structure—in this instance, in terms of Erikson's (1980) theory of psychosocial development. At the first (or oral) stage, for example, a conflict is said to exist between trust and mistrust; hence statements theoretically representing these alternatives were selected, such as "refreshingly honest and open" (trust) and "feels threatened as if expecting to be taken advantage of" (mistrust). At stage two (anal), the conflict is said to be between autonomy and shame: "spunky . . . stands up for what she believes in" (autonomy) and "lacks pride and self-assurance" (shame, doubt). And so forth down to the final stage (maturity) which pits integrity against despair: "shows great wisdom and humanity" (integrity) and "doesn't seem to care . . . completely lack-luster" (despair).

A Q sample of N = 44 items covering all eight stages was ultimately composed for use by subject 16 and the other subjects to provide Q-sort images of significant persons in their primary and secondary environments. Of central importance, of course, is any evidence which might arise indicating family-based sources of vulnerability to charismatic appeals from extrafamilial figures in the secondary world of politics. Schiffer (1973, chap. 3) described in detail the "fertile soil" of the psyche, tilled largely within the confines of the family, from which springs both the need for and mechanisms of charismatic response. Among the virtues of an intensive analysis is that it facilitates systematic inquiries into complicated domains such as this.

For the sake of continuity, we retain focus on subject 16. Richard, as he will be called, is a 22-year-old graduate student in clinical psychology, which helps explain his admiration for Freud (see Table 22.2). He was the center of domestic conflict almost from the start, since both parents insisted that he be brought up in their respective religions (Roman Catholic and Greek Orthodox). His parents were divorced when he was ten; he remained with his mother and thereafter attended Greek Orthodox services only. Richard was an above-average student academically, although he was often a disciplinary problem and at one point sported police records in three separate towns. Drug abuse became a problem through his freshman year in high school. His stepfather (from age 12 onwards) was instrumental in straightening him out and providing guidance thereafter.

Richard's relationship with his real father was always strained but became even more so during his liberal college years, when Richard began flirting with communism and discovered that his businessman-father was "a capitalist and a racist." The two of them had frequent and heated arguments. By way of contrast, Richard feels gratitude and respect for his stepfather as well as an uncle who is "conservative but open-minded." It is important to note that Richard has a history of opposing domestic sources of authority (father) and locating alternatives outside the immediate family (uncle and, ultimately, stepfather).

This thumb-nail sketch naturally excludes countless details of importance to Richard's career-line, but sufficient context has been provided to permit consideration of Table 22.3, which resulted from the factor analysis of the 12 Q-sort images Richard provided using the Erikson Q sample described above. Several prominent features immediately show themselves with unusual clarity. The first is the strong similarity between Richard's family dynamics (conditions 1 to 6) and the structure of his perceptions of the external political world (conditions 7 to 12), much as Lasswell (1930) described the situation in his celebrated

TABLE 22.3   Operant Structure of Richard's Imagery

Conditions of Instruction	Factor Loadings		
	X	Y	Z
PRIMARY			
1 self	(80)	-28	29
2 ideal self	(77)	-32	(45)
3 mother	(96)	15	12
4 father	-09	(97)	-18
5 stepfather	19	-13	(95)
6 uncle	18	-08	(94)
SECONDARY			
7 Indira Gandhi	(97)	-10	11
8 Charles Manson	(-97)	10	-13
9 Joseph McCarthy	-13	(97)	-16
10 Sigmund Freud	15	02	(80)
11 William O. Douglas	23	-19	(86)
12 Karl Marx	09	-23	(92)

( ) = significant loadings (decimals omitted).

developmental formula for political man. A second striking feature, related to the above, is the extent to which Richard stands out as mother-identified (self and mother on factor X) rather than father-identified (Little, 1973). The nurturant character of factor X, which is extended projectively to include Indira Gandhi, is clearly seen in the factor scores associated with the following statements (scores to the right for factors X, Y, and Z, respectively):

Has sympathetic concern and understanding, willing to listen.	5	-1	0
Warm and supportive.	5	1	0

However, an assertive layer appears to lie just beneath this tender exterior:

Gusty and persistent, goes after what he/she believes in.	4	1	2
Outspoken and domineering.	3	0	-4
Spunky . . . stands up for what he/she believes in.	3	0	1

Factor Y represents Richard's image of his father, with whom relations are greatly strained, and the picture that is painted is of a weak character structure covered with a rather thin layer of bravado (scores to the right for factors X, Y, and Z, respectively):

	X	Y	Z
Feels threatened, as if expecting to be taken advantage of.	−1	5	3
Unable to form a close relationship.	−5	5	3
Willing to discredit and destroy to hide his own inadequacies.	−3	5	−5
Afraid of appearing ineffectual and impotent.	−2	4	−2
Tries too hard to impress.	0	4	−1
Seems afraid he will fail.	0	4	−1

Senator Joseph McCarthy is in receipt of this same image and is apparently at the receiving end of what Winnicott (1965, p. 183) refers to as a "cul-de-sac communication"—that is, McCarthy, like a celestial black hole or a piece of abstract art, is communicatee-in-perpetuity of Richard's projections given the ambiguity of reference point and the absence of reciprocal feedback mechanisms which might serve as correctives.

Factor Z is an idealization, of Richard's self (in part) and of his stepfather and uncle. Like Y, factor Z is also masculine and may represent a search outside the family for an object (namely, the idealized father) found missing inside the family. The factor scores reveal something akin to the idealized father of childhood—remote and somewhat aloof, but stable and wise:

	X	Y	Z
Shows great wisdom and humanity.	0	−4	5
More disciplined than friendly.	−1	−3	5
Guided more by inner standards.	0	−3	4
Behaves cautiously as if every move were planned.	−2	−1	4
Withstands pressure calmly and with assurance.	2	3	4

As is obvious from Table 22.3, heroes Freud, Douglas, and Marx bask in the aura of idealization experienced initially in the more proximal interpersonal relations of the family.

As a final matter, attention is drawn to the fact that Richard's factor loadings are exceptionally high—90 percent of total variance is accounted for by factors X, Y, and Z—and that the factor matrix is in a most rigid simple structure—each

Q sort (save for no. 2) is highly defined by one factor and one factor only. This suggests a rigidly compartmentalized inner world along with hypervigilance and exaggerated concern with boundaries—that is, with making certain that internal objects of one class do not come within proximity of images of another.[3]

However, the more important matter is to ascend from the depths of this intensively analyzed case and try to indicate how Richard's experiences and characteristic ways of dealing with them have condensed into patterns that locate him in his particular position displayed in Figure 22.1. In the main, his identifications are consensual, which requires little explanation, but he is also partly in sympathy with those utopian (and almost totally non-American) figures which populate the positive pole of factor II. A summary of the main features of Richard's life history is etched in the three factors of Table 22.3 and indicates that well before he was *au fait* with Joseph McCarthy and Justice Douglas he had already experienced frustration in dealing with established authority in the home and had sought alternative sources outside the family. By analogy, the Marxs, Maos, Khomeinis, and Castros of factor II are extrasocietal alternatives who Richard calls upon to perform a "charismatic rescue operation" (Schiffer, 1973, pp. 81-82) to save him, presumably, from the uncanny feelings of *déja vu* stimulated by the Fords, Nixons, Reagans, Billy Grahams, and other guardians of the status quo. One might tentatively conclude that Richard not only learned his politics *in* the family, but that his *Weltanschauung* is a politics *of* the family (Laing, 1969).

CONCLUDING REMARKS

Persons thoroughly conversant with the issues are in general agreement that the doctrines of large and small numbers cannot be profitably regarded as in conflict with one another, at least not in any superficial, technological sense. (On the other hand, the observations which they produce, and the theories which those observations necessitate, often are in conflict.) The intensive study of single cases is not a rival data-gathering strategy destined to replace the social survey, but neither is it a nonrigorous alternative to the study of behavior which some social scientists only reluctantly accept because they cannot afford to survey a larger number of respondents. Something rather more profound is involved.

The terms *intensive* and *extensive* designate observational standpoints relative to the same political universe, and can therefore be likened to the relationship between quantum theory and classical mechanics. The latter, Cyril Burt (1958) once said, is concerned with "man-sized phenomena, i.e., with objects whose magnitudes and velocities are within range of our own sensory processes" (p. 79), and from this standpoint a rigorous determinism can be maintained. The velocities involved at both the microphysical and the galactic levels, however, are not detectable by normal sensory processes, and force us into conceptual compromises—for example, into accepting indeterminacy and uncertainty at the level of quanta. Yet no one doubts the scientific credentials of either Newton or Heisenberg.

A similar situation exists in the social sciences. At the aggregate level, a kind of Newtonian determinism is sought through the use of such devices as analysis of variance and stepwise multiple regression, and at that level of observation a certain predictability can be achieved. One can never predict the behavior of individual cases, however, and the official attitude toward them is captured in the rudeness of the term "error," by which those who fail to land on the regression line are known. (The more extreme instances are commonly referred to as "deviant.") But even single cases (like Richard's above) can be shown to be lawful, even though the precise way in which they are lawful cannot be specified ahead of time, the nature and number of operant factors which each case will produce being as uncertain as the number of quarks which will emanate from a bombarded atom.

As to the operant factors themselves, their importance for the systematic study of single cases cannot be overestimated. Stephenson (1980, p. 101) likens them to X-ray plates which reveal the vectors of lived experience as well as the joints where behaviors of one class end and others begin. Richard's factors, in both Tables 22.1 and 22.3, are therefore not categories of the transcendent kind (liberal-conservative, alienated-affiliative, and so on) to which social science has grown accustomed; rather, they are inextricably tied to the experiential specifics of Richard's career line. They are deep structures of *his* operant subjectivity which have emerged from *his* behavior, and have consequently earned their status as measures of that behavior. A more ruthless rigor would be difficult to find.

A half-century ago, Harold Lasswell (1930) characterized his *Psychopathology and Politics* as "in harmony with a trend which has been growing in strength in the social sciences . . . [namely] the intensive study of the individual's account of himself" (p. 9). At the time, Lasswell was armed with the conceptual framework of Freudian psychology and with the technique of free association, the results from which provided him with the basis for shrewd guesses. Lasswell was therefore in a position a bit like Copernicus's, with a revolutionary new vision to advance. Galileo's telescope bolstered the Copernican view enormously, however, and the advent of operant factors promises the same for Lasswell's by rendering directly demonstrable what before rested on inference.

Intensive analysis in modern political studies had its start in large measure with Lasswell, who foresaw a happy marriage and, through his *Psychopathology*, provided snapshots of what the intellectual and substantive offspring might look like. On the way to the altar, however, a fickle social science began flirting with the paramour of extensive analysis, so the original promise was never consummated. Although nearing midlife, contemporary political science still has the opportunity to reacquaint itself with earlier enticements, and, given the maturity of intervening years, perhaps even to make a successful go of it this time around.

NOTES

[1] The 1976 study produced a very weak third factor (in addition to factors comparable to I and II above) which gave prominence to then-popular celebrities such as O. J. Simpson, Richard Roundtree, Diana Ross, Robert Redford, Marlon Brando, and Raquel Welch. Only one subject, an eleven-year-old boy, had a pure loading on the factor (that is, a significant loading on that factor only), although a number of other persons had significant loadings on this factor plus one of the others.

[2] It is worth noting that various psychoanalytic writers have recently given emphasis to communicational aspects of their work, and have consequently made it more amenable to direct observation. Modell (1980), for example, states that "the communication of affects is at the centre of the psychoanalytic process" (p. 259), and Ammon and Rock (1979) regard symptoms as "a deformated mode of communication" (p. 391). Further, procedures such as Silverman's (1977) "subliminal psychodynamic activation" method render possible the experimental study of various key psychoanalytic propositions from the *objectivist* (external) standpoint, which is to be distinguished from the subjectivity inherent in the Q-methodological approach illustrated here (Brown, 1980).

[3] The only other intensive case study (of which I am aware) in which the factors were this purely defined was also of a person of Greek Orthodox background (see Brown, in press-b), which lends credibility to the exaggerated importance of honor (*philotimo*) and of the ethnic reference group which are thought to play significant roles in contemporary Greek political thought and behavior (Pollis, 1965).

REFERENCES

Ammon, G. & Rock, W. [On the unconscious structuring and group-dependent development of personality]. *Dynamische Psychiatrie*, 1979, *12*, 377-394.

Baas, L. R. & Brown, S. R. Generating rules for intensive analysis: The study of transformations. *Psychiatry*, 1973, *36*, 172-183.

Boulding, E. Deep structures and sociological analysis: Some reflections. *American Sociologist*, 1979, *14*, 70-73.

Brown, S. R. Intensive analysis in political research. *Political Methodology*, 1974, *1* (1), 1-25.

Brown, S. R. *Political subjectivity: Applications of Q methodology in political science.* New Haven, CT: Yale University Press, 1980.

Brown, S. R. Principles of intensive analysis. *Political Science Discussion Papers* (Kent State University), in press. (a)

Brown, S. R. Imagery, mood, and the public expression of opinion. *Micropolitics*, in press. (b)

Burt, C. Quantum theory and the principle of indeterminacy. *British Journal of Statistical Psychology*, 1958, *11*, 77-93.

Chassan, J. B. *Research design in clinical psychology and psychiatry* (2nd ed.). New York: Irvington, 1979.

Downton, J. V., Jr. *Rebel leadership: Commitment and charisma in the revolutionary process.* New York: Free Press, 1973.

Eckstein, H. Case study and theory in political science. In F. I. Greenstein & N. W. Polsby (Eds.), *Handbook of political science* (Vol. 7). *Strategies of inquiry.* Reading, MA: Addison-Wesley, 1975.

Edgington, E. S. Randomization tests for one-subject operant experiments. *Journal of Psychology*, 1975, *90*, 57-68.

Eisenstadt, S. N. (Ed.). *Max Weber: On charisma and institution building.* Chicago: University of Chicago Press, 1968.

Ellens, J. H. Psychodynamics in mass media society. *Journal of Psychology and Theology*, 1979, *7*, 192-201.

Erikson, E. H. *Identity and the life cycle.* New York: Norton, 1980.

Frazier, C. E. The use of life-histories in testing theories of criminal behavior: Toward reviving a method. *Qualitative Sociology*, 1978, *1*, 122-142.

Gutmann, D. The subjective politics of power: The dilemma of postsuperego man. *Social Research*, 1973, *40*, 570-616.

Hersen, M. & Barlow, D. H. (Eds.). *Single case experimental designs.* New York: Pergamon Press, 1976.

Huber, H. P. Single-case analysis. *European Journal of Behavioural Analysis and Modification*, 1977, *2*, 1-15.

Hummel, R. P. Psychology of charismatic followers. *Psychological Reports*, 1975, *37*, 759-770.

James, W. *Principles of psychology* (Vol. 1). New York: Henry Holt, 1890.

Kantor, J. R. The principle of specificity in psychology and science in general. *Revista Méxicana de Análisis de la Conducta*, 1978, *4*, 117-132.

Kazdin, A. E. Methodological and interpretive problems of single-case experimental designs. *Journal of Consulting and Clinical Psychology*, 1978, *46*, 629-642.

Kernberg, O. F. Regression in organizational leadership. *Psychiatry*, 1979, *42*, 24-39.

Kratochwill, T. R. (Ed.). *Single subject research.* New York: Academic Press, 1978.

Kratochwill, T. R. & Brody, G. H. Single subject designs: A perspective on the controversy over employing statistical inference and implications for research and training in behavior modification. *Behavior Modification*, 1978, *2*, 291-307.

Laing, R. D. *The politics of the family.* Toronto: CBC Publications, 1969.

Lasswell, H. D. *Psychopathology and politics.* Chicago: University of Chicago Press, 1930.

Lasswell, H. D. The triple-appeal principle: A contribution of psychoanalysis to political and social science. *American Journal of Sociology*, 1932, *37*, 523-538.

Lasswell, H. D. Intensive and extensive methods of observing the personality-culture manifold. *Yenching Journal of Social Studies*, 1938, *1*, 72-86.

Lasswell, H. D. & Kaplan, A. *Power and society.* New Haven, CT: Yale University Press, 1950.

Little, G. *Politics and personal style.* Melbourne: Thomas Nelson, 1973.

McIntosh, D. Weber and Freud: On the nature and sources of authority. *American Sociological Review*, 1970, *35*, 901-911.

Meyer, M. F. Review of *Handbuch der Vergleichenden Psychologie* by G. Kafka (Ed.). *Psychological Bulletin*, 1926, *23*, 261-276.

Modell, A. H. Affects and their non-communication. *International Journal of Psycho-Analysis*, 1980, *61*, 259-267.

Morris, J. E. Kierkegaard's concept of subjectivity and implications for humanistic psychology. *Journal of Humanistic Psychology*, 1979, *19* (3), 67-79.

Payne, R. W. & Jones, H. G. Statistics for the investigation of individual cases. *Journal of Clinical Psychology*, 1957, *13*, 115-121.

Pollis, A. Political implications of the modern Greek concept of self. *British Journal of Sociology*, 1965, *16*, 29-47.

Schiffer, I. *Charisma: A psychoanalytic look at mass society.* New York: Free Press, 1973.

Silverman, L. H. Experimental data on the effects of unconscious fantasy on communicative behavior. In N. Freedman & S. Grand (Eds.), *Communicative structures and psychic structures.* New York: Plenum Press, 1977.

Stephenson, W. *The study of behavior: Q-technique and its methodology.* Chicago: University of Chicago Press, 1953.

Stephenson, W. Methodology of single case studies. *Journal of Operational Psychiatry*, 1974, *5* (2), 3-16.

Stephenson, W. Concourse theory of communication. *Communication,* 1978, *3,* 21-40.

Stephenson, W. Michael Polanyi, science and belief. *Ethics in Science & Medicine,* 1980, *7,* 97-110.

Szymanski, G. G. Celebrities and heroes as models of self-perception. *Journal of the Association for the Study of Perception,* 1977, *12* (2), 8-11.

Volkan, V. D. Narcissistic personality organization and "reparative" leadership. *International Journal of Group Psychotherapy,* 1980, *30,* 131-152.

Wilson, B. R. *The noble savages: The primitive origins of charisma and its contemporary survival.* Berkeley and Los Angeles: University of California Press, 1975.

Winnicott, D. W. *The maturational processes and the facilitating environment.* London: Hogarth Press, 1965.

Wolf, M. M. Social validity: The case for subjective measurement; or, How applied behavior analysis is finding its heart. *Journal of Applied Behavior Analysis,* 1978, *11,* 203-214.

Conclusion: Constructing the Realities of a Pluralistic Field

Dan D. Nimmo and Keith R. Sanders

IN THE FIRST CHAPTER of this volume, Combs, presenting Mead's "philosophy of the present" (1959), contends that the past and the future have meaningful existence, "not in terms of what actually occurred or might occur but rather in terms of the uses of the past and the present now" (p. 42). In this concluding chapter, we hope to interpret the past and current state of the art in political communication in ways that will be stimulating to scholars as they construct the field's future. Toward this end, we have divided the chapter into three parts.

Part one reviews the contents of the previous chapters with an eye toward provocative issues and questions which ought to be taken into account as the field continues to develop. Part two points to some lines of inquiry which appear to have potential for the field but which have received little attention, and part three offers some methodological observations.

CONNECTING THE PAST, PRESENT, AND FUTURE

Setting the Political Agenda of the Future

Given the introductory paragraph of this chapter, it is propitious that we begin by noting the richness of Mead's (1959) ideas about the past, present, and future. Although they have been current in philosophy and sociology for a number of years, his point of view has only recently found its way into the literature (Nimmo & Combs, 1980) of political communication. This is unfortunate because mass communication could be playing a role in the development of the visions and the agenda of the future which are held by the public. If, for example, as the evidence presented by McCombs in Chapter 4 suggests, the mass media perform an important agenda-setting function in the present, would not one expect there to be an agenda-setting effect with regard to the past and the future?

Public officials and the mass media are constantly being presented with opportunities to be historical revisionists. Recently such opportunities presented themselves in abundance when the history of the signing of the original Panama Canal Treaty became relevant to the probity of President Carter's proposal to return the canal to its original owners. Innumerable other examples in foreign and domestic affairs immediately come to mind, including media coverage of new probes into the John F. Kennedy and Robert F. Kennedy assassinations, the ubiquitous discussion of the history of the Arab-Israeli conflict, and the history of the relationship between the United States and its allies. Public officials, the media, and the public consistently find it necessary to review the past as it develops arguments relevant to decisions that must be made in the present. To our knowledge, however, there have been no studies by scholars in political communication of this revisionist tendency and of its potential impact upon the electorate, policy-making, and the general tenor of the times.

If we have neglected studies of contemporary conceptions of the past, we have certainly neglected the future. Virtually every person in advanced countries has spent some time studying formally and thinking about the history of his or her country and culture. There are, however, relatively few opportunities to study and think about the future. This is true, not only because it is difficult to study, but also because our ways of conceiving it and of drawing upon its artifacts are primitive.

In any event, it would seem that our conceptions, hopes, fantasies, and agenda regarding the future of the nation and culture would be likely subjects for influence by the mass media: We know little about the future; it is of great concern; and there are relatively few sources of information about it. Research on the acquisition and consequences of popular conceptions about the past and future could make important contributions to the field.

Communication and Political Malaise

Have the mass media played a role in generating the pessimism and disen-chantment which are growing in the United States and other developed coun-tries? Is this feeling, as Sennett (1980) claims, nothing more or less than the inevitable decline of institutions which have served well during the immediate postindustrial period but which now must be supplanted as we move into a new era? Or is it a product, at least in part, of the media's preference for bad news, crime, violence, and sleaze? Have the media, through their news and entertainment programs, projected an image of politics, politicians, and political institutions which is likely to inspire confidence?

An answer to these questions is suggested in several of the preceding chapters. O'Keefe and Atwood in Chapter 12 provide evidence in support of the hypothesis that the press may have contributed to the decreasing esteem in which candidates and political institutions are held. They report that "the proportion of negative comment about candidates in the press has risen over the past three elections from a low of 41 percent about Humphrey in 1968 to a high of 58 percent for both Ford and Carter in 1976" (p. 332).

Zukin, in Chapter 13, discusses the impact of the media on political culture, documenting the "dramatic erosion of the public's confidence in government, trust in political leaders, and sense of political efficacy" (p. 379). Zukin cites Robinson's (1976) "theory of video malaise" as one explanation for this phenomenon. Robinson has contended that television news, by showing social and political institutions in constant conflict, has fostered cynicism and frustration. While only mixed support has been found for this position, it is provocative and deserves attention.

Zukin also cites the work of Gerbner and Gross (1976) which shows that heavy viewers of television are more likely than light viewers to give "television answers" to questions on a number of topics. Television answers are those which conform more to the "reality" of prime-time television than to the "real world." Although Gerbner and Gross's findings have been challenged by Hirsch (1980) and Hughes (1980), one cannot help but believe that entertainment television to some degree contributes to and reflects political culture, given the large amount of time the average person spends in its presence.

Prime-time television virtually never displays a political institution, a candidate, or an officeholder in anything other than an unflattering light. From the sheriff on *Carter Country* to the portrait of a governor and what governors do on *Benson* to such "docudramas" as *Washington: Behind Closed Doors,* there is little to give a viewer hope about the efficacy of the political process, the viability of democratic institutions, or the quality of political leadership. Consequently, we find plausible the argument that the content of the mass media relates in some not fully understood but important ways to knowledge and feelings regarding the political system.

Increased scholarly attention aimed at the role of communication in the development of political culture and at the influence of culture on political communication will provide dependent variables which have seldom been explored by political communication researchers. Chapter 11 by Atkin contends that political communication researchers should take more interest in such variables as conceptions of the level of political corruption in government, the amount of conflict that is present, and the amount of outright crime in government. Others come to mind. For example, how does one develop a perception of his or her status in the social and political system? How does one learn where one's opinion sits in the broad spectrum of public opinion? How does one know whether or not one is a liberal or conservative or moderate, and how does one know the extent to which one's political opinions are widely held? In other words, how does one determine whether one is a member of the moral majority or the immoral minority? Mass communication and interpersonal communication must play a role in these matters beyond that which is now understood.

The preceding chapters in this volume have opened the door to a number of new independent variables as well. Atkin's Chapter 11 suggests that we ought to pay much more attention to entertainment programs, radio news and music, cross-national and comparative political communication studies. Moreover, we should reconceptualize some formerly dependent variables, conceiving them as independent variables or as both dependent and independent, as circumstances vary. What economic, cultural, and social forces shape the content of political news and dramatic programs on television? Do changing patterns of political participation influence patterns of media consumption?

Negotiated Order and Disorder

The idea of "negotiated order" seems also to be worthy of considerable attention from political communication researchers. Advanced by Struass (1978) and reiterated by Combs in Chapter 1, it maintains that order is constantly under negotiation. This would include institutional rules, laws, conventions, conceptions of order, time, and space. Indeed, individuals tend to develop a "communication contract" with people with whom they work and constantly renegotiate the contract as demands are made upon it which its previous terms could not accommodate. It doesn't take much imagination to extend the notion of negotiated order and disorder to the larger political system and to wonder what role the political content of mass media and talk play in the establishment of communication contracts, both explicit and implicit. Has the emergence of television, its content fraught with political information, changed in any way the rules by which social/political contracts are negotiated or the contents of those contracts? Who has the power to set the agenda for such negotiations, and who actually carries out the negotiations?

The notion of negotiated order and disorder is one variant of social contract theory which has not found its way into the conceptual world of the typical political communications researcher. A natural and legitimate marriage could be arranged between social contract theorists on one hand and political communications scholars on the other. In at least one important sense, social contract theory has to do with power; who has it, how is it acquired, what can legitimately be done with it, and who monitors and comments upon its application? These, of course, are preeminently political matters.

The potential in viewing political communication from the contractual point of view is well illustrated in Chapter 17 by Blumler and Gurevitch. Regarding the source—media relationship, they conclude:

> In any continuing relationship based upon mutual dependence and need, a culture, structuring all areas of behavior in which both sides regularly interact, tends to emerge. The norms of that culture then (1) regulate the relationship, (2) get imbedded in behavioral routines which often assume the status of precedents . . . , (3) are points of reference when disputes arise over alleged failures to respect existing ground rules or demands to change them, and (4) revert back to and become absorbed into the internal role definitions of the respective actors. . . . [A] shared culture is continually reestablished, even in the face of disagreement, because it is indispensable to undergird the relationship [p. 482].

Although the above comments were written as a description of the relationship between persons who are the sources of political information and those who report such information, the underlying cultural imperative seems to have much broader application.

Smoke-Filled Rooms and Other Forbidden Places

Contemplation of the role of process in political communication leads naturally to a curiosity about informal communication habits, patterns, and environments. As Combs put it in Chapter 1, "the important processes are not found on organizational charts and in public declarations, . . . but rather in informal, subtle, but certainly not strictly structural processes" (p. 47). Because of enormous biases held about what constitutes legitimate data for study, political communication scholars have, in the main, ignored those environments in which hard empirical data are difficult to collect. It is as if we have had formalized the rule of the instrument, deciding that if our instruments could not view certain forums and data, they were not worth observing.

Any active participant in political campaigning, the legislative process, lobbying, or any of the other "real-world" activities of politics comes away with the strong feeling that the smoke-filled room, the conference committee, the caucus, are indeed among the most important arenas for the making of political decisions. However, political communication researchers have been slow to develop participant observation techniques, or other techniques, which could be utilized in these environments. In spite of the excellent example set by Leon Festinger and his colleagues (1957) as they gathered initial data for the development of the theory of cognitive dissonance, we have not followed suit. One of the great virtues of a genuinely process-oriented view of political communication is that it will lead us, kicking and screaming if necessary, into those environments and into confrontation with those data which, if we followed our current methods, we would ignore.

The Benign Neglect of Deviance

The rush toward normality and respectability exhibited by most political communication researchers takes many forms but is, perhaps, most notable in our neglect of those ideas, groups, and movements which are far to the left or right of center or which call for the overthrow of the established order.

Simons and Mechling, in Chapter 15, take up this issue, noting that "most specialized theories of communication are of the 'top-down' variety or at least assume the existence of symmetrical power/status relationships" (p. 419). There are few theories about how those in positions low in status and power exercise influence.

The authors relate part of this interest in elite institutions and individuals to the Greco-Roman rhetorical tradition. They contend that "well into the 1960s rhetoricians displayed an anticonflict, pro-'establishment' bias—manifested, for example, in the assumption that friendly, coactive forms of persuasion, useful in academic discussions or legislative debates, were equally appropriate in conflicts with repressive, recalcitrant elites" (p. 429). The study of social and political movements is clearly running against the grain of this tradition. It is an excellent example of what can be learned when one rejects, at least for the purposes of study, the basic centrist notions which currently predominate.

Time as an Object of Study

Combs's reference to Roth (1963) and his work on timetables is a reminder of the importance of time in such political communications settings as the political movement (Chapter 15), political debating (Chapter 10), and political socialization (Chapter 11). The study of time as a variable has begun to take root in even the most traditional of places. O'Keefe and Atwood in Chapter 12 refer to studies which look at where the voter stands in his or her decisional process as a way of determining how he or she is using political campaign communication. If individuals change in their needs or at least in their modes of gratification over short periods of time, such as those typically studied during a political campaign, how much more must they change over a lifetime?

We know a great deal about individuals, having studied them "extensively." Much of the research in political communication has been of a survey nature (see Chapter 21), acquiring modest amounts of information about many persons. We have randomly selected a large number of individuals, unknown to each other, and taken a snapshot of their needs, gratifications, motivations, partisan identification, voting behavior, and so on, reflecting a particular moment in each individual's life. Occasionally, we have taken two or three snapshots, and, even more rarely, we have asked our respondent to relate the moments we captured one to another. We have used the information thus acquired to build theory, to guide the decisions of candidates for office, and sometimes to aid commerce and government.

However, our narrow focus has forced great limitations on our imagination, our theories, and upon the application of knowledge. We know little about individuals, "intensively" speaking. We don't know much about people as they move onward and, perhaps, upward through political life, nor do we know much about groups of individuals as they move through their life space as groups (the work of Simon and Mechling, Chapter 15, and Brown, Chapter 22, are notable exceptions to this generalization). There must, for example, be enormous changes in the gratifications which individuals seek as they grow into maturity as a part of a political movement. There must be great changes in the groups' collective informational needs, and gratificational activities, as the group moves through the various stages outlined in Chapter 15.

In short, we are saying that while "extensive" knowledge is highly useful, and that much remains to be learned through its acquisition, it is based upon a contrived collective. The individuals who make up mean scores and standard deviations do not know each other, have not talked to each other, do not love or hate each other, and probably have in no way influenced each other in direct and immediate ways. This is not the way political life is lived. Even the best panel study, with its series of snapshots, is not a motion picture.

Alternative Views of Reality

One of the most stimulating new developments in the study of political communication is the emergence of a debate over the nature of reality. Far from being an irrelevant intellectual exercise to be pursued by philosophers only, the argument has far-reaching implications for the future of the field and for its contributions.

From the 1940s until recently, one point of view was predominant in the study of political communication in the United States: logical positivism. This school of thought held that reality existed independent of a researcher's observations of it. Variables and relationships among variables were to be discovered in a reality which was coherent, rational, lawlike, and discoverable by the application of social scientific methods. Much time and effort were spent in an attempt to develop observational techniques which were uncontaminated by the predispositions of the observer, producing, therefore, results which were potentially verifiable by other equally competent observers. The best example in this volume of this philosophical perspective can be found in Chapter 20 by Miller, in which he argues for the superiority of experimental research over other forms of research when it comes to establishing causal relationships. To deviate from this logical positivist perspective was to risk nonpublication and, perhaps worse, to risk being intellectually ostracized. (For some significant exceptions to this general observation, see the introductory chapter to this volume.) Most of the contributors to this *Handbook* are in general agreement with the tenets of logical positivism. The only clear-cut exceptions are Combs (Chapter 1), Lanigan and Strobl (Chapter 5), Bitzer (Chapter 8), Simons and Mechling (Chapter 15), Wander (Chapter 18), and Brown (Chapter 22).

Recently, however, a provocative new point of view has entered the picture. It is best summarized in Chapter 1 by Combs. Combs contends that "reality is always more complex, inchoate, contradictory, and inexplicable than our images and metaphors of it" (p. 55). Apparently quoting Watzlawick (1967, p. xi) with approval, Combs asserts that there are "many different versions of reality, some of which are contradictory but all of which are the results of communication and not reflections of eternal, objective truths." Reality is therefore not fact but hypothesis; not a set of objectifiable events, variables, and relationships, but merely our perceptions of these. Indeed, reality may be absurdly contradictory and inexplicable until the human mind organizes it and makes some sense out of it. This point of view is, of course, diametrically opposed to the views held by most contemporary political communication researchers.

It is not our task to mediate these positions. We would not want to do so even if we could. We would point out, however, that the stance one takes on this important controversy, and on related ones, will influence greatly the things he or she wishes to observe, the kinds of observations he or she will make, and the purposes to which the outcomes of research will be put. The absurdist will be interested in the perceptions, thoughts, dreams, and visions of individual human beings. The constructivist approach, as outlined by Swanson in Chapter 6, could fall, with the application of certain techniques, into this category. It has as its major reason for being the understanding of how individuals make political meaning out of the messages with which they are bombarded. Truth will not lie in the message; truth will lie in the perceptual abilities, capacities, and propensities of the individual member of the political audience. On the other hand, those who retain their logical positivist tendencies will continue to apply social scientific method much in the way that is illustrated by most of the researchers who have written for this volume. Again, without wishing to take sides, we make three observations:

The Play is the Thing. If one accepts the absurdist notions which are advanced by Combs, one must also accept the grand significance of the study of political communication and especially of political sociology. In the drama of the absurd, it is through political communication and socialization that the actors come to understand who has power, what power is, how it can be used, how it should be used, and what the consequences are of its use. If the world is indeed a drama created exclusively by its own actors, with only passing reference to an objective reality, what those actors carry on to the stage with them and what they generate in terms of their own consciousness becomes all-important.

Subjectifying the Objective. While the absurdist position of Combs in Chapter 1 and the objectivist position of Miller in Chapter 20 are miles apart philosophically, it is ironic that in practice they have come much closer together. Some behavioral scientists in the study of political communication have, without meaning to, tended to subjectify the objective in the way they have measured some key variables. The best example of this tendency is the manner in which the variable called "communication exposure" has been operationalized. As has been pointed out by a number of essayists in this volume, there have frequently not been direct measures of communication exposure; rather, the researcher has relied upon the report of the individual as to how much time he or she spent reading the newspaper, watching television, or listening to the radio. Indeed, subjective accounts given by respondents have been accepted as valid data by most political communication scholars. More objective, and more expensive, methods for measuring exposure would include mechanical methods whereby a device is placed on television sets or on the radio, observations made by a third party which could be verified, as opposed to the manifestly subjective and impossible-to-verify observations of the respondent. Thus, a considerable number of the measures of exposure which have been published in the literature on political communication are not really measures of exposure at all. They are, rather, measures of the respondent's perception of his or her exposure, which is indeed but one view of reality, and a biased one at that. This fact is frequently lost as the results of such studies are interpreted in the literature and built into theory and practice.

Objectifying the Subjective. On the other hand, some practitioners of the absurdist position have attempted successfully to objectify subjectivity. They have decided that it is not the real world of objectifiable reality that is of concern to them, but rather the dramas, perceptions, and fantasies of their subjects which are the proper objects of study. They have therefore attempted to objectify these elements by the application of behavioral and social scientific research strategies. This may have been useful in some cases, but we suspect that in the long run, phenomenologists and existentialists and all those who do not practice the logical positivist's trade will need to develop research methodologies (see Chapter 12) which capture not the mean number of fantasy themes but the intrapersonal and interpersonal significance of the events acted out in the lives of single individuals (Fransella & Bannister, 1967) and groups of individuals. It is inevitable that a relatively new approach would borrow from the methodologies of older, better-established positions. This is a forgivable tendency in the short run, but in the long run we hope that method catches up with philosophy.

Where Does Power Lie?

Another way of viewing some of the differences in emphasis which are displayed in the preceding chapters is to ask the question: Where does power lie in the political communication process? Each period in the history of the activity has presented a different answer to this question.

Classical rhetorical theorists were convinced that power lay in source and message variables. It is this orientation which allows Bitzer to assert in Chapter 8 that Senator Kennedy's speech after the incident at Chappaquidick failed because of Kennedy's "inability to find and use adequate proofs and other constraints." The assumption that power resided in source and message variables arrived full-blown (see Chapter 7) in the mid-twentieth century via neo-Aristotelian logic and propaganda analyists (see the introductory chapter).

The same view concerning the power of source and message variables can be found in the work of those who studied attitude change during the decade or so after World War II (see Introduction). Source credibility, fear appeals, and organizational patterns were all seen as sources of potential influence. However, by this point, some audience variables, such as susceptibility to persuasion, were beginning to be studied. Nevertheless, one strong and still practiced point of view is that change and resistance to change can best be induced by the skillful manipulation of source and message.

A second point of view, which will be taken up later in this essay, asserts that power lies in channel variables. This, of course, is the contention of Innis (1950, 1951) and McLuhan (1964) when they make their case for technological determinism. To these writers and to others who hold their predisposition, sources and messages become transformed as they pass through the environment of the channel, thus altering their power. The medium, indeed, becomes the message.

A third point of view is now challenging the source/message perspective. It holds that power lies within the political audience. This position is perhaps best illustrated in Chapter 2, where the argument in favor of an active, goal-directed audience is made. It can also be found in the constructivist approach taken by Swanson in Chapter 6, and it is certainly the point of view held by McCombs as he writes about communication as process in Chapter 1. Persons adhering to this position hold that the audience is the message. Reality is created within the minds of individual human beings whether they are viewed as message senders or message receivers, rejecting the more or less mechanistic views asserted by others.

A fourth point of view asserts that power does not lie within any of the elements of the communications process; rather, it lies within political, economic, and historical forces which build and carry with them the political actors of the day. This point of view was held by the limited effects theorists, who believed that one of the reasons for the impotency of mass-communicated messages was that whole societies were under inexorable and irresistible historical influences. Communication served merely to reinforce or to modify slightly these forces. Communication was never a creative force. It was recreative, operating always as the handmaiden of powerful historical trends.

All of these biases, and others, can be found in contemporary political communication studies. This is a sign of health. At no period in the study of communication's role in the political process has there been more diversity of opinion surrounding this central issue. Indeed, there is a growing recognition, perhaps best illustrated in Chapter 3 on the diffusion of information, that any element in the process can be profitably seen as exerting influence, depending upon circumstances. An eloquent political speech can have an important effect. The medium is sometimes the message. Audiences are sometimes strongly goal directed, and there are times during which the forces surrounding the moment are transcendent. Power apparently does not rest immutably in any single element of the process.

ON THE NEED FOR A BROADENED
SOCIAL/PSYCHOLOGICAL CONTEXT

The most fundamental criticism which has been offered against the hypodermic needle model of the 1920s and 1930s and the limited effects model of the 1940s and 1950s is that they failed to take into account a sufficiently broad social/psychological context. It was, for example, easy for hypodermic needle theorists to see the audience as atomistic, standing alone, without social or psychological discouragement or reinforcement, to face the propagandist's onslaught. Hypodermic needle theorists somehow could not envision families and friends seated around the radio listening to Winston Churchill, Franklin Roosevelt, or Adolph Hitler and then talking about what they had heard.

One of the contributions of the limited effects model which followed was to place individual audience members in a slightly wider social and psychological context including the acknowledgment of perceptual defenses against propaganda, and the articulation of the now questionable two-step flow of information model.

On the other hand, the limited effects theorists had their problems of context, too. They tended to define dependent variables in a way which precluded learning, and they did not have a good sense of the long-term buildup of subtle media influences.

Any reader of this volume will notice that contemporary theorists and researchers have expanded even further the variety and depth of their purview. It is clear from the essays in this volume that there is now no single dominant point of view. There is a healthy state of cacophony.

Even now, however, there remains a need for researchers to include more social and psychological context in their studies. In Chapter 2 of this volume, McLeod and Becker note rightly that some critics of the uses and gratifications model attack it for failing to identify the social structural roots of human needs, arguing for the supremacy of structural factors over the "trivial redundancy" of the gratifications people say they seek and sometimes acquire from the media. This criticism is fair and, in one form or another, could be leveled at much of the research that has been done in political communication. Merely asking persons why they are doing something at the time they are doing it, or after they have engaged in the behavior, and accepting what they say as a definitive expression of the uses to which they are putting media content ignores some other important variables. It fails to take into account the antecedents to the feeling of need and gratification. It fails to determine whether or not contextual variables affect what we say we need and what we say we feel good about having received, and it certainly fails to take into account the behavioral implications, if there are any, of the responses which have been recorded. Too much faith tends to be placed in the individual's capacity to be accurately introspective, given the objectives of the research.

Along these same lines, McLeod and Becker in Chapter 2 refer to an assumption commonly held by those who do uses and gratifications research: Audience members are sufficiently self-aware to be able to report accurately on their deepest needs and motivations. This variable is typically not viewed as a variable, but as a constant. Self-awareness is regarded as an absolute plateau which most adult members of the population have achieved. Oh, if this were only true! Individuals vary greatly in their capacity for self-awareness and in their having developed this capacity to the point where they can look into themselves and give a coherent verbal or written report of their needs and motivations.

Uses and gratifications researchers might also become more interested in the circularity of human gratification. Do individuals not learn over time where they can and cannot acquire the gratifications which they seek? Do these patterns of gratification become habitual? Is it not also logical to assume that some informational needs go ungratified?

We are in agreement with McLeod and Becker's suggestion that gratifications research would move closer to social theory if it went beyond its present, largely individual, focus to consider its relevance to social systems. They say that "surely the harsh realities of being poor, of living in decaying cities and the like, have some connection to media uses and gratifications and their effects" (pp. 95-96). This comment is in line with our call for more research which takes into account the unique life circumstances of the individuals which are the objects of study.

In Chapter 2 McLeod and Becker also remind all political communication researchers that politics is far more important to them than it is to the average subject in their experiments or surveys. Politics and information about politics are increasingly seen as less salient by members of the general public. More than two decades ago, in his book *An Economic Theory of Democracy*, Downs (1957) posited that all political behavior is utilitarian and could profitably be viewed in the context of cost effectiveness. In a provocative chapter on "The Returns from Information and Their Diminution," he contends that "it is irrational to be politically well-informed because the low returns from data simply do not justify their cost in time and other scarce resources" (p. 259). Such reasoning will shock the sensibilities of uses and gratifications researchers. They would admit, however, that it is probably time to try to understand better those who are information-poor and bent on staying that way.

Research as an Ideological Expression

Is research a dependent variable? Lanigan and Strobl's Chapter 5 is a reminder that research, like all of the other activities in which humankind is involved, is potentially an expression of something else. This essay presents a "critical" theory which argues that social scientific research in the United States, despite its claims of objectivity (indeed, partly *because* of its claims of objectivity), can be interpreted as an expression of the ideologies at work during the periods in which the research was done. Once we are reminded of this hypothesis we can find a number of supporting instances.

As we mentioned earlier, it is not by accident that the researchers of the 1920s and 1930s held a somewhat fearful, oversimplified model of the political communications process. Their theorizing and their research can be traced to the preoccupations of their day. The same can be said of the researchers who conducted the early, classic studies of voting behavior and laid the groundwork for the limited effects tradition. These researchers were interested in helping establishment personalities—that is, politicians and persons in public service—to understand how better to produce compliance on the part of selected audiences. The researcher, like his patron, was caught up in the free enterprise, democratic ethic of the day.

The ideological precepts behind the research exhibited in this volume are difficult to phanthom, but we are tempted beyond restraint to try. It is, we suspect, no accident that researchers' interests in audience variables roughly parallel the rise of consumerism in the United States and Great Britain. It is probably also no accident that the field has become much more interested in the interactions within and among the various elements in the communications process. As the world has become more complicated, so have our metaphors about it.

We have become newly self-conscious about possible ideological influences on our research and theorizing. For example, Savage in Chapter 3 contends that "diffusion researchers have often held an implicit belief that the innovations or ideas that they study have impacts upon individuals and collective welfare, typically believing that these innovations are beneficial" (p. 105). Indeed, when reluctance to participate in the innovation/diffusion process was studied, it was viewed negatively as a barrier to change. Is social and political change inevitable and, if so, is it always onward and upward? What communication patterns, functions, messages, and the like are dysfunctional for the system in which they operate? What pieces of information, what political innovations, what myths should be slowed in their movement through the diffusion process? How can the adoption of particular political innovations be slowed, allowing all participants in the process to feel good or bad, as the situation requires, about what is happening? Did we lose interest far too quickly in McGuire's (1964) inoculation theory, the only modestly well developed antipersuasion model yet to be advanced?

The most specific argument in this *Handbook* along these lines is in Chapter 5, by Lanigan and Strobl. They indicate that neo-Marxian orientations now flourishing in Germany would "point to the commodity character of media products as an instrument of manipulation via mass communications" (p. 145). This approach, they say, would also trace "the emergence of mass communications back to the needs of the capitalistic mode of production" (p. 145), contending further that "the commodity character of the media determines the selection of the content in accordance with the criteria of saleability and attractiveness to insure profit maximization" (p. 146). The solution to this problem includes nothing less radical than the "dismantling of the capitalistic system and thereby the existing structure of mass communication" (p. 146).

One does not have to go quite as far as the neo-Marxian theorist would go in order to deduce some lessons from the critical theory perspective. One might ask, for example, whether the short-term motives of maximizing production and sales are the kinds of motives which can most productively carry the United States into the twenty-first century. Is a climate of political opinion being established by the media which will allow for the proper and long-term solution to the major problems of the day, or is the opposite true?

It would be tragic if the growing self-consciousness about the ideological and cultural influences on political communication and on political communication research died before it produced more cross-cultural studies of the kind Blumler and Gurevitch report in Chapter 17, and before it lends to a deeper understanding of the influence of intellectual ethocentricity on theory and research.

Whether "Is" or "Ought" or Both?

Nowhere are social scientific and behavioral prejudices more apparent than in our obsession with the discovery of what "is." Whether we conceive of reality as does the logical positivist or the phenomenologist, or some variant of these, we are in search of what "is." We haven't collectively spent a great deal of time thinking about what "ought" to be. There has been no cultivation of some generally acceptable view of the ideal society, its politics, its political communication processes. Political communication researchers have not, for the most part, thought of themselves as philosophers. They have tended to think of themselves as empirical scholars in search of probabilistic truths from which to build theories and models toward some unspecified end.

Predictably, alienation has developed between the worlds of the humanities and the social sciences. In this volume, however, those worlds are combined, to their mutual advantage. For example, Bitzer in Chapter 8 dares to offer a conception of what "ought" to be as he talks about political competency and describes Perelman and Olbrechts-Tyteca's (1969) conception of the "universal audience." As Bitzer puts it, "the universal audience refers to a class of ideal hearers or readers to whom an arguer appeals as the perfectly reasonable and impartial audience. This audience would not be influenced by such things as flattery, prejudices, local conventions, private preferences, falsehoods, and invalid reasoning. It would be influenced instead by fact and truth, by reality, and by faultless reasoning" (p. 245). Bitzer quotes Perelman and Olbrechts-Tyteca (1969, pp. 13-14) to the effect that "in general, a speaker or writer who desires to win the adherence of the universal audience will give up arguments that this audience—as he conceives it—would find inadmissible. . . . He will deem it almost immoral to resort to an argument which is not, in his own eyes, a rational one."

There are, we should note, several other instances in this volume where authors dare to dream of how the world ought to be. To Graber, the world ought to be more rational. To Kraus and Davis, classical democratic theory, with all of its idealism, remains a good model against which to review the contribution of empirical research.

We cite this visionary tendency with the hope that it will continue. Useful theories of political communication have not and will not be derived entirely from empirical data and from the random observations of everyday experience. A theorist's conception of the way the world ought to be is a strong, guiding influence on how he or she proceeds. We are not arguing that all researchers should be philosophers. We are contending, however, that the unabashed study of what "ought" to be would serve as a useful counterpoint to our current emphasis on the search for what "is."

Technological Determinism Revisited

We were pleased to notice several essays in a recent issue of the *Journal of Communication* (Summer 1981) on Marshall McLuhan. When McLuhan (1964) made his dramatic entrance into the world of communication theory and research, refocusing and advancing Innis's (1950, 1951) ideas about the role of technology in communication and national development, he was a major topic of conversation. More than any other author, McLuhan can be credited with having reminded us of the importance of the communications channel—of technology—in the political communications process.

The vagueness of McLuhan's "probes" aided their controversiality and popularity but reduced their huristic value. The "hot-cool" continuum, for example, was never easy for empirical researchers to fathom. This extreme difficulty (some would say impossibility) of operationalizing key variables resulted in little empirical research. This is an unfortunate condition which we hope future researchers will correct.

There is some evidence in the preceding pages that political communication researchers are becoming more interested in channel variables. For example, O'Keefe and Atwood in Chapter 12 point out that "attempts to predict completeness of newspaper campaign coverage have pointed to structural factors as the best predictors . . . including (1) size of news hole, (2) number of wires, (3) number of publishing days, (4) whether morning or evening edition, and (5) size of staff." The authors conclude that "these findings support others indicating that circumstances of coverage, production necessities, and travel schedules are more likely to create distorted campaign news than is outright political bias" (pp. 331-332).

Equally interesting observations in support of McLuhan's concerns can be found in Chapter 14 by Cobb and Elder. They indicate that "specific ideational constraints on the flow of people, problems, solutions, and choice opportunities in the policy process arise from the knowledge base of society and how that knowledge is distributed" (pp. 403-404). We are inclined to wonder whether the enormous technological changes in the distribution of knowledge in advanced societies have had major political effects, including, perhaps, some contribution to voter disaffection as a result of information overload. Has technology increased rather than decreased the "information gap"?

Cobb and Elder conclude that "the development of a truly national press and communications technologies that allow members of the general public to be reached both directly and selectively has facilitated the emergence of potent new groups organized around issues and ideas rather than private interests" (p. 405). The presence of these new groups "in a policy area predictably means policy decision-making will tend to be more conflictual and command greater public visibility" (p. 406). The authors argue that the presence of such groups in the policy proces may reduce overall governmental responsiveness because such groups tend to be atypical in the intensity and extremity of their views. Their effectiveness can skew government policy away from the model preferences of the general public.

Cobb and Elder begin their argument at an unusual juncture. Most political communication researchers have strong biases in favor of sources, messages, or audiences as the beginning points in their analyses. Cobb and Elder, on the other hand, have begun, in the position presented here, with channel variables. While we are neither agreeing nor disagreeing with this analysis, we find it interesting and recommend it as the kind of thoughtful inclusion of technological considerations which has been rare and which we need more of in the future.

Political Values

Virtually every chapter in this *Handbook* implies or states that there has been a strong reaction to the narrow, linear interpretation of political communication which held sway until about 1960. A much more inclusive view of communication as process is now in vogue, including a concern for diffusion, the uses and functions of communication, what one learns as well as how one changes one's mind, and so on. Out of this broadened perspective has emerged a strong predisposition: significant attitudes, values, and behavior are not likely to be substantially or permanently changed in one-shot communication situations. If such attitudes, values, and behavior are the products of a series of interacting events which form the total personal history of the individual, it is thought to be unlikely that permanent changes can be wrought by momentarily manipulating a single stimulus among the many in each person's stimulus field.

Just as political communication scholars, especially those in speech communication, were settling comfortably into this new, broadened position, Rokeach and his colleagues (1971a, 1973, 1979) began publishing the results of a series of experiments which diametrically contradicted its basic presupposition. Rokeach was able to produce long-standing changes in attitudes, values, and behavior during a single 40-minute experimental session, concluding that "it now seems to be within man's power to alter experimentally another person's basic values and to control the direction of the change" (1971b, p. 68).

The prime assertion of the theory out of which the Rokeach experiments were drawn is that when individuals become aware, through self-confrontation, of contradictions between their conceptions of self and their values, attitudes, or behavior, they will reorganize their values and attitudes and thus their behavior in order to make them more consistent with their conceptions of self. A number of experiments have confirmed part of, or all of, this position. Recently, Rokeach has been able to replicate experimental findings in a naturalistic setting.

Even though the earliest and most stimulating of the Rokeach experiments were done using two overtly political values—freedom and equality—and even though his theory of persuasion through self-confrontation with its attitudinal and behavioral implications are of great political import, his work has been virtually ignored by political communication researchers. This condition will change, perhaps, as scholars come to appreciate the approach's content-analytic potentialities (Rokeach, Homant, & Penner, 1970), its unique explanation of the belief system, its boldness, and its growing empirical support.

The Structural/Functional/Systems Approach

Throughout most of this volume, authors have exhibited an interest in the role of communication *in* the political process, assuming the former to be a subsystem within the latter. There is another equally compelling point of view which conceives politics as communication and political systems *as* networks of communication. The assumption behind such thinking is that communication is the "infrasturcture of politics." A major book by Deutsch (1963) asserted that government and politics is an exercise in communication and control. Deutsch, in his application of cybernetic theory, emphasized such concepts as feedback, purposes, learning capacities, self-closure, and growth. It was not, however, until recently that this point of view was again given thoughtful consideration. Galnoor (1980) has elaborated Deutsch's position and has reaffirmed its value in a study of the Israeli political system (in press). It is our hope that this orientation will now be given the attention it deserves.

SOME NOTES ON METHOD

The tone of this volume is certainly one of rampant expansionism. We have said, in effect, that there is almost nothing that we are doing which we should stop doing, and, what's more, there is much that we ought to be doing which we aren't. Furthermore, we have contended that we should view our work in the largest possible theoretical, ideological, political, and methodological contexts. This kind of robust advisory calls for at least a passing comment on methodology.

Meta-Research

There is no doubt that the most prestigious single form of activity in the study of political communication is the acquisition and explanation of primary data. Whether the research be humanistic, social scientific, phenomenological, or whatever, original research based on new and exciting data is probably the quickest way to scholarly stardom. This will probably remain true for the forseeable future, but it is our hope that other forms of research will come to acquire prestige as necessity requires.

One such method has been called meta-research. In his recent presidential message before the International Communication Association, Rogers (1981) called for added respectability for the kind of research which reanalyzes data, synthesizes, reviews, and does propositional analyses and bibliographic work.

If the field is to maintain its current vitality, its cross-disciplinary approach, and if it is to continue to acquire breadth and depth, there must be a way to extract its central themes, uncover its central errors, and praise its notable advances. The haphazard procedure of piling one empirical "finding" upon another without drawing relationships, and without each project being placed in some historical stream, will produce a slow but inevitable intellectual recession.

We join Rogers in calling for the development of a meta-methodology which locates, catalogues, and analyzes primary research and other forms of relevant inquiry. We would elevate the role of the disciplinary organizer and critic to nearly that of the primary researcher. We would value sythesis and context far higher than is now the case.

Multiple Methods

We have made much in these pages of the inherently biasing nature of ideology and, by implication, of theory. We have said that researchers tend to find what they are looking for. But bias is a necessary stimulus, and we want the record to show that we do not oppose bias, so long as there is a lot of it and so long as it shows great variety! Researcher biases are only negative when there is but one or two and when they are so confining that they give their progenitors the impression that they will produce eternal truths.

Methods are no less blinding than are theories. A method is, after all, a prism through which one views a particular portion of the world, a portion which may be, in part, a reflection of the viewer. It therefore follows that we should attempt to look at the world through more than one prism. Since we will see different things with different focal lengths and different lenses, we should certainly use more than one. Some should be designed to view objective realities, and others should allow us to frame the picture and to read a lot of ourselves into it.

We would therefore suggest that instead of viewing any given research methodology as presenting *the* answer to a particular question, we view it as providing *an* answer to the question. We should cultivate a larger appreciation for laboratory experiments, which are excellent at demonstrating causal relationships, but we should also value field experiments, natural experiments, and field studies which are excellent at helping the researcher to decide which causal relationships should be tested. Thus, a constant movement from field to laboratory to field ought to be more a part of our habits. Such an approach would seem to be particularly effective in studying uses and gratifications, agenda-setting, and construct theory.

Another recent development (Atwood, 1980) which should be encouraged is the combining of content-analytic methods with survey methods. There was a long period in the history of the field during which survey research was used more as an actuarial device than as an analytic tool. As we have come to better understand and appreciate the process nature of political communication, we have come to better understand the necessity of combining different elements in the process and viewing them with whatever methodology is appropriate to their content.

Along these same lines, we can envision a study which uses content analysis (see Chapter 19), Q-methodology as described by Brown in Chapter 22, and survey research as described in Chapter 21 by Bishop. Such a study would take advantage of the ability of a survey to gather small amounts of information about a large number of people, and the ability of subjective techniques to gather a great deal of information about a small number of people. It would be possible to randomly select the subjects for the subjective study from the larger group of randomly selected subjects in the survey, thus borrowing a degree of the external validity which surveys possess. Research of this kind would pay dividends because it would teach us how much determinism sets in once we have chosen a method, quite a part from what it would teach us about the subject matter.

An Epistemology of Method

To one extent or another, every author in the methods section of this book is an epistemologist. Each one seems to be sensitive to the need to develop a theory of knowledge which is particular to the research methods and strategies which are employed in the study of political communication. Such a concern is particularly evident in Chapter 18 on cultural criticism by Wander and in Chapter 22 on intensive analysis by Brown. However, it is in Chapter 21 where it is most pronounced.

Bishop announces early in his chapter that he is going to concentrate on what he sees to be the most important single problem in the application of survey research methods in political communication: "*a lack of any explanatory model of the cognitive processes which underlie the verbal self-reports of our survey respondents*" (p. 593). He then illustrates the problems associated with the absence of such a theory, citing the well-known problem of "pseudo-opinions" passing for opinions, the enormous problems associated with question wording, and the fact that different meanings are generated by the same survey question. Bishop points out, for example, that "many of the existing difficulties in modeling political trends lies in the failure to link the shifts that occur over time in the connotations of the key symbols contained in our survey questions with a very likely causal factor: changes in the frequency and evaluative context of these symbols in the mass media."

Fortunately, Bishop does not leave us without hope. He sets forth some conceptual models of how change should be dealt with in political communication and public opinion survey research. One such model is the "audience contingent effects" model. A key proposition of this model "is that the salients of any given public affairs issue depends upon the personal attributes of respondents which may make them more or less sensitive to its emphasis and implications in the media. Being unemployed, for instance, heightens one's attention to that topic as appears in the news" (p. 610). This model requires that consideration be given to those experiences which are not related to the mass media in any particularly obvious way but which are experiences gained through direct sensory experience. One of the most substantial indictments that can be offered against survey research, and all of the other research that we have done in the empirical mode in political communication, is that we have paid far too little attention to the life experience of the respondent, assuming that somehow those experiences would wash out as we did our complicated statistical analyses.

Bishop concludes his essay with the observation that "one must begin to think of building a theory of the survey instrument itself and the larger symbolic context in which it is embedded before we make much further progress on the 'substantive' problems of the discipline" (p. 621). We would expand somewhat on this admonition. It is time that we began to think of building a theory of knowledge relating to the entire study of political communication.

Computer Simulation

Because the study of political communication will inevitably become more complicated, we must prepare to study it is a manner that allows us to deal productively with complexity. Computer simulation may offer much to the field in this regard.

We wish we were able to cite a number of examples to support the premise that computer simulation has been a productive modality in political communication research and thus have a basis for our optimism about its potential. Unfortunately, we cannot. We can point to the research by Abelson (1963), which demonstrated the value of simulation in a campaign setting, and to the volume by Shaffer (1972), which illustrates the application of simulation to the testing of two theories of political decision-making. Shaffer tested the Downsian model and the Survey Research Center's six-component model, creating a revised model which was superior to both.

Simulation has been successfully applied in the study of the economy (Orcutt, 1960), international relations (Guetzkow, Alger, Brody, & Snyder, 1963), and legislative behavior (Shapiro, 1968). We can imagine computer applications in all of the areas mentioned previously in this chapter. Simulation would have the great virtue of allowing us to manipulate variables and test models without gathering additional data. One of the reasoned responses to complexity should be technological innovation and application.

CONCLUSION

If presumptuousness is a prerequisite to scholarship, and if great presumptuousness is prerequisite to high scholarship, this book should be well received. We have attempted to place within the confines of a single volume the essence of an emerging, pluralistic activity. In the introductory chapter, we commented on the origins and background of the field, tracing the threads of rhetorical analysis, propaganda analysis, attitude change studies, voting studies, studies of the government and news media, functional and systems analysis, and studies of the influence of technological change of the field. From this beginning, various contributors presented contemporary theoretical approaches, reviewed modes and means of political persuasion, and explored political communication in a number of settings. Finally, we reviewed five current methodologies. This concluding chapter was written in an effort to help structure the future of the field.

If current trends shape the future, the field will continue to resist premature and artificial closure. For a number of years to come, political communication research will be conducted by persons who resist—indeed, defy—definition except in the most general sense. We will not use scissors too confidently, cutting ourselves off from one another and from the materials that we need to advance understanding.

Political communication research will continue to be a self-consciously cross-disciplinary enterprise. The interdisciplinary impeti set in motion in the 1950s and 1960s through the behavioral and social sciences and, to some extent, the humanities, will continue to prevail. Fortunately, political communication studies are in no danger of being compartmentalized and forced into the artifical departmental constraints of the American university system. Those interested in advancing knowledge in this domain will fight as hard to retain their initial disciplinary ties as they do to contribute to growth on this more specialized topic. In any event, it is our hope that this volume will contribute to the advancement of intellectual tolerance, diversity of thought, and to our understanding of two necessary human activities: communication and politics.

REFERENCES

Abelson, R. A computer simulation of a community referendum. *Public Opinion Quarterly,* 1963, *26,* 173-199.

Atwood, L. E. From press release to voting reasons: Tracing the agenda in a congressional campaign. In D. Nimmo (Ed.), *Communication yearbook 4.* New Brunswick, NJ: Transaction Books, 1980.

Deutsch, K. *The nerves of government.* New York: Free Press, 1963.

Downs, A. *An economic theory of democracy.* New York: Harper & Row, 1957.

Festinger, L. *When prophecy fails.* Madison: University of Wisconsin Press, 1957.

Fransella, F., & Bannister, D. A validation of repertory grid technique as a measure of construing. *Acta Psychologica,* 1967, *26,* 97-106.

Galnoor, I. Political communication and the study of politics. In D. Nimmo (Ed.), *Communication yearbook 4.* New Brunswick, NJ: Transaction Books, 1980.

Galnoor, I. *The Israeli political system.* Beverly Hills, CA: Sage, in press.

Gerbner, G., & Gross, L. Living with television: The violence profile. *Journal of Communication,* 1976, *26,* 173-199.

Guetzkow, H., Alger, C. F., Brody, R. A., & Snyder, R. C. *Simulation in international relations: Developments for research and teaching.* Englewood Cliffs, NJ: Prentice-Hall, 1963.

Hirsch, P. The "scary world" of the nonviewer and other anomolies: A reanalysis of Gerbner et al.'s findings on cultivation analysis—Part I. *Communication Research,* 1980, *7,* 403-456.

Innis, H. *Empire and communication.* London: Claredon Press, 1950.

Innis, H. *The bias of communication.* Toronto: University of Toronto Press, 1951.

Journal of Communication. The living McLuhan. Vol. 31, 1981, 116-199.

McGuire, W. Inducing resistance to persuasion. In L. Berkowitz (Ed.), *Advances in experimental social psychology* (Vol. 1). New York: Academic Press, 1964.

McLuhan, M. *Understanding media*. New York: Signet Books, 1964.

Mead, G. H. *Philosophy of the present*. LaSalle, IL: Open Court Publishing, 1959.

Nimmo, D., & Combs, J. E. *Subliminal politics: Myths & mythmakers in America*. Englewood Cliffs, NJ: Prentice-Hall, 1980.

Orcutt, G. H. Simulation of economic systems. *The American Economic Review*, 1960, *1*, 893-907.

Perelman, C., & Olbrechts-Tyteca, L. *The new rhetoric: A treatise on argumentation*. Notre Dame: Notre Dame University Press, 1969.

Robinson, M. Public affairs television and the growth of political malaise: The case of the selling of the Pentagon. *American Political Science Review*, 1976, *70*, 409-432.

Rogers, E. Importance of meta-research. *International Communication Association News*, 1981, *9*, 6-7, 12.

Rokeach, M. Long-range experimental modification of values, attitudes, and behavior. *American Psychologist*, 1971, *26*, 453-459. (a)

Rokeach, M. Persuasion that persists. *Psychology Today*, 1971, *5*, 68-73. (b)

Rokeach, M. *The nature of human values*. New York: Free Press, 1973.

Rokeach, M. (Ed.). *Understanding human values: Individual and societal*. New York: Free Press, 1979.

Rokeach, M., Homant, R., & Penner, L. A. A value analysis of the disputed Federalist Papers. *Journal of Personality and Social Psychology*, 1970, *16*, 245-250.

Roth, J. A. *Timetables*. Indianapolis: Bobbs-Merrill, 1963.

Sennett, R. *Authority*. New York: Alfred A. Knopf, 1980.

Shaffer, W. R. *Computer simulations of voting behavior*. New York: Oxford University Press, 1972.

Shapiro, J. J. The House and the Federal role: A computer simulation of roll-call voting. *The American Political Science Review*, 1968, *26*, 494-517.

Strauss, A. *Negotiations: Varieties, contexts, processes, and social order*. San Francisco: Jossey-Bass, 1978.

Appendix A:
European Research

Richard Fitchen

COMMUNICATION RESEARCHERS in the United States should not expect to discover new empirical theories in Europe. Despite occasions when Europeans have generated ideas that were developed subsequently by Americans into theories for empirical research, the flow of influence has been mostly the other way around. The European director of a communication research institute in Norway who was asked to write about any such new directions stated that "over the past three decades no discernible European theoretical tradition has emerged in empirical communication research" (Hoyer, 1977). The tendency, instead, has been to adapt empirical techniques from abroad to meet the particular circumstances of research in Europe, which nevertheless has added new cross-national and comparative perspectives to this kind of research.

Yet it should not be assumed from this that there is nothing new or different on the European scene for political communication researchers elsewhere. That would be a mistake, for Europe is considered the principal source of an alternative to the empirical approach. This European alternative is usually called "critical theory." It has grown out of a broad mix of social values and ideas and cannot be dismissed as merely a Marxist initiative. Nor should European critical theories be underestimated in terms of their geographical influence. They are already widely diffused in Africa and throughout Latin America. Yet because of the predominant flow of American techniques to Europe rather than the other way around, it is quite possible that Europeans are more aware of empirical theories than Americans are of the critical alternatives. Already in Europe there has been considerable debate about the merits of each, and this debate has carried into other parts of the world. Thus for anyone who is not familiar with theoretical work outside the United States, there should be incentive to take stock of the European experience.

This essay makes a modest contribution in that direction, though it is inevitably limited in several ways. It can serve only as a beginning. More examples could be given in each instance, sometimes as important as those cited. It is also limited by a lack of general consensus about what political communication research encompasses. Some see it only as improving techniques for winning elections, while others think it is so large as to make communication and politics virtually synonymous. Obviously, this is not a topic that can be surveyed easily. So if this chapter manages to stimulate some new interest in the different ideas and context of research in Europe, rather than despair about what remains to be said further about them, it will have served its purpose.

To start, it is worthwhile to notice the academic background in terms of which European researchers work. Communication research enjoys no traditional base in the universities. Journalism schools, when they finally came, were organized separately; and, except in a few countries, such as Germany, The Netherlands, and Finland, media research carried on in the university context was fragmented among different disciplines. Other kinds of communication study seem to have been hampered by their association with the humanities, where the style of research is different and sometimes viewed as impractical. Therefore, individuals who specialized in communication often experienced a kind of professional isolation that discouraged new theoretical efforts. Even in West Germany, where communication research was more deeply rooted, the development of empirical research methods proved difficult. On one hand, the German university system conferred full control over research institutes and personnel on the professors who headed them, which tended to discourage cross-discipline cooperation for communication research. And on the other hand, in certain disciplines, such as sociology, as a knowledgeable American has pointed out, the feeling increased that empirical research could not resolve issues about controls and freedoms affecting the press or generate theory applicable to such problems (Hardt, 1976). What growth there has been in communication studies recently has been mostly in connection with developments in the social sciences, such as political science, sociology, and psychology, but inevitably communication research did not take center stage in any of them.

The study of politics apart from the traditional faculties of law, economics, and philosophy/history has developed more definitely within the university context, though it is still a very recent development compared to its counterpart in the United States. Political science began to take hold in Germany in the 1950s, but it was late in the 1960s before it achieved full status in French and Italian universities. One of the earliest communication interests for European political scientists came in the context of political campaign and election studies. Many of them conducted attitudinal and demographic-type surveys in that connection. In addition, political scientists in Europe, in a greater proportion than in the United States no doubt, have been in the forefront of media studies investigating organizational and economic forms of control, as well as the behavior of media communicators and their audiences. In some cases there was additional interest in the media in connection with the political parties. At any rate, the scope of debate about political communication has typically gone right down to fundamental issues, and even though these debates have produced some heated antagonism, they have at least addressed vital questions that might more often be brushed over in the more compartmentalized disciplines of American universities. Perhaps it is something to do with traditional thoughtways carried over into younger disciplines in confrontation with new sophisticated methods from abroad that accounts for the passionate, yet searching, quality of recent European theoretical debate.

CRITICAL AND EMPIRICAL THEORIES

It should be noted that there is not always complete agreement about what these terms mean, or even in some cases who are the practitioners of each. But they are at least recognizable both here and abroad. Briefly, the empirical approaches are alike in emphasizing positivism, functionalist concepts, and a tendency to use quantitative methods. Critical approaches, in contrast, are oriented to broader structural issues and usually have a greater philosophical emphasis. To be sure, there is enough variety among the empirical approaches alone to produce conflicts and disagreement; and, as one would expect, there are also differences between various critical theories. One of the cleavages among critical theorists, for example, is between Marxists and non-Marxists.

Of course, it would be naive to assume that simply greater mutual exposure between critical and empirical scholars would automatically produce a more harmonious synthesis between them. For one thing, that would ignore the social contexts in which they each work. The experience in Germany is indicative. There were acrimonious debates in the 1960s between the American-style empiricists on one side and critical antipositivists on the other; but instead of ironing out into a fresh synthesis, the controversy persisted and merged into very politicized confrontations between the German New Left reformers and the universities' liberal establishments. Still, to some extent, the legitimacy acquired by empiricists in defending against the reformers may have given them greater standing in relation to a third category of established scholarship known as the normative-institutional school. And evidently exposure to the debates has also heightened awareness of various issues, which has been a benefit to contemporary writings on politics.

No doubt the roots of critical theory could be traced to factors well beyond the particular situation of European universities, particularly in view of the fact that critical theorists usually reserve their greatest concern for the well-being of whole societies rather than just selected institutions in them. Some explanations for the phenomenon of critical theory have been derived from the class-stratified nature of European societies. One view is that, insofar as empirical theories rest on assumptions of social homogeneity (for example, the melting pot), they simply are not suitable where class structure persists. But this kind of interpretation seems to disregard the coexistence in Britain of empiricism and social class, and it also dismisses the pragmatic option of deemphasizing class differences as a means to make them go away by evolution rather than revolution. Somewhat more substantial is the question of whether the class structure itself could account for critical theory—for example, whether those who have social elite status but not access to power in government may be driven inevitably to combat their rival elites with intellectual tools and positions in the universities or media. As the factors conferring elite status change, so might the arenas of conflict between competing elites.

The successful diffusion of critical theories to other parts of the world where class structures are prominent might be taken as support for the social class view of theory generation. Still another view links alternative social theories to ideological preferences. This, of course, is not entirely separate from theory as a function of social class, especially since elite fragmentation can help account for ideologies cutting across class lines. But it is a view that takes the existence of ideologies for granted and therefore hardly helps dispose of their most inconvenient social consequences. Incidentally, an empirical theorist could perhaps defer consideration of those circumstances temporarily in order to concentrate attention on a more restricted hypothesis, but a critical theorist would attack him or her for thereby ignoring the most important issue.

One of the most familiar protagonists of the critical approach in Germany is Juergen Habermas.[1] He was connected with the Frankfurt School of Max Horkheimer and Theodor W. Adorno and has published widely read theoretical writings on political sociology. Regarding communication, Habermas advocates a society of uninhibited discussion among persons with equal rational ability to distinguish appearance from reality. They must be able to engage in communication that is free of impeding restraints and thereby seek consensus in terms of a common sense of truth that is the basis of legitimate democracy. He is against anything that creates a false sense of legitimacy and against ideologies in particular because they inhibit rational discussion, and he is opposed to any form of coercion. His argument is aimed against those who propose functional concepts of decision-making as a means of explaining legitimacy in highly complex societies. Habermas initiated a debate in the late 1960s with a leading writer in sociological jurisprudence, Niklas Luhmann. A coauthored book by them, pitting social theory against social technology, came out of a seminar they conducted jointly at the University of Frankfurt. It set forth Luhmann's systems approach and Habermas' critique of it. Interestingly, given the swirl of confrontations at the time, the debate itself was carried out amicably, and Habermas and.

Luhmann remained in touch thereafter. A sort of blend between the empirical and normative-institutional schools, Luhmann's position includes explicit philosophical perspectives that deepened the debate to an extent that critical theorists do not usually reach with their straight empirical counterparts. One of Luhmann's basic concepts, as a well-informed American political scientist crystallized it, is that legitimacy in complex societies is based on following procedures that secure public support in spite of any public apprehensions about the personal motives of policymakers (Merkl, 1977). Luhmann suggests that people deal with the evolution of increasingly complex societies by selectively reducing the complexity into systems which are more meaningful and which are defined by the form of communicative action they engage in with others. In other words, meaning based on how people experience the world is less complex than social reality. Yet this does not come down to a measurement of information flows, because meaning is located in intersubjective communication. System structures, such as institutions of government, evidently gain functional legitimacy by making this kind of communication possible.

Another leading critical theorist whose writings focus on political communication is Jacques Ellul of the University of Bordeaux. His books on propaganda, technological society, and political illusion have been widely translated, though typically empiricists have tried to ignore him because his ideas reach beyond the normal limits of empirical theory. For example, he distinguishes between two types of propaganda: One is the familiar type involving a source that designs persuasive messages and purposefully manipulates their transmission in order to cause people to believe or do something they might not have otherwise done or believed. This is what Ellul calls "political propaganda," and empiricists have been content to deal with its discrete phases for some time. But it is very different from and much less worrisome than the other kind of propaganda, which he calls "sociological propaganda." In this case there is no specific source, other than the social system itself. It is propaganda that comes in through education and is subsequently reinforced by other social institutions and government. It involves an ideology, but one that penetrates sociologically to become not just dominant but established as the conventional way of seeing things. Fundamentally, it is the way a society seeks to enlarge and strengthen its internal cohesion and impose itself externally. Ellul is concerned about this rather fixed outlook as changes in society move it beyond the industrial and into a technological revolution. Ultimately, it is a question of time that concerns him most—not just change itself but the greatly increasing speed of change. His rejection of unifying bureaucracy leads to a quest for other forms of historical identity, such as might be liberated in pluralism.

Habermas and Ellul provide examples of the critical approach to social theory. There are, of course, others who could be mentioned, but no attempt at inventory is intended here. Nor is there a need to divide absolutely between critical and empirical orientations. The distinction does not really favor that. Rather than two different things, it is more like opposite ends of a spectrum. But not the simplest kind. One can consider scholars only in the United States, such as Murray Edelman in political science and Herbert Schiller in communications, to appreciate that critical scholarship converges in different ways with empiricism. It should be recognized, too, that critical scholars are not merely synthesizers but theorists who would extend the scope of social science. Yet they do not inherently diminish the stature of empirical theorists. Ideally, each counterbalances the other. Thus, centers of empirical research have developed in Europe, and some are already well established.

Empirical methods developed particularly in connection with electoral research in Germany in the 1960s. A large-scale election study led mainly by political scientists Erwin K. Scheuch and Rudolf Wildenmann at the University of Cologne, and assisted by a major commercial polling agency, was conducted in 1961. It used a social-psychological approach in the style of the University of Michigan's Survey Research Center. Data from this study subsequently were analyzed in published studies by Scheuch and Wildenmann, as well as by their colleagues and students. During this time, Wildenmann moved to the University of Mannheim, whereafter the so-called Mannheim School developed. While not all the main lines of research deriving from the initiative at Cologne are equally pertinent to political communication research, it can be suggested that research by Franz Urban Pappi on voting in different social settings leads toward understanding communication as a key variable in community cohesion. And similar variables regarding communication and community in research by Gunter D. Radtke also appear to provide some explanation for nonvoting. In another study, nonetheless, where religion clearly dominated political choice, community size and other communication-related variables were understandably of lesser importance. Many of the studies by the Cologne and Mannheim researchers involved secondary analysis of data from broad surveys, with resulting deficiencies in subsamples and suitable probes. More recently, Wildenmann and others developed an academic center for social science research in Mannheim called the Zentrum für Umfragen, Methoden und Analysen.

In France the major center for empirical study of campaigns and elections by political scientists is in Paris at the Fondation Nationale des Sciences Politiques. Again, opinion polls are used as a major source of data. Analysis based on sociological categories is sometimes carried on cooperatively with a polling agency, notably by Alain Lancelot, a scientific adviser to one of the leading agencies. Elections are also studied from the geographical viewpoint, following a tradition carried forward by François Goguel and others from the example of André Siegfried. A prominent place is given to monitoring historical patterns of voting by territorial units, especially in terms of the commune in France. There are also several persons at the FNSP who watch the role of media in elections, and others focus attention on candidates' language in campaigns. Campaign rhetoric is studied in terms of persuasion and processes of image-building by Monica Charlot. Systematic computer-based analyses of campaign speeches have also been conducted by Jean-Marie Cotteret and Jacques Gerstlé in connection with the University of Paris I.

Election studies in England have been done for years by David Butler at Nuffield College, Oxford. He has published analyses of the elections since 1952, and is also a long-time election commentator on British television. Among other things, he has helped focus attention in Europe on the important role of media in campaigns and elections, and has facilitated work by researchers interested in political functions of the media.

MEDIA-RELATED RESEARCH

Broadcast media in Europe are different from their counterparts in the United States, particularly because they are often semigovernmental or public and operate on the basis of periodically reviewed charters. Europeans therefore attach considerable importance to political and economic controls affecting media organizations. One control issue deals with financial needs and what to do about commercial advertising. Another issue centers on performance standards and professional responsibility, and still another concerns how authority should be divided between the government (executive) and the parliament. There is also a whole set of issues about conditions of access, and the list goes on. Many of these issues appear familiar to Americans, but they often tend to be somewhat different in practice due to differences in media organization and cultural surroundings. They are also different from one European country to another, since the media organizations are almost as diverse as the cultures themselves.

Questions regarding print and broadcast organization and finance in England, including those relating to political functions of the media, surface regularly during investigations by special bodies that are commissioned periodically by Parliament to examine and report on the broadcast and print media. The most recent of these was the Annan Commission report on broadcasting in 1977. These reports provide an occasion for public comment about the media by experts, including critical scholars who often raise penetrating long-range issues that broadcasters might prefer to ignore. A leading proponent of critical theory and research (in a more moderate variety than the Frankfurt School) is James D. Halloran of the University of Leicester. He has sought to shift some control over research agendas from broadcasters to the researchers, and he criticized a report on the BBC by an American researcher (Elihu Katz) as greatly impeding that effort. Halloran is also a contributor to UNESCO's cross-national studies of the media. The print media have also been studied from the critical perspective, as by Colin Seymour-Ure of the University of Kent. To be sure, there are also empirical researchers in Britain who contribute to the periodic national inquiries; these include persons widely noted for the quality of their empirical work. For example, Jay G. Blumler at the University of Leeds has conducted highly regarded panel studies of television effects on voters during campaigns. And the unique group of (Westminster) Lobby Correspondents was studied by Jeremy Tunstall of the City University, yielding previously unavailable insights about their important role in political communication.

In France, the divergence of critical theories regarding political functions of television can be represented by Jean Cazeneuve who, because of his long stewardship of the principal television channel, represents a moderate position, while Roger-Gérard Schwartzenberg projects a counterestablishment point of view by labeling television the stage of the "spectacle state." Alphons Silbermann considers media on a similar grand scale as hallmarks of a future (postindustrial) service society, with attendant adjustment problems such as information overload; Silbermann is connected with university programs in Paris and Cologne. One of the most prominent Europeans raising theory-oriented objections to the concept of "mass" that is often connected with the media is Robert Escarpit of the University of Bordeaux. Alfred Grosser of the Institut d'Etudes Politiques (and the *FNSP*) in Paris is a thoughtful critic and synthesizer of empirical media studies from a normative-historical perspective. Empirical research on the media and journalists is conducted by Roland Cayrol of the Centre d'Etude de la Vie Politique Française Contemporaine (CEVIPOF) in Paris and by Francis Balle, who directs the Institut Français de Presse et des Sciences de l'Information, also in Paris. Incidently, this institute has continued to advance the principle of individual citizens' right to information, a right that was memorably advocated by Fernand Terrou in his time.

There are, of course, numerous examples of critical and empirical analysis of political functions of media in the smaller European countries as well. Most of this work is connected with universities in The Netherlands, Belgium, Switzerland, and Austria. University departments in Scandinavia are also well known for work in this field. To single out but one example, a noted critical theorist is Kaarle Nordenstreng of the University of Tampere, Finland.

Among the currently prominent West German writers analyzing media from the critical perspective are Horst Holzer and Dieter Prokop. Both have written and edited well-known books about the German media. They and other critical scholars consider that empirical theories are too limited in dealing only with selected social phenomena. They contend that theory and methods must be advanced to reveal the interdependence of mass communication and society. Academically, the field in which they work is usually called *publizistikwissenschaft*. Its purpose has evolved over the years, and particularly in response to the influx of American research methods. The critical reaction of the Frankfurt School, mentioned above, to empirical methods of mass communication research helped stimulate a reflective period of self-evaluation by media researchers. For example, the direction taken by Wolfgang Langenbucher of the University of Munich in developing a theory of political communication is presented in the systems theoretical context formulated by Niklas Luhmann. In some ways, what Langenbucher is working on could be considered a sort of European counterpart to Stephen Chaffee's theoretical orientation based on David Easton's system theory. Langenbucher is also connected with the Institut für Kommunikationswissenschaft (formerly Zeitungswissenschaft) in Munich, where he helped develop a set of teaching materials about the role of communication in politics. *Zeitungswissenschaft*, to the extent it is still current in Germany, usually refers mainly to descriptive rather than analytic study of media (literally the "newspaper") with historical and literary methods. Media research has relatively long roots in Germany, and there are well-established journals such as *Publizistik* (coedited by Langenbucher). Other centers of media research are located in Berlin, Göttingen, Hamburg, Mainz and Münster. University programs of study extend through the doctoral level, and a number of doctoral dissertations in the field have been published over the past decade.

Critical approaches to media research are also familiar in Italy. Semiologist Umberto Eco has studied the language of journalists and politicians and analyzed his findings in terms of a larger context of communication in political society. Political scientist Giorgio Galli has examined uses of media in the context of competition among political parties. And some years ago sociologist Francesco Alberoni with his associates in Milan used survey information to analyze the role of television in Italian society and politics. These three men and others joined in the formation of a consultative committee a few years ago to launch a review, published by *Il Mulino* press in Bologna, devoted to examining issues of social and political communication from the critical perspective. The editorship of this review, called *Problemi dell'Informazione*, was assumed by Paolo Murialdi, a journalist and former president of the Italian press federation, who is also the author of a left-of-center history of the postwar Italian press. The relative scarcity of empirical media research in Italy, beyond what is done by the media organizations themselves, leaves it mainly to normative-descriptive scholars to present an alternative to critical scholarship. But the obscured debate surfaces, nevertheless, as in a series of studies by teams of specialists on juridical and organizational problems of the media directed by Paolo Barile at the University of Florence. Similarly, some of the issues present themselves, however mutedly, in cross-national media studies by Roberto Grandi of the University of Bologna. His historical and sociological analyses are aimed at improving communication policies in light of comparative experience and in preparation for new technologies. He is also a media adviser to the Council of Europe. The more isolated advances of empirical scholarship tend to be so exposed that they may be casually refuted or even ignored. For example, attention seems to have been limited for a study by Maurizio Dardano of the University of Rome, who used methods developed by American researchers and analyzed the content of political and civic affairs reporting in the major Italian dailies circulating nationally. The same seems to hold for a study by Agopik and Franca Manoukian which analyzed the content of Italian dailies with regard to the Catholic Church, including how much and what kind of attention the Church was given and what image was projected about it. In spite of these circumstances, Italian theorist Roberto Petrognani is developing an approach to political communication that is informed about American research and at the same time is addressed to issues of concern to critical scholars. Petrognani was a student of Ignazio Weiss, a pioneer of Italian media research, and he now teaches in the political science department at the University of Florence. In 1975 he cofounded a review called *Quaderni di Sociologia della Comunicazione.*

Changes in the media in Europe have produced changes in the nature of media research. As the media have moved away from direct party influence, they have been conceptualized in more organizational terms and the roles and responsibilities of journalists have been viewed in a more professional light. American approaches to studying the effects of different media have been used by a number of researchers, and studies of media communicators are under way in several countries. Some concepts, however, like that of the "gatekeeper," have attracted diminishing attention in the critical atmosphere of European scholarship. At the same time, there is a continuing search for concepts with which to assess political functions of the media in connection with other institutions in politics.

OTHER AREAS OF RESEARCH

The many different kinds of research dealing with political communication represent a field that is broad and rich in variety but also sparse because many studies do not clearly acknowledge the central importance of communication. Critical theories are beneficial in focusing more attention on communication and in pointing to the dangers of following the labels of political institutions as a basis for conceptualizing functional communication networks. In the preceding media section, at least, the central role of communication is obvious enough. What follows from here are examples of political communication research that reflect the scope of that still-emerging field.

Public Opinion Research

To be sure, some critical scholars, such as Pierre Bourdieu in Paris, have denied that public opinion exists. But public opinion research is undertaken nevertheless and for the usual reasons, such as to provide data for subsequent rigorous analysis in social research or to provide information that can be used in combination with other statistical indicators to project trends into the future. In the example mentioned earlier of empirical research at the universities of Cologne and Mannheim, the researchers worked closely with the commercial polling agency DIVO to conduct their surveys. Two other public opinion research institutes in Germany, INFAS and EMNID, have been prominent in generating information about trends that concern policymakers. One of the leading public opinion research centers connected with media research and political campaign surveys is the Institut für Demoskopie Allensbach. Its director, Elisabeth Noelle-Neumann, is also a professor of communication research at the University of Mainz and an author of scholarly articles and books contributing to theoretical development in public opinion research. She and the institute have devoted special attention to the relationship between public opinion and media. For example, one line of research focuses on journalists' attitudes and the information-processing structure of media organizations as indicators of the ways media help generate public opinion according to their agenda-setting function.

Of course, public opinion research is also carried on by media organizations themselves, both in concert with polling agencies and separately. Major centralized broadcasting organizations in particular have their own ongoing research in connection with surveying their audiences. The BBC and the Italian RAI for example, conduct surveys regularly, in addition to commissioning studies by independent researchers. They also study trends of social change, as the RAI has done using surveys by the Italian agencies DOXA and SIRM. The media sometimes take part in funding research by the polling organizations. In France, for example, this is done from time to time by *Figaro, Nouvel Observateur,* and *Express* for the agency SOFRES, and by *France-Soir, Point,* and *Europe 1* for IFOP. Other clients come from the government, civil service bureaucracies, and political candidates, although the polling agencies usually make most of their money from marketing research. In any case, the research techniques follow familiar patterns. SOFRES, for example, tends to give more emphasis to psychological variables, using small samples and in-depth interviews based on extensive interview guides, while IFOP is somewhat more oriented to large-scale samples and use of quantitative methods.

The French research organization, COFREMCA, illustrates recent applications of social science beyond straight opinion sampling in Europe. It has developed a technique for analyzing social change in terms of measurable variations in more than 30 different "sociocultural currents" in society. These currents refer to such things as decline in standing, decline in the primacy of economic security, professional expansion, rejection of authority, devaluation of national superiority, hedonism, sensitivity to manipulation, myth of nature, polysensualism, concern about personal appearance, sensitivity to violence, and so on. The analytic technique bears the code name "*3 SC,*" which stands for

Système Cofremca de Suivi des Courants Socio-Culturels. It involves four separate procedures. The first is secondary analysis of numerous studies of recent French social history, found in books, theses, and ethnographic memoires. This is the principal means of defining sociocultural currents and adding new ones as they evolve. The second part is more quantitative and consists of an annual survey since 1974 of a representative sample (n = 2500) of the French population, in which each person is asked questions pertaining to each of the currents. A chronological curve is traced of each current's evolution, and its penetration into different segments of the population is also evaluated. The third part involves continuous ethnosociological studies to find out more about how the changes monitored quantitatively are actually experienced, thereby also to detect signs of emerging new currents (and to distinguish these from mere fluctuations). This is done by interviewing key individuals and by continuously analyzing media content—it even includes attempts to explain the success or failure of certain books, films, radio and television programs, popular songs, and new products. Finally, members of COFREMCA process and analyze results of the preceding operations in concert with the organizations that use the *3 SC* information in order to respond to their clients' particular needs, define their opportunities, and elaborate scenarios for them.

This same kind of operation now works on an international scale through an organization called the International Research Institute on Social Change. COFREMCA took part in its founding in 1978, and its presiding officer is the founder and president-director general of COFREMCA, Alain de Vulpian. There are affiliated research centers in Belgium, Canada, Denmark, England, France, Finland, West Germany, Italy, Japan, Norway, South Africa, Sweden, and the United States. Others projected to take part are in Argentina, Austria, Brazil, Mexico, and Spain. Based in Lucerne, this international research center makes exchange of information and expertise more systematic, responds to the needs of such clients as multinational companies and international organizations, and organizes seminars and colloquia on social change.

Research on Communication and Government Organizations

This is an area which is less thoroughly investigated by empirical researchers. There are even fewer European studies of communication in government than in the United States of the type done on the American government by Cohen and by Bauer, Pool, and Dexter. Although gaining access to do that kind of research is hard enough anywhere, it is probably more restricted in Europe than in the United States. Thus studies that try to encompass communication on a large scale—involving different ministries and other sectors of government, for example—may incorporate at least as much speculation as research. And still, in the view of most critical scholars, it is necessary to attain increased scale in order to get a proper perspective. Fortunately, this does not mean that all macroanalyses of communication in government are merely impressionistic. On the contrary, what Michel Crozier called the "stalled society" (*sociéte bloquéé*) in France was found by him to come directly out of intractable problems in the governmental (and nonpublic) bureaucracies. Even on such a grand scale of analysis, Crozier—who, incidentally, is also familiar with American empirical research methods—was able to gather evidence and organize it into a coherent pattern. It pointed beyond the usual cliches of overcentralization with all power at the top. What he found instead was incomplete follow-through on top-generated directives by lower-echelon personnel, particularly middle-level subordinate supervisors promoted on a seniority basis. Factors of bureaucratic culture that appeared to explain this middle-level blockage—for example keeping a safe distance and avoiding face-to-face relations—were communication problems. And again, with regard to communication, Crozier saw some possibility of ameliorating the blockage through increasing contacts between interest groups and administrators. He specifically denied that technological change would in itself be the key to administrative reform, even though that proposition was attributed to him by one American student of the French civil service. Like many other critical scholars, he is suspicious of technological solutions and focuses on communication patterns to diagnose problems as well as to anticipate reform. In generalizing his analysis in *The Stalled Society,* Crozier, who is now director of the Centre de Sociologie des Organisations in Paris, warned that more procedures of political negotiation seem to be gaining legitimacy—such as strikes by workers' organizations—and hence are less and less confined within the traditional institutionalized centers of political communication (such as parliament). As an increasing number and variety of organizations achieves effective access to the political arena to negotiate directly, partly thanks to television, institutions like the administrative bureaucracy are forced to maneuver differently and more like organizations themselves in order to survive.

A rather unique study involving a civil service bureaucracy and with revelations about communication in government was carried on by Richard Crossman during the years he served in Harold Wilson's government. Impressions and experiences recorded in his diary repeatedly characterize the bureaucracy as possessing a will—and communication channels—of its own, to the extent that only a very well-informed and personally assertive minister would be capable of taking charge of a ministerial portfolio. Crossman records personal reflections about other kinds of political communication as well, such as between front- and backbench MPs of the same party, the fluid structure of communication between ministers before and during Cabinet meetings, and the importance attributed to media by policymakers. A former journalist himself, Crossman time and again indicates how carefully he worked at his relations with the press.

The external form of government communication—that is, to explain actions taken and secure public support—is a subject to which scholars and others have often turned with suspicion. There is nevertheless quite a difference between government propaganda machines from one country to the next. In England, the Central Office of Information is relatively modest and arouses little alarm, while the Federal Press and Information Office in Germany has been the subject of articles in even middle-of-the-road newspapers calling attention to its size and the potential of its computers, as well as to its proximity to the Federal Chancellor's Office and the close personal relationship between its head and the Chancellor himself. In France, the government information service has gone through numerous changes and, like government-run broadcasting, has been severely criticized in the past. Gérard Marcou of the University of Lille II has written scholarly articles that examine with misgivings the organizational movement of government information closer to the French documentation service and its upright reputation.

Communication between the government and public is one of the chief roles of parliament, as Bagehot observed long ago. While this function seems to be less and less confined to parliament, particularly given the way media provide something of an alternative forum of social and political debate, it is the parliaments after all that represent the institutional guarantee—for parties out of power as well as for the public—to continue this kind of communication. The capacity of parliaments for public communication is studied from time to time by means of analyzing structural and procedural changes over time, as, for example, in a recent study of the *Bundestag* by Leo Kissler. Of course, this leads quickly to more critical questions, such as Heinrich Oberreuter has posed about the actual communication functions of committee hearings. Also, the less familiar role of parliament in German federalism has been examined by Heinz Laufer, with some attention to communication links between the *Bundesrat* and the *Land* governments. Studies of political communication involving the parliaments are naturally different from one country to another, yet empirical studies tend to portray a general public composed of citizens in Europe (as in the United States) who are less aware and less concerned about major issues in the legislative process than critical scholars would like them to be. No doubt that helps make critical scholars even more concerned about political communication.

A good deal of critical scholarship focusing on communication issues and the institutional role of parliament includes attention to the political parties and media. Often, this includes acknowledging the important representative forum provided by parliament for right- and left-oriented parties that have little hope of taking power in the government and that get less attention (except for dramatic actions) from the media. Studies also focus on the evolution of European parties to encompass increasingly broad segments of the population, from the more empirical approach in Alf Mintzel's study of the Bavarian CSU to the more critical approach of Mauro Fotia in Rome. The broadening popular base of the parties tends to increase their dependence on the media. But in addition to familiar symbols of political conflict, such as party etiquette, others that are less predictable have emerged and are spreading through ad hoc channels of popular participation enhanced by the media and casting new and uncertain shadows over the political landscape.

As much as anything else, it is on account of changes they sense are taking place in the political arena that critical scholars have taken their counterposition to empiricism. They claim that what is needed now are theories with greater reach, more than methods with finer precision, in order to gain an understanding of the scale of transformation that is now under way.

NOTE

[1]Selected works by European writers cited hereafter can be found in the References section at the conclusion of this chapter.

REFERENCES

Alberoni, F. Presenza della tv in Italia (1954-1966). In ERI, *Televisione e vita italiana*. Turin: ERI, 1968.

Annan Commission. *Report of the committee on the future of broadcasting*. Lord Annan, Chairman. London: Her Majesty's Stationery Office, 1977.

Balle, F. *Institutions et publics des moyens d'information—presse, radiodiffusion, télévision*. Paris: Editions Montchrestien, 1973.

Barile, P., & Cheli, E. (Eds.). *La stampa quotidiana tra crisi e riforma*. Bologna: Mulino, 1976.

Blumler, J., & McQuail, D. *Television in politics: Its uses and influence*. London: Faber, 1968.

Bourdieu, P. L'opinion publique n'existe pas. *Temps modernes*, January 1973, 1292-1309.

Butler, D., & Kavanaugh, D. *The British general election of October 1974*. London: Macmillan, 1975.

Cayrol, R. *La presse, écrite et audiovisuel*. Paris: P.U.F., 1973.

Cazeneuve, J. *L'homme téléspectateur*. Paris: Editions Denoel/Gonthier, 1974.

Charlot, M. *La persuasion politique*. Paris: Colin, 1970.

Cofremca. *Description rapide des courants socio-culturels* and *Des stratégies ajustées au changement de la société* (Informational papers). Paris: COFREMCA, 1979.

Cotteret, J.-M. *Gouvernants et gouvernés, la communication politique*. Paris: P.U.F., 1973.

Crossman, R. *The diaries of a Cabinet Minister*. Vol. I: *Minister of Housing 1964-1966*. London: Book Club Associates, 1976. Vol. II: *Lord President of the Council and Leader of the House of Commons 1966-1968*. London: Hamish Hamilton and Jonathan Cape, 1976.

Crozier, M. *La société bloquée*. Paris: Seuil, 1970.

Crozier, M., & Friedberg, E. *L'acteur et le systeme*. Paris: Seuil, 1977.

Dardano, M. *Il linguaggio dei giornali italiani* (3rd ed.). Bari: Laterza, 1976.

Eco, U. Guida all'interpretazione del linguaggio giornalistico. In V. Capecchi & M. Livolsi, *La stampa quotidiana in Italia* (2nd ed.). Milan: Bompiani, 1971.

Ellul, J. [*Propaganda*] (K. Kellen & J. Lerner, trans.). New York: Alfred A. Knopf, 1965.

Ellul, J. [*The technological society*] (J. Wilkinson, trans.). New York: Alfred A. Knopf, 1964.

Escarpit, R. *Théorie générale de l'information et de la communication*. Paris: Hachette, 1976.

Fotia, M. *Partiti e movimento politico di massa*. Milan: Angeli, 1974.

Galli, G. *Dal bipartitismo imperfetto alla possibile alternativa.* Bologna: Mulino, 1975.
Goguel, F. *La politique des partis sous la IIIe République* (5th ed.). Paris: Seuil, 1975.
Grandi, R., & Richeri, G. *Le televisioni in Europa.* Milan: Feltrinelli, 1976.
Grosser, A. Réflexions sur les fonctions politiques de la presse écrite, parlée, et télévisée. *Communication,* 1980, *5,* 315-332.
Habermas, J. *Strukturwandel der offentlichkeit* (3rd ed.). Neuwied: Luchterhand, 1968.
Habermas, J., & Luhmann, N. *Theorie der gesellschaft oder socialtechnologie–was leistet die systemforschung?* Frankfurt: Suhrkamp, 1971.
Halloran, J. Further development–Or turning the clock back? *Journal of Communication,* 1978, *28,* 120-132.
Halloran, J. *Mass media and society: The challenge of research.* Leicester: Leicester University Press, 1974.
Hardt, H. The rise and problems of media research in Germany. *Journal of Communication,* 1976, *26,* 90-101.
Holzer, H. *Gescheiterte aufklärung? Politik, ökonomie, und kommunikation in der Bundesrepublik Deutschland.* Munich: Piper, 1971.
Hoyer, S. Approaches to political communication research in Europe. *Political Communication Review* (a bulletin of the International Communication Association), 1977, *2,* 1-3.
Kissler, L. *Der öffentlichkeitsfunktion des Deutschen Bundestages.* Berlin: Duncker & Humblot, 1976.
Lancelot, A. *Les attitudes politiques* (4th ed.). Paris: P.U.F., 1974.
Langenbucher, W. *Politik und kommunikation, über die öffentliche meinungsbildung.* Munich: Piper, 1979.
Langenbucher, W. *Zur theorie der politischen kommunikation.* Munich: Piper, 1974.
Laufer, H., & Wirth, J. *Die Landesvertretungen in der Bundesrepublik Deutschland.* Munich: Goldmann Verlag, 1974.
Luhmann, N. *Legitimation durch verfahren.* Neuwied: Luchterhand, 1969.
Luhmann, N. *Soziologische aufklärung, aufsätze zur theorie sozialer systeme* (3rd ed.). Opladen: Westdeutscher Verlag, 1973.
Manoukian, A., & Manoukian, F. *La Chiesa dei giornali.* Bologna: Mulino, 1968.
Marcou, G. La Délégation Générale à l'Information et la politique de l'information. *Revue du Droit public et de la science politique en France et à l'Etranger,* 1975, pp. 937-995.
Marcou, G. La nouvelle réforme de l'information Gouvernementale et de la Documentation Francaise. *La Revue Administrative,* 1976, *29,* 202-206.
Merkl, P. Trends in German political science: A review essay. *American Political Science Review,* 1977, *71,* 1097-1108.
Mintzel, A. *Die CSU: Anatomie einer konservativen partei 1945-1972.* Opladen: Westdeutscher Verlag, 1975.
Murialdi, P. *La stampa italiana del dopoguerra, 1943-1973.* Bari: Laterza, 1974.
Noelle-Neumann, E. The spiral of silence, a theory of public opinion. *Journal of Communication,* 1974, *24,* 43-51.
Noelle-Neumann, E. *Umfragen in der massengesellschaft, einfuhrung in die methoden der demoscopie.* Reinbek b. Hamburg: Rowohlt, 1967.
Nordenstreng, K., & Varis, T. *Television traffic–A one-way street? A survey and analysis of the international flow of television programme material.* Paris: UNESCO, 1974.
Oberreuter, H. Scheinpublizität oder transparenz? Zur öffentlichkeit von Parlamentsausschüssen. *Zeitschrift für Parlamentsfragen,* 1975, *6,* 77-92.
Pappi, F. *Wahlverhalten und politische kultur: Eine soziologische analyse der politischen kultur in Deutschland unter besonderer berücksichtigung von stadt-land-unterschieden.* Meisenheim am Glan: Verlag Anton Hain, 1970.
Petrognani, R. Communicazione e politica. *Quaderni di Sociologia della Comunicazione,* 1976, *1,* 33-69.
Petrognani, R. Politics as imagination. *Communication,* 1980, *5,* 239-244.
Prokop, D. (Ed.). *Massenkommunikationsforschung.* Vol. 1: *Produktion.* Vol. 2: *Konsumtion.* Frankfurt: Fischer Taschenbuch Verlag, 1972, 1973.

Radtke, G. *Stimmenthaltung bei politischen wahlen in der Bundesrepublik Deutschland.* Meisenheim am Glan: Verlag Anton Hain, 1972.

Scheuch, E., & Wildenmann, R. (Eds.). *Zur soziologie der wahl.* Cologne and Opladen: Westdeutscher Verlag, 1965.

Schwartzenberg, R. G. *L'état spectacle, essai sur et contre le star system en politique.* Paris: Flammarion, 1977.

Seymour-Ure, C. *The political impact of mass media.* London: Constable, 1974.

Silbermann, A., & Zahn, E. *Die konzentration der massenmedien und ihre wirkungen, eine wirtschafts- und kommunikations-soziologische studie.* Dusseldorf and Vienna: Econ Verlag, 1970.

Tunstall, J. *The Westminster Lobby correspondents.* London: Routledge & Kegan Paul, 1970.

Appendix B:
Guide to the Literature

Lynda Lee Kaid

STAYING ABREAST of the literature in any scholarly discipline is a difficult and time-consuming endeavor. The task is particularly difficult in political communication because of the interdisciplinary nature of the field. While this diversity of perspectives is exciting, anyone who wishes to stay current must be aware of what is transpiring and being published in the fields of political science, communication, journalism, broadcasting, business, marketing, advertising, psychology, and sociology. In addition, political communication is the subject of considerable writing and speculation in popular periodicals and newspapers. The information in this section is designed to provide assistance to anyone who wishes to know where the field has been and where it is, or is likely, to go.

BIBLIOGRAPHIES

The most comprehensive bibliography in the area of political communication is *Political Campaign Communication: A Bibliography and Guide to the Literature* (Kaid, Sanders, & Hirsch, 1974). This work contains over 1500 bibliographic citations covering scholarly and popular works published between 1950 and 1972. Annotations of major books published during that period and a section listing sources in French and German are also included. Although dated and reflecting a restrictive definition of its subject, this work continues to fulfill an important reference function.

A shorter bibliography on *Communication and Politics* (Kaid & Sanders, 1980) is available free from the Speech Communication Association as one of its ERIC modules. This bibliography was published in 1980 and provides annotations of 43 books and articles which reflect the interdisciplinary nature of the field.

SCHOLARLY JOURNALS

Although a few professional and scholarly journals could probably be said to dominate the field of political communication in terms of quantity of related articles, a wide variety of journals publish intermittently in the area. *Public Opinion Quarterly*[1] and *Journalism Quarterly* publish the largest number of articles which will interest political communication scholars. *POQ*, published by the American Association of Public Opinion Research, has an interdisciplinary emphasis and generally relies on studies which report the results of opinion polls and survey research. *JQ*, a publication of the Association for Education in Journalism, contains articles which concentrate on media content and effects in the political system. A useful aspect of *JQ* is the selected bibliography of related articles in each issue.

Other useful scholarly publications in the journalism and broadcasting area include the *Journal of Broadcasting*, published by the Broadcast Education Association; *Journalism Monographs*, published by the Association for Education in Journalism (AEJ); *Mass Comm Review*, published by the Mass Communication and Society Division of AEJ; the *Newspaper Research Journal*, published by the Newspaper Division of AEJ; and *Journalism History*, published by the History Division of AEJ. Many of the journals in the general communication area also contain articles about the media's role in politics as well as about other communication factors operating in the political system. The *Journal of Communication*, a publication of the International Communication Association, contains many relevant articles and occasionally publishes collections of articles or symposia on political communication topics. The *Quarterly Journal of Speech* and *Communication Monographs* are major outlets for the Speech Communication Association, and they carry many political communication articles, as do the journals of the regional speech associations, the *Central States Speech Journal*, the *Western Journal of Speech Communication, Communication Quarterly*, and the *Southern Speech Communication Journal.* In the past, these speech-oriented journals concentrated on political sources and messages, and their primary contribution to political communication was in the form of rhetorical and critical analyses of political speakers and speeches. Recently, these journals have become more open to articles employing quantitative methodologies and to media and interpersonal communication effects in political settings.

Several new communication journals have begun publication during the last decade. With an interdisciplinary approach to communication, *Communication Research* is published quarterly by Sage Publications. *Political Communication and Persuasion*[2] has a more international flavor. The *Revue Française de Communication*, published in France, includes important political communication articles.[3]

In the political science discipline, *American Political Science Review* is considered the premier journal and increasingly carries articles which reflect the growing awareness of political scientists about communication's role in the political system. Good articles also occasionally appear in *Western Political Quarterly, Journal of Politics, Social Science Quarterly, Political Science Quarterly, American Journal of Political Science,* and *Polity,* most of which are affiliated with regional political or social science associations. The *Annals of the American Academy of Political and Social Science* devotes an issue to political communication matters from time to time. The newer *American Politics Quarterly,* published by Sage Publications, has been particularly receptive to political communication articles. Also worthy of attention are *Presidential Studies Quarterly,*[4] and *Experimental Study of Politics.*[5]

Scholarly journals in the fields of sociology and psychology also carry relevant articles. Of particular use are the *Journal of Social Psychology, Journal of Personality and Social Psychology,* and *Journal of Sociology.* Occasionally, relevant articles can also be found in the journals of business, marketing, and advertising. Examples of such journals are the *Journal of Advertising, Journal of Advertising Research, Journal of Consumer Research,* and the *Journal of Marketing Research.* Articles appearing in these journals tend to emphasize the various aspects of political advertising and propaganda, particularly in the mass media.

PROFESSIONAL AND POPULAR PUBLICATIONS

Particularly during election years, almost all popular periodicals carry articles which may interest the political communication scholar. Weekly news magazines, such as *Time, Newsweek, Business Week,* and *United States News and World Report* emphasize campaign activities, strategies, and issues. More reflective articles are found in periodicals such as *New Republic, Nation,* and *America.* A regular search of the *Reader's Guide to Periodical Literature* will help one stay abreast of this literature.

Beyond these general publications are several more specialized popular periodicals whose contents are relevant. *Television Quarterly*[6] and *TV Guide* analyze television programming and coverage; *Columbia Journalism Review* and *Washington Journalism Review* often include discussions of press coverage of the political system; and *Congressional Quarterly Weekly Report*[7] publishes material on campaign spending reform and regulation, as well as on campaign management, media, strategy, and techniques. The *Washington Monthly*[8] contains articles of general political interest, and the relatively new *Public Opinion*[9] has many stimulating articles by scholarly as well as popular writers.

The professional news weeklies and monthlies of the media industries contain much useful information. These include *Broadcasting, Advertising Age, Editor and Publisher, Printer's Ink, Press Time,*[10] *Marketing Communications,*[11] *Marketing and Media Decisions,*[12] and *Madison Avenue Magazine.*[13] The National Association of Broadcasters also publishes helpful booklets on media regulations and conduct. Copies of the NAB Codes for Radio and Television and of their *Political Broadcast Catechism*[14] should be in every researcher's library. The *ANPA News Research Report*[15] and the research reports of the Newspaper Advertising Bureau[16] often have issues with political communication content.

A few publications designed for practicing campaign consultants are also available. *Campaign Insights*[17] is published by Campaign Associates, a large political campaign management firm in Kansas, which also sponsors seminars around the country for candidates and their staffs. Established in 1980 is a journal called *Campaigns & Elections.*[18] This interesting and practical quarterly concentrates on campaign management techniques for state, local, and national races.

Articles in newspapers are more difficult to trace. Of course, the *New York Times Index* is an annotated source of articles in that famous daily. Indexes are also available for other large metropolitan papers such as the *Washington Post* and the *Los Angeles Times.*

BOOKS, DISSERTATIONS, AND THESES

In addition to the standard sources of published books, such as *Books in Print* and *Paperback Books in Print* available in most libraries, researchers will find much current information on new books in popular and scholarly periodicals. Book publishers advertise in these publications and often exhibit new books at the annual meetings of the associations which publish them. Although there is some time lag, many journals also regularly publish reviews of new books, most of which are indexed in *Book Review Index. Book Review Digest* indexes reviews appearing in popular periodicals. For book reviews written in French, German, and English, the most comprehensive source is the *International Bibliographie der Rezensionen.*

A regular feature of *Washington Monthly*[19] is "Political Book Notes," a section which lists and sometimes annotates new books of political interest. Those who are interested in media aspects of political communication would do well to subscribe to the excellent *Mass Media Booknotes.*[20] This monthly publication is very current and publishes specific issues on government publications and film books.

Dissertations and theses often present important unpublished material in political communication. *Dissertation Abstracts* provides the best guide for unpublished doctoral dissertations in this country. *American Doctoral Dissertations* includes dissertations accepted by Canadian universities as well as those American universities which do not mandate participation in the *Dissertation*

Abstracts system. A key word search of the dissertations available on microfilm is available for a fee from University Microfilms, 313 North First Street, Ann Arbor, MI 48106. Several disciplines also catalogue the master's theses done in their areas, but no central source is available for locating such work.

INDEXES AND INDEXING SERVICES

The greatest drawback to indexes and indexing services is that they usually involve a significant time lag. However, if a researcher needs to trace an idea's development in the literature, this is not of particular concern. In addition, searches through such indexes will occasionally turn up an important citation in a lesser-known journal. It is therefore essential that one be aware of the major scholarly and popular indexes and familiar with what publications are included in each.[21]

The services of the Educational Resources Information Center (ERIC)[22] of the Office of Education are helpful in tracking down relevant citations. The ERIC system stores abstracts and copies of books, convention papers, speeches, articles, unpublished reports, and the like and is capable of doing key word searches. This system has been growing in its usefulness to political communication scholars, and a search conducted in the fall of 1980 uncovered numerous relevant citations

Several specialized publications of national associations also provide excellent indexing functions. For instance, in 1975 the Speech Communication Association published an *Index to Journals in Communication Studies through 1974.*[23] This helpful volume contains complete tables of contents for most major speech and mass communication journals from their inception through 1974, as well as a detailed subject index to these entries.

The newest entrant in the indexing field, *Communication Abstracts,*[24] commenced publication in March 1978 with broad interdisciplinary coverage. Each quarterly issue publishes book summaries and abstracts gleaned from over 100 academic journals. The yearly topical index is very useful.

PROFESSIONAL ASSOCIATIONS AND CONVENTIONS

The publication of almost all scholarly books and journals falls far behind the intellectual development of a discipline. In political communication, as in most disciplines, the only way to be aware of current trends is to participate in the annual meetings of the national associations and/or to acquire copies of papers presented at such meetings. Membership in all of the associations listed here[25] and attendance at all of their meetings would be an expensive proposition, but it is usually possible to acquire convention programs and write to authors for copies of papers when attendance is not possible.

For those concerned with political communication, the International Communication Association is the most important single organization. It is the only major professional association with a formal division in the area. Devoted exclusively to this discipline and sponsoring competitive and invited paper sessions at annual meetings, the Political Communication Division provides an opportunity for scholars, students, and practitioners to exchange ideas and to advance new points of view.

The Political Communication Division sponsors a bibliographic journal, *Political Communication Review.*[26] Published at least once a year, *PCR* contains review articles, book reviews, annotated bibliographies, and other helpful information for Political Communication Division members.

The International Communication Association has also published the *Communication Yearbook* each year since 1977. In addition to important research pieces, this yearbook includes a major overview article on developments in each of the organization's eight divisions. The overview for the Political Communication Division is always written by respected scholars and provides a review of current trends and thinking in the area.

The American Association of Political Consultants[27] holds seminars and meetings which offer more pragmatic analyses about political campaign processes. After each election, the AAPC usually hosts a symposium where pollsters, candidates, campaign staff members, consultants, and media representatives share perspectives.

NONPRINT RESOURCES

Access to nonprint materials is probably the most serious problem facing political communication researchers. There is no central location or clearinghouse for related film, videotape, audio recordings, and so on, and no comprehensive listing of such materials exists. Yet for both research and classroom use, the availability of these resources is vital.

The Presidential Libraries system is helping to fill this void. Most of these libraries have unique audiovisual collections which include records of presidential activities, foreign visits, press conferences, interviews, national addresses, television and radio commercials, and other such materials (Kaid, 1975). Only four of the libraries currently in existence have materials available for use, the libraries of Truman, Eisenhower, Kennedy, and Johnson. A library has been established in California for Nixon, but the organization of the collection is not yet sufficient to permit easy access to its materials.

The Truman Library in Missouri maintains about 200 reels of film and approximately 800 sound recordings.[28] The Eisenhower Library in Kansas also has limited holdings, but these include many campaign commercials and tapes of campaign speeches.[29] The collection at the Kennedy Library in Massachusetts is extensive—thousands of audio recordings and millions of feet of film covering campaign and congressional speeches, convention addresses, political commercials, and other important aspects of Kennedy's career.[30] The Johnson Library in Texas may have the best audiovisual collection now available to researchers. The collection houses sound recordings of LBJ speeches and press conferences, copies of official presidential activities, televised speeches, political commercials, and some network news broadcasts.[31]

The largest collection of political commercials is located in the Political Commercial Archives.[32] Archivist Julian Kanter has performed a valuable function for the political communication discipline through his collection of thousands of audio, video, and film advertisements which span over four decades.

Since the late 1960s, the Vanderbilt Television News Archive has performed a similar function for network news broadcasts. Each evening the archive staff videotapes the early evening news broadcasts of all three networks and later abstracts them for publication in the *Television News Index and Abstracts*.[33] The archives can also produce at reasonable cost duplicate and compilation tapes from the broadcasts for research use. Other television broadcasts, such as presidential addresses, are also sometimes recorded by the archive and made available.

Films are a valuable research tool, as well, and many sources exist for both nonfiction documentaries (Dybvig, 1975a, 1975b) and feature-length movies with political content. Excellent suggestions (Kranzdorf, 1977; Robinson & Ornstein, 1976) for the use of political films in political science courses have been contained in recent issues of *DEA News*.[34]

Most university and public libraries maintain a collection of film catalogues from companies which rent films, and these can provide some assistance. The standard directories and indexes may be helpful also. These include the Library of Congress's *Film and Other Materials for Projection* (and its predecessor titles), which catalogues all motion pictures and filmstrips with educational and instructional value produced in the United States. Other directories which might be useful are the *Index to 16mm Educational Films, British Film Catalogue,* and the *International Film Bibliographies.*

The suggestions contained in this guide to the literature are certainly not comprehensive, but they should provide some indication of the materials available to scholars and practitioners of political communication. The field desperately needs additional bibliographic materials which will provide easier access to both print and nonprint materials. It is hoped that the increasing recognition of the importance of political communication as a distinct field of study will encourage the production of such reference materials.

NOTES

[1] The publishing organizations and addresses of journals such as *POQ* are available in every research library and, consequently, are not provided here.

[2] *Political Communication and Persuasion* is published by Crane, Russak and Company,

3 East 44th Street, New York, NY 10017. $22 per year.

[3]*Revue Francaise de Communication,* CEEPP 38, rue de Bassano, 75008 Paris, France. $38 per year.

[4]*Presidential Studies Quarterly* is published by the Center for the Study of the Presidency, 926 Fifth Avenue, New York, NY 10021.

[5]*Experimental Study of Politics* is edited by Marilyn Dantico, Department of Political Science, Florida Atlantic University, Boca Raton, FL 33431.

[6]*Television Quarterly* is a publication of the National Academy of Television Arts and Sciences, 54 West 40th Street, New York, NY.

[7]*Congressional Quarterly Weekly Report* is produced by the Congressional Quarterly, Inc., 1735 K Street, N.W., Washington, DC 20006.

[8]*Washington Monthly* is published at 1028 Connecticut Ave., N.W., Washington, DC 20036.

[9]*Public Opinion* is a publication of the American Enterprise Institute for Public Policy Research, 1150 17th St., N.W., Washington, DC 20036. $12 per year.

[10]*Press Time* is published by the American Newspaper Association, Box 17407, Dulles International Airport, Washington, DC 20041.

[11]475 Park Avenue, South, New York, NY 10016.

[12]342 Madison Avenue, New York, NY 10017.

[13]369 Lexington Avenue, New York, NY 10017.

[14]*Political Broadcast Catechism.* 8th Edition. Washington, DC: National Association of Broadcasters, 1976. Available from the National Association of Broadcasters, 1771 N Street, N.W., Washington, DC 20036.

[15]Available from American Association of Newspapers, The Newspaper Center, Box 17407, Dulles International Airport, Washington, DC 20041.

[16]Available from the Newspaper Advertising Bureau, 485 Lexington Avenue, New York, NY 10017.

[17]Available from Campaign Associates, 516 Petroleum Building, Wichita, KS 67202.

[18]Suite 602, National Press Building, Washington, DC 20045. $48 per year.

[19]For address, see Note 8.

[20]Chris Sterling, Editor, *Mass Media Booknotes,* 4507 Airlie Way, Annandale, VA 22003. $10 per year.

[21]The following major indexes provide reasonable coverage of the journals relevant to political communication: *The Reader's Guide to Periodical Literature, The Public Affairs Information Service, Business Periodicals Index, Humanities Index, Social Sciences Index, International Political Science Abstracts, Psychological Abstracts, Education Index, News Digest Service,* and *Legal Periodicals Index.*

[22]ERIC, U.S. Office of Education, 400 Maryland Avenue, N.W., Washington, DC 20202. The Speech Communication Association (5105 Backlick Road, Suite E, Annandale, VA 22003) operates the Speech Communication Module of the ERIC Clearinghouse on Reading and Communication Skills, and this subsystem of ERIC is of the greatest potential use to political communication scholars.

[23]Ronald J. Matlon and Irene R. Matlon, *Index to Journals in Communication Studies through 1974.* Available from Speech Communication Association. See Note 22.

[24]*Communication Abstracts* is available from Sage Publications, 275 S. Beverly Drive, Beverly Hills, CA 90212. $44 per year.

[25]The major organizations include: The International Communication Association, Balcones Research Center, 10,100 Burnet Road, Austin, TX 78758; The American Association for Public Opinion Research, P.O. Box 17, Princeton, NJ 08540; Speech Communication Association, see Note 22; American Political Science Association, 1527 New Hampshire Ave., N.W., Washington, DC 20036; Broadcast Education Association, 1771 N Street, N.W., Washington, DC 20036; and the Association for Education in Journalism, School of Journalism, University of Kansas, Lawrence, KS 66045. Many of the disciplines represented

here also have active regional organizations. For instance, the Eastern Communication Association has a Political Communication Interest Group.

[26]Information on *Political Communication Review* can be obtained by writing the Editor, Professor Lynda Lee Kaid, School of Journalism and Mass Communication, University of Oklahoma, Norman, OK 73019.

[27] American Association of Political Consultants, c/o Bradley O'Leary, Treasurer, 1625 Massachusetts Ave., Suite 505, Washington, DC 20036.

[28]Harry S. Truman Library, Independence, MO 64050.

[29]Dwight D. Eisenhower Library, Abilene, KS.

[30]John F. Kennedy Library, 380 Trapelo Road, Waltham, MA 02154.

[31]Lyndon Baines Johnson Library, University of Texas, Austin, TX 78705.

[32]The Political Commercial Archives are located at 1821 Rosemary Road, Highland Park, IL 60035.

[33]Vanderbilt Television News Archive, Joint University Libraries, Nashville, TN 37203.

[34]*DEA News* is a publication of the Division of Educational Affairs of the American Political Science Association, 1527 New Hampshire Avenue, Washington, DC 10036.

REFERENCES

Dybvig, H. E. Some non-print resources on political campaign communication. *Political Communication Review,* 1975, *1*(1), 6-7. (a)

Kaid, L. L. Non-print materials in presidential libraries. *Political Communication Review,* 1975, *1*(2), 8-9. (b)

Kaid, L. L., & Sanders, K. R. *Communication and politics: A selected, annotated bibliography.* Annandale, VA: Speech Communication Association, 1980.

Kaid, L. L., Sanders, K. R., & Hirsch, R. O. *Political campaign communication: A bibliography and guide to the literature.* Metuchen, NJ: Scarecrow Press, 1974.

Kranzdorf, R. Audio-visual syllabi: Politics and film. *DEA News,* 1977, *13*, 3, 11.

Robinson, M. J., & Ornstein, N. J. Renting Dr. Strangelove: Or how I stopped worrying and learned to love the films. *DEA News,* 1976, *8*, 1, 3.

About the Authors and Editors

CHARLES K. ATKIN, professor of communication, Michigan State University, teaches courses in mass media effects, political communication, and television and children. His recent research involves adolescents' responses to alcohol advertising, the impact of televised commercials on children, and children's learning of social behaviors and roles from television. His publications on mass media effects on voting and political socialization appear in *Public Opinion Quarterly, Journalism Quarterly,* and *Journal of Broadcasting.*

L. ERWIN ATWOOD, professor of journalism, Southern Illinois University, Carbondale, has conducted various research projects in the areas of political campaign communication and international news. He helped found the Political Communication Division, International Communication Association. His publications appear in *Journalism Quarterly, Communication Yearbook,* and other scholarly organs, and he is co-author of *Circulation of News in the Third World: A Study of Asia.*

LEE B. BECKER is associate professor in the School of Journalism at Ohio State University. His research interests are in uses and effects of the media and in the professional training of journalists. He has published in such journals as *Journalism Quarterly, Communication Research,* and *Journal of Broadcasting.*

GEORGE F. BISHOP is a political social psychologist and senior research associate, Behavioral Sciences Laboratory, University of Cincinnati. His current research interests include question form effects in surveys; the relationship of changes in public affairs content in the mass media to changes in the structure of public opinion; and information-processing models of political cognition. His articles have appeared in a variety of scholarly journals in political science, sociology, social psychology, communication, and public opinion. He is co-editor of *The Presidential Debates: Media Electoral and Policy Perspectives.*

LLOYD F. BITZER is chairman of the Department of Communication Arts, University of Wisconsin-Madison. He is a past president of the Speech Communication Association and was principal investigator of The National Developmental Project on Rhetoric funded by the National Endowment for the Humanities. He is co-editor of the project's volume, The *Prospect of Rhetoric,* author of *The Philosophy of Rhetoric of George Campbell,* and co-author of *Carter Vs. Ford: The Counterfeit Debates of 1976.* His chief research areas are the history and theory of rhetoric, especially political rhetoric.

JAY G. BLUMLER is director of the Center for Television Research at the University of Leeds, England. He has written widely on political communication topics and has just concluded a cross-national study of political campaign communication in Europe. He has co-authored *Television in Politics: Its Uses and Influence* and co-edited *The Uses of Mass Communication* and several other books on related topics.

STEVEN R. BROWN, professor of political science, Kent State University, teaches and has research interests in political psychology, communication, and methodology. He is editor of *Operant Subjectivity: The Q Methodology News-letter,* and his articles appear in *Communication Yearbook, Journal of Psycho-history, American Political Science Review, Policy Sciences,* and *Psychiatry.* He is the author of *Political Subjectivity.*

ROGER W. COBB, associate professor of political science, Brown University, is author or co-author of several articles on agenda-building, belief systems, and political symbolism. He is co-author of *Participation in American Politics: The Dynamics of Agenda-Building* and of *International Community.* His research interests include public policy, political psychology, and political symbolism.

JAMES E. COMBS, associate professor of political science, Valparaiso University, is involved in teaching and research in political theory, politics and popular culture, and politics and the mass media. He is author of *Dimensions of Political Drama,* co-editor of *Drama in Life,* and co-author of *Subliminal Politics.* His book *Polpop: American Politics and Popular Culture* is forthcoming.

DENNIS K. DAVIS is associate professor and assistant chairperson in the Department of Communication at Cleveland State University. He has served as a Senior Fulbright Lecturer at the University of Amsterdam and the University of Louvain. He has co-authored two textbooks, *The Effects of Mass Communication on Political Behavior* (with S. Kraus, 1976) and *Mass Communication and Everyday Life: A Perspective on Theory and Effects.* (with S. Baran, 1981). He is currently completing work on audience comprehension of network television news (with J. P. Robinson and H. Sahin) and has begun policy research on televised presidential debates (with S. Kraus).

CHARLES D. ELDER, associate professor of political science, Wayne State University, is author or co-author of articles on agenda-building, simulation and gaming, and political symbolism. He is co-author of *Participation in American Politics: The Dynamics of Agenda Building* and of *International Community.* His research interests include public policy and program evaluation, political symbolism, and political behavior.

RICHARD FITCHEN is president of Intercom Research, a California corporation doing applied communication research for business and government. He is a student of political communication research as practiced in a number of European nations as well as the United States. He is editor of a symposium issue of *Communication* on communication and politics.

DORIS A. GRABER, professor of political science, University of Illinois, Chicago Circle, has also been a newspaper reporter, feature writer, and editor. Her research interests in political communication have resulted in such publications as *Public Opinion, the President and Foreign Policy, Verbal Behavior and Politics, Mass Media and American Politics,* and *Crime News and the Public;* and she is co-author of *Media Agenda-Setting in a Presidential Election*

MICHAEL GUREVITCH is senior lecturer in sociology at The Open University, England, and chairman of the "Mass Communication and Society" Course Team. His recent research focused on the relationship between broadcasters and political communicators in Britain. His publications include articles on media uses and gratifications and political communication and social networks; and he is co-author (with Elihu Katz) of *The Secularization of Leisure* and (with Jay Blumler) of *The Challenge of Election Broadcasting.* A book based on The Open University course which he chaired is due to be published soon.

C. RICHARD HOFSTETTER is professor of political science and chair of the department at the University of Houston, where he teaches courses in research methodology, statistics, political communication, and political behavior. He has published papers and books concerning mass media, effects of communication, message characteristics, and a variety of research methods involving multimethod approaches to studying social problems.

LYNDA LEE KAID, associate professor of journalism and mass communication, University of Oklahoma, is editor of *Political Communication Review* and co-author of *Political Campaign Communication.* Her primary research interests lie in political communication, and her articles appear in *Journalism Quarterly, Journal of Broadcasting, Journal of Advertising Research, Central States Speech Journal, Communication Research, Social Science Quarterly,* and *Communication Yearbook.*

SIDNEY KRAUS is professor and chairperson of the Cleveland State University Department of Communication. He has edited two books summarizing research on televised presidential debates, *The Great Debates: Background, Perspective, Effects* (1962) and *The Great Debates: Carter vs. Ford, 1976.* (1979). He is co-author (with D. K. Davis) of a book on political communication, *The Effects of Mass Communication on Political Behavior,* (1976) and is working on research involving the role of mass media and televised debates during the 1980 presidential campaign.

RICHARD L. LANIGAN is professor, Southern Illinois University, with cross-assignment teaching responsibilities in speech communication, philosophy, and linguistics. His research focuses on the philosophy of communication with a special interest in the camparison of analytic and phenomenological approaches to language. His publications include *Speaking and Semiology, Speech Act Phenomenology, Philosophy of Communication* (forthcoming), and *Rhetoric and Semiotic* (forthcoming).

MAXWELL E. McCOMBS is John Ben Snow Professor of Newspaper Research and director of the Communication Research Center, School of Public Communication, Syracuse University. His research specialties are agenda-setting and public opinion. He has contributed to numerous scholarly journals and volumes and is co-author of *The Emergence of American Political Issues* and *Media Agenda-Setting in a Presidential Election.*

JACK M. McLEOD is Maier-Bascom Professor of Journalism and Mass Communication and chairman of the Mass Communications Research Center at the University of Wisconsin-Madison. He teaches courses and seminars in communication research methods and theories of mass communication and social systems. His political communication research interests include family communication and adolescent political socialization, media reliance and political effects, and the impact of televised debates. Other research has examined television violence and adolescent aggressive behavior, professionalization of media occupations, coorientation, and television use and interpersonal behavior.

L. JOHN MARTIN is professor of journalism, University of Maryland, where he teaches communication research, public opinion, mass communication, and interpretation of contemporary affairs. He has worked on newspapers and was a foreign correspondent in the Near East and a research administrator for the U.S. Information Agency. He is editor of the special issue of *The Annals* on the role of the mass media in American politics, associate editor of *Journalism Quarterly*, and author of various articles and books on international propaganda.

ELIZABETH W. MECHLING, assistant professor of marketing at California State University, Hayward, teaches courses in administrative communication, marketing strategies for not-for-profit organizations, organizational relations management, campaign rhetoric, and speech communication research. Her research and consulting activities focus on image management tactics used by organizations and individuals, and on the marketing of social values. Her publications appear in *Western Journal of Speech Communication, Journal of American Culture, Quarterly Journal of Speech,* and *Communication Quarterly.*

ROY E. MILLER is associate professor of political science at Southern Illinois University at Carbondale. His teaching consists primarily of methodology courses, including survey research, causal modeling, data management, and experimental design. His principal mode of doing research is experimental; his research focus is on mass political participation, and he has conducted research on political socialization, voting behavior, and the effects of political campaign techniques. His work has appeared in *Political Communication Review, Communication Yearbook 4, Communication Yearbook 5, Teaching Political Science, Experimental Study of Politics,* and the *International Political Science Review.*

DAN D. NIMMO holds a joint appointment as professor of political science, Department of Political Science, and professor of journalism, College of Communications, University of Tennessee. Among his books in political communication are *Newsgathering in Washington, The Political Persuaders, Popular Images of Politics, Political Communication and Public Opinion in America,* and *Subliminal Politics.* He is co-editor of *Watching American Politics* and *Government and the News Media: Cross-National Perspectives,* and was editor of *Communication Yearbook,* volumes 3 and 4.

GARRETT J. O'KEEFE, professor of mass communications, University of Denver, has conducted numerous research projects in the areas of campaign effects, political socialization, and the social uses and effects of the mass media. Among his various publications is *The People Choose a President,* of which he is co-author.

KEITH R. SANDERS is professor of speech communication at Southern Illinois University at Carbondale and governmental relations officer for the Southern Illinois University System. He was the first chairperson of the Political Communication Division of the International Communication Association. He co-authored *Political Campaign Communication,* and has written widely on the role of interpersonal and mass communication in political decision-making.

ROBERT L. SAVAGE, associate professor of political science, University of Arkansas, is co-author of *Candidates and Their Images* and author or co-author of a number of articles relating to political communication appearing in such journals as *Publius, Journal of Politics, Political Methodology, Experimental Study of Politics,* and *Polity.* His research interests focus on subcultural variations in American politics, the diffusion of public policies, and popular perceptions of leaders and institutions in American society.

HERBERT W. SIMONS is professor of speech at Temple University, where he teaches persuasion, movements, conflict, and the rhetoric of science. He is author of *Persuasion: Understanding, Practice and Analysis* and co-editor (with G. R. Miller) of *Perspectives on Communication and Social Conflict.*

RUDOLF L. STROBL is assistant professor in the Department of Communication at the University of Hartford, Connecticut. His work reflects the philosophical tradition of German social thought and focuses on the epistemological, theoretical, and methodological implications of current communication research and on alternate conceptions. His main interest is the economic and political structure of the mass media with an emphasis on international communication and cultural domination. He has worked as a professional in broadcasting and for various scientific magazines.

DAVID L. SWANSON, associate professor of speech communication, University of Illinois at Urbana-Champaign, has research interests in the social effects of public communication, with a particular focus on political communication. His recent work has involved conceptual analyses of theories of mass communication and of political communication, as well as empirical studies applying agenda-setting, utility-based, and constructivist views. His published works have appeared in a variety of scholarly journals and books.

PHILIP WANDER is professor of communication studies, San Jose State University, where he teaches media criticism, argumentation, and philosophy of communication. His articles appear in the *Journal of Communication, Quarterly Journal of Speech, Journal of Popular Culture, Western Speech,* and *Southern Speech.*

CLIFF ZUKIN is associate professor of political science, Rutgers University, and director of The Eagleton Poll, Eagleton Institute of Politics. He has published articles in *Public Opinion Quarterly, Journalism Quarterly,* and the *Journal of Communication.* He teaches courses in the mass media, political behavior, and research methods and, through The Eagleton Poll, directs 10-15 New Jersey statewide surveys annually.

Index